JUSTINIAN'S
INSTITUTES

JUSTINIAN'S INSTITUTES

Translated with an Introduction by
Peter Birks & Grant McLeod

with the Latin text of
Paul Krueger

Cornell University Press

Ithaca, New York

First published 1987 by Cornell University Press

International Standard Book Number (cloth) 0-8014-1999-9
International Standard Book Number (paper) 0-8014-9400-1
Library of Congress Catalog Card Number 86-47968

Photoset in North Wales by
Derek Doyle & Associates, Mold, Clwyd
and printed in Great Britain by
Redwood Burn Limited, Trowbridge

CONTENTS

Acknowledgments

Our work has been helped by a grant made through the Edinburgh Roman Law Group by the trustees of the General Council Trust in the University of Edinburgh. We would like to take this opportunity to thank the trustees for their support. We also owe a debt of gratitude to Mrs Lisa White, our Departmental Secretary, for limitless assistance without which the speed of our work would have been halved.

April 1986

P.B.
G. McL.

Introduction

With science, religion and the liberal arts, law is one of the main elements of human culture and civilization, but in the western world only two societies have succeeded in building up a mature law library from scratch. As a result the countries of Europe, and many others to which European influence spread, have legal systems founded on either Roman or English law. There are different degrees of intermixture with indigenous materials, and different degrees of interruption by social or intellectual revolutions. But the division between the Roman and the English, or Anglo-Norman, legal families is a fact of western civilization. Some jurisdictions, such as Scotland in the United Kingdom and Louisiana in the United States, have built on a Roman base without shutting themselves off from the English materials. Such mixed systems are well placed to get the best of both worlds.

The English achievement was not completely independent of the Roman. The Anglo-Norman development began just as Roman law was starting its second European life. In the twelfth century the *Corpus Iuris* became the focus of secular intellectual life. As though a stone had been thrown into a lake, knowledge of the Roman law library spread out across Europe from the universities of northern Italy, especially Bologna. By 1150 Vacarius was teaching Roman law in England, perhaps at Oxford.[1] A hundred years later the first great book on English law, written in Latin, showed no aversion to the methods and even the substance of Roman law. That was Bracton's *De Legibus et Consuetudinibus Angliae* (On the Laws and Customs of England). We will return to it later. After Bracton English law did turn away from the Roman methods and materials. The background of the judges changed. The learning of the new men, no longer educated clerics, was in the practice of the King's courts, not in Roman law. Their medium was the Yearbooks, the robust, colloquial reports, always in French, which from Edward I to Henry VIII accumulated the matter of the common law.

But from the age of the Renaissance and Reformation onwards, despite there being no formal reception, Roman influence on common law doctrine can never be ruled out. Henry VIII founded the regius chairs of civil law in Oxford and Cambridge. Printing, and the enthusiasm of humanist scholars, made Roman materials easily available. The Inns of Court were not cut off. The career of Thomas More (1478-1535) serves as an illustration. He was the son of a judge, a barrister of Lincoln's Inn, Lord Chancellor from 1529 to 1532. But he was also the friend of Erasmus of Rotterdam (1466-1536) and a great humanist scholar in his own right. There were many points of contact, not only through the universities but also in chancery, and with the doctors of civil law who practised in the church courts and in admiralty.

All the same the division between the Roman and English legal systems is real enough. But on both sides of the divide lawyers and historians need to know their Roman law. In Scotland and on the Continent it is a matter of looking directly at the foundations of the modern law. In England and America it is more a question of keeping alert to borrowings and avoiding explanations which are blind to the Roman learning which is always in the background. For generations of lawyers Justinian's *Institutes* has been the primary vehicle of that learning. It is an elementary book. As we shall see, it is much the smallest work in the surviving body of Roman law. But it is the key or map to the whole. It has some claim to be the most important law book ever written. It could hardly be omitted from any list of the world's dozen or so most influential books. The *Institutes* was composed in Constantinople and published in AD 533. Its makers already claimed, optimistically, to look back on over fourteen hundred years of legal history. Fourteen hundred and fifty-three years later it remains essential reading for any lawyer who takes his subject seriously.[2]

We have said enough to show that when it was written the *Institutes* already looked back on a long history and forward to a second life in Europe. In this introduction we try to sketch in its present,

1. Vacarius, who had been a student and a teacher of law at Bologna, certainly came and taught in England, but there is now a doubt whether he lectured in Oxford: R.W. Southern, 'From Schools to University' in *The History of the University of Oxford*, vol.1, ed. J.I. Catto (Oxford 1984) 1,9-11.
2. 1453 is a coincidence. Constantinople fell to Mahomet II on 29th May 1453, the date traditionally taken to mark the beginning of the Renaissance. For the fourteen hundred years of legal history, see the beginning of the pronouncement 'So great is the Providence' (the *Constitutio Tanta*) by which Justinian confirmed the *Digest* on 16th December 533. On this see n.4 and n.13, below.

past, and future. We start with Justinian in sixth century Constantinople.

1. The *Corpus Iuris Civilis*

Justinian became Emperor in Constantinople in 527 at the age of 45. He reigned to the great age of 83, dying in November 565. He was born Petrus Sabbatius, in the part of Macedonia now in Yugoslavia, at Caričin Grad (*Justiniana Prima*) near Niš. His mother tongue was Latin. He rose to power under his uncle Justin I, emperor from 518 to 527 and took the name Justinian as his uncle's adopted son. He was determined to achieve greatness, zealous, unsophisticated, devoted. 'Justinian liked his labours to be noticed. He worked long hours and, presumably suffering from insomnia, often at night. Sleepless so that his subjects might sleep, he took on himself their cares that they might live without care. The aristocratic ideals of leisure and elegance he did not share. Himself austere, he expected others to work hard, produce results and abstain from enriching themselves. Not suffering fools gladly, Justinian hurried and chivvied his associates.'[3] The determination to be great and the absence of all restraint on self-congratulation are both apparent in the pronouncement 'Imperial Majesty' which promulgated, and forms the preface to, the *Institutes*.[4] Where were his energies directed? The popular mind retains his reconquest of the collapsed western empire, his buildings, in particular the great cathedral of St. Sophia, and not least his love for Theodora. Once an actress, even a prostitute, about whom Procopius could say nothing bad enough, the Empress became a pillar of respectability and power. But it is not so widely known that two less glamorous fields absorbed him. First, theology. All his life he wrestled to reconcile the factions of the early church. With characteristic lack of sensitivity, he combined an irenic theological ingenuity with the fiercest extirpation of stubborn heresy.

Next, law. Working through what we in Britain would recognize as Royal Commissions, Justinian saved and transformed the Roman law library. He compacted it. One can speak of a pocket law library, if 'pocket' is used as of battleships. Luck or skilled choice allowed Justinian to work through good agents. His achievements in war were won through the great generals Belisarius and Narses. In the law he relied on the genius of his minister Tribonian. An enthusiast and a brilliant administrator, Tribonian was also deeply learned in the law. Honoré, salvaging his reputation, makes him, despite his florid style, the worthy inheritor of the classical tradition: 'The last Roman jurist, his was the hand which preserved and renewed Rome's lawyers and its laws.'[5]

Nowadays the law library that Justinian and Tribonian saved can all be bought in three fat volumes. The print is small. It gives the right impression to think of three Bibles. That slightly understates the size. These three great volumes together make up what has come to be called the *Corpus Iuris Civilis*, literally 'The Body of the Civil Law'. 'Civil' here is a synonym for 'Roman'. This needs to be explained.

Lawyers still use the word in different oppositions, 'civil' as opposed to 'criminal', or to 'common', or to 'canon'. In the first of these the word 'civil' is a synonym for 'private', and denotes the law whose activation is left to the initiative of the individual citizen. So, crimes are wrongs which society pursues, taking action through some representative, sometimes an official, sometimes any member of the public; civil wrongs are those for which the victim must bring his own action, if he can and will. In the next opposition, between civil law and common law, 'civil' again means 'of or pertaining to a citizen' but this time with 'Roman' understood. 'Citizen' is *civis* in Latin, giving the adjective *civilis*. Henry VIII founded regius chairs of civil law. Experts and professors in Roman law are still called civilians, and Roman-based legal systems are referred to as civilian systems. English law, the mother of the other great family of western legal systems, is also called the common law. From early times the king's judges drew a distinction between the royal law which was 'common' to the whole realm and the law peculiar to a shire or other locality. Common law thus came to mean the law of England. That is how the contrast between 'civil' and 'common' expresses the difference between Roman and English law. Finally, civil law and canon law. Canon law is the law of the church. For centuries the only scholarly interest in law was in Roman law and canon law, and the highest academic distinction was to be a doctor of both laws, *utriusque iuris*. But now the contrast between civil law and canon law for the most part evokes only the difference between secular law and church law, rather than between specifically Roman law and church law. Besides these three pairs, there are further oppositions within Roman law itself. There the civil law, the *ius civile*, is the part of the law peculiar to one state (*civitas*) as opposed to the part common to all peoples, the *ius gentium*; or, in a different opposition, the part of the law derived

---

3. T. Honoré, *Tribonian* (London 1978) 22. The attributes are taken directly from the sources: ibid., notes 228-234.
4. Below, pp. 32-33. The pronouncements commissioning and confirming the parts of the *Corpus Iuris* are known by their opening words. This one in Latin is the *Constitutio Imperatoriam*.
5. Honoré, *op. cit.* n.3 above, 256.

from statute and juristic utterance in contrast with that part of the law based on the edict of a magistrate, especially the urban praetor. In these internal oppositions we decided, not without long debate, to translate *ius civile* as 'state law' or 'law of the state'. Against this was the long-standing convention in favour of 'civil law' and the slightly anachronistic ring to the word 'state'; but for it was the fact that 'civil law' has ceased to convey any message at all about the rationale behind the terminology.[6]

Novels, Codex, and Digest

The three volumes of the compacted Roman library, the *Corpus Iuris Civilis*, actually include four works, because the *Institutes* and the *Digest* are bound together. The other two are the *Codex* and the *Novels*. The *Institutes* is by far the smallest of these. The *Digest* is the biggest. It is about one and a half times the size of the Bible. The *Institutes* is one twentieth of that size.

We need not spend time on the *Novels*. They were not an original part of Justinian's great plan to remake the law library. The *Novels* are the new pronouncements of the Emperor, those which he made after the work of his commissions was complete. Most of them are in Greek. Some represent major innovations, departing from the law of the *Digest* and *Codex*. For example the law of marriage is thoroughly Christianized and codified.[7] The *Novels* now exist in a collection which was made privately. It includes legislation of some of Justinian's successors. Justinian himself had probably intended that an official collection should be made, but he never carried the plan through.

Next, the *Codex*. This is often misleadingly anglicized as the *Code*. It is better to use the Latin form. If the name were translated it would, like the Bible, become simply *The Book*. We are brought up with '*liber*' as the word for book, perhaps with '*volumen*' also in the background. Those words represent the book still in the inconvenient form of a scroll, tiresome to store and ill-adapted to quick reference. Lawyers, like theologians, often need not so much to read continuously as to search for authority. Before computers and before printing, the *codex*, the book with a spine and pages, was the first great revolution in information storage and retrieval. These books came into general use in the third century.[8] The form was much older, but the

materials held it back. Wooden pages laced together, with a waxed writing surface, served well enough for accounts, notes, or wills. Thickness limited length. Sewable parchment made possible the modern book. Even then, conservatism held the development back. The source of law dominant as the *codex* began to take over, and with no literary form of its own in the age of the scroll, was the word of the Emperor himself. Consequently the *codex* was the natural and only form for a collection of imperial utterances. In the law the word, standing alone, came to signify such a collection.

Another inconvenient anglicization needs to be mentioned here. The generic term for imperial utterances on the law is, in Latin, '*constitutio*', from the verb '*constituere*', meaning 'to decide' or 'establish'. Generations of lawyers have therefore called the emperors' determinations 'constitutions'. But this English word now refers so strongly and unequivocally to the body of rules which establishes the structure of a state or other association that we have abandoned it. The vocabulary at the end explains that we have taken 'pronouncement' as the generic term for imperial utterances. Justinian's *Codex* is a collection of imperial pronouncements.

The *Codex* which we have is the second edition. The first does not survive. It was prepared as the first stage of the plan, by a commission whose chairman was John of Cappadocia. Tribonian was a member but not chairman. John's commission was set in motion on 13th February 528, and the lost first edition was promulgated hardly more than a year later, on 7th April 529.[9] 'Imperial Majesty' refers to the successful imposition of order on the chaos in which the pronouncements were found. The task was helped by the fact that there were three earlier collections, two private ones from the reign of Diocletian (284-305), the *Codex Gregorianus* and the *Codex Hermogenianus*, which between them included pronouncements from 196 to 294, and the official collection ordered by Theodosius II and completed in 438, the *Codex Theodosianus*. John's commission had to reduce these, together with the pronouncements between 438 and Justinian's own reign, into a single volume. References in the *Institutes* to 'our *Codex*' are to the lost first edition. The second edition was produced after the *Digest* and *Institutes*. It was promulgated on 16th November 534.[10] New imperial pronouncements, especially the *Fifty Rulings* designed to settle disputes in the classical

---

6. Vocabulary, s.v. State Law.
7. Novel 22. This huge enactment has 48 substantial sections.
8. The *codex* appears to have been a Roman invention. It achieved parity with the roll about AD 300. C.H.Roberts and T.C. Skeat, *The Birth of the Codex* (London 1983) 15-35,75.
9. Its pronouncements, namely 'These matters which needed'

(*Constitutio Haec quae necessario*) of 13th February 528 and 'The chief safeguard' (*Constitutio Summa*) of 7th April 529, are prefaced to the second *Codex*, before its own 'It is always close to our heart' (*Constitutio Cordi*) of 16th November 534.
10. By *Cordi*, see preceding note.

law, had overtaken John's first edition. The work was done by a sub-committee of the Digest Commission, headed by Tribonian himself. The second edition of the *Codex Justinianus* marked the end of the great work. As we have said, the *Novels* were still to follow, but they were collected privately. But we have now run past the *Digest* itself.

The *Digest* or *Pandects* is the largest of the works. It preserves the writings of the classical jurists. Nearly everything in the book was more than three hundred years old when Justinian's commission sat. Some forty per cent of the *Digest* was taken from Ulpian, who was murdered in the summer of 223.[11] The name 'Pandects' is Greek and signifies the work's comprehensiveness – it shows everything. 'Encyclopaedia', another Greek word but one which has become English, is a good translation.[12] The name 'Digest', from the verb '*digerere*', signifies distribution under titles. If you open the work at random, you see immediately that the matter distributed under titles consists of extracts from juristic works, each extract carefully labelled with the name of the jurist and the title of the work from which it is taken. So the *Digest* is in effect an anthology of excerpts, much as though we were to make an encyclopaedia of law using scissors and paste to take extracts from the law reports and leading textbooks.

There are four hundred and thirty-two titles in the *Digest*, but they are divided up into fifty books. In Book 18 the first title is 'The Contract of Sale'. That title has eighty-one fragments, some of only a line or two, others of nearly a whole page. For example, D.18.1.28 is labelled 'Ulpian, Book 41 on Sabinus' and it says, very shortly, 'There is no doubt that a man can sell something belonging to another. The thing is indeed bought and sold, but it can be taken away from the buyer.' Then D.18.1.29 gives another excerpt, again from Ulpian but this time from the forty-third book of his commentary on Sabinus. The entire work is built up in this way, with nothing added by way of connecting commentary. In fact nothing at all is added by Justinian's commissioners, except to tidy up or abbreviate the excerpt, or occasionally to adjust it. Justinian authorized these alterations or, as they are usually called, interpolations. But early in this century the extent of doctrinal alterations was being hugely exaggerated. The pendulum has swung away from those excesses.

It is not clear whether Justinian had already decided to commit the necessary resources to the *Digest* project when he gave the order for the *Codex* in 528, or even when he began settling disputed points in 530 in the *Fifty Rulings*. At all events he gave the go-ahead on 15th December 530, when he appointed a commission under Tribonian. The members were Constantinus, a minister; Theophilus and Cratinus, two law professors from the capital; Dorotheus and Anatolius, two law professors from the great law school of Beirut; and eleven barristers. Sixteen distinguished people in all. Almost exactly three years later, on 16th December 533, the pronouncement 'So great is the Providence' – in Latin, the *Constitutio Tanta*, named from its first word – brought the *Digest* into force with effect from 30th December.[13]

It is amazing that it was finished so soon, or at all. Like many huge and imaginative projects, it was the kind of task calculated to elicit a despairing 'If only it could be done!' Three million lines had to be read; twenty times the length of the *Digest* as we have it. 'Imperial Majesty' describes the works to be read as 'an ocean of learning' and seems to picture the commissioners passing like the escaping Israelites through a sea which continually threatened to overwhelm them.[14] Theodosius had planned the same project a century earlier but had abandoned it. But some people are not deterred by daunting projects. The key in this case is the combination of Justinian's determined pursuit of glory and Tribonian's devotion to the law and administrative genius.

An inspired piece of work by the German scholar Bluhme in 1820 revealed that the commission had divided the books into three piles and a small remainder, called ever since the Sabinian, Edictal and Papinian masses – the names are taken only from the first works in each mass – and the Appendix. More recently Honoré, with Tribonianic application, has attempted to prove the detailed working methods and membership of the three sub-committees suggested by the masses. It seemed at first as though he had successfully reconstructed their operations, day by day. But questions have since been raised, and the details may not stand.[15] In the nature of things, however, Honoré's outline must be right. We have to imagine Tribonian armed above all with a tight schedule and a filing system capable of holding the *Digest* in loose leaf. The excerpts did not end in the

---

11. T. Honoré, *Ulpian* (Oxford 1982) 40-41.
12. As in *The Digest of Justinian*, eds. T. Mommsen, P. Krüger, A. Watson (Pennsylvania 1985) vol.1, xxvii and lxv. This is cited hereafter as 'The Pennsylvania *Digest*.'
13. Cf.n.4 above. *Tanta* can now be found, with parallel translation, in the Pennsylvania *Digest*, vol.1, lv-lxiv.
14. Below, pp. 32-33.
15. Honoré's theory was originally stated in A.M. Honoré

and Alan Rodger, 'How the *Digest* commissioners worked' (1970) 87 *Z.S.S.* 246, and 'The distribution of *Digest* texts into titles' (1972) 89 *Z.S.S.* 351; also A.M. Honoré, 'The editing of the *Digest* titles' (1973) 90 *Z.S.S.* 262. This work was updated in *Tribonian*, *cit.* n.3 above, esp.139-186. But very radical criticisms have been made by D.J. Osler, 'The compilation of Justinian's *Digest*' (1985) 102 *Z.S.S.* 129.

waste-paper basket. They certainly would have done if the carpenters had not first turned a room in Constantinople into a system of pigeon-holes, four hundred and thirty-two for each sub-committee's flow of excerpts.

We have now introduced all the parts of the *Corpus Iuris* except the *Institutes* themselves. It may be helpful to deal with two common misconceptions before going on. First, these books are often referred to as a code. We have already seen that the word '*codex*' does not mean 'code' but 'book', here particularly a book of imperial pronouncements. That point is out of the way. Can the whole *Corpus Iuris* be called a code? The modern notion of codification supposes a systematic restatement of the law. The mind's eye sees it in the form of a statute, whose sections and sub-sections entirely displace the old materials. The words of a code are the words of the codifiers. Such a thing would not have had much future. Fortunately for us, especially in view of the stylistic standards of the time, that was not what Justinian and Tribonian attempted. Their achievement lay in producing a collection, a compacted law library. Interpolations and tidyings up aside, the words are the words of the original materials. The reception of Roman law in Europe cannot be understood as the reception of a code; a ready-made law library, by contrast, was gift which no society could easily reject.

The other misconception is of the relationship between *Codex* and *Digest*. We are used to dividing our sources between cases and statutes – that is, between interpretative sources and legislative sources. Also, we associate closely in our minds the ideas of sovereignty and of legislation. It is easy to suppose that the *Digest* is an anthology of interpretation and the *Codex* a collection of statutes. That is not right. This is not the place for close analysis. Let it be said that the legislator is the law-maker who can overtly change the law: he makes a value-judgment and, perceiving that a given rule would be good, makes that rule law; and the interpreter is the law-maker – we do not need to pretend his role is static – whose innovation is firmly restrained by the duty to explain his conclusions as consonant with existing legal authority. Although in England and in Scotland we allow the functions of interpretation and adjudication to be combined, we expect a separation of the powers of interpretation and legislation. Judges who become too dynamic, as some thought Lord Denning occasionally was as Master of the Rolls, attract a criticism which sums this up: they are accused of usurping the function of the legislature.

This doctrine cannot be forced on the Roman emperors. They could certainly legislate, but most of their pronouncements were written answers to questions raised by individuals who wanted to know how the law applied to their cases. These imperial answers were functionally continuous with the answers of the private jurists in classical times. They are given in the same spirit, applying the law, not making it. In the transitional period at the end of the second century and the beginning of the third we can see that the same jurists whose names we know were, anonymously, the draftsmen of the imperial replies.[16] The end of the classical period is, and perhaps is no more than, the withdrawal of the great names into the anonymity of the imperial chancery. The relationship between *Digest* and *Codex* is above all chronological. There is an overlap, but the broad truth is that the *Codex* is simply later. It represents the period when the emperor, at the head of a bureaucratic machine, monopolized both the legislative and the interpretative function.

The achievement of Justinian and Tribonian in relation to these larger volumes of the *Corpus Iuris*, especially the *Digest*, can be seen in two lights. They can be portrayed as saviours of the Roman law library, brilliantly carrying through a task which seemed intellectually and administratively impossible. We have already seen that Professor Honoré takes that position. Or they can be accused of intellectual vandalism, consigning great works to oblivion and preserving an anthology in which every fragment was bound to have the instability of any quotation taken out of context. Humanist scholars, determined in law as in letters and scripture to get back to the purity of the original sources, easily took this line. They condemned Tribonian as the destroyer, not the saviour, of the precious texts. That was less than fair. It is evident that the law faced an information crisis, from the number of texts and the discrepancies between them. Douglas Osler has recently shown that not even all the legal humanists assumed the anti-Tribonianist position. Guillaume Budé (1468-1540) saw the necessity of 'cutting back to the living flesh'. Indeed he thought that the same thing needed to be done again for his own times.[17]

Osler sums up Budé's views in 1508 thus: 'The problem facing Roman law in the time of Justinian, and that facing contemporary law, were thus one and the same; the pristine majesty of the law had been overwhelmed by a vast mass of juristic writings which served only to obscure the law. The mania for juristic writing was a kind of cancer... The conclusion was plain: Tribonian's work provided a model of what was required to solve the contemporary malaise in legal studies. What was needed was another Tribonian who would carry out a similar operation to treat the cancer of

---

contemporary legal writing.'[18] The mania for writing, the *libido scribendi*, has never abated. Justinian's answer was a compacted law library and a prohibition, ultimately vain, against all further commentary on it.[19] Nowadays the answer is new technology. For the moment the computer allows us to manage a library which has grown too large, and goes on growing.

The Institutes

Translated rather than anglicized, the name of the *Institutes* would be 'Introduction' or 'Basic Principles'. The Latin '*Institutiones*' comes from the verb '*instituere*', one of whose meanings is 'to teach'. Justinian also gave the book an alternative name, '*Elementa*'. This means much the same, though there is a hint of nourishment, the basic principles on which to grow. An equivalent modern title would be 'An Introduction to Law, or First Principles of Law'. It is a book for beginners, only one twentieth the size of the *Digest*. It cannot quite be called the first year course-book, because Justinian's revised system of legal education required first year students to do more. They also had to take in their first slice of the *Digest* itself.[20]

The pronouncement 'Imperial Majesty' which promulgated the *Institutes* is dated 21st November 533, almost a month before the confirmation of the *Digest*, but it tells how the *Institutes* was commissioned only when the *Digest* had been completed, which was in March of the same year. 'Imperial Majesty' also gives the names of the commissioners who did the work and, in outline, how it was done. The task was given to Tribonian himself and the two senior law professors who had served on the *Digest* commission, Theophilus from Constantinople, and Dorotheus from Beirut.[21] Theophilus later composed a rather longer Greek version of the work, the *Paraphrase*.

The pages of the *Institutes* look different from those of the *Digest*. They do not look like a patchwork of extracts. Each title appears to be a single continuous essay. But in fact, though the *Digest*'s careful attributions have been dispensed with, the method of composition is the same, subject to two differences. First, the decision to create the impression of a continuous text must have involved rather more management of the extracts. Secondly, many Justinianic reforms are brought into the text. They stick out like baroque additions to classical buildings. The essential point is that *Institutes* were not a new invention of Justinian and Tribonian but rather an established classical genre. What was wanted was a new edition. The main contributor, both of the substance and the overall structure, was the second century jurist Gaius. 'Imperial Majesty' calls him '*Gaius noster*', 'our own Gaius'. More will be said about him below, though little is known of the man as opposed to the work. Tribonian and the two professors also drew on *Institutes* written by Marcian, Florentinus, Ulpian, and Paul. They were not limited specifically to *Institutes*. They also used Gaius' *Everyday Law* and other classical commentaries.

How did they go about the work? When he produced his edition in 1868, Huschke argued that Tribonian himself had taken a back seat.[22] He had delegated the work on the first two books and the very last title, on crime, to one professor, the rest to the other. Huschke thought that Dorotheus was probably responsible for the first stint, Theophilus for the second. The *Paraphrase*, though in Greek, provides some check on Theophilus' thought and style. Huschke's case was built up from arguments which seemed to evidence different hands in each half of the book. He thought he could detect higher colour in the modern parts of the first half, more moderation in the second, and a stronger tendency to cite the exact words of Justinian's pronouncements in the second part. He also listed repetitions in the second part of matter already handled in the first, suggesting one editor ignorant of the other's work, and internal references that never crossed the line between the two halves. Recently Honoré has shown that, while Huschke may have been right for the preparation of a first draft, he was wrong to keep Tribonian out of the limelight. Tribonian edited the draft, and it was he who modernized it by working in the Justinianic

---

18. Ibid., 201-202.

19. 'In a legal proceeding and any other contested matter where laws are applicable, let no one seek to quote or produce anything except from the aforesaid *Institutes* and our *Digest* and the *constitutiones* composed or promulgated by us, unless he wishes to be subjected to a charge of falsehood as a forger, together with the judge who permits such things to be heard...Now there is one thing which we decided from the outset...no one, of those who are skilled in the law at the present day or shall be hereafter, may dare to append any commentary to these laws, save only insofar as he may wish to translate them into the Greek language...But we do not permit them to put forward other interpretations – or rather, perversions – of the laws, for fear lest their verbosity may cause such confusion in our legislation as to bring some discredit on it. This happened in

the case of the commentators on the Perpetual Edict, who, although the compass of that work was moderate, extended it this way and that to diverse conclusions and drew it out to an inordinate length...If any should presume to do such a thing, they themselves are to be made subject to a charge of fraud, and moreover their books are to be destroyed' *Constitutio Tanta* 19,21, cf. *Constitutio Deo Auctore* 12: *Pennsylvania Digest*, vol.1, xlviii-xlix, lxii-lxiii. This quotation is taken from that translation (G.E.M. de Ste Croix).

20. Justinian's scheme for legal education is set out in the pronouncement 'That the whole body of the law' (*Constitutio Omnem*): *Pennsylvania Digest*, li.

21. Below, p.16.

22. P.E. Huschke, *Imperatoris Justiniani Institutionum libri quattuor* (Leipzig 1868) preface.

reforms and the highly coloured laudation of the Emperor, and himself.[23] Honoré's main instrument is stylistic analysis. He tests the passages which refer to Justinian against a profile of Tribonian's style and finds that they fit. His conclusions also match what he calls 'the political and psychological setting'.[24] It is obvious that the brilliant and energetic Tribonian was not a retiring scholar. He must have had the kind of central, propagandist role that Honoré gives him. The account of a first draft made by the two professors, taking half each, subsequently polished and modernized by Tribonian, the mastermind of the entire operation, is completely convincing.

The Institutional Scheme

The success and subsequent influence of the *Institutes* spring above all from their having found a way of achieving a bird's eye view of the law. It is not something to which we pay much attention these days. We throw courses at the student, and at the end the whole law will be for him the list of courses which he took, set in a rather larger list of options that he might have taken if he had chosen differently. Some courses on the list owe their place precisely to the Justinianic scheme; but, especially in common law countries, we tend to treat the list as a random one. We do not spend much time relating one part with another. When pressed to do it, even common lawyers tend to fall back on Justinian, often without knowing it. Two points about this scheme will be dealt with more fully below. One is the strength of its grip on the law of modern Europe. The other is the proper credit for it. Unless he too had predecessors whom we do not know, it was Gaius, not Justinian, who invented it. The first task is to describe it.

Like many great intellectual advances, the institutional scheme looks extremely simple. It starts from a trichotomy: all the law is about persons, things, or actions. The *Institutes* is in four books. But conceptually the division into four means nothing. It is the division into three which matters. The law of things occupies the whole of books 2 and 3, also the first part of book 4. So persons have one book, things two books and a third, actions two thirds of a book. Before even the law of persons is begun there is a short preface, which deals, rather blandly and briefly, with some jurisprudential generalities and with the sources of law. Also outside the three main parts, or perhaps tacked on, though awkwardly, to actions, is the very last title, on crime.

The heads of the trichotomy are divided and sub-divided. Persons are free or slaves. Free persons are either free-born or freed, and either independent or dependent. Independent persons either have guardians or supervisors or they are completely their own masters. The divisions and sub-divisions do not always make a perfect pyramid, but the order is always coherent. At its best the system can achieve quite remarkable feats of location and classification. A single example, fully worked through, illustrates this much better than a general description. Since in giving this example we shall for the first time have to refer to many passages in the *Institutes*, it may be helpful to draw attention to the explanation of the mode of citation in the paragraph which introduces the vocabulary at the end of this book.

Loans of Money: Their Place in the Institutional Scheme

Suppose, for example, that you borrow a sum of money. This in Roman law is an example of the loan called *mutuum*. English is weak in the vocabulary of lending and borrowing. It fails to distinguish between the loan which expects the same thing back, my pen or my umbrella, and the loan which expects the return in the same kind and quality, a pint of milk, half a dozen eggs, or such and such a sum of money. In Latin the loan of the pen is *commodatum*, of the milk or money *mutuum*.[25] Where does *mutuum* fit in the institutional scheme?

Mutuum is one of four contracts which are grouped together because they become binding by conduct, that is to say by the performance of the act identified by their names, which in each case is the delivery of a thing. They are usually called 'real contracts', using 'real' simply as an adjective formed from the Latin '*res*'. In Latin they are contracts '*re*', literally 'by a thing' or 'by a matter'. We think the matter referred to is the act identified by the name of the contract, not the thing delivered. 'Real' evades this issue. We translate '*re*' as 'by conduct', merely observing that, behind that, the conduct always entails the delivery of a thing.[26] At all events, the four are the two types of loan, *mutuum* and *commodatum*, deposit, where I give you something to keep for me and you do it not for reward but as a favour, and pledge, where I give you something, say a ring, as security for a debt. So, a loan of money is a *mutuum*, and a *mutuum* is one of four contracts classified together because their legal consequences flow from conduct, conduct

---

23. *Tribonian, cit.* n.3 above, 187-211, esp.201ff.
24. Ibid.,190.
25. J.3.14 pr,2.

26. Vocabulary, s.v. Obligation contracted by conduct. Cf. J.4.1 pr, where delictual actions are also said to arise '*ex re*', though there is no question of anything delivered.

which in each case consists in the delivery of a thing.

These in turn make up one of the four classes of contract which emerge when all contracts are classified by reference to the moment at which their legal consequences are triggered. The other three categories are contracts by words, by writing, and by mere agreement. All contracts require agreement. This fourfold classification shows that some become binding by agreement without more, some when the agreement is reduced to oral words, some when it is expressed in writing, some when the conduct principally envisaged by the contract actually takes place.[27] So, a loan of money is a *mutuum*, a *mutuum* is a contract by conduct, and contracts by conduct are one of four categories of contract which appear when contracts are sub-classified according to the events which actually make them binding.

On the next level contracts in their turn are a sub-class of obligations. Obligations also divide into four categories. The other three which co-ordinate with contracts are delicts or civil wrongs – which the common law calls torts – and a miscellany of other events which is reduced to two opaque and unsatisfactory categories, 'as though upon a contract' and 'as though upon a delict' or, more shortly, quasi-contract and quasi-delict.[28] These are the categories which emerge – though the fact is clouded by the unfortunate 'quasi' terminology – when obligations are classified by reference to their causative events, i.e. according to the facts by which they are triggered: contracts, wrongs, other events (other events then being reduced to quasi-contract and quasi-delict). What is an obligation? An obligation reduces your freedom. The metaphor of tying is inescapable. It is implicit in the word itself. '*Ligare*, to tie' gives us 'ligament', 'ligature', also 'liable'. In Justinian's definition the metaphor recurs several times. 'An obligation is a legal tie which binds us to the necessity of making some performance in accordance with the laws of our state.'[29] Without the metaphor one would have to say something like: 'An obligation supposes a relationship between two people such that one is under a duty to make a performance to the other and that other has a corresponding right to claim the performance.' The addition of words such as 'according to the laws of our state' serves to distinguish legal from merely moral obligations. In English it is certainly true that the word 'obligation' is oriented towards the

person under the duty. 'My obligation' supposes the speaker is bound, not entitled. The one entitled has a personal right – a right *in personam*, literally against a person. Stair puts this neatly: 'The same right, as it is in the creditor, it is called a personal right, but as it is in the debtor, it is called an obligation, debt, or duty...'[30] In Latin the orientation of the word is less clear. It seems to be able to comprehend the entire relationship, so that in theory '*mea obligatio*' could suppose a speaker entitled or bound, according to the context.

So obligations divided by their causative events produce four sub-classes: those from contracts, as though from contracts, from wrongs, and as though from wrongs. On the tier below, contractual obligations sub-divided on the same principle also produce four categories: contracts by conduct, by words, by writing, by mere agreement. Then, contracts by conduct break down, again into four: *mutuum*, *commodatum*, deposit, and pledge. And *mutuum* is the kind of loan involved when money is lent. But we are still some way from finding the place of a money loan on the whole map of the law. So far we have located it only in one detached region of the law, obligations.

How do obligations find a place in the overall trichotomy between persons, things, and actions? The answer is not obvious. The problem is solved by recognizing 'incorporeal things'. Corporeal things are easy. They are those which have a body and can be touched, a slave, silver, clothes, and so on. Incorporeal things are legal concepts.[31] If the owner of Blackacre has a right of way over neighbouring Whiteacre he owns no physical thing. The ground over which the track runs belongs to the owner of Whiteacre. The owner of Blackacre has an asset which cannot be touched or seen, simply an entitlement to cross Whiteacre. In Roman law such rights were called 'rights of lands' (*iura praediorum*) or 'servitudes'. They are one type of incorporeal thing. Obligations are another.

The difference between obligations and servitudes can be seen from the standpoint of the person entitled. A person entitled to a servitude – let us stay with the example of a right of way – has a real action, an action *in rem*.[32] Such an action asserts a relationship between plaintiff and thing. Here it simply affirms that the plaintiff has the right to cross Whiteacre. A person entitled to the benefit of an obligation has a personal action, an action *in personam*. Such an action asserts that a named defendant ought to make some performance

---

27. J.3.13.2; 3.22.

28. J.3.13.2; 3.27; 4.5. In the *Digest* Gaius appears to create the threefold classification – contracts, wrongs, other events – and then, himself, to break the miscellany into the two quasi categories: D.44.7.1, Gaius, *Everyday Law* or *Nuggets*, book 2; D.44.7.5, Gaius, *Everyday Law* or *Nuggets*, book 3.

29. J.3.13 pr.

30. J. Dalrymple, Viscount Stair, *Institutions of the Law of Scotland*, 1.3.1.

31. J.2.2.

32. J.4.6.1. Vocabulary, s.v. Action, real or personal.

in favour of the plaintiff. The crucial practical difference is that the plaintiff with the real action can obviously go against anyone who is preventing him from exercising his right, for the wording of the action recites a constituted relationship between him and Whiteacre, good against anyone and everyone. By contrast, the plaintiff with a personal action is limited by its very wording to a claim against the named defendant, the specific person who is under the duty to make the performance. The concepts involved in this distinction between real and personal, *in rem* and *in personam*, essentially the difference between owning and being owed, are not easy, but they are rooted in something which was originally simple and obvious. If you made a list of the early actions maintainable in the Roman courts, you would see at once from their wording that some were literally against things, not mentioning the defendant; and other actions were literally against persons. 'That cow is mine!' is literally and obviously *in rem*. My words are directed against the thing and do not mention you, my adversary, standing between me and the animal. 'You ought to give me 20!' is literally *in personam*. It is against you that I am pleading. There is of course a thing in view, the subject-matter of my claim, but only indirectly; my words reach that subject-matter only through you, only through your duty to do something in relation to it.

So the difference between a servitude and an obligation is that the man with a servitude has a real action, which makes his right exigible against anyone. A man entitled to the benefit of an obligation has a personal action, which makes his right exigible only against the person under the duty of making the performance. One secondary difference is also important in the history of the institutional scheme. In the real action the servitude is named: 'The right of crossing Whiteacre is mine!' Compare 'The cow Daisy is mine!' Though the right of way is incorporeal, it is a fairly obvious candidate to be aligned with Daisy as a 'thing'. But in a personal action nothing is said of an obligation. 'You ought to pay me 20!' No action ever said 'The obligation on you to pay 20 is mine!' So in personal actions there is no obvious incorporeal thing. To find one, you first have to make a brilliant leap. You have to see that if you could name the 'thing' that a plaintiff has when it is true of a defendant that he ought to make him some performance you would be able align the substance of all the personal actions with the 'things' named in the real actions. And then you have to find the name, obligation.

Obligations and servitudes are incorporeal things. Another example is *hereditas*, the right to inherit the estate of a deceased person. These incorporeal things co-ordinate with the corporeal things to make up the whole law of *res*, things. What is the sense of 'thing'? It is safe enough to think of the law of things as the law of property, if 'property' is taken widely as 'wealth' or 'assets'. Nowadays we usually take 'property' in a narrower sense. We notice that obligations on the one hand and all other things on the other are separated by the divide between *in personam* and *in rem*, and we think of the law of property as co-ordinated and contrasted with the law of obligations. In short we confine property to the *in rem* side of the line, excluding obligations. But the law of things in the *Institutes* includes obligations. It is the law of property in the widest sense.

We are now in a position to run through the institutional scheme from top to bottom, from the whole law right down to the loan of money. The whole law relates to persons, things or actions. Things – the law of assets, property in the large sense – divides between corporeal things and incorporeal things. Incorporeal things are servitudes, estates by inheritance, obligations. Obligations are divided by causative event, into those arising from contracts, quasi-contracts, wrongs, quasi-wrongs. Contracts divide on the same principle between those by conduct, by words, by writing, or by mere agreement. Contracts by conduct are *mutuum*, *commodatum*, deposit, pledge. And *mutuum* is the kind of loan involved when money is borrowed.

We have given this example in some detail. Standing alone it exaggerates the elegance of the scheme. It is not always so easy to pass smoothly across the map. Fragments of different patterns sometimes compete. Another warning is that the scheme, even this part of it, must not be regarded as above criticism. We have pointed out the misleading *quasi* categories in obligations, and the now strong line between obligations and the *in rem* part of the law of things. More radical criticisms have long been and still are in the field.

The Cradle of the Law

What the example does show is that the institutional goal was a map of the law. Justinian's own metaphor is a cradle of the law, *cunabula legum*. The idea of a cradle is right for a beginner's book, but there is more to it. There is also the idea of the law's being kept in, kept under control. The *Institutes* were to be the means of ordering the law library. This can only be understood by comparing the order of the *Institutes* with the lack of order in the *Digest* and the *Codex*. The four hundred and thirty-two titles in the *Digest* are not in carefully arranged genera and species. The order is pragmatic, inherited from the past, based ultimately on the praetor's edict, which was not

planned but simply grew. Matter which the *Institutes* group, and which then seems so obviously related, can be far apart in the *Digest*. For example, of the three main civil wrongs, theft, loss wrongfully caused, and contempt, the first and third are in book 47, but the second is in book 9. The role of the *Institutes* was to give the student a coherent framework. Once his mind was formed, he could expand this or that section at will. There was no need for the rest of the law library to be systematic. The enormous influence of the book is due to its having virtually monopolized that role ever since. As we shall see, some writers – Stair and Erskine in Scotland are fine examples – set out to combine the student's framework and the practitioner's library, writing on the scale of the *Digest* but using the orderly system of the *Institutes*.

Gaius, the Originator of the Institutional Scheme

Before we look forward to the book's European future, we must turn briefly to its classical past and, in particular, to the genesis of the genre. We have already observed that the *Digest* was made from works which were nearly all more than three hundred years old. They dated from the classical period, the age of the great names from Labeo (c.50 BC – AD 10), almost an exact contemporary of Augustus, to Ulpian, murdered in AD 223. There is an unending debate as to the precise qualities summed up in the word 'classical' as applied to law. The evaluation can be made from different standpoints. The law of the Principate does not score many points for social justice, political morality, or administrative efficiency. The relevant standpoint is intellectual. The qualities for which 'classical' stands are intellectual virtues, rationality, consistency, comprehensiveness. These are combined with merits which are chiefly matters of style, firm judgment, restraint, unfussy expression.

In the middle of the high classical period, though untypical of it, there lived the jurist known only by his first name, Gaius. Very little can be said of him except by inferences from his work. He lived from about 110 to 180, a contemporary of Pomponius, Africanus, and Scaevola, younger than Julian, a generation or so older than Papinian, Paul, and Ulpian. He is untypical because of his academic approach to law. He was interested in systematization and legal dogmatics. For this reason it has even been suggested that he should not be called classical. He also believed in the importance

of legal history, and he had equipped himself with the methods of Greek philosophy.[33] He also stands apart from the main stream in another way. He is not cited at all by his contemporaries and immediate successors. His fame came later, through the place he won in legal education: 'Gaius is in a true sense the architect of Justinian's codification. First, he is the teacher of the empire. He reaped the reward which comes to those who write simply. His works were known in the provinces of both East and West. Without a simple writer to whom to turn as guide, Roman law might well have been swamped or corrupted in the East, after the extension of the citizenship to all free citizens of the empire in AD 211, as it was in the West. It was Gaius more than anyone who kept it alive.'[34] In the fifth century the law of citations of Theodosius II gave special authority to the works of Papinian, Paul, Gaius, Ulpian, and Modestinus. These great law lords might have been surprised to find an academic in their midst. Justinian calls him '*Gaius noster*', 'our own Gaius', showing at the very least affection for the teacher who had become every lawyer's introduction to his subject.

There is reason to believe that Gaius had a special connexion with the provinces. One theory is that he came to Rome from the Hellenized east. Honoré thinks the movement was the other way, Rome first and then some peripatetic teaching in the east ending at Beirut.[35] If Gaius did end his career there, there may be extra depth in 'our own Gaius'. It is possible that he was involved in the establishment of the great law school at Beirut, from which Dorotheus and Anatolius were summoned to serve on Justinian's commission. But this is a speculation.

So far as we know, Gaius was the inventor of the institutional scheme and of the genre itself. His *Institutes*, written about AD 161 or perhaps revised then after having been long-standing lecture notes, were the first of their kind, and the structure we have been describing for Justinian is, with minor modifications, his. Gaius wrote many works, on the Twelve Tables, the urban edict, and the provincial edict. But his dominant place in legal education was due to his *Institutes*, a great part of which was taken into Justinian's edition by Theophilus and Dorotheus.[36]

Until 1816 we had, apart from the excerpts in the *Digest*, only a Visigothic précis of Gaius's *Institutes*, known as the *Epitome*. This entirely omitted the crucially important book 4, on actions. In 1816 Niebuhr found and Savigny identified an almost complete fifth century manuscript in the library of

---

33. A.M. Honoré, *Gaius* (Oxford 1962) 97 ff.
34. Ibid., 127.
35. Ibid., 70-96.
36. The text of Gaius's *Institutes* was divided by modern

editors into numbered paragraphs. Adding the paragraphs of all four books together there are 909. Of these 414 were taken into Justinian's edition.

the cathedral at Verona. The text had been overwritten with letters of St. Jerome and Gennadius. Later discoveries have filled some gaps, though in the meantime in the 1820s the Verona palimpsest was seriously damaged by the use of chemicals intended to improve its legibility. Nevertheless, Gaius' *Institutes*, having been so long lost, is now the only classical text to have come down to us independently of Justinian's commissioners.

Gaius's book 4 is crucial for two reasons. First, it gives a unique account of the classical and pre-classical forms of action. In Justinian's *Institutes* the bits of history which do survive are there by inertia or for propaganda. Gaius by contrast was genuinely interested in legal history and rightly believed it essential to a proper understanding of law.[37] This led him to give a full account not only of actions under the formulary system on which the classical law was founded, and which remained the normal procedure of his own time, but also of the earlier *legis actio* procedure, predecessor of formulary litigation with roots as far back as the Twelve Tables (c.450 BC). All this, even the part about the formulary system, became obsolete when the special imperial procedure, known as *extra ordinem* or *extraordinaria*, was generalized. That supercession of the Roman forms of action accounts for the much smaller space given to actions in Justinian's *Institutes*. Gaius gave them a whole book and had no appendix on crime. One critical difference between the formulary system and its successor was that under the formulary system the making of claims was still essentially a matter of choosing the right proposition from the models listed in the praetor's edict, whereas under the special judicature, as indeed today, there was no list of different pleadings but simply a general technique for making claims. Instead of choosing the ready-made proposition which he thought he could substantiate, the plaintiff had to tell his story and argue that those facts supported a claim at law. It was the change from a long list of claims to a single technique for claiming that lightened the weight of Justinian's law of actions. There are two slightly more technical ways of saying what had had happened. Using the model of a syllogism, it can be said that the formulary plaintiff began from the conclusion, while the plaintiff under the special judicature began from the minor premiss. Or, in language familiar to formulary pleaders, it can be said that the special judicature allowed everyone to plead *in factum*, on his case.

The second reason why book 4 is so important is that knowledge of the classical actions is not merely of interest for its own sake but essential for understanding the development of Roman law and of the institutional scheme itself. This is a question, above all, of understanding the evolving relationship between the law of actions and the substantive law represented in the institutional scheme by persons and things.

Gaius's law of actions is about pleading. A Roman plaintiff is the *actor*, and what he does is *agere*, giving the noun *actio*, his pleading or claim. The forms of action were prefabricated sets of words in which claims were made. If you wanted a brand new one, you could argue for it before the praetor, but in nine cases out of ten the plaintiff took his claim so to say off the peg, out of the edict of the urban praetor where models were displayed. The plaintiff had only to adjust details to fit his own facts. Let us keep to the earlier example of a loan for money. Your lawyer would know that if you proved the loan before a judge and showed that it had not been repaid, that would as a matter of law substantiate the words of the Roman action of debt, the *condictio*. The formula of that action, with the stock names of the parties, ran, 'Let Titius be judge. If it appears that Numerius Negidius ought to give 20 to Aulus Agerius, condemn Numerius Negidius to Aulus Agerius for 20; if it does not appear, exonerate him.'[38] Before the praetor you would ask for this formula. Before the judge you would show that you had advanced the money and had not been repaid. As a matter of law, your proof of these facts would substantiate the proposition implicit in the formula, 'The defendant ought to give me 20!' Other facts would also suffice, for instance stipulation, the old contract in writing described by Justinian as obsolete, mistaken payment, and a number of others. Anomalously, theft also gave rise to the *condictio*, as well as to the action for penal damages.[39]

This single example is enough to show how the law can be very fully expounded as nothing but a law of actions. If I set out the words of the action of debt and describe their scope — answering such questions as, Who may bring the claim? For what? On what facts? Against whom? — I shall in the end have explained a huge area of law. And then I can move on to another action, the action on sale, or for theft, or the *vindicatio* (which is the special name for the action for ownership) and so on, each time

---

37. 'Since I am aiming to give an interpretation of the ancient laws, I have concluded that I must trace the law of the Roman people from the very beginnings of their city. This is not because I like making extremely wordy commentaries but because I can see that in every subject a perfect job is one whose parts hang together properly. And to be sure the most important part of anything is its beginning' D.1.2.1, Gaius, *Twelve Tables*, book 1; cf. Honoré, *Gaius*, 106.

38. G.4.41,43. F. de Zulueta, *The Institutes of Gaius* (Oxford 1953, repr. 1963) part 2, 259; O. Lenel, *Das Edictum Perpetuum*, 3rd edition (Leipzig 1927) 237.

39. J.4.1.19(21); 4.6.14.

setting out the words and explaining the facts which substantiate them, the parties by and against whom they can be brought, and anything else relevant to winning or defeating that particular claim. When I have worked through the whole list of actions I shall have dealt with virtually the whole law. The action on sale begins 'Whereas Aulus Agerius sold the cow Daisy to Numerius Negidius...'[40] In expounding that clause I shall write, at whatever length I choose, on the law about the formation of the contract of sale. Does there have to be a price in money? What if the defendant gets up and says he gave, not money, but wine? Was Daisy still 'sold'? What if the price is left uncertain, to be fixed by a third party? What if the agreement is conditional? The answers to these questions can be found in the *Institutes*.[41] But, and this is the crucial point, they are not given in the law of actions as commentary on the first clause of the seller's pleading. The substance of the law has been separated from the action, and the law of actions thereby downgraded to be, not the whole law, but the law specifically about realizing rights in court. The abolition of the forms of action, allowing every plaintiff to plead his facts first and argue from the facts to his desired remedy, completes that process, turning the emphasis away from pleading to civil procedure generally.

Gaius' great achievement was to work out a classificatory system which not only allowed the substance of the law to be expounded out of its procedural envelopes but also arranged that separated substance in a coherent pattern, not just a jumble to be learned by heart. The difficulty of his task is almost impossible to recapture. It can be glimpsed in relation to the action of debt, the *condictio*. This action formed a large and well established legal category which could not be fitted easily into the scheme that Gaius decided would work best.

Most of the personal actions focused on a causative event, sale, hire, uninvited intervention, theft, and so on. We know that in relation to the substance of such actions, identified as obligations, Gaius chose to use a classification by causative events – contracts, wrongs, other events. This easily fitted the event-based actions, which only needed to be grouped under the appropriate heads. But the *condictio* was a unity of a completely different kind. It was the class of all claims arising from whatever causative event whose content was that the defendant ought to give a certain something. By a certain something is meant a specific thing or a fixed sum or quantity – the cow Daisy, so much money, or so many measures of wheat. This excludes services, such as a house to be built, clothes to be cleaned, and so on. It also excludes unliquidated sums of money such as 'the amount of my loss'. In short, the Roman action of debt was a unity based on the content of the plaintiff's claim, not on a single causative event. So Gaius, once he decided to classify by causative events, had to break up the *condictio*. He had to assign the various recognized causes of indebtedness to his new heads, *mutuum* and stipulation to contract, mistaken payment to the miscellany and thence to quasi-contract, and, in principle, theft to delict. These are examples from a longer list. It requires immense intellectual courage for a lawyer, even with logic on his side, to attack traditional categories in this way. To contemporary practitioners he will easily seem to be talking nonsense or, more charitably, to be speculating in a uselessly utopian way. The strain shows. Gaius had real trouble with mistaken payments. It still leaves a mark in Justinian's *Institutes*.[42] Another sign of the same tensions is a spectacular evasion. The action of debt against a thief, the *condictio furtiva* as opposed to the action for penal damages, is never expressly attributed to the delict column. But nor is it expressly put under quasi-contract. We are left to apply the logic of the categories, and we find it difficult to do.

Gaius is sometimes allowed only the merits of a good teacher, lucidity, order and so on. Honoré's biography is confessedly speculative, but his evaluation of the jurist is not. Honoré recognizes not only his lucidity but also his originality. Even that is perhaps too weak. The truth is that the inventor of the institutional scheme was a genius and deserves to be remembered as a Darwin among lawyers.

2. The *Institutes* and Modern Law

We turn to the strength of the *Institutes*' influence on the categories of modern legal thought. We have already mentioned the claim that it is the most influential law book ever written. Without attempting a historical explanation, we will give enough examples to show that at greater length that claim could be properly substantiated. For this purpose it is not necessary to tell even in outline the whole story of the revival and reception of Roman law in Europe. We deal with Scotland in some detail. It is our home jurisdiction, but also a fine example of the astonishing survival of the *Institutes*. After

---

40. G.4.40; de Zulueta, *loc. cit.* n.38 above; Lenel, *op. cit.* n.38 above, 299.

41. J.3.23 pr-2,4; G.3.139-141.
42. G.3.88-91; J.3.14 pr-1.

Scotland, we deal more briefly with evidence from Holland, France, and England.[43]

Scotland

'Lawyers inform us, that Law is the science *which teaches justice*, and that justice *is the constant and perpetual will to give every man his own*. They also say that law teaches us to cultivate this will by *living honestly, injuring no one, and giving every man his own*. Such is the law explained by lawyers. But law is not accustomed to figure on such lofty ground as this: for, in the first place, unfortunately for the science which the law professes to teach, man is completely the master of his own will, and the sort of will, of which it is in general his pleasure to make his choice, is not precisely that constant and perpetual will to give everyone his own, which law would inculcate, but rather a pretty constant and perpetual will to the contrary, that is, to keep all that he can. Then, in the second place, the want of the will to do what is just is in general the principal obstacle to the practice of justice, no man having an honest desire to act justly being ever much at a loss to know what it is that he ought to do.'

These are the opening words of a book of no importance, *The Pocket Lawyer*, published in Edinburgh in 1830.[44] Across a gap of thirteen hundred years, the anonymous author's scepticism is still directed at the high-flown sentiments at the beginning of Justinian's *Institutes*. Moreover, the two hundred and fifty pages of *The Pocket Lawyer* follow without acknowledgment the whole pattern of Justinian's scheme. Generalities under 'What is law?' precede pages 16 to 32 on persons, 53 to 97 on things, 197 to 245 on actions. The structure is not sign-posted in any way, and there is no division into four books. There are departures in matters of detail. The law of obligations loses its conceptual integrity; the law of civil wrongs is omitted altogether; game laws, salmon fishings, and company stock find not always easily explained places. But despite the adjustments and innovations, anyone who knows the *Institutes* can see it throughout. Sometimes it breaks the surface. For instance, the Post Office is met in a section that begins with 'shipmasters, innkeepers, stablers, masters of steam-boats, and carriers, whether by cart, mail, or stage-coach'.[45]

It is the unimportance of *The Pocket Lawyer* that shows the strength of the *Institutes*' survival. If we ask why in 1830 a little book aimed chiefly at

landowning gentry should have rested so plainly on a Justinianic foundation, the immediate answer is to be found in Erskine. The chair of Scots law in the University of Edinburgh was founded, twelve years after the chair in civil law, in 1722. John Erskine of Carnock was its second holder. He succeeded Alexander Bayne in 1737 and held the chair till 1765. In 1754 he published his *Principles of the Law of Scotland*. That work became the leading university textbook on Scots law. It went through twenty-one editions. The last, by Sir John Rankine in 1911, ran to 812 pages of text. Erskine devoted his last years to a much larger work, which appeared posthumously. This was *An Institute of the Law of Scotland*, published in 1773, five years after Erskine's death. Both the *Principles* and the *Institute* avowed on their title pages that they followed the order of Sir George Mackenzie's *Institutions of the Law of Scotland*. Mackenzie's little book, somewhat shorter even than Justinian's, had been published first in 1684 and was the leading student's introduction till it was displaced by Erskine's *Principles*.

These three books, Mackenzie's *Institutions* (1684), Erskine's *Principles* (1754), and Erskine's *Institute* (1773), all follow very closely the pattern of Justinian. It will be enough to look briefly at the last and largest of them. We noticed earlier that the institutional trichotomy has a beginning and end outside itself. Erskine's *Institute* has the same top and tail: crime occupies the last title in book 4; the first four of book 1 are given to jurisprudence and history, and then, expanding Justinian's treatment of sources, to a description of the constitution and legal system. After these introductory chapters the rest of book 1 deals with persons. The inclusion here of 'ecclesiastical persons' provides a peg for extensive treatment of the organization and rights of the church. Also included in the law of persons, replacing the old law of slavery, is the discussion of the law of master and servant, which we nowadays think of as a matter of contract, albeit much regulated, rather than of personal status.

Book 2 of Erskine's *Institute* begins: 'After having explained the legal powers, offices, and duties, of persons, which are the first objects of the law, the method proposed...naturally leads to the consideration of things, which are its second object, and to the setting forth their different kinds and legal properties.' Erskine's 2.1 then follows on

---

43. In relation to this section the reader will find especially helpful the following: (i) J.W. Cairns, 'Institutional Writings in Scotland Reconsidered' in *New Perspectives in Scottish Legal History*, eds. A. Kiralfy and H.L. MacQueen (London 1984) 76; (ii) J.W. Cairns, 'Blackstone, An English Institutist: Legal Literature and the Rise of the Nation State' (1984) 4 *Oxford Jo. Leg. St.* 318; (iii) J.W. Cairns, 'The Formation of the Scottish Legal Mind in the Eighteenth Century' in *The Legal Mind*, eds. D.N. MacCormick and P. Birks (Oxford 1986) 253; (iv) K.

Luig, 'The Institutes of National Law in the Seventeenth and Eighteenth Centuries' (1972) 17 *Jur. Rev.* 193; (v) A. Watson, *The Making of the Civil Law* (Cambridge, Mass. 1981) 62-82; (vi) A. Watson, 'Justinian's *Institutes* and Some English Counterparts' in *Studies in Justinian's Institutes*, eds. P.G. Stein and A.D.E. Lewis (London 1983) 181-186.
44. Published anonymously but by Alexander Macallan.
45. Ibid., 133.

closely parallel to Justinian's. But his law of things, which takes the whole of books 2 and 3, is differently organized. The differences of organization, no less than content, are ultimately due to the impact of feudalism on land law and succession. The main organizational difference is that the dominant distinction has to be between heritable and moveable property. Erskine also finds it convenient to bring obligations forward, dealing with them before succession. Book 3 thus begins with obligations in titles 1 to 6. It is followed by a thorough discussion of prescription, a subject postponed from book 2 – 'In treating of the several ways of acquiring rights, we delayed explaining the doctrine of prescription, because it is also a way of losing rights or obligations'. This digression is followed by three long titles on succession. In Justinian, by contrast, succession occupies the second half of book 2 and the first half of book 3, and obligations spill over from the latter part of book 3, so that delictual and quasi-delictual obligations fall in the first part of book 4.

Within Erskine's treatment of obligations, delict – he calls it 'delinquency' – appears very briefly and before contract. This new position of delict reflects Erskine's attempt to borrow some of Stair's re-classification of obligations, dispensing with the two misleading and uninformative Roman categories, 'as though from contract' and 'as though from delict'. The exiguous treatment of delict, as opposed to its new place, is more difficult to explain. In his *Principles* Erskine found no place at all for that category of obligations, unless you count one glancing reference to 'private crimes' in his final title. In the twentieth century this seems extraordinary, since actions for civil wrongs, especially for negligence, have become a centre of attention in the law reports and legal journals.

Erskine ultimately gave way to Gloag and Henderson. Their *Introduction to the Law of Scotland*[46] is this century's representative of Scottish institutional literature.[47] It seems on the face of things to have abandoned the Justinianic scheme. There is no division into four books, and the succession of chapters looks at first sight miscellaneous. But in fact blocks of the Roman scheme still survive. Sources and system still come first, and crime last. Obligations have been promoted to the front of the book, immediately after the introductory chapters. There the Roman head of quasi-contract still follows contract; and delict, divided between reparation and defamation, still follows contract and quasi-contract. This Justinianic sequence is partly concealed by the decision to place chapters

on specific contracts after rather than before quasi-contract. So there is a loop back into contracts before delict is reached. Company law is dealt with here. One of the specific contracts is partnership, and companies are handled parasitically upon partnerships. An alternative strategy is to treat companies under persons, on the ground that a company has legal personality. Like a natural person, it is an entity capable of bearing rights and duties.

After obligations Gloag and Henderson turn to property, making the division between heritable and moveable, and dividing moveables between corporeal and incorporeal. Succession, intestate and testate, follows. Then, in its proper institutional place but expanded to reach charitable trusts and holding by associations, the law of trusts concludes the block which represents the second institutional division, the law of things. The book then deals with persons: husband and wife, parent and child, guardians. There is nothing explicitly on actions, but before the final chapter on crime two on process and execution and on proceedings in bankruptcy are vestiges of the third institutional division. If Justinian's order is sources, persons, things (property, succession, obligations), actions, crime, Gloag and Henderson can be seen in the twentieth century to have done barely more than re-order his blocks: sources, things (obligations, property, succession), persons, actions (much reduced by the decision to omit civil and criminal procedure altogether), crime.

The re-ordering used by Gloag and Henderson since 1927 owes something to the innovations attempted by the greatest of Scots institutional writers, James Dalrymple, Viscount Stair. We have already seen how from the seventeenth to the nineteenth century the Justinianic scheme was made dominant by successive editions of Mackenzie and Erskine. Stair was a contemporary of Mackenzie. His great book came out first in 1681, with an expanded edition in 1693. It is the 1693 edition of the *Institutions of the Law of Scotland* which is now used, a fact brought home by the choice of the 1693 text for the tercentenary edition in 1981.[48] Despite the identical title, Stair's work is quite different from Mackenzie's. Mackenzie remained entirely true to Justinian's pedagogic purpose. Indeed his preface, invoking Euclid's *Elements*, proclaimed an intention to outdo Justinian in reducing the framework of first principle to bare essentials. Stair's book, like Erskine's *Institute* later, is not elementary or short. It derives its inspiration for good order from the *Institutes*; in bulk it more

---

46. Now in its eighth edition, eds. A.B. Wilkinson and W.A. Wilson (Edinburgh 1980). A new edition is in preparation.

47. On a larger scale but in the same tradition are the four volumes of D.M. Walker's *Principles of Scottish Private Law*, 3rd

edition, (Oxford 1982).

48. J. Dalrymple, Viscount Stair, *The Institutions of the Law of Scotland*, Tercentenary Edition, ed. D.M. Walker (Edinburgh and Glasgow 1981).

resembles the *Digest*. But Stair also differed from Mackenzie and Erskine in seeking not merely to borrow but to improve Justinian's scheme. In this his work closely resembles that of his great French contemporary Jean Domat (1625 – 1696). Admirable for their independence and intellectual power, his variations nevertheless failed for the most part to win a permanent following. Stair introduced his plan in these words:

'The Roman law taketh for its object Persons, Things, and Actions, and according to these, orders itself, but these are only the extrinsic object and matter, about which the law and right are versant. But the proper object is the right itself, whether it concerns persons, things, or actions: and, according to the several rights and their natural order, the order of jurisprudence may be taken up in a threefold consideration, First, In the constitution and nature of rights; Secondly, in their conveyance, or translation from one person to another, whether it be among the living or from the dead; Thirdly, in their cognition, which comprehends the trial, decision, and execution of every man's right by the legal remeids.'[49]

In practice Stair's programme involved two major departures from Justinian's order. He dispensed with a separate law of persons; and he enlarged, reclassified, and repositioned the law of obligations. Stair's fourth book, added in the second edition, is still actions, though without the tailpiece on crime. His first three books take the subject-matter of the law of things in a new order – obligations, property, succession. He makes explicit and dominant the Aristotelian division of obligations between voluntary and involuntary or, in his terms, conventional and obediential. Taking obediential obligations first, he starts with those which inhere in different personal conditions, husbands and wives, parents and children, guardians and wards. In this way his repositioned law of obligations does in fact cover, and in its normal place immediately after the the introductory matter, the contents of the law of persons. Stair then divides the rest of the obediential obligations in such a way as to avoid the misleading 'quasi' categories into which Justinian grouped all obligations arising neither from contract nor from delict. That exercise needed doing, and Stair's innovation here has had some enduring success. Overall, however, Stair's reclassification of obligations is open to the objection that it fails to adopt a single basis. Gaius and Justinian focused on the events which give rise to obligations. Stair's categories look now to those causative events, now to the content of the

obligations, now to a personal status to which the obligation attaches. 'A good, distinct division'[50] should not risk the logical traps which lie between badly aligned categories.

These paragraphs do scant justice to Stair's attempt to improve the institutional scheme. They are enough to show that even when the pattern of the *Institutes* is not directly borrowed it survives in the shadows as the scheme against which the author has reacted. Stair's order can only be understood in terms of the strengths and weaknesses of Justinian's. Much the same might still be said of the list of courses which make up the syllabus in a modern law school. Stair's aim was not to impose Roman law on Scotland but to raise the level of Scots law as an intelligible discipline. He wrote in English, not Latin. He drew from Roman law a standard of order, rationality and detail. It was a secondary matter that the Roman materials also constituted a corpus of learning on which to draw where domestic authority was deficient.

Holland

If we move from Stair's Scotland to the Holland of Grotius earlier in the same century we can see the same thing. For Grotius the Roman law library is also, on matters of substance, a source of authority lying behind the Dutch materials.

'When no general written laws, privileges, by-laws or customs were found touching the matter in hand, the judges were from times of old admonished by oath to follow the path of reason according to their knowledge and discretion. But since the Roman laws, particularly as codified under Justinian, were considered by men of understanding to be full of wisdom and equity, these were first received as patterns of wisdom and equity and in course of time by custom as law.'[51]

Born in 1583 Grotius was a prodigy in humanist learning, much as Mozart in music. But his glittering career as a classical scholar, lawyer and statesman was brought to an abrupt halt when he was arrested by Prince Maurice for treason. That was in 1618. He was sentenced to imprisonment for life and incarcerated in the castle of Loevestein on 6th June 1619. His scholarship remained. He was allowed books. And on 22nd March 1621 a plan devised by his wife allowed him to escape hidden in the trunk in which books were brought to him. During his imprisonment, when others might have been paralysed by despair, he wrote, in Dutch, his *Introduction to the Jurisprudence of Holland*,[52] ostensibly

---

49. *Institutions* 1.1.23.
50. Stair's own words, *Institutions* 1.3.2.
51. *Inleiding* 1.2.22. See next note.

52. This is better known as the *Inleiding*. The full Dutch title is *Inleiding tot de Hollandsche Rechtsgeleertheyd*. We have used the parallel translation by R.W. Lee (Oxford 1923, revised 1953).

for the instruction of his sons. The threat of pirated editions led him to allow its publication in 1631. It became a classic, the basis for lectures given by others and the foundation of Roman-Dutch law.

The *Introduction* has no fourth book, nothing on actions. Apart from that the order of treatment is taken directly from the *Institutes*. The names of many titles are borrowed. Much terminology is carried over into the nearest Dutch equivalent. After two introductory titles – 'Of Jurisprudence and Justice' and 'Of Different Kinds of Laws and their Operation' – Grotius devotes the rest of his book 1 to persons, all of book 2 to property and succession, and all of book 3 to obligations. This executes a plan stated at 1.3.1: 'In order to understand the rights of persons to things, since law exists between persons, to whom the right belongs, and between things, over which the right extends, we must treat first of the legal condition of persons, secondly of the legal condition of things.' His division between book 2 and book 3 allows obligations a greater independence than in the *Institutes*. It is a frequent, though not invariable, feature of modern restatements of the institutional scheme to strengthen the line between obligations and the rest of the law of things. For Gaius and Justinian the strong line came between corporeal and incorporeal things. The modern preference is to draw it between real and personal rights. We have discussed this shifting of the watershed in explaining the sense of '*res*' as 'property' in the wide sense in which it includes obligations. The inner core of the modern law school syllabus is contract, delict – called tort in common law jurisdictions – and property. Contract and delict are the main sub-classes of obligations. 'Property' is used in the narrower sense in which it includes only real rights. Hence the inner core of the curriculum is still Justinian's law of things, with obligations marked more strongly from the rest. This is already apparent in Grotius.

Before leaving seventeenth century Holland, mention should be made of the editions of Justinian's *Institutes* by Arnoldus Vinnius, professor of law at Leyden. In 1642 he published the first edition of his *Academic and Forensic Commentary*. The full title is '*In quatuor libris Institutionum imperialium Commentarius academicus et forensis*'. It gives the text of the *Institutes* and, in Latin, a very full commentary. This commentary draws on the best recent scholarship, but in addition it both goes back to the Glossators and Postglossators and also brings in modern legal practice, especially in the decisions of the 'Grand Conseil' of Malines. In the early eighteenth century the commentary was further expanded by J.G.Heineccius. The *Commentarius* is a huge and advanced work. Vinnius also produced a shorter students' version, called for short *Notae*, first published in 1646. This has Justinian's text with explanatory footnotes in which Vinnius draws on a more limited range of authorities, especially Cujas, Hotman, and Wesenbecius. Both these works went through many editions and were disseminated throughout Europe.[53] In England, Vinnius prompted an eighteenth century translation of the *Institutes* by George Harris. In the preface Harris says 'This translation of the Institutions of the civil law into English is principally intended as an introduction to Vinny's Edition.'[54] Harris added notes which show that, though his translation must have been aimed at beginners who would use Vinnius' *Notae*, he himself was drawing from the larger *Commentarius*. The great eighteenth century judge, Lord Mansfield, advised the young Duke of Portland to prepare himself for the law by reading Gravina[55] on the history of the civil law and also 'to read and study Justinian's *Institutes* without any other comment than the short one of Vinnius.'[56]

France

Vinnius was also widely read in France, and his works thus contributed to perhaps the most remarkable of the *Institutes*' survivals. It might have been expected that in late eighteenth century France, when everything traditional was thrown into the melting-pot of reason and revolution, Justinian's scheme for handling the whole law would have been repudiated and replaced. In fact, however, it defeated competition from left and right, that is to say from radical reorganizations inspired by the work of the seventeenth century natural lawyers, especially the *The Law of War and Peace* of Grotius and *The Law of Nature and Nations* of Pufendorf,[57] and from the system, or lack of system, of the *Digest* or *Pandects*, familiar to practitioners in the pays de droit écrit, for whom the *Institutes* had only a pedagogic function. When, as first consul, Napoleon established a commission on 13th August 1800 to draw up a comprehensive civil

53. R. Feenstra and C.J.D. Waal, *Seventeenth Century Leyden Law Professors and their Influence on the Development of the Civil Law* (Amsterdam and Oxford 1975) 52ff., 81-109.

54. *The Four Books of Justinian's Institutions*, translated into English, with notes, by George Harris, LL.D. (London 1756) viii.

55. This refers to the very successful *Origines Juris Civilis Libri Tres* by G.V. Gravina, published in 1701.

56. *A Treatise on the Study of the Law* (London 1797) 50, quoted by C.H.S. Fifoot, *Lord Mansfield* (London 1936) 29.

57. Grotius' *De Jure Belli ac Pacis*, published in 1625, had a fundamentally different structure from his *Inleiding*, above n.52. Its system was further developed by Pufendorf's *De Jure Naturae et Gentium libri octo* published in 1672 and later 'done into English' by Basil Kennett, President of Corpus Christi, Oxford.

code, the structure which the commissioners adopted was once again Justinian's institutional scheme. The reasons are to be found in the story of scholarship in French law in the preceding century, beginning under Louis XIV.

The teaching of French law began in earnest with the establishment of new chairs in 1679. The new courses were given in the vernacular. An Avignon advertisement of 1716-17 captures the continuing clash of old and new. It announces in Latin the lectures about to be given in French: 'gallici juris antecessor...franco exponet sermone.'[58] But the new matter needed a form, and it fell easily into the familiar scheme of the *Institutes*. François Boutaric (1672-1733) proclaimed in his *Institutes de l'empereur Justinien conférées avec le droit Français*, which was published in 1738 and then again in 1740 and 1754, that there was no better mode of operation than to abide by the classification and the order of Justinian, taking note of departures introduced by the national law. Jean-Joseph Julien (1704-1789), professor at Aix-en-Provence, recommended a slightly more emancipated approach. Publishing the outline of his course in 1785 – *Eléments de Jurisprudence sur les loix romaines et celles du royaume* – he declared in his preface that he would follow the plan of Justinian's *Institutes* without making himself a slave to them: 'Je suivroi le plan des Institutes de l'Empereur Justinien et le même ordre de matières, sans pour autant m'y assujetir absolument. Cette méthode m'a paru préférable à celle de donner simplement des notes sur les paragraphes des Institutes. Il n'y a pas dans celle-ci cet ordre, cette suite, cet enchaînement de principes qui de toutes les manières d'instruire est la plus claire, la plus sûre et la plus utile.' Christian Chêne has set out side by side the heads of Julien's course and those of the *Code civil* itself, graphically demonstrating the closeness between them. He also notes that Jean-Marie-Etienne Portalis, the Tribonian of Napoleon's commission, had been a pupil of Julien in Aix-en-Provence.[59] Similar diagrammatic representations had earlier been given by André-Jean Arnaud showing the systematic parallels between the *Code civil* and other works, especially François Bourjon's *Le Droit Commun de la France et la Coutume de Paris reduits en principes*, which had three editions between 1747 and 1773, and Gabriel-Jean Olivier's *Principes du Droit civil romain*, published in Paris in 1776.[60]

The *Code civil* itself was brought into force by enactments of 1803-4. It has nothing equivalent to Justinian's last section on actions, and of course nothing on crime. For the rest the influence of the *Institutes* is obvious. Book 1 is on persons, book 2 on property and the modifications of ownership – 'Des biens et des différentes modifications de la propriété' – and book 3 is on the acquisition of ownership – 'Des différentes manières dont on acquièrt la propriété'. Under this heading it also includes obligations. The code's failure to separate obligations from the rest of the law of things has attracted criticism. Jean Carbonnier opens his discussion of obligations with this observation:

'Obligations were not given a separate book in the *Code civil*. They were mixed with other matters provided for in book 3 under the general rubric 'The Different Modes of Acquiring Ownership'. That is hardly an instructive way of approaching the subject, since obligations, though they do sometimes lead to the acquisition of property, for example under sale, are chiefly characterized by the fact that they require an activity, a service to be performed by some person.'[61]

Carbonnier's four volumes of *Droit Civil* bring the story to the present day. Used by every student of French law, they witness the survival of the *Institutes* in modern France. The four volumes bear these titles: 1. *Introduction: Les Personnes*; 2. *La Famille, les incapacités*; 3. *Les Biens: monnaie, immeubles, meubles*; 4. *Les Obligations*. As in the code itself, there is nothing on actions, and persons overspill into a second book. For the rest, there could hardly be a more faithful adherence to the institutional patterns. At a more detailed level, many closer parallels could be given. Here is one which is particularly vivid. In stating the general nature of an obligation, Carbonnier begins, 'Dans sa notion la plus dépouillée, l'obligation apparaît comme un lien de droit existant specialement entre deux personnes, en vertu duquel l'une doit faire quelque chose pour l'autre.' This hardly goes beyond translating Justinian's definition.[62]

England

The institutional scheme is a way of comprehending the whole law. The place to look for its surviving influence is in books or codes which aim at comprehensive coverage. The English common law has never been strong in literature of that kind. Nor has it yet gone in for general codification. The textbooks which have multiplied since the mid-nineteenth century have confined themselves each to its own special subject. Only at the most

58. Quoted by C. Chêne, *L'Enseignement du droit Français en pays de droit écrit* (Geneva 1982) 283.

59. Ibid., 300-303.

60. A.-J. Arnaud, *Les origines doctrinales du Code civil français* (Paris 1969) 161, 169.

61. J. Carbonnier, *Droit Civil, 4. Les Obligations*, 11th edition (Paris 1982) 13.

62. Ibid., 15.

elementary level, for beginners or for the general reader, have authors attempted a wider coverage.[63] At the other extreme *Halsbury*,[64] the practitioner's work of reference in many volumes, sticks to the alphabet, much the commonest system of classification throughout the history of English law.

The great and obvious exception is Blackstone. He can be seen as a later part of the same development just described for France, by which national law began to be the subject of university lectures and was forced to find an orderly form.[65] Blackstone began to lecture on English law in Oxford in 1753. His hopes of becoming Regius Professor of Civil Law were disappointed. Instead, in 1758, he became the first Vinerian Professor, the first occupant of the first chair in English law in any university. The four books of his *Commentaries on the Laws of England* were published between 1765 and 1769. Thereafter they formed the minds of generations of lawyers on both sides of the Atlantic. In America they inspired James Kent's *Commentaries on American Law* which were published between 1826 and 1837 and were also based on their author's university lectures. Kent, before becoming a judge, had been a professor of law at Columbia.

Blackstone's *Commentaries* fall into four books. Book 4 is entirely devoted to crime. It is called 'Of Public Wrongs'. Book 3 is 'Of Private Wrongs'. Here private wrongs, including the wrong of breach of contract, really only occupy the first part; the last part, from chapter 18 to the end, is explicitly about procedure: 'I am now…to examine the *manner* in which these several remedies are *pursued* and applied, by action in the courts of common law; to which I shall afterwards subjoin a brief account of the proceedings in equity.'[66] This last part of Blackstone's book 3 and the whole of his book 4 together correspond to the third part of Justinian's trichotomy, i.e. to the law of actions with its addendum on crime. Of course in Blackstone the treatment of crime has swollen disproportionately, to 436 pages, a quarter of the whole work. It will be recalled that Justinian's trichotomy is spread over four books, and that its third part – actions plus crime – occupies only the last two thirds of his book 4. The first third of his book 4 deals with the last part of the last limb of the law of things: obligations from delict and as though

from delict. In other words, if we step away from the conceptual trichotomy and look instead at the four books, Justinian's book 4 looks to be about private wrongs, then procedure, then public wrongs. That, in outline, is the content of Blackstone's last two books.

The content of Blackstone's first two books can conveniently be given in the words of his own recapitulation at the start of the third:

'…we distinguished rights into two sorts: first, such as concern or are annexed to the persons of men, and are then called *jura personarum*, or *the rights of persons*; which, together with the means acquiring and losing them, composed the first book of these commentaries: and, secondly, such as a man may acquire over external objects, or things unconnected with his person, which are called *jura rerum*, or *the rights of things*; and these, with the means of transferring them from man to man, were the subject of the second book. I am therefore to proceed to the consideration of *wrongs*; which for the most part convey to us an idea merely negative, as being nothing else but a privation of right. For which reason it was necessary, that, before we entered at all into the discussion of wrongs, we should entertain a clear and distinct notion of rights: the contemplation of what is *jus* being necessarily prior to what may be termed *iniuria*, and the definition of *fas* prior to that of *nefas*.'[67]

Taken with the earlier discussion of books 3 and 4, this extract shows that the one great institutional writer of the common law still derived his structure ultimately from Justinian. The full institutional scheme is present in the *Commentaries*: generalities, persons, things, actions, crime. But the extract also serves to warn of difficulties, of departures from and transformations of the original. Further reading will confirm that the work's relationship to the *Institutes* is indeed complex. Blackstone cannot be understood without the *Institutes*, but the *Institutes* do not provide a complete key. One completely un-Roman aspect of Blackstone's scheme is his superimposition on it of a strong opposition between rights and wrongs. This is in the extract above. It is also very clearly announced early on: 'in the prosecution of these commentaries, I shall follow this very simple and obvious division; and shall in the first place consider the *rights* that are commanded, and secondly the *wrongs* that are forbidden by the laws

63. It is perhaps more accurate to say that these comprehensive books have been submerged by the indifference of English university law schools to the Justinianic theory of legal education with its insistence on a systematic overview early on. The books exist but form a sub-culture below 'serious' legal education. For example: Sir W. Markby, *Elements of Law* (Oxford 1871, sixth edtn. 1905); W. Geldart, *Elements of English Law* (Oxford 1911, ninth edtn., ed. D.C.M. Yardley, 1984); P.S. James, *Introduction to English Law* (London 1950, eleventh edtn. 1985); K. Smith and D. Keenan, *English Law* (London 1963, seventh edtn. 1982). All these show the strongest marks of the Justinianic scheme. James, in his preface, says expressly that the plan which he canvassed with his Oxford colleagues was that 'we should collaborate in the writing of a new institutional book on the Roman pattern.' In fact he wrote the book alone, after leaving Oxford.

64. Halsbury's Laws of England, fourth edition, ed. Lord Hailsham of St. Marylebone (London 1973, continuing).

65. See above, p.23.

66. *Commentaries*, book 3, p.270. Our pagination is to the first edition.

67. *Commentaries*, book 3, p.2.

of England.'[68] Early in the nineteenth century, John Austin, first professor of law in London at what is now University College, found fault with Blackstone at many points. Pursuing in Benthamite spirit the goal of reducing English law to a rationally defensible system, Austin for the most part found the Roman jurists a better guide, but in this one point, the primary division between rights and wrongs, he thought that Blackstone had outdone them.[69]

It is not far wrong to think of Blackstone as having had no predecessors, but it is an exaggeration. Thomas Wood (1661-1722) was perhaps unlucky not to win the glory that fell to Blackstone himself. Primarily a civilian, with a career at Oxford and in the church, he was an energetic advocate for finding national law a place within the university curriculum. It was partly to further that aim that he wrote his *Institute of the Laws of England*, first published in 1720. In the preface he expressed the hope that it might now be possible to order 'this heap of good learning'.[70] Wood's *Institute* is in four books, the scheme of which he expressed as follows: 'The *Object* of these Laws are 1. The *Persons* of which England is composed. 2. Their *Estates*. 3. The *Crimes* and *Misdemeanours* that may be committed by them. 4. The *Courts* of Justice, or the Jurisdiction of the Courts, and the Manner of *Proceedings* therein.' The second of these headings was expanded at the start of book 2: 'Estates are the *second* Object of our Laws; and in common signification are all Manner of Property in *Lands*, & c. *Goods*, and *Chattels*.'[71]

Justinian's scheme can be seen in this. But crime is promoted to follow the law of things, and the law of actions is expanded to include an account of the courts. Chapter 4 of book 4 is especially interesting. The subject is actions, but Wood is reduced to an alphabetical list. And his exposition of the actions remains his only vehicle for setting out the matter handled by Gaius and Justinian as the law of obligations, the last subject of the law of things. It is here that modern contract and tort are to be found. This tendency of substantive law to run back into the law of actions vividly illustrates two extremely important points.

The first is the difficulty of imposing Roman, or any, rational categories on national material which, however disordered, is plentiful and vigorous. The second is the magnitude of Gaius' original achievement in separating the substance of persons and things from the no less disordered heap of Roman actions. The most extraordinary aspect of that achievement was the identification of obligations as an entity capable of being correlated with other 'things'. That brilliant and difficult step, essential to the completion of the institutional scheme, allowed Gaius to draw off the substance of the personal actions. A complex of obstacles made it difficult for Wood, and indeed Blackstone, to achieve the same clean separation of substantive law from pleading and procedure.

Behind Blackstone and Wood we can barely do more than mention the names of those who attempted comprehensive description of English law. One, rarely noticed but deserving better, is Giles Jacob whose *Every Man His Own Lawyer* was originally a much more serious book than its innumerable later editions aimed only at a lay audience.[72] In the civilian line behind Wood stands John Cowell's *Institute of English Law – Institutiones Juris Anglicani ad Methodum et Seriem Institutionum Imperialium compositae et digestae*. This was first published in 1605 in Latin and translated into English under Cromwell. Cowell, Regius Professor of Civil Law in Cambridge from 1594 to 1611, frequently drew on an extraordinary work by the ebullient William Fulbecke called *A Parallele, or Conference of the Civil Law, the Canon Law and the Common Law*, published in 1601. Fulbecke, a barrister of Gray's Inn had been, at Oxford, a pupil of Albericus Gentilis, forerunner of Grotius and Regius Professor of Civil Law from 1587 to 1608.

On the common law side, three great names must be mentioned. Sir Edward Coke, removed by James VI and I from his position as Chief Justice of the King's Bench in 1616, divided his enforced leisure between Parliament and composition of his *Institutes of the Laws of England*. Only the first part came out in his lifetime, in 1628, the rest in the 1640s. The four massively learned volumes are not a true 'institutes', since they do not aspire to be either introductory or well ordered.[73] The first is on land law, Coke's commentary on Littleton,[74] the

---

68. *Commentaries*, book 1, p.118.
69. 'Blackstone's method, though in general greatly inferior to that of the Roman Lawyers, is here superior to it. Under the head of personal property he treats of those obligations arising from contracts and quasi-contracts which are *primary*: in his third volume, when treating of wrongs, he adverts to those obligations growing out of contracts or quasi-contracts which arise from breaches of those primary rights' J.Austin, *Lectures in Jurisprudence*, fourth edtn., ed. R. Campbell (London 1873) 796.
70. T. Wood, *An Institute of the Laws of England, or the Laws of England in their Natural Order* (London 1720) preface, p.ii.
71. Ibid.,16,191.
72. The work was published anonymously in 1741 with a preface by 'G.J.'. The sub-title was 'A Summary of the Laws of England in a New and Instructive Method'. The title page then set out seven heads in considerable detail. In abbreviated form they are: 1. Of Actions and Remedies, 2. Of Courts, 3. Of Estates and Property in Lands and Goods, 4. Of the Laws relating to Marriage, 5. Of the Liberty of the Subject, 6. Of the King and his Prerogative, 7. Of Publick Offences.
73. 'The contrast between the disorder of Coke's *Institutes* and the order of the *Institutions* of the late seventeenth century Scottish judge, Viscount Stair, is almost painful' F.H. Lawson, *The Oxford Law School 1850-1965* (Oxford 1968) 3-4.
74. Sir Thomas Littleton's *Tenures*, published in 1481 and written in French, were a uniquely straightforward 'institutional' – but not Roman – work. They were confined to land law.

second an exposition of some statutes, the third a famous and influential account of crime, and the fourth an essay on the courts. Some years earlier Sir Henry Finch had published the little book which was the nearest predecessor of Wood's *Institute*. That was the *Nomotechnia – Law, or a Discourse thereof in four Books*. That came out first in 1613. Finally, the learned and restrained Sir Matthew Hale, historian of the common law and judge under Cromwell and Charles II, left, to be published posthumously in 1713, *An Analysis of the Civil Part of the Law*. Hale's *Analysis* provides the structural link between Justinian and Blackstone.[75]

Long before these and across a chasm in the history of the common law stands that great cathedral of the thirteenth century, *Bracton on the Laws and Customs of England*. The recent work of Thorne has changed earlier beliefs about that book. It now seems that most of the work was finished in the early part of the reign of Henry III, before 1240 and not after 1250; Bracton himself was perhaps no more than the organizing editor of work done by or for two other royal judges, Martin Pattishall and William Raleigh.[76]

The book belongs to the first wave of the second life of Roman law in Europe, but it is a magnificent anticipation of the post-humanist institutes of national law. Though written in Latin, its scale and aims are close to Stair's four hundred years later, and its assumptions seem to be identical, namely that the Roman law library could be emulated, that the *Digest* set an attainable standard of detail and precision, and that the *Institutes* provided the means of order. In Thorne's edition, still using Woodbine's text, Bracton's book occupies some 1240 pages. The presence of the institutional scheme can be recognized from the following passage on page 29: 'We have now spoken of the law of nature, the law of all peoples, and the law of the state. Since all the law of which we propose to treat concerns persons, things or actions under the English laws and customs, and since persons are the most important of these three in that it was for persons that all laws were made, we must turn to persons first, starting with their various conditions and then giving the law applicable to them.' This proves the writer's intention to borrow the Justinianic structure, but another fact shows the extraordinary difficulty of making substance prevail over pleading and procedure: the law of actions is reached by page 282 and occupies more than three quarters of the entire work.

We have outlined, back to Bracton, the thin tradition of English institutional writing behind Blackstone. But Blackstone's *Commentaries* were really a new beginning. He set himself the aim as 'an academical expounder of the laws' to create 'a general map of the law, marking out the shape of the country, its connexions and boundaries, its greater divisions and principal cities' without troubling 'to describe minutely the subordinate limits, or to fix the longitude and latitude of every inconsiderable hamlet.'[77] Blackstone's map inaugurated the age of legal textbooks. These books, which we take for granted, began to proliferate in the nineteenth century. They are, in Milsom's words, 'expansions from his reduction'.[78] Blackstone also inaugurated the age of university education in the common law, though in fact Oxford itself did not take the innovation seriously till 1850. Just as Blackstone's map of the law cannot be fully understood without Justinian's *Institutes*, so also the modern list of legal textbooks or, which comes to much the same thing, the syllabus of law school courses, traces its history to the same source.

Nor can the history be ignored. Suppose for instance an ebbing of confidence in the established law school syllabus and radical proposals for reorganization, with profound implications for what the French call 'formation' of legal minds. One question to be considered, not of course decisive but not unimportant either, is how deeply rooted our current ways of thinking and teaching actually are. If it were true in the law schools that 'our basic conceptual apparatus, the fundamental characterizations and divisions which we impose on the phenomena with which we deal, do not reflect the values of our own times but *those of the last century*'[79] we might well be disposed to view them as contingent and probably mistaken. However, when the truth is that those same categories of legal thought have been surviving critical onslaughts in different jurisdictions and under different political systems since the time of Justinian in the sixth century and Gaius in the second, we are bound to approach the issue of radical reform at least with some self-doubt.

---

75. On this see J.W.Cairns, 'Blackstone' *cit.* n.43 above, esp. 340-342.

76. *Bracton on the Laws and Customs of England*, translated with revisions and notes by S.E. Thorne (Cambridge, Mass. 1968-1977), four volumes. The reassessment of the authorship issue is in the introduction to volume 3. Cf. F.B. Wiener, 'Bracton – A Tangled Web of Legal Mysteries' (1978) 2 *G.Mason Univ. L.R.* 129.

77. *Commentaries*, book 1, p.35.

78. S.F.C.Milsom, 'The Nature of Blackstone's Achievement' (1981) 1 *Oxford Jo.L.S.* 1,10.

79. P.S.Atiyah. 'Contacts, Promises and the Law of Obligations' (1978) 94 *L.Q.R.* 193,194.

3. This Translation

Whereas Gaius' *Institutes* survived in the single fifth century manuscript discovered by Niebuhr in 1816, supplemented by other fragmentary finds, Justinian's *Institutes* exist in many manuscripts, though none is earlier than the ninth century text in Berlin. The textual tradition is supported by the survival of Theophilus' Greek *Paraphrase*. Printed editions began to come out almost as soon as printing was invented. The first emanated from Mainz in 1468. A famous edition, with a much improved text, was produced by the great legal humanist Cujas in 1585. In 1817 E.Spangenberg counted six hundred and sixty-seven editions,[80] and there have been many since. Niebuhr's discovery of the Gaius text in 1816 stimulated more work on the text. In the 1860s two editions were produced which have ever since been regarded as authoritative. The first was that of P. Krüger in 1867, which is the text reproduced in this volume; the second that of P.E.Huschke in 1868.

A parallel translation, Latin on one side English on the other, is a liberating medium both for reader and translator. The reader can go fast, but as soon as doubts or questions enter his mind, he can turn to the Latin and condemn the translator's ignorance or perversity. From the translator's standpoint, the very fact that on crucial points the Latin text, not the English, will be responsible for the reader's ultimate opinion means that the English rendering can free itself from the the kind of obsessive fidelity to the original which can quickly turn the language into translationese. The freedom made possible by the parallel text is also indispensable for another reason. Latin is an intensely economical language. The English text easily expands to double its length. To keep more or less in step you need the freedom to exploit the different economies of which English is capable. Above all English can do without connecting particles, though sometimes not without a loss of nuance which a demand for formal accuracy might require to be retained.

Surprisingly there is no other Latin-English edition of the *Institutes* currently available. The lack of one has made teaching difficult. It was the urgency of this practical problem, evidence in itself of the book's miraculous capacity for remaining in demand, that originally set us to work. The appearance of the new Pennsylvania *Digest*,[81] which has transformed the accessibility of the practitioner's library, also made all the more obvious the need for a similar treatment of the student's textbook. The parallel version by the late Professor J.A.C.Thomas went quickly out of print.[82] It was never within the student price-range, and in fact it did not take full advantage of the opportunity to present the work in thoroughly modern English, because Professor Thomas preferred the accuracy of a Latinate style, laden with subjunctives. He used to lecture in the same way but so fast and with such sparkling delivery that he always struck the listener as brilliantly punctilious, not pompous and boring. Sadly only those who heard him lecture can read his translation as he would have intended.

Still more surprisingly given the importance of the book, when we began work there was not only no parallel edition still available but no English translation at all. In the meantime Lee's *Elements*, first published in 1944, has been reprinted.[83] In form that book alternates sections of translation and sections of commentary. Apart from the inconvenient absence of the Latin, Professor Lee also pruned the translation to the point of omitting some sentences and even some of the more arcane paragraphs. He also made the unfortunate decision to alter Justinian's order at some points, thus running the risk of misrepresenting the structure of the book. Out of print, though still used by students, are the editions of Sanders, first published in 1853, and of Moyle, first published in 1883. Moyle's translation, which is very good, was rather inconveniently published in a separate volume.

We have tried to give a completely modern translation, with neither Latin nor Latinate terms retained. One of the striking facts about Roman law is that, to the reader who has Latin, it does not seem in the least old-fashioned. Gaius could come back to a chair of law tomorrow, Ulpian to the House of Lords. The modernity of the translation is not false. It is a shame that old-fashioned translations should represent the subject as remote from the law of today.

The *Institutes* started life as first year lectures, notionally from the emperor himself. We have kept the idea of early lectures constantly in mind and have written so far as possible in the short, direct sentences that a good modern lecturer would use. We have often allowed ourselves to address the reader in the second person as lecturers address their audience. For the most part that style is faithful to the Latin. Gaius and Ulpian and the other classical lawyers, except Papinian whose

80. E. Spangenberg, *Einleitung in das Römisch-Justinianische Rechtsbuch* (Hanover 1817) 931ff.

81. *Cit*.12, above.

82 J.A.C. Thomas, *The Institutes of Justinian: Text, Translation and Commentary* (Cape Town 1975).

83. R.W. Lee, *The Elements of Roman Law* (London 1944, 4th edtn. 1956, repr. 1985).

works are anyhow not in question, wrote wonderfully short, clear sentences and used simple, unaffected vocabulary. Much later a change of style infected the imperial chancery. The nadir was reached in the *Codex Theodosianus*, which is full of baroque pronouncements so oblique as to be virtually inpenetrable. It is difficult to know how or why any thinking being could prefer the Theodosian froth and nonsense to the simple classical style. At all events by the time of Justinian there had been some improvement. Even so, there is a striking contrast of style in the *Institutes* between the passages taken from Gaius and the other classical writers and those, probably written by Tribonian, which tell how Justinian solved long-standing doubts or eliminated old anomalies. The Justinianic passages are grandiloquent and self-congratulatory, though the zeal which they advertise is itself admirable.

We thought at first that these purple passages could be put into a formal Victorian style. But the effect was ridiculous. There were also other difficulties. In that style they took up too much space in English. They carried the English text out of line with the Latin. Also it was not always easy to see exactly when to revert to the plainer style. We ended by taking a middle way. The contrast is, we hope, still recognizable but we have certainly made the Justinianic passages less grandiloquent than they really are. All the same we have intended not to be guilty of cutting. The one word we have consistently ignored is the honorific appellation '*divus*' given to dead emperors. 'The Divine Severus' has the wrong overtones in English. We could not think of a substitute that did not. 'Divus Severus' becomes simply 'the Emperor Severus'.

It is not to be denied that there is an element of defiance in bringing out a new edition of the *Institutes* at this time. For reasons which will not stand up to examination the recent tendency has been to reduce the number of chairs in civil law and to remove the subject to the margin of the syllabus. However, the importance of the subject guarantees that it will survive the pressures of this modernism. No self-respecting law school can permanently turn its back on the greatest manifestation of legal genius in the Western tradition. The Pennsylvania *Digest* is only one sign of a recent revival, especially in America.

Part of the difficulty has been accessibility. Latin has become ever rarer in the schools. This is being overcome, partly by translation, partly by later opportunities to learn the classical languages. A hundred and fifty years ago David Irving, librarian of the Faculty of Advocates from 1820 to 1848 was already anxious. Yet huge advances have been made in the meantime. In 1837 he said, with some sarcasm,

'A learned professor in a foreign country thought it expedient to pronounce and publish an academical oration on the excessive study of the civil law. This is a species of excess which no person, interested in the prosperity of the British universities, need at present anticipate with any painful degree of anxiety; and if too much learning should seem to have made some lawyers mad, it must at least be admitted that a very small part of their learning is drawn from the recondite sources of Roman jurisprudence. Nothing indeed is more common than to hear them declare their decided opinion as to the utter inutility of such a study: it is equally common to hear certain worthy denizens of the republic of letters profess the utmost contempt for classical learning, and both opinions rest on the same unstable foundation; they are in every instance the opinions of individuals who endeavour to derive some consolation to themselves, by pretending to despise what they do not understand.'[84]

There is still some truth in that, but it is of course a universal failing to discount the importance of learning which is hidden from oneself. We hope that this edition will contribute to the accessibility of a body of knowledge which is a corner-stone of European civilization. We would not wish to adopt Irving's tone. But his cause was just:

'The system of Roman jurisprudence has for many centuries been regarded as one of the most conspicuous monuments of human wisdom and genius; and its powerful influence on modern legislation has been felt and acknowledged by every civilized nation of Europe.'[85]

---

84. D. Irving, LL.D., *An Introduction to the Civil Law* (Edinburgh 1837) 1. The hostile oration to which he refers is H.W.Tydeman, *Oratio de eo quod nimium est studio Juris Romani* (Dewenter 1802).
85. Ibid., 2.

Further reading

This list is intended to help the reader who would like to go further into Roman law. It is restricted to works of a general kind in English which have not been cited in the course of the Introduction.

Introductory

B. Nicholas, *An Introduction to Roman Law* (Oxford 1962)

Histories of Roman Law

H.F. Jolowicz and B. Nicholas, *Historical Introduction to the Study of Roman Law*, 3rd edition (Cambridge 1972)

W. Kunkel, *An Introduction to Roman Legal and Constitutional History*, 2nd edition translated by J.M. Kelly (Oxford 1973)

H.-J. Wolff, *Roman Law: An Historical Introduction* (Norman 1951)

The Institutes of Gaius

F. de Zulueta, *The Institutes of Gaius*, part 1 Text and Translation, part 2 Commentary (Oxford 1946 and 1953)

W.M. Gordon and O.F. Robinson, *The Institutes of Gaius: A Parallel Translation* (forthcoming)

Textbooks for Reference

W.W. Buckland, *A Textbook of Roman Law*, 3rd edition edited by P.G. Stein (Cambridge 1963)

J.A.C. Thomas, *Textbook of Roman Law* (Amsterdam 1976)

Other Books

P. Birks (ed.), *A Commentary on the Institutes* (forthcoming)

J.A. Crook, *Law and Life of Rome* (London 1967)

J.P. Dawson, *The Oracles of the Law* (Ann Arbor 1968)

O.F. Robinson, T.D. Fergus, W.M. Gordon, *An Introduction to European Legal History* (Abingdon 1985)

P. Stein, *Regulae Iuris: From Juristic Rules to Legal Maxims* (Edinburgh 1966)

P. Stein, *Legal Institutions: The Development of Dispute Settlement* (London 1984)

A. Watson, *Sources of Law, Legal Change and Ambiguity* (Edinburgh 1984)

IUSTINIANI

INSTITUTIONES

RECOGNOVIT

PAULUS KRUEGER

IN NOMINE DOMINI NOSTRI JHESU CHRISTI

IMPERATOR CAESAR FLAVIUS IUSTINIANUS ALAMANNICUS GOTHICUS
FRANCICUS GERMANICUS ANTICUS ALANICUS VANDALICUS AFRICANUS
PIUS FELIX INCLITUS VICTOR AC TRIUMPHATOR SEMPER AUGUSTUS
CUPIDAE LEGUM IUVENTUTI

Imperatoriam maiestatem non solum armis decoratam, sed etiam legibus oportet esse armatam, ut utrumque tempus et bellorum et pacis recte possit gubernari et princeps Romanus victor existat non solum in hostilibus proeliis, sed etiam per legitimos tramites calumniantium iniquitates[1] expellens, et fiat tam iuris religiosissimus quam victis hostibus triumphator.
1 Quorum utramque viam cum summis vigiliis et summa providentia[2] adnuente deo perfecimus. et bellicos quidem sudores nostros barbaricae gentes sub iuga nostra deductae cognoscunt et tam Africa quam aliae innumerosae[3] provinciae post tanta temporum spatia nostris victoriis a caelesti numine praestitis[4] iterum dicioni Romanae nostroque additae imperio protestantur. omnes vero populi legibus iam a nobis 2 vel promulgatis vel compositis reguntur. Et cum sacratissimas constitutiones antea confusas in luculentam ereximus consonantiam, tunc nostram extendimus curam et ad immensa prudentiae veteris volumina, et opus desperatum quasi per medium profundum euntes caelesti favore iam adimplevimus.
3 Cumque hoc deo propitio peractum est, Triboniano viro magnifico magistro et exquaestore sacri palatii nostri nec non Theophilo et Dorotheo viris illustribus antecessoribus, quorum omnium[5] sollertiam et legum scientiam et circa nostras iussiones fidem iam ex multis rerum argumentis accepimus, convocatis specialiter mandavimus, ut nostra auctoritate nostrisque suasionibus componant institutiones: ut liceat vobis prima legum cunabula non ab antiquis fabulis discere, sed ab imperiali splendore appetere et tam aures quam animae vestrae nihil inutile nihilque perperam positum, sed quod in ipsis rerum optinet argumentis accipiant: et quod in priore tempore vix post quadriennium[6] prioribus contingebat, ut tunc constitutiones imperatorias legerent, hoc vos a primordio ingrediamini digni tanto honore tantaque reperti[7] felicitate, ut et initium vobis et finis legum eruditionis a voce principali procedat. Igitur post 4 libros quinquaginta digestorum seu pandectarum, in quos omne ius antiquum collatum est (quos per eundem virum excelsum Tribonianum nec non ceteros viros illustres et facundissimos confecimus), in hos quattuor libros easdem institutiones partiri iussimus, ut sint 5 totius legitimae scientiae prima elementa. Quibus breviter expositum est et quod antea optinebat et quod postea desuetudine inumbratum ab imperiali 6 remedio illuminatum est. Quas ex omnibus antiquorum institutionibus et praecipue ex commentariis Gaii nostri tam institutionum quam rerum cottidianarum aliisque multis commentariis compositas cum tres praedicti viri prudentes nobis optulerunt[8], et legimus et cognovimus et plenissimum nostrarum constitutionum robur eis accommodavimus.
7 Summa itaque ope et alacri studio has leges nostras accipite et vosmet ipsos sic eruditos ostendite, ut spes vos pulcherrima foveat toto legitimo opere perfecto posse etiam nostram rem publicam in partibus eius vobis credendis[9] gubernare.
Data undecimo[10] kalendas Decembres Constantinopoli domino nostro Iustiniano perpetuo Augusto tertium consule.

---

(1) sic PW cum Θ, iniquitatem BU   (2) sic PEW cum Θ, diligentia BU   (3) sic PE cum Θ. numerosae BU   (4) praestitae B   (5) sic UPWᵃ cum Θ, omnem BWᵇ   (6) μετὰ τριετῆ Θ   (7) reperti om. Bᵃ contra Θ   (8) sic BU cum Θ, contulerunt V   (9) sic VUP, credendam B   (10) sic VPE, x BU

Signorum explicatio, see p. 157.

IN THE NAME OF OUR LORD JESUS CHRIST

THE EMPEROR CAESAR FLAVIUS JUSTINIAN

CONQUEROR OF THE ALAMANNI GOTHS FRANKS GERMANS ANTES ALANI VANDALS AFRICANS

DEVOUT FORTUNATE RENOWNED VICTORIOUS AND TRIUMPHANT FOREVER AUGUSTUS

TO

YOUNG ENTHUSIASTS FOR LAW

Imperial Majesty should not only be graced with arms but also armed with laws, so that good government may prevail in time of war and peace alike. The head of the Roman state can then stand victorious not only over enemies in war but also over trouble-makers, driving out their wickedness through the paths of the law, and can triumph as much for his devotion to the law as for his conquests in battle. 1. Long hours of work and careful planning have, with God's help, given us success in both these fields. Barbarian nations brought beneath our yoke know the scale of our exertions in war. Africa and countless other provinces, restored to Roman jurisdiction and brought back within our empire after so long an interval, bear witness to the victories granted to us by the will of heaven. However, it is by the laws which we have already managed to enact and collect that all our peoples are ruled. 2. The solemn pronouncements of the emperors were in disarray. We collected them into a clear, systematic series. Then we turned our attention to the rolls of the classical law, that boundless ocean of learning, and, passing by heaven's favour as it were through the midst of the deep, we soon completed a task which seemed overwhelming. 3. When with God's help we reached the end of that, we called together Tribonian, of eminent rank, minister and former chancellor of our sacred palace, and also Theophilus and Dorotheus, professors of illustrious rank. From all three we had already received many proofs of their brilliance, their learning in the law, and their loyalty in carrying out our wishes. We gave them this specific instruction: to compose with our authority and at our instigation an edition of Institutes. Our intention was to give you an elementary framework, a cradle of the law, not based on obscure old stories but illuminated by the light of our imperial splendour; and to ensure that you hear and adopt nothing useless or out of place but only the true principles at the heart of the subject. Until now even the best students have barely begun to read imperial pronouncements after four years of study; but you have been found worthy of the great honour and good fortune of doing so from the beginning and of following a course of legal education which from start to finish proceeds from the Emperor's lips. 4. It was for these reasons that after the completion of the fifty books of the Digest or Pandects, in which all the classical law has been brought together and which we achieved through this same excellent Tribonian and other learned men of illustrious rank, we gave the order for the Institutes to be composed in these four books, to form the first principles of all learning in the law. 5. They now give a brief account both of how matters used to stand and of the imperial measures which brought light to areas darkened by disuse. 6. They have been compiled from all the books of Institutes written by the classical lawyers, and especially from the works of our own Gaius, both his Institutes and his Everyday Law, though also from many other treatises. When the work was finished, the three learned commissioners presented the books to us. We have read and examined them and have endowed them with the full force of our own pronouncements. 7. Study our law. Do your best and apply yourselves keenly to it. Show that you have mastered it. You can then cherish a noble ambition; when your course in law is finished you will be able to perform whatever duty is entrusted to you in the government of our state. Given at Constantinople on 21st November 533, the year of the third consulate of our lord Justinian, Perpetual Augustus.

DOMINI NOSTRI IUSTINIANI PERPETUO AUGUSTI

INSTITUTIONUM SIVE ELEMENTORUM

COMPOSITORUM PER TRIBONIANUM VIRUM EXCELSUM MAGISTRUM ET EX QUAESTORE
SACRI PALATII IURISQUE DOCTISSIMUM ET THEOPHILUM VIRUM MAGNIFICUM IURIS PERITUM
ET ANTECESSOREM HUIUS ALMAE URBIS ET DOROTHEUM VIRUM MAGNIFICUM
QUAESTORIUM IURIS PERITUM ET ANTECESSOREM BERYTENSIUM
INCLITAE CIVITATIS [1]

LIBER PRIMUS.

I [2]
DE IUSTITIA ET IURE.

[3]Iustitia est constans et perpetua voluntas ius suum
1 cuique tribuens. Iuris prudentia est divinarum atque humanarum rerum notitia, iusti atque iniusti scientia.
2 His generaliter cognitis et incipientibus nobis exponere iura populi Romani ita maxime videntur posse tradi commodissime, si primo levi ac simplici, post deinde diligentissima atque exactissima interpretatione singula tradantur. alioquin si statim ab initio rudem adhuc et infirmum animum studiosi multitudine ac varietate rerum oneraverimus, duorum alterum aut desertorem studiorum efficiemus aut cum magno labore eius, saepe etiam cum diffidentia, quae plerumque iuvenes avertit [4], serius ad id perducamus [5], ad quod leniore [6] via ductus sine magno labore et sine ulla diffidentia maturius perduci potuisset.
3 [7]Iuris praecepta sunt haec: honeste vivere, al-
4 terum non laedere, suum cuique tribuere. [8]Huius studii duae sunt positiones, publicum et privatum. publicum ius est, quod ad statum rei Romanae spectat, privatum, quod ad singulorum utilitatem pertinet. dicendum est igitur de iure privato, quod est tripertitum [9]: collectum est enim ex naturalibus praeceptis aut gentium aut civilibus.

II [10]
DE IURE NATURALI ET GENTIUM ET CIVILI.

[11]Ius naturale est, quod natura omnia animalia docuit. nam ius istud non humani generis proprium est, sed omnium animalium, quae in caelo, quae in terra, quae in mari nascuntur [12]. hinc [13] descendit maris atque feminae coniugatio, quam nos matrimonium appellamus, hinc liberorum procreatio et educatio: videmus etenim cetera quoque animalia istius iuris peritia censeri.
1 'Ius autem civile vel gentium ita dividitur': [14]'omnes 'populi, qui legibus et moribus reguntur, partim suo 'proprio, partim communi omnium hominum iure utun-'tur: nam quod quisque populus ipse sibi ius consti-'tuit, id ipsius proprium civitatis est vocaturque ius 'civile, quasi ius proprium ipsius civitatis: quod vero 'naturalis ratio inter omnes homines constituit, id apud 'omnes populos peraeque custoditur vocaturque ius gen-'tium, quasi quo iure omnes gentes utuntur. et populus 'itaque Romanus partim suo proprio, partim communi

'omnium hominum iure utitur. quae singula qualia
2 'sunt, suis locis proponemus.' Sed ius quidem civile ex unaquaque civitate appellatur, veluti Atheniensium: nam si quis velit Solonis vel Draconis leges appellare ius civile Atheniensium, non erraverit. sic enim et ius, quo populus Romanus utitur, ius civile Romanorum appellamus: vel ius Quiritium, quo Quirites utuntur: Romani enim a Quirino Quirites appellantur [15]. sed quotiens non addimus, cuius sit civitatis, nostrum ius significamus: sicuti cum poetam dicimus nec addimus nomen, subauditur apud Graecos egregius Homerus, apud nos Vergilius. ius autem gentium omni humano generi commune est. nam usu exigente et humanis necessitatibus gentes humanae quaedam sibi constituerunt: bella etenim orta sunt et captivitates secutae et servitutes, quae sunt iuri naturali contrariae. iure enim naturali ab initio omnes homines liberi nascebantur. ex hoc iure gentium et omnes paene contractus introducti sunt, ut emptio venditio, locatio conductio, societas, depositum, mutuum et alii innumerabiles.
3 [16]Constat autem ius nostrum aut ex scripto aut ex non scripto, ut apud Graecos: τῶν νόμων οἱ μὲν ἔγγραφοι, οἱ δὲ ἄγραφοι [17]. Scriptum ius est lex [18],
4 plebi scita, senatus consulta, principum placita, magistratuum edicta, responsa prudentium. Lex est, quod populus Romanus senatore magistratu interrogante, veluti consule, constituebat. plebi scitum est, quod plebs plebeio magistratu interrogante, veluti tribuno, constituebat. [19]plebs autem a populo eo differt, quo species a genere: nam appellatione populi universi cives significantur connumeratis etiam patriciis et senatoribus: plebis autem appellatione sine patriciis et senatoribus ceteri cives significantur. sed et plebi scita lege Hortensia lata non
5 minus valere quam leges coeperunt. [20]'Senatus 'consultum est, quod senatus iubet atque constituit.' nam cum auctus est populus Romanus in eum modum, ut difficile sit in unum eum convocare legis sanciendae causa, aequum visum est senatum vice
6 populi consuli. [21]Sed et quod principi placuit, legis habet vigorem, cum lege regia, quae de imperio eius lata est, populus ei et in eum omne suum imperium et potestatem 'concessit'. quodcumque igitur imperator per epistulam constituit vel cognoscens decrevit vel edicto praecepit, legem esse constat: haec [22] sunt, quae constitutiones appellantur. plane ex his quaedam sunt personales, quae nec ad exemplum

(1) Hanc inscriptionem restitui ex EA (2) cf. Dig. 1, 1
(3) pr. § 1 cf. Ulp. l. 1 reg. (Dig. 1, 1, 10 pr. § 2) (4) sic VAΘ, evertit B (5) sic VAB, perducemus B cum Θ
(6) sic VA, leniori P, leviore B (7) § 3 cf. Ulp. l. c. (Dig. 1, 1, 10 § 1) (8) § 4 ex Ulp. l. 1 inst. (Dig. 1, 1 § 2)
(9) sic Θ, est tripertitu V, est tripertite ABP, tripertitum est Dig. (10) cf. Gai. 1, 1..8 Dig. 1, 1 (11) pr. ex Ulp. l. 1 inst. (Dig. 1, 1, 1 § 3) (12) animalium, quae

in terra, quae in mari nascuntur, avium quoque commune est Dig. (13) hinc BP Dig., hinc enim A (14) Gai. 1, 1 (Dig. 1, 1, 9) (15) sic BΘ, appellabantur APE (16) § 3 in. ex Ulp. l. 1 inst. (Dig. 1, 1, 6. § 1) (17) id est legum aliae scriptae aliae non scriptae (18) lex] PEΘ, leges AB (19) plebs .. ceteri cives significantur simil. Gaio 1, 3 (20) Gai. 1, 4 (21) § 6 ex Ulp. l. 1 inst. (Dig. 1, 4, 1) (22) haec] AB Dig., hae V, hee P

d

THE INSTITUTES OR ELEMENTS
OF
OUR LORD JUSTINIAN,
PERPETUAL AUGUSTUS,

COMPOSED BY TRIBONIAN, MINISTER AND
FORMER CHANCELLOR OF THE SACRED
PALACE, EMINENT IN RANK, UNMATCHED IN
LEGAL KNOWLEDGE, AND THE NOBLE
THEOPHILUS, JURIST, AND PROFESSOR OF
LAW IN THIS CAPITAL CITY; AND THE NOBLE
DOROTHEUS, MINISTER, JURIST, AND
PROFESSOR OF LAW IN THE SPLENDID

BOOK ONE

1.1 JUSTICE AND LAW

Justice is an unswerving and perpetual determination to acknowledge all men's rights. 1. Learning in the law entails knowledge of God and man, and mastery of the difference between justice and injustice. 2. As we embark on the exposition of Roman law after these general statements the best plan will be to give brief, straightforward accounts of each topic. The denser detail must be kept till later. Any other approach would mean making students take in a huge number of distinctions right at the start while their minds were still untrained and short of stamina. Half of them would give up. Or else they would lose their self-confidence – a frequent source of discouragement for the young – and at the cost of toil and tears would in the end reach the very standard they could have attained earlier and without overwork or self-doubt if they had been taken along an easier road. 3. The commandments of the law are these: live honourably; harm nobody; give everyone his due. 4. There are two aspects of the subject: public and private. Public law is concerned with the organization of the Roman state, while private law is about the well-being of individuals. Our business is private law. It has three parts, in that it is derived from the law of nature, of all peoples, or of the state.

1.2 THE LAW OF NATURE, OF ALL PEOPLES, AND OF THE STATE

The law of nature is the law instilled by nature in all creatures. It is not merely for mankind but for all creatures of the sky, earth and sea. From it comes intercourse between male and female, which we call marriage; also the bearing and bringing up of children. Observation shows that other animals also acknowledge its force. 1. The law of all peoples and the law of the state are distinguished as follows. All peoples with laws and customs apply law which is partly theirs alone and partly shared by all mankind. The law which each people makes for itself is special to its own state. It is called 'state law', the law peculiar to that state. But the law which natural reason makes for all mankind is applied the same everywhere. It is called 'the law of all peoples' because it is common to every nation. The law of the Roman people is also partly its own and partly common to all mankind. Which parts are which we will explain below. 2. The name of a particular state, Athens for example, is used to identify its state law. So it is correct to refer to the legislation of Solon and Draco as the Athenian state law. Similarly, we refer to the law of the Roman people as the Roman state law. We also call it the law of the Quirites, another name for the Romans, derived from Quirinus. When we add the name of no state we mean our own law. So the poet, if his name is omitted, is great Homer to the Greeks, Vergil to ourselves. By contrast, the law of all peoples is common to all mankind. The reality of the human condition led the peoples of the world to introduce certain institutions. Wars broke out. People were captured and made slaves, contrary to the law of nature. By the law of nature all men were initially born free. Nearly all the contracts come from this law of all peoples, sale, hire, partnership, deposit, loan, and many others. 3. Next, our law is either written or unwritten. The Greeks also make this distinction between written and unwritten law. Written law includes acts, plebeian statutes, resolutions of the senate, imperial pronouncements, magistrates' edicts, and answers given by jurists. 4. An act is the type of law which the Roman people used to make on the motion of a senatorial magistrate, for instance a consul. A plebeian statute is the kind which the plebeians used to enact on the motion of a plebeian magistrate such as a tribune. Plebeians and people differ as species and genus. The people is the citizen-body including the patricians and senators, the plebeians the same minus the patricians and senators. After the Hortensian Act plebeian statutes were given the same force and effect as acts. 5. A resolution of the senate is a law decided and enacted by the senate. When the Roman people became too large to be easily called together in a body for legislative purposes, it seemed reasonable to turn to the senate instead. 6. A pronouncement of the emperor also has legislative force because, by the Regal Act relating to his sovereign power, the people conferred on him its whole sovereignty and authority. If the emperor decides a question in a written reply, or if he hears a case and gives judgment, or if he ordains something by edict, his utterance is law. These are all called pronouncements. Sometimes they are clearly personal // and cannot be

trahuntur, 'quoniam non hoc princeps vult': nam quod alicui ob merita indulsit, vel si cui poenam irrogavit, vel si cui sine exemplo subvenit, personam non egreditur. aliae autem, cum generales sunt, omnes procul
7 dubio tenent. Praetorum quoque edicta non modicam iuris optinent auctoritatem. haec etiam ius honorarium solemus appellare, quod qui honores gerunt, id est magistratus, auctoritatem huic iuri dederunt. proponebant et aediles curules edictum de quibusdam casibus, quod edictum iuris honorarii
8 portio est. ¹'Responsa prudentium sunt senten-'tiae et opiniones eorum, quibus permissum 'erat'² 'iura condere³.' nam antiquitus institutum erat, ut essent qui iura publice interpretarentur, quibus a Caesare ius respondendi datum est, qui iuris consulti appellabantur. quorum omnium sententiae et opiniones eam auctoritatem tenent, ut iudici recedere a
9 responso eorum non liceat, ut est constitutum. Ex non scripto ius venit, quod usus comprobavit. nam diuturni mores consensu utentium comprobati legem
10 imitantur. Et non ineleganter in duas species ius civile distributum videtur. nam origo eius ab institutis duarum civitatium, Athenarum scilicet et Lacedaemonis, fluxisse videtur: in his enim civitatibus ita agi solitum erat, ut Lacedaemonii quidem magis ea, quae pro legibus observarent, memoriae mandarent, Athenienses vero ea, quae in legibus scripta reprehendissent⁴, custodirent.
11 Sed naturalia quidem iura, quae apud omnes gentes peraeque servantur, divina quadam providentia constituta semper firma atque immutabilia permanent: ea vero, quae ipsa sibi quaeque civitas constituit, saepe mutari solent vel tacito consensu populi vel alia postea lege lata.
12 ⁵'Omne autem ius, quo utimur, vel ad personas 'pertinet vel ad res vel ad actiones. ac prius de per-'sonis videamus.' nam parum est ius nosse, si personae, quarum causa statutum est, ignorentur.

III ⁶
DE IURE PERSONARUM.

7 'Summa 'itaque'⁸ divizio de iure personarum haec 'est quod omnes homines aut liberi sunt aut servi.'
1 ⁹Et libertas quidem est, ex qua etiam liberi vocantur, naturalis facultas eius quod cuique facere
2 libet, nisi si quid aut vi aut iure prohibetur. Servitus autem est constitutio iuris gentium, qua quis
3 dominio alieno contra naturam subicitur. Servi autem ex eo appellati sunt, quod imperatores captivos vendere iubent ac per hoc servare nec occidere solent. qui etiam mancipia dicti sunt, quod ab hostibus
4 manu capiuntur. Servi autem aut nascuntur aut fiunt. nascuntur ex ancillis nostris: fiunt aut iure gentium, id est ex captivitate, aut iure civili, cum homo liber maior viginti annis ad pretium participandum sese venumdari passus est. in servorum
5 condicione nulla differentia est¹⁰. In liberis multae differentiae sunt. aut enim ingenui sunt aut libertini.

IV ¹¹
DE INGENUIS.

Ingenuus is est, qui statim ut natus est liber est, sive ex duobus ingenuis matrimonio editus, sive ex libertinis, sive ex altero libertino altero ingenuo. sed

---

et si quis ex matre libera nascatur, patre servo, ingennus nihilo minus nascitur: quemadmodum qui ex matre libera et incerto patre natus est, quoniam vulgo conceptus est. ¹²sufficit 'autem' liberam fuisse matrem eo tempore quo nascitur, licet ancilla conceperit. et ex contrario si libera conceperit, deinde ancilla facta pariat, placuit eum qui nascitur liberum nasci, quia non debet calamitas matris ei nocere, qui in utero est. ex his et illud quaesitum est, si ancilla praegnans manumissa sit, deinde ancilla postea facta peperit, liberum an servum pariat? et Marcellus probat liberum nasci: sufficit enim ei qui in ventre est liberam
1 matrem vel medio tempore habuisse: quod et verum est. Cum autem ingenuus aliquis natus sit, non officit illi in servitute fuisse et postea manumissum esse: saepissime enim constitutum est natalibus non officere manumissionem.

V ¹³
DE LIBERTINIS.

¹⁴'Libertini sunt, qui ex iusta servitute manumissi 'sunt.' ¹⁵manumissio autem est datio¹⁶ libertatis: nam quamdiu quis in servitute est, manui et potestati suppositus est, et manumissus liberatur potestate. quae res a iure gentium originem sumpsit, utpote cum iure naturali omnes liberi nascerentur nec esset nota manumissio, cum servitus esset incognita: sed posteaquam iure gentium servitus invasit, secutum est beneficium manumissionis. et cum uno communi¹⁷ nomine homines appellaremur¹⁸, iure gentium tria genera hominum esse coeperunt, liberi et his contrarium servi et tertium genus libertini, qui desierant
1 esse servi. 'Multis autem modis manumissio pro-'cedit: aut enim ex sacris constitutionibus in sacro-'sanctis ecclesiis aut vindicta¹⁹ aut inter amicos aut 'per epistulam aut per testamentum aut aliam quam-'libet ultimam voluntatem. sed et aliis multis modis li-'bertas servo competere potest, qui tam ex veteribus quam
2 'nostris constitutionibus introducti sunt.' ²⁰'Servi 'vero' a dominis semper manumitti solent: adeo ut 'vel in transitu manumittantur, veluti cum praetor 'aut proconsul 'aut praeses' in balneum vel in thea-'trum eat.'
3 'Libertinorum autem status tripertitus antea fuerat: 'nam qui manumittebantur, modo maiorem et iustam 'libertatem consequebantur et fiebant cives Romani, 'modo minorem et Latini ex lege Iunia Norbana fie-'bant, modo inferiorem et fiebant ex lege Aelia Sentia 'dediticiorum numero. sed dediticiorum quidem pessima 'condicio iam ex multis temporibus in desuetudinem 'abiit, Latinorum vero nomen non frequentabatur: 'ideoque nostra pietas omnia augere et in meliorem 'statum reducere desiderans in duabus constitutio-'nibus²¹ hoc emendavit et in pristinum statum reduxit, 'quia et a primis urbis Romae cunabulis una atque 'simplex libertas competebat, id est eadem, quam 'habebat manumissor, nisi quod scilicet libertinus fit²² 'qui manumittitur, licet manumissor ingenuus sit. et 'dediticios quidem per²³ constitutionem expulimus, 'quam promulgavimus inter nostras decisiones, per 'quas suggerente nobis Triboniano viro excelso quaes-'tore antiqui iuris altercationes placavimus: Latinos 'autem Iunianos et omnem quae circa eos fuerit ob-'servantiam²⁴ alia constitutione per eiusdem quaestoris 'suggestionem correximus, quae inter imperiales radiat

---

(1) *Gai.* 1, 7   (2) erat] *VAP*, est *B Gai.*   (3) concedere *VP*   (4) *sic VA*, invenissent *B*, comprehendissent *PE*   (5) *Gai.* 1, 8   (6) *Cf. Dig.* 1, 5
(7) *Gai.* 1, 9 (*Dig.* 1, 5, 3)   (8) *sic B Dig. Θ*, itaque om. *AP*, et quidem summa *Gai.*   (9) § 1..3 *ex Flor. l. 9 inst.* (*Dig.* 1, 5, 4)   (10) *sic BPE*, nullae differentiae sunt *A*   (11) *Cf. Gai.* 1, 11   (12) *pr. fin. ex Marciani l. 1 inst.* (*Dig.* 1, 5, 5 § 2. 3)   (13) *Cf. Gai.* 1, 11..34 *Dig.* 40, 1 *seqq.*

Cod. 7, 1 *seqq.*   (14) *Gai.* 1, 11 (*Dig.* 1, 5, 6)   (15) *pr. fin. ex Ulp. l. 1 inst.* (*Dig.* 1, 1, 4)   (16) *sic PEΘ Dig.*, donatio *B*   (17) communi] *PE*, naturali *Dig. Θ.* om. *B*   (18) *sic PE Dig.*, appellemur *BΘ*   (19) vindicta] *PE*, vind. manumittuntur *B*   (20) *Gai.* 1, 20   (21) *Cod.* 7, 5. 6   (22) fit] *BP*, sit *E cum Θ*   (23) per] *PEΘ*, et per *B*   (24) omnem .. observantiam] *PEΘ*, omnes quae fuerant observantia (om. circa eos) *B*

used to support a general rule because the emperor never intended them in that way. A favour rewarding one man's merit, or a punishment imposed on another, or unprecedented assistance given to a third, goes no further than that individual. Other pronouncements are general; they certainly bind everyone. 7. The edicts of the praetors are also an important source of law. They form what we call honorarian law. The term derives from the fact that the offices of the magistrates who developed this law were called 'honours'. The curule aediles also issued an edict on some topics; their edict is one part of the honorarian law. 8. Juristic answers are the opinions and advice of those entrusted with the task of building up the law. It was decided long ago that there should be official expositors of the law. They were called consultants at law, and the emperor gave them the right of replying to legal questions. When they were unanimous, their opinion had such weight that a judge could not depart from the terms of their answer. There was a ruling to that effect by imperial pronouncement. 9. Law comes into being without writing when a rule is approved by use. Long-standing custom founded on the consent of those who follow it is just like legislation. 10. The classification of the law of our state into a written part and an unwritten part acquires a certain elegance from the fact that our law was originally modelled on the law of two city-states, Athens and Sparta. Of these two, the Spartans tended to prefer laws committed to memory, while the Athenians kept to laws set out in writing. 11. The law of nature, which is observed uniformly by all peoples, is sanctioned by divine providence and lasts for ever, strong and unchangeable. The law which each state establishes for itself is often changed either by the tacit consent of the people or by later legislation. 12. All our law is about persons, things, or actions. We turn to persons first. There is little point in knowing the law if one knows nothing about the persons for whom it exists.

1.3 THE LAW OF PERSONS

The main classification in the law of persons is this: all men are either free or slaves. 1. Liberty – the Latin 'libertas' gives us 'liberi', free men – denotes a man's natural ability to do what he wants as long as the law or some other force does not prevent him. 2. Slavery on the other hand is an institution of the law of all peoples; it makes a man the property of another, contrary to the law of nature. 3. Slaves, in Latin 'servi', are so called because it is the practice of army commanders to order captives to be sold and thus saved – 'save' in Latin is 'servare' – instead of killed. Another Latin word for slaves is 'mancipia', derived from the fact that they are captured by hand from the enemy, in Latin 'manu capiuntur'. 4. They are either born slaves or enslaved afterwards. The off-spring of slave women are born slaves. Enslavement can happen under the law of all peoples, by capture; or under the law of the state, as when a free man over twenty allows himself to be sold to share the price. The legal condition of all slaves is the same. 5. Among free men there are many distinctions. Free men are either free-born or freed.

1.4 THE FREE-BORN

A person is free-born if he is free at the moment of his birth, whether he is the child of a marriage between two free-born people, or is born to freed people, or to a couple one of whom is free-born and the other freed. Equally he is free-born if his mother is free and his father a slave. The same is true if his mother is free and his father unknown because he was conceived casually. It is enough for the mother to be free at the time of the birth even though a slave at conception. Even the other way around, with the mother free at conception but a slave by the birth, it is accepted that the child is born free. The reason is that the mother's calamity should not prejudice the baby in her womb. If a mother is a slave on conception, then manumitted, then re-enslaved before giving birth, is the child born free or a slave? Marcellus concludes for freedom at birth: it is enough for the baby in the womb that he had a free mother for part of the time. That is right. 1. Once someone has been born free, later enslavement followed by manumission does not derogate from his first status. It has been decided again and again that manumission cannot displace birthrights.

1.5 FREEDMEN

A freedman is someone who has been manumitted from lawful slavery. Manumission is the grant of freedom. As the word implies, while a man is a slave he is gripped in the hand of his owner and in his power; by release from that grip he becomes free. This originated in the law common to all men. Under the law of nature all men were born free. Manumission and slavery were both unknown. But later, when the law of all peoples allowed slavery to spread, the benefit of manumission followed in its wake. We all share the single name of man but we have been put in three distinct categories by this law of all peoples: free-born; at the other extreme, slaves; and then the third class, freedmen, those who have emerged from slavery. 1. Manumission can be done in many ways. Imperial pronouncements have laid down that it can be done in church. It can be done by rod, or before friends, or by letter, or by a testamentary or other expression of the owner's last wishes. Besides these there are also many other roads to freedom, recognized in earlier pronouncements and in our own. 2. The usual thing is for slaves to be freed through manumission by their owners. It is such an everyday matter that manumissions are performed even en route from one place to another, as when the praetor or proconsul or governor is on the way to the baths or the theatre. 3. There used to be three different grades of freedman. Their manumission sometimes gave them freedom in the higher degree, making them Roman citizens, sometimes in the lower degree, making them Latins under the Junian-Norbanan Act, and sometimes in the lowest degree, making them capitulated aliens under the Aelian-Sentian Act. This last and worst condition fell out of use long ago. Even Latin status was infrequently encountered. In our concern for progress and improvement we have by two pronouncements reformed this regime and re-introduced the earliest scheme from the infancy of Rome. Then there was only one liberty attainable, single and undivided, the same as was enjoyed by the party making the manumission, except that the slave became a freedman even if the manumitting owner was free-born. We have abolished the status of capitulated alien. That was done by a pronouncement issued as one of the rulings by which, on the initiative of Tribonian our chancellor, of eminent rank, we settled certain disputes in the classical law. By another pronouncement, made at the instigation of the same chancellor and now an adornment to the imperial statute book, we reformed the status of Junian Latinity and the complex of rules surrounding it. // We

'sanctiones, et omnes libertos nullo nec aetatis manu-
'missi nec dominii [1] manumissoris nec in manumissio-
'nis modo discrimine habito, sicuti antea observaba-
'tur, civitate Romana donavimus: multis additis mo-
'dis, per quos possit libertas servis cum civitate Ro-
'mana, quae sola in praesenti est, praestari.'

VI [2]

QUI [3] EX QUIBUS CAUSIS MANUMITTERE NON POSSUNT.

[4] 'Non tamen cuicumque volenti manumittere licet.
'nam is qui in fraudem creditorum manumittit nihil
1 'agit, quia lex Aelia Sentia impedit libertatem.' Licet
autem domino, qui solvendo non est, testamento servum suum cum libertate heredem instituere, ut fiat
liber heresque ei solus et necessarius, si modo nemo
alius ex eo [5] testamento heres extiterit, aut quia nemo
heres scriptus sit, aut quia is qui scriptus est qualibet ex causa heres non extiterit. idque eadem lege
Aelia Sentia provisum est et recte: valde enim pro-
spiciendum erat, ut egentes homines, quibus alius
heres extaturus non esset, vel servum suum necessarium heredem habeant, qui satisfacturus esset creditoribus, aut hoc eo non faciente creditores res
hereditarias servi nomine vendant, ne iniuria defunc-
2 tus afficiatur. Idemque iuris est et si sine libertate servus heres institutus est. quod nostra consti-
'tutio [6] non solum in domino, qui solvendo non est,
'sed generaliter constituit nova humanitatis ratione,
'ut ex ipsa scriptura institutionis etiam libertas ei
'competere videatur, cum non est verisimile eum, quem
'heredem sibi elegit, si praetermiserit libertatis da-
'tionem, servum remanere voluisse et neminem sibi
3 'heredem fore.' [7] In fraudem autem creditorum
manumittere videtur, qui vel iam eo tempore quo
manumittit solvendo non est, vel qui datis libertatibus desiturus est solvendo esse. praevaluisse tamen
videtur, nisi animum quoque fraudandi manumissor
habuit, non impediri libertatem, quamvis bona eius
creditoribus non sufficiant: saepe enim de facultatibus suis amplius quam in his est sperant homines.
itaque tunc intellegimus impediri libertatem, cum
utroque modo fraudantur creditores, id est et consilio manumittentis et ipsa re, eo quod bona non
suffectura sunt creditoribus.
4 [8] 'Eadem lege Aelia Sentia domino minori annis
'viginti non aliter manumittere permittitur, quam si
'vindicta apud consilium iusta causa manumissionis
5 'adprobata fuerint manumissi [9]. [10] Iustae autem
'manumissionis causae sunt, veluti si quis patrem
'aut matrem aut filium filiamve aut fratrem soro-
'remve naturales aut paedagogum nutricem educato-
'rem aut alumnum alumnamve aut collactaneum
'manumittat, aut servum procuratoris habendi gratia,
'aut ancillam matrimonii causa', dum tamen intra sex
menses uxor ducatur, nisi iusta causa impediat [11], et
qui manumittitur procuratoris habendi gratia ne an-
6 nor septem et decem [12] annis manumittatur. Semel
autem causa adprobata, sive vera sive falsa sit, non
retractatur.
7 [13] 'Cum ergo [14] certus modus manumittendi mi-
'noribus viginti annis dominis per legem Aeliam Sen-
'tiam constitutus sit, eveniebat, ut, qui quattuordecim
'annos aetatis expleverit, licet testamentum facere
'possit et in eo heredem sibi instituere legataque re-
'linquere possit, tamen, si adhuc minor sit annis vi-
'ginti, libertatem servo dare non poterat.' 'quod

'non erat ferendum, si is, cui totorum bonorum in
'testamento dispositio data erat, uni servo libertatem
'dare non permittebatur. quare nos [15] similiter ei
'quemadmodum alias res ita et servos suos in ultima
'voluntate disponere quemadmodum voluerit permitti-
'mus, ut et libertatem eis possit praestare. sed cum
'libertas inaestimabilis est et propter hoc ante vicesi-
'mum aetatis annum antiquitas libertatem servo dari
'prohibebat: ideo nos mediam quodammodo viam eli-
'gentes non aliter minori viginti annis libertatem in
'testamento dare servo suo concedimus, nisi septimum
'et decimum annum impleverit et octavum decimum
'tetigerit. cum enim antiquitas huiusmodi aetati et
'pro aliis postulare concessit, cur non etiam sui iu-
'dicii stabilitas ita eos adiuvare credatur, ut et ad
'libertates dandas servis suis possint pervenire [16].'

VII [17]

DE LEGE FUFIA CANINIA SUBLATA.

[18] 'Lege Fufia Caninia certus modus constitutus erat
'in servis testamento manumittendis.' 'quam quasi liber-
'tatibus impedientem et quodammodo invidam tollen-
'dam esse censuimus, cum satis fuerat inhumanum
'vivos quidem licentiam habere totam suam familiam
'libertate donare, nisi alia causa impediat libertati,
'morientibus autem huiusmodi licentiam adimere.'

VIII [19]

DE HIS QUI SUI VEL ALIENI IURIS SUNT.

[20] 'Sequitur de iure personarum alia divisio. nam
'quaedam personae sui iuris sunt, quaedam alieno
'iuri subiectae sunt: rursus earum, quae alieno iuri
'subiectae sunt, aliae in potestate 'parentum, aliae in
'potestate dominorum' sunt. videamus 'itaque de his
'quae alieno iuri subiectae sunt: nam si cognoveri-
'mus, quae istae personae sint, simul intellegemus,
'quae sui iuris sunt. ac prius dispiciamus de his qui
'in potestate 'dominorum' sunt.
1 'In potestate itaque dominorum sunt servi. quae
'quidem potestas iuris gentium est: nam apud omnes
'peraeque gentes animadvertere possumus dominis in
'servos vitae necisque potestatem esse: et quodcum-
'que per servum adquiritur, id domino adquiritur.
2 'Sed hoc tempore 'nullis' hominibus, qui sub [21] im-
'perio 'nostro' sunt, licet sine causa 'legibus cognita'
'et supra modum in servos suos saevire. nam ex
'constitutione 'divi Pii' Antonini qui sine causa ser-
'vum suum occiderit, non minus puniri iubetur, quam
'qui servum alienum occiderit. sed et maior asperitas
'dominorum eiusdem principis constitutione coercetur.
'nam consultus a quibusdam praesidibus provincia-
'rum de his servis, qui ad 'aedem sacram' vel ad sta-
'tuas principum confugiunt, praecepit ut, si intolera-
'bilis videatur dominorum saevitia, cogantur servos
'bonis condicionibus' vendere, ut pretium dominis
'daretur', et recte: 'expedit enim rei publicae, ne quis
're sua male utatur.' [22] cuius rescripti ad Aelium
Marcianum emissi verba haec sunt: 'Dominorum qui-
'dem potestatem in suos servos illibatam esse oportet
'nec cuiquam hominum ius suum detrahi. sed domi-
'norum interest, ne auxilium contra saevitiam vel
'famem vel intolerabilem iniuriam denegetur his qui
'iuste deprecantur. ideoque cognosce de querellis
'eorum, qui ex familia Iulii Sabini ad statuam con-
'fugerunt, et [23] si vel durius habitos, quam aequum
'est, vel infami iniuria affectos cognoveris, veniri iube,

(1) sic Θ, domini *libri*   (2) *Cf. Gai.* 1, 19..21. 36..42. 47
Dig. 40, 2. 9 *Cod.* 7, 1. 11   (3) qui] *ind. V*, qui *et B index*
BΘ, *om.* E   (4) *Gai.* 1, 36. 37   (5) eo] BE, *om.* PΘ
(6) *Cod.* 6, 27, 5   (7) § 3 *in ex Gai. l.* 1 *rer. cott.* (*Dig.*
40, 9, 10)   (8) *Gai.* 1, 38. 19   (9) fuerint manumissi]
sic dett., fuerit man. *BPE*, fuerit (*om.* manumissi) *Gai.*:
fuitne quam vindicta, si ap. cons. i. c. m. adpr. fuerit
(*Savigny*)?   (10) *Cf. Gai.* 1, 39. 19   (11) *sic* PEΘ,
impediatur *B*   (12) *sic libri cum* Θ, decem et octo |

Dig. 40, 2, 13   (13) *Gai.* 1, 40   (14) *sic* PE *Gai.*,
autem *B*   (15) nos] *B*, non *PE*   (16) *sic* PE[b], invenire *B*, provenire E[a]
(17) *Cf. Gai.* 1, 42..46. *Cod.* 7, 3   (18) *Gai.* 1, 42
(19) *Cf. Dig.* 1, 6   (20) *Gai.* 1, 48..53 (*Dig.* 1, 6, 1)
(21) sub hoc *B*   (22) § 2 *fin. ex Dig.* 1, 6, 2 (*Ulp. l.* 8
de off. proc., cf. Coll. l. Mos. 3, 3)   (23) et] ut *B*

have given all freedmen Roman citizenship irrespective of shortcomings as to the age of the slave manumitted or of the owner manumitting or in the mode of manumission, all of which used to be material. We have added considerably to the ways in which slaves can acquire freedom with Roman citizenship. That is the only kind of freedom nowadays.

1.6 CASES IN WHICH MANUMISSION IS IMPOSSIBLE

The law does not allow complete freedom of manumission. A manumission in fraud of creditors is void, because the Aelian-Sentian Act bars the grant of liberty. 1. However, an insolvent owner may appoint a slave his heir by will, with a concurrent grant of freedom. The slave then becomes free as the testator's single and compulsory heir. This only happens if there is no other heir under the will, which may be because no one else is named or because for some reason the named person does not become heir. All this was allowed by the Aelian-Sentian Act. Quite rightly, since it is essential that the financially unsound, for whom no heir is likely to act, should at least have a slave to serve compulsorily. He can then negotiate arrangements with the creditors. Failing that, the creditors can sell the assets of the estate in the slave's name and avoid dishonour to the deceased. 2. The law is the same if the slave is appointed heir without a grant of freedom. Our own pronouncement, implementing a generous new principle, has laid down that in all cases, not merely in insolvency, the appointment of a slave as heir should automatically confer liberty as well. If a testator names an heir, it is contradictory to infer from the omission of a grant of freedom that he wants the appointee to stay a slave, leaving himself with no heir at all. 3. A grant of freedom amounts to fraud on creditors when the grantor is already insolvent at the time of the manumission or will become so by freeing the slaves. However, the view has prevailed that even if it reduces the estate to insolvency the grant is valid unless the grantor acted with intent to defraud. People are often over-optimistic as to the extent of their wealth. So the case in which we hold freedom barred is where the creditors are defrauded on both levels, by the grantor's intent and objectively by the deficiency of the estate. 4. The Aelian-Sentian Act also forbids manumission by an owner under twenty except where the slaves in question are given their freedom by rod for a good reason shown to a committee. 5. Such reason exists where, for instance, the grantee is the grantor's real father, mother, son, daughter, brother, or sister; or else his teacher, wet-nurse, minder, foster-child of either sex or foster-sibling; or else a slave whom he wants to make his general agent, or a slave-woman freed for marriage. In this last case he must marry the woman within six months, unless there is a legal impediment. Where a slave is freed to be a general agent, he cannot be less than seventeen years old. 6. Once the committee accepts any of these reasons, whether true or false in fact, the freedom cannot be rescinded. 7. When the Aelian-Sentian Act restricted the rights of owners under twenty to grant freedom, a consequence for those over fourteen was that despite having capacity to make a will, appoint an heir and leave legacies, they could not till twenty give freedom to a slave. It was indefensible that a person with power to dispose of all his estate by will was barred from freeing a single slave. We have given him the power over his slaves that he has over his other assets, so that he can dispose of them by his last will as he pleases. This includes freeing them. But freedom is beyond price, and for that very reason antiquity forbade its grant by owners under twenty. We have as it were trodden a middle path, allowing people under twenty to grant freedom to their slaves by will provided they are over seventeen. Since at that age antiquity allowed them even to plead for others in court, it is difficult to argue that their judgment is not well enough developed to allow them to choose whether to free their slaves.

1.7 REPEAL OF THE FUFIAN-CANINIAN ACT

The Fufian-Caninian Act restricted manumissions in wills. We decided that the Act should be repealed as a hindrance to and in a sense an enemy of freedom. It was certainly ungenerous to allow the living, in the absence of some special obstacle, to give freedom to the entire body of their slaves while withholding the same privilege from the dying.

1.8 INDEPENDENT AND DEPENDENT PERSONS

We come to another classification in the law of persons. Some people are independent and some are controlled by others. Of the latter, some are within the authority of parents, others of owners. Let us examine the dependent category. If we find out who is dependent, we cannot help seeing who is independent. We turn first to the ones in the authority of owners. 1. People in this class are slaves. Owners' authority over slaves rests on the law of all peoples. We can observe the same thing everywhere: owners hold the power of life and death over slaves, and owners get whatever slaves acquire. 2. But nowadays no one in our empire may be cruel to his slaves except on legally recognized grounds, and then only within reason. A pronouncement of the Emperor Antoninus Pius makes a man who kills his own slave without good grounds liable to the same punishment as one who kills someone else's slave. Excessive severity on the part of owners is curbed by a pronouncement of the same Emperor. He was consulted by some provincial governors about slaves who took refuge in a holy place or at a statue of the emperor. He responded by ordering that if the cruelty of the owner was found to have been intolerable such slaves should be compulsorily sold on good terms and the money paid to the owners. That was quite right. It is in the public interest that nobody should treat his property badly. These are the words of the written reply by which the Emperor replied to Aelius Marcianus: 'It is true that the power of owners over their slaves should be unfettered and that no owner's rights should be diminished, but it is in their own interest that relief against cruelty, starvation or gross abuse should not be denied to those who have reason to implore your intervention. Investigate the complaints of the slaves from the household of Julius Sabinus who took refuge at the statue. If you discover that they have been immoderately and unfairly handled or grossly abused, command that they be sold with a condition against being returned into their owner's authority. // As for

'ita ut in potestatem domini non revertantur. qui 'Sabinus[1], si meae constitutioni fraudem fecerit, sciet 'me[2] admissum severius exsecuturum.'

IX[3]
DE PATRIA POTESTATE.

[4] 'In potestate nostra sunt liberi nostri, quos ex
1 'iustis nuptiis procreaverimus.' Nuptiae autem sive matrimonium est viri et mulieris coniunctio, in-
2 dividuam consuetudinem vitae continens. [5]'Ius 'autem potestatis, quod in liberos habemus,' proprium 'est civium Romanorum: nulli enim alii sunt homi-'nes, qui talem in liberos habeant potestatem, qua-
3 'lem nos habemus.' [6]'Qui igitur ex te et uxore tua nascitur, in tua potestate est: item qui ex filio tuo et uxore eius nascitur, id est nepos tuus et nep-tis, aeque in tua sunt potestate, et pronepos et pro-neptis et deinceps ceteri. qui tamen ex filia tua nasci-tur, in tua potestate non est, sed in patris eius.

X[7]
DE NUPTIIS.

Iustas autem nuptias inter se cives Romani con-trahunt, qui secundum praecepta legum coeunt, mas-culi quidem puberes, feminae autem viripotentes, sive patres familias sint sive filii familias, dum tamen filii familias et consensum habeant parentum, quorum in potestate sunt. nam hoc fieri debere et civilis et na-turalis ratio suadet in tantum, ut iussum parentis praecedere debeat unde quaesitum est, an furiosi filia nubere aut furiosi filius uxorem ducere possit? 'cumque super filio variabatur, nostra processit de-'cisio[8], qua permissum est ad exemplum filiae furiosi 'filium quoque posse et sine patris interventu matri-'monium sibi copulare secundum datum ex constitu-'tione modum.'
1   [9]'Ergo non omnes nobis uxores ducere licet: 'nam quarundam nuptiis abstinendum est[10]. inter eas 'enim personas, quae parentum liberorumve locum 'inter se optinent, nuptiae contrahi non possunt, veluti 'inter patrem et filiam vel avum et neptem vel ma-'trem et filium 'vel aviam et nepotem et usque ad 'infinitum': et si tales personae inter se coierint, ne-'farias atque incestas nuptias contraxisse dicuntur. 'et haec adeo ita sunt, ut, quamvis per adoptionem 'parentum liberorumve loco sibi esse coeperint, non 'possint[11] inter se matrimonio iungi in tantum, ut etiam 'dissoluta adoptione idem iuris maneat: itaque eam, 'quae tibi per adoptionem filia aut neptis esse coe-'perit, non poteris uxorem ducere, quamvis eam eman-'cipaveris.'
2   [9]'Inter eas quoque personas, quae ex transverso 'gradu cognationis[12] iunguntur, est quaedam similis 'observatio, sed non tanta. sane enim[13] inter fratrem 'sororemque nuptiae prohibitae sunt, sive 'ab' eodem 'patre eademque matre nati fuerint, sive 'ex' alterutro 'eorum. sed[14] si qua per adoptionem soror tibi esse 'coeperit, quamdiu quidem constat adoptio, sane inter 'te et eam nuptiae consistere non possunt: cum vero 'per emancipationem adoptio dissoluta sit, poteris 'eam uxorem ducere: sed et tu emancipatus fueris, 'nihil est impedimento nuptiis.' et ideo constat, si quis generum adoptare velit, debere eum ante filiam suam emancipare: et si quis velit nurum adoptare,
3 debere eum ante filium emancipare. 'Fratris vel' sororis filiam uxorem ducere non licet. sed nec nep-tem 'fratris vel' sororis ducere quis potest, quamvis

quarto gradu sint[15]: cuius enim filiam uxorem du-cere non licet, eius neque neptem permittitur. eius vero mulieris, quam pater tuus adoptavit, filiam non
4 videris impediri uxorem ducere, quia neque naturali neque civili iure tibi coniungitur. Duorum autem fratrum vel sororum liberi vel fratris et sororis iungi
5 possunt. Item amitam licet adoptivam uxorem ducere non licet, item materteram, quia parentum loco habentur[16]. qua ratione verum est magnam quo-que amitam et materteram magnam prohiberi uxorem
6 ducere. Adfinitatis quoque veneratione[17] quarun-dam nuptiis abstinere necesse est. ut ecce privignam aut nurum uxorem ducere non licet, quia utraeque filiae loco sunt. quod scilicet ita accipi debeat, si fuit nurus aut privigna: nam si adhuc nurus est, id est si adhuc nupta est filio tuo[18], alia ratione uxo-rem eam ducere non possis, quia eadem duobus nupta esse non potest: item si adhuc privigna tua est[19], id est si mater eius tibi nupta est, ideo eam uxorem ducere non poteris, quia duas uxores eodem tempore
7 habere non licet. Socrum quoque et novercam prohibitum est uxorem ducere, quia matris loco sunt. quod et ipsum dissoluta demum adfinitate procedit: alioquin si adhuc noverca est, id est si adhuc patri tuo nupta est, communi iure impeditur tibi nubere, quia eadem duobus nupta esse non potest: item si adhuc socrus est, id est si adhuc filia eius tibi nupta est, ideo impediuntur nuptiae, quia duas uxores ha-
8 bere non possis. Mariti tamen filius ex alia uxore et uxoris filia ex alio marito vel contra matrimonium recte contrahunt, licet habeant fratrem sororemve ex
9 matrimonio postea contracto natos. Si uxor tua post divortium ex alio filiam procreaverit, haec non est quidem privigna tua: sed Iulianus[20] huiusmodi nuptiis abstinere debere ait: nam nec sponsam filii nurum esse nec patris sponsam novercam esse, rectius tamen et iure facturos eos, qui huiusmodi nuptiis se
10 abstinuerint. Illud certum est serviles quoque cognationes impedire esse nuptiis, si forte pater
11 et filia aut frater et soror manumissi fuerint. 'Sunt 'et aliae personae, quae propter diversas rationes nup-'tias contrahere prohibentur, quas in libris digesto-'rum seu pandectorum ex veteri iure collectarum enu-'merari permisimus.'
12   Si adversus ea quae diximus aliqui coierint, nec vir nec uxor nec nuptiae nec matrimonium nec dos intellegitur. [21]'itaque ii, qui ex eo coitu nascuntur, 'in potestate patris non sunt, sed tales sunt,' quantum ad patriam potestatem pertinet, 'quales sunt ii, quos 'mater vulgo concepit. nam nec hi patrem habere 'intelleguntur, cum is etiam incertus sit: unde so-'lent filii spurii appellari, vel a Graeca voce quasi 'σποράδην concepti vel quasi sine patre filii.' sequi-tur ergo, ut is et dissoluto tali coitu nec dotis exactioni locus sit. 'qui autem prohibitas nuptias coeunt, et 'alias poenas patiuntur, quae sacris constitutionibus 'continentur.'
13   [22]'Aliquando autem evenit, ut liberi, qui statim 'ut[23] nati sunt in potestate parentum non fiant, postea 'tamen[24] redigantur in potestatem.' qualis est is, qui, 'dum naturalis fuerat, postea curiae datus potestati 'patris subicitur. nec non is, qui a muliere libera 'procreatus, cuius matrimonium minime legibus inter-'dictum fuerat, sed ad quam pater consuetudinem 'habuerat, postea ex nostra constitutione[25] dotalibus 'instrumentis compositis in potestate patris efficitur: 'quod et aliis, si ex eodem matrimonio[26] fuerint pro-'creati, similiter nostra constitutio[27] praebuit.'

---

(1) **sabinus** *del. cum Dig. Coll.*   (2) **me**] *E Dig. Coll.*, *me hoc* AP, *me* adversum *se* B   (3) *Cf. Dig.* 1, 6 *Cod.* 8, 46 (47)   (4) *Gai.* 1, 55 (*Dig.* 1, 6, 3)   (5) *Gai. l. c.*   (6) § 3 *ex Ulp. l.* 1 *inst.* (*Dig.* 1, 6, 4)   (7) *Cf. Gai.* 1, 56..65 *Dig.* 23, 2 *Cod.* 5, 4   (8) *Cod.* 5, 4, 25   (9) *Gai.* 1, 58..61 (10) *sic* BPE, **abstinere debemus** AGai.   (11) **possint**] A, **possunt** BP Gai.   (12) **cognatione** Gai.   (13) **enim** *om. Gai.*   (14) **sed**] APΘ Gai., **sed et** BE   (15) *sic* PΘ,

quartus gradus sit *AB*, quarto gradu sit *E*   (16) *sic. dett. cum* Θ, **habetur** ABPE   (17) **ratione** *dett.*, *sed* αἰδοῖ τῆς ἀγχιστείας Θ   (18) **tuo**] PE *eius* A, *om.* B   (19) **tua est**] PE, **mevii est** A, *om.* B   (20) *cf. Dig.* 23, 2, 12 § 3   (21) *Gai* 1, 64   (22) *Gai.* 1, 65 (23) **ut**] PE *cum* Θ, *om.* AB   (24) **tamen**] *Gai.*, **autem** *libri*   (25) *Cod.* 5, 27, 10   (26) **si ex e. m.**] A, **ex e. m.** *si* BP, **qui ex e. m.** E   (27) *Cod.* 5, 27, 11

Sabinus, he will know that if he attempts to defeat the intention of my pronouncement I shall punish him severely.'

1.9 FAMILY AUTHORITY

The people within our authority are our children, the offspring of a Roman law marriage. 1. Marriage, or matrimony, is the union of a man and a woman, committing them to a single path through life. 2. Our authority over our children is a right which only Roman citizens have. Nobody else has such extreme control over children. 3. Any child born to you and your wife is in your authority. The same is true of one born to your son and his wife. That is to say, your grandson and granddaughter are equally within your authority, and your great grandson and great granddaughter, and so on. Your daughter's child is not in your authority but in its father's.

1.10 MARRIAGE

A Roman law marriage is a marriage between Roman citizens who meet the law's requirements. Males must have reached puberty. Females must be sexually mature. They may be independent persons or dependents within authority. In the latter case they must have the consent of the head of their family. Logic and law alike require this. His approval must be given in advance. Can the daughter of someone who is insane marry, or can his son take a wife? There used to be differences of opinion about the son. Our own ruling settled the matter: we took the case of the insane person's daughter as the model and extended permission to a son to contract a marriage without the father's co-operation, subject to restrictions set out in the pronouncement. 1. Next, we cannot marry any and every woman. Some unions have to be avoided. Marriage cannot be contracted between people in the relation of parent and child, for instance father and daughter or grandfather and granddaughter or mother and son or grandmother and grandson and so on up and down the line. A union within these degrees is evil and incestuous. If their relationship as parent and child is based on adoption, they still cannot marry; the same applies after the adoptive tie is broken. You cannot marry a girl who has become your daughter or granddaughter by adoption, not even if you have emancipated her. 2. A similar but less stringent regime applies to collaterals. Marriage is obviously forbidden between brother and sister, whether they have the same father and mother or are siblings with one common parent. There can be no marriage during the currency of the adoptive relationship between you and your adopted sister, but you can marry her once the adoptive tie is broken by her emancipation. If you yourself are emancipated the bar to marriage also goes. A man who wants to adopt his son-in-law must first emancipate his daughter, and one who wants to adopt his daughter-in-law should first emancipate his son. 3. One may not marry the daughter of one's brother or sister. Nor may one marry the granddaughter of one's brother or sister, despite the fact that that is a relationship in the fourth degree. A bar to marriage with a daughter always extends to the granddaughter. There is judged to be no bar to marrying the daughter of a woman adopted by your father, since in that case you are not related naturally or in the eyes of the law. 4. The children of two brothers or two sisters, or of a brother and sister, can marry. 5. Next, a man may not marry his paternal aunt even if the tie is only adoptive; nor his maternal aunt. These count as ascendants. On the same ground, marriage with a great aunt, paternal or maternal, is forbidden. 6. Respect for relationships created by marriage also obstructs some marriages. A man may not marry his step-daughter or his daughter-in-law because these both count as daughters. Obviously this bar must be taken to apply to someone who has at any time been your step-daughter or daughter-in-law. If she is still your daughter-in-law – she is married to your son – there is another bar to your marrying her: the same woman cannot be married to two men. If she is still your step-daughter – her mother is married to you – the reason you cannot marry her is that a man may not have two wives at once. 7. Marriage to a mother-in-law or step-mother is forbidden, since they count as mothers. This bar applies after the relationship through the marriage has ended. If the woman is still your step-mother, married to your father, the bar is the general rule against bigamy. If she is still your mother-in-law, in that her daughter is currently married to you, the marriage would again be bigamous. 8. The law allows a husband's son or daughter by a former wife to marry a wife's daughter or son by a former husband. This is true even if they have a brother or sister born of the later marriage. 9. If you and your wife are divorced and then she has a daughter by another man, the girl is not of course your step-daughter. Yet Julian says that you ought not to marry her. In the same way he says that though a woman engaged to your son is not a daughter-in-law and one engaged to your father is not a mother-in-law the right and proper thing is not to contemplate marrying them. 10. There is no doubt that blood-relationship among slaves is also a bar to marriage. A father and daughter or brother and sister cannot marry after being freed. 11. There are also other people who for a variety of reasons are barred from marrying. We have agreed to these being listed in the Digest or Pandects, in which the classical law has been collected. 12. In a union which breaks these rules the law recognizes no husband, no wife, no wedding, no marriage, and no dowry. Children born of such a relationship are not in the authority of their father but so far as concerns family authority are in the same position as those conceived casually. They are considered fatherless, their fathers being unknown. Such sons are called spurious. The word comes from the Greek 'sporaden', meaning 'scattered around,' or perhaps from the letters of 'sine patre filii' (sons without a father). When such a relationship breaks down there is no basis for claiming back a dowry. Those who enter these forbidden unions are also liable to punishments set out in imperial pronouncements. 13. Sometimes children excluded from family authority at birth are brought in later. One case is the natural son brought within paternal authority by virtue of being presented to his local council. Another is the son born to a free woman whom the father could lawfully have married but only lived with. Under our own pronouncement the subsequent execution of a marriage settlement brings such a son into his father's authority. Similar provision is made for other children too, so long as they are born of the same union. //

XI[1]
DE ADOPTIONIBUS.

[2]'Non solum tamen naturales liberi secundum ea quae diximus in potestate nostra sunt, verum etiam 1 'ii quos adoptamus. Adoptio autem duobus mo-'dis fit, aut 'principali rescripto' aut imperio magistra-'tus. 'imperatoris' auctoritate adoptamus eos 'easve', 'qui 'quaeve' sui iuris sunt. quae species adoptionis 'dicitur adrogatio. imperio magistratus adoptamus eos 'easve', qui 'quaeve' in potestate parentium sunt, sive 'primum gradum liberorum optinent, qualis est filius 'filia, sive inferiorem, qualis est nepos neptis, pro-2 'nepos proneptis.' [3]Sed hodie ex nostra consti-'tutione, cum filius familias a patre naturali extra-'neae personae in adoptionem datur, iura potestatis 'naturalis patris minime dissolvuntur nec quicquam 'ad patrem adoptivum transit nec in potestate eius 'est, licet ab intestato iura successionis ei a nobis 'tributa sunt. si vero pater naturalis non extraneo, 'sed avo filii sui materno, vel si ipse pater naturalis 'fuerit emancipatus, etiam paterno, vel proavo simili 'modo paterno vel materno filium suum dederit in 'adoptionem: in hoc casu, quia in unam personam 'concurrunt et naturalia et adoptionis iura, manet 'stabile ius patris adoptivi et naturali vinculo copu-'latum et legitimo adoptionis modo constrictum, ut et 'in familia et in potestate huiusmodi patris adoptivi 3 'sit.' Cum autem impubes 'per principale rescriptum' adrogatur, causa cognita adrogatio permittitur et ex-quiritur causa adrogationis[4], an honesta sit expediat-que pupillo, et cum quibusdam condicionibus adro-gatio fit, id est ut caveat adrogator personae publi-cae, hoc est tabulario, si intra pubertatem pupillus decesserit, restituturum se bona illis, qui, si adoptio facta non esset, ad successionem eius venturi essent. item non alias emancipare eos potest adrogator, nisi causa cognita digni emancipatione fuerint et tunc[5] sua bona eis reddat. sed et si decedens pater eum exheredaverit vel vivus sine iusta causa eum emanci-paverit, iubetur quartam partem ei suorum bonorum relinquere, videlicet praeter bona, quae ad patrem adoptivum transtulit et quorum commodum ei ad-4 quisivit postea. Minorem natu non posse maio-rem adoptare placet: adoptio enim naturam imitatur et pro monstro est, ut maior sit filius quam pater. debet itaque[6] is, qui sibi per adrogationem vel adop-tionem filium facit, plena pubertate, 'id est decem 5 'et octo annis' praecedere. Licet autem et in lo-cum nepotis vel neptis vel in locum pronepotis[7] vel proneptis vel deinceps adoptare, quamvis filium quis 6 non habeat. Et tam filium alienum quis in lo-cum nepotis potest adoptare, quam nepotem in locum 7 filii. Sed si quis nepotis loco adoptet vel quasi ex eo filio, quem habet iam adoptatum, vel quasi ex illo, quem naturalem in sua potestate habet: in eo casu et filius consentire debet, ne ei invito suus he-res adgnascatur[8]. sed ex contrario si avus ex filio nepotem dat in adoptionem, non est necesse filium 8 consentire. In plurimis autem causis adsimilatur is, qui adoptatus vel adrogatus est, ei qui ex legi-timo matrimonio natus est. et ideo [9]'si quis 'per impera-'torem' sive apud praetorem vel apud praesidem pro-'vinciae 'non extraneum' adoptaverit, potest eundem 9 'alii in adoptionem dare'. Sed et [9]'illud utriusque 'adoptionis commune est, quod et hi, qui generare 'non possunt, quales sunt spadones, adoptare pos-10 'sunt, castrati autem non possunt. Feminae 'quo-'que' adoptare non possunt, quia nec naturales libe-

'ros in potestate sua habent': 'sed ex indulgentia prin-'cipis ad solacium liberorum amissorum adoptare pos-11 'sunt.' [10]'Illud proprium est illius adoptionis, quae 'per 'sacrum oraculum' fit, quod is, qui liberos in po-'testate habet, si se adrogandum dederit, non solum 'ipse potestati[11] adrogatoris subicitur, sed etiam liberi 'eius in eiusdem fiunt potestate tamquam nepotes.' sic enim et[12] divus Augustus non ante Tiberium adoptavit, quam is Germanicum adoptavit: ut proti-nus adoptione facta incipiat Germanicus Augusti ne-12 pos esse. 'Apud Catonem bene scriptum refert 'antiquitas, servi si a domino adoptati sint, ex hoc 'ipso posse liberari. unde et nos eruditi in nostra 'constitutione[13] etiam eum servum, quem dominus 'actis intervenientibus filium suum nominaverit, libe-'rum esse constituimus, licet hoc ad ius filii accipien-'dum ei non sufficit.'

XII[14]
QUIBUS MODIS IUS POTESTATIS SOLVITUR[15].

[16]'Videamus nunc, quibus modis ii, qui alieno iuri 'subiecti sunt, eo iure liberantur. et quidem servi 'quemadmodum potestate liberantur, ex his intellegere 'possumus, quae de servis manumittendis superius 'exposuimus. hi vero, qui in potestate parentis sunt, 'mortuo eo sui iuris fiunt. sed hoc distinctionem re-'cipit. nam mortuo patre sane omnimodo filii filiaeve 'sui iuris efficiuntur. mortuo vero avo non omnimodo 'nepotes neptesque sui iuris fiunt, sed ita, si post 'mortem avi in potestatem patris sui recasuri non 'sunt: itaque si moriente avo pater eorum et vivit et 'in potestate patris sui est, tunc post obitum avi in 'patris sui potestate fiunt: si vero is, quo tempore 'avus moritur, aut iam mortuus est aut exiit de po-'testate patris, tunc hi, quia in potestatem eius ca-1 'dere non possunt, sui iuris fiunt. [16]Cum autem is, 'qui ob aliquod maleficium 'in insulam deportatur', 'civitatem amittit, sequitur ut, quia[17] eo modo ex nu-'mero civium Romanorum tollitur, perinde acsi mor-'tuo eo desinant liberi in potestate eius esse. pari 'ratione et si 'is', qui in potestate parentis sit, 'in in-'sulam deportatus'[18] fuerit, desinit[18] in potestate pa-2 'rentis esse.' sed si ex indulgentia principali restituti 'fuerint, per omnia pristinum statum recipiunt. [19]Re-'legati autem patres in insulam in potestate sua libe-'ros retinent: et e contrario liberi relegati in potes-3 'tate parentum remanent. Poenae servus effectus 'filios in potestate habere desinit. servi autem poenae 'efficiuntur, qui in metallum damnantur et qui bestiis 4 'subiciuntur. Filius familias si militaverit, vel si 'senator vel consul fuerit factus, manet in patris po-'testate. militia enim vel consularia[20] dignitas patris 'potestate filium non liberat. 'sed ex constitutione 'nostra[21] summa patriciatus dignitas ilico ab impe-'rialibus codicillis praestitis a patria potestate liberat. 'quis enim patiatur patrem quidem posse per eman-'cipationis modum suae potestatis nexibus filium ex-'laxare, imperatoriam autem celsitudinem non valere 'eum quem sibi patrem elegit ab aliena eximere po-5 'testate?' [22]'Si ab hostibus captus fuerit parens, 'quamvis servus hostium fiat, tamen pendet ius libe-'rorum propter ius postliminii: quia hi, qui ab hosti-'bus capti sunt, si reversi fuerint, omnia pristina iura 'recipiunt. idcirco reversus et liberos habebit in po-'testate,' quia postliminium fingit eum qui captus est 'semper in civitate fuisse: si vero ibi decesserit, ex-'inde, ex quo captus est pater, filius sui iuris fuisse 'videtur. 'ipse quoque filius neposve si ab hostibus 'captus fuerit, similiter dicimus[23] propter ius postliminii

(1) Cf. Gai. 1, 97..107 Dig. 1, 7 Cod. 8, 47 (48)   (2) Gai. 1, 97..99 (Dig. 1, 7, 2)   (3) § 2 ex Cod. 8, 47 (48), 10 (4) adoptionis B   (5) tunc] P, tunc ut B E   (6) itaque] P E, om. B   (7) neptis vel in locum pronepotis] P cum Θ, in locum (loco E) neptis B E   (8) sic E, agnoscatur P, nascatur B   (9) Gai. 1, 105. 103. 104 (Dig. 1, 7, 2 § 1)   (10) Gai. 1, 107 (Dig. 1, 7, 2 § 2)   (11) sic Gai. Dig., in potestate libri   (12) sic enim et] P E,

sed et B   (13) Cod. 7, 6, 1, 10   (14) Cf. Gai. 1, 124..141 Dig. 1, 7 Cod. 8, 48 (49)   (15) sic ind. V, dissolvitur A B E Θ   (16) Gai. 1, 124. 126..128 (17) quia] B E, qui A P Gai.   (18) sic dett. Θ, desint E, desiit A B P   (19) § 2 in. ex Marciani l. 2 inst. (Dig. 48, 22, 4)   (20) sic A P E, consularis B   (21) § 4 fin. ex Cod. 12, 3, 5   (22) Gai. 1, 129   (23) dice-mus Gai.

1.11 ADOPTIONS

We have just set out the rules under which our real children fall within our authority. This also happens with those whom we adopt. 1. Adoptions can be done in two ways, by a writ from the emperor or application to a magistrate. The imperial procedure is used where the man or woman being adopted is already an independent person. That kind of adoption is called adrogation. Adoption before a magistrate is used for persons of both sexes still within paternal authority. This applies to children in the first degree, sons or daughters, and to those below, grandchildren or great-grandchildren. 2. But now, by our own pronouncement, when a real father allows a son in his authority to be adopted by an outsider the rights implicit in the real father's authority are not affected and do not pass to the adoptive father. The son does not enter into the adoptive father's authority, although we have conceded him the right to succeed on intestacy. However, it is different where a real father allows his son to be adopted not by an outsider but by the son's maternal grandfather or, in the case in which the father has himself been emancipated, by the son's paternal grandfather, or similarly by the great-grandfather on either side. Here, with natural and legal rights combined in one person, we have left unchanged the adoptive father's legal position. The natural tie is merely strengthened by the legal procedure for adoption. This adoptive father therefore takes the son into his family and authority. 3. When a child below puberty is adrogated by imperial writ, the adrogation is only allowed after an investigation whether the reason for the change is honourable and in the child's interest. Also, the adrogation is done on terms. The adrogator must enter into an undertaking with a public official, a registrar, that in the event of the child's dying before puberty he will return all its property to the persons who would have been entitled in succession if the adoption had never taken place. Again an adrogator cannot emancipate him unless an investigation shows the emancipation to be fair. Even then, he must also restore all the property. Moreover, if he disinherits him when he dies or emancipates him in his lifetime without good cause, he must hand over a quarter of his own property. That means a quarter over and above what he brought to the adoptive father and the subsequent profit from it. 4. It is rightly held that a younger person cannot adopt an older one. Adoption imitates nature. A son older than a father would outrage nature. To adopt or adrogate a son one must be a full generation, i.e. eighteen years, older than the adoptee. 5. A man may adopt someone as grandchild or great grandchild and so on. This is so even when he has no son. 6. There is no objection to adopting another's son as grandson or grandson as son. 7. If a man adopts a grandson who becomes a son to his own son, adopted or real, he must get the consent of that son. The son would otherwise be saddled with an immediate heir against his will. But the other way around, when a grandfather gives his son's son in adoption, the son's consent is not required. 8. In most respects the position of a person who is adopted or adrogated is the same as one born in a Roman law marriage. It follows that someone who acquires a son in an intra-familial adoption, through emperor, praetor or provincial governor, can also allow him to be adopted by someone else. 9. Another feature common to both kinds of adoption is that people unable to have children – the impotent, but not castrati – can adopt. 10. Women cannot adopt. They do not hold family authority even over their real children. But by imperial favour they are allowed to adopt to make up for the loss of their own children. 11. A characteristic peculiar to adoption by imperial pronouncement is that if the person adrogated has children within his authority the children too are taken into the authority of the adrogator, as grandchildren. The Emperor Augustus did not adopt Tiberius first and then Germanicus. The one adoption immediately made Germanicus his grandson. 12. History has handed down a wise remark from Cato's works: that slaves adopted by their owner by that alone attain their freedom. We too have learned from that and have laid down in our pronouncement that a slave whom an owner names as his son in proper documents becomes free. However, that is not enough to give him the full status of a son.

1.12 EMERGENCE FROM FAMILY AUTHORITY

Now to ways in which dependent persons emerge from authority. For slaves, these can be gathered from what we have already said about manumission. By contrast free people within family authority become their own masters on the head of the family's death. But distinctions must be made. The death of a father who is head of the family makes his sons and daughters completely independent at once. The death of a grandfather does not always do so, but only if the grandchildren do not fall into their father's authority on their grandfather's death. If at the time of their grandfather's death their father is alive and within his authority, they do then pass into the authority of their father. If at the grandfather's death their father is already dead or has emerged from family authority, the grandchildren cannot pass into their father's authority. They become independent. 1. Next, since someone who is transported to an island for some crime loses his citizenship, his removal from the Roman citizen-body releases his children from his authority just as though he had died. The same logic means that a dependent person who is transported to an island passes out of the authority of the head of his family. If an imperial pardon lets such people back they completely recover their original status. 2. By contrast fathers merely detained on an island keep their children within their authority; and, vice versa, sons so detained stay within family authority. 3. Someone condemned to penal slavery ceases to hold family authority over his sons. Penal slaves are those sentenced to the mines or thrown in with wild beasts. 4. A son who has done military service or become a senator or a consul remains in his father's authority. Neither such service nor the honour of a consulate makes a man his own master. But by our own pronouncement attainment of the patriciate, the highest of honours, releases a son from family authority as soon as he is given the imperial patent. It would be intolerable for a father to be able to release a son from the bonds of his authority by emancipation while the high majesty of the emperor had no power to remove from another's authority a man he chose to rank among his fathers. 5. If the head of the family is captured by enemies the status of the children is in suspense because of his right of rehabilitation. This is true even though his captors make him a slave, because prisoners of war who come back recover all their former rights. He will have his children in his authority again when he gets back, because his right of rehabilitation allows him to be treated as if he had never stopped being a citizen. If he dies as a prisoner, the son's independence is back-dated to the moment of his father's capture. Similarly, if a son or grandson is captured by the enemy his potential for rehabilitation puts the head of the family's authority into suspense. // The Latin word for

'ius quoque potestatis parentis in suspenso esse.'
dictum est autem postliminium a limine et post,
ut[1] eum, qui ab hostibus captus[2] in fines nostros
postea pervenit, postliminio reversum recte dicimus.
nam limina sicut in domibus finem quendam faciunt,
sic et imperii finem limen esse veteres voluerunt.
hinc et limes dictus est quasi finis quidam et termi-
nus. ab eo postliminium dictum, quia eodem limine
revertebatur, quo amissus erat. [3]sed et qui victis
hostibus recuperatur, postliminio rediisse existimatur.
6 [4]'Praeterea emancipatione quoque desinunt liberi
'in potestate parentum esse.' 'sed ea emancipatio an-
'tea quidem vel per antiquam legis observationem pro-
'cedebat, quae[5] per imaginarias venditiones et inter-
'cedentes manumissiones celebrabatur, vel ex imperiali
'rescripto. nostra autem providentia et hoc in melius
'per constitutionem[6] reformavit, ut fictione pristina
'explosa recta via apud competentes iudices vel ma-
'gistratus parentes intrent et filios suos vel filias vel
'nepotes vel neptes ac deinceps sua manu dimitterunt.
'et tunc ex edicto praetoris in huius filii vel filiae,
'nepotis vel neptis bonis, qui vel quae a parente
'manumissus vel manumissa fuerit, eadem iura prae-
'stantur parenti, quae tribuuntur patrono in bonis
'liberti: et praeterea si impubes sit filius vel filia vel
'ceteri, ipse parens ex manumissione tutelam eius
7 'nanciscitur.' [7]'Admonendi autem sumus liberum
'esse arbitrium ei, qui filium et ex eo nepotem vel
'neptem in potestate habebit, filium quidem de potestate
'dimittere, nepotem vero vel neptem in potestate[8] reti-
'nere: et e diverso filium quidem in potestate retinere,
'nepotem vero vel neptem manumittere (eadem et de
'pronepote vel pronepte dicta esse intellegantur), vel
8 'omnes sui iuris efficere.' 'Sed et si pater filium,
'quem in potestate habet, avo vel proavo naturali se-
'cundum nostras constitutiones[9] super his habitas in
'adoptionem dederit, id est si hoc ipsum actis inter-
'venientibus apud competentem iudicem manifestavit,
'praesente eo qui adoptatur et non contradicente nec
'non eo qui adoptat, solvitur quidem ius potestatis
'patris naturalis, transit autem in huiusmodi paren-
'tem adoptivum, in cuius persona et[10] adoptionem
9 'plenissimam esse antea diximus.' Illud autem scire
oportet, quod, si nurus tua ex filio tuo conceperit et
filium postea emancipaveris vel in adoptionem dederis
praegnante nuru tua, nihilo minus quod ex ea nascitur in potestate tua nascitur: quod si post emancipationem vel adoptionem fuerit conceptum[11], patris
sui emancipati vel avi adoptivi potestati subicitur:
10 et quod neque naturales liberi neque adoptivi
ullo paene modo possunt cogere parentem de potestate
sua eos dimittere.

XIII[12]
DE TUTELIS.

[13]'Transeamus nunc ad aliam divisionem. nam ex
'his personis, quae in potestate non sunt, quaedam
'vel in tutela sunt vel in curatione, quaedam neutro
'iure tenentur. videamus igitur de his, quae in tutela
'vel in curatione sunt: ita enim intellegemus ceteras
'personas, quae neutro iure tenentur. ac prius dispi-
1 'ciamus de his quae in tutela sunt.' [14]Est 'autem' tutela, ut Servius definivit, ius[15] ac potestas in
capite libero ad tuendum eum, qui propter aetatem
se defendere nequit, iure civili data ac permissa.
2 Tutores autem sunt, qui eam vim ac potestatem

habent, ex qua re ipsa[16] nomen ceperunt. itaque
appellantur tutores quasi tuitores atque defensores,
3 sicut aeditui dicuntur qui aedes tuentur. [17]'Per-
'missum est itaque parentibus liberis impuberibus,
'quos in potestate habent, testamento tutores dare.'
'et hoc[18] in filio filiaque omnimodo procedit'; [19]'nepo-
'tibus tamen neptibusque ita demum 'parentes' pos-
'sunt testamento tutores dare, si post mortem eorum
'in patris sui potestatem recasuri non sunt. itaque si
'filius tuus mortis tuae tempore in potestate tua sit,
'nepotes ex eo non poterunt testamento tuo tutorem
'habere, quamvis in potestate tua fuerint; scilicet
'quia mortuo te in patris sui potestatem recasuri'
4 'sunt. [20]Cum 'autem' in compluribus aliis causis
'postumi pro iam natis habentur, et in hac causa
'placuit non minus postumis quam iam natis testa-
'mento tutores dari posse, si modo in ea causa sint,
'ut, si vivis 'parentibus' nascerentur, sui et in po-
5 'testate eorum fierent.' Sed si emancipato filio
tutor a patre testamento datus fuerit, confirmandus
est ex sententia praesidis omnimodo, id est sine inquisitione.

XIV[21]
QUI DARI TUTORES TESTAMENTO POSSUNT.

Dari autem potest tutor non solum pater familias,
1 sed etiam filius familias. Sed et servus proprius
testamento cum libertate recte tutor dari potest. sed
sciendum est eum et sine libertate tutorem datum
tacite et libertatem directam accepisse videri et per
hoc recte tutorem esse. plane si per errorem quasi
liber tutor datus sit, aliud dicendum est. servus autem alienus pure inutiliter datur testamento tutor.
sed ita 'cum liber erit' utiliter datur. proprius au-
2 tem servus inutiliter eo[22] modo datur tutor. Furiosus vel 'minor viginti quinque annis' tutor testamento datus tutor erit, cum compos mentis aut 'maior
viginti quinque annis' fuerit factus.
3 Ad certum tempus et[23] ex certo tempore vel
sub condicione vel ante heredis institutionem posse
4 dari tutorem non dubitatur. Certae autem rei
vel causae tutor dari non potest, [24]quia personae,
non causae vel rei datur.
5 [25]Si quis filiabus suis vel filiis tutores dederit,
etiam postumae vel postumo videtur dedisse, quia
filii vel filiae appellatione et postumus et postuma
continentur. quid[26] si nepotes sint, an appellatione
filiorum et ipsis tutores dati sunt? dicendum est, ut
ipsis quoque dati videantur, si modo liberos dixit.
ceterum si filios, non continebuntur: aliter enim filii,
aliter nepotes appellantur. plane si postumis dederit,
tam filii postumi quam ceteri liberi continebuntur.

XV[27]
DE LEGITIMA ADGNATORUM TUTELA.

[28]'Quibus 'autem' testamento tutor datus non sit,
'his ex lege duodecim tabularum adgnati sunt tuto-
1 'res, qui vocantur legitimi. Sunt autem adgnati[29]
'per virilis sexus cognationem[30] coniuncti, quasi a
'patre cognati, veluti frater eodem patre natus, fra-
'tris filius neposve ex eo, item patruus et patrui filius
'neposve ex eo. at qui per feminini sexus personas
'cognatione iunguntur, non sunt adgnati, sed alias
'naturali iure cognati. itaque amitae tuae filius non

---

(1) ut] $A^l BP$, et $A^u A^{bg}$ (2) captus] $B\Theta$, om. AP (3) § 5 fin. ex Flor. l. 6 inst. (Dig. 49, 15, 26)   (4) Gai. 1, 132   (5) quae] AP, om. B (6) Cod. 8, 48 (49), 6   (7) Gai. 1, 133 rest. (Dig. 1, 7, 28)   (8) in potestate] A Dig., om. BPE (9) Cod. 8, 47 (48), 11   (10) in c. persona (-nam E) et] AE, in c. persona P, c. persone B (11) sic $AB^a P^a$, conceptus $B^b P^b E$ (12) Cf. Gai 1, 142..154 Dig. 26, 1..3 Cod. 5, 28. 29 (13) Gai. 1, 142. 143 (14) § 1. 2 ex Dig. 26, 1, 1 (Paul. l. 38 ad ed.) (15) vis Dig. (16) sic Dig. Θ, ipsum B, ipsi PE

(17) Gai. 1, 144   (18) hoc P^b, haec $BP^a E$ (19) Gai. 1, 146 (20) Gai. 1, 147   (21) Cf. Dig. 26, 2 Cod. 5, 28   (22) eo] $B\Theta$, eodem T (23) et] $T\Theta$, ut B, seu P (24) quia..datur ex Marciani l. 2 inst. (Dig. 26, 2, 14)   (25) § 5 ex Dig. 26, 2, 5. 6 (Ulp. l. 15. 39 ad Sab.)   (26) quid] E^b Dig., quî B, quod PE^a

(27) Cf. Gai. 1,155..158 Dig. 26, 4 Cod. 5, 30   (28) Gai. 1, 155. 156 (Dig. 26, 4, 7)   (29) adgnati] Gai. Dig. Θ, adgnati cognati libri, cf. 3, 2, 1   (30) cognationem] BP, cognatione E, personas cognatione Gai. Dig.

this rehabilitation, 'postliminium', comes from 'limen' meaning 'threshold' and 'post' meaning 'after'. When a prisoner of war comes back to our territory we can say he has crossed the threshold again. The ancients chose to see the boundary of our sovereign territory as a threshold, as though the limit of a home. The word 'limes', 'a limit', indicating an edge or end, has the same origin. 'Postliminium' comes from the prisoner's later re-crossing the same threshold over which he was lost. If he is recovered by our going out and defeating the enemy he is still said to have re-crossed the threshold. 6. Next, children also emerge from family authority by emancipation. That used to be done by an old legal procedure involving pretended sales and intervening manumissions or else by imperial writ. Here too our meticulous pronouncement has introduced an improved regime. We have put an end to the play-acting. The head of a family can now go straight to competent judges or magistrates and there discharge sons, daughters, grandchildren, and so on, from his control. As for the property of the discharged son, daughter, or grandchild, the praetor's edict gives the head of the family the same rights as are given to a patron over the property of his freedman. If the son or daughter, and so on, is still a young child the head of the family himself becomes its guardian by virtue of the emancipation. 7. We should note that where the head of a family has a son and by that son a grandchild it is a matter entirely for him whether to discharge the son from his authority but keep the grandchild or, vice versa, to discharge the grandchild and keep the son. It is the same for great grandchildren. Equally, he is free to make them all independent. 8. The bond of the real father's authority is also broken when he allows a son within his authority to be adopted by his real grandfather or great grandfather under our legislation, i.e. where he makes a properly documented declaration of his assent before a competent judge in the presence of the adoptee and without objection voiced by the adoptor. But here the authority passes to the adoptive head of the family. As we have already said, with that category of adoptor the adoption takes full effect. 9. Note too that if your daughter-in-law conceives by your son and during her pregnancy you emancipate the son or give him in adoption the baby is still born into your authority. A baby conceived after emancipation or adoption is subject to the authority of its emancipated father or its adoptive grandfather. 10. Notice finally that children, whether real or adopted, have virtually no means of compelling the head of their family to discharge them from his authority.

1.13 GUARDIANSHIP

Now to another classification. Among those independent of family authority some are under guardianship or supervision and others are free from both these safeguards. We must look first at those under guardianship and supervision. In that way we will also see which persons are completely independent. We start with those under guardianship. 1. Guardianship, as defined by Servius, is a right and authority granted and permitted by the law of the state over the person of a free man with the object of safeguarding him while he is too young to look after himself. 2. Guardians are those who exercise this power and authority. They take their name from what they do. In Latin they are called 'tutores', as being guards – 'tuitores' – and defenders, just as wardens are called 'aeditui' from looking after churches. 3. Where the head of a family has children within his authority below the age of puberty he is allowed to appoint guardians for them by will. This is always true of his sons

and daughters. With grandchildren he can do it only if his death will not put them into the authority of their father. So, if your son is within your authority at the time of your death, your grandchildren by him cannot be given guardians in your will despite being within your authority. Obviously your death will put them into the authority of their father. 4. Since for many other intents and purposes posthumous children are treated as though born before the death, guardians should be appointed by will for them just as for those already born. This applies where, had they had been born during the life of the head of the family, they would have come into his family authority and been his immediate heirs. 5. If a father's will appoints a guardian for a son who has been emancipated, it will be confirmed as a matter of course by declaration of the governor, i.e. it should be confirmed without inquiry.

1.14 TESTAMENTARY GUARDIANS

The appointee can be the head of a family or a son within family authority. 1. A testator can also lawfully appoint one of his own slaves as guardian, combining the appointment with a grant of freedom. But note that a slave appointed as guardian without a grant of liberty is deemed automatically to have received his freedom and so to have been effectively appointed. It is different of course where he is appointed by mistake in the belief that he is a free man. An unconditional appointment by will of the slave of a third party is ineffective, but the appointment is valid if subject to the provision 'when he is free'. Appointment of one's own slave under that condition is invalid. 2. If a will appoints an insane person or a minor under twenty-five, the appointment takes effect when he becomes sane or reaches the age of twenty-five. 3. There is no doubt that a guardian's appointment can be made to or from a specified time, or subject to a condition, or ahead of the clause appointing the heir. 4. Since guardians are provided for people, not for plans or property, it is impossible for an appointment to be made for specific property or a specific venture. 5. One who appoints a guardian for his daughters and sons is deemed also to appoint for those born posthumously. Posthumous children are covered by the terms son and daughter. Are grandsons, if any, within an appointment for sons? The answer is that the appointment is good for them too if the testator appoints for descendants, not if he appoints for sons. Sons and grandsons are linguistically distinct. It is clear that an appointment for the posthumous includes posthumous sons as well as other posthumous descendants.

1.15 STATUTORY GUARDIANSHIP BY AGNATIC RELATIVES

Under the Twelve Tables agnates are made guardians when there is no appointment by will. We call them statutory guardians. 1. Agnates are relatives through the male sex, loosely relations through the father, as for instance his brother if born of the same father, that brother's son, and the grandson through that son, also his father's brother, that uncle's son, and the grandson through that son. People related through females are not agnates. They are related in a way which is recognized in the law of nature, as cognates. // If your mother's sister

'est tibi adgnatus, sed cognatus (et invicem scilicet
'tu illi eodem iure coniungeris), quia qui nascuntur
2 'patris, non matris familiam sequuntur.' Quod autem lex ab intestato vocat ad tutelam adgnatos, non
hanc habet significationem, si omnino non fecerit
testamentum is qui poterat tutores dare, sed si
quantum ad tutelam pertinet intestatus decesserit.
quod tunc quoque accidere intellegitur, cum is qui
3 datus est tutor vivo testatore decesserit. 1'Sed ad-
'gnationis quidem ius 'omnibus modis' capitis deminu-
'tione 'plerumque' perimitur': nam adgnatio 2 iuris est
nomen. 'cognationis vero ius non 'omnibus modis' com-
'mutatur, quia civilis ratio civilia quidem iura cor-
'rumpere potest, naturalia vero non 'utique'.'

XVI [3]
DE CAPITIS MINUTIONE. [4]

[5] 'Est autem capitis deminutio prioris status com-
'mutatio. eaque tribus modis accidit: nam aut maxima
'est capitis deminutio aut minor, quam quidam me-
1 'diam vocant, aut minima. [5] Maxima est capitis
'deminutio, cum aliquis simul et civitatem et liber-
'tatem amittit. quod accidit' 'in his, qui servi poenae
'efficiuntur atrocitate sententiae, vel liberti ut ingrati
'circa patronos condemnati, vel qui ad pretium par-
2 'ticipandum se venumdari passi sunt'. [5] 'Minor sive
'media est capitis deminutio, cum civitas quidem
'amittitur, libertas vero retinetur. quod accidit ei,
'cui aqua et igni [6] interdictum fuerit', 'vel ei, qui in
3 'insulam deportatus est'. [5] 'Minima est capitis demi-
'nutio, cum et civitas et libertas retinetur, sed status
'hominis commutatur. quod accidit in his, qui' 'cum
'sui iuris fuerunt, coeperunt alieno iuri subiecti esse,
4 'vel contra'. Servus autem manumissus capite
5 non minuitur, quia nullum caput habuit. Quibus
autem dignitas magis quam status permutatur, capite
non minuuntur: et ideo senatu motos [7] capite non
minui constat.
6 Quod autem dictum est manere cognationis ius
et post capitis deminutionem, hoc ita est, si minima
capitis deminutio interveniat: manet enim cognatio.
nam si maxima capitis deminutio incurrat, ius quoque cognationis perit, ut puta servitute alicuius cognati,
et ne quidem, si manumissus fuerit, recipit cognationem. sed et si in insulam deportatus quis sit,
7 cognatio solvitur. [8] 'Cum autem ad [9] adgnatos tu-
'tela pertineat, non simul ad omnes pertinet, sed ad
'eos tantum, qui proximo [10] gradu sunt', vel, si eiusdem gradus sint, ad omnes.

XVII [11]
DE LEGITIMA PATRONORUM TUTELA.

[12] 'Ex eadem lege duodecim tabularum libertorum
'et libertarum tutela ad patronos liberosque eorum
'pertinet, quae et ipsa legitima tutela vocatur: non
'quia nominatim ea lege de hac tutela cavetur, sed
'quia perinde accepta est per interpretationem, atque
'si verbis legis introducta esset. eo enim ipso, quo [13]
'hereditates libertorum libertarumque, si intestati de-
'cessissent, iusserat lex ad patronos liberosve eorum
'pertinere, crediderunt veteres voluisse legem etiam
'tutelas ad eos pertinere, cum et adgnatos, quos ad
'hereditatem vocat, eosdem et tutores esse iussit' et [14]
quia plerumque, ubi successionis est emolumentum,
ibi et tutelae onus esse debet. ideo autem diximus
plerumque, quia, si a femina impubes manumittatur,
ipsa ad hereditatem vocatur, cum alius est [15] tutor.

XVIII [16]
DE LEGITIMA PARENTIUM TUTELA.

Exemplo patronorum recepta est et alia tutela,
quae et ipsa legitima vocatur. nam si quis filium aut
filiam, nepotem aut neptem ex filio et deinceps impuberes emancipaverit, legitimus eorum tutor erit.

XIX [17]
DE FIDUCIARIA TUTELA.

Est et alia tutela, quae fiduciaria appellatur. nam
si parens filium vel filiam, nepotem vel neptem et [18]
deinceps impuberes manumiserit, legitimam nanciscitur eorum tutelam: quo defuncto si liberi virilis
sexus extant, fiduciarii tutores filiorum suorum vel
fratris vel sororis et ceterorum efficiuntur. atqui
patrono legitimo tutore mortuo, liberi quoque eius
legitimi sunt tutores: quoniam filius quidem defuncti,
si non esset a vivo patre emancipatus, post obitum
eius sui iuris efficeretur nec in fratrum potestatem
recideret ideoque nec in tutelam, libertus autem si
servus mansisset, utique eodem iure apud liberos domini post mortem eius futurus esset. 'ita tamen ii ad
'tutelam vocantur, si perfectae aetatis sint. quod nostra
'constitutio [19] generaliter in omnibus tutelis et cura-
'tionibus observari praecepit.'

XX [20]
DE ATILIANO TUTORE VEL EO QUI EX LEGE IULIA ET TITIA DABATUR.

[21] 'Si cui nullus omnino tutor fuerat, ei dabatur in
'urbe quidem Roma a praetore urbano et maiore
'parte tribunorum plebis tutor ex lege Atilia, in pro-
'vinciis vero a praesidibus provinciarum ex lege Iulia
1 'et Titia. 'Sed' et si testamento tutor sub condi-
'cione aut die certo datus fuerat, quamdiu condicio
'aut dies pendebat, 'ex isdem legibus' tutor dari po-
'terat. item si pure datus fuerit [22], quamdiu nemo 'ex
'testamento' [23] heres existat, tamdiu ex isdem legibus
'tutor petendus erat, qui desinebat tutor esse, 'si con-
'dicio existeret aut dies veniret aut heres existeret'.
2 'Ab hostibus quoque tutore capto ex his legibus
'tutor petebatur, qui desinebat esse tutor, si is qui
'captus erat in civitatem reversus fuerat: nam re-
3 'versus recipiebat tutelam iure postliminii.' Sed
ex his legibus pupillis tutores desierunt dari, posteaquam primo consules pupillis utriusque sexus tutores
ex inquisitione dare coeperunt, deinde praetores ex
constitutionibus. nam supra scriptis legibus neque
de cautione a tutoribus exigenda rem salvam pupillis
fore neque de compellendis tutoribus ad tutelae ad-
4 ministrationem quidquam cavetur. Sed hoc iure
utimur, ut Romae quidem 'praefectus urbis' vel praetor secundum suam iurisdictionem, in provinciis autem praesides ex inquisitione tutores crearent, vel
magistratus iussu praesidum, si non sint magnae
5 pupilli facultates. 'Nos autem per constitutionem
'nostram [24] et huiusmodi difficultates hominum rese-
'cantes nec exspectata iussione praesidum disposui-
'mus, si facultas pupilli vel adulti usque ad quingen-
'tos solidos valeat, defensores civitatum una cum eius-
'dem civitatis religiosissimo antistite vel apud [25] alias
'publicas personas, id est magistratus, vel iuridicum
'Alexandrinae civitatis tutores vel curatores creare,
'legitima cautela secundum eiusdem constitutionis nor-
'mam praestanda, videlicet eorum periculo qui eam
'accipiant.'

---

(1) *Gai.* 1, 158   (2) adgnatio] *PEΘ, om. B*   (3) *Cf.*
Gai. 1, 159..164 *Dig.* 4, 5   (4) *sic index V index B,*
deminutione *BEΘ*   (5) *Gai.* 1, 159..162   (6) ignis
*BP*a*E*   (7) senatu motos (*uel* motus) *P*b, a sen. motus *E*, statu mutatos *B*, senatum motum *P*a   (8) *Gai.*
1, 164   (9) ad] *P Gai.*, et ad *B*, et *E*   (10) *sic B Gai.*,
proximiore *PE* cum Θ   (11) *Cf. Gai.* 1, 165..167 *Dig.*
26, 4   (12) *Gai.* 1, 165   (13) quod *dett.*   (14) et] *B,*

om. PE   (15) est] *B*, erit *PE*

(16) *Cf. Gai.* 1, 175 *Dig.* 26, 4, 3 § 10   (17) *Cf. Gai.*
1, 166..175 *Dig.* 26, 4, 3. 4   (18) et] *BP*, vel *E*
(19) *Cod.* 5, 30, 5   (20) *Cf. Gai.* 1, 185..191 *Dig.* 26, 5
Cod. 5, 34   (21) *Gai.* 1, 185..187   (22) *sic B*a *Gai.*,
fuerat *B*a *TP*   (23) ex testamento *om. Gai.*   (24) *Cod.*
1, 4, 30   (25) apud] *B*, συνόντων Θ, *om. TP*: etiam
apud *cum* Θ et *Cod. scr.*

has a son he is not your agnate. To you he is a cognatic relative, as of course in the same system you are to him. On birth babies enter the family of their father, not of their mother. 2. The statutory requirement that agnates take the guardianship on intestacy does not mean that they become guardians only when someone who could have appointed makes no will at all. They also act if he dies intestate specifically as regards guardianship, including the case where the appointed guardian predeceases the testator. 3. The agnatic tie is often broken by status-loss of any degree. Agnation is a creature of the law. Cognatic relationship, by contrast, is not affected by all degrees of status-loss. While the logic of state law can destroy rights founded on the state law, it cannot so easily affect rights founded on the law of nature.

1.16 STATUS-LOSS

Status-loss is the exchange of one status for another and happens in three ways, namely in the first, the second – also called intermediate – or the third degree. 1. Status-loss in the first degree happens when a person loses his citizenship and his liberty together, as by the very harsh sentence of penal slavery, or where a freedman is found guilty of ingratitude to his patron, or where a man allows himself to be sold to share the price. 2. Second degree or intermediate status-loss means loss of citizenship but not liberty, as where a man is banished from home and hearth or transported to an island. 3. Third degree status-loss occurs where a man keeps both citizenship and freedom but alters his personal standing, as where an independent person passes into the authority of another, or vice versa. 4. A slave's manumission does not count as a status-loss, because as a slave he had no standing at all. 5. Where people suffer a set-back in honour rather than status, there is no status-loss. So, removal from the senate is accepted not to be a status-loss. 6. The proposition that cognate ties survive status-loss holds good only for the third degree. Then the tie does survive. But a status-loss in the first degree destroys even the cognatic link. This happens for instance where one's relative is enslaved. It does not even revive if he is manumitted. Transportation to an island also breaks cognatic relationship. 7. Though guardianship belongs to the agnatic relations, it does not devolve on all of them at once but only on the closest, or on all of them if they do all happen to be of the same degree.

1.17 STATUTORY GUARDIANSHIP BY PATRONS

Again by virtue of the Twelve Tables, guardianship of freedmen and freedwomen is vested in their patrons and their patrons' descendants. This too is called statutory guardianship, not because provisions for it are spelled out in that code but because it has been evolved by an interpretation which treats it as though there were express provisions for it. The old jurists held that the fact that the code vested the estates of intestate freedmen and freedwomen in their patrons and their patrons' descendants meant that it intended to vest the guardianship in them too. They inferred this from its treatment of agnates: the code made them heirs and also imposed guardianship upon them. Generally the burden of guardianship ought to go with the benefit of succession. 'Generally' is used advisedly, because if a child is given his freedom by a woman she is made heir but another person becomes guardian.

1.18 STATUTORY GUARDIANSHIP BY HEADS OF FAMILIES

Modelled on the case of patrons, another species of guardianship, also called statutory, has been evolved. If someone emancipates his son, or his daughter, or his grandchild through his son, and so on, and the person emancipated is still a young child, he himself becomes its statutory guardian.

1.19 FIDUCIARY GUARDIANSHIP

There is yet another case of guardianship, called fiduciary. If the head of the family emancipates his son, his daughter, or his grandchild, and the person emancipated is still a young child, he himself becomes statutory guardian. When he dies, his male children, if any, then become fiduciary guardians of their own son or sister or brother, and so on. By contrast where a patron is a statutory guardian and dies his children follow him as statutory guardians. The son of a person now dead, had he not been emancipated by his father in the father's life, would have become independent after the father's death. Authority over him would not have passed to the brother. Nor can the guardianship. By contrast if the freedman had stayed a slave the children of the owner would have stepped into the same relationship to him as their father before his death. The people in this category are only called upon to act as guardians if they are of full age. That is a rule which by our own pronouncement we have extended to every kind of guardianship and supervision.

1.20 GUARDIANS UNDER THE ATILIAN ACT OR THE JULIAN-TITIAN ACT

If someone had no guardian, the practice in the city of Rome was for him to be given one under the Atilian Act by the urban praetor and a majority of the tribunes of the people. In the provinces it was done by the provincial governors under the Julian-Titian Act. 1. If there was a guardian appointed by will but subject to a condition or from a specified day, an appointment could be made under the same statutes to cover the interval till the condition was satisfied or the day came. Even if there was an unconditional appointment, a guardian was needed under these acts until the position of heir under the will was accepted. The appointees ceased to act when the condition was fulfilled, the day arrived, or an heir accepted. 2. Another case for a petition under these acts arose if a guardian became a prisoner of war. Here the appointee ceased to act if the prisoner came back and resumed his guardianship by virtue of his right of rehabilitation. 3. However, guardians stopped being appointed for children under these acts after two developments: first, the consuls began to appoint guardians for children of both sexes after a simple inquiry; later imperial pronouncements allowed the praetors to do the same. The two acts had failed to make any provision for demanding security from a guardian for the safety of the child's property or for compelling them to manage the guardianship properly. 4. The current position is that in Rome the city prefect or a praetor in the exercise of his jurisdiction appoints guardians after an inquiry, while in the provinces the governors do the same, or else, if the child's property is not substantial, the magistrates do it with the governors' authorization. 5. We have made a simplifying pronouncement: without insisting on the authorization of the governors where the child's or supervisee's property is worth less than 500 solidi, we have provided for the appointment of guardians and supervisors by city ombudsmen acting with the city's most reverend bishop or before other

6 [1]'Impuberes 'autem' in tutela esse naturali iuri[2] 'conveniens est, ut is qui perfectae aetatis non sit 7 'alterius tutela regatur.' 'Cum igitur' [3]'pupillorum 'pupillarumque tutores negotia 'gerunt', post puberta-'tem tutelae iudicio rationem reddunt[4].'

XXI[5]
DE AUCTORITATE TUTORUM.

Auctoritas autem tutoris in quibusdam causis ne-cessaria pupillis est, in quibusdam non est necessa-ria. ut ecce si quid dari sibi stipulentur[6], non est necessaria tutoris auctoritas: quod si aliis pupilli promittant, necessaria est: namque placuit meliorem quidem suam condicionem licere eis facere etiam sine tutoris auctoritate[7], deteriorem vero non aliter quam tutore auctore[8]. unde in his causis, ex quibus mu-tuae obligationes nascuntur, in emptionibus venditio-nibus, locationibus conductionibus, mandatis, deposi-tis, si tutoris auctoritas non interveniat, ipsi quidem qui cum his[9] contrahunt obligantur, at invicem pu-1 pilli non obligantur. [10]Neque tamen hereditatem adire neque bonorum possessionem petere neque he-reditatem ex fideicommisso suscipere aliter possunt nisi tutoris auctoritate, quamvis lucrosa sit neque 2 ullum damnum habeat[11]. Tutor autem statim in ipso negotio praesens debet auctor fieri, si hoc pu-pillo prodesse existimaverit. post tempus vero aut per 3 epistulam interposita auctoritas[12] nihil agit. [13]Si inter tutorem pupillumve iudicium agendum sit, quia ipse tutor in rem suam auctor esse non potest, non praetorius tutor ut olim constituitur, sed curator in locum eius datur, quo interveniente iudicium peragi-tur et eo peracto curator esse desinit.

XXII[14]
QUIBUS MODIS TUTELA FINITUR.

Pupilli pupillaeque[15] 'cum puberes esse coeperint, tutela liberantur'. 'pubertatem autem veteres quidem 'non solum ex annis, sed etiam ex habitu corporis in 'masculis aestimari volebant. nostra autem maiestas 'dignum esse castitate temporum nostrorum bene pu-'tavit, quod in feminis et[16] antiquis impudicum esse 'visum est, id est inspectionem habitudinis corporis, 'hoc[17] etiam in masculos extendere: et ideo sancta 'constitutione promulgata[18] pubertatem in masculis 'post quartum decimum annum completum ilico ini-'tium accipere disposuimus, antiquitatis normam in 'femininis personis bene positam suo ordine relin-'quentes, ut post duodecimum annum completum viri-1 'potentes esse credantur.' [19]Item finitur tutela, si adrogati sint adhuc impuberes vel deportati: item si in servitutem pupillus redigatur[20] vel ab hostibus 2 fuerit captus. [21]Sed et si usque ad certam con-dicionem datus sit testamento, aeque evenit, ut desi-3 nat esse tutor existente condicione. Simili modo 4 finitur tutela morte vel tutorum vel pupillorum. Sed et capitis deminutione tutoris, per quam libertas vel civitas eius amittitur, omnis tutela perit. minima au-tem capitis deminutione tutoris, veluti si se in adop-tionem dederit, legitima tantum tutela perit, ceterae non pereunt: sed pupilli et pupillae capitis demi-5 nutio licet minima sit, omnes tutelas tollit. Prae-terea qui ad certum tempus testamento dantur tu-6 tores, finito eo deponunt tutelam. Desinunt au-tem esse tutores, qui vel removentur a tutela ob id quod suspecti visi sunt, vel[22] ex iusta causa sese

excusant et onus administrandae[23] tutelae deponunt secundum ea quae inferius proponemus.

XXIII[24]
DE CURATORIBUS.

Masculi puberes et feminae viripotentes usque ad vicesimum quintum annum completum curatores ac-cipiunt: qui, licet puberes sint, adhuc tamen huius 1 aetatis sunt, ut negotia sua tueri non possint[25]. Dan-tur autem curatores ab isdem magistratibus, a qui-bus et tutores. sed curator testamento non datur, sed datus confirmatur decreto praetoris vel praesidis. 2 Item inviti adulescentes curatores non accipiunt prae-terquam in litem: curator enim ad certam causam 3 dari potest. Furiosi quoque et prodigi, licet maiores viginti quinque annis sint, tamen in curatione sunt adgnatorum ex lege duodecim tabularum. sed solent Romae praefectus[26] urbis vel praetor et in provin-ciis[27] praesides ex inquisitione eis dare curatores. 4 Sed et mente captis et surdis et mutis et qui morbo perpetuo laborant, quia rebus suis superesse 5 non possunt, curatores dandi sunt. Interdum au-tem et pupilli curatores accipiunt, ut puta si legi-timus tutor non sit idoneus, quia habenti[28] tutorem tutor dari non potest. item si testamento datus tu-tor vel a praetore vel a praeside idoneus non sit ad administrationem nec tamen fraudulenter negotia ad-ministrat, solet ei curator adiungi. item in locum tutorum, qui non in perpetuum, sed ad tempus a 6 tutela excusantur, solent curatores dari. Quodsi tutor adversa valetudine vel alia necessi-tate impeditur, quo minus negotia pupilli administrare possit, et pupillus vel absit vel infans sit, quem velit actorem periculo ipsius[29] praetor vel qui provinciae praeerit decreto constituet.

XXIV[30]
DE SATISDATIONE TUTORUM ET CURATORUM.

[31]'Ne tamen pupillorum 'pupillarumve' et eorum, qui 'quaeve' in curatione sunt, negotia a tutoribus cura-'toribusve consumantur aut deminuantur[32], curat prae-'tor, ut et tutores et curatores eo nomine satisdent. 'sed hoc non est perpetuum: nam tutores testamento 'dati satisdare non coguntur, quia fides eorum et 'diligentia ab ipso testatore probata est': item ex in-quisitione tutores vel curatores dati satisdatione non 1 onerantur, quia idonei electi sunt. Sed et si ex testamento vel inquisitione duo pluresve dati fuerint, potest unus offerre satis de indemnitate pupilli 'vel adulescentis' et contutori 'vel concuratori' praeferri, ut solus administret, vel ut contutor satis offerens praeponatur ei, ut[33] ipse solus administret. itaque per se non potest petere satis a contutore 'vel con-curatore' suo, sed offerre debet, ut electionem det contutori suo, utrum velit satis accipere an satis dare. quodsi nemo eorum satis offerat, si quidem adscriptum fuerit a testatore, quis gerat, ille gerere debet: quodsi non fuerit adscriptum, quem maior pars elegerit, ipse gerere debet, ut edicto praetoris cavetur. sin autem ipsi tutores dissenserint circa eli-gendum eum vel 'eos qui gerere debent, praetor par-tes suas interponere debet. idem et in pluribus ex inquisitione datis probandum est, id est ut maior pars eligere possit, per quem administratio fieret. 2 [34]Sciendum autem est non solum tutores vel cu-ratores pupillis et adultis ceterisque personis ex ad-

---

(1) *Gai*. 1, 189   (2) iuri] *PΘ*, iure *BT*, rationi *Gai*. (3) *Gai*. 1, 191   (4) sic *TGai*., reddent *B*   (5) *Cf. Dig*. 26, 8 *Cod*. 5, 59   (6) sic *dett*., stipuletur *BTP*   (7) sic *BΘ*, tu-tore auctore *T*   (8) sic *B*, tutoris auctoritate (-tatis *T*ᵃ) *T* (9) qui cum his] *TΘ*, cum quo *B*   (10) § 1. 2 similes *Dig*. 26, 8, 9 § 3..5 (*Gai. l*. 12 *ad ed. prov*.) (11) sic *B Dig. Θ*, habeant *T* (12) auctoritas] *B*, tutoris auct. *T*, eius auct. *Dig*.   (13) § 3 *in. simile Gaio* 1, 184   (14) *Cf. Gai*. 1, 170. 173. 182. 187. 194. 196 *Dig*. 26, 1, 12. 14..17 *Cod*. 5, 60   (15) *Gai*. 1, 196 (16) et] *B*, *om. T*   (17) hoc] *T*, h. nos *B*   (18) *Cod*. 5, 60, 3   (19) § 1 *similis Dig*. 26, 1, 14 *pr.* § 1. 2 (*Ulp. l*. 37 *ad Sab*.)   (20) sic *P*,

ut ingratus a patrono *add. cum Θ post* redigatur *T*, *post* servitutem *B*   (21) § 2 *similis Dig*. 26, 1, 14 § 5 (*Ulp. l*. 37 *ad Sab*.)   (22) vel] *dett. cum Θ*, vel quod *BT*   (23) sic *T*, administratae *B*   (24) *Cf. Gai*. 1, 197. 198 *Dig*. 26, 5 (25) possunt *libri*   (26) sic *Θ*, praefecti *libri* (27) sic *Θ*, provincia *libri*   (28) quia habenti] qui habet *B*   (29) ipsius] *B*, ipsius tutoris *T*   (30) *Cf. Dig*. 27, 7. 46, 6 *Cod*. 5, 42..57   (31) *Gai*. 1, 199. 200 (32) aut dem.] *dett. cum Gai*., vel dem. *TP*ᵇ, *om. BP*ᵃ (33) ut] *B*, et *T*   (34) § 2..4 *fere Iustinianorum esse vidit Kuebler*

public officials – that is to say, before magistrates – or by the high judge of the city of Alexandria. And we have further laid down in the pronouncement the amounts of the obligatory security, to be taken in the usual way at the risk of the person accepting it. // 6. The institution of guardianship is approved by the law of nature to meet a young child's need for someone to protect him. 7. So the guardians manage the boy's or girl's affairs; and then, when the wards grow up, the action on guardianship calls the guardians to account.

1.21 GUARDIAN'S ENDORSEMENT

A child needs his guardian's endorsement in some matters but not in others. If he takes a stipulation for a conveyance to himself he needs no endorsement. But if he makes a promise to someone else he must have it. The principle which applies is that he may improve his position without his guardian's endorsement but cannot make it worse without that backing. Where reciprocal obligations arise, as from sale, hire, mandate, and deposit, the outsider contracting with the child therefore becomes bound but the child incurs no obligation unless the guardian endorses. 1. A child cannot accept an inheritance, apply for estate-possession, or receive an inheritance under a trust without his guardian's endorsement, even though they may be profitable and not involve him in loss. 2. The guardian must be present when the business is done and give his backing there and then if he thinks it to the child's advantage. An endorsement given after an interval or by letter is a nullity. 3. A guardian cannot give his endorsement where his own interest is involved. If a matter between the child and the guardian has to go to trial the former practice was for the praetor to appoint someone to act as guardian, but now a supervisor is assigned instead. The case can proceed once he has taken over, and when it is finished his office ends.

1.22 TERMINATION OF GUARDIANSHIP

Guardianship ends for both girls and boys when they reach puberty. In the case of boys the old jurists chose to make puberty not merely a matter of age but also of physical development. We ourselves have thought it better suited to the propriety of our imperial reign to extend to boys the ancient ruling as to girls, which condemned bodily inspection as immoral. By solemn pronouncement we have laid down: that for boys puberty shall be considered as beginning from the completion of the fourteenth year; that for girls the well considered ancient standard shall be retained, deeming them sexually mature on completion of their twelfth year. 1. Guardianship is also ended if the child is adrogated before puberty; on transportation; on reduction to slavery; and on capture by an enemy. 2. If a guardian is appointed by will to act until a specified condition is satisfied, the happening of that event ends his office. 3. The same where the child or guardian dies. 4. Even a status-loss on the part of the guardian, if it involves liberty or citizenship, ends every type of guardianship. But a status-loss by the guardian in the third degree, as where he has himself adopted, terminates statutory guardianship but not the other kinds. Status-loss on the child's part, boy or girl, terminates every kind, even if only in the third degree. 5. Anyone appointed by will for a fixed time stops being guardian on the expiry of that period. 6. Guardianship also ends for those who are removed after being found untrustworthy or who excuse themselves for a sufficient reason and retire from the burden of administration which guardianship involves.

We shall return to this below.

1.23 SUPERVISORS

From sexual maturity to the age of twenty-five young men and young women have supervisors because, though grown-up, they are still not old enough be able look after their own affairs. 1. Supervisors are appointed by the same magistrates as guardians, but not by will. If one is named in a will his appointment is confirmed by a decree of the praetor or governor. 2. Next, these minors are not given supervisors without their consent, except for the purpose of litigation. It is possible to appoint a supervisor for a particular purpose. 3. The insane and the wasteful, even over twenty-five, are put under the supervision of their agnates by the Twelve Tables. However, the practice is for the city praetor in Rome and the governors in the provinces to make inquiries and appoint the supervisors. 4. Supervisors should also be appointed for the mentally handicapped, the deaf, the dumb, and the chronically ill, because such people cannot stand up for themselves. 5. Sometimes even a young child is given a supervisor, for instance where his statutory guardian is unsuitable; another guardian cannot be appointed for someone who already has one. Again, if a guardian appointed by will or by the praetor or the governor cannot cope with the management duties but is not guilty of fraud in his administration, the practice is to add a supervisor as his colleague. Also, where a guardian is temporarily excused from office it is usual to appoint a supervisor to fill the gap. 6. And if the guardian is hindered by bad health or some emergency from administering the ward's affairs, and the ward is away or is an infant, the praetor or the provincial governor will appoint a representative to act for him and at his risk.

1.24 SECURITY FROM GUARDIANS AND SUPERVISORS

To prevent guardians and supervisors from wasting and depleting the estates of wards and others under them, the praetor takes steps to make them give security. But the practice is not uniform. Guardians appointed by will are not compelled to give security. It is assumed that the testator will have satisfied himself of their honesty and application. Guardians and supervisors appointed after an inquiry are spared this burden because they will have been chosen for their suitability. 1. If there are two or more appointees under a will or after an official inquiry, one of them can offer security to indemnify the ward or minor and thus take priority over his colleague as sole administrator, or he can offer to let his colleague give security and go in as sole administrator. He cannot himself directly demand security from his co-guardian or co-supervisor but should make an offer allowing the colleague a choice whether to give security or take it. If neither of them offers security, the management should devolve on the one the testator named to do it, if one was named; if none was named, on the one chosen by the majority, as is provided in the praetor's edict. If the guardians fail to agree on the election of one or more of their number to conduct the administration, the praetor must intervene himself. The same applies where there is more than one appointee after an official inquiry, i.e. the majority should choose the one to do the administration. 2. Note that the liabilities arising out of the administration // give the wards, minors, and others, a

ministratione teneri, sed etiam in eos qui satisdationes[1] accipiunt subsidiariam actionem esse, quae ultimum eis praesidium possit afferre. subsidiaria autem actio datur in eos, qui vel omnino a tutoribus vel curatoribus satisdari non curaverint aut non idonee passi essent caveri. quae quidem tam ex prudentium responsis quam ex constitutionibus impe3 rialibus et in heredes eorum extenditur. [2]Quibus constitutionibus et illud exprimitur, ut, nisi caveant tutores vel curatores, pignoribus captis coerceantur. 4 [2]Neque autem praefectus urbis neque praetor neque praeses provinciae neque quis alius cui tutores dandi ius est hac actione tenebitur, sed hi tantummodo qui satisdationem exigere solent.

XXV[3]
DE EXCUSATIONIBUS.

Excusantur autem tutores vel curatores variis ex causis: plerumque autem propter liberos, sive in potestate sint sive emancipati. si enim tres liberos quis superstites Romae habeat vel in Italia quattuor vel in provinciis quinque, a tutela vel cura possunt excusari exemplo ceterorum munerum: nam et tutelam et[4] curam placuit publicum munus esse. sed adoptivi liberi non prosunt, in adoptionem autem dati naturali patri prosunt. item nepotes ex filio prosunt, ut in locum patris succedant, ex filia non prosunt. filii autem superstites tantum ad tutelae vel curae muneris excusationem prosunt, defuncti non prosunt. sed si in bello amissi sunt, quaesitum est, an prosint. 'et 'constat eos solos prodesse qui in acie amittuntur: 'hi enim, quia pro re publica ceciderunt, in perpe1 'tuum per gloriam vivere intelleguntur.' Item divus Marcus in semestribus rescripsit eum, qui res fisci administrat, a tutela vel cura quamdiu administrat 2 excusari posse. Item qui rei publicae causa absunt[5], a tutela et cura excusantur. sed et si fuerunt tutores vel curatores, deinde rei publicae causa abesse coeperunt, a tutela et cura excusantur, quatenus rei publicae causa absunt, et interea curator loco eorum datur. qui si reversi fuerint, recipiunt onus tutelae nec anni habent vacationem, ut Papinianus responsorum libro quinto scripsit: nam hoc spatium 3 habent ad novas tutelas vocati. Et qui potestatem aliquam habent, excusare se possunt, sed coeptam tutelam deserere non 4 possunt. [6]Item propter litem, quam cum pupillo 'vel adulto tutor vel curator' habet, excusare se 'nemo' potest: nisi forte de omnibus bonis vel hereditate 5 controversia sit. Item tria onera tutelae non affectatae vel curae praestant vacationem, quamdiu administrantur: ut tamen plurium pupillorum[7] tutela vel cura eorundem bonorum, veluti fratrum, pro una 6 computetur. Sed et propter paupertatem excusationem tribui tam divi fratres quam per se divus Marcus rescripsit, si quis imparem se oneri iniuncto 7 possit docere. Item propter adversam valetudinem, propter quam nec suis quidem negotiis interesse 8 potest, excusatio locum habet. Similiter eum qui litteras nesciret excusandum esse divus Pius rescripsit: quamvis et imperiti litterarum possunt ad 9 administrationem negotiorum sufficere. Item si propter inimicitiam[8] aliquem testamento tutorem pater dederit, hoc ipsum praestat ei excusationem: sicut per contrarium non excusantur, qui se tutelam patri 10 pupillorum administraturos promiserunt. Non esse autem admittendam excusationem eius, qui hoc

solo utitur, quod ignotus patri pupillorum sit, divi 11 fratres rescripserunt. Inimicitiae[9], quas quis cum patre pupillorum vel adultorum[10] exercuit, si capitales fuerunt nec reconciliatio intervenit, a tu12 tela[11] solent excusare[12]. Item si quis[13] status controversiam a pupillorum patre passus est, excu13 satur a tutela. Item maior septuaginta annis a tutela vel cura se potest excusare. 'minores autem 'viginti et quinque annis olim excusabantur: 'a nostra autem constitutione[14] prohibentur ad tute'lam vel curam adspirare, adeo ut nec excusatione 'opus fiat. qua constitutione[15] cavetur, ut nec pu'pillus ad legitimam tutelam vocetur nec adultus: cum 'erat incivile eos, qui alieno auxilio in rebus suis ad'ministrandis egere noscuntur et sub aliis reguntur, 14 'aliorum tutelam vel curam subire'. Idem et in milite observandum est, ut nec volens ad tutelae mu15 nus[16] admittatur. Item Romae grammatici rhetores et medici et qui in patria sua id[17] exercent et intra numerum sunt, a tutela vel cura habent vacationem. 16 [18]Qui autem se vult excusare, si plures habeat excusationes et de quibusdam non probaverit, aliis uti intra tempora non prohibetur. qui[19] excusare se volunt, non appellant: sed intra dies quinquaginta continuos, ex quo cognoverunt, excusare se debent (cuiuscumque generis sunt, id est qualitercumque dati fuerint tutores), si intra centesimum lapidem sunt ab eo loco, ubi tutores dati sunt: si vero ultra centesimum habitant, dinumeratione facta viginti milium diurnorum et amplius triginta dierum. quod tamen, ut[20] Scaevola dicebat, sic debet computari, ne minus 17 sint quam quinquaginta dies. Datus autem tutor 18 ad universum patrimonium datus esse creditur. Qui tutelam alicuius gessit, invitus curator eiusdem fieri non compellitur, in tantum ut, licet pater, qui testamento tutorem dederit, adiecit se eundem curatorem dare, tamen invitum eum curam suscipere non cogendum divi Severus et Antoninus rescripserunt. 19 Idem rescripserunt[21] maritum uxori suae curatorem datum excusare se posse, licet se immisceat. 20 Si quis autem falsis allegationibus excusationem tutelae meruit, non est liberatus onere tutelae.

XXVI[22]
DE SUSPECTIS TUTORIBUS ET CURATORIBUS.

[23]Sciendum est suspecti crimen e lege duodecim 1 tabularum descendere. Datum est autem ius removendi suspectos tutores Romae praetori et in pro2 vinciis praesidibus earum et legato proconsulis. Ostendimus, qui possunt de suspecto cognoscere: nunc videamus, qui suspecti fieri possunt. Et quidem omnes tutores possunt, sive testamentarii sint sive non, sed[24] alterius generis tutores. quare et si legitimus sit tutor, accusari poterit. quid[25] si patronus? adhuc idem erit dicendum: dummodo meminerimus famae patroni parcendum, licet ut suspectus remotus 3 fuerit. Consequens est, ut videamus, qui possint suspectos postulare. et sciendum est quasi publicam esse hanc actionem, hoc est omnibus patere. quin immo et mulieres admittuntur ex rescripto divorum Severi et Antonini, sed[26] hae solae, quae pietatis necessitudine ductae ad hoc procedunt, ut puta mater: nutrix quoque et avia possunt, potest et soror: sed et si qua mulier fuerit, cuius praetor perpensam[27] pietatem intellexerit non sexus verecundiam egredientis, sed pietate productam[28] non continere iniuriam 4 pupillorum, admittit eam ad accusationem. Im-

(1) sic T, satisdationem BΘ   (2) cf. p. 8 not. 34   (3) Cf. Dig. 27, 1 Cod. 5, 62..69   (4) et]TΘ, vel B   (5) sic T[b]Θ, causam assumunt B, causa ab●●●unt T[a]   (6) § 4 ex Marciani l. 2 inst. (Dig. 27,1,21 pr.).   (7) pupillorum del.   (8) sic B, inimicitias T   (9) sic T, inimicitias B   (10) sic TΘ, pupilli vel adulti B   (11) sic BΘ, a tut. vel cura T   (12) sic T, excusari B (13) sic Θ, si qui B, is qui T   (14) Cod. 5, 30, 5   (15) sic P, cui constitutioni BE   (16) sic PE[b], onus B, in unius

E[a]   (17) id] PEΘ, artem B   (18) § 16 in. ex Marciani l. 2 inst. (Dig. 27, 1, 21 § 1)   (19) qui PE[a], qui enim B (20) ut om. B   (21) idem rescr. om. B   (22) Cf. Dig. 26, 10 Cod. 5, 43   (23) pr. .. § 3 ex Dig. 26, 10, 1 § 2..7 (Ulp. l. 35 ad ed.)   (24) non sed] BP, n. s. sint Dig., om. E   (25) quid] B[b]P[b] Dig., quod B[a]P[a]E (26) sed] P Dig. Θ, sed et BT   (27) sic libri cum Dig (28) sic P Dig., producta BT

e

claim not only against the guardians or supervisors but also a subsidiary claim against the officials whose business it is to take the security. That subsidiary claim is their last resort. It lies against those who have not bothered to take any security from the guardians or supervisors or who have been satisfied with too little. Both juristic opinions and imperial pronouncements make the claim lie against their heirs as well. 3. The same imperial pronouncements also lay down that pressure should be put on guardians and supervisors who do not give the necessary undertakings by taking property from them as pledges. 4. This action does not lie against a city prefect, praetor, provincial governor or anyone else with the power to appoint guardians; it lies only against the persons whose job it is to take the security.

1.25 EXCUSES

People can be excused acting as guardian or supervisor for a variety of reasons. Frequently it is on account of their children, whether within their authority or emancipated. Someone who has three surviving children in Rome, four in Italy, or five in the provinces can be excused from these duties as from other public duties. It is accepted that the office of guardian or supervisor is a public duty. Adoptive children do not count for this purpose, though their real father can count them. Grandchildren by a son do count when they succeed to the son's place; those by a daughter do not. Only sons still living can be included in the case for an excuse from these offices, not those who have died. Is this true of those who have fallen in war? Those killed in combat count, but only those. They live on for ever in the glory of giving their lives for their country. 1. Next, the six-monthly series of pronouncements of the Emperor Marcus contains a writ allowing someone working in the administration of the imperial exchequer to be excused while so engaged from both guardianship and supervision. 2. The same is true of those away on state business. If they are already guardians or supervisors when called away they are excused for the duration of their absence, and a supervisor is appointed to stand in for them. When they return they resume the burden; nor do they qualify for a one year's break, as Papinian holds in Answers, Book 5. That postponement is only allowed when someone comes back to a new guardianship. 3. Those in a senior office can also excuse themselves, as is stated in a written reply of the Emperor Marcus; but they cannot give up guardianships already begun. 4. Again, nobody can escape being guardian or supervisor on the ground that he is involved in litigation against the child or minor, unless perhaps the issue relates to the latter's entire estate or inheritance. 5. Next, the burden of administering three guardianships or supervisions, if they were not voluntarily acquired, is an excuse as long as they last. But a guardianship of a number of children or supervision of property common to several people, for example brothers, only counts once. 6. Again, replies of the Imperial Brothers, and of the Emperor Marcus alone, held that poverty was a good excuse where the person could show that he could not cope with the burden imposed on him. 7. Again, bad health preventing the management even of one's own affairs is a good excuse. 8. A written reply of the Emperor Pius holds that a person who cannot read or write is to be excused, despite the fact that an illiterate person need not be regarded as disqualified from managing business. 9. Again, if the appointment in a father's will was made out of spite, that in itself affords an excuse. On the other hand, someone who made a promise to the father that he would take on the guardianship of the children is barred from excusing

himself. 10. A reply of the Imperial Brothers holds that it is not an excuse merely to say that you did not know the father of the child in question. 11. The practice is to accept hostility between the appointee and the father of the child or minor and the others as a good excuse if it is grave and implacable. 12. The same is true if the appointee was involved in a dispute with the child's father over his status. 13. People over seventy can also excuse themselves. People under twenty-five used to be excused; under our own pronouncement they are forbidden even to aspire to these offices. There is no longer any place for an excuse. That pronouncement provides that these children, minors, and others shall not be called to act as statutory guardians. It was inappropriate that people should take on the guardianship or supervision of others when they were known to have to rely on the support and control of a third party to manage their own affairs. 14. A similar ban applies to soldiers; they may not be appointed to the office of guardian even if they want to be. 15. In Rome teachers of grammar and rhetoric and doctors are relieved from guardianship and supervision, as also those who practise these professions in their own localities. 16. Someone who wants to plead an excuse and has several possibilities, some of which he fails to make out, is not prevented from advancing the others within the time-limit. To plead an excuse, you need not issue a summons but must advance the excuse within fifty consecutive days of discovering the appointment. This limit applies whatever the kind of guardianship – i.e. whatever the manner of appointment – provided you are within one hundred miles of a place where the business of appointing guardians is done. Further away, the time is calculated at one day for every twenty miles plus thirty days, with, as Scaevola established, a minimum of fifty days. 17. A guardian's appointment is deemed to be for the child's entire estate. 18. One who served as guardian cannot be continued as supervisor for the same person without his consent. This is carried to the point of holding, as did a written reply of the Emperors Severus and Antoninus, that, even if the father's will appointed the guardian and expressly said that he was to continue as supervisor, still he could not be compelled to take on the supervision if he did not want to. 19. Another reply of theirs held that a husband appointed as supervisor for his wife can excuse himself even though he has involved himself in her estate. 20. If someone obtains his excuse from guardianship by making false statements, his discharge from the burden of the office is void.

1.26 UNTRUSTWORTHY GUARDIANS AND SUPERVISORS

It is to be noted that this charge of untrustworthiness derives from the Twelve Tables. 1. The power to remove distrusted guardians has been given to the praetor in Rome, and in the provinces to the governor or the legate of the proconsul. 2. So much for the jurisdiction to investigate. Who can be charged as untrustworthy? All guardians can be, whether testamentary or appointed in one of the other ways. Even a statutory guardian is open to the accusation. What about a patron? The same answer must be given, so long as we remember that the reputation of a patron must be spared even when he is removed as distrusted. 3. Next, who can accuse the untrustworthy? The important point is that the action is in effect public, i.e. it can be brought by anyone, even a woman, as held in a written reply of the Emperors Severus and Antoninus. But a woman can only take these proceedings when duty-bound. For example a mother can. A foster-mother and a grandmother also can. And a sister too. In fact the praetor will allow any woman to make the charge if he considers that her behaviour is not

puberes non possunt tutores suos suspectos postulare: puberes autem curatores suos ex consilio necessariorum suspectos possunt arguere: et ita divi
5 Severus et Antoninus rescripserunt. Suspectus est autem, qui non ex fide tutelam gerit, licet solvendo est, ut et Iulianus quoque scripsit. sed et [1] ante, quam incipiat gerere tutelam tutor, posse eum quasi suspectum removeri idem Iulianus scripsit et
6 secundum eum constitutum est. Suspectus autem remotus, si quidem ob dolum, famosus est: si ob
7 culpam, non aeque. Si quis autem suspectus postulatur, quoad cognitio finiatur, interdicitur ei administratio, ut Papiniano visum est. Sed si su-
8 specti cognitio suscepta fuerit posteaque tutor vel
9 curator decesserit, extinguitur cognitio suspecti. Si quis tutor copiam sui non faciat, ut alimenta pupillo decernantur, cavetur epistula divorum Severi et Antonini [2], ut in possessionem bonorum eius pupillus

mittatur: et quae mora deteriora futura sunt, dato curatore distrahi iubentur. ergo ut suspectus remo-
10 veri poterit qui non praestat alimenta. Sed si quis praesens negat propter inopiam alimenta posse decerni, si hoc per mendacium dicat, remittendum eum esse ad praefectum urbis puniendum placuit, sicut ille remittitur, qui data pecunia ministerium
11 tutelae redemit. [3] Libertus quoque, si fraudulenter gessisse tutelam filiorum vel nepotum patroni probetur, ad praefectum urbis remittitur puniendus.
12 Novissime sciendum est eos, qui fraudulenter tutelam vel curam administrant, etiamsi satis offerant, removendos a tutela, [4] quia satisdatio propositum tutoris malevolum [5] non mutat, sed diutius grassandi in
13 re familiari facultatem praestat. [6] Suspectum 'enim' eum putamus, qui moribus talis est, ut suspectus sit: enimvero tutor 'vel curator' quamvis pauper est, fidelis tamen et diligens, removendus non est quasi suspectus.

LIBER SECUNDUS.

I [7]

DE RERUM DIVISIONE

[8] 'Superiore libro de iure personarum exposuimus: 'modo videamus de rebus. quae vel in nostro patri- 'monio vel extra nostrum patrimonium habentur.'
[9] quaedam enim naturali iure communia sunt omnium, quaedam publica, quaedam universitatis, quaedam nullius, pleraque singulorum, quae variis ex causis cuique adquiruntur, sicut ex subiectis apparebit.
1 [9] Et quidem naturali iure communia sunt omnium haec: aer et aqua profluens et mare et per hoc litora maris. nemo igitur ad litus [10] maris accedere prohibetur, dum tamen villis et monumentis et aedificiis abstineat, quia non sunt iuris gentium, sicut et mare.
2 [9] Flumina autem omnia et portus publica sunt: ideoque ius piscandi omnibus commune est in portu-
3 bus [11] fluminibusque. Est autem litus maris, quate-
4 nus hibernus fluctus maximus excurrit. [12] Riparum quoque usus publicus est iuris [13] gentium, sicut ipsius fluminis: itaque navem [14] ad eas appellere [15], funes ex arboribus ibi natis religare, onus aliquid in his reponere cuilibet liberum est, sicuti per ipsum flumen navigare. sed proprietas earum illorum [16] est, quorum praediis haerent [17]: quia de causa arbores quo-
5 que in iisdem natae eorundem sunt. Litorum quoque usus publicus iuris gentium est, sicut ipsius maris: et ob id quibuslibet liberum est casam ibi imponere, in qua se recipiant, sicut retia siccare et ex mare deducere. proprietas autem eorum potest intellegi nullius esse, sed eiusdem iuris esse, cuius et mare et quae subiacent mari, terra vel harena.
6 [18] Universitatis sunt, non singulorum veluti quae in civitatibus sunt, ut [19] theatra stadia et similia et si qua alia sunt communia civitatium.
7 Nullius autem sunt res sacrae et religiosae et sanctae: quod enim divini iuris est, id nullius in bo-
8 nis est. Sacra sunt, quae rite et per pontifices

deo consecrata sunt, veluti aedes sacrae et dona, quae rite ad ministerium dei dedicata sunt, 'quae 'etiam per nostram constitutionem [20] alienari et obli- 'gari prohibuimus, excepta causa redemptionis capti- 'vorum.' [21] si quis vero auctoritate sua quasi sacrum sibi constituerit, sacrum non est, sed profanum. locus autem, in quo sacrae aedes aedificatae sunt, etiam diruto aedificio adhuc sacer manet, ut et Papinianus
9 scripsit. [22] [23] Religiosum locum unusquisque sua voluntate facit, dum mortuum infert in locum suum. in communem autem locum purum invito socio inferre non licet: 'in commune vero sepulcrum etiam invitis ceteris licet inferre'. item si alienus usus fructus est, proprietarium placet nisi consentiente usufructuario locum religiosum non facere. in alienum locum concedente domino licet inferre: et licet postea ratum habuerit [24], quam illatus est mortuus, tamen
10 religiosus locus fit. [25] 'Sanctae quoque res, veluti 'muri et portae, quodammodo divini iuris sunt et 'ideo nullius in bonis sunt.' ideo autem muros sanctos dicimus, quia poena capitis constituta sit in eos, qui aliquid in muros deliquerint. ideo et legum eas partes, quibus poenas constituimus adversus eos qui contra leges fecerint, sanctiones vocamus.
11 [26] Singulorum autem hominum multis modis res fiunt: quarundam enim rerum dominium nanciscimur iure naturali, quod, sicut diximus, appellatur ius gentium, quarundam iure civili. commodius est itaque a vetustiore iure incipere. palam est autem vetustius esse naturale ius, quod cum ipso genere humano rerum natura prodidit: civilia enim iura tunc coeperunt esse [27], cum et civitates condi et magistratus creari et leges scribi coeperunt.
12 [28] Ferae igitur bestiae et volucres et pisces, id est omnia animalia, quae in terra mari caelo [29] nascuntur [30], simulatque ab aliquo capta fuerint, iure gentium statim illius esse incipiunt: quod enim ante nullius est, id naturali ratione occupanti conceditur.

---

(1) sic Θ, et om. libri   (2) Cf. Dig. 26, 10, 7 § 2   (3) § 11 ex Dig. 26, 10, 2 (Ulp. l. 1 de omnib. trib.)   (4) quia... praestat ex Dig. 26, 10, 6 (Callistr. l. 4 de cogn.)   (5) male voluntatis B   (6) § 13 ex Dig. 26, 10, 8 (Ulp. l. 61 ad ed.) (7) Cf. Gai. 2, 1..11. 19..21. 41. 65..79. Dig. 1, 8. 41, 1 (8) Gai. 2, 1   (9) pr. fin. § 1. 2 ex Marciani l. 3 inst. (Dig. 1, 8, 2. 4)   (10) sic A Dig. Θ, litora BT   (11) sic A Θ, portu BT   (12) § 4. 5 ex Gai. l. 2 rer. cott. (Dig. 1, 8, 5)   (13) iure Dig.   (14) sic A Dig. Θ, naves BT   (15) sic A Dig. Θ, applicare BT   (16) earum illorum] dett., eorum illorum A, illorum eorum B, illarum eorum T, illorum Dig.   (17) sic A Dig., adhaereat BT   (18) § 6 ex Marciani l. 3 inst. (Dig. 1, 8, 6 § 1)   (19) ut om. Dig. Θ   (20) Cod. 1, 2, 21   (21) § 8 fin. ex Marciani l. 3 inst. (Dig. 1, 8, 6 § 3)   (22) Dig. 18, 1, 73 pr.)   (23) § 9 ex Marc. l. c. (Dig. 1, 8, 6 § 4)   (24) sic A Dig. Θ, non habuerit BT   (25) Gai. 2, 8. 9 (Dig. 1, 8, 1 pr.) (26) § 11 in. similis Dig. 41, 1, 1 pr. (Gai. l. 2 rer. cott.) (27) esse] T, om. AB   (28) § 12..17 ex Gai. l. 2 rer. cott. (Dig. 41, 1. 3. 5. 7 pr.)   (29) sic A bg Ap Dig., caeloque A I BT   (30) sic et Θ, capiuntur Dig.

an affront to the natural quietness of the female character but stems from a dutiful concern to right an injustice to the ward. // 4. A young child cannot charge his own guardian with untrustworthiness, but after puberty a supervisee acting on the advice of his relations can bring the charge against his supervisor. So held in a reply of the Emperors Severus and Antoninus. 5. An untrustworthy guardian is one who is guilty of unreliable management. It does not matter that he is not insolvent. Julian wrote that removal is possible even before the guardian begins to act. Imperial pronouncements have followed him in that. 6. A guardian removed on this ground becomes infamous if guilty of deliberate wickedness. It is different if he is guilty only of unintentional fault. 7. Once accused and until the trial is over, he is suspended from his duties. Papinian so held. 8. But if a trial for untrustworthiness is under way and the guardian or supervisor then dies, the proceedings terminate. 9. If the guardian cannot make sufficient resources available to maintain the child, a written reply of the Emperors Severus and Antoninus provides that the child must be put into possession of his property; that a supervisor must be appointed, and anything likely to lose value by further delay must then be put up for sale; that the failure to provide maintenance is a ground for removing the guardian as untrustworthy. 10. If he comes and says that lack of means makes it impossible to provide the maintenance, and if that is a lie, he must be handed over to the the city prefect to be punished, just as must anyone who uses bribery to obtain the management of a ward's estate. 11. A freedman is similarly sent off for punishment by the city prefect if he is guilty of fraudulently managing the guardianship of his patron's sons or grandsons. 12. Finally, note that a guardian or supervisor found to be dishonest in the conduct of his office must be removed even if he offers security. Giving security does nothing to reform the unscrupulous intentions of such a guardian but wins him more time to plunder the family property. 13. We consider a man to be untrustworthy when his behaviour is such as to make him seem unreliable. A guardian or a supervisor who is poor but loyal and attentive to business must not be removed as untrustworthy.

BOOK TWO

2.1 THE CLASSIFICATION OF THINGS

After persons in the previous book, we turn to things. They are either in the category of private wealth or not. Things can be: everybody's by the law of nature; the state's; a corporation's; or nobody's. But most things belong to individuals, who acquire them in a variety of ways, described below. 1. The things which are naturally everybody's are: air, flowing water, the sea, and the sea-shore. So nobody can be stopped from going on to the sea-shore. But he must keep away from houses, monuments, and buildings. Unlike the sea, rights to those things are not determined by the law of all peoples. 2. Rivers and harbours are state property. So everybody shares the right to fish in them. 3. The sea-shore extends as far as the highest winter tide. 4. The law of all peoples allows public use of river banks, as of the rivers themselves: everybody is free to navigate rivers, and they can moor their boats to the banks, run ropes from trees growing there, and unload cargo. But ownership of the banks is vested in the adjacent landowners. That also makes them owners of the trees which grow there. 5. The law of all peoples gives the public a similar right to use the sea-shore, and the sea itself. Anyone is free to put up a hut there to shelter himself. He can dry his nets, or beach his boat. The right view is that ownership of these shores is vested in no one at all. Their legal position is the same as that of the sea and the land or sand under the sea. 6. Corporate, as opposed to individual, property consists in things in towns like theatres, race-courses and so on, in fact in all the things vested in the citizen-body. 7. Sacred, religious, and sanctified things are owned by nobody. Things under divine law cannot belong to individuals. 8. Sacred things are those which have been ceremonially consecrated to God by priests, for instance churches, and also gifts solemnly dedicated to the service of God. Under our pronouncement such things must not be alienated or charged except for redeeming prisoners. If anyone tries to make something sacred himself for his own purposes, it does not become sacred but remains secular. The ground on which a church has been built remains sacred even after the building comes down. That is in Papinian. 9. Anyone can make a site religious by deciding to bury a dead body on land which he owns. A co-owner of land which is not religious cannot use it as a burial place without his colleague's consent. With a shared tomb it is different: burial by one does not need the others' consent. Where someone has a usufruct in the land the law is that the owner cannot make it religious unless the usufructuary consents. The land of a third party may be used for burial if its owner consents; the site does become religious even if his approval is given after the burial. 10. Sanctified things, such as city walls and gates, are also in a certain sense under divine law; they cannot become private property. We call them sanctified because anyone who offends against them faces a capital penalty. We use the word 'sanctions' to describe the parts of statutes which specify the punishment for those who break their provisions. 11. Things become the property of individuals in many ways, some by the law of nature, which, as we have said, can be described as the law of all peoples, and others by our state law. It is easier to begin with the older law. Obviously natural law is earlier. It is the product of the natural order, as old as man himself. Systems of state law did not start to develop until cities were founded, magistracies were established, and law began to be written. 12. Wild animals, birds and fish, the creatures of land, sea and sky, become the property of the taker as soon as they are caught. Where something has no owner, it is reasonable that the person who takes it should have it. // It is immaterial whether

nec interest, feras bestias et volucres utrum in suo fundo quisque capiat, an in alieno: plane qui in alienum fundum ingreditur venandi aut aucupandi gratia, potest a domino, si is providerit, prohiberi ne ingrediatur. quidquid autem eorum ceperis, eo usque tuum esse intellegitur, donec tua custodia coercetur: cum vero evaserit custodiam tuam et in naturalem libertatem se receperit, tuum esse desinit et rursus occupantis fit. naturalem autem libertatem recipere intellegitur, cum vel oculos tuos effugerit vel ita sit in conspectu tuo, ut difficilis sit eius perse-13 cutio. [1] Illud quaesitum est, an, si fera bestia ita vulnerata sit, ut capi possit, statim tua esse intellegatur. 'quibusdam' placuit statim tuam esse et eo usque tuam videri, donec eam persequaris [2], quodsi desieris persequi, desinere tuam esse et rursus fieri occupantis. 'alii' non aliter putaverunt tuam esse, quam si ceperis. 'sed posteriorem sententiam non confirmamus', quia multa accidere 'solent', ut eam non 14 capias. [1] Apium quoque natura fera est. itaque quae in arbore tua consederint, antequam a te alveo includantur, non magis tuae esse intelleguntur, quam volucres, quae in tua arbore nidum fecerint: ideoque si alius eas incluserit, is earum dominus erit. favos quoque si quos hae fecerint [3], quilibet eximere potest. plane integra re si provideris ingredientem in fundum tuum, potes eum iure prohibere ne ingrediatur. examen, quod ex alveo tuo evolaverit, eo usque tuum esse intellegitur, donec in conspectu tuo est nec difficilis eius persecutio est: alioquin occupantis fit. 15 [1] Pavonum et columbarum fera natura est. nec ad rem pertinet, quod ex consuetudine avolare [4] et revolare solent: nam et apes idem faciunt, quarum constat feram esse naturam: cervos quoque ita quidam mansuetos habent, ut in silvas ire et redire soleant, quorum [5] et ipsorum feram esse naturam nemo negat. in his autem animalibus, quae ex consuetudine abire et redire solent, talis regula comprobata est, ut [6] eo usque tua esse intellegantur, donec animum revertendi habeant: nam [7] 'si revertendi animum 'habere desierint, etiam tua esse desinunt et fiunt 'occupantium. revertendi autem animum videntur de-'sinere habere, cum revertendi consuetudinem dese-16 'ruerint.' [1] Gallinarum et anserum non est fera natura idque ex eo possumus intellegere, quod aliae sunt gallinae, quas feras vocamus, item alii anseres, quos feros appellamus. ideoque si anseres tui aut gallinae tuae aliquo casu turbati turbataeve evolaverint, licet conspectum tuum effugerint, quocumque tamen loco sint, tui tuaeve esse [8] intelleguntur: et qui lucrandi animo ea animalia retinet, furtum 17 committere intellegitur. [2] Item ea, quae ex hostibus capimus, iure gentium statim nostra fiunt: adeo quidem, ut et liberi homines in servitutem nostram deducantur, qui tamen, si evaserint nostram potestatem et ad suos reversi fuerint, pristinum statum re-18 cipiunt. [9] Item lapilli gemmae et cetera, quae in litore inveniuntur, iure naturali statim 'inventoris' 19 fiunt. [9] Item ea, quae ex animalibus dominio tuo subiectis nata sunt, eodem iure tibi adquiruntur. 20 [10] Praeterea quod per alluvionem agro tuo flumen adiecit, iure gentium tibi adquiritur. est autem alluvio incrementum latens [11]. per alluvionem autem id videtur adici, quod ita paulatim adicitur, ut intellegere non possis, quantum quoquo momento tem-21 poris adiciatur. [10] Quodsi vis fluminis partem aliquam ex tuo praedio detraxerit et vicini praedio appulerit, palam est eam tuam permanere. plane si longiore [12] tempore fundo vicini haeserit arboresque, quas secum traxerit, in eum fundum radices egerint,

ex eo tempore videntur vicini fundo adquisitae [13] esse. 22 [10] Insula quae in mari nata est, quod raro accidit, occupantis fit: nullius enim esse creditur. at in flumine nata, quod frequenter accidit, si quidem mediam partem fluminis teneat, communis est eorum, qui ab utraque parte fluminis prope ripam praedia possident, pro modo latitudinis cuiusque fundi, quae latitudo prope ripam sit. quodsi alteri parti proximior sit, eorum est tantum, qui ab ea parte prope ripam praedia possident. quodsi aliqua parte divisum flumen, deinde infra unitum agrum alicuius in formam insulae redegerit, eiusdem permanet is ager, 23 cuius et fuerat. [10] Quodsi naturali alveo in universum derelicto alia parte fluere [14] coeperit, prior quidem alveus eorum est, qui prope ripam eius praedia possident, pro modo scilicet latitudinis cuiusque agri, quae latitudo prope ripam sit, novus autem alveus eius iuris esse incipit, cuius et ipsum flumen, id est publicus [15]. quodsi post aliquod tempus ad priorem alveum reversum fuerit flumen, rursus novus alveus eorum esse incipit, qui prope ripam eius prae-24 dia possident. [10] Alia sane causa est, si cuius totus ager inundatus fuerit. neque enim inundatio speciem fundi commutat et ob id, si recesserit aqua, palam est eum fundum eius manere, cuius et fuit. 25 [16] Cum ex aliena materia species aliqua facta sit ab aliquo, quaeri solet, quis [17] eorum naturali ratione dominus sit, utrum is qui fecit, an ille potius qui materiae dominus fuerit: ut ecce si quis ex alienis uvis aut olivis aut spicis vinum aut oleum aut frumentum fecerit, aut ex alieno auro vel argento vel aere vas aliquod fecerit, vel ex alieno vino et melle mulsum miscuerit, vel ex alienis medicamentis emplastrum aut collyrium composuerit, vel ex aliena lana vestimentum fecerit, vel ex alienis tabulis navem vel armarium vel subsellium fabricaverit. et post 'multas Sabinianorum et Proculianorum ambiguitates 'placuit media sententia existimantium', si ea species ad materiam reduci [18] possit, eum videri dominum esse, qui materiae dominus fuerat, si non possit reduci, eum potius intellegi dominum qui fecerit: ut ecce vas conflatum potest ad rudem massam aeris vel argenti vel auri reduci, vinum autem aut oleum aut frumentum ad uvas et olivas et spicas reverti non potest [19] ac ne mulsum quidem ad vinum et mel resolvi potest. quodsi partim ex sua materia, partim ex aliena speciem aliquam fecerit quisque, veluti ex suo vino et alieno melle mulsum aut ex suis et alienis medicamentis emplastrum aut collyrium aut ex sua et aliena lana vestimentum fecerit, dubitandum non est hoc casu eum esse dominum qui fecerit: cum non solum operam suam dedit, sed et partem 26 eiusdem materiae praestavit. Si tamen alienam purpuram quis intexuit suo vestimento, licet pretiosior est purpura, accessionis vice cedit vestimento: et qui dominus fuit purpurae, adversus eum qui subripuit habet furti actionem et condictionem, sive ipse est qui vestimentum fecit, sive alius. nam '[20] extin-'ctae res licet vindicari non possint, condici tamen a 'furibus et [21] a quibusdam aliis possessoribus pos-27 'sunt.' Si duorum materiae ex voluntate dominorum confusae sint, totum id corpus, quod ex confusione fit, utriusque commune est [22], veluti si qui vina sua confuderint aut massas argenti vel auri conflaverint. sed [23] si diversae materiae sint et ob id propria species facta sit, forte ex vino et melle mulsum aut ex auro et argento electrum, idem iuris est: nam et eo casu communem esse speciem non dubitatur. quodsi fortuito et non voluntate dominorum confusae fuerint vel diversae materiae vel quae eius-

---

(1) § 13..17 *ex Gai l. 2 rer. cott.* (*Dig.* 41, 1, 5 § 1..7. 7) (2) *sic B*, persequamur *A cum Dig.*, persequeris *T* (3) hae fecerint] *Dig.*, effecerint *libri* (4) *sic AB Dig. Θ*, advolare *T* (5) quorum] *BT Dig.*, quamvis *A* (6) ut] ut et *T* (7) *Gai.* 2, 68 (8) esse] *BT*, om. *A* (9) § 18. 19 *ex Flor. l. 6 inst.* (*Dig.* 1, 8, 3 *et* 41, 1, 6) (10) § 20..24 *ex Gai. l. 2 rer. cott.* (*Dig.* 41, 1, 7 § 1..6) (11) est ... latens *om. Dig.* (12) *sic Dig. Θ*, longiori *T*, longo *AB* (13) *sic TΘ*, videtur ... adquisita *Dig.*, videntur ..adquisita *AB* (14) *sic A Dig. Θ*, defluere *BT* (15) *sic* (publicis *F*[1]) *Dig.*, publicum *libri*, publici *legisse videtur Θ* (16) § 25 *similis Dig.* 41, 1, 7 § 7 (*Gai. l. c.*) (17) quis *BT*[t], uter *AT*[v] (18) redigi *B* (19) *sic ABΘ*, reduci non possunt *T* (20) *Gai.* 2, 79 (21) et] *ABΘ Gai.*, vel *T* (22) est] *AT*, fit *B* (23) sed] *libri cum Θ: fuitne* sed et (*edd.*)?

*

he catches the wild animal or bird on his own land or someone else's. Suppose a man enters someone else's land to hunt or to catch birds. If the landowner sees him, he can obviously warn him off. If you catch such an animal it remains yours so long as you keep it under your control. If it escapes your control and recovers its natural liberty, it ceases to be yours. The next taker can have it. It is held to have regained its natural freedom when it is out of your sight or when, though still in sight, it is difficult for you to reach it. 13. Does an animal become yours when it is wounded and ready to be caught? Some jurists thought it became yours at once and stayed yours till you gave up the chase, only then becoming available again to the next taker. Others thought that it became yours only when you caught it. We confirm that view. After all, many things can happen to stop you catching the animal. 14. Bees are also wild by nature. If they swarm in your tree they are not yours till you manage to contain them. They are in the same position as birds nesting in the same tree. If another person hives them, he becomes their owner. Also, anyone can take their honey, if they have made any. If you see someone coming on your land, you can obviously stop him before anything is done. A swarm which leaves your hive remains yours while it is within your sight and can be followed without difficulty. Otherwise someone else can take it. 15. Peacocks and pigeons are wild by nature. It is immaterial that their habit is usually to keep flying off and coming back. Bees do that too and there is no doubt that they are wild. Some people also keep deer so domesticated that they regularly go back and forth to the woods. Nobody suggests that they are not wild by nature. There is a special rule for these animals which come and go: they stay yours so long as they keep their homing instinct. It is only when they lose it that they stop being yours. They then vest in the next taker. They are judged to lose the homing instinct when they stop coming back. 16. Ducks and geese are not wild by nature. That is apparent from the existence of separate wild species. If your ducks or geese are disturbed and fly off, they stay yours wherever they are, even when out of your sight. Anyone who takes such animals with intent to gain commits theft. 17. The law of all peoples also instantly makes us owner of things captured from an enemy. This even makes slaves of free captives. If they escape and get back to their own people they recover their former status. 18. Stones and gems and so on found on the sea-shore immediately become the finder's by the law of nature. 19. The offspring of animals you already own also become yours under the law of nature. 20. The law of all peoples makes yours any alluvial accretion which a river adds to your land. An alluvial accretion is one which goes on so gradually that you cannot tell at any one moment what is being added. 21. If the river's current rips away a piece of your land and carries it down to your neighbour, it clearly remains yours. If after a while it attaches itself to the neighbour's land, and trees which it took with it drive roots into that land, it will then have become part of his land and as such his. 22. If, as does happen, an island arises in the sea, it vests in the first taker because it has no owner. But when, as commonly happens, an island is formed in a river, then, if it is in mid-stream, it becomes the common property of those with land each side, in shares proportionate to the frontage along the river of each estate; but if it is nearer one side it goes to the owners on that side. If the river turns a man's land into an island by splitting at one point and joining up again lower down, ownership remains unchanged. 23. Suppose the river entirely abandons its original course and flows along a new bed. The deserted river-bed goes to the adjacent landowners, according to the frontage of their estates on the old bed. The new bed becomes state property, the same status as the river itself. If the river ever returns to the old bed, the new bed is again divided between the adjacent landowners. 24. It is different, of course, if a land is flooded. A flood does not change the geography. If the water recedes the land is obviously still the property of the person who owned it before. 25. Suppose one man makes something out of another's materials. Who is it reasonable to see as owner, the maker or the owner of the materials? Suppose, for example, that one man makes wine, oil, or grain from another's grapes, olives, or corn; or a pot of some kind from another's gold, silver, or bronze; or mead from another's wine and honey; or a plaster or ointment from another's medicines; or clothes from another's wool; or a ship, a chest, or a chair from another's timber. Debates between Sabinians and Proculians left this unresolved. A middle view has been upheld: if the thing can be turned back into its materials, its owner is the one who owned the materials; if not, the maker. The completed pot can be turned back into a raw ingot of bronze, or silver, or gold; wine, or oil, or grain cannot be made back into grapes, olives, or corn, and even mead cannot be turned back into wine and honey. If someone makes something partly out of his own material and partly out of another's — mead from his wine and another's honey, or a plaster or ointment from some medicines belonging to himself and others belonging to someone else, or clothes out of his own and someone else's wool — ownership vests, without a doubt, in the maker. He contributes not only his work but also even part of the material. 26. Suppose someone weaves another's purple thread into his own garment. It merges with the garment by accession, even if the thread is more valuable than all the rest. The former owner of the thread then has the action for theft and the action of debt against the taker, whether he was the one who made the clothes or not. When something has ceased to exist it is no longer possible to bring a vindication, but the action of debt can still be used against thieves and certain other types of possessor. 27. If materials owned by two people are deliberately blended together, the resultant mass becomes the common property of both. Examples are where two people blend together their wine, or melt together their ingots of silver or of gold. The same applies where the materials are different and their fusion produces a new substance, for instance mead from wine and honey, or electrum from gold and silver. Even if the blend occurs by chance and not by design, the same rule applies where the materials are different and where they are the same. // 28. But suppose that corn owned by

28 dem generis sunt, idem iuris esse placuit. Quodsi frumentum Titii tuo frumento mixtum fuerit, si quidem ex voluntate vestra, commune erit, quia singula corpora, id est singula grana, quae cuiusque propria fuerunt, ex consensu vestro communicata sunt. quodsi casu id mixtum fuerit vel Titius id miscuerit sine voluntate tua, non videtur commune esse, quia singula corpora in sua substantia durant nec magis istis casibus commune fit frumentum, quam grex communis esse intellegitur, si pecora Titii tuis pecoribus mixta fuerint: sed ab alterutro vestrum id totum frumentum retineatur, in rem quidem actio pro modo frumenti cuiusque competat, arbitrio autem iudicis continetur, ut is[1] aestimet, quale cuius-
29 que frumentum fuerit. [2]Cum in suo solo aliquis aliena materia aedificaverit, ipse dominus intellegitur aedificii, quia omne quod inaedificatur solo cedit. nec tamen ideo is, qui materiae dominus fuerat, desinit eius dominus esse: sed tantisper neque vindicare eam potest neque ad exhibendum de ea re agere propter legem duodecim tabularum, qua cavetur, ne quis tignum alienum aedibus suis iunctum eximere cogatur, sed duplum pro eo praestet per actionem quae vocatur de tigno iuncto (appellatione autem tigni omnis materia significatur, ex qua[3] aedificia fiunt): quod ideo provisum est, 'ne aedificia rescindi necesse sit'. sed si aliqua ex causa dirutum sit aedificium, poterit materiae dominus, 'si non fuerit duplum iam persecutus', tunc eam vindicare et ad
30 exhibendum agere[4]. [2]Ex diverso si quis in alieno solo sua materia domum aedificaverit, illius fit domus, cuius et solum est. sed hoc casu materiae dominus proprietatem eius amittit, qua voluntate eius alienata intellegitur, utique si[5] non ignorabat in alieno solo se aedificare: et ideo, licet diruta sit domus, vindicare materiam non possit[6]. certe illud constat, si in possessione constituto aedificatore soli dominus petat domum suam esse nec solvat pretium materiae et mercedes fabrorum, posse eum per exceptionem doli mali repelli, utique si bonae fidei possessor fuit qui aedificasset: nam scienti alienum esse solum potest culpa obici, quod temere aedificaverit in eo solo,
31 quod intellegeret alienum esse. [2]Si Titius alienam plantam in suo solo posuerit, ipsius erit: et ex diverso si Titius suam plantam in Maevii solo posuerit, Maevii planta erit, si modo utroque casu radices egerit. antequam autem radices egerit, eius permanet, cuius et fuerat. adeo autem ex eo, ex[7] quo radices agit planta, proprietas eius commutatur, ut, si vicini arborem ita terra[8] Titii presserit[9], ut in eius fundum radices ageret, Titii effici arborem dicimus[10]: rationem etenim non permittere[11], ut alterius arbor esse intellegatur, quam cuius in fundum radices egisset. et ideo prope confinium arbor posita si etiam in vicini fundum radices egerit, communis
32 fit. [12]Qua ratione autem plantae, quae terra coalescunt, solo cedunt, eadem ratione frumenta quoque, quae sata sunt, solo cedere intelleguntur. ceterum sicut is qui in alieno solo aedificaverit, si ab eo dominus petat aedificium, defendi potest per exceptionem doli mali secundum ea quae diximus: ita eiusdem exceptionis auxilio tutus esse potest is, qui alienum[13] fundum sua impensa[14] bona fide consevit.
33 [12]Litterae quoque, licet aureae sint, perinde chartis membranisque cedunt, acsi[15] solo cedere solent ea quae inaedificantur aut inseruntur: ideoque si in chartis membranisve tuis carmen vel historiam vel

orationem Titius scripserit, huius corporis non Titius, sed tu dominus esse indiceris[16]. sed si a Titio petas tuos libros tuasve membranas esse nec impensam scripturae solvere paratus sis, poterit se Titius defendere per exceptionem doli mali, utique si bona fide earum chartarum membranarumve possessionem
34 nanctus est. Si quis in aliena tabula pinxerit, 'quidam putant' tabulam picturae cedere: 'aliis' videtur picturam[17], qualiscumque sit, tabulae cedere. 'sed nobis videtur melius esse tabulam picturae cedere: 'ridiculum est enim picturam Apellis vel Parrhasii[18] 'in accessionem vilissimae tabulae cedere. unde'[19] 'si 'a domino tabulae imaginem possidente is qui pinxit 'eam petat nec solvat pretium tabulae, poterit per 'exceptionem doli mali summoveri: at si is qui pinxit 'possideat, consequens est, ut utilis actio domino 'tabulae adversus eum detur, quo casu, si non solvat 'impensam picturae, poterit per exceptionem doli mali 'repelli, utique si bona fide possessor fuerit 'ille qui 'picturam imposuit'. illud 'enim' palam est, quod, sive 'is qui pinxit' subripuit tabulas sive alius, competit 'domino tabularum' furti actio.'
35 Si quis a non domino, quem dominum esse crederet, bona fide fundum emerit vel ex donatione aliave qua iusta causa aeque bona fide acceperit: naturali ratione placuit fructus quos percepit eius esse pro cultura et cura. et ideo si postea dominus supervenerit et fundum vindicet, de fructibus ab eo 'consumptis' agere non potest. ei vero, qui sciens alienum fundum possederit, non idem concessum est. itaque cum fundo etiam fructus, 'licet consumpti sint',[20]
36 cogitur restituere. Is, ad quem usus fructus fundi pertinet, non aliter fructuum dominus efficitur, quam si eos ipse perceperit. et ideo licet maturis fructibus, nondum tamen perceptis decesserit, ad heredem eius non pertinent, sed[21] domino proprietatis adquiruntur. eadem fere et de colono dicuntur.
37 [22]In pecudum fructu etiam fetus est, sicuti lac et pilus et lana: itaque agni et haedi et vituli et equuli[23] statim naturali iure dominii[24] sunt fructuarii. partus vero ancillae in fructu non est itaque ad dominum proprietatis pertinet: absurdum enim videbatur hominem in fructu esse, cum omnes fructus
38 rerum natura hominum gratia comparavit. Sed si gregis usum fructum quis habeat, in locum demortuorum capitum ex fetu fructuarius summittere debet, ut et Iuliano visum est, et in vinearum demortuarum vel arborum locum alias debet substituere. recte enim colere et quasi bonus pater familias uti debet[25].
39 Thesauros, quos quis in suo loco invenerit, divus Hadrianus naturalem aequitatem secutus ei concessit qui invenerit. idemque statuit, si quis in sacro aut in religioso loco fortuito casu invenerit. at si quis in alieno loco non data ad hoc opera, sed fortuitu invenerit, dimidium domino soli concessit. et convenienter, si quis in Caesaris loco invenerit, dimidium inventoris, dimidium Caesaris esse statuit. cui conveniens est, ut, si quis in publico loco vel fiscali invenerit, dimidium ipsius esse[26], dimidium fisci vel civitatis.
40 [27]Per traditionem quoque iure naturali[28] res nobis adquiruntur: nihil enim tam conveniens est naturali aequitati, quam voluntatem domini, volentis rem suam in alium transferre, ratam haberi. 'et ideo 'cuiuscumque generis sit corporalis res, tradi potest[29] 'et a domino tradita alienatur. itaque stipendiaria

(1) is] A, id B, ipse T   (2) § 29..31 ex Gai l. 2 rer. cott. (Dig. 41, 1, 7 § 10. 12. 13)   (3) sic AT (sed significat T), omnes materiae significantur ex quibus (ex qua B) B Dig. (4) agere] Dig. Θ, de ea re (re om. T^a) ag. AT, de eis ag. B (5) si om. T^a   (6) sic A, potest BT   (7) ex om. A (8) terram BT et in Dig. F[1]   (9) Titius presserit expectes: presserim Dig., ut cogitandum sit de arbore propagata, qua de re cf. Plin. h. n. 17, 13 Dig. 43, 24, 22 pr. (10) dicamus edd.   (11) sic ATDig., ratio enim non permittit B   (12) § 32. 33 ex Gai l. c. (Dig. 41, 1, 9 pr. § 1)

(13) sic AT, in alienum BDig.   (14) suam impensam B (15) ac Dig.   (16) sic AB, videris T, intellegeris Dig. (17) sic AT^a, pictura BT^b   (18) parrasis libri   (19) Gai. 2, 78   (20) '> Justinianis tribuit Pernice   (21) sed] ABΘ, sed omnino T   (22) § 37 ex Gai l. 2 rer. cott. (Dig. 22, 1, 28)   (23) et equuli] TΘ, et equuleia A, et equi B, om. Dig.   (24) sic AT, dominio B, om. Dig.   (25) uti debet] AT, om. B   (26) sic BT, esset A   (27) § 40 in. ex Gai l. c. (Dig. 41, 1, 9 § 3)   (28) iure naturali] naturalem B   (29) sic T, possit AB

Titius is mixed with yours. If you both wanted the mixing done, you own the mass in common, because every particle you each owned, i.e. every grain of corn, is by your agreement made common to you both. But if the mixture happens accidentally or is done by Titius against your will, the whole is not held in common, because the individual particles retain their own identity. The corn is not made common property here any more than flocks become common if the animals get mixed up. If one of you keeps the whole lot, a real action lies for the quantity of the other's individual contribution. The judge has power to allow for the quality of each contribution in assessing his award. 29. Suppose that someone builds on his own land with materials owned by another. He owns the building. The reason is that anything built on land becomes part of the land. This does not mean that the owner of the materials loses his ownership of them; but for the time being he cannot vindicate them or bring an action for their production. A rule of the Twelve Tables provides that nobody can be compelled to remove another's beams set into his house; instead he must pay double the timber's value under the claim called the action for beams set in. 'Beams' includes all materials which go into the building of a house. The provision was designed to stop buildings being demolished. If for some reason the building does come down, then, provided he has not already claimed his double damages, the owner of the materials can vindicate them or bring the action for their production. 30. Conversely if someone builds a house with his own materials on another's land, the landowner still becomes owner of the house. Here the owner of the materials does lose his ownership because he is taken to have parted with them voluntarily. That assumes he knew he was building in another's land. In that case, even if the house comes down he cannot vindicate the materials. Suppose the builder is in possession and the owner of the land vindicates. He asserts the house is his but will not pay the cost of labour and materials. His action can be defeated by the plea of deceit. That assumes, though, that the builder acquired possession in good faith. Where he knew the land was not his, it can be replied that it was his fault for taking the risk of building on land which he knew was not his. 31. If Titius puts someone else's plants into his land, they becomes his. And, the other way around, his own plants placed in Maevius's land vest in Maevius. But they must have rooted. Until then they continue to be owned by their original owner. Roots are critical. If a neighbouring tree close by Titius' land drives its roots into his land, Titius becomes its owner. It would be unreasonable for the law to give ownership of a tree to anyone except the owner of the land in which it is rooted. A tree by a boundary is owned in common if it drives roots into your land and your neighbour's. 32. Just as plants become part of the land in which they are rooted, so corn which is sown also becomes part of the land. And just as we have shown that a builder on another's land can defeat the owner's vindication with the plea of deceit, so one who in good faith has incurred the expense of sowing another's land is protected by the same defence. 33. Writing, even in letters of gold, becomes part of the paper or parchment, just as fixtures on or in land merge in the land. Suppose Titius writes a poem or a history or a speech on your paper or parchment. A judge will find

that you, not Titius, are owner. But if you vindicate the books or papers and are not prepared to pay him the expenses of the writing, Titius will have the plea of deceit. That assumes he acquired possession of the paper or parchment in good faith. 34. If someone paints on another person's board, some jurists think the board's identity is absorbed by the picture, others the picture's by the board, whatever the quality of the picture. Our view makes the picture prevail over the board. It would be ridiculous for a picture by Apelles or Parrhasius to accede to a board worth almost nothing. If the owner of the board is in possession of the picture and the painter claims without paying the its price, his claim can be defeated by the plea of deceit. If the painter is in possession, the owner of the board is given a policy action. In that claim, assuming good faith on the part of the painter, the plaintiff will again be defeated by the plea of deceit if he fails to pay the painter's costs. Finally an obvious point: if the painter or a third party stole the board, its owner has the action for theft. 35. Suppose you believe that someone is owner of a piece of land when in fact he is not, and you buy it from him in good faith or, still on the assumption of good faith, receive it as a gift or on some other legally sufficient ground. The law decided, true to first principles, that fruits which you harvest become yours because of your work in growing and looking after them. So if the owner appears and vindicates the land, he cannot claim in respect of fruits you have consumed. You cannot benefit by this rule if you knew you were taking possession of another's land. In that case you have to make restitution of the land and the fruits, even the fruits already consumed. 36. A usufructuary becomes owner of the fruits of the land only by harvesting them himself. If he dies when the fruit is ready but unpicked, his heir is not entitled to it. It goes to the landowner. Much the same rules apply for tenants. 37. With livestock, offspring are included in fruits along with milk, hair and wool. Natural law gives lambs, kids, calves, and foals to the usufructuary. The offspring of slave-women do not count as fruits. They go to the owner. It would be absurd for human beings to be counted as fruits when it is for man that nature provides all fruits. 38. If someone has a usufruct in a flock, he must replace those which die from his lambs and so on. Julian so holds. Similarly the usufructuary of a vineyard must replace dead vines and trees. That is implied by his duty to farm properly, using the land as a good owner. 39. The Emperor Hadrian, deciding in accordance with natural justice, allowed treasure found by a man on his own land to go to the finder, with the same ruling for chance finds on sacred or religious land. For a find on land of a private owner, so long as the treasure was found by chance and not by deliberate search, he allowed the owner half; and, correspondingly, for a find on imperial property he ruled that half should go the finder and half to the emperor. A natural extension for a find on public or fiscal land gives half to the finder and half to the exchequer or to the town. 40. Another natural law mode of acquisition is delivery. What could be more in line with natural justice than to give effect to a man's intention to transfer something of his to another? That is why the law allows all corporeal things to be delivered and all deliveries by owners to pass the property in the thing delivered. //

'quoque et tributaria praedia eodem modo alienantur.
'vocantur autem stipendiaria et tributaria praedia,
'quae in provinciis sunt, inter quae nec non Italica
'praedia ex nostra constitutione [1] nulla differentia est.'
41 Sed si quidem ex causa donationis aut dotis aut
qualibet alia ex causa tradantur, sine dubio transferuntur: venditae vero et traditae non aliter emptori adquiruntur, quam si is venditori pretium solverit vel alio modo ei satisfecerit, veluti expromissore
aut pignore dato. quod cavetur quidem etiam lege
duodecim tabularum: tamen recte dicitur et iure
gentium, id est [2] iure naturali, id effici. sed si is qui
vendidit fidem emptoris secutus fuerit [3], dicendum
42 est [4] statim rem emptoris fieri.' [5] Nihil autem interest, utrum ipse dominus tradat alicui rem, an vo-
43 luntate eius alius [6]. [5] Qua ratione, si cui [7] libera negotiorum [8] administratio a domino permissa fuerit isque ex his negotiis rem vendiderit et tradiderit, facit
44 eam accipientis. [5] Interdum etiam sine traditione
nuda voluntas sufficit domini ad rem transferendam,
veluti si rem, quam tibi aliquis commodavit aut lo-
cavit aut apud te deposuit, vendiderit tibi [9] aut donaverit. quamvis enim ex ea causa tibi eam non
tradiderit, eo tamen ipso, quod patitur tuam esse,
statim adquiritur tibi proprietas perinde ac si eo no-
45 mine tradita fuisset. [5] Item si quis merces in
horreo depositas vendiderit, simul atque claves horrei
tradiderit emptori, transfert proprietatem mercium ad
46 emptorem. [5] Hoc amplius interdum et in incertam
personam collocata [10] voluntas domini transfert rei
proprietatem: ut ecce praetores vel consules, qui missi-
lia iactant in vulgus, ignorant, quid eorum quisque
excepturus sit, et tamen, quia volunt quod quisque
exceperit eius esse, statim eum dominum efficiunt.
47 Qua ratione verius esse videtur et, si rem pro
derelicto a domino habitam occupaverit quis, statim
eum dominum effici. pro derelicto autem habetur,
quod dominus ea mente abiecerit, ut id rerum suarum esse nollet, ideoque statim dominus esse desinit.
48 [11] Alia causa est earum rerum, quae in tem-
pestate maris levandae navis causa eiciuntur. hae
enim dominorum permanent, quia palam est eas non
eo animo eici, quo [12] quis eas habere non vult, sed
quo magis cum ipsa nave periculum maris effugiat:
qua de causa si quis eas fluctibus expulsas vel etiam
in ipso mari nactus lucrandi animo abstulerit, furtum
committit. nec longe discedere videntur ab his, quae
de rheda currente [13] non intellegentibus dominis ca-
dunt.

II
DE REBUS INCORPORALIBUS.

[14] 'Quaedam praeterea res corporales sunt, quae-
1 'dam incorporales. Corporales hae sunt, quae sui
'natura tangi possunt: veluti fundus homo vestis au-
'rum argentum et denique aliae res innumerabiles.
2 'Incorporales autem sunt, quae tangi non possunt.
'qualia sunt ea, quae in iure consistunt: sicut heri-
'ditas, usus fructus [15], obligationes quoquo modo con-
'tractae. nec ad rem pertinet, quod in hereditate res
'corporales continentur: nam et fructus, qui ex fundo
'percipiuntur, corporales sunt et id, quod ex aliqua
'obligatione nobis debetur, plerumque corporale est,
'veluti fundus homo pecunia: nam ipsum ius heredita-
'tis [16] et ipsum ius utendi fruendi et ipsum ius obli-
3 'gationis incorporale est. Eodem numero sunt iura

'praediorum urbanorum et rusticorum', quae etiam
servitutes vocantur.

III [17]
DE SERVITUTIBUS

[18] Rusticorum praediorum iura sunt haec: iter actus
via aquae ductus. iter est ius eundi ambulandi homini, non etiam iumentum agendi vel vehiculum:
actus est ius agendi vel iumentum vel vehiculum.
itaque qui iter habet, actum non habet. qui actum
habet, et [19] iter habet eoque uti potest etiam sine iumento. via est ius eundi et agendi 'et ambulandi':
nam et iter et actum in se via continet. aquae ductus
1 est ius aquae ducendae per fundum alienum. [20] Praediorum urbanorum sunt servitutes, quae aedificiis in-
haerent, ideo urbanorum praediorum dictae, quoniam
aedificia omnia urbana praedia appellantur, etsi in
villa aedificata sunt. item praediorum urbanorum
servitutes sunt hae: ut vicinus onera vicini sustineat:
ut in parietem eius liceat vicino tignum immittere:
ut stillicidium vel flumen recipiat quis in aedes suas
vel in aream [21], vel non recipiat: et ne altius tollat
2 quis aedes suas, ne luminibus vicini officiatur. [22] In
rusticorum praediorum servitutes [23] quidam computari
recte putant aquae haustum, pecoris ad aquam ad-
pulsum, ius pascendi, calcis coquendae, harenae fo-
diendae.
3 [22] Ideo autem hae servitutes praediorum appellantur, quoniam sine praediis constitui non possunt.
nemo enim potest servitutem adquirere urbani vel
rustici praedii, nisi qui habet praedium, nec quis-
4 quam debere, nisi qui habet praedium. Si quis
velit vicino aliquod ius constituere, pactionibus atque stipulationibus id efficere debet. [24] potest etiam
in testamento quis heredem suum damnare, ne altius
tollat [25], ne luminibus aedium vicini officiat: vel ut
patiatur eum tignum in parietem immittere vel stillicidium habere: vel ut patiatur eum per fundum ire
agere aquamve ex eo ducere.

IV [26]
DE USU FRUCTU.

[27] Usus fructus est ius alienis rebus utendi fruendi
salva rerum substantia. est enim ius in corpore: quo
1 sublato et ipsum tolli necesse est. Usus fructus
a proprietate separationem recipit idque plurimis [28]
modis accidit. ut ecce si quis alicui usum fructum
legaverit: nam heres nudam habet proprietatem,
legatarius usum fructum: et contra si fundum legaverit deducto usu fructu, legatarius nudam habet
proprietatem, heres vero usum fructum: item alii
usum fructum, alii deducto eo fundum legare potest.
[29] sine testamento vero si quis velit alii usum fructum
constituere, pactionibus et stipulationibus id efficere
debet. ne tamen in universum inutiles essent pro-
prietates semper abscedente usu fructu, placuit certis modis extingui usum fructum et ad proprietatem
2 reverti. Constituitur autem usus fructus non tantum in fundo et aedibus, verum etiam in servis et
iumentis ceterisque rebus exceptis his quae ipso usu
consumuntur: nam eae [30] neque naturali ratione neque civili recipiunt usum fructum. quo numero sunt
vinum oleum frumentum vestimenta. quibus proxima
est pecunia numerata: namque in ipso usu adsidua

(1) Cod. 7, 31, 1   (2) id est] AT, et B   (3) secutus
fuerit] BT, secuturus (secutus A¹) est A   (4) dic. est
om. B   (5) § 42..46 ex Gai l. 2 rer. cott. (Dig. 41, 1, 9
§ 4..7)   (6) alius] AΘ, aliquis Dig., alius aut possessio
eius rei permissa sit (sit om. B) BT   (7) cui om. A
(8) negotiorum] B Dig. Θ, universorum neg. AT   (9) tibi
om. B   (10) sic A Dig., collata BT   (11) § 48 ex Gai
l. 2 rer. cott. (Dig. 41, 1, 9 § 8)   (12) quod Dig.   (13) cur-
rente] AT, om. B
(14) Gai. 2, 12..14 Dig. 1, 8, 1 § 1   (15) sic Gai. Dig. Θ,
usus fructus usus libri   (16) successionis Gai. Dig.

(17) Cf. Dig. 8 Cod. 3, 34   (18) pr. ex Ulp. l. 2 inst.
(Dig. 8, 3, 1 pr.)   (19) et] T Dig. Θ, om. B   (20) § 1 in.
ex Ulp. l. c. (Dig. 8, 4, 1 pr.)?   (21) sic BTªΘ, vel in
cloacam add. dett.   (22) § 2..3 ex Ulp. l. c. (Dig. 8, 3, 1 § 1
et 8, 4, 1 § 1)   (23) sic TΘ, servitute B   (24) § 4 fin. ex
Gai l. 2 rer. cott. (Dig. 8, 4, 16)   (25) tollat] BTª, aedes
suas tollat Dig.
(26) Cf. Gai. 2, 30. 33 Dig. 7, 1. 4. 5; 33, 2 Cod. 3, 33   (27) pr.
ex Dig. 7, 1, 1. 2 (Paul. l. 3 ad Vitell. et Cels. l. 18 dig.)   (28) sic
BT, pluribus dett., πολλοῖς Θ   (29) § 1 fin. § 2 in. ex Gai
l. 2 rer. cott. (Dig. 7, 1, 3 pr. § 1)   (30) eae] B, eae res T

Stipendiary and tributary lands can be alienated in this way. These terms are used of land in the provinces. As a result of our pronouncement there is now no difference between them, nor between them and land in Italy. 41. If delivery rests on gift or dowry or any other sufficient basis, the property certainly passes. But things which have been sold and delivered only become the buyer's if he has paid the price to the seller or satisfied him in some other way, as by providing a guarantor or a pledge. There is even a provision on this in the Twelve Tables, though it is true that it is also a rule of the law of all peoples, i.e. of the law of nature. But if the seller gives credit to the buyer, the property in the thing does pass immediately to the buyer. 42. It makes no difference whether the delivery is made by the owner or by another with his consent. 43. A slave whose owner has allowed him full management powers can transfer to a recipient the property in a thing which he sells and delivers in the course of that management. 44. Sometimes the owner's mere intention, even without delivery, is enough to transfer the property in the thing. Examples are where someone sells or gives you something which he has lent or hired you or deposited with you. Even though he makes no actual delivery, the property immediately passes to you. His consent to your holding as owner here works just as though he had delivered with that in view. 45. If someone sells goods deposited in a warehouse, the property in them passes to the buyer as soon as the keys of the warehouse are delivered to him. 46. A more extreme case is where the intention of the owner is not directed to an identifiable person but the property still passes. When praetors or consuls throw largesse to a crowd they have no idea who will take what. Despite this, because their intention is that anyone is to have what he takes, the property passes to every taker. 47. The logic of this supports the view that if an owner abandons a thing the property passes straight away to anyone who takes possession of it. The law sees a thing as abandoned when its owner throws it away intending that it shall cease at once to be his property. 48. It is different with things thrown overboard in a storm to lighten ship. They continue to belong to their owners. They are definitely not thrown away with the intention to be rid of them but to help both owner and ship escape the dangers of the sea. Anyone who finds them driven ashore by the waves or still on the sea commits theft if he takes them with intent to gain. Such things are in much the same position as those which drop out of moving vehicles without their owners' knowledge.

2.2 INCORPOREAL THINGS

Some things are corporeal, some incorporeal. 1. Corporeal things can actually be touched – land, a slave, clothes, gold, silver, and of course countless others. 2. Incorporeal things cannot be touched. They consist of legal rights – inheritance, usufruct, obligations however contracted. It is irrelevant that an inheritance may include corporeal things. What a usufructuary takes from the land will also be corporeal. And what is owed to us by virtue of an obligation is usually corporeal, such as land, a slave, or money. The point is that the actual right of inheritance is incorporeal, as is the actual right to the use and fruits of a thing, and the right inherent in an obligation. 3. The rights which belong to urban and rustic estates also come under this heading. These are also called servitudes.

2.3. SERVITUDES

The following are rights belonging to rustic land: passage, drive, way, aqueduct. Passage is the right for a man to pass or walk without taking either a beast or a vehicle; drive is the right to take a beast or vehicle. One who has passage does not have drive; but one who has drive has passage too and can exercise his right even without his beast. Way is the right to pass and drive and walk. Way includes passage and drive. Aqueduct is the right of leading water over another's land. 1. The servitudes belonging to urban land are those to do with buildings. They are said to belong to urban land because all buildings are referred to as urban property, even out on a farm. These are examples: that one neighbour support the weight of another's building; that he allow his neighbour to insert a beam in his party-wall; that he receive run-off or a stream on to his buildings or his site – or, that he not receive it; that a man raise his building no higher, to prevent obstruction of his neighbour's light. 2. In the category of servitudes belonging to rustic land some correctly put drawing water, driving cattle to water, pasturage, burning lime, and digging sand. 3. The reason these rights are called servitudes belonging to land is that they cannot exist independently of land. Nobody can acquire a servitude of urban or rustic land unless he has land; nor can one without land bear the liability implicit in a servitude. 4. An owner who intends to grant such a right to his neighbour should do it by pacts and stipulations. He can also impose the liability on his heir by will, for instance not to build higher so as to obstruct the light of his neighbour's building, or to allow the neighbour to put a beam in the party-wall, or accept his run-off, or allow him to pass or drive over the land or lead water from it.

2.4 USUFRUCT

Usufruct is the right to the use and fruits of another person's property, with the duty to preserve its substance. It is a right in a corporeal thing. It must end if its corporeal object ceases to exist. 1. Usufruct has to be split off from ownership. This can happen in many ways. One person may leave another a legacy of a usufruct. The heir then gets bare ownership, the legatee the right to the use and fruits. Conversely, a legacy of land with usufruct deducted gives the legatee bare ownership and the heir the use and fruits. There can be a legacy of usufruct to one and of the land with usufruct deducted to another. Anyone wanting to create a non-testamentary usufruct for another should do it by pacts and stipulations. To prevent ownership being rendered useless by permanent usufructs the law makes usufruct terminate in certain conditions. That revives the rights of the owner. 2. There can be a usufruct in slaves, beasts, and other things, as well as land and buildings. But not in things used up by being used. Logic and law argue against the possibility of a usufruct in these, for instance wine, oil, corn, and clothes. Money is a similar case, which is in a certain sense used up by the continual exchange involved in using it. // But convenience led the

permutatione quodammodo extinguitur. sed utilitatis causa senatus censuit posse etiam earum rerum usum fructum constitui, ut tamen eo nomine heredi utiliter caveatur. itaque si pecuniae usus fructus legatus sit, ita datur legatario, ut eius fiat, et legatarius satisdat heredi de tanta pecunia restituenda, si morietur aut capite minuetur. ceterae quoque res ita traduntur legatario, ut eius fiant: sed aestimatis his satisdatur, ut, si morietur aut capite minuetur, tanta pecunia restituatur, quanti eae fuerint aestimatae. ergo senatus non fecit quidem earum rerum usum fructum (nec enim poterat), sed per cautionem quasi usum 3 fructum constituit. Finitur autem usus fructus morte fructuarii et 'duabus capitis deminutionibus, maxima et media', et non utendo 'per modum et tem-'pus. quae omnia[1] nostra statuit constitutio[2]. item finitur usus fructus, si domino proprietatis ab usufructuario cedatur (nam extraneo cedendo nihil agitur): vel ex contrario si fructuarius proprietatem rei adquisierit, quae res consolidatio appellatur. eo amplius constat, si aedes incendio consumptae fuerint vel etiam terrae motu aut vitio suo corruerint, extingui usum fructum et ne areae quidem usum fructum 4 deberi. Cum autem finitus fuerit usus fructus, revertitur scilicet ad proprietatem et ex eo tempore nudae proprietatis dominus incipit plenam habere in re potestatem.

V[3]
DE USU ET HABITATIONE.

[4]Isdem istis modis, quibus usus fructus constituitur, etiam nudus usus constitui solet isdemque illis modis 1 finitur, quibus et usus fructus desinit. Minus autem scilicet iuris in usu est quam in usu fructu. namque is, qui fundi nudum usum habet, nihil ulterius habere intellegitur, quam ut oleribus pomis floribus feno stramentis lignis ad usum cottidianum utatur: [5]in eoque fundo hactenus ei morari licet, ut neque domino fundi molestus sit neque his, per quos opera rustica fiunt, impedimento sit: nec ulli alii ius quod habet aut vendere aut locare aut gratis concedere potest, 'cum is qui usum fructum habet potest 2 haec omnia facere'[6]. Item is, qui aedium usum habet, hactenus iuris habere intellegitur, ut ipse tantum habitet, nec hoc ius ad alium transferre potest: et vix receptum videtur, ut hospitem ei recipere liceat. et cum uxore sua liberisque suis, item libertis 'nec non aliis liberis personis, quibus non minus quam servis utitur', habitandi ius habeat, et convenienter si ad mulierem usus aedium pertinet, cum marito 3 ei[7] habitare liceat. Item is[8], ad quem servi usus pertinet, ipse tantum operis[9] atque ministerio eius uti potest: ad alium vero nullo modo ius suum transferre ei concessum est. idem scilicet iuris est et in 4 iumento. Sed[10] si pecoris vel ovium usus legatus fuerit, neque lacte neque agnis neque lana utetur usuarius, quia ea in fructu sunt. plane ad stercorandum agrum suum pecoribus uti potest. ƀ Sed si cui habitatio legata 'sive aliquo modo constituta' sit, neque usus videtur neque usus fructus sed quasi proprium aliquod ius. 'quam habitationem 'habentibus propter rerum utilitatem secundum Mar-'celli sententiam nostra decisione[11] promulgata[12] per-'misimus non solum in ea degere, sed etiam aliis lo-'care.' 6 Haec de servitutibus et usu fructu et usu et habitatione dixisse sufficiat. de hereditate autem et de obligationibus suis locis proponamus. exposuimus summatim, quibus modis iure gentium res adquirun-

tur: modo videamus, quibus modis legitimo et civili iure adquiruntur.

VI[13]
DE USUCAPIONIBUS ET LONGI TEMPORIS POSSESSIONIBUS.

Iure civili constitutum fuerat, ut, ut, qui bona fide ab eo, 'qui dominus non erat, cum crediderit eum dominum 'esse, rem emerit vel ex donatione aliave qua iusta 'causa acceperit, is eam rem, si mobilis erat, anno 'ubique, si immobilis, biennio tantum in Italico solo 'usucapiat, ne rerum dominia in incerto essent. et 'cum hoc placitum erat, putantibus antiquioribus[14] 'dominis sufficere ad inquirendas res suas praefata 'tempora, nobis melior sententia resedit[15], ne domini 'maturius suis rebus defraudentur neque certo loco 'beneficium hoc concludatur. et ideo constitutionem[16] 'super hoc promulgavimus, qua cautum est, ut res 'quidem mobiles per triennium usucapiantur, immo-'biles vero per longi temporis possessionem, id est 'inter praesentes decennio, inter absentes viginti annis 'usucapiantur et his modis non solum in Italia, sed 'in omni terra, quae nostro imperio gubernatur, do-'minium rerum iusta causa possessionis praecedente 'adquiratur.' 1 [17]Sed aliquando etiamsi maxime quis bona fide rem possederit, non tamen illi usucapio 'ullo tempore' procedit, veluti si quis liberum hominem vel rem sacram vel religiosam vel servum fugitivum possideat. 2 Furtivae quoque res et quae vi possessae sunt, nec si 'praedicto longo tempore' bona fide possessae fuerint, usucapi possunt: nam furtivarum rerum lex duodecim tabularum et lex Atinia[18] inhibet usucapio-3 nem, vi possessarum lex Iulia et Plautia. [19]'Quod 'autem' dictum est furtivarum et vi possessarum rerum 'usucapionem per legem[20] prohibitam esse, non eo 'pertinet, ut ne ipse fur quive per vim possidet usu-'capere possit: nam his alia ratione usucapio non 'competit, quia scilicet mala fide possident: sed ne 'ullus alius, quamvis ab eis bona fide emerit 'vel ex 'alia causa acceperit,' usucapiendi ius habeat[21]. unde 'in[22] rebus mobilibus non facile procedit, ut bonae 'fidei possessori[23] usucapio competat. nam qui alie-'nam rem vendidit 'vel ex alia causa' tradidit, furtum 4 'eius committit. [19]Sed tamen id aliquando aliter se 'habet. nam si heres rem defuncto commodatam aut 'locatam vel apud eum depositam existimans here-'ditariam esse 'bona fide accipienti' vendiderit aut do-'naverit' aut dotis nomine dederit, quin is qui acce-'perit usucapere possit, dubium non est, quippe ea 'res in furti vitium non ceciderit, 'cum utique heres, 'qui bona fide tamquam suam alienaverit, furtum non 5 'committit'[24]. [25]Item si is, ad quem ancillae usus 'fructus pertinet, partum suum esse credens vendi-'derit aut donaverit, furtum non committit: furtum 6 'enim sine affectu furandi non committitur. [25]Aliis 'quoque modis accidere potest, ut quis sine vitio furti 'rem alienam ad aliquem transferat et efficiat, ut a 7 'possessore usucapiatur.' Quod autem ad eas res, quae solo continentur[26], expeditius procedit, ut[27] quis loci vacantis possessionem propter absentiam aut neglegentiam domini, aut quia sine successore decesserit, sine vi nanciscatur. [28]qui quamvis ipse mala fide possidet, quia intellegit se alienum fundum occupasse, tamen, si alii bona fide accipienti tradi-derit, poterit 'ei longa possessione res adquiri', quia neque furtivum neque vi possessum 'accepit'. abolita est enim quorundam veterum sententia existimantium etiam fundi locive usum furtum fieri 'et[29] eorum, qui res

(1) quae omnia] *TΘ*, quod *B*   (2) *Cod.* 3, 33, 16   (3) *Dig.* 7, 8; 33, 2 *Cod.* 3, 33   (4) *pr. simile Dig.* 7, 1, 3 § 3 (*Gai. l.* 2 *rer. cott.*)   (5) § 1 *fin. ex Gai l.* 2 *rer. cott.* (*Dig.* 7, 8, 11)   (6) ‹ › *Iustinianis tribuit Ferrini*   (7) ei] *P*, om. *BTᵇ*, deficit *Tᵉ*   (8) is] ei *libri*   (9) *sic Tᵛ Θ*, opere *BTᵇ*   (10) sed] *BCᵇ Θ*, sed et *TCᵃ*   (11) *Cod.* 3, 33, 13   (12) promulgatam *B*   (13) *Gai* 2, 41..61 *Dig.* 41, 3..10; 44, 3 *Cod.* 7, 26..40   (14) *sic ATC, anti-*quissimis *B*   (15) *sic B,* resederit *TCᵇ,* sederit *ACᵃ*

(16) *Cod.* 7, 31, 1   (17) § 1 *in. simile Gaio* 2, 45   (18) Ἀτίλιος νόμος Θ   (19) *Gai.* 2, 49. 50   (20) *sic ATᵛ,* per leges *BTCᵇ,* per lege[m] XII tabularum *Gai.*   (21) *sic Gai.,* habet *libri*   (22) in] *ATC Gai,* et in *B*   (23) pos-sessoribus *Tᵃ*   (24) ‹ › *Iustinianis adscripsit Kuebler*   (25) *Gai.* 1, 50   (26) *sic ATᵛ,* pertinet *add. BTᵇ*   (27) ut] *A,* ut si *BT*   (28) qui .... furtum fieri *ex Gai l.* 2 *rer. cott.* (*Dig.* 41, 3, 38)   (29) et] *AB,* om. *T*

senate to resolve that it should be possible to arrange a usufruct even in these things, subject to the heir's being given security. So a legacy of a usufruct in money means the money becomes the legatee's and he gives security for the return of the same amount in the event of death or status-loss. Other things in this category are also handed over so as to become the legatee's with him giving security at a valuation. This means that if he dies or suffers a status-loss money to the amount of the valuation must be returned. In fact the senate did not actually create a usufruct in these things, something it could not do. It introduced a quasi-usufruct based on this security. 3. Usufruct comes to an end by the death of the fructuary; by the two higher degrees of status-loss; by non-use defined by mode and time. Our pronouncement has covered all this. Also, usufruct ends if the fructuary assigns his interest to the person in whom the property is vested. An assignment to a third party achieves nothing at all. And, vice versa, the usufruct is extinguished if the fructuary acquires ownership. This is called consolidation. Besides this, it is accepted that if a building is destroyed by fire or earthquake or inherent defect a usufruct over it is ended. The site is not covered by the usufruct. 4. When usufruct comes to an end, the rights revert to the owner. From that moment, bare ownership becomes full beneficial entitlement.

2.5 USE AND HABITATION

The ways in which a usufruct is created, and ended, also apply to the simple right of use. 1. Use is a more restricted right than usufruct. Someone with a use in land may only take vegetables, fruit, flowers, hay, straw, and firewood for day to day needs. He can only stay on the land himself if he does not cause trouble to the owner or get in the way of those doing the farm work. He has no power to sell what he is entitled to, or to hire it out, or grant a gratuitous licence. A usufructuary can do all these things. 2. One who has a use in a house has only a personal right of habitation. He cannot transfer this right to anyone else. There was a certain amount of hesitation before it was admitted that he could take in a guest or that his right covered his wife, children, and freedmen, and also other free persons, not unlike slaves, employed as servants; or, correspondingly, that a woman with a use in a house might live there with her husband. 3. Someone who has a use in a slave has only a personal right to his work and service. He may not in any way transfer this right to another. The same applies to an animal. 4. A legacy of a use in cattle or sheep does not give the usuary the milk, lambs, or wool, since they count as fruits. He can definitely use the cattle to manure his land. 5. A right of habitation given to someone by legacy or in some other way is not construed as either use or usufruct but as an independent right. To those entitled to habitation we have granted the right not only of dwelling in the place themselves but also of letting it out to others. That was announced in one of our rulings. In the interests of convenience it adopted the opinion of Marcellus. 6. Enough has now been said of servitudes and of usufruct, use, and habitation. There are separate discussions later of inheritance and obligations. We have given a short explanation of the ways in which things are acquired under the law common to all peoples. We must now turn to modes of acquisition under statutory and state law.

2.6 USUCAPION AND LONG-TERM POSSESSION

To prevent uncertainty over title, the old state law laid down that, where someone dealt with a non-owner in the belief that he was dealing with an owner, and obtained something in good faith by purchase or gift or on some other legally sufficient basis, he should become owner by usucapion, i.e. possession over time. For movables the requirement was one year, with no geographical restriction; for immovables, two years, with a restriction to land in Italy. This seemed right once, when people could accept that these periods gave owners long enough to discover their property. But better opinions prevailed with us, namely that owners should not be stripped of their property so soon, and that the benefit should not be confined to any specific area. We therefore promulgated an enactment on this subject providing that movable things should be acquired by usucapion in three years, and that immovables should be acquired by long-term possession, that is to say, that they should be usucapted in ten years as between people present and in twenty years as between people apart; and that not only in Italy but in every land in our empire these should be the terms for acquiring ownership through well founded possession. 1. Sometimes no period of usucapion will work to the advantage of the possessor, even though his possession is definitely in good faith. Examples are where he possesses a free person, a sacred or religious thing, or a runaway slave. 2. Things which have been stolen or taken by force cannot be usucapted even if possessed in good faith for the long period mentioned above. The reason is that the Twelve Tables and the Atinian Act forbid usucapion of stolen things, and the Julian-Plautian Act does the same for things taken by force. 3. The point of the statutory prohibition against usucapion of things stolen or taken by force is not to exclude the thief or the violent taker himself from the right to usucapt. They are excluded anyhow for another reason: they possess in bad faith. It is rather that a third party has no right to usucapt, even after buying or acquiring them properly in good faith. So with movable things such a possessor cannot often rely on usucapion, because someone who sells another's property or delivers it on some other basis commits theft. 4. Yet sometimes the result is different. Suppose that an heir transfers something by way of sale, gift, or dowry to a recipient who is in good faith, and that the heir's belief is that the thing was part of the inheritance, when in fact it had been lent to the deceased, or hired to him, or deposited with him. Here there is no doubt that the recipient can usucapt, because the thing does not become tainted with theft. Obviously the heir does not commit theft when he alienates the thing honestly, believing it to be his. 5. A person with a usufruct in a female slave who sells or gives away the offspring in the belief that they are his does not commit theft. Theft is not committed without intent to steal. 6. There are also other ways that someone can transfer a third party's property to another without the taint of theft and leave it possible for the recipient to usucapt the thing. 7. With land, there are fewer obstacles. A man can for instance take land without force where it is unoccupied because the owner is away or neglects it or dies with no successor. The taker is a possessor in bad faith because he knows that he has taken possession of land belonging to another. But if he delivers it to another who receives in good faith that other can acquire by long possession. What he has received is not tainted by theft or violent taking. This follows from the rejection of the opinion held by some early jurists that immovable property could be stolen. // Also it is

'soli possident, principalibus constitutionibus prospici-
'tur, ne cui longa et indubitata possessio auferri de-
8 'beat.' Aliquando etiam furtiva vel vi possessa res
usucapi potest: veluti si in domini potestatem reversa
fuerit. tunc enim vitio rei purgato procedit eius usu-
9 capio. Res fisci 'nostri' usucapi non potest. sed
Papinianus scribit[1] bonis vacantibus fisco[2] nondum
nuntiatis bona fide emptorem sibi traditam rem ex
his bonis usucapere posse: et ita divus Pius et divus[3]
10 Severus et Antoninus rescripserunt. Novissime
sciendum est rem talem esse debere, ut in se non
habeat vitium, ut a bona fide emptore usucapi possit
vel qui ex alia iusta causa possidet.
11 Error autem falsae causae usucapionem non
parit. veluti si quis, cum non emerit, emisse se existimans possideat[4]: vel cum ei donatum non fuerat,
quasi ex donatione possideat.
12 'Diutina possessio', quae prodesse coeperat defuncto, et heredi et bonorum possessori continuatur,
licet ipse sciat praedium alienum: quodsi ille initium
iustum non habuit, heredi et bonorum possessori
licet ignoranti possessio non prodest. 'quod nostra
'constitutio[5] similiter et in usucapionibus observari
13 'constituit, ut tempora continuentur.' Inter ven-
ditorem quoque et emptorem coniungi tempora divus
Severus et Antoninus rescripserunt.
14 Edicto divi Marci cavetur eum, qui a fisco
rem alienam emit, si post venditionem quinquennium
praeterierit, posse dominum rei per exceptionem[6] re-
pellere. 'constitutio autem divae memoriae Zenonis[7]
'bene prospexit his, qui a fisco per venditionem vel
'donationem vel alium titulum aliquid accipiunt, ut
'ipsi quidem securi statim fiant et victores existant,
'sive conveniantur sive experiantur: adversus sacra-
'tissimum autem aerarium usque ad quadriennium li-
'ceat intendere his, qui pro dominio vel hypotheca
'earum rerum, quae alienatae sunt, putaverint sibi
'quasdam competere actiones. nostra autem divina
'constitutio[8], quam nuper promulgavimus, etiam de
'his, qui a nostra vel venerabilis Augustae domo ali-
'quid acceperint, haec statuit, quae in fiscalibus alie-
'nationibus praefatae Zenonianae constitutioni[9] con-
'tinentur.'

VII[10]

DE DONATIONIBUS.

Est etiam aliud genus adquisitionis donatio. donationum autem duo genera sunt: mortis causa et non
1 mortis causa. Mortis causa donatio est, quae
propter mortis fit suspicionem[11], cum quis ita donat,
ut, si quid humanitus ei contigisset, haberet is qui
accepit: sin autem supervixisset qui donavit, reci-
peret, vel si eum donationis paenituisset aut prior
decesserit is cui donatum sit. 'hae[12] mortis causa
'donationes ad exemplum legatorum redactae sunt per
'omnia. nam cum prudentibus ambiguum fuerat, utrum
'donationis an legati instar eam optineret[13] oporteret[14],
'et utriusque causae quaedam habebat insignia et alii
'ad aliud genus eam retrahebant: a nobis constitutum
'est[15], ut per omnia legatis connumeretur et sic
'procedat, quemadmodum eam nostra formavit con-
'stitutio.' [16]et in summa mortis causa donatio est,
cum magis se quis velit habere, quam eum cui donatur, magisque eum cui donat, quam heredem suum.
sic et apud Homerum Telemachus donat Piraeo.[17]
2 'Aliae autem donationes sunt, quae sine ulla
'mortis cogitatione fiunt, quas inter vivos appellamus.

quae omnino non comparantur legatis: quae si fue-
'rint perfectae, temere revocari non possunt. per-
'ficiuntur autem, cum donator suam voluntatem scrip-
'tis aut sine scriptis manifestaverit: et ad exemplum
'venditionis nostra constitutio[18] eas etiam in se ha-
'bere necessitatem traditionis voluit, ut, et si non tra-
'dantur, habeant plenissimum et perfectum robur et
'traditionis necessitas incumbat donatori. et cum retro
'principum dispositiones insinuari eas actis interveni-
'entibus volebant, si maiores ducentorum fuerant soli-
'dorum, nostra constitutio[19] et quantitate usque ad
'quingentos solidos ampliavit, quam stare et sine in-
'sinuatione statuit, et quasdam donationes invenit,
'quae penitus insinuationem fieri minime desiderant,
'sed in se plenissimam habent firmitatem. alia insuper
'multa ad uberiorem exitum donationum invenimus,
'quae omnia ex nostris constitutionibus, quas super
'his posuimus, colligenda sunt. sciendum tamen est,
'quod, etsi plenissimae sint donationes, tamen si in-
'grati existant homines, in quos beneficium collatum
'est, donatoribus per nostram constitutionem[20] licen-
'tiam praestavimus certis ex causis eas revocare, ne,
'qui suas res in alios[21] contulerunt, ab his quandam
'patiantur iniuriam vel iacturam, secundum enumera-
3 'tos in nostra constitutione modos. Est et aliud
'genus inter vivos donationum, quod veteribus quidem
'prudentibus penitus erat incognitum, postea autem a
'iunioribus divis principibus introductum est, quod
'ante nuptias vocabatur et tacitam in se condicionem
'habebat, ut tunc ratum esset, cum matrimonium fue-
'rit[22] insecutum: ideoque ante nuptias appellabatur,
'quod ante matrimonium efficiebatur et nusquam post
'nuptias celebratas talis donatio procedebat. sed pri-
'mus quidem divus Iustinus pater noster, cum augeri
'dotes et post nuptias fuerat permissum, si quid tale
'evenit, etiam ante nuptias donationem augeri et con-
'stante matrimonio sua constitutione[23] permisit: sed
'tamen nomen inconveniens remanebat, cum ante nup-
'tias quidem vocabatur, post nuptias autem tale ac-
'cipiebat incrementum. sed nos plenissimo fini tradere
'sanctiones cupientes et consequentia nomina rebus
'esse studentes constituimus[24], ut tales donationes
'non augeantur tantum, sed et constante matrimonio
'initium accipiant et non ante nuptias, sed propter
'nuptias vocentur et dotibus in hoc exaequentur, ut,
'quemadmodum dotes et constante matrimonio non
'solum augentur, sed etiam fiunt, ita et istae dona-
'tiones, quae propter nuptias introductae sunt, non
'solum antecedant matrimonium, sed etiam eo con-
'tracto et augeantur et constituantur.
4 'Erat olim et alius modus civilis adquisitionis
'per ius adcrescendi, quod est tale: si communem ser-
'vum habens aliquis cum Titio solus libertatem ei im-
'posuit vel vindicta vel testamento, eo casu pars eius
'amittebatur et socio adcrescebat. sed cum pessimo
'fuerat exemplo[25] et libertate servum defraudari et
'ex ea humanioribus quidem dominis damnum inferri,
'severioribus autem lucrum adcrescere: hoc quasi in-
'vidiae plenum pio remedio per nostram constitutio-
'nem[26] mederi necessarium duximus et invenimus viam,
'per quam et manumissor et socius eius et qui liber-
'tatem accepit nostro fruantur beneficio, libertate cum
'effectu procedente (cuius favore et antiquos legis-
'latores multa et contra communes regulas statuisse
'manifestissimum est) et eo qui[27] eam imposuit suae
'liberalitatis stabilitate gaudente et socio indemni con-
'servato pretiumque servi secundum partem dominii,
'quod nos definivimus, accipiente.'

---

(1) sic AT[a]?, scripsit B (2) fisco] AT, et f. B (3) Θειό-
τατοι Θ (4) sic A, possidet B[a], possidea**T[a] (5) Cod.
7, 31, 1 (6) per exceptionem] T, exceptione AB (7) Cod.
7, 37, 2 (8) Cod. 7, 37, 3 (9) sic T[v], constitutionis
ABT[b] (10) Cf. Dig. 24, 1; 39, 5. 6 Cod. 5, 3, 16;
8, 53..56 (11) sic B, suspectionem T (12) hae]
TΘ, om. B (13) optinere] T, ponere B (14) oportet
T[a] (15) Cod. 8, 56, 4 (16) § 1 fin. ex Marciani

l. 9 inst. (Dig. 39, 6, 1) (17) Homeri versus Od. 17,
78—83 hic inscrunt edd. (18) Cod. 8, 53, 35 § 5
(19) Cod. 8, 53, 36 (20) Cod. 8, 55, 10 (21) sic
TΘ, alienos B (22) sic T, fuerat B (23) Cod.
5, 3, 19 (24) Cod. 5, 3, 20 (25) sic BW[a], pessimum f. exemplo W[b], pessimum f. exemplum E, κά-
κιστον ἦν τοῦτο παράδειγμα Θ (26) Cod. 7, 7, 1
(27) quia B

laid down in imperial pronouncements that long and unchallenged possession of land should not be disturbed. 8. Sometimes even a thing which has been stolen or violently taken can be usucapted, as where it has returned into the power of its owner. That clears the taint and usucapion can go ahead. 9. Things belonging to our exchequer cannot be usucapted. But Papinian writes that, where ownerless property has lapsed to the exchequer but no notice has yet been given, an honest buyer who takes delivery of something from it can usucapt. There are written replies of the Emperor Pius and the Emperors Severus and Antoninus to the same effect. 10. Lastly, it must be understood that, if a possessor in good faith by purchase or on other sufficient basis is to be able to usucapt, the thing itself must not be inherently tainted in any way. 11. Usucapion cannot run if there is a mistake as to its basis, as where someone who has not actually bought a thing takes possession in the belief that he has, or where he possesses under the mistaken impression that he has received a gift. 12. Once long possession has begun to work to the advantage of a person who then dies it continues to run in favour of his heir or estate-possessor, even if the successor knows the land is another's. If the deceased's possession was bad at its inception, it will not run to the advantage of the heir or estate-possessor even if they are unaware of the problem. Our pronouncement has applied the same rule for aggregating the time-periods to ordinary usucapion. 13. The Emperors Severus and Alexander issued a reply allowing the time to be aggregated as between seller and buyer. 14. The Emperor Marcus ordained by edict that, once five years elapsed from the sale, a purchaser of a thing belonging to a third party from the exchequer could defeat that owner's claim by means of a plea in defence. On the other hand Zeno of blessed memory made a pronouncement providing that recipients from the exchequer, whether by purchase or gift or other title, should become immediately secure and should win as plaintiffs or defendants; that those who claim to be entitled to actions as owners or mortgagees of the property thus alienated should have four years in which to advance their claims against the imperial treasury. The solemn pronouncement we ourselves recently promulgated addresses the case in which someone receives something from our palace or that of our revered Augusta; it prescribes the same rules as Zeno's constitution just mentioned provides for fiscal alienations.

2.7 GIFTS

Another type of acquisition is gift. There are two kinds: those made in contemplation of death and those not so made. 1. A gift in contemplation of death is one where the donor anticipates dying. He gives the thing on the understanding that if he passes away the donee shall keep it, but if he survives, and equally if he changes his mind or the donee dies first, he shall have it back. Gifts in contemplation of death have been completely assimilated to legacies. The jurists debated whether the correct model for them was gift or legacy. They had characteristics of each, and different authorities classified them differently. We have enacted that in virtually every respect they should be counted as legacies and handled as required by the pronouncement. In sum, a gift in contemplation of death is one where the donor's intention is to prefer himself to the donee, the donee to his heir. There is an example of this in Homer, where

Telemachus makes such a gift to Piraeus. 2. Now to gifts not in contemplation of death. These are gifts inter vivos. This time there is no comparison with legacies. Once these gifts are complete they cannot simply be revoked. They are complete when the donor makes his intention clear, in writing or without writing. Our pronouncement recognizes, following the analogy of sale, that gift also implies an inherent duty to make delivery: gifts are complete even before delivery and put their donor under an obligation to make the delivery. Earlier emperors made provisions requiring gifts worth more than 200 solidi to be recorded in registers prepared for the purpose. Our pronouncement has raised the registration threshold to 500 solidi and lists some gifts which are to be given effect without any registration requirement. We have also introduced many other reforms to bring gifts to better fruition. These can be studied in our pronouncements on the subject. But note that even where a gift has actually been given if donees prove ungrateful after the kindness done them, our pronouncement does allow donors a right of revocation on specified grounds. The aim is to ensure that someone who has endowed others with his property should not suffer any wrong or prejudice at the latter's hands. The conditions are listed in our pronouncement. 3. There is even another class of inter vivos gift, unknown to the old jurists but introduced by more recent emperors. This came to be called a gift before marriage and was held to include an implied condition for taking effect only if the marriage did take place. The name 'before marriage' came from the custom of settling it before the wedding; it was never done afterwards. Then for the first time a pronouncement of our father the Emperor Justin, in view of the fact that it was already permissible to increase dowries after marriage, allowed that, in response to an increase in dowry, a gift before marriage could also be augmented during the marriage. The inconvenient name survived: the transaction was called 'gift before marriage' although it could be increased after marriage. We were anxious to uphold whatever could be upheld and to find clearer terminology; and we have enacted that these gifts may not only be increased but also created during the marriage. The gift shall be called, not 'gift before marriage', but 'gift on account of marriage'. It shall be assimilated to dowry in this way: just as dowries can both be increased and constituted during the marriage, these gifts on account of marriage may not only precede the marriage but also be increased and newly constituted after the marriage has been contracted. 4. There was once yet another mode of acquisition recognised in state law, namely accrual. Suppose one person owns a slave in common with Titius. He alone grants him freedom, whether by rod or by will. On those facts he used simply to forfeit his share, which accrued to his co-owner. This was a shocking situation, cheating the slave of his freedom, and giving more severe masters a windfall at the expense of the more generous. We concluded that this troublesome situation required to be remedied by our pronouncement, and we found a path to lead each party to the fruits of our benevolence, the manumittor, his co-owner, and the man given his freedom. Our solution gives full effect to the grant of liberty – in many rules and exceptions to rules the old law-givers also leaned heavily in favour of liberty; to the grantor we give the happiness of knowing that his generosity has achieved its end; the co-owner we keep free from loss, our scheme ensuring that he is given, in proportion to his interest, a share of the slave's value. //

VIII [1]
QUIBUS ALIENARE LICET VEL NON.

[2]'Accidit aliquando, ut qui dominus sit alienare 'non possit et contra qui dominus non [3] sit alienan-'dae rei potestatem habeat. nam dotale praedium 'maritus invita muliere per legem Iuliam prohibetur 'alienare, quamvis ipsius sit dotis causa ei datum.' 'quod nos legem Iuliam corrigentes in meliorem sta-'tum deduximus [4]. cum enim lex in soli tantummodo 'rebus locum habebat, quae Italicae fuerant, et alie-'nationes inhibebat, quae invita muliere fiebant, hypo-'thecas autem earum etiam volente: utrisque [5] reme-'dium imposuimus, ut etiam in eas res, quae in pro-'vinciali solo [6] positae sunt, interdicta fiat alienatio 'vel obligatio et neutrum eorum neque consentientibus 'mulieribus procedat, ne sexus muliebris fragilitas in
1 'perniciem substantiae earum converteretur. [7]'Con-'tra autem' 'creditor pignus ex pactione, quamvis eius 'ea res non sit, 'alienare potest.' sed hoc forsitan ideo 'videtur fieri, quod voluntate debitoris intellegitur 'pignus alienare [8], qui 'ab initio contractus' pactus est, 'ut liceret creditori pignus vendere, si pecunia non 'solvatur.' 'sed ne creditores ius suum persequi im-'pedirentur neque debitores temere suarum rerum do-'minium amittere videantur, nostra constitutione [9] con-'sultum est et certus modus impositus est, per quem 'pignorum distractio possit procedere, cuius tenore 'utrique parti creditorum et debitorum satis abunde-
2 'que provisum est.' [10]'Nunc admonendi sumus ne-'que pupillum 'neque pupillam' ullam rem sine tutoris 'auctoritate alienare posse. ideoque si mutuam pecu-'niam alicui sine tutoris auctoritate dederit, non con-'trahit obligationem, quia pecuniam non facit acci-'pientis. ideoque vindicare nummos possunt, sicubi 'extent': sed si nummi, 'quos mutuos dedit [11], ab eo 'qui accepit' bona fide consumpti sunt, condici pos-'sunt, si mala fide, ad exhibendum de his agi potest. 'at ex contrario omnes res pupillo et pupillae sine 'tutoris auctoritate recte dari possunt. ideoque si de-'bitor pupillo solvat, necessaria est [12] tutoris auctori-'tas: alioquin non liberabitur. 'sed etiam hoc eviden-'tissima ratione statutum est in constitutione, quam 'ad Caesareenses [13] advocatos ex suggestione Tribo-'niani viri eminentissimi quaestoris sacri palatii nostri 'promulgavimus [14], qua dispositum est ita licere tutori 'vel curatori debitorem pupillarem solvere, ut prius 'sententia iudicialis sine omni damno celebrata hoc 'permittat. quo subsecuto, si e iudex pronuntiaverit 'et debitor solverit, sequitur [15] huiusmodi solutionem 'plenissima [16] securitas. sin autem aliter quam dispo-'suimus solutio facta fuerit et pecuniam salvam ha-'beat pupillus aut ex ea locupletior sit et adhuc ean-'dem summam pecuniae petat, per exceptionem doli 'mali summoveri poterit: quodsi aut male consumpserit 'aut furto amiserit, nihil proderit debitori doli mali 'exceptio, sed nihilo minus damnabitur, quia temere 'sine tutoris auctoritate et non secundum nostram 'dispositionem solverit.' sed ex diverso pupilli vel pu-pillae solvere sine tutore auctore non possunt, quia id quod solvunt non fit accipientis, cum scilicet [17]'nullius 'rei alienatio eis sine tutoris auctoritate concessa est.'

IX [18]
PER QUAS PERSONAS NOBIS ADQUIRITUR.

[19]'Adquiritur nobis [20] non solum per nosmet ipsos, 'sed etiam per eos quos in potestate habemus: item

'per eos servos, in quibus usum fructum habemus: 'item per homines liberos et servos alienos quos 'bona fide possidemus. de quibus singulis diligentius
1 'dispiciamus. [19]Igitur liberi vestri 'utriusque sexus,' 'quos in potestate habetis,' 'olim quidem, quidquid ad 'eos pervenerat (exceptis videlicet castrensibus pecu-'liis), hoc parentibus suis adquirebant sine ulla dis-'tinctione: et hoc ita parentum fiebat, ut esset eis 'licentia, quod per unum vel unam eorum adquisitum 'est, alii [21] vel extraneo donare vel vendere vel que-'cumque modo voluerant applicare. quod nobis inhu-'manum visum est et generali constitutione [22] emissa 'et liberis pepercimus et patribus debitum reservavi-'mus [23]. sancitum etenim a nobis est, ut, si quid ex 're patris ei obveniat, hoc secundum antiquam obser-'vationem totum parenti adquirat (quae enim invidia 'est, quod ex patris occasione profectum est, hoc ad 'eum reverti?): quod autem ex alia causa sibi filius 'familias [24] adquisivit, huius usum fructum quidem 'patri adquiret, dominium autem apud eum rema-'neat, ne, quod ei suis laboribus vel prospera fortuna 'accessit, hoc in alium perveniens luctuosum ei pro-
2 'cedat. Hocque a nobis dispositum est et in ea 'specie, ubi parens emancipando liberum [25] ex rebus 'quae adquisitionem effugiunt sibi partem tertiam re-'tinere si voluerat licentiam ex anterioribus constitu-'tionibus habebat quasi pro pretio quodammodo emanci-'pationis et inhumanum quid [26] accidebat, ut filius 'rerum suarum ex hac emancipatione dominio pro 'parte defraudetur et, quod honoris ei ex emancipa-'tione additum est, quod sui iuris effectus est, hoc 'per rerum deminutionem decrescat. ideoque statui-'mus, ut parens pro tertia bonorum parte dominii, 'quam retinere poterat, dimidiam non dominii rerum, 'sed usus fructus retineat: ita etenim et res intactae 'apud filium remanebunt et pater ampliore summa
3 'fruetur pro tertia dimidia potiturus.' [27]'Item vobis 'adquiritur, quod servi vestri ex traditione nancis-'cuntur sive quid stipulentur vel ex [28] qualibet alia 'causa adquirunt.' hoc enim vobis et ignorantibus et invitis obvenit. 'ipse enim 'servus' qui in potestate 'alterius est nihil suum habere potest. 'sed' si heres 'institutus sit, 'non alias' nisi iussu vestro hereditatem 'adire potest: et si iubentibus vobis adierit, vobis 'hereditas adquiritur, perinde ac si vos ipsi heredes 'instituti essetis. et convenienter scilicet legatum per 'eos vobis adquiritur. non solum autem proprietas 'per eos quos in potestate habetis adquiritur vobis, 'sed etiam possessio: cuiuscumque enim rei posses-'sionem adepti fuerint, id vos possidere videmini. unde 'etiam per eos usucapio 'vel longi temporis possessio
4 'vobis' accedit [29]. [27]De his autem servis, in quibus 'tantum usum fructum habetis, ita placuit, ut, quid-'quid ex re vestra vel ex operibus [30] suis adquirant, id 'vobis adiciatur, quod vero extra eas causas perse-'cuti sunt, id ad dominum proprietatis pertineat. ita-'que si is servus heres institutus sit legatumve quid 'ei aut donatum fuerit, non usufructuario, sed do-'mino proprietatis adquiritur. idem placet et [31] de eo, 'qui a vobis bona fide possidetur, sive is liber sit 'sive alienus servus: quod enim placuit de usufructua-'rio [32], idem 'placet' et de bonae fidei possessore. ita-'que quod extra duas istas causas adquiritur, id vel 'ad ipsum pertinet, si liber est, vel ad dominum, si 'servus est. sed bonae fidei possessor cum usuceperit 'servum, quia eo modo dominus fit, ex omnibus cau-'sis per eum sibi adquirere potest: fructuarius vero

(1) *Cf. Gai. 2, 62..64. 80..85*   (2) *Gai. 2, 62. 63*   (3) *non om. B*   (4) *Cod. 5, 13, 1 § 15*   (5) *sic B, utrisque T*[a] (6) provinciali solo] *T, provincia B*   (7) *Gai. 2, 64* (8) *sic BT*[a]*, alienari T*[b] *Gai.*   (9) *Cod. 8, 33, 3* (10) *Gai. 2, 80..82*   (11) dedit] *BT*[b]*, minor d. T*[a] (12) est] *T*[a]*, est debitori BT*[b]   (13) *Caesarenses BT* (14) *Cod. 5, 37, 25*   (15) *sic P Cod., sequatur BT* (16) plenissimam *B*   (17) *Gai. 2, 84*   (18) *Cf. Gai.* 2, 86..100 *Dig. 41, 1 Cod. 4, 27*   (19) *Gai. 2, 86. 87* (*Dig.* 41, 1, 10)   (20) vobis *et similiter deinceps PE*   (21) alii]

P, id est filio alii *B,* filio alii *E*   (22) *Cod. 6, 61, 6* (23) *sic B,* servavimus *PE*   (24) familias] *PEΘ,* filiave *B*   (25) liberum] *PE,* l. suum *B,* τὸν παῖδα *Θ*   (26) *sic BΘ,* quidem *PE*   (27) *Gai. 2, 87. 89. 91..93* (*Dig. 41, 1, 10*)   (28) vel ex] *Gai. Dig. cum Θ,* vel ex donatione et legato ex *B,* vel ex don. leg. vel ex *T*[a]   (29) vobis accedit] *BT*[b]*,* vobis accidit *T*[a] *P,* procedit *Gai. Dig.*   (30) operis *Gai. Dig.* *Θ*   (31) et] *BT*[b]*Θ,* om. *T*[a] *Gai. Dig.*   (32) *sic P Gai. Dig.,* fruc-tuario *BT*

2.8 THE POWER TO ALIENATE

It sometimes happens that an owner does not have power to alienate and, vice versa, that a non-owner does. Under the Julian Act a husband may not alienate land forming part of the dowry without his wife's consent. Yet it is his, having been given to him as dowry. In this matter we have introduced reforms to improve the regime of the Julian Act. It applied only to Italian land and forbade alienations without the woman's consent and mortgages even with her consent. Our reform has extended the ban to land in the provinces and has forbidden both alienations and charges even with the woman's consent. The aim is to stop men exploiting the weakness of the female sex and ruining them financially. 1. On the other side of the line, a creditor, under his contract, has power to alienate a pledge despite not being its owner. But here the explanation is perhaps that he alienates the pledge with the debtor's authority, given by a term of the contract allowing the creditor the right to sell on failure to repay. In our pronouncement on this subject our concern was both that creditors should not be impeded in realizing their rights and that debtors should not be too easily deprived of their property. We have fixed the conditions under which the sale of pledges may proceed. The terms of our pronouncement amply protect the interest of each party, both creditor and debtor. 2. Next we must note that boys and girls with guardians cannot alienate anything without the guardian's endorsement. If they lend money to someone without that backing they create no obligation because they fail to pass the property in the money to the recipient. They can vindicate the coins wherever they are; if the borrower spends all the money which was lent and does so in good faith, an action of debt lies against him; if in bad faith, an action for production can be brought for it. When the boys and girls in guardianship are the recipients, the property in every kind of thing can be passed to them even without the guardian's endorsement. But the guardian's endorsement is essential when a debtor pays a ward; otherwise he will not get his discharge. This is made very clear in the pronouncement which, prompted by Tribonian, of highest rank, chancellor of our sacred palace, we promulgated to the Bar of Caesarea. It provides that a debtor to a ward may make payment to the guardian or supervisor so long as a judgment of a court, obtained without abuse of process, first gives permission. Once these steps are taken – the judicial pronouncement and the payment – that mode of payment gives absolute protection. If payment is not made according to these provisions, a ward who sues again for the same sum can be defeated by the plea of deceit if he still has the money or remains enriched by it; but if the ward has wasted the money or lost it to a thief, the plea of deceit will achieve nothing for the debtor, and despite the earlier payment he will be condemned. The reason is that he was rash to pay the ward without the guardian's endorsement and not to keep to the machinery we have provided. Children in guardianship cannot pay debts without endorsement because the property in what they pay does not pass to the payee. Without the guardian's endorsement they do not have power to alienate property.

2.9 ACQUISITION THROUGH OTHER PEOPLE

Property passes to us not only through our own acts but through those of the people within our authority. This is true of slaves in whom we have a usufruct, also of free people and slaves belonging to others whom we possess in good faith. We must consider each of these more closely. 1. First, male and female descendants within your authority. The old rule was that everything which came to them, with the exception of the military fund, was acquired for the head of the family. No distinctions were drawn. The property vested in the head so absolutely that he was free to take what one member of his family had acquired and give it away to another or to an outsider or sell or use it in any way he pleased. To us that seemed harsh. We have made a general pronouncement both easing the lot of children and preserving the rights of fathers. We have laid down that anything which comes to a child from using the father's property shall become the father's absolutely in the old way – for what could be wrong with the father getting the return on his own capital? – but anything which a son acquires in any other way shall vest in himself as owner, subject to a usufruct in the father. The aim is to ensure that what he obtains by his own work or good fortune does not bring profit to another and bitterness to himself. 2. We have also dealt with this problem in another situation. A father in emancipating a child was entitled under earlier imperial pronouncements to keep back, if he wanted to, as a kind of price for the emancipation, one third of the child's assets which had escaped his automatic right of acquisition. Here the harshness consisted in the possibility of the son's being stripped of some of his assets, losing in wealth the value of the enhanced, independent status conferred by his emancipation. We have enacted that instead of ownership in the third the head should be allowed a usufruct over half. This will keep the son's property intact, while the father will enjoy a larger sum by gaining control of a half rather than a third. 3. Next, you acquire things when your slaves obtain them by delivery, when they take stipulations, and when things come to them on any other basis. These acquisitions vest in you even without your knowledge or against your will; a slave is always in the authority of another and can have nothing of his own. Where he is instituted heir he cannot accept the inheritance unless you tell him to do so. When he does accept on your command, you acquire the inheritance, just as if you had been made heir yourself. Correspondingly a legacy to him accrues to you. It is not only ownership but also possession that comes to you through those in your authority. Whatever things they possess you possess. So usucapion and long-term possession also run in your favour through them. 4. With slaves in whom you only have a usufruct, the received opinion is that whatever they get through your property or by their work accrues to you but what they obtain by other means goes to their owner. Thus, if such a slave is instituted heir or is given a legacy or gift, the owner, not the usufructuary, acquires. The law solves the problem in the same way in the case of someone possessed by you in good faith, whether free or another's slave. The solution adopted for the usufructuary as applied to the honest possessor means that acquisitions outside the two named cases accrue to the man himself if he is free, or to his owner if he is a slave. The honest possessor becomes owner of the slave when usucapion is completed and then has power to take all types of acquisition through him. // By

'usucapere non potest, primum quia non possidet, sed 'habet ius utendi fruendi, deinde quia scit servum 'alienum esse.' 'non solum autem proprietas per eos 'servos, in quibus usum fructum habetis vel quos 'bona fide possidetis, vel per liberam personam, quae 'bona fide vobis servit, adquiritur vobis[1], sed etiam 'possessio': [2]'loquimur autem in utriusque persona secundum definitionem, quam proxime exposuimus, 'id est si 'quam possessionem' ex re vestra vel ex 5 'operibus suis 'adepti fuerint'. [2]'Ex his itaque ap- 'paret per liberos homines, quos neque iuri vestro 'subiectos habetis neque bona fide possidetis, item 'per alienos servos, in quibus neque usum fructum 'habetis neque iustam possessionem, nulla ex causa 'vobis adquiri posse. et hoc est, quod dicitur per 'extraneam personam nihil adquiri posse': excepto eo, quod per liberam personam veluti per procura- torem placet non solum scientibus, sed etiam igno- rantibus vobis adquiri possessionem secundum divi Severi constitutionem[3] et per hanc possessionem etiam dominium, si dominus fuit qui tradidit, vel usucapio- nem aut longi temporis praescriptionem, si dominus non sit. 6   [4]'Hactenus tantisper admonuisse sufficiat, quem- 'admodum singulae res adquiruntur: nam legatorum 'ius, quo et ipso[5] singulae res vobis adquiruntur, 'item fideicommissorum, ubi singulae res vobis relin- 'quntur', opportunius 'inferiori' loco referemus. videa- 'mus itaque nunc, quibus modis per universitatem 'res vobis adquiruntur. si cui ergo heredes facti sitis 'sive cuius bonorum possessionem petieritis 'vel si[6] 'quem adrogaveritis vel si cuius bona libertatum 'servandarum causa vobis addicta fuerint', 'eius res 'omnes ad vos transeunt. ac prius de hereditatibus 'dispiciamus. quarum duplex condicio est: nam vel 'ex testamento vel ab intestato ad vos pertinent. et 'prius est, ut de his dispiciamus, quae vobis ex testa- 'mento obveniunt.' 'qua in re necessarium est initio[7] de ordinandis testamentis exponere.'

X [8]
DE TESTAMENTIS ORDINANDIS.

Testamentum ex eo appellatur, quod testatio men- tis est. 1   'Sed ut nihil antiquitatis penitus ignoretur, scien- 'dum est olim quidem duo genera testamentorum in 'usu fuisse, quorum altero in pace et in otio uteban- 'tur, quod calatis comitiis appellabatur[9], altero, cum 'in proelium[10] exituri essent, quod procinctum[11] dice- 'batur. accessit deinde tertium genus testamentorum, 'quod dicebatur per aes et libram, scilicet quia per 'emancipationem, id est imaginariam quandam vendi- 'tionem, agebatur quinque testibus et libripende civi- 'bus Romanis puberibus praesentibus et eo qui fami- 'liae emptor dicebatur. sed illa quidem priora duo 'genera testamentorum ex veteribus temporibus in de- 'suetudinem abierunt: quod vero per aes et libram 'fiebat, licet diutius permansit, attamen partim et hoc 2 'in usu esse desiit. Sed praedicta quidem nomina 'testamentorum ad ius civile referebantur. postea vero 'ex edicto praetoris alia forma faciendorum testamen- 'torum introducta est: iure enim honorario nulla eman- 'cipatio[12] desiderabatur[13], sed septem testium signa 'sufficiebant, cum iure civili signa testium non erant 3 'necessaria. Sed cum paulatim tam ex usu homi- 'num quam ex constitutionum emendationibus coepit 'in unam consonantiam ius civile et praetorium iungi, 'constitutum est, ut uno eodemque[14] tempore, quod

'ius civile quodammodo exigebat, septem testibus ad- 'hibitis et subscriptione testium, quod ex constitutio- 'nibus inventum est, et ex edicto praetoris signacula 'testamentis imponerentur: ut hoc ius tripertitum esse 'videatur, ut testes quidem et eorum praesentia uno 'contextu testamenti celebrandi gratia[15] a[16] iure civili 'descendant[17], subscriptiones autem testatoris et tes- 'tium ex sacrarum constitutionum observatione adhi- 'beantur, signacula autem et numerus testium ex edicto 4 'praetoris. Sed his omnibus ex[18] nostra consti- 'tutione[19] propter testamentorum sinceritatem, ut nulla 'fraus adhibeatur, hoc additum est, ut per manum 'testatoris vel testium nomen heredis exprimatur et 'omnia secundum illius constitutionis tenorem pro- 'cedant.' 5   Possunt autem testes omnes et uno anulo signare testamentum (quid enim, si septem anuli una sculptura fuerint?) secundum quod Pomponio[20] visum est. sed 6 et alieno quoque anulo licet signare. Testes au- tem adhiberi possunt ii, cum quibus testamenti factio est. sed neque mulier neque impubes neque servus neque mutus neque surdus neque furiosus nec cui bonis interdictum est nec is, quem leges iubent im- probum intestabilemque esse, possunt in numero tes- 7 tium adhiberi. Sed cum aliquis ex testibus testa- menti quidem faciendi tempore liber existimabatur, postea vero servus apparuit, tam divus Hadrianus Catonio Vero[21] quam divi Severus et Antoni- nus rescripserunt subvenire se ex sua liberalitate testamento, ut sic habeatur, atque si ut oportet factum esset, cum eo tempore, quo testamentum signaretur, omnium consensu hic testis liberorum loco fuerit nec quisquam esset, qui ei status quaestionem moveat. 8   [22]Pater nec non is, qui in potestate eius est, item duo fratres, qui in eiusdem patris potestate sunt, utrique[23] testes in unum testamentum fieri possunt: quia nihil nocet ex una domo plures testes alieno 9 negotio adhiberi. [24] 'In testibus autem non debet 'esse qui in potestate testatoris est. sed si filius fa- 'milias de castrensi peculio post missionem faciat 'testamentum, nec pater eius recte testis adhibetur 'nec is qui in potestate eiusdem patris est: reproba- 'tum est 'enim in ea re domesticum testimonium.' 10   'Sed neque heres scriptus neque is qui in po- 'testate eius est neque pater eius qui habet eum in 'potestate neque fratres qui in eiusdem patris potes- 'tate sunt testes adhiberi possunt', [24] 'quia totum hoc 'negotium, quod agitur testamenti ordinandi gratia, 'creditur 'hodie inter heredem et testatorem agi. licet 'enim totum ius tale conturbatum fuerat et veteres, 'qui familiae emptorem et eos, qui per potestatem ei 'coadunati fuerant, testamentariis testimoniis repelle- 'bant, heredi et his, qui coniuncti ei per potestatem 'fuerant, concedebant testimonia in testamentis prae- 'stare, licet hi, qui id permittebant, hoc iure minime 'abuti debere eos suadebant: tamen nos eandem ob- 'servationem corrigentes et, quod ab illis suasum est, 'in legis necessitatem transferentes ad imitationem 'pristini familiae emptoris merito nec heredi, qui ima- 'ginem vetustissimi familiae emptoris optinet, nec aliis 'personis, quae ei ut dictum est coniunctae sunt, li- 'centiam concedimus sibi quodammodo testimonia prae- 'stare: ideoque nec eiusmodi veterem constitutionem 11 'nostro codici inseri permisimus. Legatariis au- 'tem et fideicommissariis, quia[25] non iuris[26] succes- 'sores sunt, et aliis personis eis coniunctis testimo- 'nium non denegamus, immo in quadam nostra con- 'stitutione[27] et hoc specialiter concessimus, et multo 'magis his, qui in eorum potestate sunt, vel qui eos 'habent in potestate, huiusmodi licentiam damus.'

(1) vobis om. T[a]   (2) Gai 2, 94. 95   (3) Cod. 7, 32, 1 (4) Gai. 2, 97..100   (5) ipso] Gai. Θ, ipso iure libri (6) si] si cuius B   (7) sic BΘ, initium T   (8) Cf. Gai. 2, 101..108. 119 Dig. 28, 1 Cod. 6, 23   (9) sic TΘ, appellabant B   (10) sic T, proelio B   (11) sic TΘ, procinctu B   (12) sic BT[b]Θ, mancipatio T[a]   (13) sic TΘ, desideratur B   (14) eodemque] TΘ, eo quidem B   (15) celebrandi gratia] T, celebranda B   (16) a om. BT   (17) descendat BT   (18) ex] TΘ, a B   (19) Cod. 6, 23, 29   (20) sic BΘ, papiniano T   (21) Cod. 6, 23, 1   (22) § 8 = Ulp. l. sing. reg. 20, 6 (Dig. 22, 5, 17)   (23) utrius- que B   (24) Gai. 2, 105. 106   (25) quia] BΘ, qui T   (26) sic T[r]Θ, iure BT[l]   (27) hanc constitutionem Codicis libri non servarunt

contrast the usufructuary cannot usucapt, first because he does not possess but has a right to the use and fruits, and secondly because he knows the slave belongs to another. Possession, as well as ownership, can be acquired for you by slaves in whom you have a usufruct; also by slaves and free people whom you honestly possess. But only in the cases mentioned, i.e. only possession obtained through your property or their work. 5. So you never acquire through a free person except where you have family authority over him or honestly possess him. And never through a third party's slave, unless you have a usufruct in him or honestly possess him. That justifies the maxim 'No acquisition through an outsider'. But there is an exception. A pronouncement of the Emperor Severus lets you acquire possession through a free person such as a general agent even without your knowledge. With possession comes ownership, provided the party delivering was himself owner; if he was not, ownership will follow by usucapion or long-term possession. 6. No more need be said for the moment about acquiring single things. It is convenient to postpone legacies, which also involve acquisition of individual things, and also trusts of particular things. We are now going to deal with the ways in which you acquire a man's property in its entirety. Suppose you are made someone's heir, or you petition to be his estate-possessor, or you adrogate someone, or you become his assignee for preserving freedom. On these facts his whole estate goes to you. We must deal first with inheritance. This happens in two ways. The estate comes to you either by will or on intestacy. We will start with those which come by will. The first thing to explain is how a will should be drawn up.

2.10 MAKING A WILL

The Latin for a will, 'testamentum', is formed from 'testatio mentis', testimony to the mind or intention. 1. Some history is essential. In the old days there were two kinds of will, one for times of peace and leisure, the other when battle was imminent. The first was called the will before the convocation, the second the will in battle-line. Later a third kind developed, called the will by bronze and scales. Its name comes from the pretended sale which it involved, called mancipation. There had to be five witnesses and a person to hold a pair of scales, all six being adult Roman citizens, and someone in the role of 'property-purchaser'. The first two types of will went out of use early. The one by bronze and scales lasted longer but some aspects of it were also abandoned. 2. All these were created by the old state law. Later a new type was introduced under the edict of the praetor. Under praetorian law the requirement of a mancipation was dropped; the seals of seven witnesses were enough. State law did not require the witnesses to seal anything. 3. The combined effect of the practice of testators and reforms introduced by imperial pronouncements gradually brought the praetorian and state methods closer together. This led to these rules: on one and the same occasion, a unity in a certain sense required by the law of the state, seven witnesses should be present and should subscribe, a requirement introduced by pro-

nouncements, and, as the praetor's edict laid down, they should seal the will. The law here has three sources: from the old state law witnesses and presence at a single will-making occasion; from imperial pronouncements the requirement that testator and witnesses subscribe; from the praetorian edict the seals and the number of the witnesses. 4. However, to make wills unassailable and to prevent fraud, our own pronouncement also requires that the name of the heir must be expressed in the handwriting of the testator or of the witnesses and that the procedure must be as laid down in the pronouncement. 5. As Pomponius held, the witnesses can all seal with the same ring. Otherwise what could be said of seven rings with the same motif? The rings need not be their own. 6. Witnesses must themselves have capacity to make a will. They must not include any woman, child, or slave; nor anyone who is dumb, deaf, or insane; nor anyone under a ban from dealing with his property; nor anyone whom the law declares infamous and unfit to be a witness. 7. Suppose a witness was thought a free man when the will was made but later turned out to have been a slave. Both the Emperor Hadrian by a written reply to Catonius Verus and later the Emperors Severus and Antoninus by another written reply generously held that such a will would be upheld: it should be treated as though everything had been done properly, so long as when it was sealed everyone thought the witness was free and nobody questioned his status. 8. A father and a son within his authority, or again two sons within the authority of the same father, can both be witnesses to the same will. There is nothing wrong with having several witnesses from one family so long as that family's business is not in question. 9. But among the witnesses there should not be anyone who is within the authority of the testator himself. If a son within authority wants to make a will after his demobilization in respect of his military fund, it is wrong for his father or any person in his father's authority to be a witness. In this context there are objections to evidence from within the family. 10. The following are also disqualified as witnesses: the heir named in the will, anyone within his authority, his father if his father still has authority over him, his brothers if still within that same authority. The making of a will is nowadays looked on as a transaction at arm's length between the testator and the heir. Here the law has had to be turned upside down. The old jurists held that it was the property-purchaser and everyone connected with him in family authority who were disqualified as witnesses to wills; they allowed the heir and his relatives to act, subject only to a warning that in doing so they ought at all costs to avoid abusing their position. We have reformed this scheme of things and have turned their urging into a legal prohibition, so that now it is the heir who is in the position of the old property-purchaser, and the law has disqualified him and his relatives from witnessing what are in effect their own acts. We could not allow any pronouncement in favour of the old scheme to appear in our Codex. 11. On the other hand, because they are not in the legal position of successors to the deceased, we do not disqualify legatees and trustees and their families. Indeed in one pronouncement we expressly permit it; and a fortiori we allow it to those within their authority or with authority over them. // 12. It does not matter whether a will is

12   Nihil autem interest, testamentum in tabulis an in chartis membranisve vel in alia materia fiat.

13   [1] Sed et unum testamentum pluribus codicibus conficere[2] quis potest, 'secundum optinentem tamen observationem omnibus factis'. quod interdum et necessarium est, si quis navigaturus et secum ferre et domi relinquere iudiciorum suorum contestationem velit, 'vel propter alias innumerabiles causas, quae

14   humanis necessitatibus imminent. Sed haec quidem de testamentis, quae in scriptis conficiuntur. si 'quis autem voluerit sine scriptis ordinare iure civili 'testamentum, septem testibus adhibitis et sua voluntate coram eis nuncupata sciat hoc perfectissimum 'testamentum iure civili firmumque constitutum'.

XI [3]
DE MILITARI TESTAMENTO.

[4] 'Supra dicta diligens observatio in ordinandis testa'mentis militibus propter nimiam imperitiam consti'tutionibus principalibus remissa est. nam quamvis 'hi neque legitimum numerum testium adhibuerint 'neque 'aliam testamentorum sollemnitatem observa'verint', recte nihilo minus testantur,' 'videlicet cum in 'expeditionibus occupati sunt: quod merito nostra con'stitutio[5] induxit. quoquo enim modo voluntas eius 'suprema sive scripta inveniatur sive sine scriptura, 'valet testamentum ex voluntate eius. illis autem tem'poribus, per quae citra expeditionem necessitatem in 'aliis locis vel in suis sedibus[6] degunt, minime ad 'vindicandum tale privilegium adiuvantur: sed testari 'quidem et si filii familias sunt propter militiam con'ceduntur, iure tamen communi, ea[7] observatione et 'in eorum testamentis adhibenda, quam et in testa-
1 'mentis paganorum proxime exposuimus'. [8]Plane de militum testamentis divus Traianus Statilio Severo ita rescripsit: 'Id privilegium, quod militantibus da'tum est, ut quoquo modo facta ab his testamenta 'rata sint, sic intellegi debet, ut utique prius con'stare debeat testamentum factum esse, quod et sine 'scriptura a non militantibus quoque fieri potest. is 'ergo miles, de cuius bonis apud te quaeritur, si con'vocatis ad hoc hominibus, ut voluntatem suam tes'taretur, ita locutus est, ut declararet[9], quem vellet 'sibi esse heredem et cui libertatem tribuere, potest 'videri sine scripto hoc modo esse testatus et volun'tas eius rata habenda est. ceterum si, ut plerum'que sermonibus fieri solet, dixit alicui: 'ego te here'dem facio' aut 'tibi bona mea relinquo', non oportet 'hoc pro testamento observari. nec ullorum magis 'interest quam ipsorum, quibus id privilegium datum 'est, eiusmodi exemplum non admitti: alioquin non 'difficulter post mortem alicuius militis testes existe'rent[10], qui adfirmarent se audisse dicentem aliquem 'relinquere se bona, cui visum sit, et per hoc iudicia
2 'vera subvertantur.' Quin immo et mutus et sur-
3 dus miles[11] testamentum facere possunt. Sed hactenus hoc illis a principalibus constitutionibus conceditur, quatenus militant et in castris degunt: post missionem vero veterani vel extra castra si faciant adhuc militantes testamentum, communi omnium civium Romanorum iure facere debent: et quod in castris fecerint testamentum non communi iure, sed quomodo voluerint, post missionem intra annum tantum valebit. quid igitur, si intra annum quidem decesserit, condicio autem heredi adscripta post annum extiterit? an quasi militis testamentum valeat? et
4 placet valere quasi militis. Sed et si quis[12] ante

militiam non iure fecit testamentum et miles factus et in expeditione degens resignavit illud et quaedam adiecit sive detraxit vel alias manifesta est militis voluntas hoc valere volentis, dicendum est valere
5 testamentum quasi ex nova militis voluntate. [13]Denique et in adrogationem datus fuerit miles vel filius familias emancipatus est, testamentum eius quasi militis ex nova voluntate valet nec videtur capitis deminutione inritum fieri.
6 'Sciendum tamen est, quod ad exemplum castren'sis peculii tam anteriores leges quam principales con'stitutiones quibusdam quasi[14] castrensia dederunt pe'culia, quorum[15] quibusdam permissum erat etiam in 'potestate degentibus testari. quod nostra constitu'tio[16] latius extendens permisit omnibus in his tan'tummodo peculiis testari quidem, sed iure communi: 'cuius constitutionis tenore perspecto[17] licentia est 'nihil eorum quae ad praefatum ius pertinent ignorare.'

XII [18]
QUIBUS NON EST PERMISSUM TESTAMENTA FACERE [19]

[20]Non tamen omnibus licet facere testamentum. statim enim hi, qui alieno iuri subiecti sunt, testamenti[21] faciendi ius non habent, adeo quidem ut, quamvis parentes eis permiserint, nihilo magis iure testari possint[22]: exceptis his quos antea enumeravimus et praecipue militibus qui in potestate parentum sunt, quibus de eo quod in castris adquisierint permissum est ex constitutionibus principum testamentum facere. quod quidem initio[23] tantum militantibus datum est tam ex auctoritate divi Augusti quam Nervae nec non optimi imperatoris Traiani, postea vero subscriptione divi Hadriani etiam dimissis militia, id est veteranis, concessum est. itaque si quidem fecerint de castrensi peculio testamentum, pertinebit hoc ad eum quem heredem reliquerint: si vero intestati decesserint nullis liberis vel fratribus superstitibus, ad parentes[24] eorum iure communi pertinebit. ex hoc intellegere possumus, quod in castris adquisierit miles, qui in potestate patris est, neque ipsum patrem adimere posse neque patris creditores id vendere vel aliter inquietare neque patre mortuo cum fratribus esse commune, sed scilicet proprium eius esse id quod in castris adquisierit, quamquam iure civili omnium qui in potestate parentum sunt peculia perinde in bonis parentum computantur, acsi servorum peculia in bonis dominorum numerantur: 'exceptis videlicet his, quae ex sacris constitutionibus 'et praecipue nostris propter diversas causas non ad'quiruntur'. praeter hos igitur, qui castrense peculium 'vel quasi castrense' habent, si quis alius filius familias testamentum fecerit, inutile est, licet suae pote-
1 statis factus decesserit. Praeterea testamentum facere non possunt impuberes, quia nullum eorum animi iudicium est: item furiosi, quia[25] mente carent. nec ad rem pertinet, si impubes postea pubes factus aut furiosus postea compos mentis factus fuerit et decesserit. furiosi autem si per id tempus fecerint testamentum, quo furor eorum intermissus est, iure testati esse videntur, 'certe eo quod ante 'furorem fecerint testamento valente': nam neque testamenta recte facta neque aliud ullum negotium recte
2 gestum postea furor interveniens peremit. Item prodigus, cui bonorum suorum administratio interdicta est, testamentum facere non potest, sed id quod ante fecerit, quam 'interdictio ei bonorum fiat[26]', ratum

(1) § 13 *similis Dig.* 28, 1, 24 (*Flor. l.* 10 *inst.*)   (2) *sic BC*, perficere *T*

(3) Cf. *Gai.* 2, 109..111 *Dig.* 29, 1; 37, 13 *Cod.* 6, 21   (4) *Gai.* 2, 109   (5) *Cod.* 6, 21, 17   (6) *sic BΘ*, edibus *TC* (7) ea] *BTᵃC*, 'eadem *Tᵇ*   (8) § 1 *ex Flor. l.* 10 *inst.* (*Dig.* 29, 1, 24)   (9) *sic Dig.* Θ, declaret *libri*   (10) *sic Dig.*, existent *libri*   (11) *sic BCΘ*, muti et surdi milites *T* (12) quis] *TC*, quod *B*   (13) § 5 *similis Dig.* 29, 1, 22 (*Marcian. l.* 4 *inst.*)   (14) quasi] *dett. cum Θ*, om. *libri*

(15) quorum] *Cᵇ*, ex quorum *B*, et quorum *TP*, inc. *Cᵃ* (16) *Cod.* 3, 28. 37 § 1ᶜ. 1ᶠ= 6, 22, 12   (17) prospecto *BT* (18) Cf. *Gai.* 2, 111..114 *Dig.* 28, 1 *Cod.* 6, 22   (19) *sic Θ et indd. VB*, testamentum facere *C*, facere testamentum *BT* (20) *pr. in. simile Dig.* 28, 1, 6 *pr.* (*Gai. l.* 17 *ad ed. prov.*) (21) *sic BDig.*, testamentum *T*   (22) possunt *libri*   (23) initio] *BΘ*, ius initio *T*, initio ius *C*   (24) *sic Θ*, parente *B*, parentem *TC*   (25) qui *B*   (26) bonorum fiat] *C cum Θ*, bonorum suorum fiat *T*, bonorum ma *Bᵃ*, bonorum *Bᵇ*

made on a writing tablet, on paper, on parchment, or on some other material. 13. Copies can be made as long as they are all executed according to the prevailing requirements. Sometimes people who have to go abroad and want to have evidence of their intentions with them and back at home need copies. But all kinds of pressures can suggest the same precaution. 14. This has all been about wills in writing. A man can make a will without writing which the law of the state will recognize. If he collects seven witnesses and declares his wishes before them, that counts as an absolutely valid will, binding under the law of the state.

2.11 MILITARY WILLS

The detailed scheme for making wills which has just been discussed has been relaxed for soldiers by imperial pronouncements. Soldiers know little of such matters. Their wills are good despite defects in number of witnesses or testamentary formalities. Of course, this applies only when they are on active service. All this was very properly confirmed by our own pronouncement. A soldier's will takes its validity from his intention, and it does not matter how his last wishes are evidenced, whether in writing or not. But the military are not to be encouraged to claim this privilege in times when they are on the march or in their barracks but not actually on campaign. They can then make wills under the general law, by applying the rules just described for civilians. This is even true of sons in authority, by virtue of their military service. 1. A written reply of the Emperor Trajan replying to Statilius Severus contains a clear decision on soldiers' wills: 'The privilege conceded to troops which upholds their wills however they are made is to be applied in this way: it must always first be clear that a will has been made, on the lines a civilian can follow to make a will without writing. In the case of the soldier whose property is in question before you, if he collected people together for the specific purpose of making a will and declared the heir whom he wished to appoint and named a person to be freed, he has made a will of this kind. His wishes should then be given effect. On the other hand if he merely said in normal conversation 'I make you my heir' or 'I leave you my goods' you should not treat these words as a will. Those entitled to this privilege have more interest than anyone in excluding cases like these. Otherwise witnesses might easily come forward after a soldier's death and throw over his true dispositions by affirming that they heard him say he wanted his property to go to anyone they choose.' 2. The deaf or dumb soldier can make a will. 3. Under imperial pronouncements the military privilege is limited to time on active service and life in camp. If a veteran after his release or a soldier still in service but out of camp wants to make a will he must do it according to the general law binding on all Roman citizens. A will made in camp by his own chosen method and not in conformity with the ordinary rules remains valid only for one year after his release. What if he dies within the year but a condition for the heir's entry is not fulfilled till the year is up? Is it still a valid military will? It has been decided that it is. 4. Suppose someone makes an irregular will before military service and then, as a soldier on campaign, opens it and adds to or subtracts from it or in some other way shows that he wants it to take effect. The will is valid, as a new expression of his wishes. 5. The military will of a soldier who is adrogated or a son who is emancipated from authority is also effective as the expression of his wishes and does not lapse for status-loss. 6. Notice that earlier acts and imperial pronouncements allowed some people to hold a quasi-military fund, extending the analogy of the military fund. Then to some of those they conceded the privilege of disposing of it by will even while still within family authority. Our own pronouncement took this further and allowed everyone to dispose of these funds by will if they followed the rules of the general law. Study of its terms will leave no excuse for not knowing all the law about this right.

2.12 PERSONS INCAPABLE OF MAKING A WILL

Not everyone has the capacity to make a will. First, someone within another's authority has no power to do so, not even with the consent of the head of the family. There are exceptions which we have already spelled out, notably soldiers in family authority, to whom imperial pronouncements have given the power to make a will of their military acquisitions. This was originally granted to serving soldiers, by the authority of the Emperor Augustus, then of Nerva, and then of Trajan, best of emperors. Later it was extended by the Emperor Hadrian in an answer appended to a petition from soldiers who had been demobilized, i.e. veterans. If they make a will relating to their military fund it will go to the heirs they name. But if they die intestate, survived by neither children nor brothers, it will go to the head of the family in accordance with the general law. So a father cannot take away a dependent son's acquisitions gained on active service. Similarly, the father's creditors cannot sell them or disturb them in any way. And he does not have to share them with his brothers on the father's death. They are his own property. This is despite the fact that the old state law counted the personal funds of those within authority as belonging entirely to the head of the family, just as much as slaves' possessions belonged to their owners. Some things are excluded. By virtue of imperial pronouncements, our own in particular, they cannot for various reasons become owners of certain types of property. Apart from those who do have a military or quasi-military fund, any other son within authority who makes a will achieves nothing at all, even if he becomes his own master before he dies. 1. Next, a young child cannot make a will: he can understand but lacks judgment. The same is true of a man who is insane: he cannot even understand. It makes no difference that the child becomes adult before dying, or the madman recovers his senses. An insane person's will is considered valid if it is made in a lucid interval. And there is no doubt that a will made before the onset of madness is valid. Neither a will nor any other transaction validly executed is subsequently rescinded by supervening insanity. 2. Again, the wasteful who are banned from dealing with their own property cannot make a will, though their acts before the ban are valid. // 3. Again,

3 est. Item mutus et surdus 'non semper'[1] facere
testamentum possunt. utique autem de eo surdo loquimur, qui omnino non exaudit, non qui tarde exaudit:
nam et mutus is intelligitur, qui eloqui nihil potest, non
qui tarde loquitur. 'saepe autem etiam litterati et eru-
'diti homines variis casibus et audiendi et loquendi fa-
'cultatem amittunt: unde nostra constitutio[2] etiam his
'subvenit, ut certis casibus et modis secundum nor-
'mam eius possint testari aliaque facere quae eis per-
'missa sunt'. [3]sed si quis post testamentum factum
valetudine aut quolibet alio casu mutus aut surdus
esse coeperit, ratum nihilo minus eius remanet testa-
4 mentum. 'Caecus autem non potest facere testa-
'mentum nisi per observationem, quam lex[4] divi Iustini
5 'patris mei introduxit'. [5]'Eius, qui apud hostes est',
testamentum quod ibi fecit non valet, quamvis red-
ierit: sed quod dum in civitate fuerat fecit, sive red-
ierit, valet iure postliminii, sive illic decesserit, valet
ex lege Cornelia.

XIII [6]
DE EXHEREDATIONE LIBERORUM.

[7]'Non tamen, ut 'omnimodo' valeat testamentum',
'sufficit haec observatio, quam supra exposuimus.
'sed' qui filium in potestate habet, curare debet, ut
'eum heredem instituat vel 'exheredem' nominatim 'fa-
'ciat': alioquin si eum silentio praeterierit, inutiliter
'testabitur, adeo quidem ut, etsi vivo patre filius 'mor-
'tuus' sit, nemo ex eo testamento heres existere pos-
'sit, quia scilicet ab initio non constiterit' 'testamen-
'tum. sed non ita de[8] filiabus vel aliis per virilem
'sexum descendentibus liberis utriusque sexus fuerat
antiquitati observatum: sed si iure nostro heredes
'scripti scriptaeve vel exheredati exheredataeve, testa-
'mentum quidem non infirmabatur, ius autem adcre-
'scendi eis ad certam portionem[9] praestabatur. sed
'nec nominatim eas personas exheredare parentibus
'necesse erat, sed licebat et inter ceteros hoc facere'.
1 [10]'Nominatim autem exheredari quis videtur, sive
'ita exheredetur 'Titius filius meus exheres esto', sive
'ita 'filius meus exheres esto' non adiecto proprio
'nomine', 'scilicet si alius filius non extet'. [11]'postumi
'quoque liberi vel heredes institui debent vel exhere-
'dari. et in eo par omnium condicio est, quod et in
'filio postumo et in quolibet ex ceteris liberis sive
'feminini sexus sive masculini praeterito[12] valet qui-
'dem testamentum, sed postea adgnatione postumi
'sive postumae rumpitur et ea ratione totum infirma-
'tur: ideoque si mulier, ex qua postumus aut postuma
'sperabatur, abortum fecerit, nihil impedimento est
'scriptis heredibus ad hereditatem adeundam. sed femi-
'nini quidem sexus personae vel nominatim vel inter
'ceteros exheredari solebant, dum tamen, si inter ce-
'teros exheredentur, aliquid eis legetur, ne videantur
'per oblivionem praeteritae esse, masculos vero postu-
'mos, 'id est filium et deinceps,' placuit non aliter
'recte exheredari, 'nisi' nominatim exheredentur, hoc
'scilicet modo: 'quicumque mihi filius genitus fuerit,
2 'exheres esto'. [13]Postumorum autem loco sunt et
'hi, qui in sui heredis locum succedendo quasi adgnas-
'cendo fiunt parentibus sui heredes. ut ecce si quis
'filium et ex eo nepotem neptemve in potestate ha-
'beat, quia filius gradu praecedit, is solus iura sui
'heredis habet, quamvis nepos quoque et neptis ex eo
'in eadem potestate sunt: sed si filius eius vivo eo
'moriatur aut qualibet alia ratione exeat de potestate

'eius, incipit nepos neptisve in eius locum succedere
'et eo modo iura suorum heredum quasi adgnatione
'nanciscuntur. ne ergo eo modo rumpatur eius testa-
'mentum, sicut ipsum filium vel heredem instituere
'vel nominatim exheredare debet testator, ne non iure
'faciat testamentum, ita et nepotem neptemve ex filio
'necesse est ei vel heredem instituere vel exheredare,
'ne forte vivo eo filio mortuo, succedendo in locum
'eius nepos neptisve quasi adgnatione rumpant testa-
'mentum. idque lege Iunia[14] Vellaea provisum est,
'in qua simul exheredationis modus 'ad similitudinem
3 postumorum demonstratur.' [15]'Emancipatos liberos
'iure civili neque heredes instituere neque exheredare
'necesse est, quia non sunt sui heredes. sed praetor
'omnes tam feminini quam masculini sexus, si here-
'des non instituantur, exheredari iubet, virilis sexus
'nominatim, feminini 'vero et' inter ceteros. quodsi
'neque heredes instituti fuerint neque ita ut diximus
'exheredati[16], promittit praetor eis contra tabulas
4 'testamenti bonorum possessionem.' 'Adoptivi liberi
'quamdiu sunt in potestate patris adoptivi, eiusdem
'iuris habentur, cuius sunt iustis nuptiis quaesiti: ita-
'que heredes instituendi vel exheredandi sunt secun-
'dum ea quae de naturalibus exposuimus: [17]'emanci-
'pati vero a patre adoptivo neque iure civili neque
'quod ad edictum praetoris attinet inter liberos nu-
'merantur. qua ratione accidit, ut ex diverso quod
'ad naturalem parentem attinet, quamdiu quidem sint
'in adoptiva familia, extraneorum numero habeantur',
'ut eos neque heredes instituere neque exheredare
'necesse sit: 'cum vero emancipati fuerint ab adop-
'tivo patre, tunc incipiant in ea causa esse, in qua
'futuri essent, si ab ipso naturali patre emancipati
5 'fuissent.' 'Sed haec vetustas introducebat. nostra
'vero constitutio[18] inter masculos et feminas in hoc
'iure nihil interesse existimans, quia utraque persona[19]
'in hominum procreatione similiter naturae officio fun-
'gitur et lege antiqua duodecim tabularum omnes simi-
'liter ad successiones ab intestato vocabantur, quod
'et praetores postea secuti esse videntur, ideo[20] sim-
'plex ac simile ius et in filiis et in filiabus et in ce-
'teris descendentibus[21] per virilem sexum personis
'non solum natis, sed etiam postumis introduxit[22], ut
'omnes, sive sui sive emancipati sunt, et[23] nominatim
'exheredentur et eundem habeant effectum circa testa-
'menta parentum suorum infirmanda et hereditatem
'auferendam, quem filii sui vel emancipati habent, sive
'iam nati sunt sive adhuc in utero constituti postea
'nati sunt. circa adoptivos autem certam induximus
'divisionem, quae constitutioni nostrae[24], quam super
6 'adoptivis tulimus, continetur. Sed si 'expeditione
'occupatus' miles testamentum faciat et liberos suos
'iam natos vel postumos nominatim non exheredaverit,
'sed silentio praeterierit non ignorans, an habeat libe-
'ros, silentium eius pro exheredatione nominatim facta
7 valere constitutionibus principum cautum est.[29] Mater
'vel avus maternus necesse non habent liberos suos
'aut heredes instituere aut exheredare, sed possunt
'eos omittere. nam silentium matris aut avi materni
'ceterorumque per matrem ascendentium tantum facit,
'quantum exheredatio patris. [25]'neque enim matri filium
'filiamve neque avo maternum nepotem neptemve ex
'filia, si cum eamve heredem non instituat, exhere-
'dare necesse est, sive de iure civili quaeramus, sive
'de edicto praetoris, quo[26] praeteritis liberis contra
'tabulas bonorum possessionem promittit'. 'sed aliud
'eis adminiculum servatur, quod paulo post[27] vobis
'manifestum fiat[28]'.

---

(1) semper] $TC\Theta$, per se B (2) *Cod.* 6, 22, 10   (3) § 3
fin. ex Dig. 28, 1, 6 § 1 (*Gai. l.* 17 *ad ed. prov.*)   (4) *Cod.*
6, 22, 8   (5) § 5 *in. ex Dig.* 28, 1, 8 *pr.* (*Gai. l. c.*)
(6) *Cf. Gai.* 2, 123..143 *Dig.* 28, 2, 3 *Cod.* 6, 28. 29   (7) *Gai.* 2,
115. 123   (8) de] *B*, et de *TC*   (9) *sic TC*, eis certe portionis *B*
(10) *Gai.* 2, 127   (11) *Gai.* 2, 130. 131 *rest.*   (12) praeterito]
TC Gai., pr. postumo *B*   (13) *Gai.* 2, 133. 134 *rest. ex Dig.*
28, 3, 13   (14) iulia $C^a\Theta$ (15) *Gai.* 2, 135 *   (16) *sic*
$C^1 E$ *cum Gai.* Θ, instituantur neque i. u. d. exheredentur

BTC^v (17) *Gai.* 2, 136. 137   (18) *Cod.* 6, 28, 4   (19) *sic*
CE, utraeque personae *B*, in utramque personam T^b, *inc.*
T^a (20) ideo] *B*, et i. *T*   (21) *sic T*, descendentium *B*
(22) introduximus *T*   (23) et] *BC*, aut heredes instituantur aut T^bWE, *inc.* T^a, *ut tamen appareat afuisse*
verba aut her. inst.   (24) *Cod.* 8, 47, 10   (25) *Gai.*
3, 71   (26) quo] BT *Gai.* 3, 71. quod T^a (27) post]
P, om. BTC   (28) 2, 18   (29) *Cod.* 6, 21, 9. 10

the dumb and the deaf do not always have testamentary capacity. By deaf we mean completely unable to hear, not hard of hearing, and by dumb unable to speak at all, not having difficulty in speaking. Yet it often happens that educated and literate people lose their speech or hearing for one reason or another. To help them our pronouncement has provided certain ways and means for them to be able to make wills and perform other acts. If someone makes a will and is then struck deaf or dumb through illness or some other cause, his will remains valid. 4. A blind man cannot make a will except under the scheme laid down by my father, the Emperor Justin. 5. A will made by a prisoner of war while in enemy hands is a nullity even if he later returns. But one made before he lost his citizenship is valid, under his right of rehabilitation if he returns, under the Cornelian Act if he dies in enemy hands.

2.13 DISINHERITING CHILDREN

A will's validity is not conclusively determined by the conditions set out above. Someone with a son within his authority must be sure to appoint him heir or to disinherit him specifically. If he passes over him in silence his will becomes a nullity. Even if the son dies before the father it will be impossible for anyone to become heir under it, for the obvious reason that the will failed from the outset to come into existence. However, the old rules did not apply with the same rigour to daughters or to other male or female members of the family descended through the male line. If they were neither appointed heirs nor disinherited the will was not wholly invalidated. Instead they had a right to come in for their proper shares. The head of the family was also not obliged to disinherit them by name but could do it by a general clause. 1. The requirement for specific removal is satisfied by 'Let Titius my son be disinherited' and also by 'Let my son be disinherited' with his actual name omitted. This will only do, of course, if there is no other son. Posthumous children must also be appointed heirs or disinherited. The rules are the same for all: if a posthumous son or any other posthumous offspring, male or female, is passed over, the will is good, but the birth of the posthumous child then vitiates it, overthrowing it completely. This means that if a woman carrying a posthumous child happens to miscarry nothing prevents the heirs appointed in the will from accepting the inheritance. In the case of females the practice grew up of removing them either by a specific or by a general exclusion. If a general exclusion was used they were then given something by way of legacy in order to show that they had not simply been forgotten. But in the case of posthumous males, sons and so on, it was held that an effective removal must be specific. Of course, it has to be of this kind: 'Let any son begotten hereafter by me be disinherited.' 2. Next, the rules on posthumous children also apply to those who by succeeding to the immediate heir of the head of the family become his immediate heirs as it were on the second tier. Suppose for example that a man has a son within his authority and through him a grandchild also within authority. Here the son is a degree higher and he alone has the rights of the immediate heir, despite the fact that they are within authority together. If the son dies before the the father, or leaves his authority for some other reason, the grandchild

succeeds to his place and assumes the rights of the immediate heir on as it were the second tier. To guard against the nullification of his will, the testator, just as he must appoint or specifically remove his son, must also appoint or remove his grandchildren by the son. That way he will avoid making an ineffective will. The danger is that his son may die in his lifetime and let in these second-tier heirs, whose succession will overthrow the will. This was anticipated in the Junian-Vellaean Act, which also contains a model exclusion drafted on the lines of the one for posthumous children. 3. Children who have been emancipated do not according to the law of the state have to be appointed or excluded, because they are not immediate heirs. But the praetor requires that all of them, male and female, must be disinherited if they are not appointed. He requires males to be excluded specifically but allows a general exclusion of females. If they are neither appointed nor excluded in the way described above, the praetor gives them estate-possession counter to the will. 4. Adoptive children still in the authority of their adoptive father are in the same legal position as those born to the marriage. They must be appointed or excluded just as we have said for real descendants. An adoptee who is emancipated by the adoptive father no longer counts as a descendant either in state law or under the praetor's edict. The logic of this applies conversely to the real father. His son in the adoptive family counts as a stranger. He need not appoint or exclude him. But if the son is emancipated by the adoptive father he assumes the position that he would have had if emancipated by his own father. 5. But all this is history. Our pronouncement has taken the position that no difference should be made between males and females in this connexion: each sex plays its own part in the procreation of mankind, and from early times the Twelve Tables gave them equal rights of intestate succession, an approach the praetors appear to have followed later. Our pronouncement has introduced a single and simple rule for sons and daughters alike and for the next generations through the male line, and for both the born and the posthumous. Disinheriting exclusions of immediate heirs and emancipated persons shall all be specific. The effects for the nullification of wills and ademption of inheritances shall be as for sons, whether within authority or emancipated, and whether born or in the womb. As for adoptees we have introduced a categorization which is set out in our pronouncement on adoption. 6. Suppose a soldier makes a will on campaign and fails to make a specific exclusion of his children, born or unborn. If he passes over them in silence but not because he is unaware of having children, his silence will be construed as an effective specific exclusion. This is laid down by imperial pronouncements. 7. A mother or maternal grandmother need not appoint or exclude her children but can just omit them. A mother's silence has the same effect as a disinheriting exclusion by a father. The same applies to a grandmother or other ascendant on the mother's side. Whether we turn to the law of the state or the part of praetor's edict which promises estate-possession counter to the will to descendants who have been overlooked, we find that a mother need not exclude a son or daughter whom she does not appoint, and that a maternal grandmother has the same freedom in respect of a grandchild by her daughter. But as you will see later these people have another remedy.//

XIV [1]
DE HEREDIBUS INSTITUENDIS.

Heredes instituere permissum est tam liberos homines quam servos tam proprios quam [2] alienos. proprios autem 'olim quidem secundum plurium sententias' non aliter quam cum libertate recte instituere licebat. 'hodie vero etiam sine libertate ex nostra 'constitutione [3] heredes eos instituere permissum est. 'quod non per innovationem induximus, sed quoniam 'et aequius erat et Atilicino placuisse Paulus suis 'libris, quos tam ad Massurium Sabinum quam ad 'Plautium scripsit, refert'. proprius autem servus etiam is intellegitur, in quo nudam proprietatem testator habet, 'alio usum fructum habente'. [4] est autem casus, in quo nec cum libertate utiliter servus a domina heres instituitur, ut constitutione divorum Severi et Antonini cavetur, cuius verba haec sunt: 'Servum 'adulterio maculatum non iure testamento manumis-'sum ante sententiam ab ea muliere videri, quae rea 'fuerat eiusdem criminis postulata, rationis est: quare 'sequitur, ut in eundem a domina collata institutio [5] 'nullius momenti habeatur.' alienus servus etiam is intellegitur, in quo usum fructum testator habet.
1 [6]Servus autem a domino suo 'heres institutus, si 'quidem in eadem causa 'manserit', fit ex testamento 'liber heresque necessarius. si vero a vivo testatore 'manumissus fuerit, suo arbitrio adire hereditatem 'potest, 'quia non fit necessarius, cum utrumque ex domini testamento non consequitur'. 'quodsi alienatus 'fuerit, iussu novi domini adire hereditatem debet et 'ea ratione per eum dominus fit heres: nam ipse 'alie-'natus' neque liber neque heres esse potest', 'etiamsi 'cum libertate heres institutus fuerit: destitisse etenim 'a libertatis datione videtur dominus qui eum alie-'navit'. 'alienus quoque servus heres institutus si in 'eadem causa duraverit, iussu domini [7] adire heredi-'tatem debet. si vero alienatus ab eo [8] fuerit aut vivo 'testatore aut post mortem eius antequam 'adeat', debet 'iussu novi domini 'adire'. at si manumissus est 'vivo testatore, vel mortuo antequam adeat', suo arbitrio
2 'adire hereditatem potest'. Servus alienus post domini mortem recte heres instituitur, quia et cum hereditariis servis est testamenti factio: nondum enim adita hereditas personae vicem sustinet, non heredis futuri, sed defuncti, cum et eius, qui in utero est,
3 servus recte heres instituitur. Servus plurium, cum quibus testamenti factio est, ab extraneo institutus heres unicuique dominorum, cuius iussu adierit, pro portione dominii adquirit hereditatem.
4 Et unum hominem et plures in infinitum [9], quot
5 quis [10] velit, heredes facere licet. [11]Hereditas plerumque dividitur in duodecim uncias, quae assis appellatione continentur [12]. habent autem et hae partes propria nomina ab uncia usque ad assem, ut puta haec: sextans [13], quadrans, triens, quincunx, semis, septunx, bes, dodrans, dextans, deunx, as. non autem utique duodecim uncias esse oportet. nam tot unciae assem efficiunt [14], quot testator voluerit, et si unum tantum quis ex semisse verbi gratia heredem scripserit, totus as in semisse erit: neque enim idem ex parte testatus et ex parte intestatus decedere potest, nisi sit miles, cuius sola voluntas in testando spectatur. et e contrario potest quis in quantascumque voluerit 'plurimas' uncias suam hereditatem divi-
6 dere. Si plures instituantur, ita demum partium distributio necessaria est, si nolit [15] testator eos ex

aequis partibus heredes esse: satis enim constat nullis partibus nominatis aequis ex partibus eos heredes esse. partibus autem in quorundam personis expressis, si quis alius sine parte nominatus erit, si quidem aliqua pars assi deerit, ex ea parte heres fit: et si plures sine parte scripti sunt, omnes in eadem parte concurrent. si vero totus as completus sit, in partem dimidiam vocatur [16] et ille vel illi omnes in alteram dimidiam. nec interest, primus an medius an novissimus sine parte scriptus sit: ea enim pars data
7 intellegitur quae vacat. Videamus, si pars aliqua vacet nec tamen quisquam sine parte heres institutus sit, quid iuris sit? veluti si tres ex quartis partibus heredes scripti sunt. et constat vacantem partem singulis tacite pro hereditaria parte accedere et perinde haberi, ac si ex tertiis partibus heredes scripti essent: et ex diverso si plus in portionibus sit [17], tacite singulis decrescere, ut, si verbi gratia quattuor ex tertiis partibus heredes scripti sint, perinde habeantur, ac si unusquisque ex quarta parte scriptus
8 fuisset. Et si plures unciae quam duodecim distributae sunt, is, qui sine parte institutus est, quod dipondio deest habebit: idemque erit, si dipondius expletus sit. quae omnes partes ad assem postea revocantur, quamvis sint plurium unciarum.
9 Heres et pure et sub condicione institui potest, ex certo tempore aut ad certum tempus non potest, veluti 'post quinquennium quam moriar' vel 'ex ka-'lendis illis' aut 'usque ad kalendas illas heres esto': diemque [18] adiectum pro supervacuo haberi placet et
10 perinde esse, ac si pure heres institutus esset. Impossibilis condicio in institutionibus et legatis nec non in [19] fideicommissis et libertatibus pro non scripto
11 habetur [20]. Si plures condiciones institutioni adscriptae sunt, si quidem coniunctim, ut puta 'si illud 'et illud factum erit', omnibus parendum est: si separatim, veluti 'si illud aut illud factum erit', cuilibet obtemperare satis est.
12 Hi, quos numquam testator vidit, heredes institui possunt. veluti si fratris filios peregri natos ignorans qui essent heredes instituerit: ignorantia enim testantis inutilem institutionem non facit.

XV [21]
DE VULGARI SUBSTITUTIONE.

[22]Potest autem quis in testamento suo plures gradus heredum facere, ut puta 'si ille heres non erit, 'ille heres esto': et deinceps in quantum velit testator substituere potest et novissimo loco in subsidium
1 vel servum necessarium heredem instituere. [22]Et plures in unius locum possunt substitui, vel unus in plurium, vel singuli singulis [23], vel invicem ipsi qui
2 heredes instituti sunt. Et si ex disparibus partibus heredes scriptos invicem substituerit et nullam mentionem in substitutione habuerit partium, eas videtur partes in substitutione dedisse, quas in insti-
3 tutione expressit: et ita divus Pius rescripsit [24]. Sed si instituto heredi et coheredi suo substituto dato alius substitutus fuerit, divi Severus et Antoninus sine distinctione rescripserunt ad utramque partem
4 substitutum admitti. Si servum alienum quis patrem familias arbitratus heredem scripserit et, si heres non esset, Maevium ei substituerit isque servus iussu domini adierit hereditatem, Maevius in partem admittitur. illa enim verba 'si heres non erit' in eo quidem, quem alieno iuri subiectum esse testator scit,

(1) *Cf.* Gai. 2, 185..190 *Dig.* 28, 5 *Cod.* 6, 24   (2) tam pr.quam] tam pr. quamque *T*, pr. vel *B*, et tam pr. quam *C* (3) *Cod.*6,27,5 §1^b   (4) *pr. fin. ex Marciani l.* 4 *inst.* (*Dig.* 28, 5, 49 § 2)   (5) institutio] *C^a Dig.*, hereditas inst. *B*, hereditatis inst. *TC^bP*   (6) *Gai.* 2, 188. 189   (7) domini] *Gai.*, eius domini *CP*, domini eius *BT*   (8) ab eo] *TC Gai.*, om. *B*θ   (9) infinito *BTC^a*   (10) quot (quod *C^a*) quis] *CT^b*, quo quis *B*, ** *T^a*   (11) § 5 *in. simile Dig.* 28, 5, 51 § 2 (*Ulp. lib.* 6 *reg.*)   (12) *sic TC Dig.*, continetur *AB*   (13) sextans] *AB Dig.*, sexunx vel sextans

T^a, secunx sextans *C*   (14) *sic T^b*, efficerent *AB*, efficere *C^a*, efficint *T^a*   (15) *sic AB*, noluerit *T*   (16) *sic ABC*, vocantur *T*   (17) *sic A*, si plus in p. sint *B*, si plures in p. sint (sit *C*) *TC*   (18) *sic BTC*, denique *A*   (19) nec non in] *AC*, vel *BT*   (20) *sic B*, habeatur *AT*, habentur *C^a*   (21) *Cf. Gai.* 2, 174..178 *Dig.* 28, 6 *Cod.* 28, 6   (22) *pr.* § 1 *ex Marciani l.* 4 *inst.* (*Dig.* 28, 6, 36)   (23) singuli in singulis *libri*   (24) *Cod.* 6, 26, 1

2.14 APPOINTMENT OF HEIRS

It is possible to appoint as heir either a free man or a slave, one's own or another's. At one time a man could only appoint his own slave if he also made him free. This was based on the opinions of many jurists. Nowadays the appointment can be made even without a grant of freedom, under the terms of our own pronouncement. We did not approve this as an innovation but because it seemed more reasonable and because Paul in his works on Massurius Sabinus and on Plautius says that Atilicinus took the same position. A slave is counted as the testator's own if he has the bare title, even where someone else holds the usufruct. There is one situation in which a female owner cannot effectively appoint her own slave as heir even with a grant of freedom. This is established by a pronouncement of the Emperors Severus and Antoninus: 'It is right that a slave stained by adultery cannot be treated as lawfully freed before his sentence by the will of the woman co-accused, and so her appointment of him as her heir should be regarded as a nullity.' A slave in whom the testator has a usufruct counts as belonging to another. 1. Where an owner appoints his own slave as heir and the man's position remains unchanged, the will operates to make him free and compulsory heir. If he has been freed during the testator's lifetime, he has a choice whether to accept the inheritance or not. Because his master's will does not combine both grants, he does not become compulsory heir. Suppose he has been conveyed to another. He must accept the inheritance if his new owner tells him to; his owner then becomes heir through him. He cannot, after his transfer, become free or heir, not even if appointed with an express grant of freedom, because his former owner's power to free him ends with the change of ownership. Where the testator appoints as heir a slave belonging to another, and that slave's position then remains unchanged, he must accept the estate if his owner orders. If he has been transferred in the testator's lifetime, or after the latter's death but before acceptance of the inheritance, his acceptance depends on his new owner's order. If he has been manumitted in the testator's lifetime or between death and acceptance, the choice is his own. 2. An appointment of another's slave can take effect even if his owner has just died, since testamentary capacity holds good as regards slaves vested in an inheritance. In the interval before acceptance the estate itself assumes the legal personality of the deceased, not of the future heir. But the slave of a person still in the womb can be appointed. 3. Suppose someone appoints a slave belonging to co-owners, who all have capacity to take under his will. The slave acquires the estate for each of his owners who authorizes his acceptance, in shares measured by their shares in him. 4. The law allows the appointment of a single heir or of as many co-heirs as the testator wants, without limit. 5. It is common to divide the estate into the twelve ounces which in the language of coinage make up a pound. From ounce to pound the fractions have their own names: two twelfths make a *sextans*, three a *quadrans*, four a *triens*, five a *quincunx*, six a *semis*, seven a *septunx*, eight a *bes*, nine a *dodrans*, ten a *dextans*, and eleven a *deunx*. Twelve make the whole pound, the *as*. A testator does not have to deal in the twelve ounces; he can divide his pound into as many ounces as he likes. If he appoints a single heir to one fraction, say to a *semis*, the half will carry the whole pound, because it is impossible for anyone to die partly testate and partly intestate. The exception is a soldier. His will is governed exclusively by his intention. The opposite case is division into many shares; the testator can use just as many fractions as he wants. 6. The testator need only specify shares among co-heirs if he does not want them to take equally. It is accepted that co-heirs take equally in the absence of express provision to the contrary. Suppose that the will spells out the shares for some but leaves another with no specified share. If some fraction of the pound is left over, that heir will get that slice. If several are left without specified shares, they will get equal shares in that remainder. On the other hand, if the heirs given specified shares take up the whole pound, they are remitted to one half, and the one or ones with no specified share will take the other half. It makes no difference whether the one without a share is named first, last, or in the middle; the construction is that he takes the vacant remainder. 7. What happens if one part is unallotted and there is no heir appointed without a specified share? For example, suppose three heirs are appointed, each to a quarter share. The vacant quarter implicitly accrues to each of them in the shares in which they are heirs. It is as if they had been appointed to thirds. The principle applies in reverse, so that each takes a proportionate decrease if the shares exceed the whole. If four are appointed to thirds, each is treated as though appointed to a quarter. 8. When more than twelve ounces are allotted, an heir appointed without a share gets the remainder that brings the total to two pounds; and if the shares exhaust a two pound module, the calculation advances pound by pound in the same way. The shares are all in the end scaled down to a single pound, however many ounces are allocated. 9. An heir can be appointed conditionally or unconditionally but not to or from a given time, for example not 'from five years after my death' or 'from the first of such and such a month' or 'to the first of that month'. The correct approach to a time limit is to treat it as superfluous, leaving the appointment absolute. 10. An impossible condition attached to the appointment of an heir, to a legacy, to a trust or a grant of freedom, is ignored. 11. If an appointment is subject to multiple conditions, all have to be satisfied if they are concurrent, as say 'if such and such and so and so occurs'. With disjunctive conditions, say 'If such and such or so and so occurs', it is enough if one is satisfied. 12. A testator can appoint people he has never met. For instance, without knowing the identity of his nephews born abroad he can appoint them as his heirs. The validity of the appointment is unaffected by his not knowing them.

2.15 ORDINARY SUBSTITUTES

A will can make appointments in tiers, in this way: 'If X does not become heir, let Y be heir.' The testator can go on to make as many of these substitutions as he wants. At the end as a last resort he can make a slave compulsory heir. 1. The substitution can be of several people for one person, one for several, or one for one; or it can make co-appointees substitutes for each other. 2. If the testator appoints co-heirs to unequal shares and then substitutes them to each other without saying anything more about the shares, he is construed to have given the same share in the substitution as in the appointment. So held in a written reply of the Emperor Pius. 3. Suppose an heir is instituted and his co-heir is made his substitute and then another person is put in as substitute to the co-heir. A reply of the Emperors Severus and Antoninus holds that the substitute here takes both shares, merged together. 4. Suppose a testator appoints as his heir, with Maevius as his substitute, a man who is a another's slave but whom the testator thinks is a free head of a family, and the slave then accepts the estate on his owner's command. Here Maevius is let into the slave's place. Where the testator knows his appointee is not independent, the words 'If he does not become heir' are construed to mean, 'If he himself does not become heir,

sic accipiuntur: si neque ipse heres erit neque alium heredem effecerit: in eo vero, quem patrem familias esse arbitratur, illud significant[1]: si hereditatem sibi cive, cuius iuri postea subiectus esse coeperit, non adquisierit. [2]idque Tiberius[3] Caesar in persona Parthenii servi sui constituit.

XVI[4]
DE PUPILLARI SUBSTITUTIONE.

[5]'Liberis suis impuberibus, quos in potestate quis 'habet, non solum ita ut supra diximus substituere 'potest, id est ut, si heredes ei non extiterint, alius 'ei sit heres, sed eo amplius ut et, si heredes ei ex-'titerint et adhuc impuberes mortui fuerint, sit eis 'aliquis heres. veluti 'si quis dicat' hoc modo: 'Titius "filius meus heres mihi esto: si filius meus heres "mihi non erit, sive heres erit et prius moriatur, quam "in suam tutelam venerit" '(id est pubes factus sit)', "tunc Seius heres esto.' quo casu si quidem non ex-'titerit heres filius, tunc substitutus patri fit heres: 'si vero extiterit heres filius et ante pubertatem de-'cesserit, ipsi filio fit heres substitutus.' nam mori-bus[6] institutum est, ut, cum eius aetatis sunt, in qua ipsi sibi testamentum facere non possunt, parentes eis faciant. 'Qua ratione excitati etiam constitu-'tionem[7] in nostro posuimus codice, qua prospectum 'est, ut, si mente captos habeant filios vel nepotes vel 'pronepotes cuiuscumque sexus vel gradus, liceat eis, 'etsi puberes sint, ad exemplum pupillaris substitu-'tionis certas personas substituere: sin autem resi-'puerint, eandem substitutionem infirmari, et hoc ad 'exemplum pupillaris substitutionis, quae postquam 'pupillus adoleverit infirmatur. Igitur in pupil-'lari substitutione secundum praefatum modum ordi-'nata'[8] 'duo quodammodo sunt testamenta, alterum pa-'tris, alterum filii, tamquam si ipse filius sibi here-'dem instituisset: aut certe unum est testamentum 'duarum causarum, id est duarum hereditatum.' Sin autem quis ita formidolosus sit, ut timeret, ne filius eius pupillus adhuc ex eo, quod palam substitutum accepit, post obitum eius periculo insidiarum subi-ceretur[9]: [10]'vulgarem quidem substitutionem palam 'facere' et in primis testamenti partibus debet, 'illam 'autem substitutionem, per quam et si heres extiterit 'pupillus et intra pubertatem decesserit substitutus 'vocatur, separatim in inferioribus 'partibus' scribere "eamque partem' proprio lino propriaque cera con-'signare'[11] 'et in 'priore parte' testamenti cavere, ne 'inferiores tabulae vivo filio et adhuc impubere ape-'riantur.' illud palam est non ideo minus valere sub-'stitutionem impuberis filii, quod in iisdem tabulis scripta sit, quibus sibi quisque heredem instituisset, quamvis hoc pupillo periculosum sit. [12]'Non solum autem 'heredibus institutis impuberibus liberis ita substi-'tuere parentes possunt, ut et[13] si heredes eis extite-'rint et ante pubertatem mortui fuerint, sit eis heres 'is quem ipsi voluerint, sed etiam exheredatis. ita-'que eo casu si quid pupillo ex hereditatibus legativeve 'aut donationibus propinquorum atque amicorum ad-'quisitum fuerit, id omne ad substitutum pertineat. quae-'cumque diximus de substitutione impuberum libero-'rum vel heredum institutorum vel exheredatorum, 'eadem etiam de postumis intellegimus.' Liberis autem suis testamentum facere nemo potest, nisi et sibi faciat: nam pupillare testamentum pars et se-quela est paterni testamenti, adeo ut, si patris testa-mentum non valeat, ne filii quidem valebit. [14]'Vel

singulis autem liberis vel qui eorum novissimus im-pubes morietur substitui potest. singulis quidem, si neminem eorum intestato decedere voluit: novissimo, si ius legitimarum hereditatum integrum inter eos custodiri velit. Substituitur autem impuberi[15] aut nominatim, veluti 'Titius', aut generaliter 'quisquis[16] 'mihi[17] heres erit': quibus verbis vocantur ex sub-stitutione impubere filio mortuo, qui et[18] scripti sunt heredes et extiterunt, et pro qua parte heredes facti sunt. Masculo igitur usque ad quattuordecim annos substitui potest, feminae usque ad duodecim annos: et si hoc tempus excesserit, substitutio eva-nescit. [19]'Extraneo vero vel filio puberi heredi[19] 'instituto ita substituere nemo potest, ut, si heres 'extiterit et intra aliquod tempus decesserit, alius ei 'sit heres: sed hoc solum permissum est, ut eum per 'fideicommissum testator obliget alii hereditatem eius 'vel totam vel pro parte restituere: quod ius quale 'sit, suo loco trademus'[21]

XVII[22]
QUIBUS MODIS TESTAMENTA INFIRMANTUR.

Testamentum iure factum usque eo valet, donec rumpatur irritumve fiat. Rumpitur autem testa-mentum, cum in eodem statu manente testatore ipsius testamenti ius vitiatur. [23]'si quis 'enim' post factum 'testamentum adoptaverit sibi filium 'per imperatorem' 'eum, qui sui iuris est, aut per praetorem 'secundum 'nostram constitutionem' eum, qui in potestate paren-'tis fuerit, testamentum eius rumpitur quasi adgna-'tione sui heredis. [24]Posteriore quoque testamento, 'quod iure 'perfectum' est, superius rumpitur. nec in-'terest, an extiterit aliquis heres ex eo, an non ex-'titerit: hoc enim solum spectatur, an 'aliquo casu' 'existere potuerit[25]. ideoque si quis aut noluerit he-'res esse, aut vivo testatore aut post mortem eius 'antequam hereditatem adiret decesserit, aut condi-'cione, sub qua heres institutus est, defectus sit, 'in-'his' casibus pater familias intestatus moritur: nam 'et prius testamentum non valet ruptum a posteriore 'et posterius aeque nullas vires habet, cum ex eo 'nemo heres extiterit.' [26]Sed si quis priore testa-mento iure 'perfecto' posterius aeque iure fecerit, etiamsi ex certis rebus in eo heredem instituerit, superius testamentum sublatum esse divi Severus et Antoninus rescripserunt. cuius constitutionis inseri verba 'iussi-mus[27], cum aliud quoque praeterea in ea constitu-tione expressum est. 'Imperatores Severus et An-'toninus Cocceio Campano. Testamentum secundo 'loco factum, licet in eo certarum rerum heres scri-'ptus sit, iure valere, perinde ac si rerum mentio facta 'non esset, sed teneri heredem scriptum, ut conten-'tus rebus sibi datis aut suppleta quarta ex lege Fal-'cidia hereditatem restituat his, qui in priore testa-'mento scripti fuerant, propter inserta verba secundo 'testamento, quibus ut valeret prius testamentum ex-'pressum est, dubitari non oportet.' 'et ruptum qui-'dem testamentum hoc modo efficitur'. [28]'Alio quo-'que modo testamenta iure facta infirmantur, veluti 'cum is qui fecit testamentum capite deminutus sit. quod quibus modis accidit, primo libro rettulimus[32]. [28]'Hoc autem casu irrita fieri testamenta dicuntur, 'cum alioquin et quae rumpuntur irrita fiant et quae 'statim ab initio non iure fiunt irrita sunt: et[29] ea, 'quae iure facta sunt[30], postea[31] propter capitis demi-'nutionem irrita fiunt, possumus nihilo minus rupta 'dicere. sed quia sane commodius erat singulas cau-

---

(1) significat *libri*   (2) *cf. Dig.* 28, 5, 42   (3) *sic B Dig.*, titus *TC,* Πιος (*al.* Ἀντωνινος) Θ
   (4) *Cf. Gai.* 2, 179..184 *Dig.* 28, 6 *Cod.* 6, 26   (5) *Gai.* 2, 179. 180   (6) moribus] *T*ªΘ, a maioribus *B*   (7) *Cod.* 6, 26, 9   (8) *Gai.* 2, 180   (9) *sic P,* subicietur *B,* subicitur *E*   (10) *Gai.* 2, 181   (11) *sic P cum Gaio,* signare *BE*   (12) *Gai.* 2, 182. 183   (13) et *om. dett. cum Gaio* (14) § 6 *ex Flor. l.* 10 *inst.* (*Dig.* 28, 6, 37)   (15) *sic PE*Θ, impuberibus *B*

(16) quisquis] *B,* ut quisquis *PE,* patri *PE*   (17) mihi] *B,* et] *BP*Θ, ei *E*   (19) *Gai.* 2, 184 (20) *sic T*ᵇ *Gai.* Θ, pubere herede *BT*ᵃ   (21) 2, 23
   (22) *Cf. Gai.* 2, 138..151 *Dig.* 28, 3   (23) *Gai.* 2, 138 (24) *Gai.* 2, 144   (25) *sic Gai.,* poterit *BT*   (26) § 3 *ex Marciani l.* 4 *inst.* (*Dig.* 36, 1, 30)   (27) inseri verba iussimus] *B,* verba inscrimus *T*   (28) *Gai.* 2, 145. 146 (29) sint: sed *et scr.*   (30) sunt *del.*   (31) postea] *T,* om. *B, deficit Gai. Veron.*   (32) 1, 16

nor another through him'; // but where the testator does think him independent their effect is 'If he does not take the estate himself, nor any other within whose authority he hereafter passes.' Tiberius Caesar decided this in the case of his slave Parthenius.

2.16 SUBSTITUTES FOR CHILDREN

A testator who has a young child within his authority can draft one of these ordinary substitutions for him: 'If he does not become my heir, let so and so be heir'. But he can also put in a substitute in case the child becomes heir but dies before puberty, in effect: 'Let my son Titius be my heir. If he does not become my heir or if being heir he dies before taking control of his own affairs (meaning before puberty) let Seius be heir.' Here if the son fails to become heir the substitute comes in as the father's heir; if the son does become heir but dies in childhood the substitute takes as the son's heir. The father thus makes a will for him to cover the time while he is too young to make one for himself. This was introduced simply by practice. 1. The good sense of it has led to a pronouncement in our Codex providing that those with insane children, grandchildren or great grandchildren, of either sex and any degree, may nominate people as substitutes for them even when adult, on the model of the substitution for children; and that, on the same model, the substitution should cease to operate if they recover their sanity, as one for a child drops away at puberty. 2. Where these substitutions for children are encountered there are in a sense two wills, the father's and the son's, as though the son had appointed an heir himself. Alternatively there is one will with double contents, namely the two estates. 3. Any testator worried that after his death an open substitution may expose his young son to foul play should make an ordinary substitution publicly in the top part of the will and then at the back, sewn up and sealed independently, should make the substitution for his son's becoming heir but dying in childhood. He should provide in the first part that the other must remain sealed so long as the son lives and remains under age. Obviously the nomination of a substitute for the boy is equally valid if done all in one document along with the appointment of his father's own heir. But to do it that way is dangerous for the child. 4. By one of these substitutions against death in childhood the head of the family can impose any heir on a child appointed as his own heir. He can also do it for a child whom his will disinherits. The effect is to pass all the boy's acquisitions – inheritances, legacies and gifts from his relatives and friends – to the substitute. These rules about grafting substitutions for children on to appointments and exclusions also apply to posthumous issue. 5. Nobody can make a will for his children except in making one for himself. The will for the child is part and parcel of the parent's own. If the parent's will is not valid the other falls too. 6. The substitution can be made for every child or only for the last to reach puberty – for every child where the testator wants to displace the rules of intestacy for all of them, for only the youngest when he is content to let the statutory rules to operate between them. 7. The substitute can be appointed specifically – 'Titius' – or generally – 'Whoever is then my heir'. The latter words let into the dead boy's place those who were appointed and did become my heirs, in proportion to their original shares. 8. Substitutions can be made for boys up to fourteen, girls up to twelve. At that age, the substitution falls away. 9. Substitutions cannot be grafted on the appointment of an outside heir or of a son above puberty so as to let in another heir if the appointee becomes heir but dies within a given time. But a testator is allowed to impose a trust on such an heir to make him transfer all or part of the estate to someone else. We will deal with trusts later.

2.17 WILLS: SUPERVENING INVALIDITY

A properly made will remains valid until it is nullified or frustrated. 1. It is nullified where the will is is deprived of legal effect despite the testator's status remaining unchanged. Suppose that after making his will the testator adopts a son, by imperial grant if the adoptee is independent or by the praetorian procedure as approved in our legislation if he is not. Here the will is nullified. It is destroyed, just as if a new immediate heir had been born. 2. Also, a later will, properly made, nullifies an earlier one. It does not matter whether an heir actually takes under it or not, since the only relevant question is whether an heir could ever do so. Suppose he declines, or he dies before the testator, or he dies after the testator but before he can accept the estate, or a condition of his appointment fails. The head of this family dies intestate: his earlier will is invalid, nullified by the later; and the later will is ineffective because it produces no heir. 3. Suppose a testator makes a will which is perfectly good and then follows it with another, also good but appointing an heir only to certain items. Here too the first will goes. This is in a written reply of the Emperors Severus and Antoninus. We have required its words to be set out because it also carries the point a step further: 'The Emperors Severus and Antoninus in reply to Cocceius Campanus. There can be no doubt that the second will, even though it covers only a part of the property, takes effect in law, just as if it had not been restricted. The heir must either be content with what is actually left him or claim his supplemented quarter under the Falcidian Act. He must then hand over the rest of the estate to those appointed under the previous will. This is because the express wording of the second will shows that the testator intended the first to take effect.' Even a will that has been nullified can in this way have some effect. 4. Another way in which a will, good when made, can become invalid is by the testator's status-loss. We discussed this in Book 1. 5. In this case the will is said to be frustrated, though nullified wills could equally be referred to as frustrated, as could those bad from the beginning. Similarly wills which are good as made but are frustrated by status-loss could also be described as nullified. // All the same, because it is useful to have

'sas singulis appellationibus distingui, ideo quaedam
'non iure facta dicuntur, quaedam iure facta rumpi
6 (5) 'vel irrita fieri: [1]Non tamen per omnia inutilia
'sunt ea testamenta, quae ab initio iure facta 'propter
'capitis deminutionem' irrita facta sunt. nam si septem
'testium signis signata sunt, potest scriptus heres se-
'cundum tabulas testamenti bonorum possessionem
'agnoscere', si modo defunctus et civis Romanus et
'suae potestatis mortis tempore fuerit: nam si ideo
'irritum factum sit testamentum, quod civitatem vel
'etiam libertatem testator amisit, aut quia in adoptio-
'nem se dedit et mortis tempore in adoptivi patris
'potestate sit, non potest scriptus heres secundum
7 (6) 'tabulas bonorum possessionem petere. [2]Ex
'eo autem solo non potest infirmari testamentum, quod
'postea testator id noluit valere: usque adeo ut' et,
'si quis post factum prius testamentum posterius fa-
'cere coeperit et aut mortalitate praeventus, aut quia
'eum eius rei paenituit, id[3] non perfecisset, divi Per-
'tinacis oratione cautum est, ne alias tabulae priores
'iure factae irritae fiant, nisi sequentes iure ordina-
'tae et perfectae[4] fuerint. nam imperfectum testa-
8 (7) 'mentum sine dubio nullum est. Eadem oratione expressit non admissurum se hereditatem eius,
qui litis causa principem heredem reliquerit, neque
tabulas non legitime factas, in quibus ipse ob eam
causam heres institutus erat, probaturum neque ex
nuda voce heredis nomen admissurum neque ex ulla
scriptura, cui iuris auctoritas desit, aliquid adeptu-
rum. secundum haec divi quoque Severus et Antoninus saepissime rescripserunt: 'licet enim' inquiunt
'legibus soluti sumus, attamen legibus vivimus'.

XVIII[5]
DE INOFFICIOSO TESTAMENTO

    Quia plerumque parentes sine causa liberos suos
vel exheredant vel omittunt, inductum est, ut de inofficioso testamento agere possint liberi, qui querun-
tur aut inique se exheredatos aut inique praeteritos,
'hoc colore, quasi non sanae mentis fuerunt, cum
testamentum ordinarent. sed hoc dicitur, non quasi
vere furiosus sit, sed recte quidem fecit testamentum, non autem ex officio pietatis: nam si vere fu-
1 riosus est, nullum est testamentum. Non tantum
autem liberis permissum est parentum testamentum
inofficiosum accusare, verum etiam[7] parentibus liberorum. 'soror autem et frater turpibus personis scri-
'ptis heredibus ex sacris constitutionibus[8] praelati sunt:
'non ergo contra omnes heredes agere possunt. ultra
'fratres et sorores cognati nullo modo aut agere pos-
2 'sunt aut agentes vincere'. Tam autem naturales
liberi, quam 'secundum nostrae constitutionis[9] divisionem' adoptati ita demum de inofficioso testamento
agere possunt, si nullo alio iure ad bona defuncti
venire possunt. nam qui alio iure veniunt ad totam
hereditatem vel partem eius, de inofficioso agere non
possunt. postumi quoque, qui nullo alio iure venire
3 possunt, de inofficioso agere possunt. 'Sed haec
'ita accipienda sunt, si nihil eis penitus a testatori-
'bus testamento relictum est. quod nostra constitutio[10]
'ad verecundiam naturae introduxit. sin vero quanta-
'cumque pars hereditatis vel res eis fuerit relicta, de
'inofficiosi querela quiescente id quod eis deest usque
'ad quartam legitimae partis repletur, licet non fuerit
4 'adiectum boni viri arbitratu debere eam repleri'. Si
tutor nomine pupilli, cuius tutelam gerebat, ex testamento patris ius legatum acceperit, cum nihil erat
ipsi tutori relictum a patre suo, nihilo minus possit
nomine suo de inofficioso patris testamento agere.
5 Sed et si e contrario pupilli nomine, cui nihil re-

lictum fuerit, de inofficioso egerit et superatus est,
ipse quod sibi in eodem testamento legatum relictum
6 est non amittit. Igitur quartam quis debet habere, ut de inofficioso testamento agere non possit:
sive iure hereditario sive iure legati vel fideicommissi,
'vel si mortis causa ei quarta donata fuerit, vel inter
'vivos in his tantummodo casibus, quorum nostra
'constitutio mentionem facit, vel aliis modis qui con-
7 'stitutionibus continentur'. Quod autem de quarta
diximus, ita intellegendum est, ut, sive unus fuerit
sive plures, quibus agere de inofficioso testamento
permittitur, una quarta eis dari possit, ut pro rata
distribuatur eis, id est pro virili portione quarta.

XIX[11]
DE HEREDUM QUALITATE ET DIFFERENTIA.

    [12]'Heredes autem aut necessarii dicuntur aut sui et
1 'necessarii aut extranei. Necessarius heres est
'servus heres institutus: ideo sic appellatus[13], quia,
'sive velit sive nolit, omnimodo post mortem testa-
'toris protinus liber et necessarius[14] heres fit. unde
'qui facultates suas suspectas habent, solent servum
'suum primo aut secundo vel etiam ulteriore gradu
'heredem instituere, ut, si creditoribus satis non fiat,
'potius eius heredis bona quam ipsius testatoris' 'a
'creditoribus possideantur vel distrahantur vel inter
'eos dividantur'. 'pro hoc tamen incommodo illud ei
'commodum praestatur, ut ea, quae post mortem pa-
'troni sui sibi adquisierit, ipsi reserventur: et quam-
'vis 'non sufficiant[15] bona defuncti creditoribus', ite-
'rum ex 'ea' causa 'res eius, quas sibi adquisierit', non
2 'veneunt. [16]Sui autem et necessarii heredes sunt
'veluti filius filia nepos neptisque ex filio et deinceps
'ceteri 'liberi', qui modo in potestate morientis fue-
'rint. sed ut nepos neptisve sui heredes sint, non
'sufficit eum eamve in potestate avi mortis tempore
'fuisse, sed opus est, ut pater eius vivo patre suo
'desierit suus heres esse aut morte interceptus aut
'qualibet alia ratione liberatus potestate: tunc enim
'nepos neptisve in locum patris sui succedit. sed sui
'quidem heredes ideo appellantur, quia domestici he-
'redes sunt et vivo quoque patre quodammodo domini
'existimantur. unde etiam, si quis intestatus mortuus
'sit, prima causa est in successione liberorum. ne-
'cessarii vero ideo dicuntur, quia omnimodo, sive
'velint sive nolint, tam ab intestato quam ex testa-
'mento heredes fiunt. sed his praetor permittit vo-
'lentibus abstinere se ab hereditate, ut potius paren-
'tis 'quam ipsorum' bona 'similiter a creditoribus pos-
'sideantur'.
3   [17]'Ceteri, qui testatoris iuri subiecti non sunt,
'extranei heredes appellantur. itaque liberi quoque
'nostri, qui in potestate nostra non sunt, heredes a
'nobis instituti extranei heredes videntur. qua de
'causa et qui heredes a matre instituuntur, eodem
'numero sunt, quia feminae in potestate liberos non
'habent. servus quoque a domino heres institutus et
'post testamentum factum ab eo manumissus eodem
4 'numero habetur.' [18]In extraneis heredibus illud
observatur, ut sit cum eis testamenti factio, sive ipsi
heredes instituantur sive hi qui in potestate eorum
sunt. et id duobus temporibus inspicitur, testamenti
quidem facti, ut constiterit institutio, mortis vero
testatoris, ut effectum habeat. hoc amplius et cum
adit hereditatem, esse debet cum eo testamenti factio,
sive pure sive sub condicione heres institutus sit:
nam ius heredis eo vel maxime tempore inspiciendum
est, quo[19] adquirit hereditatem. medio autem tempore inter factum testamentum et mortem testatoris
vel condicionem institutionis existentem mutatio iuris

---

(1) *Gai.* 2, 147   (2) *Gai.* 2, 151   (3) *sic scripsi sec.* Θ, peni-
tui •• set id *T*[a], penituit se id *T*[b], id *om.* B   (4) *sic* BΘ,
factae *T*

   (5) *Cf. Dig.* 5, 2 *Cod.* 3, 28   (6) *pr. fin. ex Marciani
l.* 4 *inst.* (*Dig.* 5, 2, 2)   (7) etiam et *BT*   (8) *Cod.*
3, 28, 27   (9) *Cod.* 8, 47, 10   (10) *Cod.* 3, 28, 30

   (11) *Cf. Gai.* 2, 152..173 *Dig.* 29, 2 *Cod.* 6, 30. 31   (12) *Gai.*
2, 152..155   (13) *sic dett. Gai.* Θ, appellatur *BT*   (14) ne-
cess. tuetur Θ, *om. Gai.*   (15) sufficiunt*BT*   (16) *Gai.* 2,
156. 158   (17) *Gai.* 2, 161   (18) § 4 *in. ex Flor. l.* 10 *inst.*
(*Dig.* 28, 5, 50. § 1)   (19) quod *BT*[a]

different terms for different things, we say some are invalid as made, others nullified, and others frustrated. 6.(5) Wills which are valid as made and then frustrated by a status-loss are not absolutely ineffective for all purposes. If the will bears the seals of seven witnesses the appointed heir can claim estate-possession in support of the will. There are conditions: the deceased must have been a Roman citizen and independent at the time of his death. If the will was frustrated by a status-loss which deprived the testator of citizenship or liberty as well, or which happened because he was adopted and at the time of his death was within the authority of his adoptive father, the appointee cannot seek estate-possession in support of the will. 7.(6) A will does not become invalid merely because the testator wants to rescind it. Suppose a testator has made one will and then begins to make a second but does not finish it, either because death overtakes him or because he changes his mind. There is an address of the Emperor Pertinax which provides that once the first will has been effectively executed it is not frustrated until the second has been validly drawn up and completed. An incomplete will is certainly a nullity. 8.(7) In the same address he said that he would not allow himself to accept an estate from anyone who made the emperor his heir to improve his prospects in litigation; he would not uphold improperly executed testamentary documents naming him as heir with a view to the same end; he would not accept nomination as heir by mere word of mouth; and he would not take any benefit at all from any document insufficient in law. In similar vein are many written replies of the Emperors Severus and Antoninus: 'Although we stand above the law,' they say, 'we live by it.'

2.18 IRRESPONSIBLE WILLS

Heads of families often disinherit or omit their children without good reason. Those aggrieved at being unfairly cut out or passed over are allowed the complaint of an irresponsible will. The form of this is that the balance of the testator's mind was disturbed when he made his will. But the suggestion is not that he really was insane, rather that in making an otherwise valid will he failed to keep his mind on his family responsibilities. The will of someone really insane is of course a nullity. 1. The right to complain of an irresponsible will is not only given to children against parents but also vice versa. A brother or sister is allowed to challenge disreputable appointees. That is laid down in imperial pronouncements. They cannot go against every type of heir. Relatives remoter than brother or sister cannot sue, or if they do cannot win. 2. Real children and adopted children covered by our pronouncement can make this complaint provided they have no other claim to some of the deceased's property. Those who have some other right to all or part of the estate can never bring the complaint of an irresponsible will. Posthumous children too may use this claim if they have no other. 3. That must be construed as meaning they can do so if the testator made no provision for them in the will. Our pronouncement on this subject maintains respect for natural ties. If some part – however small – of the estate or its contents is left to someone in the will, he cannot bring the complaint of irresponsibility. Instead he can claim supplementation to a quarter of his entitlement on intestacy. This supplementation, worked out by the standards of the reasonable man, is an automatic right, not dependent on the intention of the testator. 4. Suppose a guardian administering a ward's affairs is given a legacy for the child in his own father's will. This does not bar him from challenging his father's will for irresponsibility, since his father left him nothing

for himself. 5. Again, suppose the child is left nothing and has a claim for irresponsibility which the guardian makes and loses. This defeat does not forfeit a legacy left to himself under the will. 6. The bar to a complaint for irresponsibility is receipt of your quarter entitlement. It can come to you as heir, legatee, beneficiary under a trust, donee in contemplation of death, or – though here only in the cases specified in our pronouncement – as donee inter vivos, or in any other way specified in imperial pronouncements. 7. Our references to the quarter share are to be taken in this way: whether there is one person in the category allowed to make the complaint of irresponsibility or more than one, it is enough to give a single quarter for proportionate division between them. That works out at one quarter of the intestate entitlement for each claimant.

2.19 TYPES OF HEIR

There are compulsory heirs, immediate and compulsory heirs, and outside heirs. 1. A slave appointee is a compulsory heir, so called because the testator's death automatically makes him free and and compels him to be heir whether he likes it or not. People who doubt their solvency make an appointment in the first or second tier, or lower down, to one of their slaves. If the creditors' claims cannot be met, it is then his property and not the testator's which is seized, sold up or divided by the creditors. A plus compensates him for this minus: acquisitions after his patron's death are his and, even if the property of the deceased cannot meet the creditors' claims, the wealth he acquires for himself is immune from a second sale on the same account. 2. The immediate and compulsory heirs are the sons and daughters, also grandchildren through a son and so on down the line, who were within the authority of the deceased on his deathbed. But grandchildren do not qualify on that condition alone; their father must have vacated the position of immediate heir in his father's lifetime, either through death or through some other discharge from paternal authority. It is then that the grandchild steps into his father's place. These heirs are called immediately the testator's own because they come from inside the family and are in a certain sense thought of as owners even while their father is alive. That is why, in the event of intestacy, these descendants have the first entitlement. They are called compulsory because they have no choice in the matter: whether there is a will or not, they become heirs automatically. But, to deflect creditors to the father's estate rather than to their own, the praetor gave them a right to stand off from the estate. 3. All other heirs, not being within the testator's authority, are called outsiders. The appointment of one of our own children, if outside our authority, makes even him an outside heir; the same with every appointment by a mother, since women never have children within their authority. If an owner appoints a slave and then frees him after making the will, he too is an outside heir. 4. With an outsider a matter to watch is whether there is testamentary capacity in relation to him. Sometimes he is the actual appointee, sometimes the appointed heir is a person in his authority. Capacity has first to be tested at two points, at the making of the will in order to validate the appointment, and at the death to give it effect. Then a third time: whether the appointment is absolute or conditional, the testamentary capacity must hold good when the estate is accepted. The heir's position must be examined with special care at the time when he acquires. He is not affected by changes in the legal position between the making of the will and the death or falling in of a condition of the appointment. // The reason is that

heredi non nocet, quia ut diximus tria tempora inspici debent[1]. testamenti autem factionem non solum
is habere videtur, qui testamentum facere potest, sed
etiam qui ex alieno testamento vel ipse capere potest vel alii adquirere, licet non potest facere testamentum. [2]et ideo et[3] furiosus et mutus et postumus et infans et filius familias et servus alienus testamenti factionem habere dicuntur: 'licet enim testamentum facere non possunt, attamen ex testamento
5 'vel sibi vel alii adquirere possunt'. [4]'Extraneis
'autem heredibus deliberandi potestas est de adeunda
'hereditate vel non adeunda. sed sive is, cui absti-
'nendi potestas est, immiscuerit se bonis heredita-
'riis[5], sive 'extraneus', cui de adeunda hereditate de-
'liberare licet, adierit, postea relinquendae hereditatis
'facultatem non habet, nisi minor sit annis viginti
'quinque: nam huius aetatis hominibus sicut in cete-
'ris omnibus causis deceptis, ita et si temere dam-
'nosam hereditatem susceperint, praetor succurrit.
6 'Sciendum tamen est divum Hadrianum etiam maiori
'viginti quinque annis veniam dedisse, cum post adi-
'tam hereditatem grande aes alienum, quod aditae
'hereditatis tempore latebat', emersisset. 'sed hoc di-
'vus quidem Hadrianus speciali beneficio cuidam prae-
'stitit: divus autem Gordianus postea in militibus
(6) 'tantummodo hoc extendit: sed nostra benevolen-
'tia commune omnibus subiectis imperio nostro hoc
'praestavit beneficium et constitutionem tam aequissi-
'mam quam nobilem scripsit[6], cuius tenorem si ob-
'servaverint homines, licet eis adire hereditatem et in
'tantum teneri, in[7] quantum valere bona hereditatis
'contingit[8]: ut ex hac causa neque deliberationis
'auxilium eis fiat necessarium, nisi omissa observa-
'tione nostrae constitutionis et deliberandum existi-
'maverint et sese veteri gravamini aditionis suppone-
7 'maluerint. Item extraneus' [9]'heres 'testamento' in-
'stitutus aut ab intestato 'ad legitimam hereditatem'
'vocatus potest aut pro herede gerendo vel etiam
'nuda voluntate suscipiendae hereditatis heres fieri.'
pro herede autem gerere quis videtur, si rebus hereditariis tamquam heres utatur vel vendendo res hereditarias aut praedia colendo locandove et quoquo
modo si voluntatem suam declaret vel re vel verbis
de adeunda hereditate, dummodo sciat eum, in cuius
bonis pro herede gerit, testato intestatove obiisse et
se ei heredem esse. pro herede enim gerere est pro
domino gerere: veteres enim heredes pro dominis
appellabant. [10]'sicut autem nuda voluntate 'extraneus'
'heres fit, ita et contraria destinatione statim ab he-
'reditate repellitur.' eum, qui mutus vel surdus natus
est vel postea factus, nihil prohibet pro herede gerere et adquirere sibi hereditatem, si tamen intellegit
quod agitur.

XX [11]
DE LEGATIS.

[12]'Post haec videamus de legatis. quae pars iuris
'extra propositam quidem materiam videtur: nam
'loquimur de his iuris figuris, quibus per universita-
'tem res nobis adquiruntur. sed cum omnino de
'testamentis deque heredibus qui testamento insti-
'tuuntur locuti sumus, non sine causa sequenti loco
'potest haec iuris materia tractari.'
1 Legatum itaque est donatio quaedam a defuncto
2 relicta. 'Sed olim quidem erant legatorum genera
'quattuor: per vindicationem, per damnationem, si-
'nendi modo, per praeceptionem: et certa quaedam
'verba cuique generi legatorum adsignata erant, per
'quae singula genera legatorum significabantur. sed
'ex constitutionibus divorum principum [13] sollemnitas

huiusmodi verborum penitus sublata est. nostra autem
'constitutio [14], quam cum magna fecimus lucubratione,
'defunctorum voluntates validiores esse cupientes et
'non verbis, sed voluntatibus eorum faventes, dispo-
'suit, ut omnibus legatis una sit natura et, qui-
'buscumque verbis aliquid derelictum sit, liceat le-
'gatariis id persequi non solum per actiones per-
'sonales, sed etiam per in rem et per hypothecariam:
'cuius constitutionis perpensum modum ex ipsius te-
3 'nore perfectissime accipere possibile est. Sed
'non usque ad eam constitutionem standum esse ex-
'istimavimus. cum enim antiquitatem invenimus legata
'quidem stricte concludentem, fideicommissis autem,
'quae ex voluntate magis descendebant defunctorum,
'pinguiorem naturam indulgentem: necessarium esse
'duximus [15] omnia legata fideicommissis exaequare,
'ut nulla sit inter ea differentia, sed quod deest lega-
'tis, hoc repleatur ex natura fideicommissorum et, si
'quid amplius est in legatis, per hoc crescat fidei-
'commissi natura. sed ne in primis legum cunabilis
'permixte de his exponendo studiosis adulescentibus
'quandam introducamus difficultatem, operae pretium
'esse duximus interim separatim prius de legatis et
'postea de fideicommissis tractare, ut natura utrius-
'que iuris cognita facile possint permixtionem eorum
'eruditi suptilioribus auribus accipere.'
4   Non solum autem testatoris vel heredis res, sed
et aliena legari potest: ita ut heres cogatur redimere
eam et praestare vel, si non potest redimere, aestimationem eius dare. sed si talis res sit, cuius non
est commercium, nec aestimatio eius debetur, sicuti
si [16] campum Martium vel basilicas vel templa vel
quae publico usui destinata sunt legaverit: nam nullius momenti legatum est. quod autem diximus alienam rem posse legari, ita intellegendum est, si defunctus sciebat alienam rem esse, non et [17] si ignorabat: forsitan enim, si scisset alienam, non legasset.
et ita divus Pius rescripsit. [18]et verius est [19] ipsum
qui agit, id est legatarium, probare oportere scisse
alienam rem legare [20] defunctum, non heredem probare oportere ignorasse alienam, quia semper neces-
5 sitas probandi incumbit illi qui agit. Sed et si
rem obligatam creditori aliquis legaverit, necesse habet heres luere. et hoc quoque casu idem placet,
quod in re aliena, ut ita demum luere necesse habeat heres, si sciebat defunctus rem obligatam esse:
et ita divi Severus et Antoninus rescripserunt. si
tamen defunctus voluit legatarium luere et hoc ex-
6 pressit, non debet heres eam luere. Si res aliena
legata fuerit et eius vivo testatore legatarius dominus factus fuerit, si quidem ex causa emptionis, ex
testamento actione pretium consequi potest: si vero
ex causa lucrativa, veluti ex donatione vel ex alia
simili causa, agere non potest. nam traditum est
duas lucrativas causas in eundem hominem et in
eandem rem concurrere non posse. hac ratione si
ex duobus testamentis eadem res eidem debeatur,
interest, utrum rem an aestimationem ex testamento
consecutus est: nam si rem, agere non potest, quia [21]
habet eam ex causa lucrativa, si aestimationem, agere
7 potest   [22]'Ea quoque res, quae in rerum natura
'non est, si modo futura est, 'recte legatur', veluti
'fructus qui in illo fundo nati erunt, aut quod ex
8 'illa ancilla natum erit.' Si eadem res duobus
legata sit sive coniunctim sive disiunctim, si ambo
perveniant ad legatum, scinditur inter eos legatum:
si alter deficiat, quia aut spreverit legatum aut vivo
testatore decesserit aut alio quolibet modo defecerit,
totum ad collegatarium pertinet. coniunctim autem
legatur veluti si quis dicat 'Titio et Seio hominem
'Stichum do lego': disiunctim ita 'Titio hominem

---

(1) *sic B*, inspici deberent *T*, inspicimus *Dig. Θ*   (2) § 4
fin. similis Dig. 28, 1, 16 *pr.* (*Pomp. l. sing. reg.*)   (3) et]
BΘ, om. T   (4) *Gai.* 2, 162. 163   (5) *sic Gai.*, hereditatis *libri*   (6) *Cod.* 6. 30, 22   (7) in] *PEΘ*,
om. B   (8) *sic PEΘ*, contigit *B*   (9) *Gai.* 2, 167
(10) *Gai.* 2, 168. 169

(11) *Cf. Gai.* 2, 191..223. 229..245 *Dig.* 30..32 *Cod.* 6, 37. 43
(12) *Gai.* 2, 191   (13) *Cod.* 6, 37, 21   (14) *Cod.* 6, 43, 1
(15) *Cod.* 6, 43, 2   (16) si *om. BT*   (17) et] *B, om. T*
(18) § 4 *fin. ex Marciani l.* 6 *inst.* (*Dig.* 22, 3, 21)
(19) est] *T cum Θ*, esse *B*   (20) *sic B Dig.*, legasse *T*,
(21) quia] *T*, qui *B*   (22) *Gai.* 2, 203

only three times are critical, as we have said. This requirement of testamentary capacity is satisfied not only in a person who can make a will but in one who can take for himself or another under a will but not make one of his own. A person qualifies even if insane, dumb, or posthumous; or a baby; or a dependant, free or unfree. Though these people cannot make wills, they can take by will, for themselves or for others. 5. Outsiders have a choice whether to accept the estate or not. If an heir with a right to decline meddles in the estate, or an outsider entitled to take time to think it over does accept, he loses the power to renounce. The exception is someone under twenty-five. The praetor relieves people under that age who rashly accept a debt-ridden inheritance, just as he helps them when they make mistakes in all other contexts. 6. But it is essential to note that the Emperor Hadrian absolved even someone over twenty-five when large debts appeared which lay hidden at the time of his acceptance. For Hadrian this was an individual favour. The Emperor Gordian later generalized it but only to soldiers (6) We in our concern for the general welfare have extended the privilege to everyone in the empire by a pronouncement which is both just and admirable. Keeping to its terms a person can accept an inheritance with liability limited to the value realizable from the estate. This means that an heir does not need time to think except where the conditions of our pronouncement are not met and he decides to take his time and face the liabilities of acceptance under the old law. 7. An outsider appointed by will or inheriting on intestacy can become heir by acting as heir or merely by showing an intention to accept the estate. You act as heir if you behave towards the assets of the estate as though you were heir, selling them, cultivating the land or letting it, and by doing or saying anything which shows that you intend to accept the estate. If this conduct is to be decisive you must be aware that the owner of the property has died testate or intestate and believe that you are his heir. Acting as heir is acting as owner. In fact in the old days the word for heir signified owner. Just as an outside appointee makes himself heir simply by coming to that decision, so a decision against accepting makes for an immediate exclusion from the estate. Provided he understands what he is doing, a person who is dumb or deaf, whether born with the disability or overtaken by it, can perfectly well accept an estate by acting as heir.

2.20 LEGACIES

We turn next to legacies. This might appear to be a digression from our theme, namely the rules on acquisition of entire estates. But the discussion has been all about wills and heirs appointed under wills. That justifies going on to legacies. 1. A legacy is a gift left by someone who has died. 2. There used to be four kinds: proprietary, obligatory, permissive, and preceptive. Special forms of words were reserved for each kind, one set of words serving to identify a single type of legacy. But these formalities were abolished by imperial legislation. Our own pronouncement, to which we devoted long hours in the effort to give better effect to the deceased's wishes and to respect his intention rather than his words, has laid down that all legacies should be

of one kind and that legatees, whatever the wording of the bequest, should be able to sue by personal action, and real action, and the action on a mortgage. The care taken in drafting this enactment can best be gathered from its actual words. 3. We thought it wrong to stop at the point reached in that pronouncement. We found that the old approach had been to construe legacies very tightly but that trusts, more directly based on the deceased's intention, were generously interpreted. We concluded that it was essential to assimilate legacies and trusts, to eliminate the differences between them, and to bring to the weaknesses of each the strengths of the other. However, if we were to fuse the accounts of both of these here, when we are trying to create a framework of first principle, our cradle of the law, we might confuse young students. To avoid this we have decided that it is best for the time being to deal first with legacies and then separately with trusts. Later, when he has learned the basic rules, the student will easily be able to cope with their fusion. By then he will have a subtler understanding. 4. A testator can give a legacy not only of his own property or his heir's but also of a third party's. This is done by obliging the heir to buy the thing and hand it over or, if he cannot get it, to pay its value. If the legacy is of something excluded from private dealing, the heir is under no obligation to pay its value – e.g. a public place of assembly like the Campus Martius, a public building, a church, or something else reserved for public use. Such a legacy is a nullity. To say that a testator can bequeath property which is a third party's means he can if he knows; not if he does not. In the latter case perhaps he would have withheld it had he known the truth. There is a written reply of the Emperor Pius to that effect. The law is that it is for the claimant, i.e. the legatee, to prove the deceased knew, not for the heir to prove he did not. The onus of proof always lies on the party claiming. 5. If the legacy is of property charged to a creditor, the heir must redeem it. The same rule applies as with things belonging to a third party: the heir need only redeem if the deceased knew the thing was charged. That was decided in a reply of the Emperors Severus and Antoninus. If the deceased intended and said that the legatee should redeem, the heir is under no obligation to do it. 6. Suppose property of a third party is bequeathed and then, before the testator dies, the legatee becomes its owner. If he bought it, he can sue on the will for the price; if it was a case of straight gain, for instance a gift or something like that, he has no claim. The rule is that a man cannot take two gratuitous bites at the same thing. The logic of this is that if one thing is left to a legatee under two wills the critical question is whether he has obtained the actual thing under one of the wills or only its value. If the actual thing, since he has it, and gratuitously, he cannot sue again; if the value, he can. 7. A legacy of non-existent things is valid if they are likely to come into being, as crops from that land, or the offspring of that slave-woman. If one thing is left to two people, jointly or severally, and both claim it, it is shared between them. If rejection of the legacy, death before the testator, or some other obstacle prevents one of them coming forward, the other gets it all. A joint example is 'I give and bequeath the slave Stichus to Titius and Seius.' A several example is 'I give and bequeath the slave Stichus to Titius. I give and bequeath Stichus to Seius.'

'Stichum do lego, Seio Stichum do lego'. sed et[1] si expresserit 'eundem hominem Stichum', aeque dis-
9 iunctim legatum intellegitur. Si cui fundus alienus legatus fuerit et emerit proprietatem detracto[2]
usu fructu et usus fructus ad eum pervenerit et
postea ex testamento agat, recte eum agere 'et fundum petere' Iulianus[3] ait, 'quia usus fructus in petitione servitutis locum optinet[4]: sed officio iudicis contineri, 'ut deducto usu fructu iubeat aestimationem
10 praestari'[5]. Sed si rem legatam quis ei legaverit,
inutile legatum est, quia quod proprium est ipsius,
amplius eius fieri non potest: et licet alienaverit
11 eam, non debetur nec ipsa nec aestimatio eius. Si
quis rem suam quasi alienam legaverit, valet legatum: nam plus valet, quod in veritate est, quam
quod in opinione. sed et si legatarii putavit, valere
constat, quia exitum voluntas defuncti potest habere.
12 Si rem suam legaverit testator posteaque eam
alienaverit, Celsus existimat, si non adimendi animo
vendidit, nihilo minus deberi, idque divi Severus et
Antoninus rescripserunt. idem rescripserunt[6] eum,
qui post testamentum factum praedia quae legata
erant pignori dedit, ademisse legatum non videri et
ideo legatarium cum herede agere posse, ut praedia
a creditore luantur. si vero quis partem rei legatae
alienaverit, pars quae non est alienata omnimodo
debetur, pars autem alienata ita debetur, si non adi-
13 mendi animo alienata sit. Si quis debitori suo
liberationem legaverit, legatum utile est et neque ab
ipso debitore neque ab herede eius potest heres petere nec ab alio qui heredis loco est: sed et potest
a debitore conveniri, ut liberet eum. potest autem
14 quis vel ad tempus iubere, ne heres petat. Ex
contrario si debitor creditori suo quod debet legaverit, inutile est legatum, si nihil plus est in legato
quam in debito, quia nihil amplius habet per legatum. quodsi in diem vel sub condicione debitum ei
pure legaverit, utile est legatum propter repraesen-
tationem: quodsi vivo testatore dies venerit aut condicio exititerit, Papinianus scripsit[7] utile esse nihilo
minus legatum, quia semel constitit. 'quod et verum
est: non enim placuit sententia existimantium' ex-
tinctum esse legatum, quia in eam causam pervenit,
15 a qua incipere non potest. Sed si uxori maritus dotem legaverit, valet legatum, quia plenius est
legatum quam 'de dote' actio. sed si quam non acceperit dotem legaverit, divi Severus et Antoninus
rescripserunt, si quidem simpliciter legaverit, inutile
esse legatum: si vero certa pecunia[8] vel certum corpus aut instrumentum dotis in praelegando demon-
16 strata sunt, valere legatum. Si res legata sine
facto heredis perierit, legatario decedit. et si servus
alienus legatus sine facto heredis manumissus fuerit,
non tenetur heres. si vero heredis servus legatus
fuerit et ipse eum manumiserit, teneri eum Iulianus
scripsit, [9]nec interest[10], scierit an ignoraverit a se
legatum esse. sed et si alii donaverit servum et is
cui donatus[11] est eum manumiserit, tenetur heres,
17 quamvis ignoraverit a se eum legatum esse. Si
quis ancillas cum suis natis legaverit, etiamsi ancillae
mortuae fuerint, partus legato cedunt. idem est, si
ordinarii servi cum vicariis legati fuerint, ut, licet
mortui sint ordinarii, tamen vicarii legato cedant[12].
sed si servus cum peculio fuerit legatus, mortuo
servo vel manumisso vel alienato et peculii legatum
extinguitur. idem est, si fundus instructus cum
instrumento legatus fuerit: nam fundo alienato et
18 instrumenti legatum extinguitur. Si grex legatus
fuerit posteaque ad unam ovem pervenerit, quod su-
perfuerit vindicari potest. Grege autem legato etiam

eas oves, quae post testamentum factum gregi adi-
ciuntur, legato cedere Iulianus ait: esse[13] enim gregis unum corpus ex distantibus capitibus, sicuti aedium unum corpus est ex cohaerentibus lapidibus::
19 aedibus denique legatis columnas et marmora,
quae post testamentum factum adiecta sunt, legato
20 cedere. Si peculium legatum fuerit, sine dubio
quidquid peculio accedit vel decedit vivo testatore,
legatarii lucro vel damno est. quodsi post mortem
testatoris ante aditam hereditatem servus adquisierit,
Iulianus ait, si quidem ipsi manumisso peculium legatum fuerit, omne, quod ante aditam hereditatem
adquisitum est, legatario cedere, quia dies huius legati adita[14] hereditate cedit: sed si extraneo peculium legatum fuerit, non cedere ea legato, nisi ex
rebus peculiaribus auctum fuerit peculium[15]. peculium autem nisi legatum fuerit, manumisso non debetur, quamvis si vivus manumiserit, sufficit, si non
adimatur: et ita divi Severus et Antoninus rescripserunt. idem rescripserunt[22] peculio legato non videri
id relictum, ut petitionem habeat pecuniae, quam in
rationes dominicas impendit. idem rescripserunt peculium videri legatum, cum rationibus redditis liber
21 esse iussus est et ex eo reliquas inferre. Tam
autem corporales res quam incorporales legari possunt. et ideo et[16] quod defuncto debetur, potest alicui legari, ut actiones suas heres legatario praestet,
nisi exegerit vivus testator pecuniam: nam hoc casu
legatum extinguitur. sed et tale legatum valet: 'dam-
'nas[17] esto heres domum illius reficere' vel 'illum
22 'aere alieno liberare'. Si generaliter servus vel
alia res legetur, electio legatarii est, nisi aliud testa-
23 tor dixerit. Optionis legatum, 'id est ubi testa-
'tor ex servis suis vel aliis rebus optare legatarium
'iusserat, habebat in se condicionem, et ideo nisi ipse
'legatarius vivus optaverat, ad heredem legatum non
'transmittebat. sed ex constitutione nostra[18] et hoc
'in meliorem statum reformatum est et data est licen-
'tia et heredi legatarii optare, licet vivus legatarius
'hoc non fecit. et diligentiore tractatu habito et hoc
'in nostra constitutione additum est, ut, sive plures
'legatarii existant, quibus optio relicta est, et dissen-
'tiant in corpore eligendo, sive unius legatarii plures
'heredes, et inter se circa optandum dissentiant alio
'aliud corpus eligere cupiente, ne pereat legatum
'(quod plerique prudentium contra benivolentiam in-
'troducebant), fortunam esse huius optionis iudicem
'et sorte esse hoc dirimendum, ut, ad quem sors per-
'veniat, illius sententia in optione praecellat.'
24 Legari autem illis solis potest, cum quibus
25 testamenti factio est. Incertis vero personis neque legata neque fideicommissa 'olim' relinqui 'concessum erat': nam nec miles quidem incertae personae poterat relinquere, ut divus Hadrianus rescripsit. [19]'incerta autem persona videbatur, quam in
'certa opinione animo suo testator subiciebat, veluti
''si quis ita dicat': 'quicumque filio meo in matrimo-
''nium filiam suam collocaverit[20], ei heres meus illum
''fundum dato': illud quoque, quod his relinquebatur,
'qui post testamentum scriptum primi consules de-
'signati erunt, aeque incertae personae legari vide-
'batur: et denique multae aliae huiusmodi species
'sunt. libertas quoque non videbatur posse incertae
'personae dari, quia 'placebat' nominatim servos libe-
'rari. tutor quoque certus dari debebat[21]. sub certa
'vero demonstratione, 'id est ex certis personis in-
'certae personae', recte legabatur, veluti 'ex cognatis
''meis qui nunc sunt 'si quis filiam meam uxorem
''duxerit', ei heres meus 'illam rem' dato'. incertis
autem personis legata vel fideicommissa relicta et

(1) et Θ, om. libri (2) detractio B, deducto Θ (3) Dig. 30, 82 § 2 (4) '*Iustinianorum esse vidit Longo* (5) '*Iust. (Faber col-lata l.* 82 § 2 *cit.*) (6) Cod. 6, 37, 3 (7) Dig. 35, 2, 5 (*Pap. l.* 5 *resp.*) (8) sic PE, certam pecuniam B (9) § 16 *fin. ex Mar-ciani l.* 6 *inst.* (Dig. 30, 112 § 1) (10) sic W Θ Dig., interesse BPE (11) sic E[b] Dig. Θ, donatum BE[a], donatur P (12) ut ...cedant] *scripsi:* ...cedant (*om.* ut) B, et...cedunt PE (13) esse] BE[a], est PE[b] (14) adita] BP[a], ab ad P[b]E (15) pe-

culium] PE, om. B (16) et] B, om. PE (17) damnatus B (18) Cod. 6, 43, 3 (19) Gai. 2, 238...240? (20) collocaverit] Gai., de-derit id est collocaverit libri (21) tutor q. c. d. debebat] W[a] Gai., om. BPEW[b] cum Θ, qui tamen consulto ea omisisse vi-detur suae expositioni non congrua (ἀλλὰ ταῦτα πάντα κατὰ τὸ παλαιόν) neque hoc quidem loco apte retenta a compilatoribus 22) cf. Dig. 33, 8, 6 § 4

// Even if he says 'the same slave Stichus' this disposition remains several. 9. Suppose the legatee of a third party's land buys the title minus the usufruct, and then the usufruct falls to him. If he later brings his action on the will, Julian holds that he wins his claim. Here the usufruct is only treated like any other servitude. But it is part of the judge's duty to deduct the value of the usufruct from his award of the value of the land. 10. A legacy of something belonging to the legatee is a nullity. What is one's own cannot be made more so. That legatee has no claim for the thing or its value, not even if he has meanwhile conveyed it to another. 11. Suppose a legacy of property which is the testator's but which he thinks belongs to a third party. The legacy is valid. In fact it is more obviously valid objectively than as perceived. Suppose he thought it the legatee's. It is valid again, because the end-result is what he wanted. 12. If a testator bequeaths a thing of his own and later conveys it away, Celsus says it remains due to the legatee unless the conveyance was made with intent to revoke. Celsus was upheld in a written reply of the Emperors Severus and Antoninus, who added that where a testator later mortgaged land he had bequeathed he was not assumed to have revoked the legacy, and the legatee could sue the heir to redeem the land from the mortgagee. If someone alienates part of the thing bequeathed, the part kept is due to the legatee in all events, the other only if the transfer was not made with intent to revoke. 13. If a testator bequeaths to his debtor his release from the debt, the legacy is effective, and neither the heir nor anyone in his shoes can sue the debtor or the debtor's heir. The debtor can in addition sue him for his discharge. A testator can also require his heir not to sue till a given time. 14. If, the other way around, a debtor makes a bequest to his creditor of what he owes, the legacy is a nullity unless it adds something to what was due already, since the legatee otherwise gets nothing by the legacy. On the other hand if the debt is suspended for a time or against a condition, and the bequest is absolute, the legacy is valid because of the acceleration. Suppose the condition is fulfilled or the time passes before the testator dies. Papinian says the legacy, once valid, stays valid. That is right. Some thought a legacy became void if facts supervened that would have vitiated it at the outset, but that view has not prevailed. 15. If a husband leaves his wife's dowry to her, the legacy is good, because her position is stronger as legatee than under the action on dowry. However, a reply of the Emperors Severus and Antoninus makes void a legacy to her of a dowry not actually received by the husband, at least when there is nothing more to it. But if he gives her a preferential legacy which names a specific sum of money or specific item or a deed relating to the dowry, they uphold the legacy. 16. If the subject-matter perishes independently of any act done by the heir, the loss falls on the legatee. In a legacy of a slave belonging to a third party, if the slave is freed independently of anything done by the heir, the heir is not liable. But if the legacy is of the heir's own slave and the heir has freed him, Julian holds him liable, whether or not he knew the slave was covered by the legacy. Suppose he gave the slave away and the donee freed him. He is still liable, again whether he knew or not. 17. If a testator leaves a slave-woman and her offspring, the offspring pass to the legatee even if the woman is dead. Similarly with slaves of slaves: a legacy of both together carries the sub-slaves to the legatee even if the head-slaves are dead. But a legacy of a slave with his personal fund lapses even as to the fund if the slave dies or is freed or alienated. The same of a farm with its equipment: the legacy of the equipment lapses if the farm is alienated. 18. In a legacy of a flock, if its size afterwards falls to a single sheep, that one survivor can be claimed; and here Julian says that if sheep are added to the flock after the will is made they too go to the legatee. He holds that a flock is a single entity made of distinct units as a building is one entity from many stones. 19. It is certain that a legacy of a house gives the legatee columns and marble fittings added after the will was made. 20. In a legacy of a personal fund there is no doubt that additions and subtractions during the lifetime of the testator are taken and borne by the legatee. Suppose a slave makes acquisitions after the death of the testator but before the estate is accepted. Julian says that if the fund was left to the slave himself, now freed, every acquisition before the heir's acceptance falls to him as legatee, since the critical moment for such a legacy is the heir's acceptance. On the other hand, he says, if the legatee of the fund is an outsider these acquisitions are not added to the legacy unless the fund is increased by earnings from its own assets. A slave freed by will is not entitled to his personal fund unless it is given to him as a legacy, despite the fact that if freed in his master's life he would get the fund unless expressly deprived of it. This is in a written reply of the Emperors Severus and Antoninus, who also held that a legacy of the fund does not carry the right to reclaim money laid out on the master's business. They added that the fund is impliedly bequeathed if the will makes him free on rendering accounts and paying arrears. 21. There can be a legacy of corporeal or of incorporeal things. So a man can leave to another debts owed to himself, compelling his heir to assign the actions to the legatee unless he, the testator, already claimed the money before he died. If he has, the legacy becomes void. These examples are also valid: 'Let my heir be obliged to repair so and so's house' or 'to discharge so and so's debts'. 22. In the case of an open alternative between a slave and some other thing, the choice is the legatee's unless the testator says something to the contrary. 23. A legacy of a choice, i.e. where the testator requires the legatee to select from his slaves or from his other property, is inherently conditional. If the legatee died before making the choice, the right used not to pass to his heir. But a reforming pronouncement of our own has allowed the legatee's heir to make the choice if he himself fails to do so. After anxious reconsideration a further provision was added to our pronouncement. Where a number of legatees with the right to choose cannot agree what to select, and similarly where co-heirs of one legatee want to make different choices and cannot decide, to prevent failure of the legacy – which many jurists rather callously accepted – chance shall be judge and the argument be settled by lot. The person on whom the lot falls shall have the right to make the choice. 24. Legacies can only be given when there is testamentary capacity as between testator and legatee. 25. The creation of legacies and trusts in favour of unidentifiable persons was once not possible. A written reply of the Emperor Hadrian held that not even a soldier could do it. A beneficiary counted as unidentifiable when the testator left his identity open to guesswork. For example, suppose he said 'Let my heir give such and such a farm to the person who marries his daughter to my son.' A legacy to the first persons designated consuls after the making of the will had the same flaw; and many other examples could be given. Freedom cannot be granted to unidentifiable persons either. It has been held that the grant must be to specified slaves. The appointment of a guardian must also satisfy the requirement of certainty. But it was always possible to give a legacy within a specified class, i.e. to an unidentified person within an identifed group, as 'Let my heir give such and such to anyone among my relatives now living who marries my daughter.' Where legacies and trusts are made which break the rules of certainty // and are paid out by

per errorem soluta repeti non posse sacris constitu-
26 tionibus cautum erat[1]. [2]'Postumo quoque alieno
'inutiliter legabatur: est autem alienus postumus, qui
'natus inter suos heredes testatoris futurus non est:
'ideoque ex emancipato filio conceptus nepos extra-
27 'neus erat postumus avo.' 'Sed nec huiusmodi
species penitus est sine iusta emendatione derelicta,
'cum in nostro codice constitutio[3] posita est, per
'quam et huic parti medevimus[4] non solum in here-
'ditatibus, sed etiam in legatis et fideicommissis: quod
'evidenter ex ipsius constitutionis lectione clarescit.
'tutor autem nec per nostram constitutionem incertus
'dari debeat, quia certo iudicio debet quis pro tutela
28 'suae posteritati cavere. Postumus autem alienus
'heres institui et antea poterat et nunc potest, nisi
'in utero eius sit, quae iure nostra[5] uxor esse non
29 'potest.' Si quid[6] in nomine cognomine prae-
nomine legatarii erraverit testator, si de persona constat, nihilo minus valet legatum: idem in heredibus
servatur et recte: nomina enim significandorum hominum gratia reperta sunt, qui si quolibet alio modo
30 intellegantur, nihil interest. Huic proxima est
illa iuris regula falsa demonstratione legatum non
peremi. veluti si quis ita legaverit 'Stichum servum
'meum vernam do lego': licet enim non verna, sed
emptus sit, de servo tamen constat, utile est legatum. et convenienter si ita demonstraverit 'Stichum
'servum, quem a Seio emi', sitque ab alio emptus,
31 utile legatum est, si de servo constat. Longe
magis legato[7] falsa causa non nocet. veluti cum ita
quis dixerit: 'Titio, quia[8] absente me negotia mea
'curavit, Stichum do lego', vel ita: 'Titio, quia pa-
'trocinio eius capitali crimine liberatus sum, Stichum
'do lego': licet enim neque negotia testatoris umquam gessit Titius neque patrocinio eius liberatus
est, legatum tamen valet. sed si condicionaliter enun-
tiata fuerit causa, aliud iuris est, veluti hoc modo:
'Titio, si negotia mea curaverit, fundum do lego'.
32 An servo heredis recte legamus, quaeritur. et
constat pure inutiliter legari nec quicquam proficere,
si vivo testatore de potestate heredis exierit, quia
quod inutile foret legatum, si statim post factum
testamentum decessisset testator, hoc non debet ideo
valere, quia diutius testator vixerit. sub condicione
vero recte legatur, ut requiramus, an, quo tempore
33 dies legati cedit, in potestate heredis non sit. Ex
diverso herede instituto servo quin domino recte etiam
sine condicione legetur, non dubitatur. nam et si
statim post factum testamentum decesserit testator,
non tamen apud eum qui heres sit dies legati cedere
intellegitur, cum hereditas a legato separata sit et
possit per eum servum alius heres effici, si prius,
quam iussu domini adeat, in alterius potestatem trans-
latus sit, vel manumissus ipse heres efficitur: quibus
casibus utile est legatum: quodsi in eadem causa
permanserit et iussu legatarii adierit, evanescit lega-
34 tum. [9]'Ante heredis institutionem inutiliter an-
'tea legabatur, scilicet quia testamenta vim ex insti-
'tutione heredum accipiunt et ob id veluti caput at-
'que fundamentum intellegitur totius testamenti here-
'dis institutio. pari ratione nec libertas ante heredis
'institutionem dari poterat.' 'sed quia incivile esse
'putavimus ordinem quidem scripturae sequi (quod et
'ipsi antiquitati vituperandum fuerat visum), sperni
'autem testatoris voluntatem: per nostram constitu-
'tionem[10] et hoc vitium emendavimus, ut liceat et
'ante heredis institutionem et inter medias heredum
'institutiones legatum relinquere et multo magis liber-
35 'tatem, cuius usus favorabilior est.' [11]'Post mor-
'tem quoque heredis aut legatarii simili modo inuti-
'liter legabatur: 'veluti si quis ita dicat': 'cum heres

'meus mortuus erit, do lego': 'item' 'pridie quam heres
'"aut legatarius" morietur'.' 'sed simili modo et hoc
'correximus[12] firmitatem huiusmodi legatis ad fidei-
'commissorum similitudinem praestantes, ne vel in hoc
'casu deterior causa legatorum quam fideicommisso-
36 'rum inveniatur.' [13]'Poenae quoque nomine in-
'utiliter legabatur' et adimebatur vel transferebatur.
'poenae autem nomine legari videtur, quod coercendi
'heredis causa relinquitur, quo magis is[14] aliquid faciat
'aut non faciat: veluti 'si quis ita scripserit': 'heres
'"meus si filiam suam in matrimonium Titio colloca-
'"verit' (vel ex diverso 'si non collocaverit'), 'dato de-
'"cem aureos' Seio', aut si ita scripserit 'heres meus
'si servum Stichum alienaverit' (vel ex diverso 'si
'non alienaverit'), "Titio decem 'aureos' dato". et in
tantum haec regula observabatur, ut 'perquam pluri-
'bus' principalibus constitutionibus significetur nec
principem quidem agnoscere, quod ei poenae nomine
legatum sit. nec ex militis quidem testamento talia
legata valebant, quamvis aliae[15] militum voluntates in
ordinandis testamentis valde observantur. quin etiam
nec libertatem poenae nomine dari posse placebat.
eo amplius nec heredem poenae nomine adici posse
Sabinus existimabat, veluti si quis ita dicat: 'Titius
'heres esto: si Titius filiam suam Seio in matrimo-
'nium collocaverit, Seius quoque heres esto': nihil
enim intererat, qua ratione Titius coerceatur, utrum
legati datione an coheredis adiectione. 'at huiusmodi
'scrupulositas nobis non placuit et generaliter ea quae
'relinquuntur, licet poenae nomine fuerint relicta vel
'adempta vel in alios[16] translata, nihil distare a ce-
'teris legatis constituimus[17] vel in dando vel in ad-
'imendo vel in transferendo: exceptis his videlicet,
'quae impossibilia sunt vel legibus interdicta aut alias
'probrosa: huiusmodi enim testatorum dispositiones
'valere secta temporum meorum non patitur.'

XXI[18]
DE ADEMPTIONE LEGATORUM ET TRANS-
LATIONE.

Ademptio legatorum, sive eodem testamento adiman-
tur sive codicillis, firma est, 'sive' contrariis verbis fiat
ademptio, veluti si, quod ita quis legaverit 'do lego',
ita adimatur 'non do non lego', 'sive non contrariis,
1 'id est aliis quibuscumque verbis'. Transferri quoque legatum ab alio ad alium potest, veluti si quis ita
dixerit: 'hominem Stichum, quem Titio legavi, Seio do
'lego', sive in eodem testamento sive in codicillis hoc
fecerit: quo casu simul Titio adimi videtur et Seio dari.

XXII[19]
DE LEGE FALCIDIA.

Superest, ut de lege Falcidia dispiciamus, qua modus novissime legatis impositus est. cum enim olim
lege duodecim tabularum libera erat legandi potestas,
ut liceret vel totum patrimonium legatis erogare
(quippe ea lege ita cautum esset: 'uti legassit suae
'rei, ita ius esto'): visum est hanc legandi licentiam
coartare, idque ipsorum testatorum gratia provisum
est ob id, quod plerumque intestati[20] moriebantur,
recusantibus scriptis heredibus pro nullo aut minimo
lucro hereditates adire. et cum super hoc tam lex
Furia quam lex Voconia latae sunt, quarum neutra
sufficiens ad rei consummationem videbatur: novissime lata est lex Falcidia, qua cavetur, ne plus legare liceat, quam dodrantem totorum bonorum, id
est ut, sive unus heres institutus esset sive plures,
1 apud eum eosve pars quarta remaneret. Et cum
quaesitum esset, duobus heredibus institutis, veluti

---

(1) erat] *BE*, est *P cum* Θ   (2) *Gai.* 2, 240. 241   (3) *Cod.* 6, 48, 1   (4) *sic BE*[b], medebimur *PE*[a]   (5) nostra] *E*, nostro *BP*   (6) quid] *E*[b] Θ   (7) *sic PE* Θ, legatum *B*   (8) quia] *W*[b] Θ, qui *BPEW*[a]   (9) *Gai.* 2, 229. 230   (10) *Cod.* 6, 23, 24   (11) *Gai.* 2, 232   (12) *Cod.* 8, 37, 11   (13) § 36 *in. similis Gaio* 2, 235   (14) is] *B*, heres *Gai.*, om. *PE*   (15) alias *dett. cum* Θ   (16) *sic W*[a] *cum* Θ, alio *BEW*[b]   (17) *Cod.* 6, 41, 1   (18) *Cf. Dig.* 34, 4   (19) *Cf. Gai.* 2, 224..228 *Dig.* 35, 2 *Cod.* 6, 50   (20) *sic E*Θ, intestato *BP*

mistake imperial pronouncements have ruled that they cannot be recovered. 26. A legacy to a posthumous outsider used also to be void. Within this description fell one who when born would not count as an immediate heir of the testator. Thus, a grandson of an emancipated son was a posthumous outsider to the grandfather. 27. However, this case too was not neglected when we placed in our Codex the pronouncement by which we remedied the condition of this unfortunate figure as heir, legatee, and trust beneficiary. If you read the pronouncement itself, you will find this becomes perfectly clear. We have not relaxed the requirement of certainty for the appointment of a guardian. A man should use unambiguous language in the care of his posterity. 28. You could and still can appoint a posthumous outsider to be your heir, but not if the pregnant mother could not lawfully have been your wife. 29. If the testator makes a mistake in the first, second or third name of the legatee, so long as there is no mistake as to the person meant, the legacy is good. The same of heirs, quite rightly. Names were invented to identify; if identification can be done some other way, well and good. 30. On the same lines is the maxim for legacies, 'False descriptions are not fatal.' Take 'I give and bequeath my slave Stichus, born in my household.' If Stichus was not born there but was bought, the legacy is still good as long as there is agreement on his identity. Similarly, if the description says 'Stichus, the slave I bought from Seius', when in fact he was bought from someone else, the legacy is valid if the identity of the slave is not in doubt. 31. Still less does it matter if a the testator discloses a false belief in the background. Take 'I give and bequeath Stichus to Titius because he managed my affairs in my absence' or 'I give and bequeath Stichus to Titius because by his advocacy I was acquitted of a capital charge.' Here the legacy is valid even if Titius never managed his affairs or secured his acquittal. It is different if it is put conditionally: 'I give and bequeath land to Titius, if it was he who managed my affairs in my absence.' 32. Can a legacy be left to a slave of the heir? Such a legacy framed absolutely is void. The fact that the slave is freed while the testator is alive does not help. A legacy which would be void if the testator died straight after making the will cannot be made good by his living longer. Framed conditionally, the legacy is good, provided that on the critical day he is not within the heir's authority. 33. The other way, where the slave is the appointed heir, there is no doubt that an absolute legacy to the owner is valid. Even if the testator dies the moment after the will there is no merger of identity between heir and legatee on the critical day. The legacy and estate are separate. The slave can bring in a different heir if he is alienated before the order to accept the estate, or if he is granted freedom, becoming heir himself. The legacy is good in these cases. However, if these changes do not happen and he accepts the estate at the command of the legatee, the legacy is extinguished. 34. A legacy ahead of the heir's appointment used to be bad. The force of the will flows from the heir's appointment, which is its foundation or cornerstone. Similarly a grant of freedom could not precede his appointment. Yet it seemed to us to be primitive – even in ancient times it was sharply condemned – to cling to the order of words and ignore the testator's intention. We corrected this defect. We provided that legacies could be given and slaves freed even before, or among, appointments of heirs. The principle in favour of liberty is an extra argument. 35. Legacies designed to take effect after the death of heir or legatee used also to be bad. Examples are 'I give and bequeath after my heir's death,' or 'on the day before my heir, or legatee, dies.' But here too we have reformed the law, extending to such legacies the validity enjoyed by trusts. Our aim was that legacies should not prove

weaker in this than trusts. 36. It also used to be impossible to enforce penal legacies, revocations and transfers. A penal legacy was one calculated to compel an heir to do or not to do something. For example, a clause saying 'If my heir marries his daughter to Titius – or, does not marry, etc – let him pay 10 to Seius,' or 'If my heir alienates – or, does not alienate – the slave Stichus, let him pay 10 to Titius.' This rule was closely followed. There were many imperial pronouncements affirming that not even the emperor would accept anything that came to him through the operation of a penalty. Such legacies failed even in soldiers' wills, though the intentions soldiers express in drawing up their wills are in other respects given paramount importance. It was decided that a grant of freedom arranged as a penalty could also not be enforced. Nor could an additional heir be let in as a penalty, as by this clause, 'Let Titius be heir. If Titius marries his daughter to Seius, let Seius also be heir.' Sabinus so held. It made no difference what means was used to coerce Titius, whether the imposition of a legacy or the addition of a co heir. However, we could not sympathize with these scruples. We laid down a general rule that bequests which, by way of penalties, are left, revoked, or forfeited to others, are to be treated no differently from all other bequests given, revoked, or transferred from one person to another. Naturally those which are impossible or illegal or in other ways disgraceful are excluded. To uphold dispositions of that kind would be out of keeping with the spirit of my reign.

2.21 REVOCATION AND TRANSFER OF LEGACIES

Legacies can be revoked. This can be done either in the same will or in a codicil. It can be done by exactly contrary words. For example, where a legacy has been given in the words 'I give and bequeath,' it is revoked by the words 'I do not give and do not bequeath.' Or else it can be done in any words at all. 1. A legacy can also be transferred from one person to another. For example, you can say 'I give and bequeath to Seius the slave Stichus whom I bequeathed to Titius.' This can be done either in the same will or in a codicil. The effect is at one and the same time to revoke the legacy to Titius and to give it to Seius.

2.22 THE FALCIDIAN ACT

We still have to discuss the Falcidian Act. This was the measure that finally put a limit on legacies. Earlier, under the Twelve Tables, a man had power to make what bequests he liked. He could use up his whole estate. Indeed the code provided, 'As a man bequeaths, so let the law be.' Later it was decided on a restraint. This was in the interest of testators themselves, since intestacies were commonly produced by the refusal of heirs to accept estates offering little or no gain. The Furian Act and the Voconian Act addressed the problem but were judged not to have achieved a solution. The last step was taken by the Falcidian Act, which made it unlawful to give legacies of more than nine twelfths of the whole estate. That is, whether one or more heirs were appointed, a quarter was to be kept for them. 1. Suppose two heirs, Titius and Seius. // The legacies expressly

Titio et Seio, si Titii pars aut tota exhausta sit legatis, quae nominatim ab eo data sunt, aut supra modum onerata, a Seio vero aut nulla relicta sint legata, aut quae partem eius dumtaxat in partem dimidiam minuunt, an, quia is quartam partem totius hereditatis aut amplius habet, Titio nihil ex legatis, quae ab eo relicta sunt, retinere liceret: placuit retinere licere, ut quartam partem suae partis salvam habeat[1]: [2]etenim in singulis heredibus ratio 2 legis Falcidiae ponenda est. [3]Quantitas autem patrimonii, ad quam ratio legis Falcidiae redigitur, mortis tempore spectatur. itaque si verbi gratia is, qui centum 'aureorum' patrimonium habebat, centum 'aureos' legaverit, nihil legatariis prodest, si ante aditam hereditatem per servos hereditarios aut ex partu ancillarum hereditariarum aut ex fetu pecorum tantum accesserit hereditati, ut centum 'aureis' legatorum nomine erogatis heres quartam partem hereditatis habiturus sit, sed necesse est, ut nihilo minus quarta pars legatis detrahatur. ex diverso si septuaginta quinque legaverit et ante aditam hereditatem in tantum decreverint bona incendiis forte aut naufragiis aut morte servorum, ut non amplius quam septuaginta quinque 'aureorum' substantia vel etiam minus relinquatur, solida legata debentur[4]. nec ea res damnosa est heredi, cui liberum est non adire hereditatem: quae res efficit, ut necesse sit legatariis, ne destituto testamento nihil consequantur, cum herede 3 in portione pacisci. Cum autem ratio legis Falcidiae ponitur, ante deducitur aes alienum, item funeris impensa et pretia servorum manumissorum, tunc deinde in reliquo ita ratio habetur, ut ex eo quarta pars apud heredes remaneat, tres vero partes inter legatarios distribuantur, pro rata scilicet portione eius, quod cuique eorum legatum fuerit. [5]itaque si fingamus quadringentos 'aureos' legatos esse et patrimonii quantitatem, ex qua legata erogari oportet, quadringentorum esse, quarta pars singulis legatariis detrahi debet. quodsi trecentos quinquaginta legatos fingamus, octava debet detrahi. quodsi quingentos legaverit, initio quinta, deinde quarta detrahi debet: ante enim detrahendum est, quod extra bonorum quantitatem est, deinde quod ex bonis apud heredem remanere oportet.

XXIII[6]

DE FIDEICOMMISSARIIS HEREDITATIBUS.

[7]'Nunc transeamus ad fideicommissa. et prius de 'hereditatibus 'fideicommissariis' videamus.'
1 Sciendum itaque est omnia fideicommissa primis temporibus infirma esse, quia nemo invitus cogebatur praestare id de quo rogatus erat: quibus enim non poterant hereditates vel legata relinquere, si relinquebant, fidei committebant eorum, qui capere ex testamento poterant: et ideo fideicommissa appellata sunt, quia nullo vinculo iuris, sed tantum pudore eorum qui rogabantur continebantur. postea primus divus Augustus semel iterumque gratia personarum motus, vel quia per ipsius salutem rogatus quis diceretur, aut ob insignem quorundam perfidiam iussit consulibus auctoritatem suam interponere. quod quia iustum videbatur et populare erat, paulatim conversum est in adsiduam iurisdictionem: tantusque favor eorum factus est, ut paulatim etiam praetor proprius crearetur, qui fideicommissis ius diceret, quem fideicommissarium appellabant.
2 [8]'In primis igitur sciendum est opus esse, ut 'aliquis recto iure testamento heres instituatur eius-'que fidei committatur, ut eam hereditatem alii resti-'tuat: alioquin inutile est testamentum, in quo nemo 'heres instituitur. cum igitur aliquis scripserit: 'Lu-'"cius Titius heres esto', poterit adicere: 'rogo te, '"Luci Titi, ut, cum primum possis hereditatem meam '"adire, eam Gaio Seio reddas restituas'. potest au-'tem quisque et de parte restituenda heredem rogare: 'et liberum est vel pure vel sub condicione relinquere 'fideicommissum vel ex die certo.
3 [9]'Restituta autem hereditate is quidem qui re-'stituit nihilo minus heres permanet: is vero qui re-'cipit hereditatem aliquando heredis aliquando lega-4 'tarii loco 'habebatur. [10]Et in Neronis quidem tem-'poribus' 'Trebellio Maximo et Annaeo Seneca con-'sulibus[11] senatus consultum factum est, quo cautum 'est, ut, si[12] hereditas ex fideicommissi causa resti-'tuta sit, omnes actiones, quae iure civili heredi et 'in heredem competerent, ei et in eum darentur, 'cui ex fideicommisso restituta esset[13] hereditas. post 'quod senatus consultum praetor utiles actiones ei et 'in eum qui recepit hereditatem quasi heredi et in 5 'heredem dare coepit. Sed quia heredes scripti, 'cum aut totam hereditatem aut paene totam ple-'rumque restituere rogabantur, adire hereditatem ob 'nullum vel minimum lucrum recusabant atque ob id 'extinguebantur fideicommissa: postea 'Vespasiani Au-'gusti temporibus' Pegaso et Pusione consulibus[14] 'senatus censuit[15], ut ei, qui rogatus esset heredita-'tem restituere, perinde liceret quartam partem reti-'nere, atque lege Falcidia ex legatis retinere conce-'ditur. ex singulis quoque rebus, quae per fideicom-'missum relinquuntur, eadem retentio permissa est. 'post quod senatus consultum ipse heres onera here-'ditaria sustinebat: ille autem, qui ex fideicommisso 'recepit partem hereditatis, legatarii partiarii loco 'erat, id est eius legatarii, cui pars bonorum lega-'batur. quae species legati partitio vocabatur, quia 'cum herede legatarius partiebatur hereditatem. unde 'quae solebant stipulationes inter heredem et partia-'rium legatarium interponi, eaedem interponebantur 'inter eum, qui ex fideicommisso recepit hereditatem, 'et heredem, id est ut et lucrum et damnum heredi-6 'tarium pro rata parte inter eos commune sit. Ergo 'si quidem non plus quam dodrantem hereditatis scrip-'tus heres rogatus sit restituere, tunc ex Trebelliano 'senatus consulto restituebatur hereditas et in utrum-'que actiones hereditariae pro rata parte dabantur: 'in heredem quidem iure civili, in eum vero qui re-'cipiebat hereditatem ex senatus consulto Trebelliano 'tamquam in heredem. at[16] si plus quam dodrantem 'vel etiam totam hereditatem restituere rogatus sit, 'locus erat Pegasiano senatus consulto, 'et heres,' qui 'semel adierit hereditatem, si modo sua voluntate 'adierit, sive retinuerit quartam partem sive noluerit 'retinere, ipse universa onera hereditaria sustinebat. 'sed[17] quarta quidem retenta quasi partis et pro parte 'stipulationes interponebantur tamquam inter partia-'rium legatarium et heredem: si vero totam heredi-'tatem restituerit, [18]emptae et venditae hereditatis 'stipulationes interponebantur. sed si recuset scrip-'tus heres adire hereditatem ob id, quod dicat eam 'sibi suspectam esse quasi damnosam, cavetur Pega-'siano senatus consulto, ut desiderante eo, cui resti-'tuere rogatus est, iussu praetoris adeat et restituat 'hereditatem perindeque ei et in eum qui recipit he-'reditatem actiones dentur, acsi iuris est ex Trebel-'liano senatus consulto: quo casu nullis stipulationi-'bus opus est, quia simul et huic qui restituit secu-'ritas datur et actiones hereditariae ei et in eum 'transferuntur qui recipit hereditatem', 'utroque sena-7 'tus consulto in hac specie concurrente. Sed quia 'stipulationes ex senatus consulto Pegasiano descen-'dentes et ipsi antiquitati displicuerunt et quibusdam

---

(1) placuit ret. lic. ut...habeat] *scripsi*. plac. ret. lic. *om. B*, placuit ut...habeat et pl. posse ret. *CPE* (2) § 1 *fin. similis Dig.* 35, 2, 77 (3) § 2 *similis Dig.* 35, 2, 73 *pr.* (*Gai. l.* 18 *ad ed. prov.*) (4) *sic Dig.*, dentur *libri* (5) *cf. Dig.* 35, 2, 73 § 5 (*Gai. l. c.*) (6) *Cf. Gai.* 2, 246..259 *Dig.* 36, 1 *Cod.* 6, 49 (7) *Gai.* 2, 246. 247 (8) *Gai.*

2, 248. 250. 251 (9) *Gai.* 2, 251 (10) *Gai.* 2, 253..258 (11) *anno p. Chr.* 56? (12) si] si cui *Gai.* Θ (13) *sic Gai.*, est *libri* (14) *anno incerto* (15) *sic Gai. PE*, constituit B (16) at] T* *PGai.* Θ, *ac B*, aut T*, inter alia om. T* (17) sed] *T Gai.*, sed si B (18) *sic libri cum* Θ, *ad exemplum ins. Gai.*

payable from Titius' share use it up completely or exceed the limit. The legacies on Seius' share are either non-existent or leave at least half. Since a quarter or more of the inheritance does survive in Seius' share, can Titius keep back nothing from the legacies charged on him? He can. He can keep a quarter of his own share. This shows that the Falcidian principle is to be applied heir by heir. 2. The Act operates on the estate as at the time of the death. Suppose a man dies with an estate of 100, leaving legacies of 100. It will not help the legatees if, during the period up to acceptance, the value of the estate is raised by its slaves or by slave or animal offspring to a level where legacies of 100 would leave the heir a full quarter. It follows that the legacies must be reduced by a quarter. Suppose things run the other way: there are legacies of 75 but fire, shipwreck and slave deaths reduce the estate to 75 or less before acceptance of the inheritance. Here the legacies still have to be met in full. But the heir need not suffer loss. He is free not to accept the inheritance. This will force the legatees to settle with him for a reduced share, since if the will is thrown over they will get nothing. 3. Before the Falcidian calculation, debts, funeral expenses, and the value of slaves freed must all be deducted. It is to the balance that the Act applies, saving a quarter for the heirs and leaving three quarters available for distribution to the legatees in proportion to their original legacies. Suppose the case of an estate of 400 charged with legacies of 400. Every legacy must be scaled down by a quarter. Supposing instead legacies of 350, the reduction must be an eighth. If the legacies come to 500, there must be a reduction first of a fifth, then of a quarter. The right way to proceed is first to cut off the excess over the value of the estate, then to subtract the share reserved for the heir.

2.23 TRUSTS OF ESTATES

We now move on to trusts, and first to trusts of the whole estate. 1. Note that trusts were originally unenforceable. Nobody could be compelled to carry out the request made to him. Some people lack the capacity to take under a will. If you wanted such a person to get your estate, or a legacy, the way to do it was to leave it to someone who did have capacity and rely on his honour. Trusts, in Latin 'fideicommissa', are so called because the trustee was bound only by his conscience, not at law. The Emperor Augustus was the first to order the consuls to intervene. He did this time and again, as a favour to petitioners, either because his own name had been invoked in the charge to the trustee or because there had been outrageous breaches of trust. Just and popular, this gradually settled into a regular jurisdiction. The demand became so strong that a special praetor was created to preside over trust litigation, the praetor for trusts. 2. The crucial starting point is a valid will with an appointment of an heir charged as trustee to hand over the estate to an third person. Without an appointment of an heir, the will is void. Once the testator has written 'Let Lucius Titius be heir,' he can then add, 'and I ask you, Lucius Titius, as soon as you can accept the estate, to give it to Gaius Seius.' Alternatively he can ask the heir to hand over part of the estate. He is free to make the trust absolute or conditional or post-dated. 3. After the transfer, the heir remains heir. The recipient used to be treated sometimes as heir, sometimes as legatee. 4. In Nero's reign, in the consulship of Trebellius Maximus and Annaeus Seneca, a Resolution was passed by the senate providing that after transfer of a trust estate the transferee should be entitled to and liable under all those actions which by the law of the state lay for or against an heir. After that Resolution the praetor began to allow policy actions by and against the transferee as though by and against the heir. 5. However, appointed heirs who were asked to give up all or most of the estate saw little or no prospect of profit to themselves and began to refuse inheritances. The effect was to bring down the trusts. Consequently, in the Emperor Vespasian's reign, in the consulship of Pegasus and Pusio, the senate resolved that an heir required to transfer the estate should have the same right to retain a quarter as the Falcidian Act allowed in relation to legacies. The same retention was allowed where a single thing was caught by the trust. Under this Resolution, the burdens of an heir were again shouldered by the heir, but the beneficiary under the trust, as recipient of part of the estate, was placed in the position of a cut in legatee. That kind of legatee was one who was left a share of the whole estate. Such a legacy was called a cut, in Latin 'partitio', because the legatee was cut in for a share of the estate with the heir. As a result the stipulations customarily required between heir and cut-in legatee were required between the heir and the beneficiary under the trust. These undertakings bound the parties to share profit and loss from the estate in proportion to their interests. 6. Suppose the appointed heir was required to transfer less than nine twelfths of the estate. Here the transfer fell under the Trebellian regime. The actions for and against heirs were proportionately distributed, to the heir under state law, to the recipient as though he were heir under the Trebellian Resolution. Suppose instead that the heir was to make over more than nine twelfths or even the whole estate. Here the Pegasian regime applied. Once the heir accepted, provided it was by his own wish, he had to bear all the burdens of an heir, whether he retained his quarter or chose not to. If he did keep his quarter, the share-and-share stipulations were made, as between heir and cut-in legatee. If he made over the whole estate, the undertakings were those used between buyer and seller of an estate. Suppose again that the appointed heir refused to accept, claiming that the estate was unsound and likely to bring him loss. Here the Pegasian Resolution required him to accept and to convey over if the praetor so decreed on the petition of the trust beneficiary, the distribution of actions then being controlled as though the Trebellian applied. Here there was no need for any stipulations. The trustee was instantly protected; at the same moment the transferee acquired the claims and liabilities belonging to an heir. Here the two senatorial resolutions worked together. 7. The Pegasian stipulations were criticized even in the old days; // the brilliant Papinian called them

ʿcasibus captiosas eas homo excelsi ingenii Papinianus
ʿappellat et nobis in legibus magis simplicitas quam
ʿdifficultas placet, ideo omnibus nobis suggestis tam
ʿsimilitudinibus quam differentiis utriusque senatus
ʿconsulti placuit exploso senatus consulto Pegasiano,
ʿquod postea supervenit, omnem auctoritatem Trebel-
ʿliano senatus consulto praestare, ut ex eo fideicom-
ʿmissariae hereditates restituantur, sive habeat heres
ʿex voluntate testatoris quartam sive plus sive minus
ʿsive penitus nihil, ut tunc, quando vel nihil vel mi-
ʿnus quarta apud eum remaneat, liceat ei vel quar-
ʿtam vel quod deest ex nostra auctoritate retinere vel
ʿrepetere solutum, quasi ex Trebelliano senatus con-
ʿsulto pro rata portione actionibus tam in heredem
ʿquam in fideicommissarium competentibus. si vero
ʿtotam hereditatem sponte restituerit, omnes heredi-
ʿtariae actiones fideicommissario et adversus eum
ʿcompetunt. sed etiam id, quod praecipuum Pegasiani
ʿsenatus consulti fuerat, ut, quando recusabat heres
ʿscriptus sibi datam hereditatem adire, necessitas ei
ʿimponeretur totam hereditatem volenti fideicommis-
ʿsario restituere et omnes ad eum et contra eum
ʿtransire[1] actiones, et hoc transponimus ad senatus
ʿconsultum Trebellianum, ut ex hoc solo et necessi-
ʿtas heredi imponatur, si ipso nolente adire fideicom-
ʿmissarius desiderat restitui sibi hereditatem, nullo
ʿnec damno nec commodo apud heredem manente.ʾ
§ [2]ʿNihil autem interest, utrum aliquis ex asse he-
ʿres institutus aut totam hereditatem aut pro parte
ʿrestituere rogatur, an ex parte heres institutus aut
ʿtotam eam[3] partem aut partis partem restituere ro-
ʿgatur: nam et hoc casu' ʿeadem observari praecipi-
ʿmus, quae in totius hereditatis restitutione diximus.ʾ
9 Si quis una aliqua re deducta sive praecepta,
quae quartam continet, veluti fundo vel alia re rogatus sit restituere hereditatem, simili modo ex Trebelliano senatus consulto restitutio fiat, perinde ac
si quarta parte retenta rogatus esset reliquam hereditatem restituere. sed illud interest, quod altero
casu, id est cum deducta sive praecepta aliqua re
restituitur hereditas, in solidum ex eo senatus consulto actiones transferuntur et res quae remanet
apud heredem sine ullo onere hereditario apud eum
manet quasi ex legato ei adquisita, altero vero casu,
id est cum quarta parte retenta rogatus est heres
restituere hereditatem et restituit, scindantur actiones
et pro dodrante quidem transferantur ad fideicommissarium, pro quadrante remaneant apud heredem.
quin etiam licet in una re, qua deducta aut praecepta restituere aliquis hereditatem rogatus est,
maxima pars hereditatis contineatur, aeque in solidum transferuntur actiones et[4] secum deliberare debet is, cui restituitur hereditas, an expediat sibi restitui. eadem scilicet interveniunt et si duabus pluri-
busve rebus deductis praeceptisve restituere hereditatem rogatus sit. sed et[5] si certa summa deducta
praeceptave, quae quartam vel etiam maximam partem hereditatis continet, rogatus sit aliquis hereditatem restituere, idem iuris est. quae diximus de eo
qui ex asse heres institutus est, eadem transferimus
et ad eum qui ex parte heres scriptus est.
10 Praeterea intestatus[6] quoque moriturus potest
rogare eum, ad quem bona sua vel legitimo iure vel
honorario pertinere intellegit, ut hereditatem suam
totam partemve eius aut rem aliquam, veluti fundum
hominem pecuniam, alicui restituat: cum alioquin
11 legata nisi ex testamento non valeant. Eum quoque, cui aliquid restituitur, potest rogare, ut id rursus
alii totum aut pro parte[7] vel etiam aliud aliquid re-
12 stituat. ʿEt quia prima fideicommissorum cuna-
ʿbula a fide heredum pendent et tam nomen quam
ʿsubstantiam acceperunt et ideo divus Augustus ad

ʿnecessitatem iuris ea detraxit: nuper et nos eundem
ʿprincipem superare contendentes ex facto, quod Tri-
ʿbonianus vir excelsus quaestor sacri palatii sugges-
ʿsit, constitutionem[8] fecimus, per quam disposuimus:
ʿsi testator fidei heredis sui commisit, ut vel heredi-
ʿtatem vel speciale fideicommissum restituat, et neque
ʿex scriptura neque ex quinque testium numero, qui
ʿin fideicommissis legitimus esse noscitur, res possit
ʿmanifestari, sed vel pauciores quam quinque vel nemo
ʿpenitus testis intervenerit, tunc sive pater heredis
ʿsive alius quicumque sit, qui fidem elegit heredis et
ʿab eo aliquid restitui voluerit, si heres perfidia ten-
ʿtus adimplere fidem recusat negando rem ita esse
ʿsubsecutam, si fideicommissarius iusiurandum ei de-
ʿtulerit, cum prius ipse de calumnia iuraverit, necesse
ʿeum habere vel iusiurandum subire, quod nihil tale
ʿa testatore audivit, vel recusantem ad fideicommissi
ʿvel universitatis vel specialis solutionem coartari, ne
ʿdepereat ultima voluntas testatoris fidei heredis com-
ʿmissa. eadem observari[9] censuimus et si a legatario
ʿvel fideicommissario aliquid similiter relictum sit.
ʿquod si is, a quo relictum dicitur, confiteatur qui-
ʿdem aliquid a se relictum esse, sed ad legis suptili-
ʿtatem decurrat, omnimodo cogendus est solvere.ʾ

XXIV [10]
DE SINGULIS REBUS PER FIDEICOMMISSUM RELICTIS.

[11]ʿPotest autem quis etiam singulas res per fidei-
ʿcommissum relinquere, veluti fundum hominem vestem
ʿargentum pecuniam numeratam, et vel ipsum here-
ʿdem rogare, ut alicui restituat, vel legatarium, quamvis
1 ʿa legatario legari non possit. [11]Potest autem non
ʿsolum proprias testator res per fideicommissum re-
ʿlinquere, sed et heredis aut legatarii ʿaut fideicom-
ʿmissariiʾ aut cuiuslibet alterius. itaque et legatarius
ʿet fideicommissariusʾ non solum de ea re rogari po-
ʿtest, ut eam alicui restituat, quae ei ʿrelictaʾ sit, sed
ʿetiam de alia, sive ipsius sive aliena sit. hoc solum
ʿobservandum est, ne plus quisquam rogetur alicui
ʿrestituere, quam ipse ex testamento ceperit: nam
ʿquod amplius est, inutiliter relinquitur. cum autem
ʿaliena res per fideicommissum relinquitur, necesse
ʿest ei qui rogatus est aut ipsam redimere et praestare
2 ʿaut aestimationem eius solvere. [11]Libertas quoque
ʿservo per fideicommissum dari potest, ut heres eum[12]
ʿrogetur manumittere vel legatarius ʿvel fideicommis-
ʿsarius.ʾ nec interest, utrum de suo proprio servo
ʿtestator roget, an de eo qui ipsius heredis aut lega-
ʿtarii vel etiam extranei sit. itaque[13] alienus servus
ʿredimi et manumitti debet: quod si dominus eum
ʿnon vendat', [14]ʿsi modo nihil ex iudicio eius qui reli-
ʿquit libertatem percepit, non statim extinguitur fidei-
ʿcommissaria libertas, sed differtur, quia possit tem-
ʿpore procedente, ubicumque occasio redimendi servi
ʿfuerit, praestari libertas.ʾ [15]ʿqui autem ex causa fidei-
ʿcommissi manumittitur, non testatoris fit libertus,
ʿetiamsi testatoris servus sit, sed eius qui manumittit:
ʿat is, qui directo testamento liber esse iubetur, ipsius
ʿtestatoris fit libertus', qui etiam orcinus appellatur.
ʿnec alius ullus directo ex testamento libertatem ha-
ʿbere potest, quam qui utroque tempore testatoris
ʿfuerit, et quo faceret testamentum et quo morere-
tur.ʾ directo autem libertas tunc dari videtur, cum
ʿnon ab alio servum manumitti rogat, sed velut ex
3 ʿsuo testamento libertatem ei competere vult.
[16]ʿVerba autem fideicommissorum haec maxime in usu
ʿhabeantur: peto, rogo, volo, mando, fidei tuae com-
ʿmitto. quae perinde singula firma sunt, atque si
ʿomnia in unum congesta essent.ʾ

---

(1) transirent *Huschke* (2) *Gai.* 2, 259 (3) eam] *T*ᵇ *P*ᵇ *E
Gai.,* ••••tem *P*ᵃ, om. *B*Θ, inc. *T*ᵃ (4) et] sed *B* (5) sed
et] *T*ᵇ*C*, sed *B*, et *T*ᵃ (6) sic *B*, intestato *TC* (7) sic *BC*,
aut partem *T*Θ (8) *Cod.* 6, 42, 32 (9) sic *CP*, observare *BT*

(10) *Cf. Gai.* 2, 260..267 *Cod.* 6, 42 (11) *Gai.* 2, 260..265
(12) heres eum *BTC*, eum heres *P*, vel heres *Gai.* (13) ita-
que] *libri cum* Θ, itaque et dett. cum Gaio (14) *sequentia
ex Cod.* 7, 4, 6 *addita sunt* (15) *Gai.* 2, 266 (16) *Gai.* 2, 249

g*

treacherous on some facts; and we ourselves prefer simplicity in law to complexity. We have compared and contrasted the senate's two resolutions and have decided to abolish the Pegasian, the later of the two, and to apply the Trebellian in all cases. Trust estates are to be made over under the Trebellian rules whether the testator gives the heir his quarter, or more, or less, or absolutely nothing. In these last cases, where the heir has nothing or less than a quarter, he may retain or make up his quarter, or reclaim an excess already transferred. The actions for and against heirs are to be distributed on the Trebellian principle between the heir and the beneficiary in proportion to their interests. If the heir hands over the whole estate of his own accord, the actions for and against an heir are all transferred to the trust beneficiary. A special concern of the Pegasian Resolution was that an appointed heir who refused to accept the inheritance should be compelled to convey it to the beneficiary if he so desired, and with it all the relevant actions. We have incorporated this into the Trebellian scheme. The heir who does not want to accept is now bound solely under that Resolution to convey over to the trust beneficiary who does want the estate. In this scheme the heir is immunized from profit and loss. 8. There is no difference for these purposes between an heir appointed to the whole pound and asked to make over the whole or part, or an heir appointed to a share and asked to make over that whole share or part of it. In the second case we intend the same rules to be applied as for transfers of the whole estate. 9. If an heir is asked to make over an estate after the deduction or preselection of some single thing valued at a quarter of the whole, a farm or some similar asset, the transfer falls under the Trebellian resolution, just as though the trust was for him to keep his quarter and transfer the rest. But there is a distinction. In the one case – where the transfer is made after the subtraction or preselection of some asset – the Trebellian resolution passes the actions to the transferee with no apportionment, and the asset which stays with the heir does so free of all the burdens of an heir, as though it were a legacy. In the other case – where the trust is to retain a quarter and transfer the rest of the estate and the heir has done so – the Resolution requires the apportionment of the actions, nine twelfths to the transferee, a quarter to the heir. Further, even if the specific asset to be deducted or preselected ahead of the transfer which the trustee is required to make itself takes up the bulk of the estate, still the actions pass unapportioned to the transferee. Here he will have to ask himself whether it is in his interest that the transfer should go through. The same rules certainly apply if the trustee is to transfer the estate after deduction or pre-selection of more than one asset. The same is true if a specified sum of money, running to a quarter or the bulk of the estate, is to be deducted or preselected before the transfer. What we have said of an heir appointed to the entire estate applies equally to one given a share. 10. Someone who is about to die intestate can impose a trust on the person whom he expects to inherit his estate under either the old state law or the honorarian law. He can require him to transfer the whole or part of his estate to another, or a single thing such us a farm, a slave, or a sum of money. This is despite the fact that normally legacies can take effect only under a will. 11. The recipient of the first trust transfer can also be required to make another transfer of the whole or part, or of a specific asset. 12. The Emperor Augustus brought trusts within the law. He recognized that they were founded in reliance on the heir and took their name and substance from trust in his good faith. We, seeking to emulate the

Emperor Augustus in a measure proposed by Tribonian, eminent in rank and chancellor of our sacred palace, have lately pronounced as follows: where any testator has relied on his heir's good faith to transfer his estate or perform any particular trust, and there is no proof in writing or from five witnesses, the number which the law is acknowledged to require for trusts, but only evidence from fewer than five or none at all, then, whether it was the heir's father or another who relied on the heir as trustee for some performance, if the heir is tempted to treachery and refuses performance, denying the trust, the beneficiary must first swear the oath against abuse of process and then challenge the heir to swear that he never received any instruction from the testator. The heir must take the oath or, if he declines, must be compelled to make the performance, general or specific as the case may be, so that the last wishes of the testator entrusted to the heir's good faith may be respected. We have applied the same machinery where, on similar lines, an obligation to transfer is imposed on a legatee or a trust beneficiary. Anyone who admits that an obligation to transfer was imposed upon him and then seeks to escape it by legalistic quibbling must definitely be made to perform.

2.24 TRUSTS OF SINGLE THINGS

It is also possible for specific things to be left on trust, for example land, a slave, clothes, silver, or a sum of money. The trust can be imposed on the heir or on a legatee. That is despite the normal rule that one legacy cannot be grafted on another. 1. The testator can leave on trust not only his own property but also that of the heir, the legatee, the trust beneficiary, or of anyone at all. The legatee or trust beneficiary can be called upon to transfer not just what the testator leaves them but also something else, something belonging to themselves or a third party. The limit to be watched is this: nobody can be subjected to a trust to transfer more than he receives under the will. The disposition is void as to the excess. In a trust of property belonging to a third party the trustee must either buy it and hand it over or pay its value. 2. A slave can be given his freedom under a trust, as where an heir, legatee or trust beneficiary is called upon to manumit him. It makes no difference whether the trust obligation is imposed in relation to the testator's own slave, the heir's, legatee's, or a third party's. So he can have an obligation to buy and free someone else's slave. Suppose the owner will not sell. Though it is true that the slave gets nothing from the disposition made by the person who wanted him to be free, the trust freedom is not nullified but rather postponed, since in time there may be an opportunity for him to be purchased and freed. A slave freed under a trust does not become the freedman of the testator, even if he is the testator's slave, but of the person who does the manumission. By contrast those made free by the will itself do become the testator's freedmen, also called 'dead man's men'. But the will itself can directly free only those owned by the testator at both of two critical times, when the will is made and when the testator dies. A direct grant of freedom is one where the testator's intention is not to ask another to free the slave but to make him free immediately by his own will. 3. In creating trusts the following words are very commonly used: I ask, I call upon, I wish, I require, I rely on your honour. Using them all achieves no more than using one. //

XXV[1]
DE CODICILLIS

Ante Augusti tempora constat ius codicillorum non fuisse, sed primus Lucius Lentulus, ex cuius persona etiam fideicommissa coeperunt, codicillos introduxit. nam cum decederet in Africa[2], scripsit codicillos testamento confirmatos, quibus ab Augusto petiit per fideicommissum, ut faceret aliquid: et cum divus Augustus voluntatem eius implesset, deinceps reliqui auctoritatem eius secuti fideicommissa praestabant et filia Lentuli legata, quae iure non debebat, solvit. dicitur Augustus convocasse prudentes, inter quos Trebatium quoque, cuius tunc auctoritas maxima erat, et quaesisse, an possit hoc recipi nec absonans a iuris ratione codicillorum usus esset: et[3] Trebatium suasisse Augusto, quod diceret utilissimum et necessarium hoc civibus esse propter magnas et longas peregrinationes, quae apud veteres fuissent[4], ubi, si quis testamentum facere non posset, tamen codicillos posset. post quae tempora cum et Labeo codicillos

fecisset, iam nemini dubium erat, quin codicilli iure optimo admitterentur.

1 Non tantum autem testamento facto potest quis codicillos facere, sed et[5] intestatus quis decedens fideicommittere codicillis potest. sed cum ante testamentum factum codicilli facti erant, Papinianus[6] ait non aliter vires habere, quam si speciali postea voluntate confirmentur. sed divi Severus et Antoninus rescripserunt ex his codicillis qui testamentum praecedunt posse fideicommissum peti, si appareat eum, qui postea testamentum fecerat, a voluntate quam 2 codicillis expresserat non recessisse. Codicillis autem hereditas neque dari neque adimi potest, ne confundatur ius testamentorum et codicillorum, et ideo nec exheredatio scribi. directo autem hereditas codicillis neque dari neque adimi potest: nam per fideicommissum hereditas codicillis iure relinquitur. [7]nec condicionem heredi instituto codicillis adicere neque 3 substituere directo potest. Codicillos autem etiam plures quis facere potest: 'et nullam sollemnitatem ordinationis desiderant'.

LIBER TERTIUS.

I[8]
DE HEREDITATIBUS QUAE AB INTESTATO DEFERUNTUR

Intestatus decedit, qui aut omnino testamentum non fecit aut non iure fecit[9] aut id quod fecerat ruptum irritumve factum est aut[10] nemo ex eo heres extitit.
1 [11]'Intestatorum autem hereditates ex lege duo-'decim tabularum primum ad suos heredes pertinent.
2 'Sui autem heredes existimantur, ut et supra dixi-'mus[12], qui in potestate morientis fuerunt: veluti 'filius filia, nepos neptisve ex filio, pronepos pro-'neptisve ex nepote filio nato, prognatus prognatave. 'nec interest, utrum naturales sunt liberi an adoptivi. 2a 'Quibus connumerari necesse est etiam eos, qui 'ex legitimis quidem matrimoniis non sunt progeniti, 'curiis tamen civitatum dati secundum divalium con-'stitutionum, quae super his positae sunt, tenorem 'suorum iura nanciscuntur: nec non eos, quos nostrae 'amplexae sunt constitutiones[13], per quas iussimus, [14]'si quis mulierem in suo contubernio copulaverit 'non ab initio affectione maritali, eam tamen, cum 'qua poterat habere coniugium, et ex ea liberos sus-'tulerit, postea vero affectione procedente etiam nup-'tialia instrumenta cum ea fecerit filiosque vel filias 'habuerit: non solum eos liberos, qui post dotem editi 'sunt, iustos et in potestate esse patribus, sed etiam 'anteriores, qui et his[15] qui postea nati sunt occa-'sionem legitimi nominis praestiterunt: quod optinere 'censuimus, etiamsi non progeniti fuerint post dotale 'instrumentum confectum liberi vel etiam nati ab hac 2b 'luce subtracti fuerint.' [16]'Ita demum tamen ne-'pos neptisve et pronepos proneptisve suorum here-'dum numero sunt, si praecedens persona desierit in 'potestate parentis esse, sive morte id acciderit sive 'alia ratione, veluti emancipatione: nam si per id 'tempus, quo quis moreretur, filius in potestate eius

'sit, nepos ex eo suus heres esse non potest. idque 'et in ceteris deinceps liberorum personis dictum in-'tellegemus. postumi quoque, qui, si vivo parente nati 'essent, in potestate futuri forent, sui heredes sunt.'
3 Sui autem etiam ignorantes fiunt heredes et, licet furiosi sint, heredes possunt existere: quia quibus ex causis ignorantibus adquiritur nobis, ex his causis et furiosis adquiri potest. et statim morte parentis quasi continuatur dominium: et ideo nec tutoris auctoritate opus est in pupillis, cum etiam ignorantibus adquiritur suis heredibus hereditas: nec curatoris con-4 sensu adquiritur furioso, sed ipso iure. Interdum autem, licet in potestate mortis tempore suus heres non fuit, tamen suus heres parenti efficitur, veluti si ab hostibus quis reversus fuerit post mortem patris 5 sui: ius enim postliminii hoc facit. Per contrarium evenit ut, licet quis in familia defuncti sit mortis tempore, tamen suus heres non fiat, veluti si post mortem suam pater iudicatus fuerit reus perduellionis ac per hoc memoria eius damnata fuerit: suum enim heredem habere non potest, cum fiscus ei succedit. sed potest dici ipso iure esse suum heredem, 6 sed desinere. [17]'Cum filius filiave et ex altero 'filio nepos neptisve extant, pariter ad hereditatem 'vocantur nec qui gradu proximior est ulteriorem ex-'cludit: aequum enim esse videtur nepotes neptesque 'in patris sui locum succedere. pari ratione et si ne-'pos neptisque sit ex filio et ex nepote pronepos pro-'neptisve, simul vocantur. et quia placuit nepotes 'neptesque, item pronepotes proneptesque in parentis 'sui locum succedere, conveniens esse visum est non 'in capita, sed in stirpes hereditatem dividi, ut filius 'partem dimidiam hereditatis habeat et ex altero filio 'duo pluresve nepotes alteram dimidiam. item si ex 'duobus filiis nepotes extant et ex altero unus forte 'aut duo, ex altero tres aut quattuor, ad unum aut 'duos dimidia pars pertinet, ad tres vel ad quattuor 7 'altera dimidia.' Cum autem quaeritur, an quis

---

(1) Cf. *Dig.* 29, 7 *Cod.* 6, 36   (2) sic *B* cum Θ, qui *codicillos mortis tempore in Africa factos fingit*, africam *T* (3) esset et] esset *B*, est et *TC*   (4) crebuissent *scr.*, cf. Θ συνεχεῖς ἦσαν (similiter Huschke)   (5) sed et] Θ, sed *libri* (6) *Dig.* 29, 7, 5 (*Pap. l.* 7 *resp.*)   (7) § 2 *fin.* 3 *ex Marciani l.* 7 *inst.* (*Dig.* 29, 7, 6 *pr.* § 1)

(8) Cf. *Gai.* 3, 1..8 *Dig.* 38, 16 *Cod.* 6, 55   (9) facit *B*, testamentum fecit *TC*[a]   (10) aut] *T?C*[a], aut si *BC*[b] (11) *Gai.* 3, 1. 2   (12) 2, 19, 2   (13) *Cod.* 5, 27, 10. 11 (14) si quis...fuerint *ex Cod.* 5, 27, 11   (15) qui et his] *BΘ Cod.*, quia et his *T*   (16) *Gai.* 3, 2. 4   (17) *Gai.* 3, 7. 8

2.25 CODICILS

Everyone accepts that before the reign of Augustus codicils had no legal effect. Lucius Lentulus was responsible for their introduction, as also for the first trusts. Dying in Africa, he wrote some codicils, validated by his will, in which he asked something of Augustus, in the nature of a trust. Augustus carried out his wishes. The weight of his example encouraged others to carry out trust requests, and Lentulus' daughter honoured legacies which were not legally binding. It is said that Augustus called together the jurists, including Trebatius, the greatest authority of the time, and asked them whether this practice should be adopted, and whether the use of codicils was contrary to legal principle. Trebatius urged on Augustus the view that codicils would be immensely useful and convenient to people on long and far-flung journeys, a problem unknown to the ancients. On these travels a man might be able to make a codicil when he could not make a will. From then on,

since even Labeo made codicils, nobody entertained any doubt that they had full legal effect. 1. It is not only after making a will that a man can draw up a codicil; someone dying intestate can also create trusts in one. When they are made before a will Papinian says that they are validated only by a subsequently expressed intention to confirm them. But a written reply of the Emperors Severus and Antoninus holds that a trust can be established from codicils which antedate a will where the person who subsequently made the will did not resile from the intention declared in the codicils. 2. The inheritance itself cannot be given or taken away by codicil. Otherwise the line between the law of wills and the law of codicils would be lost. So a codicil cannot disinherit anyone. Though codicils cannot give or take the estate directly, a man can lawfully dispose of his estate by codicil behind a trust. A codicil cannot add a condition to the appointment of an heir. Nor can it effect a direct substitution. 3. One can make more than one codicil. No formalities are required

BOOK 3

3.1 INHERITANCE ON INTESTACY

Intestacy occurs if a man dies without any will, if the will he did make was invalid, if it was later nullified or frustrated, or if no heir takes under it. 1. The Twelve Tables give the estate of an intestate first to his immediate heirs. 2. The immediate heirs are, as has been said, those in his authority at the time of his death: son or daughter, grandchild by the son, great grandchild by a grandson through the son. It makes no difference if they are adoptive. 2a. With these must be included the illegitimates who, under the relevant provisions of imperial pronouncements, obtain the rights of immediate heirs by entering the ranks of local councillors. Other cases are covered by our pronouncements. We have made provision for the man who lives with and has children by a woman who could lawfully be his wife. If he does not at first intend to marry her but later changes his mind and executes a marriage deed, then has more sons and daughters by her, not only the children born after the marriage are to count as legitimate and in family authority but also those earlier ones who provided the occasion for the later children's legitimate birth. We have extended this even to the case in which no children are born after the marriage settlement or are born but die. 2b. Grandchildren or great grandchildren only count as immediate heirs if people ahead of them have left the head of the family's authority. This can happen by death, or for some other reason, like emancipation. If a man has a son in his authority on his death, a grandson by that son cannot be an immediate heir. The same applies to other descendants. Posthumous children count as immediate heirs if, had the father been alive at their birth, they would have been in his authority. 3. Immediate heirs inherit even if they know nothing about

it. The insane are not debarred. They can always acquire rights which accrue independently of the acquirer's knowledge. It is as though ownership is continued without the death causing a moment's interruption. A child has no need here of his guardian's endorsement because of the rule that the estate vests in immediate heirs independently of their knowledge; and the insane heir takes automatically, not by virtue of his supervisor's assent. 4. It can happen that someone not in his father's authority at his death can become an immediate heir. An example is where he comes back from enemy captivity after his father's death. This effect is a function of his right of rehabilitation. 5. It can also happen, the other way around, that someone may not qualify although he was within the deceased's authority. Suppose a father after his death is found guilty of treason, and his memory is condemned. There can be no immediate heirs; the imperial exchequer is his successor. One might admittedly say that the son did automatically become heir, only to be removed. 6. Suppose the survivors are a son or daughter and a grandson or granddaughter by the other son. They take equally. The nearer degree does not displace the more remote. Justice requires grandchildren to be stood in their father's shoes. The same reasoning applies if the survivors are a grandson or granddaughter by one son and a great grandson or great granddaughter by a grandson: they take equally. Since grandchildren and great grandchildren stand in their ascendants' places, the estate is correspondingly divided by stems, not by heads: the son takes half, the two or more grandsons by the other son take the other half. If the survivors from two sons are, say, one or two grandsons from one, and three or four from the other, a half goes to the one or two, the other half to the three or four. // 7. The time to ask

suus heres existere potest: eo tempore quaerendum est, quo certum est aliquem sine testamento decessisse: quod accidit et[1] destituto testamento. hac ratione si filius exheredatus fuerit et extraneus heres institutus est, filio mortuo postea certum fuerit heredem institutum ex testamento non fieri heredem, aut quia noluit esse heres aut quia non potuit: nepos avo suus heres existet, quia quo tempore certum est intestatum decessisse patrem familias, solus invenitur nepos. et hoc certum est. Et licet post mortem avi natus sit, tamen avo vivo conceptus, mortuo patre eius posteaque deserto avi testamento suus heres efficitur. plane si et conceptus et natus fuerit post mortem avi, mortuo patre suo desertoque postea avi testamento suus heres avo non existit, quia nullo iure cognationis patrem sui patris tetigit. sic nec ille est inter liberos avo, quem filius emancipatus adoptaverat. hi autem cum non sunt quantum ad hereditatem liberi, neque bonorum possessionem petere possunt quasi proximi cognati. haec de suis heredibus.

9 Emancipati autem liberi iure civili nihil iuris habent: neque enim sui heredes sunt, quia in potestate esse desierunt parentis, neque alio ullo iure per legem duodecim tabularum vocantur. sed praetor naturali aequitate motus dat eis bonorum possessionem unde liberi, perinde ac si in potestate parentis mortis tempore fuissent, sive soli sint sive cum suis heredibus concurrant. itaque duobus liberis extantibus, emancipato et qui mortis tempore in potestate fuerit, sane quidem is qui in potestate fuerit solus iure civili heres est, id est solus suus heres est: sed cum emancipatus beneficio praetoris in partem admittitur[2], evenit, ut suus heres pro parte heres fiat. At
10 hi, qui emancipati a parente in adoptionem se dederunt, non admittuntur ad bona naturalis patris quasi liberi, si modo cum is moreretur in adoptiva familia sint. nam vivo eo emancipati ab adoptivo patre perinde admittuntur ad bona naturalis patris, ac si emancipati ab ipso[3] essent nec umquam in adoptiva familia fuissent: et convenienter quod ad adoptivum patrem pertinet extraneorum loco esse incipiunt. post mortem vero naturalis patris emancipati ab adoptivo et quantum ad hunc aeque extraneorum loco fiunt et quantum ad naturalis parentis bona pertinet nihilo magis liberorum gradum nanciscuntur: quod ideo sic placuit, quia iniquum erat esse in potestate patris adoptivi, ad quos bona naturalis patris pertinerent,
11 utrum ad liberos eius an ad adgnatos. Minus ergo iuris habent adoptivi quam naturales. namque naturales emancipati beneficio praetoris gradum liberorum retinent, licet iure civili perdunt: adoptivi vero emancipati et iure civili perdunt gradum liberorum et a praetore non adiuvantur[4]. et recte: naturalia enim iura civilis ratio peremere non postest nec, quia desinunt sui heredes esse, desinere possunt filii filiaeve aut nepotes neptesve esse: adoptivi vero emancipati extraneorum loco incipiunt esse, quia ius nomenque filii filiaeve, quod per adoptionem consecuti sunt, alia civili ratione, id est emancipatione, perdunt.
12 Eadem haec observantur et in ea bonorum possessione, quam contra tabulas testamenti parentis liberis praeteritis, id est neque heredibus institutis neque ut oportet exheredatis, praetor pollicetur. nam eos quidem, qui in potestate parentis mortis tempore fuerunt, et emancipatos vocat praetor ad eam bonorum possessionem: eos vero, qui in adoptiva familia fuerunt per hoc tempus, quo naturalis parens moreretur, repellit. item adoptivos liberos emancipatos ab adoptivo patre sicut ab intestato, ita longe minus contra tabulas testamenti ad bona eius admittit, quia

13 desinunt in liberorum numero esse. Admonendi tamen sumus eos, qui in adoptiva familia sunt quive post mortem naturalis parentis ab adoptivo patre emancipati fuerint, intestato parente naturali mortuo licet ea parte edicti, qua liberi ad bonorum possessionem vocantur, non admittantur, alia tamen parte vocari, id est qua cognati defuncti vocantur. ex qua parte ita admittuntur, si neque sui heredes liberi neque emancipati obstent neque adgnatus quidem ullus interveniat: ante enim praetor liberos vocat tam suos heredes quam emancipatos, deinde legitimos heredes,
14 deinde proximos cognatos. 'Sed ea omnia anti'quitati quidem placuerunt: aliquam autem emenda'tionem a nostra constitutione[5] acceperunt, quam 'super his personis posuimus, quae a patribus suis 'naturalibus in adoptionem aliis dantur. invenimus 'etenim nonnullos casus, in quibus filii et naturalium 'parentum successionem propter adoptionem amitte'bant et adoptione facile per emancipationem soluta 'ad neutrius patris successionem vocabantur. hoc so'lito more corrigentes constitutionem scripsimus, per 'quam definivimus, quando parens naturalis filium 'suum adoptandum alii dederit, integra omnia iura ita 'servari, atque si in patris naturalis potestate per'mansisset nec penitus adoptio fuerit[6] subsecuta: nisi 'in hoc tantummodo casu, ut possit ab intestato ad 'patris adoptivi venire successionem. testamento au'tem ab eo facto neque iure civili neque praetorio 'aliquid ex hereditate eius persequi potest neque con'tra tabulas bonorum possessione agnita neque in'officiosi querella instituta, cum nec necessitas patri 'adoptivo imponitur vel heredem eum instituere vel 'exheredatum facere utpote nullo naturali vinculo 'copulatum. neque si ex Afiniano[7] senatus consulto 'ex tribus maribus fuerit adoptatus: nam et in huius'modi casu neque quarta ei servatur nec ulla actio 'ad eius persecutionem ei competit. nostra autem con'stitutione exceptus est is, quem parens naturalis 'adoptandum susceperit: utroque enim iure tam natu'rali quam legitimo in hanc personam[8] concurrente 'pristina iura tali adoptioni[9] servavimus, quemadmo'dum si pater familias sese dederit adrogandum. quae 'specialiter et singillatim ex praefatae constitutionis 'tenore possunt colligi.'
15 'Item vetustas ex masculis progenitos plus dili'gens solos nepotes vel neptes, qui ex virili sexu 'descendunt, ad suorum vocabat successionem et iuri 'adgnatorum eos anteponebat: nepotes autem, qui ex 'filiabus nati sunt, et pronepotes ex neptibus cogna'torum loco numerans post adgnatorum lineam eos 'vocabat tam in avi vel proavi materni quam in aviae 'vel proaviae sive paternae sive maternae successio'nem. divi autem principes[10] non passi sunt talem 'contra naturam iniuriam sine competenti emendatione 'relinquere: sed cum nepotis et pronepotis nomen 'commune est utrisque[11], qui tam ex masculis quam 'ex feminis descendunt, ideo eundem gradum et ordi'nem successionis eis donaverunt: sed ut aliquid am'plius sit eis, qui non solum naturae, sed etiam vete'ris iuris suffragio muniuntur, portionem nepotum et 'neptium vel deinceps, de quibus supra diximus, paulo 'minuendam esse existimaverunt, ut minus tertiam 'partem[12] acciperent, quam mater eorum vel avia 'fuerat accepta, vel pater eorum vel avus paternus 'sive maternus, quando femina mortua sit cuius de 'hereditate agitur, hisque, licet[13] soli sint, adeuntibus 'adgnatos minime vocabant. et quemadmodum lex 'duodecim tabularum filio mortuo nepotes vel neptes[14] 'vel pronepotes et proneptes in locum patris sui ad[15] 'successionem avi[16] vocat: ita et principalis disposi'tio[17] in locum matris suae vel aviae eos cum iam

(1) et] T^v P cum Θ, ex B, •••• (vel et?) ex T^t (2) sic B, in parte admittatur T   (3) ipso] P, ipso patre BT   (4) adiuvantur] BΘ, adhibentur T   (5) Cod. 8, 47 (48), 10   (6) sic T, fuerat B   (7) afiniano] B Cod. Θ (τὸ Afinianion δόγμα), afabiniano W, papiniano E. sabiniano TC   (8) sic B, hac persona TC   (9) sic P cum Θ, adoptione   BTC   (10) Cod. 6, 55, 9   (11) sic C, utriusque BT^a (12) sic TC, tertia parte B   (13) hisque licet] C, his qui licet B, his qui licet si (si add. man. 2?) T^a, hisque scilicet T^b (14) nepotem vel nepotes BT^a, nepotes vel neptem C^b (15) ad] P, et B, et ad T   (16) avi] B, avi sui T   (17) Cod. 6, 55, 9

whether a deceased has an immediate heir is when intestacy is inevitable. This may be when the will is abandoned. Applying this: suppose a son is disinherited and an outsider is appointed; the son dies and afterwards it becomes certain that the appointee is not going to become heir, because he does not want to or because he cannot. The grandson becomes immediate heir because now it is certain that the head of the family has died intestate and the grandson is the only one left. There is no doubt about this. 8. Suppose him born after the grandfather's death though conceived before. With his father dead and his grandfather's will subsequently thrown over, he becomes immediate heir. Clearly, if he was conceived and born after the grandfather's death, the death of his father and the later abandonment of the grandfather's will cannot make him his grandfather's immediate heir: his birth here puts him in no legal relationship with his father's father. The adoptee of an emancipated son is also not counted among the grandfather's issue. Discounted in the quest for an heir, such a person also cannot qualify in the class of nearest cognates for estate-possession. That concludes the discussion of immediate heirs. 9. Emancipated children have no claims under the law of the state. They are not immediate heirs because not within family authority, and the Twelve Tables give them no other rights. The praetor, in pursuit of natural justice, does allow them estate-possession as children, on their own or concurrently with immediate heirs, just as if they were still within authority at the time of the death. If there are two survivors, one emancipated and one within authority on the death, the latter is certainly the sole heir at state law, the only immediate heir. But the other's praetorian right means that the immediate heir actually gets only a share. 10. A son who is emancipated and then adopted gets no share of his real father's estate as one of his father's descendants, not at least if in his adoptive family on the death. If he is emancipated by the adoptive father while the real father is alive he does get a share, as though emancipated by his father and never adopted. Correspondingly he then becomes an outsider in relation to the adoptive father. Emancipated by the adoptive father after his real father's death, he still becomes an outsider to the adoptive family. But here he remains disqualified from the class of descendants able to claim his real father's estate. This was decided because it seemed unjust that the adoptive father should have the power to control the destination of the real father's estate, as between his issue and his agnatic relatives. 11. Adoptive rights are weaker than natural: by virtue of his praetorian claim an emancipated son retains his rank among his father's issue, despite the destruction of his state law rights; an emancipated adoptive son loses his state law ranking and gets no praetorian relief. That is right. The rules of state law cannot destroy natural ties. People do not cease to be sons and daughters and grandchildren just because they stop being immediate heirs. Emancipated adoptees become outsiders because they only get their status as sons and daughters from a rule of law, by adoption, and lose it through another, by emancipation. 12. The same principle applies in the estate-possession granted by the praetor counter to the parental will where descendants have been passed over, neither appointed heirs nor properly disinherited. The praetor allows those within authority on the death and those previously emancipated to claim that estate-possession. He bars those who are in adoptive families at the time of the real father's death. With adoptees emancipated by the adoptive father – whom he excludes from estate-possession on intestacy – he all the more excludes them from estate-possession in contradiction of the will, because they have ceased to be descendants. 13. Although adoptees still in the adoptive family or emancipated by the adoptive father after the death of the head of their real family have no claim on his intestacy under the part of the edict which entitles descendants to estate-possession, note that they do have rights under another part, where cognates of the deceased may claim: they can come in if there are no descendants who are immediate heirs or their emancipated equivalents and if no agnate claims. The praetor's ranking is: first, descendants whether immediate heirs or emancipated; next, statutory heirs; next, nearest cognatic relatives. 14. But these were the old rules. They have been improved by our pronouncement on the law of adoption. We identified some cases in which a son lost his rights of succession to his real father through adoption and then, since the adoptive tie was easily cut by emancipation, found himself entitled to inherit from neither. In our usual way we set out to correct this and laid down that when a real father lets his son be adopted the son keeps all his rights, just as though he had stayed within his real father's authority and the adoption had never happened, except only that he acquires a right of succession to the adoptive father in the event of the latter's intestacy. If the adoptive father leaves a will the adoptee is given no entitlement at state law or at praetorian law to obtain any share of the estate, whether by estate-possession counter to the will or by the complaint of irresponsibility. Since there is no natural tie between them, the adoptive father is not bound to appoint or exclude the adoptee as his heir, not even where the adoption is of one of three brothers under the Afinian Resolution. No quarter-share is reserved for the adoptee and no action to demand it is available to him. The exception is the adoption by a real ascendant. Here natural and legal ties concur, and we have preserved the old regime, as also for the case in which the head of a family is adrogated. The details can be read in the pronouncement itself. 15. The earlier law was biased in favour of males. It recognized the priority over agnates of grandchildren by sons; but as for grandsons and great grandsons through daughters and granddaughters, it treated them as cognates and ranked them after the line of agnates in the succession to their grandfathers and great grandfathers on their mother's side, and their grandmothers and great grandmothers on both sides. The emperors could not allow such an injustice to continue without some appropriate remedy. Since grandsons and great grandsons had the same name on both sides of the family, the emperors recognized both groups as having the same degree and rank in the law of succession. However, they decided that, to give rather more to the ones who had the support both of nature and the old law, the shares of these grandsons, granddaughters, and so on, mentioned above, should be slightly reduced: they should take a third less than their mother or grandmother had been qualified to get, or than their father or their paternal and maternal grandfathers had been qualified to get where the estate in question was a woman's. If members of this class took, even they alone, the agnates were excluded. The Twelve Tables, if the father was dead, put the grandchildren in his place, then the great granchildren in theirs and so on. Similarly the imperial scheme gives these claimants their mother's rights, or their grandmother's, subject to the one third reduction already mentioned. // 16. However,

16 'designata partis tertiae deminutione vocat. Sed 'nos, cum adhuc dubitatio manebat inter adgnatos et 'memoratos nepotes, partem quartam defuncti sub- 'stantiae adgnatis sibi vindicantibus ex cuiusdam con- 'stitutionis[1] auctoritate, memoratam quidem constitu- 'tionem a nostro codice segregravimus neque inseri 'eam ex Theodosiano codice in eo concessimus. nostra 'autem constitutione[2] promulgata toti iuri eius dero- 'gatum est: et sanximus talibus nepotibus ex filia vel 'pronepotibus ex nepte et deinceps superstitibus ad- 'gnatos nullam partem mortui successionis sibi vindi- 'care, ne hi, qui ex transversa linea veniunt, potiores 'his habeantur, qui recto iure descendunt. quam con- 'stitutionem nostram optinere secundum sui vigorem 'et tempora et nunc sancimus: ita tamen ut[3], quem- 'admodum inter filios et nepotes ex filio antiquitas 'statuit non in capita sed in stirpes dividi heredita- 'tem, similiter nos inter filios et nepotes ex filia distri- 'butionem fieri iubemus, vel inter omnes nepotes et 'neptes[4] et alias deinceps personas, ut utraque pro- 'genies matris suae vel patris, aviae vel avi portio- 'nem sine ulla deminutione consequantur, ut, si forte 'unus vel duo ex una parte, ex altera tres aut quat- 'tuor extent, unus aut duo dimidiam, alteri[5] tres aut 'quattuor alteram dimidiam hereditatis habeant.'

II[6]
DE LEGITIMA ADGNATORUM SUCCESSIONE.

Si nemo suus heres 'vel eorum, quos inter suos he- redes praetor vel constitutiones vocant', extat 'et[7] 'successionem quoquo modo amplectatur': tunc ex lege duodecim tabularum ad adgnatum proximum heredi- 1 tas pertinet. Sunt autem adgnati, ut primo quo- que libro[8] tradidimus, cognati per virilis sexus per- sonas cognatione iuncti, quasi a patre cognati. [9]'ita- 'que eodem patre nati fratres adgnati sibi sunt, qui 'et consanguinei vocantur, nec requiritur, an etiam 'eandem matrem habuerint. item patruus fratris filio 'et invicem is illi adgnatus est. eodem numero sunt 'fratres patrueles, id est qui ex duobus fratribus pro- 'creati sunt, qui etiam consobrini vocantur. qua ra- 'tione etiam ad plures gradus adgnationis pervenire 'poterimus.' hi quoque, qui post mortem patris nas- cuntur, nanciscuntur consanguinitatis iura. [10]'non ta- 'men omnibus simul adgnatis dat lex hereditatem, sed 'his, qui tunc proximo gradu sunt, cum certum esse 2 'coeperit aliquem intestatum decessisse.' Per adop- tionem quoque adgnationis ius consistit, veluti inter filios naturales et eos quos pater eorum adoptavit (nec dubium est, quin proprie consanguinei appel- lentur): item si quis ex ceteris adgnatis tuis[11], veluti frater aut patruus aut denique is qui longiore gradu est, aliquem adoptaverit, adgnatos inter suos[12] esse 3 non dubitatur. Ceterum inter masculos quidem adgnationis iure hereditas etiam longissimo gradu ultro citroque capitur. quod ad feminas vero ita placebat, ut ipsae consanguinitatis iure tantum ca- piant hereditatem, si sorores sint, ulterius non ca- piant: masculi vero ad earum hereditates, etiam si longissimo gradu sint, admittantur. qua de causa fratris tui aut patrui tui filiae vel amitae tuae here- ditas ad te pertinet[13]. tua vero ad illas non pertine- bat. quod ideo ita constitutum erat, quia commodius videbatur[14] ita iura constitui, ut plerumque heredi- tates ad masculos confluerent. sed quia sane ini- quum erat in universum eas quasi extraneas repelli, praetor eas ad bonorum possessionem[15] admittit[16] ea parte, qua proximitatis nomine bonorum posses- sionem pollicetur: ex qua parte ita scilicet admit-

tuntur, si neque adgnatus ullus nec proximior cogna- 3a tus interveniat. Et haec quidem lex duodecim tabularum nullo modo introduxit, sed simplicitatem legibus amicam amplexa simili modo omnes adgnatos sive masculos sive feminas cuiuscumque gradus ad similitudinem suorum invicem ad successionem voca- bat: media autem iurisprudentia, quae erat lege qui- dem duodecim tabularum iunior, imperiali autem dispositione anterior, suptilitate quadam excogitata praefatam differentiam inducebat et penitus eas a successione adgnatorum repellebat, omni alia succes- sione incognita, donec praetores, paulatim asperitatem iuris civilis corrigentes sive quod deest adimplentes, humano proposito alium ordinem suis edictis addi- derunt et cognationis linea proximitatis nomine intro- ducta per bonorum possessionem eas adiuvabant et pol- licebantur his bonorum possessionem, quae unde cognati 3b appellantur. Nos vero legem duodecim tabularum sequentes et eius vestigia in hac parte conservantes laudamus quidem praetores suae humanitatis, non tamen eos in plenum causae mederi invenimus: quare etenim uno eodemque gradu naturali concurrente et adgnationis titulis tam in masculis quam in feminis aequa lance constitutis masculis quidem dabatur ad successionem venire omnium adgnatorum, ex adgnatis autem mulieribus nullis penitus nisi soli sorori ad adgnatorum successionem patebat aditus? ideo in plenum omnia reducentes et ad ius duodecim tabu- larum eandem dispositionem exaequantes nostra con- stitutione[17] sanximus omnes legitimas personas, id est per virilem sexum descendentes, sive masculini sive feminini generis sunt, simili modo ad iura suc- cessionis legitimae ab intestato vocari secundum gra- dus sui praerogativam nec ideo excludendas, quia consanguinitatis iura sicuti germanae non habent.' 4 'Hoc etiam addendum nostrae constitutioni existi- 'mavimus, ut transferatur unus tantummodo gradus a 'iure cognationis in legitimam successionem, ut non 'solum fratris filius et filia secundum quod iam defi- 'nivimus ad successionem patrui sui vocentur, sed 'etiam germanae consanguineae vel sororis uterinae 'filius et filia soli et non deinceps personae una cum 'his ad iura avunculi sui perveniant et mortuo eo, qui 'patruus quidem est fratris sui filiis[18], avunculus au- 'tem sororis suae suboli[19], simili modo ab utroque 'latere succedant, tamquam si omnes ex masculis 'descendentes legitimo iure veniant, scilicet ubi frater 'et soror superstites non sunt (his etenim personis 'praecedentibus et successionem admittentibus ceteri 'gradus remanent penitus semoti): videlicet hereditate 5 'non ad[20] stirpes, sed in capita dividenda.' Si plures sint gradus adgnatorum, aperte lex duo- decim tabularum proximum vocat: itaque si verbi gratia sit frater defuncti et alterius fratris filius aut patruus, frater potior habetur. et quamvis singulari numero usa lex proximum vocet, tamen dubium non est, quin et, si plures sint eiusdem gradus, omnes admittan- tur: nam et proprie proximus ex pluribus gradibus intelligitur et tamen dubium non est, quin, licet unus sit gradus adgnatorum, pertineat ad eos hereditas. 6 Proximus autem, si quidem nullo testamento facto quisque decesserit, per hoc tempus requiritur, quo mortuus est is cuius de hereditate quaeritur. quod si facto testamento quisquam decesserit, per hoc tempus requiritur, quo certum esse coeperit nullum ex testamento heredem extaturum: tum enim pro- prie quisque intelligitur intestatus[21] decessisse. quod quidem aliquando longo tempore declaratur: in quo spatio temporis saepe accidit, ut proximiore mortuo proximus esse incipiat, qui moriente testatore non

---

(1) *non extat*   (2) *Cod.* 6, 55, 12   (3) *ut del. Huschke* (4) **omnes nepotes et neptes**] *WΘ*, nepotes vel inter ne- **potes et neptes** *BT*   (5) *alteri*] *T, et B*

(6) *Cf. Gai.* 3, 9..16. 23..30 *Dig.* 38, 7. 16 *Cod.* 6, 15. 55 (7) et] *T,* ut *B*   (8) 1, 15, 1   (9) *Gai.* 3, 10   (10) *Gai.* 3, 11   (11) tuis] *B,* om. *T*   (12) adgnatos (agnatus *B*) inter suos] *BTPW^b,* agnatus suus *W^a,* ἀδγνατιῶν μεταξὺ

ἡμῶν συνίσταται Θ, secundum quem *B* aut adgnationem inter vos *scr.*   (13) *sic T,* pertinebat *B* cum Θ   (14) *sic T,* videbantur *B*   (15) *sic P,* possessiones *BT^a*?   (16) *sic T,* admittebat *B*   (17) *Cod.* 6, 58, 14, *ubi* §3 *fin. et* §4 *ad verbum redeunt* (18) filii *BT* (19) sob- oles *BT^b*   (20) ad] *TE,* in *B*   (21) *sic BΘ,* in- testato *T*

there remained unresolved disputes between the agnates and these grandchildren. On the strength of a particular imperial pronouncement agnates claimed to be entitled to a quarter of the deceased's estate. We chose to keep that pronouncement out of our Codex and forbade its being taken over from the Theodosian Codex. It was finally repealed by our own pronouncement. We enacted that where these grandsons by daughters, great grandsons by granddaughters, and so on, survive, the agnates are to have no right to any share in the deceased's estate, so that collateral claimants do not displace any true descendants. We now confirm that our pronouncement is effective from the time set out in its provisions, but with this addition: the old law divided estates between sons and grandsons by sons according to stems, not heads; we ordain division on the same principle between sons and grandsons by daughters and between all grandsons and granddaughters down the line, with the effect that the issue of any mother or father or grandmother or grandfather shall take that predecessor's share without any reduction whatever. It follows that if, say, one share of the estate is represented by one or two, the other by three or four, the one or two take a half, while the other three or four take the other half.

3.2 STATUTORY SUCCESSION BY AGNATIC RELATIVES

Suppose there is no immediate heir and also nobody from the equivalent class in praetorian or imperial law able one way or another to take. Here the code of the Twelve Tables gives the succession to the nearest agnate. 1. As we said in Book 1, agnates are relatives in the male line, loosely relations through the father. Two brothers born to one father are agnatically related – they are also called full agnates – and it is immaterial whether they also have the same mother. An uncle and his brother's son are agnatically related. So are the sons of two brothers, called cousins. We could run through many degrees on the same principle. Those born after a father's death come in as full agnates. The code does not give the estate to them all, only the closest at the time intestacy becomes certain. 2. Adoption also creates an agnatic tie, for example between a son and his brother by adoption, certainly full agnates. Again, if another of your agnates adopts – your brother, paternal uncle, or remoter – he undoubtedly brings the adoptee into the agnatic network. 3. Males qualify to inherit agnatically even in a very remote degree. Females came to qualify only by the full agnatic tie: sisters could take but none more remote. By contrast remote male agnates could claim women's estates. You have a claim to a woman's estate if she is your brother's daughter or paternal uncle's, or your aunt; but they have no claim to yours. This regime reflects a conviction that the best policy was generally for men to inherit. But it was obviously unjust for women to be invariably excluded as rank outsiders. The praetor therefore gave them a claim under the edict offering estate-possession to nearest cognates. That, of course, let them in only if there was no agnate at all and no nearer cognate. 3a. This regime was not sanctioned by the Twelve Tables. That code, making simplicity the handmaid of the law, treated male and female agnates all alike. The degrees were ranked and allowed to succeed on the same lines as immediate heirs. The jurists of the intervening period, after the Twelve Tables and before the imperial legislation, refined the arguments and introduced the distinction. In effect it eliminated women from agnatic succession. They had no other avenue of succession until the praetors slowly began to correct the severity of the old state law and mend its deficiencies. Aiming at a more liberal scheme, they added a new edictal class, cognates in order of proximity. By this promise of estate-possession to cognates, the praetors came to women's assistance. 3b. We ourselves, anxious to follow the scheme of the Twelve Tables and preserve its outline, applaud the sensitivity of the praetors but find their remedy inadequate. Given that in a single natural category the agnatic claims of males and females are balanced equally, why was it that the males of the class were given the right to succeed any agnate while the females, except the deceased's sister, were completely excluded? Our pronouncement has redesigned the system and made it conform to the scheme of the Twelve Tables. All persons envisaged by the that code – those related through males whether themselves male or female – shall have title to succeed to an intestate, taking their priority from their degree; none shall be excluded because not a full agnate of, and in particular not a sister of, the deceased. 4. We also added one cognatic class to the statutory scheme of succession: to a paternal uncle shall succeed, not only his brother's son and daughter, as above, but also, though going no further than this, the son and daughter of his sister, whether fully agnatic or born of the same mother. This means that on the death of a man who was paternal uncle to his brother's children and maternal uncle to his sister's, the children on both sides shall succeed as though all were statutorily qualified by male relationship. Clearly this will only happen if his brother and sister are dead, since they have priority; if they go in, the rest are excluded. Division of the estate in this case must naturally be by heads, not stems. 5. Where there are agnates in different degrees the Twelve Tables expressly entitle the closest. Suppose the survivors are his brother and another brother's son or his father's uncle. The brother takes. Though the code uses the singular, the nearest agnate, it is clear that a number of people in the same degree all take together. In fact nearest strictly speaking supposes several classes, but if all the claimants come from a single class there is no doubt that that they take as members of that class. 6. To find the nearest agnate, the question must be put at the death if the intestate made no will at all. If he did make a will, it must be put at the time when it becomes certain that there will be no heir under the will. Strictly, that is always the moment of intestacy. Sometimes there is a long gap, and someone turns out to be nearest only because someone nearer at the time of death has died. //

7 erat proximus. Placebat autem in eo genere percipiendarum hereditatum successionem non esse, id est ut, quamvis proximus, qui secundum ea quae diximus vocatur ad hereditatem, aut spreverit hereditatem aut antequam adeat decesserit, nihilo magis legitimo iure sequentes admittuntur. 'quod iterum 'praetores imperfecto iure corrigentes non in totum 'sine adminiculo relinquebant, sed ex cognatorum or- 'dine eos vocabant, utpote adgnationis iure eis re- 'cluso. sed nos nihil deesse perfectissimo iuri cu- 'pientes nostra constitutione¹ sanximus, quam de iure 'patronatus humanitate suggerente protulimus, succes- 'sionem in adgnatorum hereditatibus non esse eis 'denegandam, cum satis absurdum erat, quod cogna- 'tis a praetore apertum est, hoc adgnatis esse reclu- 'sum, maxime cum in onere quidem tutelarum et 'primo gradu deficiente sequens succedit et, quod in 'onere optinebat, non erat in lucro permissum.'

8   Ad legitimam successionem nihilo minus vocatur etiam parens, qui contracta fiducia filium vel filiam, nepotem vel neptem ac deinceps emancipat. 'quod ex nostra constitutione² omnimodo inducitur, 'ut emancipationes liberorum semper videantur con- 'tracta fiducia fieri, cum apud antiquos non aliter 'hoc optinebat, nisi specialiter contracta fiducia pa- 'rens manumisisset.'

III³
DE SENATUS CONSULTO TERTULLIANO.

'Lex duodecim tabularum ita stricto iure utebatur 'et praeponebat masculorum progeniem et eos', ⁴'qui 'per feminini sexus necessitudinem sibi iunguntur, adeo 'expellebat', 'ut ne quidem inter matrem et filium 'filiamve ultro citroque hereditatis capiendae ius' 'daret, 'nisi quod praetores ex proximitate cognatorum eas 'personas ad successionem bonorum possessione unde 1 'cognati accommodata vocabant.' ⁴'Sed hae iuris' 'angustiae postea' 'emendatae sunt.' et primus quidem divus Claudius matri ad solacium liberorum amisso- 2 rum legitimam eorum detulit hereditatem. Postea autem senatus consulto Tertulliano, quod divi Ha- driani temporibus factum est, 'plenissime de tristi⁵ 'successione matri, non etiam viae deferenda' cautum est: ut mater ingenua trium liberorum ius habens, libertina quattuor ad bona filiorum filiarumve ad- mittatur intestatorum mortuorum, licet in potestate parentis sit, ut scilicet, cum alieno iuri subiecta est, 3 iussu eius adeat, cuius iuri subiecta est. Prae- feruntur autem matri liberi defuncti, qui sui sunt quive⁶ suorum loco, sive primi gradus sive ulterioris. 'sed 'et filiae suae mortuae filius vel filia opponitur ex 'constitutionibus matri defunctae, id est aviae suae.' pater quoque utriusque, non etiam avus vel proavus matri anteponitur, scilicet cum inter eos solos de hereditate agitur. frater autem consanguineus tam filii quam filiae excludebat matrem: soror autem con- sanguinea pariter cum matre admittebatur: sed si fuerat frater et soror consanguinei et mater liberis honorata, frater quidem matrem excludebat, commu- nis autem erat hereditas ex aequis partibus fratri et 4 sorori. 'Sed nos constitutione⁷, quam in codice 'nostro nomine decorato posuimus, matri subvenien- 'dum esse existimavimus, respicientes ad naturam et 'puerperium et periculum et saepe mortem ex hoc 'casu matribus illatam. ideoque impium esse credidi- 'mus casum fortuitum in eius admitti detrimentum: 'si enim ingenua ter vel libertina quater non peperit⁸, 'immerito defraudabatur successione suorum libero- 'rum: quid enim peccavit, si non plures, sed paucos 'pepererit? et dedimus ius legitimum plenum matri- 'bus sive ingenuis sive libertinis, etsi non ter enixae 'fuerint vel quater, sed eum tantum vel eam, qui

'quaeve morte intercepti sunt, ut et sic vocentur in 5 'liberorum suorum legitimam successionem. Sed 'cum antea constitutiones iura legitima perscrutantes 'partim matrem adiuvabant, partim eam praegrava- 'bant et non in solidum eam vocabant, sed in qui- 'busdam casibus tertiam partem ei abstrahentes certis 'legitimis dabant personis, in aliis autem contrarium 'faciebant: nobis⁹ visum est recta et simplici via ma- 'trem omnibus legitimis personis anteponi et sine ulla 'deminutione filiorum suorum successionem accipere, 'excepta fratris et sororis persona, sive consanguinei 'sint sive sola cognationis iura habentes, ut quemad- 'modum eam toto alio ordini legitimo praeposuimus, 'ita omnes fratres et sorores, sive legitimi sint sive 'non, ad capiendas hereditates simul vocemus, ita 'tamen ut, si quidem solae sorores cognatae vel ad- 'gnatae et mater defuncti vel defunctae supersint, di- 'midiam quidem mater, alteram vero dimidiam partem 'omnes sorores habeant, si vero matre superstite et 'fratre vel fratribus solis vel etiam cum sororibus sive 'legitima sive sola cognationis iura habentibus inte- 'status quis vel intestata moriatur, in capita distribua- 6 'tur eius hereditas. Sed quemadmodum nos ma- 'tribus prospeximus, ita eas oportet suae suboli con- 'sulere: scituris eis, quod, si tutores liberis non 'petierint vel in locum remoti vel excusati intra annum 'petere neglexerint, ab eorum impuberum morientium 7 'successione merito repellentur.' Licet autem vulgo quaesitus sit filius filiave, potest ad bona eius mater ex Tertulliano senatus consulto admitti.

IV¹⁰
DE SENATUS CONSULTO ORFITIANO.

Per contrarium autem ut liberi ad bona matrum intestatarum admittantur¹¹, senatus consulto Orfi- tiano effectum est, quod latum est¹² Orfito et Rufo consulibus¹³, divi Marci temporibus. et data est tam filio quam filiae legitima hereditas, etiamsi alieno iuri subiecti sunt: et praeferuntur et consanguineis et 1 adgnatis defunctae matris. 'Sed cum ex hoc sena- 'tus consulto nepotes ad aviae successionem legitimo 'iure non vocabantur, postea hoc constitutionibus 'principalibus¹⁴ emendatum est, ut ad similitudinem 'filiorum filiarumque et nepotes et neptes vocentur.' 2 Sciendum autem est huiusmodi successiones, quae a Tertulliano et Orfitiano deferuntur, capitis demi- nutione non peremi propter illam regulam, qua no- vae hereditates legitimae capitis deminutione non per- eunt, sed illae solae quae ex lege duodecim tabularum 3 deferuntur. Novissime sciendum est etiam illos liberos, qui vulgo quaesiti sunt, ad matris heredita- tem ex hoc senatus consulto admitti. 4   ¹⁵Si ex pluribus legitimis heredibus quidam omiserint hereditatem vel morte vel alia causa im- pediti fuerint quominus adeant, reliquis qui adierint adcrescit illorum portio et, licet ante decesserint qui adierint, ad heredes tamen eorum pertinet.

V¹⁶
DE SUCCESSIONE COGNATORUM.

Post suos heredes eosque, quos inter suos heredes praetor 'et constitutiones' vocant, et post legitimos ('quo numero sunt adgnati et hi, quos in locum ad- 'gnatorum tam supra dicta senatus consulta quam 'nostra erexit constitutio¹⁷') proximos cognatos praetor 1 vocat. Qua parte naturalis cognatio spectatur. nam adgnati capite deminuti quique ex his progeniti sunt ex lege duodecim tabularum inter legitimos non habentur, sed a praetore tertio ordine vocantur, 'ex- 'ceptis solis tantummodo fratre et sorore emancipatis,

(1) *Cod.* 6, 4, 4 § 20   (2) *Cod.* 8, 48, 6   (3) *Cf. Gai.* 3, 24. 33 *Dig.* 38, 17 *Cod.* 6, 56 (4) *Gai.* 3, 24. 25 (5) de tristi] *P.* der insti *B*, ex tristi *T* (6) quive] *T*, sive *B* (7) *Cod.* 8. ... (8) sic *P*, pepererit *BT*   (9) *Cod.* 6, 56, 7 ... *Dig.* 38, 17 *Cod.* 6, 57   (11) ut lib. ...admit-

tantur] *B*, lib. ...admittuntur *T*   (12) *anno p. Chr.* 178 (13) effectum...consulibus] *Russardus cum* Θ, quod orphito et rufo conss. eff. est quod latum est *BT* (14) *Cod.* 6, 55, 9 (15) § 4 *ex Marciani l.* 5 *inst.* (*Dig.* 38, 16, 9) (16) *Cf. Gai.* 3, 21. 24. 27..31 *Dig.* 38, 8 *Cod.* 6, 15   (17) 3, 2, 4

7. In this type of inheritance, the choice went against allowing a qualified claimant to be replaced: if the nearest agnate as defined above rejected, or died before accepting the estate, the people in the next nearest class of agnates were not entitled to replace him. Here the praetor again offered some remedy, though an incomplete one. He recognized the remoter agnates, their agnatic claims now barred, in his cognatic category. Anxious not to leave the law short of a complete solution, we ourselves have provided, in our liberal pronouncement on patrons' rights, that in agnatic inheritance the succession of one degree to another should be permitted. It was absurd that the praetor's regime for cognates should have been unavailable to agnates. This was aggravated by the fact that when it came to allocating the duties of guardianship subsequent degrees were made to succeed if the earlier dropped out: the rules of replacement operated as to burdens but not benefits. 8. The head of a family retains his statutory rights of succession despite a fiduciary emancipation of his son, daughter, grandchild, and so on. Under our pronouncement every emancipation has that character. Under the old law it depended on there being an express agreement to that effect.

3.3 THE TERTULLIAN RESOLUTION

The Twelve Tables were strict in favouring the male line and excluding those connected through females. They did not even recognize rights of succession between a mother and her children. A limited departure was made by the praetors, who allowed them to succeed each other as close relations in the species of estate-possession open to cognates. 1. This restrictive attitude was later relaxed. The Emperor Claudius was the first to console a mother's loss by giving her the estates of her children. 2. Afterwards, in the reign of the Emperor Hadrian, the senate passed the Tertullian Resolution. This made full provision for the mother's sad succession. It gave no right to the grandmother. It enacted that free-born mothers with the honour of three children, and freedwomen with four children, should have the right to their sons' and daughters' estates on intestacy. This applied even to a mother within family authority provided the head of her family agreed to her accepting the estate. 3. The following have priority over the deceased's mother: immediate heirs and those replacing them in the first or a subsequent degree; with deceased daughters, under imperial pronouncements, their own sons and daughters, who thus defeat their grandmother; with sons and daughters, the father – but as between the mother and a grandfather or great grandfather the mother wins; again with sons and daughters, a fully agnatic brother. A mother takes equally with a fully agnatic sister, but where there is a mother honoured with children and a surviving brother and such a sister, the mother is again excluded; and the brother and sister take equal shares. 4. By a pronouncement in the Codex which our name adorns, we determined to improve the mother's position. We took into consideration her natural love, her labour in child-birth, and the danger, often of death. We concluded that it was wicked to allow her to be prejudiced by chance events, cheated of the succession if she happened not to bear three children if free-born, four if freed. How could she be blamed for not having many children? We therefore granted all mothers the full statutory right of succession to their children, whether free-born or freed and whether having three or four children or perhaps only the one whose death has raised the issue. 5. Earlier pronouncements sifting through these statutory rights conferred on the mother a confusion of benefits and burdens. They sometimes allowed her less than the whole estate and gave a third away within the class of statutory heirs, and sometimes took exactly the opposite course. Our own decision was the straight and simple one: we ruled that the mother should take priority over every other member of the statutory class and should receive her son's or daughter's estate without any deduction. There is an exception for brothers and sisters, whether fully agnatic or cognatic. Just as we give the mother priority over the entire statutory class, so we bring to the estate with her all brothers and sisters, whether entitled under the statutory scheme or not. This is then worked out as follows: if the survivors of the deceased are his or her mother and sisters, agnatic or cognatic, the mother takes one half and all the sisters take the other half; if the intestate dies leaving his or her mother and a brother, or only brothers, or brothers with sisters, whether entitled in the statutory class or as cognates, the estate must be divided by heads. 6. We have safeguarded the interests of mothers; they must look to the protection of their children. They should note that failure to obtain a guardian for them or to replace within a year a guardian who has gone abroad or been removed or excused will quite rightly disqualify them from succession to those children. 7. Even if the son or daughter was conceived casually the mother can succeed to the estate under the Tertullian resolution.

3.4 THE ORFITIAN RESOLUTION

The senate passed the Orfitian Resolution to deal with the converse case, to allow a mother to be succeeded by her children. It was passed in the reign of the Emperor Marcus, in the consulship of Orfitus and Rufus. It gave sons and daughters a statutory right of succession even when within family authority, with priority over the deceased mother's agnates full and otherwise. 1. This Resolution did not give grandchildren any statutory right to succeed grandmothers. Later imperial pronouncements changed that and gave them a right similar to sons and daughters. 2. Note that succession under the Tertullian and Orfitian resolutions is not barred by status-loss. This is because of the rule that, while statutory rights of succession under the Twelve Tables are destroyed by status-loss, those under the new regimes are not. 3. Finally, notice that even children conceived casually can succeed under this resolution. 4. When there are several statutory heirs, if some fail to take or are prevented from accepting by death or some other cause, their share enlarges the shares of those who do accept; if any die early, but after acceptance, their shares go to their own heirs.

3.5 SUCCESSION OF COGNATIC RELATIVES

After immediate heirs and their equivalents under praetorian and imperial law, and after statutory heirs, namely agnates and their equivalents under the resolutions discussed above and our own legislation, the praetor brings in the nearest cognates. 1. Here it is natural relationship that counts. The Twelve Tables exclude agnates who suffer status-loss, and their issue. The praetor brings them back in this third category. Emancipated brothers and sisters are in an exceptional position. // Under the Anastasian Act they, but not their

'non etiam liberis eorum, quos lex Anastasiana[1] cum
'fratribus integri iuris constitutis vocat quidem ad
'legitimam fratris hereditatem sive sororis, non aequis
'tamen partibus, sed cum aliqua deminutione, quam
'facile est ex ipsius constitutionis verbis colligere,
'aliis vero adgnatis inferioris gradus, licet capitis de-
'minutionem passi non sunt, tamen eos anteponit et
2 (1) 'procul dubio cognatis.' Hos etiam, qui per
feminini sexus personas ex transverso cognatione iunguntur, tertio gradu proximitatis nomine praetor ad
3 (2) successionem vocat. [2]'Liberi quoque, qui in
'adoptiva familia sunt, ad naturalium parentum here-
4 (3) 'ditatem hoc eodem gradu vocantur.' Vulgo
quaesitos nullum habere adgnatum manifestum est,
cum adgnatio a patre, cognatio sit a matre, hi autem nullum patrem habere intelleguntur. eadem ratione nec inter se quidem possunt videri consanguinei
esse, quia consanguinitatis ius species est adgnationis: tantum igitur cognati sunt sibi, sicut et matris
cognati[3]. itaque omnibus istis ea parte competit
bonorum possessio, qua proximitatis nomine cognati
5 (4) vocantur. Hoc loco et illud necessario admonendi sumus adgnationis quidem iure admitti aliquem
ad hereditatem et si decimo gradu sit, sive de lege
duodecim tabularum quaeramus, sive de edicto quo
praetor legitimis heredibus daturum se bonorum possessionem pollicetur. proximitatis vero nomine his
solis praetor promittit bonorum possessionem, qui
usque ad sextum gradum cognationis sunt, et ex
septimo a sobrino sobrinaque nato nataeve[4].

VI[5]

DE GRADIBUS COGNATIONIS.

Hoc loco necessarium est exponere, quemadmodum
gradus cognationis numerentur. qua in re inprimis
admonendi sumus cognationem aliam supra nume-
rari, aliam infra, aliam ex transverso, quae etiam
a[6] latere dicitur. superior cognatio est parentium,
inferior liberorum, ex transverso fratrum sororumve
eorumque, qui ex his progenerantur, et convenienter
patrui amitae avunculi materterae. et superior quidem et inferior cognatio a primo gradu incipit: at ea,
1 quae ex transverso numeratur, a secundo. [7]Primo
2 gradu est supra pater mater, infra filius filia. Secundo supra avus avia, infra nepos neptis, ex trans-
3 verso frater soror. Tertio supra proavus proavia,
infra pronepos proneptis, ex transverso fratris sororisque filius filia et convenienter patruus amita avunculus matertera. patruus est patris frater, qui Graece
πάτρως vocatur: avunculus est matris frater, qui
apud Graecos proprie μήτρως appellatur: et pro-
miscue θεῖος dicitur. amita est patris soror, matertera vero matris soror: utraque θεῖα vel apud quos-
4 dam τηθίς appellatur. Quarto gradu supra ab-
avus abavia, infra abnepos abneptis, ex transverso
fratris sororisque nepos neptis et convenienter patruus magnus amita magna (id est avi frater et soror), item avunculus magnus matertera magna (id
est aviae frater et soror), consobrinus consobrina (id
est qui quaeve ex fratribus aut sororibus progenerantur). sed quidam recte consobrinos eos proprie
putant dici, qui ex duabus sororibus progenerantur,
quasi consororinos: eos vero, qui ex duobus fratribus progenerantur, proprie fratres patrueles vocari
(si autem ex duobus fratribus filiae nascantur, sorores patrueles appellantur): at eos, qui ex fratre et

sorore propagantur, amitinos proprie dici (amitae
tuae filii consobrinum te appellant, tu illos amitinos).
5 Quinto supra atavus atavia, infra adnepos ad-
neptis, ex transverso fratris sororisque pronepos proneptis et convenienter propatruus proamita (id est
proavi frater et soror), proavunculus promatertera
(id est proaviae frater et soror), item fratris patruelis
sororis patruelis, consobrini et consobrinae, amitini amitinae filius filia, proprior[8] sobrinus[9] so-
brina (hi sunt patrui magni amitae magnae avunculi
6 magni materterae magnae filius filia). [10]Sexto gradu
sunt supra tritavus tritavia, infra trinepos trineptis,
ex transverso fratris sororisque abnepos abneptis et
convenienter abpatruus abamita (id est abavi frater
et soror) abavunculus abmatertera (id est abaviae
frater et soror), [11]item sobrini sobrinaeque[12] (id est
qui quaeve ex fratribus vel sororibus patruelibus vel
7 consobrinis vel amitinis progenerantur). Hactenus
ostendisse sufficiet, quemadmodum gradus cognationis numerentur. namque ex his palam est intellegere, quemadmodum ulterius quoque gradus numerare debemus: quippe semper generata quaeque persona gradum adiciat, ut longe facilius sit respondere,
quoto quisque gradu sit, quam propria cognationis
8 appellatione quemquam denotare. Adgnationis quo:
9 que gradus eodem modo numerantur. Sed cum
magis veritas oculata fide quam per aures animis
hominum infigitur, ideo necessarium duximus post
narrationem graduum etiam eos praesenti libro in-
scribi, quatenus possint et auribus et inspectione
adulescentes perfectissimam graduum doctrinam adipisci[13].
10   [14]Illud certum est ad serviles cognationes illam
partem edicti, qua proximitatis nomine bonorum possessio promittitur, non pertinere: nam nec ulla aliqua lege talis cognatio computabatur. 'sed nostra
'constitutione[15], quam pro iure patronatus fecimus
'(quod ius usque ad nostra tempora satis obscurum
'atque nube plenum et undique confusum fuerat) et
'hoc humanitate suggerente concessimus, ut si quis
'in servili consortio constitutus liberum vel liberos
'habuerit sive ex libera sive servilis condicionis mu
'liere, vel contra serva mulier ex libero vel servo ha-
'buerit liberos cuiuscumque sexus, et ad libertatem
'his pervenientibus et hi, qui ex servili ventre nati
'sunt, libertatem meruerunt, vel dum mulieres liberae
'erant, ipsi in servitutem eos habuerunt[16] et postea
'ad libertatem pervenerunt, ut hi omnes ad succes-
'sionem vel patris vel matris veniant, patronatus iure
'in hac parte sopito: hos enim liberos non solum in
'suorum parentium successionem, sed etiam alterum
'in alterius mutuam successionem vocavimus, ex illa
'lege specialiter eos vocantes, sive soli inveniantur
'qui in servitute nati et postea manumissi sunt, sive
'una cum aliis. qui post libertatem parentium con-
'cepti sunt sive ex eadem matre vel eodem patre sive
'ex aliis nuptiis, ad similitudinem eorum qui ex iustis
'nuptiis procreati sunt.'
11   Repetitis itaque omnibus quae iam tradidimus
apparet non semper eos, qui parem gradum cognationis optinent, pariter vocari eoque amplius nec eum
quidem, qui proximior sit cognatus, semper potiorem
esse. cum enim prima causa sit suorum heredum
quosque inter suos heredes iam enumeravimus, apparet pronepotem vel abnepotem defuncti potiorem
esse quam fratrem aut patrem matremque defuncti,
cum alioquin pater quidem et mater, ut supra quo-

---

(1) *in Cod. repet. praelect. recepta non est: cf. ad Cod.* 5, 70, 5
(2) *Gai.* 3, 31   (3) *sic BΘ,* cognati sunt *T*   (4) natave *libri*
   (5) *Cf. Dig.* 38, 10   (6) a] *BT[i], ex AT[v]*   (7) § 1..5
similes Dig. 38, 10, 1 § 3..7 *(Gai. l.* 8 *ad ed. prov.)*   (8) *sic*
libri Θ et in Dig. F[1], propior *Dig. F[2]*   (9) *sic BTΘ,* sobrino *A Dig.*   (10) § 6 *similis Dig.* 38, 10, 3 *pr. (Gai. l. c.)*
(11) *sic libri cum Θ:* item patrui magni amitae magnae
avunculi magni materterae magnae nepos neptis, item
fratris patruelis sororis patruelis consobrini consobrinae
amitini amitinae nepos neptis, propatrui proamitae pro-

avunculi promaterterae filius filia *ins. Dig.*   (12) *sic*
BT cum Dig., consobrini consobrinaeque *A cum Paulo*
4, 11, 6 *et Θ*

   (13) *stemma cognationum libri boni omittunt, dett. alii*
alia proferunt. id quod ex A[l] edidit Conrat Geschichte
der Quellen des Röm. Rechts I p. 634, *ab A olim afuisse*
videtur testibus libris optimis A[u] A[bg]

   (14) *rubricam h. l. dett. inserunt* de servili cognatione
(15) *Cod.* 6, 4, 4 § 10. 11   (16) eos habuerunt] abierunt
Mommsen

descendants, are given a statutory right of succession to the estate of another brother, together with brothers still within the family. They do not get an equal share. There is a deduction. The details can be easily read in the pronouncement. But they are given priority over remoter agnates, even those who have not suffered a status-loss, and certainly over all cognates. 2 (1). Collaterals related through females are also brought into this third praetorian rank based on near relationship. 3 (2). Descendants in adoptive families are also qualified in this class to claim the estates of their real ascendants. 4 (3). Children conceived casually are treated as having no father and obviously have no agnates. Agnatic relationship is through the father, cognatic through the mother too. Logically this prevents their being full agnates to each other, that being merely a special degree of agnatic relationship. They are cognates to each other, as to their mother. All such persons can claim this type of estate-possession open to cognates on the basis of close relationship. 5 (4). Finally it is important to note that agnatic claims can run to the tenth degree, whether the question arises under the Twelve Tables or under the praetor's edictal offer of estate-posession to statutory heirs. But the praetor's offer of estate-possession to near cognates runs only to six degrees, or seven with the children of maternal cousins.

3.6 DEGREES OF COGNATIC RELATIONSHIP

The business here is to explain how to count the cognatic degrees. Note first that these relationships can run up, down, or across, i.e. collaterally. Up, to ascendants, down, to descendants; across, to their issue, and correspondingly to uncles and aunts on both sides. Up and down, the degrees begin at one; across, at two. 1. The first degree up gives father and mother; down, son and daughter. 2. The second up gives grandparents; down, grandchildren; across, brother and sister. 3. The third up gives great grandparents; down, great grandchildren; across, son and daughter of brother and sister, also uncles and aunts on both sides. The father's brother is 'patruus' in Latin, 'patros' in Greek; the mother's brother is 'avunculus' and in Greek 'metros'. The Greek 'theios' is used for both these uncles. The father's sister is 'amita', the mother's 'matertera', both being 'theia' in Greek, or, as some prefer, 'tethis'. 4. The fourth degree up gives great great grandparents; down, great great grandchildren; across, brother's and sister's grandchildren, and correspondingly great uncles and great aunts on both sides. A grandfather's brother and sister are 'patruus magnus' and 'amita magna'; a grandmother's 'avunculus magnus' and 'matertera magna'. Cousins, i.e. the sons or daughters of brothers or sisters, are also related in the fourth degree. Some say quite rightly that the word for cousin 'consobrinus'

strictly applies to the children of two sisters, and that the children of brothers are 'fratres patrueles' or, if girls, 'sorores patrueles'. 'Consobrinus' is really 'consororinus', i.e. co-sisterish. The children of a brother and sister are strictly speaking 'amitini'. The sons of your father's sister, your 'amita', will call you 'consobrinus'; to you they will be 'amitini'. 5. The fifth degree up gives great grandparents' grandparents; down, great grandchildren's grandchildren; across, great grandchildren of a brother or sister, and correspondingly great great uncles and aunts – i.e. great grandparents' brothers and sisters: 'propatruus', 'proamita', 'proavunculus' and 'promatertera' – and also the sons and daughters of all cousins, including the sons and daughters of great uncles and great aunts. 6. The sixth degree up gives great grandparents' great grandparents; down, great grandchildren's great grandchildren; across, great great grandchildren of a brother or sister, and correspondingly great great great uncles and aunts, i.e the brothers and sisters of great great grandparents, and also second cousins. 7. This is enough to show how to count cognatic degrees. It is plain to see how to go on. Every generation adds a degree. In fact it is much easier to count out the degree of one person's relation to another than it is to give the name of the relationship. 8. Agnatic relationship is calculated in the same way. 9. One showing is worth a hundred sayings; we decided that we should describe the degrees in words and give a diagram as well. Learning by eye and ear, you will be able to master the whole system of the family tree. 10. Relationships through slaves certainly do not count for the purposes of the edict offering estate-possession to near relatives. In fact such relationships were never taken into account under any of the old laws. However, our legislation on the rights of patrons, a subject obscure and deeply confused until our reign, has made a liberal concession: where a man in slavery has a child or children by a slave or free woman, or a woman in slavery has sons or daughters by a slave or free man, if the parents attain freedom, and the children, if of slave mothers, also earn their liberty or, if of free mothers but themselves enslaved, recover their liberty, these children are entitled to succeed to the estates of their mothers and fathers, displacing the patron's rights. Also, we have there expressly entitled such children to succeed not only their parents but also each other. This holds good whether the only children in question are those born in slavery and later freed or whether there are also others, who were conceived after the parent became free, either with the same mother or father or from the parent's marriage with someone else. Similar principles apply here as for children born to ordinary married couples. 11. A review of all we have said shows that an equal degree of cognatic relationship does not always carry an equal right of succession; the nearer relative may not have the stronger claim. Since immediate heirs and their equivalents have first claim, a great grandson or great great grandson of the deceased has a better claim than the dead man's brother or father or mother.

que tradidimus, primum gradum cognationis opti-
neant, frater vero secundum, pronepos autem tertio
gradu sit cognatus et abnepos quarto: nec interest,
in potestate morientis fuerit an non fuerit, quod vel
emancipatus vel ex emancipato aut ex feminino sexu
12 propagatus est. Amotis quoque suis heredibus
'quosque inter suos heredes vocari diximus'[1], adgnatus,
qui integrum ius adgnationis habet, etiamsi longissimo
gradu sit, 'plerumque' potior habetur quam proximior
cognatus: nam patrui nepos vel pronepos avunculo
vel materterae praefertur. totiens igitur dicimus aut
potiorem haberi eum qui proximiorem gradum cognationis optinet, aut pariter vocari eos qui cognati sint,
quotiens neque suorum heredum iure 'quique inter
'suos heredes sunt' neque adgnationis iure aliquis
praeferri debeat secundum ea quae[2] tradidimus, 'ex-
'ceptis fratre et sorore emancipatis, qui ad succes-
'sionem fratrum vel sororum vocantur, qui etsi ca-
'pite deminuti sunt, tamen praeferuntur ceteris ulte-
'rioris gradus adgnatis'.

VII[3]
DE SUCCESSIONE LIBERTORUM

[4]'Nunc de libertorum bonis videamus. olim itaque
'licebat liberto patronum suum impune testamento
'praeterire: nam ita demum lex duodecim tabularum
'ad hereditatem liberti vocabat patronum, si intesta-
'tus mortuus esset libertus nullo suo herede relicto.
'itaque intestato quoque mortuo liberto, si is suum
'heredem reliquisset, nihil in bonis eius patrono ius
'erat. et si quidem ex naturalibus liberis aliquem
'suum heredem reliquisset, nulla videbatur querella:
'si vero adoptivus filius esset[5], aperte iniquum erat
1 'nihil iuris patrono superesse. [4]Qua de causa post-
'ea praetoris edicto haec iuris iniquitas emendata
'est. sive enim faciebat testamentum libertus, iube-
'batur ita testari, ut patrono partem dimidiam bono-
'rum suorum relinqueret: et si aut nihil aut minus
'partis dimidiae reliquerat, dabatur patrono contra
'tabulas testamenti partis dimidiae bonorum posses-
'sio. si vero[6] intestatus moriebatur suo herede re-
'licto filio adoptivo, dabatur aeque patrono contra
'hunc suum heredem partis dimidiae bonorum pos-
'sessio. prodesse autem liberto 'solebant' ad exclu-
'dendum patronum naturales liberi, non solum quos
'in potestate mortis tempore habebat, sed etiam
'emancipati et in adoptionem dati, si modo ex aliqua
'parte heredes scripti erant aut praeteriti contra tabu-
'las bonorum possessionem ex edicto petierant: nam
2 'exheredati nullo modo repellebant patronum.[4] Post-
'ea lege Papia adaucta sunt iura patronorum, 'qui'
'locupletiores libertos 'habebant'. cautum est enim, ut
'ex bonis eius, qui sestertiorum centum milium patri-
'monium reliquerit et pauciores quam tres liberos
'habebat, sive is testamento facto sive intestato mor-
'tuus erat, virilis pars patrono debebatur. itaque cum
'unum filium filiamve heredem reliquerit libertus, per-
'inde pars dimidia patrono debebatur, ac si is sine
'ullo filio filiave[7] 'decessisset': cum duos duasve he-
'redes reliquerat, tertia pars debebatur patrono: si
3 'tres reliquerat, repellebatur patronus.' 'Sed nostra
'constitutio[8], quam pro omnium notione Graeca lingua
'compendioso tractatu habito composuimus, ita huius-
'modi causas definivit, ut si quidem libertus vel liberta
'minores centenariis[9] sint, id est minus centum aureis
'habeant substantiam (sic enim legis Papiae summam
'interpretati sumus, ut pro mille sestertiis unus au-
'reus computetur), nullum locum habeat patronus in
'eorum successionem, si tamen testamentum fecerint.
'sin autem intestati decesserint nullo liberorum re-
'licto, tunc patronatus ius, quod erat ex lege duo-
'decim tabularum, integrum reservavit. cum vero

'maiores centenariis sint, si heredes vel bonorum pos-
'sessores liberos habeant sive unum sive plures cuius-
'cumque sexus vel gradus, ad eos successionem pa-
'rentum deduximus, omnibus patronis una cum sua
'progenie semotis. sin autem sine liberis decesserint,
'si quidem intestati, ad omnem hereditatem patronos
'patronasque vocavimus: si vero testamentum quidem
'fecerint, patronos autem vel patronas praeterierint,
'cum nullos liberos haberent vel habentes eos exhere-
'daverint, vel mater sive avus maternus eos praeter-
'ierit, ita ut non possint argui inofficiosa eorum testa-
'menta: tunc ex nostra constitutione per bonorum
'possessionem contra tabulas non dimidiam, ut ante,
'sed tertiam partem bonorum liberti consequantur,
'vel quod deest eis ex constitutione nostra repleatur,
'si quando minus tertia parte bonorum suorum liber-
'tus vel liberta eis reliquerint, ita sine onere, ut nec
'liberis liberti libertaeve ex ea parte legata vel fidei-
'commissa praestentur, sed ad coheredes hoc onus red-
'undaret: multis aliis casibus a nobis in praefata
'constitutione congregatis, quos necessarios esse ad
'huiusmodi iuris dispositionem perspeximus: ut tam
'patroni patronaeque quam liberi eorum nec non qui
'ex transverso latere veniunt usque ad quintum gra-
'dum ad successionem libertorum vocentur, sicut ex
'ea constitutione intellegendum est: ut si eiusdem
'patroni vel patronae vel duorum duarum pluriumve
'sint liberi, qui proximior est, ad liberti sive libertae
'vocetur successionem et in capita, non in stirpes
'dividatur successio, eodem modo et in his qui ex
'transverso latere veniunt servando. paene enim con-
'sonantia iura ingenuitatis et libertinitatis in succes-
4 'sionibus fecimus. Sed haec de his libertinis hodie
'dicenda sunt, qui in civitatem Romanam pervenerunt,
'cum nec sunt alii liberti simul et dediticiis et Latinis
'sublatis, cum Latinorum legitimae successiones nullae
'penitus erant, qui[10] licet ut liberi vitam suam per-
'agebant, attamen ipso ultimo spiritu simul animam
'atque libertatem amittebant, et quasi servorum ita
'bona eorum iure quodammodo peculii ex lege Iunia
'manumissores detinebant. postea vero senatus con-
'sulto Largiano cautum fuerat, ut liberi manumissoris
'non nominatim exheredati facti extraneis heredibus
'eorum in bonis Latinorum praeponerentur. quibus
'supervenit etiam divi Traiani edictum, quod eundem
'hominem, si invito vel ignorante patrono ad civita-
'tem venire ex beneficio principis festinavit, faciebat
'vivum quidem civem Romanum, Latinum autem mo-
'rientem. sed nostra constitutione[11] propter huiusmodi
'condicionum vices et alias difficultates cum ipsis La-
'tinis etiam legem Iuniam et senatus consultum Lar-
'gianum et edictum divi Traiani in perpetuum deleri
'censuimus, ut omnes liberti civitate Romana fruan-
'tur, et mirabili modo quibusdam adiectionibus ipsas
'vias, quae in Latinitatem ducebant, ad civitatem Ro-
'manam capiendam transposuimus.'

VIII[12]
DE ADSIGNATIONE LIBERTORUM.

In summa quod ad bona libertorum admonendi
sumus senatum censuisse, ut quamvis ad omnes patroni liberos, qui eiusdem gradus sint, aequaliter
bona libertorum pertineant, tamen liceret[13] parenti
uni ex liberis adsignare libertum, ut post mortem
eius solus est patronus habeatur, cui adsignatus est,
et ceteri liberi, qui ipsi quoque ad eadem bona nulla
adsignatione interveniente pariter admitterentur, nihil
iuris in his bonis habeant. sed ita demum pristinum
ius recipiunt, si is cui adsignatus est decesserit nullis
1 liberis relictis. Nec tantum libertum, sed etiam
libertam, et non tantum filio nepotive, sed etiam filiae
2 neptive adsignare permittitur. Datur autem haec

---

(1) 3, 1, 2ᵃ   (2) ea quae] B, id quod iam T
(3) Cf. Gai. 3, 39..76 Dig. 38, 2 Cod. 6, 4. 13   (4) Gai.
3, 39..42   (5) esset] T Gai., fuisset B   (6) si vero]
T Gai. Θ, sive B   (7) sic scripsi cum Gaio et Θ,

testatus ins. B, intestatus ins. T   (8) Cod. 6, 4, 4
(9) centenarii BT   (10) qui] T, quia B   (11) Cod.
7, 6, 1
(12) Cf. Dig. 38, 4   (13) sic T, licere B

h

// Yet we have shown that the father and mother are related to him in the first degree, the brother in the second, the great grandson in the third, and the great great grandson in the fourth. The example holds good even if our claimant is outside the authority of the deceased at his death, for instance because he or his parent was emancipated, or because he traces his relationship through the female line. 12. In the absence of claims from immediate heirs and their equivalents, a remote agnate whose relationship remains intact is frequently better placed than a nearer cognate. So, a paternal uncle's grandson or great grandson has a better claim than a maternal uncle or aunt. General statements such as that the nearer cognate has the stronger claim, or that all cognates are entitled on an equal footing, are only good on the assumption that there is nobody with priority as an immediate heir or equivalent, or as an agnate, under the rules we have given. Even then there is the exception for an emancipated brother or sister: they have a claim to the estate of their brother or sister, and, despite their status-loss, that claim takes priority over all remoter agnates.

3.7 SUCCESSION TO FREEDMEN

The next subject is the property of freedmen. A patron could once be freely ignored in his freedman's will. The Twelve Tables only gave him a claim if the freedman died intestate and without immediate heirs. If a freedman died intestate but with an immediate heir the patron got nothing. There was no cause for complaint if the heir was really the freedman's son or daughter, but it was wrong that an adoptive child should displace the patron's claims. 1. The praetor's edict later cured this injustice. If the freedman made a will, he had to leave his patron half his estate. If left nothing or less than half, the patron was entitled to estate-possession counter to the will for his half. If the freedman died intestate leaving an adoptive immediate heir, the patron was again entitled to estate-possession for a half. Real children sufficed to exclude the patron. This was so even if they had been emancipated or given in adoption as long as the will made them heirs or if they obtained estate-possession counter to the will because of their omission. But disinherited issue did not displace the patron. 2. The Papian Act then enlarged the patron's rights in relation to rich freedmen. It gave the patron an equal share in the estate of one who died, testate or intestate, with an estate of a hundred thousand sesterces and less than three children. If he left one son or daughter, the patron thus took his half just as if there had been none; if two, a third; if three, nothing. 3. This type of case is now governed by a long pronouncement of our own, issued in Greek so as to be accessible to all. If the freedperson dies testate and – converting the Papian figure at one aureus to a thousand sesterces – with an estate below one hundred aurei, the patron shall be excluded completely; if he dies intestate without children, the patron shall keep his rights under the Twelve Tables. If the estate exceeds the hundred, and the freedperson has one or more descendants of either sex and any degree as heirs or estate-possessors, the succession shall go to them, and the patron and his issue shall again be excluded. If such a freedperson dies intestate and childless the whole estate shall go to the patron or patroness. If he dies testate and childless, or with only disinherited children, and ignores his patron or patroness, or his mother or maternal grandfather ignores them, but in such a way that there can be no complaint against an irresponsible will, then under our pronouncement the patron or patroness shall be entitled to estate-possession counter to the will, not for a half as before but for one third, or, where left less than a third, for the balance. Their share is to be free from burdens, so that the other heirs must from their part meet liabilities to pay legacies and honour trusts, even to the freedperson's issue. Many other eventualities which we had to deal with to settle this area of law are addressed in our pronouncement. For instance, the entitlement of patrons, patronesses, their descendants and collaterals to succeed freedpersons runs to five degrees of relationship, as can be seen in the pronouncement. Also, if there are descendants of the one or more than one patron or patroness, those in the nearest degree take, and any division is done by heads, not stems. This holds good even for collaterals. We have virtually unified the law of succession in relation to freedmen and persons born free. 4. All this applies nowadays to freedmen who become Roman citizens. This means all of them. That is the effect of eliminating capitulated alien status and Latinity. Actually there was no law of succession to Latins because they were free during their lives but gave up their freedom with their lives. Under the Junian Act those who had manumitted them kept their property as though it was the personal fund of one of their slaves. Then the Largian Resolution provided that the descendants of the manumitter, unless expressly disinherited, took priority over outsider heirs in relation to the property of Latins. On top of this came the Emperor Trajan's edict to the effect that one who snatched at a grant of citizenship from the emperor without the knowledge or consent of his patron should have citizenship for life but revert to Latinity at death. These twists and turns moved us to abolish Latinity and to repeal the Junian Act, the Largian Resolution and Trajan's edict, so as to give every freedman the benefit of citizenship. With a little work on the paths that used to lead to Latinity we have almost miraculously made them issue in Roman citizenship.

3.8 ASSIGNING FREEDMEN

There is a last point about the property of freedmen. The senate resolved that, despite the general rule that their estates go equally to a patron's descendants of the same degree, the head of a family can assign a freedman to a particular descendant. That makes him patron after the father's death and excludes the other issue who would have shared equally but for the assignment. They only recover their original rights if the assignee dies childless. 1. A freedman or woman can be assigned, and to a daughter or granddaughter as well as a son or grandson.

adsignandi facultas ei, qui duos pluresve liberos in potestate habebit, ut eis, quos in potestate habet, adsignare ei [1] libertum libertamve liceat. unde quaerebatur, si eum cui adsignaverit postea emancipaverit, num evanescat adsignatio? sed placuit evanescere, 3 quod et Iuliano et aliis plerisque visum est. Nec interest, testamento quis adsignet an sine testamento: sed etiam quibuscumque verbis hoc patronis permittitur facere ex ipso senatus consulto, quod Claudianis temporibus factum est Suillo Rufo et Ostorio Scapula consulibus [2].

IX [3]
DE BONORUM POSSESSIONIBUS.

Ius bonorum possessionis introductum est a praetore emendandi veteris iuris gratia. nec solum in intestatorum hereditatibus vetus ius eo modo praetor emendavit, sicut supra dictum est, sed in eorum quoque, qui testamento facto decesserint. nam si alienus postumus heres fuerit institutus, quamvis hereditatem iure civili adire non poterat, cum institutio non valebat, honorario tamen iure bonorum possessor efficiebatur, videlicet cum a practore adiuvabatur: 'sed et 'hic a [4] nostra constitutione [5] hodie recte heres insti-
1 'tuitur, quasi et iure civili non incognitus.' [6]'Aliquando tamen neque emendandi neque impugnandi 'veteris iuris, sed magis confirmandi gratia pollicetur 'bonorum possessionem. nam illis quoque, qui recte 'facto testamento heredes instituti sunt, dat secundum 'tabulas bonorum possessionem: item ab intestato suos 'heredes et adgnatos ad bonorum possessionem vocat: 'sed et' remota quoque bonorum possessione ad eos
2 'hereditas pertinet iure civili. [7]Quos autem praetor 'solus' vocat ad hereditatem, heredes quidem ipso 'iure non fiunt (nam praetor heredem facere non po'test: per legem tantum vel similem iuris con'stitutionem heredes fiunt, veluti per senatus consul'tum et constitutiones principales): sed cum eis prae'tor dat bonorum possessionem, loco heredum con'stituuntur et vocantur bonorum possessores. adhuc 'autem et alios complures gradus praetor fecit in bo'norum possessionibus dandis, dum id agebat, ne quis 'sine successore moriatur'. 'nam angustissimis finibus 'constitutum per legem duodecim tabularum ius per'cipiendarum hereditatum praetor ex bono et aequo
3 'dilatavit'. Sunt autem bonorum possessiones ex testamento quidem hae. prima, quae praeteritis liberis datur vocaturque contra tabulas. secunda, quam omnibus iure scriptis heredibus praetor pollicetur ideoque vocatur secundum tabulas. et cum de testamentis prius locutus est, ad intestatos transitum fecit. et primo loco suis heredibus et his, qui ex edicto praetoris suis connumerantur, dat bonorum possessionem quae vocatur unde liberi: secundo legitimis heredibus: tertio decem personis, quas extraneo manumissori praeferebat (sunt autem decem personae hae: pater mater, avus avia tam paterni quam materni, item filius filia, nepos neptis tam ex filio quam ex filia, frater soror atque consanguinei sive uterini): quarto cognatis proximis: quinto tum quam [8] ex familia: sexto patrono et patronae liberisque eorum et parentibus: septimo viro et uxori: octavo cognatis
4 manumissoris. 'Sed eas quidem praetoria induxit 'iurisdictio. nobis tamen nihil incuriosum praetermis'sum est, sed nostris constitutionibus omnia corrigentes 'contra tabulas quidem et secundum tabulas bonorum 'possessiones admisimus utpote necessarias constitutas, 'nec non ab intestato unde liberi et unde legitimi
5 'bonorum possessiones. Quae autem in praetoris 'edicto quinto loco posita fuerat, id est unde decem 'personae, eam pio proposito et compendioso sermone 'supervacuam ostendimus: cum enim praefata bono-

'rum possessio decem personas praeponebat extraneo 'manumissori, nostra constitutio [9], quam de emanci'patione liberorum fecimus, omnibus parentibus eis'demque manumissoribus contracta fiducia manumis'sionem facere dedit, ut ipsa manumissio eorum hoc 'in se habeat privilegium et supervacua fiat praedicta 'bonorum possessio. sublata igitur praefata quinta 'bonorum possessione in gradum eius sextam antea 'bonorum possessionem reduximus et quintam fecimus,
6 (5) 'quam praetor proximis cognatis pollicetur. Cum'que antea septimo loco fuerat bonorum possessio, 'tum quam [10] ex familia et octavo unde liberi patroni 'patronaeque et parentes eorum, utramque per con'stitutionem nostram [11], quam de iure patronatus feci'mus, penitus vacuavimus: cum enim ad similitudinem 'successionis ingenuorum libertinorum successiones po'suimus, quas usque ad quintum tantummodo gradum 'coartavimus, ut sit aliqua inter ingenuos et libertos 'differentia, sufficiunt [12] eis tam contra tabulas bono'rum possessio quam unde legitimi et unde cognati, 'ex quibus possint sua iura vindicare, omni scrupu'lositate et inextricabili errore duarum istarum bono-
7 (6) 'rum possessionum resoluta. Aliam vero bo'norum possessionem, quae unde vir et uxor appella'tur et nono loco inter veteres bonorum possessiones 'posita fuerat, et in suo vigore servavimus et altiore 'loco, id est sexto, eam posuimus, decima veteri bo'norum possessione quae erat unde cognati manumis'soris propter causas enarratas merito sublata: ut 'sex tantummodo bonorum possessiones ordinariae
8 (7) 'permaneant suo vigore pollentes. Septima eas 'secuta, quam optima ratione praetores introduxerunt. 'novissime enim promittitur edicto hanc etiam bonorum 'possessio, quibus ut detur lege vel senatus consulto 'vel constitutione comprehensum est, quam neque bo'norum possessionibus quae ab intestato veniunt ne'que eis quae ex testamento sunt praetor stabili iure 'connumeravit, sed quasi ultimum et extraordinarium 'auxilium, prout res exigit, accommodavit scilicet his, 'qui ex legibus senatus consultis constitutionibus prin'cipum ex novo iure vel ex testamento vel ab intes'tato veniunt.'
9 (8) Cum igitur plures species successionum praetor introduxisset easque per ordinem disposuisset et in unaquaque specie successionis saepe plures extent dispari gradu personae: ne actiones creditorum differantur, sed haberent quos convenirent, et ne facile in possessionem bonorum defuncti mittantur et eo modo sibi consulerent, ideo petendae bonorum possessioni
(9) certum tempus praefinivit. liberis itaque et parentibus tam naturalibus quam adoptivis in petenda bonorum possessione anni [13] spatium, ceteris [14] centum
10 (5) dierum dedit. Et si intra hoc tempus aliquis bonorum possessionem non petierit, eiusdem gradus personis adcrescit: vel si nemo sit, deinceps ceteris proinde bonorum possessionem ex successorio edicto pollicetur, ac si is qui praecedebat ex eo numero non esset. si quis itaque delatam sibi bonorum possessionem repudiaverit, non quousque tempus bonorum possessioni praefinitum excesserit exspectatur, sed statim ceteri ex eodem edicto admittuntur. In petenda
11 (6) autem bonorum possessione dies utiles singuli considerantur. 'Sed bene anteriores principes et huic
12 (7) 'causae providerunt, ne quis pro petenda bo'norum possessione curet, sed, quocumque modo si 'admittentis eam indicium intra statuta tamen tem'pora ostenderit, plenum habeat earum beneficium.'

X [15]
DE ADQUISITIONE PER ADROGATIONEM.

[16]'Est et alterius generis per universitatem suc'cessio, quae neque lege duodecim tabularum neque

---

(1) *ei om.* T   (2) *inter a. p. Chr.* 41—47   (3) *Cf. Gai.* 3, 25..38 *Dig.* 37, 1..13 *Cod.* 6, 9..20   (4) *scr.* e   (5) *Cod.* 6, 48, 1   (6) *Gai.* 3, 33ᵇ? 34   (7) *Gai.* 3, 32. 33   (8) tum quam] Θ, tunc qua B, qua T   (9) *Cod.*

(10) tum quam] Θ, tum qua B, qua T   (11) *Cod.* 6, 4, 4   (12) *sic* B, sufficit T   (13) *sic* B, annuum T   (14) autem *ins.* T   (15) *Cf. Gai.* 3, 82..84   (16) *Gai.* 3, 82

// 2. The right to assign is given to anyone with two or more descendants in his authority. It allows him to assign a freedman or woman to those in his authority. Suppose he subsequently emancipates the assignee. Is the assignment rescinded? It has been accepted that it is. So Julian and many other jurists. 3. It does not matter whether the assignment is made by will or not. It can be done by the patron in any words. That was in the Resolution itself, passed in the reign of Claudius in the consulship of Suillus Rufus and Ostorius Scapula.

3.9 ESTATE-POSSESSION

Estate-possession was introduced by the practor to improve the old law. He aimed to reform not only the old law of intestate succession, as indicated above, but also the law relating to wills. Suppose someone appointed as heir the unborn issue of an outsider. At state law such an heir could not accept; the appointment was a nullity. But honorarian law would give him estate-possession. In short the praetor would help him. Nowadays our pronouncement makes such an appointment valid, within the ambit of the state law. 1. Some cases of estate-possession are designed to re-inforce the old law, not to improve or oppose it. For instance, it is available to heirs validly appointed in the will. This is estate-possession in support of the will. Again, on intestacy the practor entitles immediate heirs and agnates to estate-possession. Yet, if this were out of the question, the estate would go to the same people at state law. 2. A person entitled to the estate only by the praetor does not become heir by operation of law. The praetor cannot make an heir. That has to be done under an act or an equivalent source — a resolution of the senate or an imperial pronouncement. But such a person, with estate-possession from the praetor, is in as good a position as an heir and is called an estate-possessor. In pursuit of his policy that the deceased should not be left without a successor, the praetor also enlarged the number of classes qualified to claim. He widened the very narrow right to inherit recognized in the Twelve Tables by appealing to reasonableness and fairness. 3. The cases of estate-possession where there is a will are as follows: first, for descendants who have been passed over — this is 'counter to the will'; second, for all the appointed heirs — this is 'in support of the will'. After wills he turned to intestacy: first, for the immediate heirs and their equivalents under the edict — this is 'for descendants'; second, for statutory heirs; third, for the ten persons given priority over an extra-familial emancipator — these ten are father, mother, grandparents on both sides, son, daughter, grandchildren by son or daughter, brother and sister with either father or mother in common; fourth, for nearest cognates; fifth, for nearest members of the patron's family; sixth, for the patron, male or female, their ascendants or descendants; seventh, for husband and wife; eighth, for cognates of the person who granted freedom to the deceased. 4. These categories were introduced by the praetor. Attentive to every detail and legislating to remedy all defects, we have found essential and have confirmed estate-possession counter to and in support of the will, also the intestate categories for descendants and for statutory heirs. 5. As for the fifth edictal category, for the ten, we have composed a brief but well-constructed address showing it superfluous. Its purpose was to give ten persons priority ahead of an outside emancipator. But our legislation on the subject of emancipating descendants allowed such emancipation to be done by a fiduciary arrangement between parents and manumitters in such a way as to attach the same privileges to the emancipation itself, making superfluous the priority achieved by a special case of estate-possession. With the abolition of that fifth category we moved back the sixth — for nearest cognates — to fill the vacant fifth place. 6(5). Our pronouncement on the rights of patrons emptied the old seventh and eighth categories of all significance — namely the patron's family case and the patron's ascendants and descendants. We harmonized succession to freedmen and free-born, subject to an upper limit of five degrees imposed to make some difference between the two. Claimants here only need estate-possession counter to the will, for statutory heirs, and for nearest cognates. So we eliminated the seventh and eighth categories, both of them complex and incurably prone to error. 7(6). The next case, husband and wife, put by the old lawyers at ninth place, we retained and promoted to sixth place. The tenth case, cognates of a manumitter, we abolished for good reasons, already discussed. We have thus retained six strong categories of estate-possession. 8(7). A seventh category follows, which with admirable logic the praetor also introduced This last edictal estate-possession is for those entitled under the will, resolutions or pronouncements. This category was not included along with the regular cases on intestacy or under a will. It was brought in as an exceptional category to cover new entitlements under acts, resolutions, and imperial pronouncements, whether on testacy or intestacy. 9(8). Various factors led the praetor to fix time-limits for taking estate-possession. The rights of succession introduced by him were marshalled in ranks, often with one rank stretching over different degrees; and there was also the need to be sure that creditors were not delayed in bringing actions or finding defendants, while at the same time not letting them too easily take over and have their own way with the estate. (9). So he gives a year to ascendants and descendants, real and adoptive. To everyone else he gives one hundred days. 10(5). If a qualified claimant fails to claim estate-possession within the time-limit, the shares of the others of his degree are enlarged. If there are no others, the praetor offers the estate to the next edictal class as though there never had been anyone with priority over them. If someone is entitled but refuses there is no need to wait to the end of the time-limit. The rest of the same rank are let in at once. 11(6). In calculating the time for applying for estate-possession every court day is counted. 12(7). Earlier emperors rightly provided in this context that nobody needs to go to any trouble over an application for estate possession. As long as he shows within the time-limit that this is what he intends, he becomes fully entitled, no matter how he expresses it.

3.10 ACQUISITION THROUGH ADROGATION

There is another way in which an entire estate can be acquired. It did not originate in the Twelve Tables // or

'praetoris edicto, sed eo iure, quod consensu recep-
1 'tum est, introducta est. '1Ecce enim cum pater
'familias sese in adrogationem dat, omnes res eius
'corporales et incorporales quaeque ei debitae sunt
''adrogatori ante quidem pleno iure' adquirebantur.
'exceptis his quae per capitis deminutionem pereunt,
'quales sunt operarum obligationes' 'et ius adgnatio-
'nis. usus etenim et usus fructus, licet his antea
'connumerabantur, attamen capitis deminutione minima
2 'eos tolli nostra prohibuit constitutio². Nunc autem
'nos eandem adquisitionem, quae per adrogationem
'fiebat, coartavimus³ ad similitudinem naturalium pa-
'rentum: nihil etenim áliud nisi tantummodo usus
'fructus tam naturalibus patribus quam adoptivis per
'filios familias adquiritur in his rebus quae extrinsecus
'filiis obveniunt, dominio eis integro servato: mortuo
'autem filio adrogato in adoptiva familia etiam domi-
'nium eius ad adrogatorem transit⁴, nisi supersint
'aliae personae, quae ex nostra constitutione⁵ patrem
3 'in his quae adquiri non possunt antecedunt. Sed'
'⁶ex diverso 'pro eo', quod is debuit qui se in adoptio-
'nem dedit', ipso quidem iure adrogator non tenetur,
'sed nomine filii convenietur et, si noluerit eum defeu-
'dere, permittitur creditoribus per competentes nostros
'magistratus' 'bona, quae eorum 'cum usu fructu' futura
'fuissent, si se alieno iuri non subiecissent', 'possidere
'et legitimo modo ea disponere.'

XI
DE EO CUI LIBERTATIS CAUSA BONA ADDICUNTUR.

Accessit novus casus successionis ex constitutione
divi Marci. nam si hi, qui libertatem acceperunt a
domino in testamento, ex quo non aditur hereditas,
velint bona sibi addici libertatium conservandarum
causa, audiuntur. et ita rescripto divi Marci ad Po-
1 pilium Rufum continetur. Verba rescripti ita se
habent: 'Si Virginio Valenti, qui testamento suo liber-
'tatem quibusdam adscripsit, nemine successore ab
'intestato existente in ea causa bona esse coeperunt,
'ut veniri debeant: is cuius⁷ de ea re notio est
'aditus rationem desiderii tui habebit, ut libertatium
'tam earum, quae directo, quam earum, quae per
'speciem fideicommissi relictae sunt, tuendarum gratia
'addicantur tibi, si idonee creditoribus caveris de so-
'lido quod cuique debetur solvendo. et hi quidem,
'quibus directa libertas data est, perinde liberi erunt,
'ac si hereditas adita esset: hi autem, quos heres
'rogatus est manumittere, a te libertatem consequan-
'tur: ita ut si non⁸ alia condicione velis bona tibi
'addici, quam ut⁹ etiam qui directo libertatem acce-
'perunt tui liberti fiant, nam huic etiam voluntati
'tuae, si ii de quorum statu agitur consentiant, aucto-
'ritatem nostram accommodamus. et ne huius rescrip-
'tionis nostrae emolumentum alia ratione irritum
'fiat, si fiscus bona agnoscere voluerit: et hi qui
'rebus nostris attendunt scient commodo pecuniario
'praeferendam libertatis causam et ita bona cogenda,
'ut libertas his salva sit, qui eam adipisci potuerunt,
2 'si hereditas ex testamento adita esset.' Hoc rescripto subventum est et libertatibus et defunctis, ne
bona eorum a creditoribus possideantur et veneant.
certe si fuerint ex hac causa bona addicta, cessat
bonorum venditio: extitit enim defuncti defensor, et
quidem idoneus, qui de solido creditoribus cavet.
3 Inprimis hoc rescriptum totiens locum habet, quotiens testamento libertates datae sunt. quid ergo¹⁰ si
quis intestatus decedens codicillis libertates dederit
neque adita sit ab intestato hereditas? favor constitutionis debet¹¹ locum habere. certe si testatus de-
cedat et codicillis dederit libertatem, competere eam

4 nemini dubium est. Tunc constitutioni locum esse
verba ostendunt, cum nemo successor ab intestato
existat: ¹²ergo quamdiu incertum sit, utrum existat
an non, cessabit constitutio: si certum esse coeperit
5 neminem extare, tunc erit constitutioni locus. ¹²Si
is, qui in integrum restitui potest, abstinuit se ab
hereditate, an, quamvis¹³ potest in integrum restitui,
potest admitti constitutio et addictio bonorum fieri?
quid ergo, si post addictionem libertatum conservandarum causa factam in integrum sit restitutus? utique non erit dicendum revocari libertates, quae¹⁴
6 semel competierunt. Haec constitutio libertatum
tuendarum causa introducta est: ergo si libertates
nullae sint datae, cessat constitutio. quid ergo, si
vivus dedit libertates vel mortis causa et, ne de hoc
quaeratur, utrum in fraudem creditorum an non factum sit, idcirco velint addici sibi bona, an audiendi
sunt? et magis est, ut audiri debeant, etsi deficiant
7 verba constitutionis. 'Sed cum multas divisiones
'eiusmodi constitutioni deesse perspeximus, lata est a
'nobis plenissima constitutio¹⁵, in quam multae spe-
'cies collatae¹⁶ sunt, quibus ius huiusmodi successio-
'nis plenissimum est effectum: quas ex ipsa lectione
'constitutionis potest quis cognoscere.'

XII¹⁷
DE SUCCESSIONIBUS SUBLATIS, QUAE FIEBANT PER BONORUM VENDITIONEM ET EX SENATUS CONSULTO CLAUDIANO.

'Erant ante praedictam successionem olim et aliae
'per universitatem successiones. qualis fuerat bono-
'rum emptio, quae de bonis debitoris vendendis per
'multas ambages fuerat introducta et tunc locum habe-
'bat, quando iudicia ordinaria in usu fuerunt: sed
'cum extraordinariis iudiciis posteritas usa¹⁸ est, ideo
'cum ipsis ordinariis iudiciis etiam bonorum vendi-
'tiones exspiraverunt et tantummodo creditoribus datur
'officio iudicis bona possidere et prout eis utile visum
'fuerit ea disponere, quod ex latioribus digestorum
1 'libris perfectius apparebit. Erat et ex senatus
'consulto Claudiano miserabilis per universitatem ad-
'quisitio, cum libera mulier servili amore bacchata
'ipsam libertatem per senatus consultum amittebat et
'cum libertate substantiam: quod indignum nostris
'temporibus esse existimantes et a nostra civitate de-
'leri et non inseri nostris digestis concessimus¹⁸ᵃ.'

XIII¹⁹
DE OBLIGATIONIBUS.

²⁰'Nunc transeamus ad obligationes.' obligatio est
iuris vinculum, quo necessitate adstringimur alicuius
1 solvendae rei secundum nostrae civitatis iura. Omnium autem obligationum summa divisio in duo genera diducitur: namque aut civiles sunt aut praetoriae. civiles sunt, quae aut legibus constitutae aut
certe iure civili comprobatae sunt. praetoriae sunt,
quas praetor ex sua iurisdictione constituit, quae
2 etiam honorariae vocantur²¹. Sequens divisio in
quattuor species diducitur: aut enim ex contractu
sunt aut quasi ex contractu aut ex maleficio aut
quasi ex maleficio. prius est, ut de his quae ex contractu sunt dispiciamus. harum aeque quattuor species sunt: aut enim re contrahuntur aut verbis aut
litteris aut consensu. de quibus singulis dispiciamus.

XIV²²
QUIBUS MODIS RE CONTRAHITUR OBLIGATIO.

²³Re contrahitur obligatio veluti mutui datione²⁴.
mutui autem obligatio in his rebus consistit, quae

---

(1) *Gai.* 3, 83　　(2) *Cod.* 3, 33, 16　　(3) *Cod.* 6, 61, 6
(4) pertransit *T*　　(5) *Cod.* 6, 59, 11　　(6) *Gai.* 3, 84
(7) cui *T*　　(8) si non] non nisi *B*　　(9) quam ut
del. Mommsen　　(10) si quis..habere *ex Dig.* 40, 5, 2
(*Ulp. l.* 60 *ad ed.*)　　(11) debebit *T*　　(12) § 4 *fin.* § 5 *ex*
Dig. 40, 5, 4 *pr.* § 1. 2 (*Ulp. l.* 60 *ad ed.*)　　(13) quamvis] *libri*
cum Θ, quamdiu *Dig.* Θ, quia *libri*　　(15) *Cod.*
7, 2, 15　　(16) collectae *T*　　(17) *Cf. Gai.* 3, 77..81　　(18) usa]
W*ᵇ*, nisa *BT*, uisa W*ᵃ*　　(18ᵃ) *Cod.* 7, 24　　(19) *Cf. Gai.* 3, 88, 89
Dig. 44, 7 *Cod.* 4, 10　　(20) *Gai.* 3, 88　　(21) dicuntur *T*
(22) *Cf. Gai.* 3, 90. 91　　(23) *pr. in. ex Gaii l.* 2 *rer. cott.*
(*Dig.* 44, 7, 1 § 2)　　(24) datione] *Dig.*, obligatione *BT*
h*

the praetor's edict but in the law accepted by convention. 1. On the adrogation of the head of a family, the adrogator used to become fully entitled to all his corporeal and incorporeal assets and claims, except those destroyed by status-loss such as claims to services and rights implicit in agnatic relationship – previously including use and usufruct, though our pronouncement has now ruled that they are not to be extinguished by status-loss in the third degree. 2. However, we have harmonized the law of aquisition by an adrogator and by ordinary heads of families. Real and adopted fathers both now get no more than a usufruct in property acquired by a son from outside the family, with ownership reserved for the son himself. If an adrogated son dies in his adoptive family, ownership does pass to the adrogator, unless he is survived by people who, under our rules, take priority over the father as regards the class of assets not covered by his automatic right of acquisition. 3. On the other side, the adrogator does not succeed automatically to the liabilities of the adoptee. But he can be sued on the son's account. If he chooses not to defend him, the magistrates in our courts will allow the creditors to take possession of the son's assets and to sell them off in the proper way. These assets are the things over which he now has a usufruct but would have owned if had stayed independent.

3.11 ASSIGNEES TO PRESERVE FREEDOM

A pronouncement of the Emperor Marcus added a new kind of succession. Suppose a testator frees slaves by will and then nobody accepts the inheritance. Here they save their freedom by getting the estate awarded to themselves. This is the effect of a written reply of Marcus in answer to Popilius Rufus. It runs as follows. 1. 'If Virginius Valens, who granted freedom to certain persons by his will, has no successor even as an intestate, and matters have reached the stage at which his assets must now be sold up, then, provided you give sound security to the creditors for full payment of their claims, the official with jurisdiction in this matter will hear your request that the estate be assigned to you in order to save both the freedoms directly conferred and those given through trusts imposed on the heir. Those whom the will itself directly freed shall take their freedom as though the inheritance had been accepted; those whom the heir was trusted to free shall obtain their freedom from yourself. If you want the assignment only on condition that even the directly freed shall become your freedmen, we lend our authority to your wishes in that respect as well, provided those whose status is in issue consent. To those in charge of our finances we say, to prevent the benefit of this reply being frustrated for a different reason, namely the interest of our exchequer in the estate: freedom must be put before finance, and to save the freedom of those to whom this device can give it the assets must be marshalled just as though an heir had accepted the estate.' 2. This reply was a benefit to the people freed and to the deceased, saving his assets from being taken and sold up by creditors. It is certain that an assignment under this head does exclude a selling up, since it gives the deceased a backer, indeed a sound one, willing to satisfy the creditors in full. 3. The reply deals expressly with the case of freedom given by will. What of an intestate's grant by codicil, followed by non-acceptance of the estate on the intestacy? It should be possible to take the benefit of the pronouncement. There is no doubt at all that that is so where the deceased dies testate but makes the grants of freedom by codicil. 4. The wording shows that the reply holds where there is no intestate heir. So long as this remains uncertain, the reply is

inapplicable. Once it is certain, the pronouncement operates. 5. Suppose the potential heir who declines is a person qualified to seek the remedy of restitution to the status quo. Is the reply applicable, and can the assignment be made even though he may subsequently obtain the remedy? What if after the assignment of the estate to preserve freedom he is in fact restored to his former rights? The answer will be in each case that freedom once given cannot be rescinded. 6. This pronouncement was introduced to preserve liberty. It has no place if no grants of freedom are given. What then if the deceased made grants of freedom while alive or in contemplation of death, and the donees petition for the assignment to themselves to avoid a contest on the issue whether the manumissions were in fraud of creditors? The better view is that they should be heard, though outside the letter of the reply. 7. We ourselves saw that many different cases were not covered by this pronouncement and we therefore introduced one of our own, dealing comprehensively with many situations and completing the picture of this type of succession. The details can be read in the pronouncement itself.

3.12 OBSOLETE SUCCESSIONS: SALES IN EXECUTION; THE CLAUDIAN RESOLUTION

There were other cases of succession to an entire estate, earlier than this last case. One was the sale of assets in execution against a debtor. This was introduced in an involved way and was used so long as the formulary system of litigation lasted. Later we went over to the special judicature. Along with the old forms of action, execution by sale of the estate also became obsolete. Instead the judge has power to allow the creditors to take possession of the assets and to sell off as much as they think necessary. The Digest gives the complete picture. 1. There was another wretched case under the Claudian Resolution. The senate resolved that a free woman led astray by love for a slave should lose her freedom and with it her property. We judged this unworthy of our reign. We have agreed to its repeal and its omission from the Digest.

3.13 OBLIGATIONS

We turn to obligations. An obligation is a legal tie which binds us to the necessity of making some performance in accordance with the laws of our state. 1. They divide first into two: legal and praetorian. Legal obligations are those recognized by statute or, of course, by the state law. Praetorian obligations are those which the praetor recognized in the exercise of his own jurisdiction. These are also called honorarian. 2. The next classification is into four: obligations arise from a contract, as though from a contract, from a wrong, or as though from a wrong. Those from contract are our first concern. They also fall into four classes: they are contracted by conduct, by words, by writing, or by agreement. We will take these in turn.

3.14 OBLIGATIONS CONTRACTED BY CONDUCT

One case where an obligation is contracted by conduct is when a loan is made, of the kind called mutuum. // This

pondere numero mensurave constant, veluti vino oleo frumento pecunia numerata aere argento auro. [1]'quas 'res aut numerando aut metiendo aut pendendo in [2] 'hoc damus, ut accipientium fiant et quandoque nobis 'non eaedem res, sed aliae eiusdem naturae' et quali- tatis 'reddantur. unde etiam mutuum appellatum sit [3], 'quia ita a me tibi datur, ut ex meo tuum fiat.' 'ex [4] 'eo contractu nascitur actio quae vocatur condictio.'

1   [5]'Is quoque, qui non debitum accepit ab eo qui 'per errorem solvit, re obligatur': 'daturque agenti 'contra eum propter repetitionem condicticia actio.' 'nam proinde ei [6] condici potest 'si paret eum dare '"oportere" ac si mutuum accepisset: unde pupillus, 'si ei sine tutoris auctoritate non debitum per erro- 'rem datum est, non tenetur indebiti condictione non 'magis quam mutui datione. sed haec species obli- 'gationis non videtur ex contractu consistere, cum is 'qui solvendi animo dat magis distrahere voluit nego- 2 'tium quam contrahere.' [7]'Item is cui res aliqua utenda datur, id est commodatur, re obligatur 'et tenetur commodati actione.' sed is ab eo qui mu- tuum accepit longe distat: namque non ita res datur, ut eius fiat, et ob id de ea re ipsa restituenda tene- tur. et is quidem qui mutuum accepit, si quolibet fortuito casu quod accepit amiserit, veluti incendio ruina naufragio aut latronum hostiumve incursu, ni- hilo minus obligatus permanet. at is qui utendum accepit sane quidem exactam diligentiam custodien- dae rei praestare iubetur nec sufficit ei tantam dili- gentiam adhibuisse, quantam suis rebus adhibere soli- tus est, si modo alius diligentior poterit eam rem custodire: sed propter maiorem vim maioresve casus non tenetur, si modo non huius [8] culpa is casus inter- venerit: alioquin si id quod tibi commodatum est peregre ferre tecum malueris et vel incursu hostium praedonumve vel naufragio amiseris, dubium non est, quin de restituenda ea re tenearis. commodata autem res tunc proprie intellegitur, si nulla mercede ac- cepta vel constituta res tibi utenda data est. alio- quin mercede interveniente locatus tibi usus rei vide- 3 tur: gratuitum enim debet esse commodatum. [7]'Prae- terea et is, apud quem res aliqua deponitur, re obli- gatur 'et [9] actione depositi', qui et ipse de ea re quam accepit restituenda tenetur. sed is ex eo solo tene- tur, si quid dolo commiserit, culpae autem nomine, id est desidiae atque neglegentiae, non tenetur: ita- que securus est qui parum diligenter custoditam rem furto amisit, 'quia, qui neglegenti amico rem custo- diendam tradit [10], suae facilitati id [11] imputare debet'. 4 [7]'Creditor quoque qui pignus accepit re obligatur, qui et ipse de ea ipsa re quam accepit restituenda tenetur 'actione pigneraticia.' sed quia pignus utrius- que gratia datur, et debitoris, quo magis ei pecunia crederetur, et creditoris, quo magis ei in tuto sit creditum, placuit sufficere, quod ad eam rem custo- diendam exactam diligentiam adhiberet: quam si prae- stiterit et aliquo fortuitu casu rem amiserit, securum esse nec impediri creditum petere.

XV [12]
DE VERBORUM OBLIGATIONE.

[13]Verbis obligatio contrahitur ex interrogatione et responsu [14], cum quid dari fierive nobis stipulamur. ex qua duae proficiscuntur actiones, tam condictio, si certa sit stipulatio, quam ex stipulatu, si incerta. quae hoc nomine inde utitur, quia stipulum apud veteres firmum appellabatur, forte a stipite descen- dens.

1   In hac re olim talia verba tradita fuerunt: spon- des? spondeo, promittis? promitto, fidepromittis? fide-

promitto, fideiubes? fideiubeo, dabis? dabo, facies? faciam. utrum autem Latina an Graeca vel qua alia lingua stipulatio concipiatur, nihil interest, scilicet si uterque stipulantium intellectum huius linguae ha- beat: nec necesse est eadem lingua utrumque uti, sed sufficit congruenter ad interrogatum respondere: quin etiam duo Graeci Latina lingua obligationem contrahere possunt. 'sed haec sollemnia verba olim 'quidem in usu fuerunt: postea autem Leoniana [15] 'constitutio lata est, quae sollemnitate verborum sublata 'sensum et consonantem intellectum ab utraque parte 'solum desiderat, licet quibuscumque verbis expres- 'sus est.'

2   Omnis stipulatio aut pure aut in diem aut sub condicione fit. pure veluti 'quinque aureos dare spon- 'des?' idque confestim peti potest. in diem, cum adi- ecto die quo pecunia solvatur stipulatio fit: veluti 'decem aureos primis kalendis Martiis dare spondes?' id autem, quod in diem stipulamur, statim quidem debetur, sed peti prius quam dies veniat non potest: ac ne eo quidem ipso die, in quem stipulatio facta est, peti potest, quia totus [16] dies arbitrio solventis tribui debet. neque enim certum est eo die, in quem promissum est, datum non esse, priusquam [17] prae- 3 tereat. At si ita stipuleris 'decem aureos annuos 'quoad vivam dare spondes?', et pure facta obligatio intellegitur et perpetuatur, quia ad tempus deberi non potest. sed heres petendo pacti exceptione sub- 4 movebitur. Sub condicione stipulatio fit, cum in aliquem casum differtur obligatio, ut, si aliquid fac- tum fuerit aut non fuerit, stipulatio committatur, veluti 'si Titius consul factus fuerit, quinque aureos 'dare spondes?' si quis ita stipuletur 'si in Capito- 'lium non ascendero, dare spondes?' perinde erit, ac si stipulatus esset cum morietur dari sibi. ex condi- cionali stipulatione tantum spes est debitum iri, eam- que ipsam spem transmittimus, si, priusquam condicio 5 existat, mors nobis contigerit. Loca etiam inseri stipulationi solent, veluti 'Carthagine dare spondes?' quae stipulatio licet pure fieri videatur, tamen re ipsa habet tempus iniectum, quo promissor utatur ad pecuniam Carthagine dandam. et ideo si quis ita Romae stipuletur 'hodie Carthagine dare spondes?' inutilis erit stipulatio, cum impossibilis sit repromis- 6 sio. Condiciones, quae ad praeteritum vel ad praesens tempus referuntur, aut statim infirmant obli- gationem aut omnino non differunt: veluti 'si Titius 'consul fuit' vel 'si Maevius vivit, dare spondes?' nam si ea ita non sunt, nihil valet stipulatio: sin autem ita se habent, statim valet. quae enim per rerum naturam certa sunt, non morantur obligatio- nem, licet apud nos incerta sint.

7   Non solum res in stipulatum deduci possunt, sed etiam facta: ut si [18] stipulemur fieri aliquid vel non fieri. et in huiusmodi stipulationibus optimum erit poenam subicere, ne quantitas stipulationis in incerto sit ac necesse sit actori probare, quid eius intersit. itaque si quis ut fiat aliquid stipuletur, ita adici poena debet: 'si ita factum non erit, tum poe- 'nae nomine decem aureos dare spondes?' sed si quaedam fieri, quaedam non fieri una eademque con- ceptione stipuletur, clausula erit huiusmodi adicienda: 'si adversus ea factum erit sive quid ita factum non 'erit, tunc poenae nomine decem aureos dare spondes?'

XVI [19]
DE DUOBUS REIS STIPULANDI ET PROMITTENDI.

Et stipulandi et promittendi duo pluresve rei fieri possunt. stipulandi ita, si post omnium interrogatio- nem promissor respondeat 'spondeo'. ut puta cum

---

(1) *Gai.* 3, 90   (2) in] *T Gai.*, ob *B*   (3) est *Gai.*   (4) ex] *BΘ*, et ex *T*   (5) *Gai.* 3, 91   (6) ei] *Gai.*, ei ab eo *BT* (7) § 2..4 *in. ex Gaii l. 2 rer. cott. (Dig. 44, 7, 1 § 3..6)* (8) *huius*] *T*, h. ipsius *B*   (9) et] *TΘ*, om. *B*   (10) tradit] *B*, committit *Dig.*, ✱✱✱it✱✱t tradidit *T*ᵘ   (11) id] *E*, ad *B*, om. *T*ᵘ

(12) Cf. *Gai.* 3, 92. 93 *Dig.* 45, 1 *Cod.* 8, 37   (13) *pr. in. ex Gaii l. 2 rer. cott. (Dig. 44, 7, 1 § 7)*   (14) responsu] *Dig. F* ¹, responso *AB*, responsione *T et in Dig. F* ² ? (15) *Cod.* 8, 37, 10   (16) totus] *A*, totus is *T*, totus ille *B*   (17) sic *A*, is ins. *BT*   (18) si om. *libri* (19) *Cf. Dig.* 45, 2 *Cod.* 8, 40

arises only with things identified by weight, number or measure, such as wine, oil, corn, money, bronze, silver, and gold. When we lend such things by number, measure, or weight we intend that they should become the property of the recipient and that when the time comes for getting them back we should receive not the very things we gave but others of the same kind and quality. This is the origin of the term 'mutuum': I give so as to make my property your property: 'ex meo tuum'. This contract gives rise to the action of debt. 1. A person also incurs an obligation by conduct if he receives something not due to him from a person who pays him by mistake. When the payor sues to get it back he also has the action of debt. This recipient is just as much caught by the words of that action – 'If it appears that he ought to give' – as if he had been given a loan. If a child receives a mistaken payment not due to him without getting his guardian's endorsement, he is no more liable to the action of debt for something not due than he is when the same action is brought on a loan. But here the obligation cannot be said to arise from contract. Someone who gives intending to discharge a debt means, not to tie up a deal, but to untie one, 'distrahere' not 'contrahere'. 2. Next, someone who is given something to use – that is to say, who receives a loan of the kind called commodatum – also comes under an obligation by conduct. He is liable to the action on loan for use. His position is quite different from the borrower of a mutuum. Here the thing does not become the property of the borrower, which means he must restore the very thing borrowed. With mutuum, if the borrower loses the thing through some catastrophe such as fire, collapse, shipwreck, or attack by bandits or an enemy force, he remains liable. By contrast the borrower for use is under a duty to conform to the highest standard of care in keeping the thing safe, a requirement not satisfied by his own habitual standard if others could do better. But he is not liable for overwhelming forces and disasters so long as they strike without fault on his part. On the other hand suppose you borrow something for use and you choose to take it away with you. If you end up losing it in an enemy assault or an attack by bandits or in a shipwreck, there is no doubt that you remain liable for its return. The loan of a thing is properly called commodatum only when it is given to you to use with no charge paid or agreed. Where there is a charge the contract for the use of the thing is hire: commodatum must be free. 3. A depositee also incurs an obligation by conduct. His liability is realized by the action on deposit. He too is bound to return the very thing received. In his case the liability extends only to deliberate wickedness, not to fault such as laziness or negligence. He will be safe even if he looks after the thing with insufficient care and loses it to a thief. A person who gives something to a negligent friend to look after should blame his loss on his own complacency. 4. A creditor who takes a pledge also comes under an obligation by conduct. He too is liable for the return of the very thing received. He can be sued by the action on pledge. Pledge benefits both parties, the debtor because it helps him get credit, and the creditor because it helps him give credit safely. The benefit to the creditor puts him under the highest standard of care in looking after the thing. If he keeps to that standard and still loses it in some catastrophe he should neither be liable nor barred from reclaiming his money.

3.15 OBLIGATIONS BY WORDS

An obligation by words is contracted by question and answer. This happens when we stipulate for something to be given to us or done for us. The obligation gives rise to two actions, to an action of debt if the stipulation is for a fixed thing or quantity, and to the action on a stipulation if the stipulation is not for something fixed. The name 'stipulation' is used because in the old days the word for 'firm' was 'stipulus', coming perhaps from 'stipes' which is the trunk of a tree. 1. For making the exchange – 'Do you promise?' 'I do so promise' – the traditional Latin words are spondere, promittere, fidepromittere, fideiubere, dare and facere. But it makes no difference whether it is done in Latin, Greek, or any other language, so long as both parties understand. Nor is it necessary to use the same language on both sides. It is enough if the content of the answer corresponds with that of the question. And two Greeks can contract the obligation in Latin. Once only the special words could be used. But later a pronouncement of Leo abolished that verbal solemnity and required no more than that the parties understand each other's meaning and agree, whatever words they used. 2. A stipulation is either absolute or postponed or conditional. An absolute example is 'Do you promise to give me 5?' There the promisee can sue at once. A postponed stipulation is made by specifying a day for money to be paid: 'Do you promise to pay me 10 on 1st March?' In a postponed stipulation, the obligation comes into being immediately but no action lies till the specified time. Actually the claim cannot even be made on that day, because the debtor can choose any time during it. So it will not be certain until the day has passed that he has in fact failed to pay on time. 3. If you stipulate in these terms, 'Do you promise to give 10 every year so long as I live?' an obligation comes into existence which is both absolute and perpetual, because owing cannot run for a limited time. Nevertheless if your heir sued he would be defeated by the plea of contrary agreement. 4. A conditional stipulation is one suspended against some event, with the effect that it is triggered if something is done or not done. One example is a stipulation like this, 'Do you promise to give me 5 if Titius is made consul?' If someone stipulates, 'Do you promise to give if I never go up to the Capitol?' the result is exactly as though he had stipulated for the thing to be given on his deathbed. A conditional stipulation only gives rise to an expectation of a debt. We pass on that expectation to our heirs if we die before the condition is fulfilled. 5. It is common to insert a place of performance, as for instance 'Do you promise to give at Carthage?' This looks absolute, but in the nature of the undertaking it must allow enough time for the promissor to make the payment at Carthage. A stipulation made at Rome like this, 'Do you promise to give at Carthage today?' is void, since the answering promise is impossible. 6. Conditions which refer to the past or present either destroy the obligation immediately or do not suspend it at all. For example, 'Do you promise to give if Titius has been consul?' or 'if Maevius is alive?' If these things are not so, the stipulation has no effect; if they are, it is instantly valid. Facts which are objectively certain do not suspend an obligation just because they look uncertain from our own standpoint. 7. Not only things but also services can be made the subject of stipulations, as where we stipulate for something to be done or not to be done. The best plan here is to insert a penalty to avoid leaving the value of the stipulation uncertain, which would put the onus on the plaintiff to prove the quantum of his interest. If someone stipulates for something to be done, he ought to attach a penalty in this way: 'If it is not done, do you promise to pay me a penalty of 10?' If a single stipulation is drafted to include obligations both to do and not to do, the clause to add is this: 'If anything is done contrary to the foregoing or not done as the foregoing requires, do you promise to give me a penalty of 10?'

duobus separatim stipulantibus ita promissor respondeat 'utrique vestrum dare spondeo': nam si prius Titio spoponderit, deinde alio interrogante spondeat, alia atque alia erit obligatio nec creduntur duo rei stipulandi esse. duo pluresve rei promittendi ita fiunt: 'Maevi, quinque aureos dare spondes? Sei, eosdem 'quinque aureos dare spondes?' respondeant[1] singuli 1 separatim 'spondeo'. Ex huiusmodi obligationibus et stipulantibus solidum singulis debetur et promittentes singuli in solidum tenentur. in utraque tamen obligatione una res vertitur: et vel alter debitum accipiendo vel alter solvendo omnium peremit obliga-2 tionem et omnes liberat. [2]Ex duobus reis promittendi alius pure, alius in diem vel sub condicione obligari potest: nec impedimento erit dies aut condicio, quo minus ab eo qui pure obligatus est petatur.

XVII[3]
DE STIPULATIONE SERVORUM.

Servus ex persona domini ius stipulandi habet. sed[4] hereditas in plerisque personae defuncti vicem sustinet: ideoque quod servus hereditarius ante aditam hereditatem stipulatur, adquirit hereditati ac per hoc 1 etiam heredi postea facto adquiritur. [5]Sive autem domino sive sibi sive conservo suo sive impersonaliter servus stipuletur, domino adquirit. idem iuris est et in liberis, qui in potestate patris sunt, ex quibus cau-2 sis adquirere possunt. Sed cum factum in stipulatione continebitur, omnimodo persona stipulantis continetur, veluti si servus stipuletur, ut sibi ire agere liceat: ipse enim tantum prohiberi non debet, 3 non etiam dominus eius. Servus communis stipulando unicuique dominorum pro portione dominii adquirit, nisi si unius eorum iussu aut nominatim cui eorum stipulatus est: tunc enim soli ei adquiritur. quod servus communis stipulatur, si alteri ex dominis adquiri non potest, solidum alteri adquiritur, veluti si res quam dari stipulatus est unius domini sit.

XVIII
DE DIVISIONE STIPULATIONUM.

[6]Stipulationum aliae iudiciales sunt, aliae praetoriae, aliae conventionales, aliae communes tam prae-1 toriae quam iudiciales. [6]Iudiciales sunt dumtaxat, quae a mero iudicis officio proficiscuntur: veluti de dolo cautio vel de persequendo servo qui in fuga 2 est restituendove pretio. [6]Praetoriae, quae a mero praetoris officio proficiscuntur, veluti damni infecti vel legatorum. praetorias autem stipulationes sic exaudiri oportet, ut in his contineantur etiam aedili-3 ciae: nam et hae ab iurisdictione veniunt. [6]Conventionales sunt, quae ex conventione utriusque partis concipiuntur, 'hoc est neque iussu iudicis neque 'iussu praetoris, sed ex conventione contrahentium.' quarum totidem genera sunt, quot paene dixerim 4 rerum contrahendarum. [6]Communes sunt stipulationes veluti rem salvam fore pupilli: nam et praetor iubet rem salvam fore pupillo caveri et interdum iudex, si aliter expediri haec res non potest: vel de rato stipulatio.

XIX[7]
DE INUTILIBUS STIPULATIONIBUS.

Omnis res, quae dominio nostro subicitur, in stipulationem deduci potest, sive illa mobilis sive soli sit. 1 At[8] si quis rem, quae in rerum natura non est aut esse non potest, dari stipulatus fuerit, veluti

Stichum, qui mortuus sit, quem vivere credebat, aut hippocentaurum, qui esse non possit, inutilis erit 2 stipulatio. Idem iuris est, si rem sacram aut religiosam, quam humani iuris esse credebat, vel publicam, quae usibus populi perpetuo exposita sit. ut forum vel theatrum, vel liberum hominem, quem servum esse credebat, vel cuius commercium non habuit, vel rem suam dari[9] quis stipuletur. nec in pendenti erit stipulatio ob id, quod publica res in privatum deduci et ex libero servus fieri potest et commercium adipisci stipulator potest et res stipulatoris esse desinere potest, sed protinus inutilis est. item contra licet initio utiliter res in stipulatum deducta sit, si postea in earum qua causa[10], de quibus supra dictum est, sine facto promissoris devenerit, extinguitur stipulatio. ac ne[11] statim ab initio talis stipulatio valebit 'Lucium Titium cum servus 'erit dare spondes?' et similia: quia natura sui dominio nostro exempta in obligationem deduci nullo 3 modo possunt. Si quis alium daturum facturumve quid spoponderit, non obligabitur, veluti si spondeat Titium quinque aureos daturum. quodsi effecturum 4 se, ut Titius daret, spoponderit, obligatur. Si quis alii, quam cuius iuri subiectus sit, stipuletur, nihil agit. plane solutio etiam in extranei personam conferri potest (veluti[12] si quis ita stipuletur 'mihi 'aut Seio dare spondes?'), ut obligatio quidem stipulatori adquiratur, solvi tamen Seio etiam invito eo recte possit, ut liberatio ipso iure contingat, sed ille adversus Seium habeat mandati actionem. quod si quis sibi et alii, cuius iuri subiectus non sit, decem dari[13] 'aureos' stipulatus est, valebit quidem stipulatio: sed utrum totum debetur quod in stipulatione deductum est, an vero pars dimidia, dubitatum est: sed 'placet' non plus quam partem dimidiam ei adquiri. ei qui tuo iuri subiectus est si stipulatus sis, tibi adquiris, quia vox tua tamquam filii sit, sicuti filii vox tamquam tua intellegitur 'in his rebus quae 5 tibi adquiri possunt.' [14]'Praeterea inutilis est sti-'pulatio, si quis ad ea quae interrogatus erit non 'responderit, veluti si decem 'aureos' a te dari[15] sti-'puletur, tu quinque promittas,' vel contra: 'aut si 'ille pure stipuletur, tu sub condicione promittas,' vel contra, si modo scilicet id exprimas, id est si cui sub condicione vel in diem stipulanti tu respondeas: 'praesenti die spondeo.' nam si hoc solum respondeas 'promitto', breviter videris in eandem diem aut 6 condicionem spopondisse: nec enim necesse est in respondendo eadem repeti, quae stipulator expresserit. [16]'Item inutilis est[17] stipulatio, si ab 'eo stipuleris, qui iuri tuo subiectus est, vel si is a 'te stipuletur. sed servus quidem non solum domino 'suo obligari non potest, sed ne alii quidem ulli': filii 7 vero familias aliis obligari possunt. [18]'Mutum ne-'que stipulari neque promittere posse palam est. quod 'et in surdo receptum est, quia et is qui stipulatur 'verba promittentis et is qui promittit verba stipu-'lantis audire debet.' [19]'unde apparet non de eo nos 'loqui qui tardius exaudit, sed de eo qui omnino non 8 exaudit. [20]'Furiosus nullum negotium gerere po-9 'test, quia non intellegit quid agit. [20]'Pupillus omne 'negotium recte gerit: ut tamen, sicubi tutoris aucto-'ritas necessaria sit, adhibeatur tutor, veluti si ipse 'obligetur: nam alium sibi obligare etiam sine tutoris 10 'auctoritate potest. [20]'Sed quod diximus de pu-'pillis, utique de his verum est, qui iam aliquem in-'tellectum habent: nam infans et qui infanti proxi-'mus est non multum a furioso distant, quia huius 'aetatis pupilli nullum intellectum habent: sed in 'proximis infanti propter utilitatem eorum benignior

---

(1) respondeant] *BP*, et r. *T*, si r. *E*: ut interroget stipulator *vel simile quid inter* fiunt *et* Maevi *a compilatoribus male deletum censet* Mommsen   (2) § 2 *ex Flor. l.* 8 *inst.* (*Dig.* 45, 2, 7)

(3) *Cf. Gai.* 3, 114. 167 *Dig.* 45, 3   (4) sed] *T*, sed et *B* (5) § 1 *in. ex Flor. l.* 8 *inst.* (*Dig.* 45, 3, 15)

(6) *pr...* § 4 *ex Dig.* 45, 1, 5 *pr.* (*Pomp. l.* 26 *ad Sab.*)

(7) *Cf. Gai.* 3, 97..109 *Cod.* 8, 38   (8) at] *ATΘ*, itaque *B* (9) dare *libri*   (10) qua causa] *Tª?*, qua alii causa *Aᵘ ante emend. Aᵇᵍ*, aliqua causa *AˡAᵘ ex emend.*, causa *B*   (11) ne] *AT*, nec *B*   (12) veluti] *TΘ*, om. *AB*   (13) dare *libri* (14) *Gai.* 3, 102   (15) dari] *BGai.*, dari sibi *AT*   (16) *Gai.* 3, 104 (17) est] *BT*, erit *A*   (18) *Gai.* 3, 105   (19) § 7 *fin. ex Gai. l.* 2 *rer. cott.* (*Dig.* 44, 7, 1 § 15)   (20) *Gai* 3, 106. 107. 109

3.16 MULTI-PARTY STIPULATIONS

Two or more persons can take or make a stipulatory promise. To get a plurality on the stipulator's side, the promissor must reply, 'I promise,' after the question has been put by every stipulator. // For example, two people separately put the stipulatory question, and the promissor answers, 'To each of you I promise to give.' If he made his promise first to Titius and then again in reply to the second person's question, there would be two different obligations. It would not then be a case of two parties on the promisee's side. The way to get two promissors is this: 'Maevius, do you promise to give 5? Seius, do you promise to give the same 5?' They should reply each to his own question. 1. Where obligations are created in this way each stipulator is owed the whole amount, and each promissor is liable for the whole amount. Yet in both obligations only one performance is in question. If one of the parties receives what is owed, or one on the other side makes the performance, the obligation is extinguished and all are discharged. 2. Where there are two promissors, one can be put under an absolute obligation and another under an obligation either conditional or postponed. Neither the deferment nor the condition obstructs the claim against the one who is liable absolutely.

3.17 STIPULATIONS TAKEN BY SLAVES

The legal personality of his owner gives a slave a derivative capacity to take stipulations. When people die their personality is generally assumed by their estate. It follows that a slave of the deceased's estate acquires for the estate itself anything for which he stipulates before the heir accepts. Afterwards the heir acquires it with the estate. 1. Whether the slave stipulates for his owner, for himself, for another of his owner's slaves, or for no named person, he acquires for his owner. The law is the same for an owner who is still within family authority if the transaction is one in which he can acquire for himself. 2. However, when a stipulation requires an act, the implication is that it shall by done for the stipulator. For example, if a slave stipulates for permission to walk and drive over land, it is he who must not be prevented, not his owner. 3. If a slave in common ownership takes a stipulation, the right accrues to each owner in proportion to his share unless he stipulates by command of one of them or for one of them by name. If it is impossible for one of his owners to acquire under its terms, the right accrues entirely to the other, as, for example, where he stipulates for something to be conveyed and that thing is already owned by one of his masters.

3.18 CLASSIFICATION OF STIPULATIONS

Some are judicial, some are praetorian, some are conventional, some are hybrid between praetorian and judicial. 1. Judicial stipulations are those which are made solely on the authority of a judge, for example the undertaking against fraud or the one for pursuit of a fugitive slave or restoration of his price. 2. Praetorian stipulations are those made on the authority of the praetor, for instance the one against imminent loss or in respect of legacies. The category of praetorian stipulations should be understood as including aedilician stipulations, which also rest on jurisdictional authority. 3. Conventional stipulations are those which emanate simply from the agreement of parties. That is to say, they are made by agreement of parties as opposed to the order of judge or praetor. There are about as many kinds of these as there are matters to contract about. 4. Hybrid stipulations are exemplified by the undertaking for the preservation of a ward's property. The praetor sometimes requires that undertaking to be given; sometimes also a judge, if there is no alternative. Another such example is the stipulation for ratification by one's principal.

3.19 INEFFECTIVE STIPULATIONS

Everything we own – land or goods – can be the subject of a stipulation. 1. But if someone stipulates for the giving of something which does not or cannot exist, for instance for the slave Stichus believed alive but actually dead, or for a hippocentaur, a creature which cannot exist, the stipulation has no effect. 2. The law is the same if a man stipulates to be given a sacred or religious thing believing it governed by human law; or a public thing dedicated permanently to civic purposes such as a city square or a theatre; or a free man whom he believes to be a slave; or something outside his commercial capacity; or something already his. There is no question of such stipulations being treated as suspended against the possibility that the public thing may become private, the free man become a slave, the defective capacity be made good, or the thing owned by the stipulator stop being his. On the contrary, such a stipulation is immediately void. Conversely, if the stipulation is effective as made but the subject-matter then falls into one of the categories just mentioned and does so without any act on the part of the promissor, the contract is discharged. Again, initial validity is not instantly secured by a putting the stipulation in these or similar terms: 'Do you promise to give Lucius Titius when he becomes a slave?' When a thing simply cannot be owned there is no way of making it the subject of an obligation. 3. If a person promises that a third party will give or do, he incurs no obligation, as for instance if he promises that Titius will give five. But if he promises that he will see to it that Titius gives, he does incur the obligation. 4. If someone takes a stipulation for a third party, other than for the head of his family, he achieves nothing. But it is clearly possible to confer on a third party a power to accept performance, as where a stipulator asks, 'Do you promise to give to me or to Scius ?' Here the obligation accrues to the stipulator but even without his consent the performance can properly be made to Seius, automatically discharging the promissor. Against Seius the stipulator has the action on mandate. If someone takes a stipulation for 10 to be given to himself and to a third party, that third party not being the head of the stipulator's family, the stipulation is valid. But does the whole or half the amount have to be paid? The answer is that the stipulator only acquires a right to half. If you stipulate for the benefit of someone within your authority, the right accrues to you. You speak for him here – and he for you as when acquiring property on your behalf. 5. Next, a stipulation is ineffective if the answer fails to match the question, as where the other party asks whether you promise to give 10, and you answer 5, or vice versa; or if he puts the question absolutely, and you promise conditionally, or vice versa. Only express discrepancies matter, as where he puts the stipulation subject to a condition or postponement and you answer, 'I promise it for this very day.' If you just say 'I promise,' your short reply will be construed as matching his condition or deferment. It is not necessary in answering to repeat the stipulator's every word. 6. A stipulation taken from the head of your family is a nullity. So also one by him from you. A slave cannot incur an obligation to his owner or to any other person at all, but a son under family authority can incur obligations to outsiders. 7. It is obvious that a person who is dumb cannot stipulate or promise. The same has been accepted of the deaf. The stipulator must

'iuris interpretatio facta est,' ut idem iuris habeant, quod pubertati proximi. sed qui in parentis potestate est impubes, nec auctore quidem patre obligatur. 11 Si impossibilis condicio obligationibus adiciatur, nihil valet stipulatio. impossibilis autem condicio habetur[1], cui natura impedimento est, quo minus existat, veluti si quis ita dixerit: 'si digito caelum attigero, 'dare spondes?' at si ita stipuletur, 'si digito caelum 'non attigero, dare spondes?' pure facta obligatio 12 intellegitur ideoque statim petere potest. Item verborum obligatio inter absentes concepta inutilis est. 'sed cum hoc materiam litium contentiosis ho- 'minibus praestabat, forte post tempus tales allega- 'tiones opponentibus et non praesentes esse vel se 'vel adversarios suos contendentibus: ideo nostra con- 'stitutio[2] propter celeritatem dirimendarum litium intro- 'ducta est, quam ad Caesarienses[3] advocatos scripsi- 'mus, per quam disposuimus tales scripturas, quae 'praesto esse partes indicant, omnimodo esse creden- 'das, nisi ipse, qui talibus utitur improbis allegatio- 'nibus, manifestissimis probationibus vel per scriptu- 'ram vel per testes idoneos approbaverit in ipso toto 'die quo conficiebatur instrumentum sese vel adver- 13 'sarium suum in aliis locis esse.' Post mortem suam dari sibi nemo stipulari poterat, non magis quam post eius mortem a quo stipulabatur. ac ne is, qui in alicuius potestate est, post mortem eius stipulari poterat, quia patris vel domini voce loqui videtur. sed et si quis ita stipuletur, 'pridie quam mo- riar' vel 'pridie quam morieris dari[4]?' inutilis erat stipulatio. 'sed cum, ut iam dictum est, ex consensu 'contrahentium stipulationes valent, placuit nobis[5] 'etiam in hunc iuris articulum necessariam inducere 'emendationem, ut, sive post mortem sive pridie quam 'morietur stipulator sive promissor stipulatio concepta 14 'est, valeat stipulatio.' Item si quis ita stipulatus erat: 'si navis ex Asia venerit, hodie dare spondes?' inutilis erat stipulatio, quia praepostere concepta est. 'sed cum Leo inclitae recordationis in dotibus ean- 'dem stipulationem quae praepostera nuncupatur non 'esse reiciendam existimavit, nobis[6] placuit et huic 'perfectum robur accommodare, ut non solum in do- 'tibus, sed etiam in omnibus valeat huiusmodi con- 15 'ceptio stipulationis.' Ita autem concepta stipu- latio, veluti si Titius dicat 'cum moriar, dare spon- 'des?' vel 'cum morieris', 'et apud veteres' utilis erat 16 'et nunc valet.' Item post mortem alterius recte 17 stipulamur.[7] Si scriptum fuerit in instrumento promisisse aliquem, perinde habetur, atque si inter- 18 rogatione praecedente responsum sit. Quotiens plures res una stipulatione comprehenduntur, si qui- dem promissor simpliciter respondeat 'dare spondeo', propter omnes tenetur: si vero unam ex his vel quas- dam daturum se spoponderit, obligatio in his pro quibus spoponderit contrahitur. ex pluribus enim stipulationibus una vel quaedam videntur esse per- fectae: singulas enim res stipulari ad singulas re- 19 spondere debemus.[8] Alteri stipulari, ut supra dictum est, nemo potest: inventae sunt enim huius- modi obligationes ad hoc, ut unusquisque sibi ad- quirat quod sua interest: ceterum si[9] alii detur, nihil interest stipulatoris. plane si quis velit hoc facere, poenam stipulari conveniet, ut, nisi ita factum sit, ut comprehensum esset[10], committetur[11] poenae sti- pulatio etiam ei cuius nihil interest: poenam enim cum stipulatur quis, non illud inspicitur, quid inter- sit eius, sed quae sit quantitas in condicione stipu- lationis. 'ergo si quis stipuletur Titio dari, nihil agit, 'sed si addiderit de poena 'nisi dederis, tot aureos 20 "dare spondes?' tunc committitur stipulatio.'[12] Sed

et si quis stipuletur alii, cum eius interesset, 'placuit' stipulationem valere. 'nam si' is, qui pupilli tutelam administrare coeperat, cessit administratione contu- tori suo et stipulatus est rem pupilli salvam fore, 'quoniam' interest stipulatoris fieri quod stipulatus est, cum obligatus futurus esset pupillo, si male res ges- serit, 'tenet obligatio. ergo' et si quis procuratori suo dari stipulatus sit, stipulatio vires habebit. et si cre- ditori suo, quod sua interest, ne forte vel poena com- mittatur vel praedia distrahantur quae pignori data 21 erant, 'valet stipulatio.' Versa vice qui alium facturum promisit, videtur in ea esse causa, ut non 22 teneatur, nisi poenam ipse promiserit. [13]Item nemo rem suam futuram in eum casum quo[14] sua 23 fit utiliter stipulatur. Si de alia re stipulator senserit, de alia promissor, perinde nulla contrahitur obligatio, ac si ad interrogatum responsum non esset, veluti si hominem Stichum a te stipulatus quis fuerit, tu de Pamphilo senseris, quem Stichum vocari cre- 24 dideris. Quod turpi ex causa promissum est, veluti si quis homicidium vel sacrilegium se facturum promittat, non valet. 25 Cum quis sub aliqua condicione fuerit stipu- latus, licet ante condicionem decesserit, postea ex- istente condicione heres eius agere potest. idem est 26 et a promissoris parte. [15]Qui hoc anno aut hoc mense dari stipulatus sit, nisi omnibus partibus prae- 27 teritis anni vel mensis non recte petet[16]. Si fundum dari[17] stipuleris vel hominem, non poteris continuo agere, nisi tantum spatii praeterierit, quo traditio fieri possit.

XX[18]

DE FIDEIUSSORIBUS.

[19]'Pro eo qui promittit solent alii obligari qui fide- 'iussores appellantur, quos homines accipere solent, 1 'dum curant, ut diligentius sibi cautum sit. [20]'In 'omnibus autem obligationibus 'adsumi possunt,' id est 'sive re sive verbis sive litteris sive consensu con- 'tractae fuerint. ac ne illud quidem interest, utrum 'civilis an naturalis sit obligatio, cui adiciatur fide- 'iussor, adeo quidem, ut pro servo quoque obligetur, 'sive extraneus sit qui fideiussorem a servo accipiat, 'sive ipse dominus in id quod sibi 'naturaliter' debe- 2 'tur.'[21] Fideiussor non tantum ipse obligatur, sed 3 etiam heredem obligatum relinquit. Fideiussor et 4 praecedere obligationem et sequi potest. [22]Si plures sint fideiussores, 'quotquot erunt numero, singuli 'in solidum tenentur. itaque liberum est creditori a 'quo velit solidum petere. sed ex epistula divi Ha- 'driani compellitur creditor a singulis, qui modo sol- 'vendo sint 'litis contestatae tempore,' partes petere. 'ideoque si quis ex fideiussoribus eo tempore sol- 'vendo non sit, 'hoc' ceteros 'onerat. sed et' si ab uno 'fideiussore creditor totum consecutus fuerit, huius 'solius detrimentum erit, si is pro quo fideiussit[23] 'solvendo non sit: 'et sibi imputare debet, cum po- 'tuerit adiuvari' ex epistula divi Hadriani 'et' deside- 5 'rare, ut pro parte in se detur actio. [24]Fideius- 'sores ita obligari non possunt, ut plus debeant, quam 'debet is pro quo obligantur: nam eorum obligatio 'accessio est principalis obligationis nec plus in ac- 'cessione esse potest quam in principali re. at ex 'diverso, ut minus debeant, obligari possunt.' [25]itaque si reus decem 'aureos' promiserit, fideiussor in quin- que recte obligatur: contra vero non potest obligari. item si ille pure promiserit, fideiussor sub condicione promittere potest: contra vero non potest. [26]'non so- 'lum enim in quantitate, sed etiam in tempore minus

---

(1) habetur] *AB*, appellatur *T*   (2) *Cod.* 8, 37, 14
(3) caesarienses *libri*   (4) dari] *BT*, dabis *A*   (5) *Cod.*
8, 37, 11   (6) *Cod.* 6, 23, 25   (7) § 17 *similis Paulo*
5, 7, 2   (8) § 19 *in. ex Dig.* 45, 1, 38 § 17 (*Ulp. l.* 49 *ad Sab.*)
(9) si] ut *Dig.*   (10) *sic AB*, est *TDig.*   (11) *sic ATDig.*,
committeretur *B* (12) § 20 *ex Dig.* 45, 1, 38 § 20. 23 (*Ulp. l. c.*)
(13) § 22 *similis Dig.* 45, 1, 87 (*Paul. l.* 75 *ad ed.*)   (14) quo]

A, quod *BT*, qua *Dig.*   (15) § 26 *ex Dig.* 45, 1, 42 (*Pomp.
l.* 27 *ad Sab.*)   (16) *sic TⵀDig.*, petit *AB*   (17) dare *libri*
(18) Cf. *Gai.* 3, 115..127 *Dig.* 46, 1 *Cod.* 8, 40   (19) *Gai.*
3, 115. 117   (20) *Gai.* 3, 119ᵃ   (21) § 2 *similis Dig.* 46, 1, 4 § 1
(*Ulp. l.* 45 *ad Sab.*)   (22) *Gai.* 3, 121. 122   (23) *sic TE
Gai.*, fideiussor accessit *B*   (24) *Gai.* 3, 126   (25) *Cf.
Gai.* 3, 113   (26) *Gai.* 3, 113

hear the words of the promissor, and the promissor must hear the words of the stipulator. Obviously we exclude only those who cannot hear at all, not those who have difficulty hearing. 8. An insane person cannot perform any transaction because he does not know what he is doing. 9. A child under guardianship has capacity to perform any act so long as he gets his guardian's endorsement when that is required, as when he puts himself under an obligation. He can put another under an obligation towards himself even without his guardian's endorsement. 10. What we have said of a child is only true of one who has attained some understanding. A baby and a child barely past infancy hardly differ from the insane, in that they are too young to understand anything. With those just past infancy, convenience has encouraged a generous interpretation of the law, // so that they are treated as having the same capacity as those near puberty. A young child still within his family incurs no obligation even with the endorsement of the head of the family. 11. If obligations are made subject to an impossible condition, the stipulation is void. A condition is considered to be impossible when in the nature of things it cannot be fulfilled. One example is where the question is put, 'Do you promise to give if I touch the sky?' But a stipulation the other way round, 'Do you promise to give if I do not touch the sky?' is construed as absolute and can be enforced at once. 12. Next, an obligation by words is void if the parties are not in each other's presence. But this rule used to provide argumentative people with too much grist for the mill of litigation. They would snatch at allegations – probably long after the event – that they or their adversary had not been present. That was why, to speed up litigation, we made the pronouncement addressed to the advocates of Caesarea. We there provided that documents which indicate that the parties were present are to be regarded as conclusive unless the person who makes this suspect defence proves by the clearest evidence in writing or from respectable witnesses that for the entire day on which the document was made he or his adversary was in another place. 13. It used to be impossible to take a stipulation for something to be given to the stipulator after his death. The same with one for performance after the promissor's death. Also a person within authority could not take a stipulation to operate after the death of the head of his family, he being considered to speak with his father's or his owner's voice. It was equally ineffective to stipulate for a giving 'the day before I die' or 'the day before you die'. But given the modern principle, already mentioned, that stipulations are based on agreement between the parties, we decided to introduce yet another necessary reform: we made the stipulation valid even if framed for performance after the death of, or on the day before the death of, the stipulator or promissor. 14. Next, a stipulation used to be void if framed like this: 'If the ship arrives from Asia sometime, do you promise to give today.' That kind of stipulation has its times back to front. But Leo, of glorious memory, held in relation to dowry that a similar stipulation framed with a temporal contradiction should not be rejected, and we have extended that ruling, so that not only in the context of dowry but in all cases stipulations like these shall be valid. 15. A stipulation of this kind, as for intance where Titius says 'Do you promise to give as I lie dying?' or 'as you lie dying?' was held to be valid even by the classical jurists and is also valid nowadays. 16. A valid stipulation can also be made for a performance after the death of a third party. 17. If the document says that someone gave a promise, it is assumed that he promised in response to a question put beforehand. 18. Whenever many things are demanded in one stipulation, a promissor who simply answers 'I promise to give' is bound for all of them. If he

promises to give one of them or some of them, he contracts an obligation for those he actually promises. The one stipulation is then deemed to have been put as several demands for single things, some of which were accepted. The basic rule is that we should stipulate for things one by one and answer in the same way. 19. As has been said above, nobody can take a stipulation for a third party. Obligations of this sort were introduced to allow every person to secure his own interest, and a stipulator has no interest in a giving to a third party. Plainly, if someone does want to achieve this end, the way to do it is to stipulate for a penalty. If the specified performance is not made the penal stipulation will then be triggered despite the stipulator's lack of an interest. In penal stipulations no inquiry is made into the stipulator's underlying interest in the condition. The question is only as to the sum made to turn on it. So, if someone stipulates for a giving to Titius, he achieves nothing, but if he adds 'If you do not give, do you promise to give me such and such a sum of money?' the stipulation is effective. 20. If someone takes a stipulation for another when he does have an interest in the performance, the stipulation is valid. Suppose a man begins to act as guardian to a child and then renounces the administration in favour of his fellow guardian. If he takes a stipulation from the latter for the safety of the child's property, he has an interest in the the promise being kept since he himself will be liable to the child in the event of maladministration. Consequently, the obligation is valid. A stipulation is similarly valid if it requires something to be given to the stipulator's general agent. The same is true of a stipulation in favour of his creditor, since the stipulator then has an interest, say, in avoiding a penalty which he might incur or in saving mortgaged lands from being sold off. 21. The other way around, one who promises that another will do something is in the same position. He is not liable unless he promises a penalty. 22. Again, nobody can effectively take a stipulation to ensure that something which is actually his own will be in a condition to be conveyed to him. 23. If the stipulator has one thing in mind and the promissor another, there is no obligation, no more than if the question met with no answer at all. An example is where the stipulator asks you for Stichus and you have in mind Pamphilus, whose name you think is Stichus. 24. A promise arising from an immoral contract is void, as for instance when someone promises to commit murder or sacrilege. 25. If someone takes a stipulation subject to a condition and dies before the condition is fulfilled, his heir can sue if the condition is satisfied afterwards. It is the same on the side of the promissor. 26. One who stipulates for something to be given this year or this month cannot sue till every part of the year or month has gone. 27. If you stipulate for a conveyance of land or of a slave, you cannot sue at once. Time for delivery must be allowed.

3.20 GUARANTORS

It is common for others to bind themselves on behalf of the promissor. They are then called guarantors. They are invoked by stipulators anxious for greater security. 1. But in fact guarantors can be taken for all sorts of obligations, by conduct, by words, by writing, or by agreement. It does not even matter whether the obligation is legal or natural. The use of guarantors for natural obligations allows a slave's obligation to be guaranteed. The party requiring the slave to provide a guarantor can be an outsider or the slave's owner securing a natural debt owed to himself. 2. A guarantor not only binds himself but also his heir. 3. The guarantee can be taken before or after the principal obligation. 4. When there is a number of guarantors, however many there are each of them is

'et plus intellegitur. plus est enim statim aliquid dare,
6 'minus est post tempus dare. [1]Si quid 'autem
'fideiussor' pro reo solverit, eius reciperandi causa
7 'habet cum eo mandati iudicium.' [2]Graece fideiussor 'plerumque' ita accipitur: τῇ ἐμῇ πίστει κελεύω,
λέγω, θέλω sive βούλομαι[3]: sed et si φημί dixerit,
8 pro eo erit, ac si dixerit λέγω. In stipulationibus
fideiussorum sciendum est generaliter hoc accipi, ut,
quodcumque scriptum sit quasi actum, videatur etiam
actum: ideoque constat, [4]si quis se scripserit fideius-
sisse[5], videri omnia sollemniter acta.

XXI[6]
DE LITTERARUM OBLIGATIONE.

'Olim scriptura fiebat obligatio, quae nominibus
'fieri dicebatur, quae nomina hodie non sunt in usu.
'plane si quis debere se scripserit, quod numeratum
'ei non est, de pecunia minime numerata post mul-
'tum temporis exceptionem opponere non potest: hoc
'enim saepissime constitutum est. sic fit, ut et hodie,
'dum queri non potest, scriptura obligetur: et ex ea
'nascitur condictio, cessante scilicet verborum obli-
'gatione. multum autem tempus in hac exceptione
'antea quidem ex principalibus constitutionibus usque
'ad quinquennium procedebat: sed ne creditores diu-
'tius possint suis pecuniis forsitan defraudari, per
'constitutionem nostram[7] tempus coartatum est, ut
'ultra biennii metas huiusmodi exceptio minime ex-
'tendatur.'

XXII
DE CONSENSU OBLIGATIONE.

[8]'Consensu fiunt obligationes in emptionibus ven-
'ditionibus, locationibus conductionibus, societatibus,
1 'mandatis. [8]Ideo autem istis modis consensu dici-
'tur obligatio contrahi, quia neque 'scriptura neque
'praesentia omnimodo opus est, ac ne dari quicquam
necesse est, ut substantiam capiat obligatio,' 'sed suf-
2 'ficit eos qui negotium gerunt consentire. [8]Unde
'inter absentes quoque talia negotia contrahuntur,
3 'veluti per epistulam aut per nuntium. Item in
'his contractibus alter alteri obligatur 'in id', quod
'alterum alteri ex bono et aequo praestare oportet,
'cum alioquin in verborum obligationibus alius stipu-
'letur, alius promittat.'

XXIII[9]
DE EMPTIONE ET VENDITIONE.

[10]'Emptio et venditio contrahitur, 'simulatque' de
'pretio convenerit, quamvis nondum pretium nume-
'ratum sit ac ne arra quidem data fuerit. nam quod
'arrae nomine datur, argumentum est emptionis et
'venditionis contractae.' 'sed haec quidem de emptio-
'nibus et venditionibus, quae sine scriptura consistunt,
'optinere oportet. nam nihil a nobis in huiusmodi
'venditionibus innovatum est. in his autem quae scrip-
'tura conficiuntur non aliter perfectam esse emptio-
'nem et venditionem constituimus[11], nisi et instru-
'menta emptionis fuerint conscripta vel manu propria
'contrahentium, vel ab alio quidem scripta, a contra-
'hente autem subscripta et, si per tabellionem fiunt,
'nisi et completiones acceperint et fuerint partibus
'absoluta. donec enim aliquid ex his deest, et paeni-
'tentiae locus est et potest emptor vel venditor sine
'poena recedere ab emptione. ita tamen impune re-
'cedere eis concedimus, nisi iam arrarum nomine ali-
'quid fuerit datum: hoc etenim subsecuto, sive in scrip-
'tis sive sine scriptis venditio celebrata est, is qui re-
'cusat adimplere contractum, si quidem emptor est,

'perdit quod dedit, si vero venditor', duplum resti-
'tuere compellitur, licet nihil super arris expressum
1 'est.' Pretium autem constitui oportet: nam nulla
(1) emptio sine pretio esse potest. sed et [12]'certum
'pretium esse debet. alioquin si ita inter aliquos con-
'venerit, ut, quanti Titius rem aestimaverit, tanti sit
'empta': 'inter veteres satis abundeque hoc dubita-
'batur, sive constat venditio sive non. sed nostra de-
'cisio[13] ita hoc constituit, ut, quoties sic composita
'sit venditio 'quanti ille aestimaverit', sub hac condi-
'cione staret contractus, ut, si quidem ipse qui no-
'minatus est pretium definierit, omnimodo secundum
'eius aestimationem et pretium persolvatur et res tra-
'datur, ut[14] venditio ad effectum perducatur, emptore
'quidem ex empto actione[15], venditore autem ex ven-
'dito agente. sin autem ille qui nominatus est vel
'noluerit vel non potuerit pretium definire, tunc pro
'nihilo esse venditionem quasi nullo pretio statuto.
'quod ius cum in venditionibus nobis placuit, non est
'absurdum et in locationibus et conductionibus tra-
2 'here.' [16]'Item pretium in numerata pecunia con-
'sistere debet. nam in ceteris rebus an pretium esse
'possit, veluti homo aut fundus aut toga alterius rei
'pretium esse possit, valde quaerebatur. 'Sabinus et
'Cassius' etiam in alia re putant posse pretium con-
'sistere: unde illud est, quod vulgo 'dicebatur' per
'permutationem rerum emptionem et venditionem con-
'trahi eamque speciem emptionis venditionisque ve-
'tustissimam esse: argumentoque utebantur Graeco
'poeta Homero, qui aliqua parte 'exercitum Achivo-
'rum vinum sibi comparasse' ait 'permutatis quibus-
'dam rebus, his verbis'[17]:

ἔνθεν ἄρ' οἰνίζοντο καρηκομόωντες Ἀχαιοί,
ἄλλοι μὲν χαλκῷ, ἄλλοι δ' αἴθωνι σιδήρῳ,
ἄλλοι δὲ ῥινοῖς, ἄλλοι δ' αὐτῇσι βόεσσι,
ἄλλοι δ' ἀνδραπόδεσσι[18].

'Diversae scholae auctores 'contra' sentiebant aliud-
'que esse existimabant permutationem rerum, aliud
'emptionem et venditionem. alioquin non posse rem
'expediri permutatis rebus, quae videatur res venisse
'et quae pretii nomine data esse: 'nam' utramque
'videri et venisse et pretii nomine datam esse' rationem non pati. 'sed Proculi sententia dicentis per-
'mutationem propriam esse speciem contractus a ven-
'ditione separatam merito praevaluit, cum et ipsa
'aliis[19] Homericis versibus[20] adiuvatur et validioribus
'rationibus argumentatur. quod et anteriores divi prin-
'cipes admiserunt et in nostris digestis latius signi-
3 'ficatur[21].' Cum autem emptio et venditio contracta sit (quod effici diximus, simulatque de pretio
convenerit, 'cum sine scriptura res agitur'), periculum
rei venditae statim ad emptorem pertinet, tametsi
adhuc ea res emptori tradita non sit. itaque si res
mortuus sit vel aliqua parte corporis laesus fuerit,
aut aedes totae aut aliqua ex parte incendio consumptae fuerint, aut fundus vi fluminis totus vel
aliqua ex parte ablatus sit, sive etiam inundatione
aquae aut arboribus turbine deiectis longe minor aut
deterior esse coeperit: emptoris damnum est, cui necesse est, licet rem non fuerit nactus, pretium solvere. quidquid enim sine dolo et culpa venditoris
accidit, in eo venditor securus est. sed et si post
emptionem fundo aliquid per alluvionem accessit, ad
emptoris commodum pertinet: nam et commodum eius
3a esse debet, cuius periculum est. Quod si fugerit
homo qui veniit aut subreptus fuerit, ita ut neque
dolus neque culpa venditoris interveniat, animadver-
tendum erit, an custodiam eius usque ad traditionem
venditor susceperit. sane enim, si susceperit, ad
ipsius periculum is casus pertinet: si non susceperit,

(1) *Gai.* 3, 127   (2) § 7 *ex Dig.* 46, 1, 8 *pr.* (*Ulp. l. 47 ad
Sab.*)   (3) *id est* fide mea iubeo dico volo   (4) § 8 *fin.
ex Dig.* 45, 1, 30 (*Ulp. l. 47 ad Sab.*)   (5) *sic* T *Dig.*, fideiussorem esse B   (6) *Cf. Gai.* 3, 128..138 *Cod.* 4, 30
(7) *Cod.* 4, 30, 14   (8) *Gai.* 3, 135..137 (*Dig.* 44, 7, 2)
   (9) *Cf. Dig.* 18, 1..19, 1 *Cod.* 4, 38..49   (10) *Gai.* 3, 139

(11) *Cod.* 4, 21, 17   (12) *Gai.* 3, 140   (13) *Cod.* 4, 38, 15
(14) ut] *TΘ*, et B   (15) actionem *BT*   (16) *Gai.* 3, 141
(17) *Il.* 7, 472 seqq.   (18) *id est:* inde vinum comparabant
comantes Achivi, alii aere, alii splendido ferro, alii pelli-
bus, alii ipsis bobus, alii mancipiis   (19) aliis| *TC*, ex
aliis B   (20) *Il.* 6, 235. *cf. Dig.* 18, 1, 1 § 1   (21) *Dig.* 19, 4

liable for the whole amount. So the creditor can sue whichever he pleases. But under a written reply of the Emperor Hadrian the creditor can be compelled to divide the burden of his demand between all the guarantors solvent at the time issue is joined. This means that one who is then insolvent increases the burden on the rest. If the creditor does get the whole amount from one guarantor he alone must bear the loss if the principal debtor is insolvent. He has only himself to blame, since he could have invoked the benefit of Hadrian's reply and asked for the action against him to be limited to his share. 5. The guarantor's obligation cannot be greater than the principal debtor's. His obligation is accessory to the principal obligation, and an accessory cannot be greater than its principal. The guarantor can have a lesser obligation. If the principal promises 10, a guarantor can properly be taken for 5, but not the other way round; if the principal promises absolutely, a guarantor can be asked to promise conditionally, but not the other way round. The notions of more and less are applied not only to amount but also to time. // Thus it is more to give something at once, less to give it after an allowance of time. 6. If a guarantor pays anything for the principal, he can recoup by bringing an action on mandate against him. 7. In Greek a guarantee is generally given in words for 'I wish (or, desire), say, and order on my credit...' But if the word for 'say' is varied the effect is just the same. 8. It should be observed that when stipulations are taken from guarantors the general rule is that whatever the writing says was done is deemed to have been done. There is no doubt that if someone states in writing that he has given a guarantee, the formalites will be presumed.

3.21 OBLIGATIONS BY WRITING

In the old days there was an obligation which was created by written words called 'account entries', but these are obsolete. Of course, if someone states in writing that he owes a sum of money which was in fact never paid to him, there will come a time when he will no longer be able to resist a claim by using the plea of money not paid. This has frequently been the subject of imperial pronouncements. Even today, when a man can no longer advance this plea, he comes under an obligation by writing, realized by the action of debt. Naturally, the obligation only rests on the writing itself when it is not founded on a stipulation. Imperial pronouncements previously allowed a considerable period for this defence, even up to five years. Such a long period increases the danger of creditors being cheated of their money. Our own pronouncement has restricted the time limit, strictly confining it to two years.

3.22 OBLIGATIONS BY AGREEMENT

Obligations are created by agreement in sale, hire, partnership, and mandate. 1.They are said to arise by agreement in these cases because for the obligation to come into being there is absolutely no need for anything in writing, for the parties to meet, or for anything to be transferred. It is enough if the parties to the transaction merely come to an agreement. 2. Consequently contracts of this kind can be made by people at a distance, by letter or messenger for example. 3. Another feature of these contracts is that both parties come under reciprocal obligations to conform to the standard of what is fair and reasonable. By contrast, in obligations by words, only one party promises, in response to the other's question.

3.23 SALE

The contract of sale is concluded the moment the parties agree on the price. It makes no difference if it is not then paid, or if no down-payment is made. A down-payment only goes towards proving that a contract has been made. However, these rules apply to unwritten sales. We have made no changes to them. For those made in writing we have laid down that the sale remains incomplete unless the documents of sale have been drawn up, either in the parties' own writing or in a third person's writing subscribed by the parties. When a notary is used, the documents must have been completed and delivered to the parties. So long as any of these steps still has to be taken there is room for a change of mind, and both buyer and seller can withdraw from the sale without any penalty. We allow them this right of free withdrawal only if no down-payment has been made. Once it has, then, whether the sale has been made in writing or without writing, the party who refuses to fulfil his part, if buyer, forfeits what he has given, and, if seller, must return double what he received. This rule applies even in the absence of any express term about the down-payment. 1. A price must be settled, since there can be no sale without a price. The price must be certain. There was an all too vigorous debate among the classical jurists as to whether a contract of sale was concluded when the parties agreed that the buyer could have the thing at a price to be fixed in a valuation by Titius. We settled this issue: every sale at a price to be fixed by third party valuation is to be construed conditionally, so that if the appointee fixes the price, the thing is to be delivered and the price paid exactly according to his valuation, the buyer now having the action on purchase and the seller the action on sale; but if the appointee will not or cannot fix a price, the sale must fail, as though never concluded for want of agreement on the price. Having decided that this was the right rule for sale, it seemed reasonable to extend it to hire as well. 2. The price must be in money. There used to be a considerable dispute whether the price could consist in other things, a slave, a piece of land, or a toga. Sabinus and Cassius thought it could. That was their inference from the common belief that an exchange of things is a sale, actually the oldest type. They appealed for support to Homer, who at one place says that the Achaean army bought wine by giving goods in exchange: 'Then the long-haired Achaeans bought wine, some with bronze and others with shining steel, some with hides and some with live oxen, others with slaves.' The authorities of the other school took the opposite position and held that exchange and sale were different contracts. In particular they thought it was impossible in an exchange of goods to settle which thing had been sold and which given as price; they held that logic did not allow each side to be regarded as both selling and paying the price. This opinion of Proculus that exchange was a contract quite distinct from sale rightly prevailed. He could also rely on some other lines of Homer, and his view was more logical. His position was accepted by earlier emperors and is more fully explained in our Digest. 3. When a contract of sale is made, which as we have said happens as soon as the price is agreed if the contract is not in writing, the risk passes immediately to the buyer. This is so even if the thing has not yet been delivered. Suppose that a slave dies or suffers injury, or a building is wholly or partly destroyed by fire, or a parcel of land is wholly or partly washed away by the current of a river or is made much smaller or worse by a flooding or by having its trees blown down in a gale. In such cases the buyer must bear the loss, and he must pay the price despite not having obtained the thing. The seller will be immune from

securus erit. idem et in ceteris animalibus ceterisque rebus intellegimus. utique tamen vindicationem rei et condicionem exhibere debebit emptori, quia sane, qui rem nondum emptori tradidit, adhuc ipse dominus est. idem est etiam de furti et de damni 4 iniuriae actione. Emptio tam sub condicione quam pure contrahi potest. sub condicione veluti 'si Sti-'chus intra certum diem tibi placuerit, erit tibi em-5 'ptus aureis tot.' Loca sacra vel religiosa, item publica, veluti forum basilicam, frustra quis sciens emit, quas tamen si pro privatis vel profanis deceptus a venditore emerit, habebit actionem ex empto, quod non habere ei liceat, ut consequatur, quod sua interest deceptum eum non esse. idem iuris est, si hominem liberum pro servo emerit.

XXIV[1]
DE LOCATIONE ET CONDUCTIONE.

[2]Locatio et conductio proxima est emptioni et venditioni isdemque iuris regulis consistunt. nam ut emptio et venditio ita contrahitur, si de pretio convenerit, sic etiam locatio et conductio ita contrahi intellegitur, si merces constituta sit. 'et competit loca-'tori quidem locati actio, conductori vero conducti.' 1 Et quae supra diximus[3], si alieno arbitrio pretium permissum fuerit, eadem et de locatione et conductione dicta esse intellegamus, si alieno arbitrio merces permissa fuerit. [4]'qua de causa si fulloni po-'lienda curandave aut sarcinatori sarcienda vestimenta 'quis dederit nulla statim mercede constituta, sed 'postea tantum daturus, quantum inter eos convene-'rit,' 'non proprie locatio et conductio contrahi intel-'legitur, sed eo nomine praescriptis verbis actio datur.' 2 Praeterea sicut vulgo quaerebatur, an permutatis rebus emptio et venditio contrahitur: ita quaeri solebat de locatione et conductione, si forte rem aliquam tibi utendam sive fruendam quis dederit et invicem a te aliam utendam sive fruendam acceperit. 'et[5] 'placuit non esse locationem et conductionem, sed 'proprium genus esse contractus.' [6]veluti si, cum unum quis bovem haberet et vicinus eius unum, placuerit inter eos, ut per denos dies invicem boves commodarent, ut opus facerent, et apud alterum bos periit: neque locati vel conducti neque commodati competit actio, quia non fuit gratuitum commodatum, verum 3 praescriptis verbis agendum est. [7]'Adeo autem 'familiaritatem aliquam inter se habere videntur em-'ptio et venditio, item locatio et conductio, ut in 'quibusdam causis quaeri soleat, utrum emptio et 'venditio contrahatur, an locatio et conductio. 'ecce de praediis, quae perpetuo quibusdam fruenda 'traduntur, id est ut, quamdiu pensio sive reditus 'pro his domino praestetur, neque ipsi conductori 'neque heredi eius,' cuive conductor heresve eius id praedium vendiderit aut donaverit aut dotis nomine dederit aliove quo modo alienaverit, auferre liceat. 'sed talis contractus, quia inter veteres dubitabatur 'et a quibusdam locatio, a quibusdam venditio existi-'mabatur: lex Zenoniana[8] lata est, quae emphyteu-'seos contractui[9] propriam statuit naturam neque ad 'locationem neque ad venditionem inclinantem, sed 'suis pactionibus fulciendam, et si quidem aliquid 'pactum fuerit, hoc ita optinere, ac si naturalis[10] esset 'contractus, sin autem nihil de periculo rei fuerit 'pactum, tunc si quidem totius rei interitus acces-'serit, ad dominum super hoc redundare periculum, 'sin particularis, ad emphyteuticarium huiusmodi dam-4 'num venire. quo iure utimur.' [11]'Item quaeritur, 'si cum aurifice Titio[12] convenerit, ut is ex auro suo 'certi ponderis certaeque formae anulos ei faceret et 'acciperet verbi gratia 'aureos' decem, utrum emptio et

'venditio an locatio et conductio contrahi videatur? 'Cassius[13] ait materiae quidem emptionem venditio-'nemque contrahi, operae autem locationem et con-'ductionem. sed placuit tantum emptionem et vendi-'tionem contrahi. 'quodsi' suum aurum Titius dederit 'mercede pro opera constituta,' 'dubium non est, quin 'locatio et conductio sit.' 5 Conductor omnia secundum legem conductionis facere debet, et si quid in lege praetermissum fuerit, id ex bono et aequo debet praestare. qui pro usu aut vestimentorum aut argenti aut iumenti mercedem aut dedit aut promisit, ab eo custodia talis deside-ratur, qualem diligentissimus pater familias suis rebus adhibet. quam si praestiterit et aliquo casu rem ami-6 serit, de restituenda ea non tenebitur. Mortuo conductore intra tempora conductionis heres eius eodem iure in conductionem succedit.

XXV[14]
DE SOCIETATE.

[15]'Societatem coire solemus aut totorum bonorum,' quam Graeci specialiter κοινοπραξίαν appellant, 'aut 'unius alicuius negotiationis, veluti mancipiorum emen-'dorum vendendorumque,' aut olei vini frumenti emendi 1 vendendique. Et quidem si nihil de partibus lucri et damni nominatim convenerit, aequales scilicet par-tes et in lucro et in damno spectantur. quod si ex-pressae fuerint partes[16], hae servari debent: nec enim umquam dubium fuit, quin valeat conventio, si duo inter se pacti sunt, ut ad unum quidem duae partes et damni et lucri pertineant, ad alium tertia. 2 [17]De illa sane conventione quaesitum est, si Titius et Seius inter se pacti sunt, ut ad Titium lucri duae partes pertineant, damni tertia, ad Seium duae par-tes damni, lucri tertia, an rata debet haberi con-ventio? Quintus Mucius contra naturam societatis talem pactionem esse existimavit et ob id non esse ratam habendam. Servius Sulpicius, cuius sententia praevaluit, contra sentit, quia saepe quorundam ita pretiosa est opera in societate[18], ut eos iustum sit meliore condicione in societatem admitti: nam et ita coiri posse societatem non dubitatur, ut alter pecu-niam conferat, alter non conferat et tamen lucrum inter eos commune sit, quia saepe opera alicuius pro pecunia valet. et adeo contra Quinti Mucii senten-tiam optinuit, ut illud quoque constiterit posse con-venire, ut quis lucri partem ferat, damno non tenea-tur, quod et ipsum Servius convenienter sibi existi-mavit: quod tamen ita intellegi oportet, ut, si in aliqua re lucrum, in aliqua damnum allatum sit, com-pensatione facta solum quod superest intellegatur 3 lucri esse. Illud expeditum est, si in una causa pars fuerit expressa, veluti in solo lucro vel in solo damno, in altera vero omissa: in eo quoque quod 4 praetermissum est eandem partem servari. [19]'Ma-'net autem societas eo usque, donec in eodem con-'sensu perseveraverint: at cum aliquis renuntiaverit 'societati, solvitur societas. sed plane si quis callide 'in hoc renuntiaverit societati, ut obveniens aliquod 'lucrum solus habeat, veluti si totorum bonorum so-'cius, cum ab aliquo heres esset relictus, in hoc re-'nuntiaverit societati, ut hereditatem solus lucriface-'ret, cogitur hoc lucrum communicare: si quid vero 'aliud lucrifaceret, quod non captaverit, ad ipsum 'solum pertinet: ei vero, cui renuntiatum est, quid-'quid omnino post renuntiatam societatem adquirit, 5 'soli conceditur. [19]Solvitur adhuc societas etiam 'morte socii, quia qui societatem contrahit certam 'personam sibi eligit.' [20]sed et si consensu plurium societas coita sit, morte unius socii solvitur, etsi plures supersint, nisi si in coeunda societate aliter

---

(1) Cf. Gai. 3, 142..147 Dig. 19, 2 Cod. 4, 65   (2) pr. ex Gaii l. 2 rer. cott. (Dig. 19, 2, 2)   (3) 3, 23, 1   (4) Gai. 3, 143 (5) et] TΘ, om. B   (6) § 2 fin. ex Dig. 19, 5, 17 § 3 (Ulp. l. 28 ad ed.)   (7) Gai. 3, 145   (8) Cod. 4, 66, 1   (9) sic BΘ, con-tractus T   (10) natura talis Ferrettus ad Θ   (11) Gai. 3, 147

(12) sic B, mihi Gai., titius T   (13) cassius] BGai., et c. TΘ (14) Cf. Gai. 3, 148..154 Dig. 17, 2 Cod. 4, 37   (15) Gai. 3, 148   (16) partes om. B   (17) cf. Gai. 3, 149   (18) sic PE, societatem B   (19) Gai. 3, 151. 152   (20) § 5 fin. 6. 7 similes Dig. 17, 2, 65 § 9. 10. 12 (Paul. l. 32 ad ed.)

liability for any disaster which arises other than through his malice or fault. If something is added to the land after the sale the advantage accrues to the buyer. The chance of profit must go with the risk of disaster. 3a. If a slave who has been sold escapes or is stolen in circumstances not involving malice or fault on the seller's part, check whether the seller assumed an insurance liability for the period up to delivery. Obviously, if he did, the risk of the disaster lies with him; if he did not, he will be safe. The same applies with other animals and other things. // Naturally, he has to assign his vindication and his claim in debt to the buyer. As one who has not yet made delivery to his buyer, he himself is still the owner. The same duty to assign applies to the actions for theft and wrongful loss. 4. Sale can be contracted absolutely or subject to a condition. One example of a conditional sale is this: 'Stichus is yours at such and such a price if by such and such a day he proves satisfactory to you.' 5. A buyer who knows he is buying a sacred or religious place, or a public one, for instance a city square or a church, achieves nothing at all. However, if he is misled by the seller and buys them as private or secular he can bring an action on purchase against the seller, on the ground that he has not been allowed to remain in possession. That action will allow him to recover his interest in not being misled. The law is the same where a purchaser buys a slave who turns out to be free.

3.24 HIRE

Hire is closely related to sale and controlled by the same rules. Just as sale is contracted when a price is agreed, so hire is concluded when the charge is fixed. The party who hires out has the action for hiring out; the other has the action for taking on hire. 1. What has been said above about the price being left to a third party should be read as also applying where the hire charge is to be decided by another. If a man gives clothes to a cleaner to be cleaned or to have some other treatment, or to a tailor to be mended, and the charge is not fixed then and there but left till later, the contract cannot be described as hire. An action with a special preface is given on those facts. 2. Just as there was a discussion whether exchange was an instance of sale, there was also a debate whether it was hire if two people exchanged things for temporary use and enjoyment. The answer is that this is not hire but a distinct type of contract. Suppose one person has a single ox and his neighbour has another; they agree that to get their work done each will lend the other his ox for periods of ten days. One of the oxen then dies when with one or other of the neighbours. Here actions on hire are excluded; so also the action on loan for use, because the lending here was not free. The action to bring is one with a special preface. 3. The relationship between hire and sale is so close that on some facts it has been difficult to say which of the two contracts is made. Take, for example, the case where land is transferred to be enjoyed in perpetuity. That is to say, the agreement is that if the owner receives his rent or other return he will always be barred from disturbing not only the tenant and his heir but also any assignee from them, whether the alienation arises from sale, gift, dowry or any other reason. Doubts about this contract, with some of the classical jurists coming down for hire and others for sale, led the Emperor Zeno to establish its independence under the name of emphyteusis. It no longer leans towards sale or hire but stands apart, with its own implied terms. Zeno's enactment also provided for express terms to be given effect, as in other contracts recognized by the law of nature. It also ruled that in the absence of an express provision as to risk the owner bears the risk of total destruction, while partial loss is borne by the

emphyteutic tenant. This is the law today. 4. Another borderline case: a goldsmith agrees with Titius to make him rings of a given weight and design. The goldsmith is to use his own gold, and the charge is to be, say, 10. Cassius held that this was sale of the material and hire of the work. But the decision has been taken to treat the whole transaction as sale. Suppose Titius brought his own gold and a charge was fixed for the work. The contract would undoubtedly be hire. 5. The person who takes something on hire must keep to all the terms of the hiring. Where the terms are silent he must conform to the standard of what is fair and reasonable. Anyone who pays or promises to pay a charge for the use of clothes or silver or a beast of burden is under a duty to keep it as carefully as the most careful owner would keep his own property. If he observes that standard and still loses the thing through some accident, he will not be liable for its return. 6. If someone who has something on hire dies before the period of the hire expires, his heir steps into his shoes with the same rights.

3.25 PARTNERSHIP

Partnerships usually cover either all the partners' worldly wealth, something for which the Greeks have a special name, koinopraxia, or else a single line of business, for instance buying and selling slaves or buying and selling oil, wine, and corn. 1. If nothing is expressly agreed about the shares of profit and loss, equal division will be implied. If the shares are expressly agreed, the agreed proportions apply. It has never been doubted that two partners can validly agree that one shall have two thirds of profit and loss, and the other one third. 2. But there certainly was a question about the pattern of agreement in which Titius and Seius decided that Titius should have two thirds of profit but bear one third of loss, Seius bearing two thirds of loss and getting one third of profit. Would such an agreement be upheld ? Quintus Mucius said not, because it was contrary to the nature of partnership. But the view of Servius Sulpicius prevailed. He went the other way, on the ground that there are often people whose participation in a partnership is so valuable that it is reasonable to bring them in on relatively advantageous terms. There is no doubt that a partnership agreement can validly require one party to put up money but not the other, while still giving both parties equal shares of profit. Some people's services are often as valuable as a money contribution. The law went so far against the Mucian position that it even upheld agreements giving one party a share in profit but immunity from loss. Servius consistently maintained that that too was acceptable. But such a term has to be construed as applying only to the net profit, the balance after loss-making and profitable transactions have been set off against each other. 3. If the share for one side of the account is stated but nothing is said for the other, for instance only for the profit side or only for the loss side, the convenient solution has been to carry over the stated share to the other side as well. 4. A partnership lasts as long as the partners remain of the same mind but ends when one party renounces. Clearly though, if someone is sharp to withdraw with an eye to a profit for himself, for example where a partner in all worldly wealth is left heir to somebody's estate and renounces the partnership in order to take the inheritance himself, he will be compelled to share his profit. But if he makes some gain without having snatched at it, it goes to him alone. The other partner, the victim of the renunciation, keeps for himself anything at all which he receives after it. 5. Partnership is dissolved by the death of a partner, because when one enters a partnership one does so with a specifically chosen person. Even where the partnership is made between

6 convenerit. [1]Item si alicuius rei contracta societas sit et finis negotio impositus est, finitur societas.
7 [1]Publicatione quoque distrahi societatem manifestum
est, scilicet si universa bona socii publicentur: nam
cum in eius locum alius succedit, pro mortuo habe-
8 tur. [2]Item si quis ex sociis mole debiti praegra-
vatus bonis suis cesserit et ideo propter publica aut
propter privata debita substantia eius veneat, solvitur societas. sed hoc casu si adhuc consentiant in
9 societatem, nova videtur incipere societas. Socius
socio utrum eo nomine tantum teneatur pro socio
actione, si quid dolo commiserit, sicut is qui deponi
apud se passus est, an etiam culpae, id est desidiae
atque neglegentiae nomine, quaesitum est: praevaluit
tamen etiam culpae nomine teneri eum. [3]culpa autem non ad exactissimam diligentiam dirigenda est:
sufficit enim talem diligentiam in communibus rebus
adhibere socium[4], qualem suis rebus adhibere solet.
nam qui parum diligentem socium sibi adsumit[5], de
se queri debet[6].

XXVI[7]
DE MANDATO.

[8]Mandatum contrahitur quinque modis, sive sua
tantum gratia aliquis tibi mandet, sive sua et tua,
sive aliena tantum, sive sua et aliena, sive tua et
aliena. at si tua tantum gratia tibi mandatum sit,
supervacuum est mandatum et ob id[9] nulla ex eo ob-
1 ligatio 'nec mandati inter vos actio' nascitur. [8]Man-
dantis tantum gratia intervenit mandatum, veluti
si quis tibi mandet, ut negotia eius gereres, vel ut
2 fundum ei emeres, vel ut pro eo sponderes. [8]Tua
et mandantis, veluti si mandet tibi, ut pecuniam sub
usuris crederes ei, qui in rem ipsius mutuaretur, aut
si volente te agere cum eo ex fideiussoria causa mandet tibi, ut cum reo agas periculo mandantis, vel ut
ipsius periculo stipuleris ab eo, quem tibi deleget in
3 id quod tibi debuerat. [8]Aliena autem[10] causa intervenit mandatum, veluti si tibi mandet, ut Titii negotia gereres, vel ut Titio fundum emeres, vel ut pro
4 Titio sponderes. [8]Sua et aliena, veluti si 'de com-
'munibus suis et Titii negotiis gerendis' tibi mandet,
vel ut sibi et Titio fundum emeres, vel ut pro eo et
5 Titio sponderes. [8]Tua et aliena, veluti si tibi
mandet, ut Titio sub usuris crederes. quodsi ut[11] sine
usuris crederes[12], aliena tantum gratia intercedit man-
6 datum. [8]Tua gratia intervenit mandatum, veluti
si tibi mandet, ut pecunias tuas potius in emptiones
praediorum colloces, quam feneres, vel ex diverso
ut[13] feneres potius, quam in emptiones praediorum
colloces. cuius generis mandatum magis consilium
est quam mandatum et ob id non est obligatorium,
quia nemo ex consilio 'mandati'[14] obligatur, etiamsi
non expediat ei cui dabitur, cum liberum cuique
sit apud se explorare, an expediat consilium. [15]itaque
si otiosam pecuniam domi te habentem hortatus
fuerit aliquis, ut rem aliquam emeres vel eam cre-
das, quamvis non expediet tibi eam emisse vel
credidisse, non tamen tibi mandati tenetur. et adeo
haec ita sunt, ut quaesitum sit, an mandati teneatur
qui mandavit tibi, ut Titio pecuniam fenerares: sed
optinuit Sabini sententia obligationem esse in hoc
casu mandati, quia non aliter Titio credidisses,
7 quam si tibi mandatum esset. Illud quoque mandatum non est obligatorium, quod contra bonos mores est, veluti si Titius de furto aut[16] damno fa-
ciendo aut de iniuria facienda tibi mandet. licet
enim poenam istius facti nomine praestiteris, non
tamen ullam habes adversus Titium actionem.

8 Is qui exsequitur mandatum non debet exce-
dere fines mandati. ut ecce si quis usque ad centum
'aureos' mandaverit tibi, ut fundum emeres vel ut pro
Titio sponderes, neque pluris emere debes neque in
ampliorem pecuniam 'fideiubere', alioquin non habebis
cum eo mandati actionem: adeo quidem, ut Sabino
et Cassio placuerit, etiam si usque ad centum 'aureos'
cum eo agere velis, inutiliter te acturum: [17]diversae
scholae auctores recte te[18] usque ad centum 'aureos'
acturum existimant: 'quae sententia sane benignior
est.' [19]'quod si minoris emeris, habebis scilicet cum eo
'actionem, 'quoniam' qui mandat, ut sibi centum 'au-
'reorum' fundus emeretur, is utique mandasse intelle-
'gitur, ut minoris si posset emeretur.'
9 [20]'Recte quoque mandatum 'contractum', si, dum
'adhuc integra res sit, revocatum fuerit, evanescit.
10 [20]Item si adhuc integro mandato mors alterutrius[21]
'interveniat, id est vel eius qui mandaverit, vel eius[22]
'qui mandatum susceperit, solvitur mandatum. sed
'utilitatis causa receptum est, si[23] mortuo eo, qui
'tibi mandaverit, tu ignorans eum decessisse exsecu-
'tus fueras mandatum, posse te agere mandati actione:
'alioquin iusta et probabilis ignorantia damnum tibi
'afferat. et huic simile est, quod placuit, si debi-
'tores manumisso dispensatore Titii per ignorantiam
'liberto solverint, liberari eos: cum alioquin stricta
'iuris ratione non possent liberari, quia alii solvis-
11 'sent, quam qui solvere deberent.' Mandatum
non suscipere liberum est: susceptum autem con-
summandum aut quam primum renuntiandum est, ut
aut per semet ipsum aut per alium eandem rem mandator exsequatur. nam nisi ita renuntiatur, ut integra causa mandatori reservetur eandem rem ex-
plicandi, nihilo minus mandati actio locum habet,
nisi si[24] iusta causa intercessit aut non renuntiandi
aut intempestive renuntiandi.
12 Mandatum et in diem differri et sub condi-
13 cione fieri potest. In summa sciendum est mandatum, nisi gratuitum sit, in aliam formam negotii
cadere: nam mercede constituta incipit locatio et
conductio esse et ut generaliter dixerimus: quibus
casibus sine mercede suscepto officio mandati aut
depositi contrahitur negotium, his casibus interveniente
mercede locatio et conductio contrahi intellegitur.
et ideo si fulloni polienda curandave vestimenta dederis[25] aut sarcinatori sarcienda nulla mercede constituta neque promissa, mandati competit actio.

XXVII
DE OBLIGATIONIBUS QUASI EX CONTRACTU.

Post genera contractuum enumerata dispiciamus
etiam de his obligationibus, quae non proprie quidem ex contractu nasci intelleguntur, sed tamen,
quia non ex maleficio substantiam capiunt, quasi ex
1 contractu nasci videntur. [26]Igitur cum quis ab-
sentis negotia gesserit, ultro citroque inter eos nascuntur actiones, quae appellantur negotiorum gestorum:
sed domino quidem rei gestae adversus eum qui gessit directa competit actio, negotiorum autem gestori
contraria. quas ex nullo contractu proprie nasci
manifestum est: quippe ita nascuntur istae actiones,
si sine mandato quisque alienis negotiis gerendis se
optulerit: ex qua causa ii quorum negotia gesta fuerint etiam ignorantes obligantur. idque utilitatis causa
receptum est, ne absentium, qui subita festinatione
coacti nulli demandata negotiorum suorum administratione peregre profecti essent, desererentur negotia: quae sane nemo curaturus esset, si de eo quod

---

(1) cf. p. 40 not. 20   (2) cf. Gai. 3, 154   (3) § 9 fin. ex
Gai l. 2 rer. cott. (Dig. 17, 2, 72)   (4) socium] T?Θ,
socio B, om. Dig.   (5) sic B^b T, adscivit B^a, adquirit Dig.
(6) sic Dig., hoc est sibi imputare debet addunt libri
{7) Cf. Gai. 3, 155...162 Dig. 17, 1 Cod. 4, 35 (8) pr... § 6
in. ex Gai l. 2 rer. cott. (Dig. 17, 1, 2)   (9) ob id] T Dig.,
ideo B   (10) tantum Dig. Θ   (11) ut] Dig. Θ, om. libri
{12) sic Dig. BC^a, credideris TC^b   (13) ut] B Dig. Θ,

ut pecunias tuas T^aC   (14) mandati] libri cum Θ, om.
Dig.   (15) cf. Gai. 3, 156   (16) aut] BC, aut de T
(17) ex Gai l. 2 rer. cott. (Dig. 17, 1, 4)   (18) te] et B,
•• T, te post aureos collocat C (19) Gai. 3, 161 (20) Gai.
3, 159. 160   (21) sic T, alterius BC^a, alterius utrius P,
alterutrius alicuius Gai.   (22) illius T   (23) si] BT^a,
ut si T^bC Gai.   (24) si] B, ita T   (25) dederis] B, quis
dederit TC   (26) cf. Dig. 44, 7, 5 pr. (Gai l. 3 rer cott.)

i

more than two people, it ends with the death of one, despite the survival of a plurality of others. This applies unless there was an agreement to the contrary when the partnership was made. // 6. If the partnership is made in relation to a specific matter and that business is concluded, the partnership ends. 7. Confiscation obviously ends a partnership, at least where all a partner's wealth is confiscated. Since another has succeeded to all that partner's rights, the effects in law are the same as if he had died. 8. Again, if a partner is borne down by the weight of his debts and has to surrender his property to be sold up for public or private debts, the partnership is dissolved. If after such a disaster the people still want to be partners, a new partnership is held to come into being. 9. Does the liability of one partner to another in the action on partnership extend only to malice, as with a person who accepts a deposit? Or does it run to unintentional fault such as laziness and negligence? The opinion which has prevailed makes a partner liable for fault as well. But the measure is not the very highest standard of care. It is enough if the partner shows in the partnership affairs the same care as he usually displays in his own. Someone who chooses a careless partner has only himself to blame.

3.26 MANDATE

There are five kinds of mandate. The mandator's commission to you may be: solely for him; for both you and him; solely for a third party; for both him and a third party; for both you and a third party. In contrast a commission to you solely in your own interest is superfluous. No obligation arises from it, and no actions on mandate lie. 1. The contract is solely for the mandator where he tells you to carry out some business for him, to buy him some land or to act as guarantor for him. 2. It is for you and him when he tells you to lend at interest to a person who is to borrow the money for his, the mandator's, own purposes; or if, when you propose to call in his liability as guarantor, he tells you to sue the principal debtor and undertakes to bear the risk of failure; or if he tells you, again at his risk, to take a stipulation from a substitute debtor for the amount which he now owes you. 3. The mandate is for a third party when the mandator tells you to conduct some business which concerns Titius or buy land for him or stand as guarantor for him. 4. It is for both him and a third party when he tells you to conduct some business which concerns both himself and Titius, or buy land for both of them or stand as guarantor for both of them. 5. It is for you and a third party when he tells you to make an interest-bearing loan to Titius. However, if the loan is to be interest-free, the mandate becomes one that is solely for a third party. 6. The mandate is solely for you where the mandator tells you to employ your money in buying land rather than in lending at interest; or, vice versa, to lend it out rather than invest it in land. This type of mandate is more a piece of advice than a commission to act. That is why it creates no obligation. For nobody becomes liable under the action on mandate for advice, even if it turns out badly for the person advised. Everyone can work out for himself whether advice he receives is likely to be to his advantage. So, if you have money lying idle at home and someone encourages you to buy something or to lend it out, even if the purchase or loan then turns out not to have been to your advantage, your adviser will not be liable in the action on mandate. This has been carried so far as to raise a question whether the action on mandate can lie against someone who asks you to lend money at interest to Titius. But here the opinion of Sabinus prevailed, which was that the mandate does generate an obligation in this case, because but for the mandate you would not have chosen to lend to Titius. 7. An immoral mandate is not obligatory either, as where Titius gives you a mandate to commit theft, wrongful loss, or contempt. Even if you have to pay the penal damages for one of these wrongs, you will have no action against Titius. 8. In performing a mandate you must not exceed its limits. So, for instance, if someone asks you, subject to a limit of 100, to buy land or stand as guarantor for Titius, you must not buy or give a guarantee for more. Otherwise you will have no action on mandate against your mandator. This is so strong a principle that in the view of Sabinus and Cassius even if you were willing to restrict your claim to the 100 you still could not win. But the authorities of the other school correctly hold that you can sue up to the agreed limit. That position is certainly more liberal. If you buy below the limit you will of course have your action against the mandator, because a person who gives a mandate for land to be bought at 100 indisputably asks for it to be got for less if possible. 9. A contract of mandate, though properly made, is dissolved by a revocation before any change of position. 10. It is similarly discharged by the death of either party – that is, of either the mandator or the person who accepted the mandate – before the task is performed. But convenience has required that if your mandator dies and you carry through his commission in ignorance of his death you should none the less have the action on mandate. Otherwise you would suffer loss through a reasonable mistake. This is a similar case to that in which debtors to Titius make their payments to his cashier without knowing he has been freed. They are discharged by their payments to the freedman, despite the fact that strictly they could not release themselves by paying the wrong person. 11. Everyone is free not to accept a mandate. Once having accepted, he must perform it or must renounce as soon as possible, so as to allow the mandator to achieve his purpose himself or through some other person. If the renunciation does not leave the mandator in as good a position as ever to achieve his end, the action on mandate will lie in the absence of some sufficient reason for your not telling him of your withdrawal or telling him too late. 12. A mandate can be subject to a postponement or a condition. 13. Lastly, it is important to notice that a mandate which is not gratuitous falls under a different contractual head. Once a charge is made, the transaction becomes hire. As we have said, the general rule is that if a contract of mandate or deposit is formed when a task is undertaken without charge, on the same facts if a charge is made the contract becomes hire. So, if clothes are given to a cleaner for cleaning or for some other treatment, or to a tailor for repair, the action which lies if no charge is fixed or promised is the action on mandate.

3.27 OBLIGATIONS AS THOUGH FROM CONTRACT

After the classification of contracts, we come to obligations which cannot strictly be seen as arising from contract but which, because they do not owe their existence to wrongdoing, are said to arise as though from a contract. 1. When a person is absent and someone looks after his affairs, actions arise reciprocally between them. These are known as the actions on uninvited intervention. The direct action lies for the principal, the person whose business is managed; the intervener has the counter-action. It is obvious that they are not really contractual, because they only lie when the intervener has no mandate. The beneficiary of the intervention incurs his obligations without even knowing the facts. This was accepted as good policy, to ensure that the affairs of the absent were not left untended if they suddenly had to set off abroad without having time to

quis impendisset nullam habiturus esset actionem.
sicut autem is qui utiliter gesserit negotia habet obligatum dominum negotiorum, ita et contra iste quoque tenetur, ut administrationis rationem reddat. quo
casu ad exactissimam quisque diligentiam[1] compellitur reddere rationem: nec sufficit talem diligentiam
adhibere, qualem suis rebus adhibere soleret, si modo
alius diligentior commodius administraturus esset neg-
2 otia. [2]Tutores quoque, qui tutelae iudicio tenentur, non proprie ex contractu obligati intelleguntur (nullum enim negotium inter tutorem et pupillum
contrahitur): sed quia sane non ex maleficio tenentur, quasi ex contractu teneri videntur. et hoc autem
casu mutuae sunt actiones: non tantum enim pupillus cum tutore habet tutelae actionem, sed et[3] ex
contrario tutor cum pupillo habet contrariam tutelae,
si vel impenderit aliquid in rem pupilli vel pro eo
3 fuerit obligatus aut rem suam creditori eius obliga-
3 verit. Item si inter aliquos communis sit res sine
societate, veluti quod pariter eis legata donatave esset,
et alter eorum alteri ideo teneatur communi dividundo iudicio, quod solus fructus ex ea re perceperit, aut quod socius eius[4] in eam rem necessarias
impensas fecerit: non intellegitur proprie ex contractu obligatus esse, quippe nihil inter se contraxe-
runt: sed quia non ex maleficio tenetur, quasi ex con-
4 tractu teneri videtur. Idem iuris est de eo, qui
coheredi suo familiae erciscundae iudicio ex his cau-
5 sis obligatus est. [5]Heres quoque legatorum nomine non proprie ex contractu obligatus intellegitur
(neque enim cum herede neque cum defuncto ullum
negotium legatarius gessisse proprie dici potest[6]): et
tamen[7], quia ex maleficio non est obligatus heres,
6 quasi ex contractu debere intellegitur. [5]Item is,
cui quis per errorem non debitum solvit, quasi ex
contractu debere videtur. adeo enim non intellegitur
proprie ex contractu obligatus, ut, si certiorem rationem sequamur, magis ut supra diximus ex distractu,
quam ex contractu possit dici obligatus esse: nam
qui solvendi animo pecuniam dat, in hoc dare videtur, ut distrahat potius negotium quam contrahat.
sed tamen proinde is qui accepit obligatur, ac si
mutuum illi daretur, et ideo condictione tenetur.
7 Ex quibusdam tamen causis repeti non potest,
quod per errorem non debitum solutum sit. sic[8]
namque definuerunt veteres: ex quibus causis in-
fitiando lis crescit, ex his causis non debitum solutum repeti non posse, veluti ex lege Aquilia, item
ex legato. 'quod veteres quidem in his legatis locum
'habere voluerunt, quae certa constituta per damna-
'tionem cuicumque fuerant legata: nostra autem con-
'stitutio[9] cum unam naturam omnibus legatis et fidei-
'commissis indulsit, huiusmodi augmentum in omnibus
'legatis et fideicommissis extendi voluit: sed non omni-
'bus legatariis[10] praebuit, sed tantummodo in his le-
'gatis et fideicommissis, quae sacrosanctis ecclesiis
'ceterisque venerabilibus locis, quae religionis vel pie-
'tatis intuitu honorificantur, derelicta sunt, quae si
'indebita solvantur, non repetuntur.'

XXVIII[11]
PER QUAS PERSONAS NOBIS OBLIGATIO ADQUIRITUR.

[12] 'Expositis generibus obligationum, quae ex con-
'tractu 'vel quasi ex contractu' nascuntur, admonendi

'sumus adquiri vobis non solum per vosmet ipsos,
'sed etiam per eas 'quoque' personas, quae in vestra
'potestate sunt,' veluti per servos vestros et filios[13]:
'ut tamen, quod per servos quidem[14] vobis adquiri-
'tur, totum vestrum fiat, quod autem per liberos, quos
'in potestate habetis, ex obligatione fuerit adquisitum,
'hoc dividatur secundum imaginem rerum proprietatis
'et usus fructus, quam[15] nostra discrevit constitutio[16]:
'ut, quod ab actione commodum[17] perveniat, huius
'usum fructum quidem habeat pater, proprietas au-
'tem filio servetur, scilicet patre actionem movente
'secundum novellae nostrae constitutionis divisionem.'
1 [18]'Item' 'per liberos homines et alienos servos, quos
'bona fide possidetis, adquiritur vobis, sed tantum ex
'duabus causis, id est si quid ex operis suis vel ex
2 're vestra adquirant.' [19]'Per eum quoque servum,
'in quo usum fructum 'vel usum' habetis, similiter ex
3 'duabus istis causis vobis adquiritur. [19a]Communem
'servum pro dominica parte dominis adquirere cer-
'tum est, excepto eo, quod uni nominatim stipulando
'aut 'per traditionem' accipiendo illi soli adquirit, veluti
'cum ita stipuletur: 'Titio domino meo dare spon-
'des?'' 'sed si unius domini iussu servus fuerit sti-
'pulatus, licet antea dubitabatur, tamen post nostram
'decisionem[20] res expedita est, ut illi tantum adqui-
'rat, qui hoc ei facere iussit, ut supra[21] dictum est.'

XXIX[22]
QUIBUS MODIS OBLIGATIO TOLLITUR.

[23]'Tollitur autem 'omnis' obligatio solutione eius quod
'debetur, 'vel' si quis consentiente creditore aliud pro
'alio solverit.' nec tamen interest, quis solvat, utrum
ipse qui debet an alius pro eo: liberatur enim et[24]
alio solvente, sive sciente debitore sive ignorante vel
invito solutio fiat. item si reus solverit, etiam ii qui
pro eo intervenerunt liberantur. idem ex contrario
contingit, si fideiussor solverit: non enim solus ipse
1 liberatur, sed etiam reus. [25]'Item per acceptila-
'tionem tollitur obligatio. est autem acceptilatio ima-
'ginaria solutio. quod enim ex verborum obligatione
'Titio debetur, id si velit Titius remittere, poterit sic
'fieri, ut patiatur haec verba debitorem dicere: 'quod
'"ego tibi promisi habesne acceptum?' et Titius re-
'spondeat 'habeo'': [26]sed et Graece potest acceptum
'fieri, dummodo sic fiat, ut Latinis verbis solet: [27]Ἔχεις
'λαβὼν δηι ἀρια τόσα; ἔχω λαβών. [28]quo genere ut
'diximus tantum eae obligationes solvuntur, quae ex
'verbis consistunt, non etiam ceterae: consentaneum
'enim visum est verbis factam obligationem posse
'aliis verbis dissolvi: sed[29] id, quod ex alia causa
'debetur, potest in stipulationem deduci et per ac-
'ceptilationem dissolvi.' [30]sicut autem quod debetur pro
parte recte solvitur, ita in partem debiti acceptilatio
2 fieri potest. Est prodita stipulatio, quae vulgo
Aquiliana appellatur, per quam stipulationem contingit, ut omnium rerum obligatio in stipulatum deducatur et ea per acceptilationem tollatur. stipulatio
enim Aquiliana novat omnes obligationes et a Gallo
Aquilio ita composita est: [31]'quidquid te mihi ex
'quacumque causa dare facere oportet oportebit prae-
'sens in diem[32] quarumque rerum mihi tecum actio
'quaeque abs te petitio vel adversus te persecutio
'erit quodque[33] tu meum habes tenes possides possi-
'deresve[34] dolove malo fecisti, quo minus possideas:

---

(1) de (?) exactissima q. diligentia T   (2) § 2 ex Gai l. 3
rer. cott. (Dig. 44, 7, 5 § 1)   (3) et] Dig. Θ, om. libri   (4) eius]
dett. cum Θ, solus Tᵃ, eius solus BTᵇ   (5) ad § 5. 6 cf. Dig.
44, 7, 5 § 2. 3 (Gai. l. 2 rer. cott.)   (6) sic T (ubi tamen
dici potest incerta sunt) P, legatarium pr. gess. posse B
(7) et tamen] sed T   (8) sic] T, om. B   (9) Cod. 1, 3, 45, 7?
(10) legatariis] Cᵇ E, legatis Cᵃ, l. hoc B, hoc l. T
    (11) Cf. Gai. 3, 163..167 Cod. 4, 27   (12) Gai. 3, 163
(13) filios] CΘ, filios vestros BTᵃ   (14) quidem] TCᵃ,
om. BCᵇ   (15) quam] BΘ, quae T, quem Cᵇ, inc. Cᵃ
(16) Cod. 6, 61, 6   (17) commodum] BΘ, quoquo modo TC

(18) Gai. 3, 164   (19) Gai. 3, 165   (19ᵃ) Gai. 3, 167
(20) Cod. 4, 27, 2   (21) 3, 17, 8
    (22) Cf. Gai. 3, 168..181 Dig. 46, 2..4 Cod. 8, 41. 43   (23) Gai.
3, 168   (24) et] TCΘ, om. B   (25) Gai. 3, 169   (26) sed...λα-
βών ex Dig. 46, 4, 8 § 4 (Ulp. l. 48 ad Sab.)   (27) id est:
habesne acceptos tot denarios? habeo   (28) Gai. 3, 170
(29) sed] Gai. Θ, sed et libri   (30) cf. Gai. 3, 172   (31) cf.
Dig. 46, 4, 18 § 1   (32) diemve] Tᵘ Dig. Θ, diem vel sub
condicionem BTᵇ, diesve (vel sub condicione add. Cᵇ)
oportebit oportetve C   (33) sic libri cum Θ, quodve Dig.
(34) possideresve] sic libri cum Θ, recte om. Dig.

make proper arrangements. // Plainly no one would intervene on their behalf without an action to recoup his outlay. Just as a useful intervention by the intervener puts the principal under an obligation, so the intervener too becomes liable to render an account. He must give that account on the basis of the highest standard of care. It is not enough for him to have kept to his own habitual standard if a more attentive person would have managed the business better. 2. Guardians liable in the trial on guardianship also cannot properly be said to owe their obligations to contract. There is no contract between a guardian and his ward. Since the liability certainly does not derive from wrongdoing, it is said to arise as though from contract. Here too there are reciprocal actions. The child has the action on guardianship against the guardian. On the other side the guardian has the counter-action against the ward if he has incurred expense or entered into obligations for him or charged his own property to the ward's creditor. 3. Next, suppose something is held in common by two people other than under a contract of partnership, for instance as joint legatees or donees; then, in a trial for division of common property, one of them is found liable to the other on the ground that he alone took the fruits of the thing or that his colleague incurred necessary expenses on it. He cannot properly be said to have incurred his obligations by contract, because these co-owners made no contract. Since his liability is not from wrongdoing, it is held to arise as though from contract. 4. The law is the same where, in the trial for division of an estate, one co-heir is found to be under similar obligations to another. 5. An heir bound to pay legacies also does not really owe his obligation to contract. It is impossible to see the legatee as dealing in any any way with the heir or the deceased. Since the heir's obligation does not derive from wrongdoing, it is classed as arising as though from contract. 6. Next, a person to whom someone mistakenly pays what he does not owe also incurs his debt as though from contract. It is quite incorrect to think of him as bound by contract; in fact, as we have already said, stricter analysis shows that he is bound 'ex distractu' rather than 'ex contractu', because such a person means to discharge a debt, not to contract one. The recipient is bound as though he had been given a loan, and he thus becomes liable to the action of debt. 7. On some facts it is impossible to recover a mistaken payment which was not due. This point was summed up by the classical jurists thus: if the cause of action is one in which liability enlarges on denial, the law denies recovery of a payment not due. This happens under the Aquilian Act and in respect of legacies. Here the classical jurists chose to confine the rule to those legacies which were both obligatory and fixed; but our own pronouncement unifying the law of all legacies and trusts generalized this liability-enlarging rule to all kinds of legacy and trust, though only as concerns some donees, namely holy churches and other sacred places honoured for the sake of religion and piety. If such legatees get payments which are not due, recovery is barred.

3.28 OBLIGATIONS ACQUIRED THROUGH OTHERS

So much for obligations from contract and as though from contract. Now we must note that you can acquire rights through your own acts and also through the agency of people within your authority, your slaves and sons. There is a difference: what you acquire through your slaves becomes entirely yours; with sons, what you acquire under obligations through them is split in accordance with the scheme of our legislation, which divides ownership and usufruct. If an action brings a gain, it will vest in the son, but his ownership will be subject to a usufruct in the father. That was the principle of our recent pronouncement. The father of course remains responsible for initiating the litigation. 1. You acquire also through persons whom you hold in good faith as your slaves, whether they are in fact free or slaves of third parties. But here you acquire only in two circumstances, namely where they obtain something by their labour or from your capital. 2. You acquire in the same two circumstances through a slave in whom you have a usufruct or use. 3. A slave held in co-ownership acquires for his owners in proportion to their shares. That does not apply to something the slave acquires for one of the owners by taking a stipulation in his name alone or by receiving in his name a conveyance by delivery, as where for instance he takes a stipulation in these words: 'Do you promise to give to my owner Titius?' Further, where the slave takes a stipulation by order of one of his owners, a dispute in earlier times has been settled by ourselves. As we have already mentioned, he then acquires solely for the owner who gave him that order.

3.29 DISCHARGE OF OBLIGATIONS

Every obligation is discharged by performance or, with the consent of the creditor, by a substituted performance. It makes no difference who performs, whether the debtor or someone else for him. The discharge is complete even when a third party performs, with or without the knowledge of the debtor, or even against his will. If a principal debtor performs, his guarantors are discharged; the same is true the other way around, so that a guarantor's performance releases himself and the principal debtor. 1. Next, obligations are discharged by verbal release, which involves a pretence of performance. Suppose Titius has a debtor under a stipulation and wants to release him from his obligation. It can be done in this way: Titius should get the debtor to say, 'What I have promised, do you hold received?' and then Titius should answer, 'I do.' A verbal release can also be effected in Greek, so long as it is done just as in the Latin form, so that the exchange runs, in Greek: 'Do you hold received such and such a sum of money?' 'I do hold it received.' This type of discharge, as we have indicated, is only applicable to verbal obligations, not to the others. It is appropriate that an obligation created by words should be dissoluble by other words. But other obligations can be converted to a stipulation and then released verbally. Just as there can be genuine performance as to part of what is due, so there can also be a verbal release of part of a debt. 2. There is a stipulation, commonly called the Aquilian stipulation, which has been devised for converting all kinds of obligations into one based on stipulation, ready to be extinguished verbally. It novates all obligations. It was drafted by Gallus Aquilius in these words: 'Whatever you are or shall be under a duty to do for me or give to me now or in the future for any reason whatsoever, every cause of action which I have or shall have against you, every demand from you, every suit against you, every asset of mine which you have, hold, do or may possess, or would possess but for fraud, // as regards all these

'quanti quaeque earum rerum res erit, tantam pe-
'cuniam dari stipulatus est Aulus Agerius, spopondit
'Numerius Negidius.' item e diverso Numerius Negidius interrogavit Aulum Agerium: 'quidquid tibi
'hodierno die per Aquilianam stipulationem spopondi,
'id omne habesne acceptum?' respondit Aulus Age-
3 rius: 'habeo[1] acceptumque tuli.'[2] 'Praeterea nova-
tione tollitur obligatio. veluti si id, quod tu Seio
'debeas, a Titio dari stipulatus sit. nam interventu
'novae personae nova nascitur obligatio et prima tol-
'litur translata in posteriorem, adeo ut interdum, licet
'posterior stipulatio inutilis sit, tamen prima nova-
'tionis iure tollatur[3]. veluti si id, quod Titio tu debe-
'bas, a pupillo sine tutoris auctoritate stipulatus fue-
'rit, quo casu res amittitur: nam et prior debitor
'liberatur et posterior obligatio nulla est. non idem
'iuris est, si a servo quis stipulatus fuerit: nam tunc
'prior proinde obligatus manet, ac si postea a nullo[4]
'stipulatus fuisset. sed si eadem persona sit, a qua
'postea stipuleris, ita demum novatio fit, si quid in
'posteriore stipulatione novi sit, forte si condicio aut
'dies aut 'fideiussor' adiciatur aut detrahatur. quod
'autem diximus, si condicio adiciatur, novationem
'fieri, sic intellegi oportet, ut ita dicamus factam

'novationem, si condicio extiterit: alioquin si defece-
3a 'rit, durat prior obligatio.' 'Sed cum hoc quidem
'inter veteres constabat tunc fieri novationem, cum
'novandi animo in secundam obligationem itum fue-
'rat: per hoc autem dubium erat, quando novandi
'animo videretur[5] hoc fieri et quasdam de hoc prae-
'sumptiones alii in aliis casibus introducebant: ideo
'nostra processit constitutio[6], quae apertissime defini-
'vit tunc solum fieri novationem, quotiens hoc ipsum
'inter contrahentes expressum fuerit, quod propter
'novationem prioris obligationis convenerunt, alioquin
'manere et pristinam obligationem et secundam ei ac-
'cedere, ut maneat ex utraque causa obligatio secun-
'dum nostrae constitutionis definitiones, quas licet ex
4 'ipsius lectione apertius cognoscere.' Hoc amplius
eae obligationes, quae consensu contrahuntur, contraria voluntate dissolvuntur. nam si Titius et Seius
inter se consenserunt, ut fundum Tusculanum emptum
Seius haberet centum 'aureorum', deinde re nondum
secuta, id est neque pretio soluto neque fundo tra-
dito, placuerit inter eos, ut discederetur ab emptione
et venditione, invicem liberantur. idem est et in conductione et locatione et omnibus contractibus, qui
ex consensu descendunt, sicut iam dictum est.

LIBER QUARTUS.

I[7]

DE OBLIGATIONIBUS QUAE EX DELICTO NASCUNTUR[8].

Cum expositum sit superiore libro de obligationibus ex contractu et quasi ex contractu, sequitur ut
de obligationibus ex maleficio dispiciamus. [9]sed illae
quidem, ut suo loco tradidimus, in quattuor genera
dividuntur: hae vero unius generis sunt, nam omnes
ex re nascuntur, id est ex ipso maleficio, veluti ex
furto aut rapina aut damno aut iniuria.
1 [10]Furtum est contrectatio rei fraudulosa vel ipsius
rei vel etiam usus eius possessionisve, quod lege na-
2 turali prohibitum est admittere. [11]Furtum autem
vel a furvo id est nigro dictum est, quod clam et
obscure fit et plerumque nocte: vel a fraude: vel a
ferendo, id est auferendo: vel a Graeco sermone, qui
φῶρας appellant fures. immo etiam Graeci ἀπὸ τοῦ
3 φέρειν[12] φῶρας dixerunt. [13]Furtorum autem genera duo sunt, manifestum et nec manifestum. nam
'conceptum et oblatum species potius actionis sunt
'furto cohaerentes quam genera furtorum, sicut in-
'ferius apparebit.' [14]manifestus fur est, quem Graeci
ἐπ' αὐτοφώρῳ appellant: nec solum is qui in ipso
furto deprehenditur, sed etiam is qui eo loco deprehenditur, quo fit, veluti qui in domo[15] furtum fecit
et nondum egressus ianuam deprehensus fuerit, et
qui in oliveto olivarum aut in vineto uvarum furtum
fecit, quamdiu in eo oliveto aut in vineto fur deprehensus sit: immo ulterius furtum manifestum exten-
dendum est, quamdiu eam rem fur tenens visus vel
deprehensus fuerit sive in publico sive in privato vel
a domino vel ab alio, antequam eo perveniret, quo
perferre ac deponere rem destinasset. [16]sed si pertulit
quo destinavit, tametsi deprehendatur cum re furtiva, non est manifestus fur. [17]nec manifestum

'tum quid sit, ex his quae diximus intellegitur: nam
'quod manifestum non est, id scilicet nec manifestum
4 'est. Conceptum furtum dicitur, cum apud ali-
'quem testibus praesentibus furtiva res quaesita et
'inventa sit: nam in eum[18] propria actio constituta
'est, quamvis fur non sit, quae appellatur concepti.
'oblatum furtum dicitur, cum res furtiva ab aliquo
'tibi oblata sit eaque apud te concepta sit, utique si
'ea mente tibi data fuerit, ut apud te potius quam
'apud eum qui dederit conciperetur: nam tibi, apud
'quem concepta sit, propria adversus eum qui optu-
'lit, quamvis fur non sit, constituta est actio, quae
'appellatur oblati. est etiam prohibiti furti actio ad-
'versus eum, qui furtum quaerere testibus praesenti-
'bus volentem prohibuerit.' praeterea poena constituitur edicto praetoris per actionem furti non exhibiti adversus eum, qui furtivam rem apud se quaesi-
tam et inventam non exhibuit. 'sed hae actiones, id
'est concepti et oblati et furti prohibiti nec non furti
'non exhibiti, in desuetudinem abierunt. cum enim
'requisitio rei furtivae hodie secundum veterem obser-
'vationem non fit: merito ex consequentia etiam prae-
'fatae actiones ab usu communi recesserunt, cum
'manifestissimum est, quod[19] omnes, qui scientes rem
'furtivam susceperint et celaverint, furti nec mani-
5 'festi obnoxii sunt.' [20]Poena manifesti furti quadrupli est tam ex servi persona quam ex liberi, nec
manifesti dupli.
6 [21]Furtum autem fit non solum, cum quis inter-
'cipiendi causa rem alienam amovet, sed generaliter
'cum quis alienam rem invito domino contrectat. ita-
'que sive creditor pignore sive is apud quem res de-
'posita est ea re utatur sive is qui rem utendam
'accepit in alium usum eam transferat, quam cuius
'gratia ei data est, furtum committit. veluti si quis
'argentum utendum acceperit quasi amicos ad cenam
'invitaturus et id peregre secum tulerit, aut si quis

---

(1) acceptum *ins. dett.*: ἔχω λαβὼν ἢ καὶ ληφϑὲν ἀπη-
νεγκάμην (quasi esset habeo acceptum acceptumve tuli) Θ
(2) *Gai.* 3, 176. 177. 179   (3) *sic Gai.*, tollitur *BT*?
(4) a nullo] *Gai.*, nullus *libri*   (5) videtur *B*, videatur *T*[b],
inc. T[a]   (6) *Cod.* 8, 41 (42). 6   (7) *Cf. Gai.* 3, 182..208 *Dig.*
47, 2 *Cod.* 6, 2   (8) *sic APΘ*, et de furto *add. B*   (9) *cf.
Dig.* 44, 7, 4 (*Gai l.* 3 *rer. cott.*)   (10) § 1 *ex Dig.* 47, 2, 1 § 3

(*Paul. l.* 39 *ad ed.*)   (11) § 2 *ex Dig.* 47, 2, 1 *pr.* (*Paul.
l.* 39 *ad ed.*)   (12) id est: a ferendo   (13) *Gai.* 3, 183; *similia
Dig.* 47, 2, 2 (*Gai. l.* 13 *ad ed.*)   (14) manif. ...appellant *ex
Dig.* 47, 2, 3 *pr.* (*Ulp. l.* 41 *ad Sab.*)   (15) in domo] *W*,
domo *A*, domi *BC*, *inc. T*[a]   (16) sed ... fur = *Dig.* 47,
2, 5 § 1   (17) *Gai.* 3, 185..188   (18) eo *TC*[a]   (19) quin
libri (20) § 5 *similis Gaio* 3, 189. 190   (21) *Gai.* 3, 195. 196

i*

matters aforesaid, whatever any shall be worth in money, do you promise that so much money shall be given? Aulus Agerius put the question, Numerius Negidius gave the promise.' Numerius Negidius then puts a question to Aulus Agerius: 'Whatever I have this day promised you in the terms of the Aquilian stipulation, do you hold it all received?' To which Aulus Agerius replies: 'I hold it and have entered it received.' 3. Obligations are also discharged by novation, where, for example, a stipulation is taken from Titius for what you owe to Seius. With the intervention of a new person, a new obligation is created; the earlier obligation is merged with the later and extinguished. Sometimes this happens even though the later stipulation is unenforceable. Suppose a child, acting without his guardian's endorsement, undertakes by stipulation to give what you owe Titius. The right is lost. The first debtor is released; the subsequent obligation is void. It is different where the stipulation is taken from a slave. There the first debtor remains bound as if there had been no subsequent stipulation at all. When the later stipulation is taken from the same person, novation only happens if the second stipulation has some new feature, as for instance the addition, or subtraction, of a condition, a postponement, or a guarantor. But

when we say that adding a condition achieves a novation, we mean only that the novation happens if and when the condition is fulfilled. The old obligation survives if it fails. 3a. Although the classical jurists were agreed that novation occurred when and only when the second obligation was entered with the intent that it should have novatory effect, there were doubts as to what circumstances indicated such an intent. Different jurists introduced different presumptions. That was why we issued our own pronouncement. We restricted novation to the case in which parties expressly declare that the purpose of their agreement is to novate an earlier obligation. In other cases the first obligation is to survive and the second is added to it, each enduring on its own basis as provided in the enactment. The pronouncement itself sets this out more fully. 4. Next, obligations by mere agreement can be dissolved by contrary agreement. Suppose Titius and Seius agree on the sale of a Tusculan estate to Seius at 100; then, while the contract remains unexecuted – i.e. before the price is paid or the land is transferred – they decide that the sale should be called off. Both are discharged. As has been said, the law is the same for hire and for all contracts which become binding by agreement.

BOOK FOUR

4.1 OBLIGATIONS FROM DELICT

The last book dealt with obligations from contract and as though from contract. Now come those from wrong-doing. We showed that contractual obligations divide into four categories. Delictual obligations are all of one kind. They arise from conduct. They all spring from the wrongdoing itself, from theft, robbery, loss wrongfully caused, or contempt. 1. Theft is the handling of a thing with fraudulent intention in relation to the thing itself or even its use or its possession. It is against the law of nature. 2. The word, in Latin 'furtum', comes from 'furvus', which means 'black', from the wrong's being committed secretly and in the dark, in fact mostly at night; or else from 'fraus', meaning 'fraud'; or from 'ferre', in the sense of 'auferre', which means 'to carry off'; or from the Greek word for thief, which is 'phor'. The Greeks themselves take this from their word for carrying, which is 'pherein'. 3. Theft is of two kinds, manifest and non-manifest. As we shall see, there are also 'theft by receiving' and 'theft by planting'. These are not really kinds of theft so much as ancillary actions. A manifest thief, whom the Greeks call 'self-detected', is not just one caught in the act. It is enough if he is caught in the place: if the theft is in a house, before he gets out of the door; if the theft is of olives in a grove or grapes in a vineyard, while he is in the grove or vineyard. But the accepted definition is wider still: if he is seen or caught with the stolen thing, in public or private, by the owner or anyone else, before he reaches the place where he planned to stow it. Once there, he is no longer a manifest thief, not even if caught with the stolen thing. The definition of non-manifest theft must now be clear: any theft which is not manifest is obviously non-manifest.

4. 'Theft by receiving' is where a stolen thing is found in someone's premises after a search before witnesses. A special action, the action for theft by receiving, was given against such a person, even if not the thief. 'Theft by planting' is where a stolen thing is planted on you and found in your premises. The liability arises when the planter intended that it be found with you rather than him. Again the name comes from the special action available against him even where he was not the thief, the action for theft by planting. Another action, for theft by prohibition, lay for preventing someone from making a search before witnesses. The praetor's edict also penalized a refusal to hand over a stolen thing found in a search. That gave the action for theft by retention. These actions – i.e. for receiving, planting, prohibiting, and retaining – have become obsolete. Searches for stolen things are no longer conducted in the old way, and these actions have disappeared with them. This is reasonable enough, given that it is perfectly clear that anyone who knowingly receives or conceals a stolen thing is liable for non-manifest theft. 5. For manifest theft the penalty is fourfold damages whether the culprit is a slave or free; for non-manifest, double. 6. Theft is committed not only when someone removes something belonging to another to have it for himself but, more comprehensively, whenever someone handles something belonging to another without the owner's consent. Creditors and depositees commit theft if they use the pledge or the thing deposited. A borrower of a thing for use commits theft if he puts it to a use other than that for which it was lent. So, it is theft if a person borrows silver saying he wants it for a dinner for his friends and takes it off with him on a journey, // or borrows a horse for a ride and

'equum gestandi causa commodatum sibi longius ali-
'quo duxerit, quod veteres scripserunt de eo, qui in
7 'aciem equum perduxisset [1]. [2]Placuit tamen eos,
'qui rebus commodatis aliter uterentur, quam uten-
'das acceperint, ita furtum committere, si se intelle-
'gant id invito domino facere eumque si intellexisset
'non permissurum, ac si permissurum credant, extra
'crimen videri: optima sane distinctione, quia furtum
8 'sine affectu furandi non committitur. [2]Sed et[3] si
'credat aliquis invito domino se rem commodatam
'sibi[4] contrectare, domino autem volente id fiat, dici-
'tur furtum non fieri. unde illud quaesitum est, cum
'Titius servum Maevii sollicitaverit, ut quasdam res
'domino subriperet et ad eum perferret, et servus id
'ad Maevium pertulerit, Maevius, dum vult Titium in
'ipso delicto deprehendere, permisit servo quasdam
'res ad eum perferre, utrum furti an servi corrupti
'iudicio teneatur Titius, an neutro?' 'et cum nobis
'super hac dubitatione suggestum est et antiquorum
'prudentium super hoc altercationes perspeximus, qui-
'busdam neque furti neque servi corrupti actionem
'praestantibus, quibusdam furti tantummodo: nos huius-
'modi calliditati obviam euntes per nostram decisio-
'nem[5] sanximus non solum furti actionem, sed etiam
'servi corrupti contra eum dari: licet enim is servus
'deterior a sollicitatore minime factus est et ideo non
'concurrant regulae, quae servi corrupti actionem
'introducerent, tamen consilium corruptoris ad perni-
'ciem probitatis servi introductum est, ut sit ei poe-
'nalis actio imposita, tamquam re ipsa fuisset servus
'corruptus, ne ex huiusmodi impunitate et in alium
'servum, qui possit corrumpi, tale facinus a quibus-
9 'dam perpetretur.' [6]Interdum etiam liberorum
'hominum furtum fit, veluti is quis liberorum nostro-
'rum, qui in potestate nostra sit[7], subreptus fuerit.
10 [6]Aliquando autem etiam suae rei quisque furtum
'committit, veluti is debitor rem quam creditori pigno-
'ris causa dedit subtraxerit.
11 [8]Interdum furti tenetur, qui ipse furtum non
'fecerit: qualis est, cuius ope et consilio furtum factum
'est. in quo numero est, qui tibi nummos excussit,
'ut alius eos raperet, aut obstitit tibi, ut alius rem
'tuam exciperet, vel oves aut boves tuas fugaverit,
'ut alius eas exciperet: et hoc veteres scripserunt de
'eo, qui panno rubro fugavit armentum. sed si quid
'eorum per lasciviam et non data opera, ut furtum
'admitteretur, factum est, 'in factum actio' dari de-
'beat.' at ubi ope Maevii Titius furtum fecerit, ambo
'furti tenentur. ope consilio eius quoque furtum ad-
'mitti videtur, qui scalas forte fenestris supponit aut
'ipsas fenestras vel ostium effringit, ut alius furtum
'faceret, quive ferramenta ad effringendum aut scalas
'ut fenestris supponerentur commodaverit, sciens cuius
(12) gratia commodaverit. certe qui nullam operam
'ad furtum faciendum adhibuit, sed tantum consilium
'dedit atque hortatus est ad furtum faciendum, non
12 (13) 'tenetur furti. Hi, qui in parentium vel do-
'minorum potestate sunt, si rem eis subripiant, fur-
'tum quidem illis faciunt et res in furtivam causam
'cadit nec ob id ab ullo usucapi potest, antequam in
'domini potestatem revertatur, sed furti actio non
'nascitur, quia nec ex alia ulla causa potest inter eos
(14) actio nasci: si vero ope consilio alterius fur-
'tum factum fuerit, quia utique furti committitur,
'convenienter ille furti tenetur, quia verum est ope
'consilio eius furtum factum esse.
13 (15) [9]Furti autem actio ei competit, cuius in-
'terest rem salvam esse, licet dominus non sit: ita-
'que nec domino aliter competit, quam si eius inter-
14 (16) 'sit rem non perire. [9]Unde constat credito-
'rem de pignore subrepto furti agere posse,' etiamsi
'idoneum debitorem habeat, quia expedit ei pignori
'potius incumbere quam in personam agere: 'adeo

'quidem ut, quamvis ipse debitor eam rem subri-
'puerit, nihilo minus creditori competit actio furti.
15 (17) [9]Item si fullo polienda curandave aut sarci-
'nator sarcienda vestimenta mercede certa acceperit
'eaque furto amiserit, ipse furti habet actionem, non
'dominus, quia domini nihil interest eam rem non
'perire, quia iudicio locati a fullone aut sarcinatore
'rem suam persequi potest.' sed et bonae fidei emp-
'tori subrepta re quam emerit, quamvis dominus non
'sit, omnimodo competit furti actio, quemadmodum et
'creditori. fulloni vero et sarcinatori non aliter furti
'competere placuit, quam si solvendo sint, hoc est si
'domino rei aestimationem solvere possint: [10]nam si
'solvendo non sunt, tunc quia ab eis suum dominus
'consequi non possit, ipsi domino furti actio compe-
'tit, quia hoc casu ipsius interest rem salvam esse.'
'idem est et si in parte solvendo sint fullo aut sarcinator.
16 (18) [11]Quae de fullone et sarcinatore diximus,
'eadem et ad eum cui commodata res est transferenda
'veteres existimabant: nam ut ille fullo mercedem
'accipiendo custodiam praestat, ita is quoque, qui
'commodum utendi percipit, similiter necesse habet
'custodiam praestare.' 'sed nostra providentia etiam[12]
'hoc in decisionibus nostris emendavit, [13]ut in domini
'sit voluntate, sive commodati actionem adversus eum
'qui rem commodatam accepit movere desiderat, sive
'furti adversus eum qui rem subripuit, et alterutra
'earum electa dominum non posse ex paenitentia ad
'alteram venire actionem. sed si quidem furem ele-
'gerit, illum qui rem utendam accepit penitus liberari.
'sin autem commodator veniat adversus eum qui rem
'utendam accepit, ipsi quidem nullo modo competere
'posse adversus furem furti actionem, eum autem, qui
'pro re commodata convenitur, posse adversus furem
'furti habere actionem, ita tamen, si dominus sciens
'rem esse subreptam adversus eum cui res commo-
'data fuit pervenit: sin autem nescius et dubitans rem
'non esse apud eum commodati actionem instituit,
'postea autem re comperta voluit remittere quidem
'commodati actionem, ad furti autem pervenire, tunc
'licentia ei concedatur et adversus furem venire nullo
'obstaculo ei opponendo, quoniam incertus constitutus
'movit adversus eum qui rem utendam accepit com-
'modati actionem (nisi domino ab eo satisfactum est:
'tunc etenim omnimodo furem a domino quidem furti
'actione liberari, suppositum autem esse ei, qui pro re
'sibi commodata domino satisfecit), cum manifestissi-
'mum est, etiam si ab initio dominus actionem instituit
'commodati ignarus rem esse subreptam, postea autem
'hoc ei cognito adversus furem transivit, omnimodo
'liberari eum qui rem commodatam accepit, quem-
'cumque causae exitum dominus adversus furem ha-
'buerit: eadem definitione optinente, sive in partem
'sive in solidum solvendo sit is qui rem commodatam
17 (19) 'accepit.' [14]Sed is, apud quem res deposita
'est, custodiam non praestat, sed tantum in eo ob-
'noxius est, si quid ipse dolo malo fecerit: qua de
'causa si res ei subrepta fuerit, quia restituendae
'eius[15] nomine depositi non tenetur nec ob id eius
'interest rem salvam esse, furti agere non potest, sed
18 (20) 'furti actio domino competit. [14]In summa
'sciendum est quaesitum esse, an impubes rem alie-
'nam amovendo furtum faciat. et placet, quia fur-
'tum ex affectu consistit, ita demum obligari eo cri-
'mine impuberem, si proximus pubertati sit et ob id
19 (21) 'intellegat se delinquere.' Furti actio sive
'dupli sive quadrupli tantum ad poenae persecutionem
'pertinet: nam ipsius rei persecutionem extrinsecus
'habet dominus, quam aut vindicando aut condicendo
'potest auferre. sed vindicatio quidem adversus pos-
'sessorem est, sive fur ipse possidet sive alius qui-
'libet: condictio autem adversus ipsum furem here-
'demve eius, licet non possideat, competit.

---

(1) sic AB^bC^b Gai., produxisset TC^a, perduxerit B^a (2) Gai.
3, 197. 198   (3) et] $AT^bC\Theta$ Gai., om. BT^a (4) commodatam sibi om. Gai.   (5) Cod. 6, 2, 20   (6) Gai. 3, 199. 200
(7) sit] AB, st C^a, sunt T^bC^b Gai., inc. T^a (8)   Gai.

3, 202   (9) Gai. 3, 203..205   (10) Gai. 3, 205   (11) Gai.
3, 206   (12) etiam om. T   (13) § 16 fin. ex Cod. 6, 2,
22 § 1. 2   (14) Gai. 3, 207. 208   (15) eius] A Gai., eius
rei BP

uses it to go somewhere far away. The case in the old books is the horse borrowed and taken into into battle. 7. But it was accepted that borrowers who put the thing to an extra use only commit theft if they know the owner does not consent and would not consent if he knew; if they believe that he would allow the extra use, they are not liable. This is an excellent distinction. Theft cannot be committed without intent to steal. 8. There is no theft if a person believes that he is handling a borrowed thing without the owner's consent but in fact the owner does consent. That gives rise to the following problem. Titius approaches a slave of Maevius and urges him to take some things from his owner and bring them out to him. The slave reveals the plan to Maevius. Maevius wants to catch Titius in the act of committing the delict. He therefore allows the slave to take some things to him. Is Titius liable for theft? Or for corruption of a slave? Or for neither? The difficulties of this problem were put to us. We analysed the arguments between the classical jurists, some giving neither the action for theft nor the action for corruption, some giving only the action for theft, and we settled the controversy. In order to combat this type of wickedness, not only the action for theft but also the action for corruption shall be given against the rogue. Though the slave was not in fact corrupted by the approach, so that the conditions for the action for corruption are not all satisfied, the corrupter did act on his plan to destroy the slave's character. The slave's corruption is implied, and this penal action is now given. Otherwise this kind of defence might encourage the same mischief with more susceptible slaves. 9. There can even be theft of free people, as where one of our children, still under family authority, is kidnapped. 10. Sometimes an owner can commit theft of his own property, as where a debtor takes back something which he has given his creditor as a pledge. 11. Sometimes a man is liable to the action for theft who has not himself committed theft, for example where a theft has been committed with his help and advice: someone knocks coins from your hand so that another can snatch them, or obstructs you so that another may relieve you of some valuable, or drives off your sheep or cattle so that another can take them. The case in the old books is the herd stampeded with a red rag. Where this is mindless hooliganism, not aimed at theft, an action on the case should be given. But where Titius has committed a theft with Maevius' help, both are liable to the action. Further examples of theft 'with help and advice' are: where someone puts a ladder to a window or breaks a window or door to help another to steal, or he lends tools for breaking in or ladders to reach a window knowing the intended purpose. (12) Of course if someone urges and encourages a theft, but offers no help, he is not liable to the action for theft. 12 (13) Dependent persons do commit theft against parents or owners if they take things from them. The thing in question becomes stolen property, incapable of usucapion by anyone until it has been back in its owner's control. But no action for theft lies, because no action at all can arise between such parties. (14) What if such a theft is committed with the help and advice of another person? Since a theft is committed, that other is certainly liable under the action. It is perfectly true that with his help and advice a theft has been committed. 13 (15) The action for theft can be brought by anyone with an interest in the safety of the thing, even if he is not the owner; and it cannot be brought by the owner if he does not have such an interest. 14 (16) So a creditor can sue for theft if a pledge is taken from him. This holds good even if his debtor is solvent, since he has an interest in controlling the thing pledged rather than being put to a personal action against the debtor. Even if it is the debtor himself who takes it the creditor can bring the action for theft. 15 (17) Suppose a laundryman charges a given sum for washing clothes or giving them some other treatment, or a tailor for repairing them. If he loses the clothes to a thief, he, not the owner, has the action. The owner has no interest in the safety of the clothes, since he can recover from the laundryman or the tailor in the action on hire. Like the pledge-creditor, someone who buys a thing in good faith always has the action for theft if it is taken, despite not being owner. But it has been decided that the laundryman and the cleaner only have the action for theft if they are solvent, i.e. if they can pay the owner the value of the thing. If they are insolvent, the owner cannot recover from them. So the action for theft reverts to him, since now he has an interest in the safety of the thing. The same rule applies where they are partly unable to meet his claim. 16 (18) What we have said of laundrymen and tailors was held by the classical jurists to apply equally to the borrower for use. The laundryman incurs an insurance liability because he receives a reward. Similarly the borrower attracts the same liability, because he gets the advantage of using the thing. Our concern led us to address this matter too, in our rulings on controverted issues. We provided as follows. An owner has a choice between bringing the action on loan for use against the borrower or the action for theft against the thief; once he makes the choice, he may not change his mind and go back to the other action. If he sues the thief, the borrower is absolutely discharged. If he goes as lender against the borrower, he bars himself from the action for theft; and the borrower then acquires the right to bring the action for theft against the thief. But this supposes that the owner begins his action against the borrower knowing that the thing has been taken. He may begin without that knowledge, simply unsure whether the thing is or is not with the borrower, only later discovering its whereabouts. If he then wants to give up the action on the loan and turn to the action for theft, permission should be given to him to proceed against the thief. No obstacle should then be put in his way, because he began to sue the borrower in a state of uncertainty. But this in turn supposes that the owner's claim has not been settled by the borrower. If it has, the thief is absolutely discharged from the owner's action for theft and must face instead the same action from the borrower who has met the owner's claim. Nothing could be more obvious than that, if the owner originally began his action against the borrower without knowing that the thing had been stolen and only later, when this became known to him, transferred to his action against the thief, the borrower is still absolutely discharged, whatever the result of the owner's suit against the thief. That ruling applies whether the borrower has funds enough to cover the whole value of the thing or only part of it. 17 (19) By contrast a depositee has no insurance liability but is answerable only for his own wilful defaults. Suppose the thing is taken from him. He has no interest in its safety: his obligation to restore the thing in the action on deposit is discharged. So he cannot sue for the theft, and the owner consequently has that action. 18 (20) Finally, does a child commit theft if he removes something belonging to another? The answer is that, since theft depends on intent, a child only incurs the liability if he is near puberty. He can then understand that he is doing wrong. 19 (21) The action for theft, for double or fourfold, is entirely penal. The owner has separate means of restoring his wealth. He can get it back by a vindication or an action of debt. The vindication lies against someone in possession, the thief or anybody else. The action of debt lies against the thief or his heir, in possession or not. //

II[1]

VI[2] BONORUM RAPTORUM.

[3]'Qui res alienas rapit, tenetur quidem etiam furti '(quis enim magis alienam rem invito domino con-'trectat, quam qui vi rapit? ideoque recte dictum est 'eum improbum furem esse): sed tamen propriam 'actionem eius delicti nomine praetor introduxit, quae 'appellatur vi bonorum raptorum et est intra annum 'quadrupli, post annum simpli. quae actio utilis est, 'etiamsi quis unam rem licet minimam rapuerit.' quadruplum autem non totum poena est et extra poenam rei persecutio, sicut in actione furti manifesti diximus: sed in quadruplo inest et rei persecutio, ut poena tripli sit, sive comprehendatur raptor in ipso delicto sive non. ridiculum est enim levioris esse condicionis eum qui vi rapit, quam qui clam amovet. 1 Quia tamen ita competit ea actio, si dolo malo quisque rapuerit: qui aliquo errore inductus suam rem esse et imprudens iuris eo animo rapuit, quasi domino liceat rem suam etiam per vim auferre possessoribus, absolvi debet. cui scilicet conveniens est nec furti teneri eum, qui eodem hoc animo rapuit. 'sed ne, dum talia excogitentur, inveniatur via, per 'quam raptores impune suam exerceant avaritiam: 'melius divalibus constitutionibus[4] pro hac parte pro-'spectum est, ut nemini liceat vi rapere rem mobilem 'vel se moventem, licet suam eandem rem existimet: 'sed si quis[5] contra statuta fecerit, rei quidem suae 'dominio cadere, sin autem aliena sit, post restitutio-'nem[6] etiam aestimationem eiusdem rei praestare. quod 'non solum in mobilibus rebus, quae rapi possunt, 'constitutiones optinere censuerunt, sed etiam in in-'vasionibus, quae circa res soli fiunt, ut ex hac causa 2 'omni rapina homines abstineant.' [7]'In hac actione non utique exspectatur rem in bonis actoris esse: nam sive in bonis sit sive non sit, si tamen ex bonis sit, locum haec actio habebit. quare sive commodata sive locata sive etiam pignerata sive deposita sit apud Titium sic, ut intersit eius eam non auferri, veluti si in re deposita culpam quoque promisit, sive bona fide possideat, sive usum fructum in ea quis habeat vel quod aliud ius, ut intersit eius non rapi: dicendum est competere ei hanc actionem, ut non dominium accipiat, sed illud solum, quod ex bonis eius qui rapinam passus est, id est. quod ex substantia eius ablatum esse proponatur. et generaliter dicendum est, ex quibus causis furti actio competit in re clam facta, ex isdem causis omnes habere hanc actionem.

III[8]

DE LEGE AQUILIA.

[9]'Damni iniuriae actio constituitur per legem Aqui-'liam. cuius primo capite cautum est, ut si quis ho-'minem alienum alienamve quadrupedem quae pecu-'dum numero sit iniuria occiderit, quanti ea res in 'eo anno plurimi fuit, tantum domino dare damne-1 'tur.' Quod autem non praecise de quadrupede, sed de ea tantum quae pecudum numero est cavetur, eo pertinet, ut neque de feris bestiis neque de canibus cautum esse intellegamus, sed de his tantum, quae proprie pasci dicuntur, quales sunt equi muli asini boves oves caprae. de suibus quoque idem placuit: nam et sues pecorum appellatione continentur, quia et hi gregatim pascuntur: sic denique et Homerus in Odyssea[10] ait, 'sicut Aelius Marcianus in suis institutionibus[11] refert':

δήεις τόν γε σύεσσι παρήμενον· αἱ δὲ νέμονται
πὰρ Κόρακος πέτρῃ, ἐπί τε κρήνῃ Ἀρεθούσῃ[12].

2 Iniuria autem occidere intellegitur, qui nullo iure occidit. itaque qui latronem occidit, non tene-

tur, utique si aliter periculum effugere non potest. 3 Ac ne is quidem hac lege tenetur, qui casu occidit, si modo culpa eius nulla invenitur: nam aloquin non minus ex dolo quam ex culpa quisque hac 4 lege tenetur. Itaque si quis, dum iaculis ludit vel exercitatur, transeuntem servum tuum traiecerit, distinguitur. nam si a milite quidem[13] in campo eoque, ubi solitum est exercitari, admissum est, nulla culpa eius intellegitur: si alius tale quid admisit, culpae reus est. idem iuris est de milite, si is in alio loco, quam qui exercitandis militibus destinatus 5 est, id admisit. Item si putator ex arbore deiecto ramo servum tuum transeuntem occiderit, si prope viam publicam aut vicinalem id factum est neque praeclamavit, ut casus evitari possit, culpae reus est: si praeclamavit neque ille curavit cavere, extra culpam est putator. aeque extra culpam esse intellegitur, si seorsum a via forte vel in medio fundo caedebat, licet non praeclamavit, quia 6 eo loco nulli extraneo ius fuerat versandi. Praeterea si medicus, qui servum tuum secuit, dereliquerit curationem atque ob id mortuus fuerit servus, 7 culpae reus est. Imperitia quoque culpae adnumeratur, veluti si medicus ideo servum tuum occiderit, quod eum male secuerit aut perperam ei 8 medicamentum dederit. Impetu quoque mularum, quas mulio propter imperitiam retinere non potuerit, si servus tuus oppressus fuerit, culpae reus est mulio. sed et si propter infirmitatem retinere eas non potuerit, cum alius firmior retinere potuisset, aeque culpae tenetur. eadem placuerunt de eo quoque, qui, cum equo veheretur, impetum eius aut propter infirmitatem aut propter imperitiam suam retinere non 9 potuerit. His autem verbis legis 'quanti id[14] in 'eo anno plurimi fuerit' illa sententia exprimitur, ut si quis hominem tuum, qui hodie claudus aut luscus aut mancus erit, occiderit, qui in eo anno integer aut pretiosus fuerit, non tanti teneatur, quanti is hodie erit, sed quanti in eo anno plurimi fuerit. qua ratione creditum est poenalem esse huius legis actionem, quia non solum tanti quisque obligatur, quantum damni dederit, sed aliquando longe pluris: ideoque constat in heredem eam actionem non transire, quae transitura fuisset, si ultra damnum numquam 10 lis aestimaretur. Illud non ex verbis legis, sed ex interpretatione placuit non solum perempti corporis aestimationem habendam esse secundum ea quae diximus, sed eo amplius quidquid praeterea perempto eo corpore damni[15] vobis adlatum fuerit, veluti si servum tuum heredem ab aliquo institutum ante quis occiderit, quam is iussu tuo adiret: nam hereditatis quoque amissae rationem esse habendam constat. item si ex pari mularum unam vel ex quadriga equorum unum occiderit, vel ex comoedis unus servus fuerit occisus: non solum occisi fit aestimatio, sed eo amplius id quoque computatur, quanto depretiati 11 sunt qui supersunt. Liberum est autem ei, cuius servus fuerit occisus, et privato iudicio legis Aquiliae damnum persequi et capitalis criminis eum reum facere.

12 'Caput secundum legis Aquiliae in usu non est.'
13 [16]'Capite tertio de omni cetero damno cavetur. Ita-'que si quis servum vel eam quadrupedem quae pe-'cudum numero est vulneraverit, sive eam quadru-'pedem quae pecudum numero non est, veluti canem 'aut feram bestiam, vulneraverit aut occiderit, hoc 'capite actio constituitur. in ceteris quoque omnibus 'animalibus, item in omnibus rebus quae anima ca-'rent damnum iniuria datum hac parte vindicatur. si 'quid enim ustum aut ruptum aut fractum fuerit, 'actio ex hoc capite constituitur: quamquam poterit 'sola rupti appellatio in omnes istas causas sufficere:

(1) Cf. Dig. 47, 8 Cod. 9, 33   (2) vi] A, de vi B utr. l. (3) Gai. 3, 209   (4) Dig. 4, 2, 13. 48, 7, 7 Cod. 3, 39, 4. 8, 4, 7. 10 (5) quis] AW, quid B, quidem E   (6) restitutionem] A, rest. eius BW (7) § 2 ex Dig. 47, 8, 2 § 22. 23 (Ulp. l. 56 ad ed.) (8) Cf. Gai. 3, 210..219 Dig. 9, 2 Cod. 3, 35   (9) Gai.

3, 210   (10) Od. 13, 407 sq.   (11) Dig. 32, 65, 4   (12) id est: invenies eum apud sues sedentem. hae vero pascuntur ad Coracis clivum et apud fontem Arethusam   (13) quidem] dett., qui libri   (14) id] APΘ, om. B   (15) damni] P, d. quid ABC   (16) Gai. 3, 217

4.2 THINGS TAKEN BY FORCE

A robber is of course liable to the action for theft. Who can more truly be said to handle the property of another without his consent than one who forcibly seizes it? So it is a good description of a robber to say that he is disgraceful even among thieves. But the praetor introduced a special action to deal with this wrong, the action for things taken by force. It lies for fourfold damages within one year, for single damages after the year is up. It can be used even where a single thing is taken, however small. Here the fourfold award is not all penalty, so as to leave the victim separate means of restoring his wealth as we have just seen for manifest theft. The fourfold award includes restoration, so that the penalty is in fact threefold, whether the robber is caught in the act or later. It would be absurd for one who takes by force to be in a less serious position than one who takes in secret. 1. This action only lies where a person takes something with wicked intent. A defendant must be absolved if he mistakenly thought the thing was his and took it because, not knowing the law, he supposed that an owner was allowed to recover his property by violent self-help against the person in possession. One who takes in that state of mind is also not liable even for theft. But steps have been taken to ensure that violent men cannot exploit these rules to cover their rapaciousness. Imperial pronouncements have wisely provided that nobody may take by force any movable or living thing even if he thinks it his; that anyone who breaks these these enactments shall, if the thing is his, lose his ownership, and, if the thing is another's, shall restore it and its money value over again. They have also extended these rules from movable things which can be carried off to invasions of landed property. The purpose is to induce men to renounce every type of violent seizure. 2. In this action there is no requirement that the thing must belong to the plaintiff. Whether it is numbered among his own goods or not, the action will lie so long as the absence of the thing in some degree reduces his substance. So the action must be given where the thing was lent or hired to Titius; or pledged to him; or deposited with him, if on terms which give him an interest in its not being carried off, for example a warranty against non-intentional fault in relation to the thing deposited; or where he was a possessor in good faith; or where he had a usufruct in it; or any other right sufficient to give him an interest in its not being taken away. However, the action lies to these victims of violence to recover, not for the general property in the thing, but for what went from them, i.e. the amount by which the taking diminished their substance. The general proposition can be made that the people entitled to this action include all those who would have the action for theft if the same wrong were committed secretly.

4.3 THE AQUILIAN ACT

The action for wrongful loss is founded on the Aquilian Act. Its first section provides that if anyone wrongfully kills another's slave, male or female, or another's livestock-quadruped he must pay the owner the highest value which the thing had in that year. 1. The section specifies, not simply quadrupeds, but quadruped livestock. This is to exclude wild animals and dogs. The animals covered are those which can properly be said to graze. Horses, mules, donkeys, cows, sheep, and goats all fall in this class. Pigs have been included. Pigs do qualify as livestock because they too go to pasture in herds.

Aelius Marcianus notes in his Institutes that the Odyssey supports this where Homer says 'You will find him sitting with his pigs grazing by the Raven's Crag near the spring of Arethusa.' 2. A person kills wrongfully when he kills without justification. Someone who kills a robber is not liable, at least if he could not otherwise escape danger. 3. Even one who kills by accident escapes liability under the Act if not at fault; malicious intent or fault form the basis of the liability. 4. So, if someone engaged in sport or practice with javelins transfixes your slave, a distinction has to be taken. Suppose first that it was done by a soldier and in a field where it was usual to practise. Here there is no fault on his part. Suppose some other person does the same thing. He is guilty of fault. It is the same with the soldier if the act is done in some place other than one designated for military exercise. 5. Suppose someone pruning a tree throws down a branch and kills your slave passing below. If that is done near a public highway or a path between neighbours and no shout is given to enable the victim to avoid the disaster, the pruner is at fault. If he shouts and the other does not watch out for himself he is not at fault. The same if he is pruning away from the road, say in the middle of the field, and gives no warning shout. No stranger has any right to be walking about there. 6. Suppose again a doctor who cuts into your slave and then neglects the aftercare, so that the slave dies. He is at fault. 7. Lack of skill also counts as fault, as where a doctor kills your slave by operating on him badly or by giving him the wrong medicine. 8. A muledriver is at fault if he lacks the skill to control his mules and they knock down and crush your slave. He is equally at fault if it is weakness that makes him unable to control them, if anyone would have the strength to hold them. Similar conclusions are reached when a rider fails to control his horse's gallop, whether from want of skill or want of strength. 9. The statutory words 'the highest value which the thing had in that year' show that, if someone kills one of your slaves who is now lame or without an eye or maimed but within the year was well and more valuable, he is liable not for today's price but for the price at its highest during the year. This is the basis for saying that the statutory action is penal, since a defendant is not liable merely for the loss he has inflicted but sometimes for a much larger sum. So it is accepted that the action does not lie against the wrongdoer's heir, which it would if the amount of judgment never exceeded the loss. 10. By juristic interpretation, though not of any words in the Act, this valuation has come to be directed not merely to the dead body but to any additional loss caused to the plaintiff by the death. If someone kills your slave when he has been appointed heir but before he can obey your order to accept the estate, account must be taken of the lost inheritance. If one member is killed out of a pair of mules or a team of horses or a company of actors, the valuation must cover not only the one who has been killed but the depreciation of the survivors. 11. One whose slave has been killed can bring a civil suit to recover his loss under the Aquilian Act and also prosecute the killer criminally on a capital charge. 12. The second section of the Aquilian Act is obsolete. 13. The third section provides for all other loss. If someone wounds a slave or livestock-quadruped, or if he wounds or kills a quadruped not classed as livestock, such as a wild beast or a dog, an action lies under this section. It gives a remedy for loss wrongfully caused when any animal or any inanimate thing is burned or damaged or broken. The word 'damaged' – the Latin verb 'rumpere' – could have covered all these cases, since it is construed to include every kind of spoiling, // in Latin 'corrumpere'.

'ruptum enim intellegitur, quod quoquo [1] modo corrup-
'tum est. unde non solum usta aut fracta, sed etiam
'scissa et collisa et effusa et quoquo modo perempta at-
'que deteriora facta hoc verbo continentur': denique responsum est, si quis in alienum vinum aut oleum id
immiserit, quo naturalis bonitas vini vel olei cor-
14 rumperetur, ex hac parte legis eum teneri. Illud
palam est, sicut ex primo capite ita demum quisque
tenetur, si dolo aut culpa eius homo aut quadrupes
occisus occisave fuerit, ita ex hoc capite ex dolo aut
culpa de cetero damno quemquam teneri. [2]'hoc tamen
'capite non quanti in eo anno, sed quanti in diebus
'triginta proximis res fuerit, 'obligatur' is qui damnum
15 'dederit. [2]Ac ne plurimi quidem verbum adicitur.
'sed Sabino 'recte' placuit perinde habendam aesti-
'mationem, ac si etiam hac parte plurimi verbum ad-
'iectum fuisset: nam' plebem Romanam, quae Aquilio
tribuno rogante hanc legem tulit, 'contentam fuisse,
'quod prima parte eo verbo usa est'.
16 [2]'Ceterum placuit ita demum ex hac lege actio-
'nem esse, si quis 'praecipue' corpore suo damnum
'dederit. ideoque in eum, qui alio modo damnum
'dederit, utiles actiones dari solent: veluti si quis
'hominem alienum aut pecus ita incluserit, ut fame
'necaretur, aut iumentum tam vehementer egerit, ut
'rumperetur, aut pecus in tantum exagitaverit, ut
'praecipitaretur [3], aut si quis alieno servo persuaserit,
'ut in arborem ascenderet vel in puteum descenderet,
'et is ascendendo vel descendendo aut mortuus fuerit
'aut aliqua parte corporis laesus erit', utilis in eum
actio datur. 'sed si quis alienum servum de ponte
'aut ripa in flumen deiecerit et is suffocatus fuerit,
'eo quod proiecerit corpore suo damnum dedisse non
'difficiliter intellegi poterit' ideoque ipsa lege Aquilia
tenetur. 'sed si non corpore damnum fuerit datum
'neque corpus laesum fuerit, sed alio modo damnum
'alicui contigit, cum non sufficit neque directa neque
'utilis Aquilia, placuit eum qui obnoxius fuerit in
'factum actione teneri': [4]veluti si quis misericordia
ductus alienum servum compeditum solverit, ut fu-
geret.

IV [5]

DE INIURIIS.

[6]Generaliter iniuria dicitur omne quod non iure
fit: specialiter alias contumelia, quae a contemnendo
dicta est, quam Graeci ὕβριν appellant, alias culpa,
quam Graeci ἀδίκημα dicunt, sicut in lege Aquilia
damnum iniuria accipitur, alias iniquitas et iniustitia,
quam Graeci ἀδικίαν vocant. cum enim praetor vel
iudex non iure contra quem pronuntiat, iniuriam ac-
1 cepisse dicitur. [7]'Iniuria autem committitur non
'solum, cum quis pugno puta aut fustibus caesus vel
'etiam verberatus erit, sed etiam si cui convicium
'factum fuerit, sive cuius bona quasi debitoris [8]' pos-
'sessa fuerint ab eo, qui intellegebat 'nihil eum sibi
'debere, vel si quis ad infamiam alicuius libellum aut
'carmen scripserit' composuerit ediderit dolove malo
fecerit, quo quid eorum fieret, 'sive quis matrem fa-
'milias aut praetextatum praetextatamve adsectatus
'fuerit', sive cuius pudicitia attemptata esse dicatur: 'et
'denique aliis pluribus modis' admitti iniuriam mani-
2 festum est. [7]Patitur autem quis iniuriam non so-
'lum per semet ipsum, sed etiam per liberos suos
'quos in potestate habet: item per uxorem suam', id
enim magis praevaluit. 'itaque si filiae alicuius, quae
'Titio nupta est, iniuriam feceris, non solum filiae
'nomine tecum iniuriarum agi potest, sed etiam pa-
'tris quoque et mariti nomine.' contra autem, si viro
iniuria facta sit, uxor iniuriarum agere non potest:
defendi enim uxores a viris, non viros ab uxoribus

aequum est. sed et socer nurus nomine, cuius vir in
3 potestate est, iniuriarum agere potest. [9]'Servis
'autem ipsis quidem nulla iniuria fieri intellegitur,
'sed domino per eos fieri videtur: non tamen isdem
'modis, quibus etiam per liberos et uxores, sed ita
'cum quid atrocius commissum fuerit et [10] quod aperte
'ad contumeliam domini' respicit. 'veluti si quis alie-
'num servum verberaverit, et in hunc casum actio
'proponitur: at si quis servo convicium fecerit vel
'pugno eum percusserit', 'nulla in eum actio domino
4 'competit.' Si communi servo iniuria facta sit,
aequum est non pro ea parte, qua dominus quisque
est, aestimationem iniuriae fieri, sed ex dominorum
5 persona, quia ipsis fit iniuria. Quodsi usus fructus
in servo Titii est, proprietas Maevii est, magis Maevio
6 iniuria fieri intellegitur. Sed si libero, qui tibi
bona fide servit, iniuria facta sit, nulla tibi actio
dabitur, sed suo nomine is experiri poterit: nisi in
contumeliam tuam pulsatus sit, tunc enim competit
et tibi iniuriarum actio. [11]idem ergo est et in servo
alieno bona fide tibi serviente, ut totiens admittatur
iniuriarum actio, quotiens in tuam contumeliam iniuria ei facta sit.
7 [12]'Poena autem iniuriarum ex lege duodecim
'tabularum propter membrum quidem ruptum talio
'erat: propter os [13] vero fractum' 'nummariae poenae
'erant constitutae quasi in magna veterum pauper-
'tate. sed postea praetores permittebant' ipsis qui
'iniuriam passi sunt eam aestimare, ut iudex vel tanti
'condemnet, quanti iniuriam passus aestimaverit, vel
'minoris, prout ei visum fuerit.' sed poena quidem
iniuriae, quae ex lege duodecim tabularum introducta
est, in desuetudinem abiit: quam autem praetores
introduxerunt, quae etiam honoraria appellatur, in
iudiciis frequentatur. nam secundum gradum digni-
tatis vitaeque honestatem crescit aut minuitur aestimatio iniuriae: qui gradus condemnationis et in servili persona non immerito servatur, ut aliud in servo
actore, aliud in medii actus homine, aliud in vilis-
8 simo vel compedito constituatur. Sed et lex Cornelia de iniuriis loquitur et iniuriarum actionem introduxit. quae competit ob eam rem, quod se pul-
satum quis verberatumve domumve suam vi introitum
esse dicat. domum autem accipimus, sive in propria
domo quis habitat sive in conducta vel gratis sive
9 hospitio receptus sit. [14]'Atrox iniuria aestimatur
'vel ex facto, veluti si quis ab aliquo vulneratus fue-
'rit vel fustibus caesus: vel ex loco, veluti si cui in
'theatro vel in foro vel in conspectu praetoris iniuria
'facta sit: vel ex persona, veluti si magistratus in-
'iuriam passus fuerit, vel si senatori ab humili in-
'iuria facta sit,' aut parenti patronoque fiat a liberis
vel libertis: aliter enim senatoris et parentis patroni-
que, aliter extranei et humilis personae iniuria aestimatur. nonnumquam et locus vulneris atrocem iniuriam facit, veluti si in oculo quis percussus sit [15].
[16]parvi autem refert, utrum patri familias an filio
familias talis iniuria facta sit: nam et haec atrox
10 aestimabitur. In summa sciendum est de omni
iniuria eum qui passus est posse vel criminaliter
agere vel civiliter. et si quidem civiliter agatur, aestimatione facta secundum quod dictum est poena imponitur. sin autem criminaliter, officio iudicis extraordinaria poena reo irrogatur: 'hoc videlicet observando, quod Zenoniana constitutio [17] introduxit, ut
viri illustres quique supra eos sunt et per procuratores possint actionem iniuriarum criminaliter vel
persequi vel suscipere secundum eius tenorem, qui
11 ex ipsa manifestius apparet'. [18]Non solum autem
is iniuriarum tenetur qui fecit iniuriam, hoc est qui
percussit: verum ille quoque continebitur, qui dolo

---

(1) quod quoquo] $A^l C^b$, quod quo $A^u A^{bq}$, quo B^a, quoquo $B^b C^a P$ (2) Gai. 3, 218. 219   (3) aut pecus in . . .
praecip.] $BCP\Theta$, om. A Gai.   (4) cf. Dig. 4, 3, 7 § 7
  (5) Cf. Gai. 3, 220..225 Dig. 47, 10 Cod. 9, 35   (6) pr.
simile Coll. l. Mos. 2, 5 (Paul. l. sing. et tit. de iniuriis)
(7) Gai. 3, 220. 221   (8) debitoris] Gai., deb. qui nihil de-

beret libri   (9) Gai. 3, 222   (10) et] $A^l BP\Theta$, om. $A^u A^{bq}$
Gai.   (11) § 6 fin. similis Dig. 47, 10, 15 § 48 (Ulp. l. 57 ad ed.)
(12) Gai. 3, 223. 224   (13) os] P Gai., ossum ABC
(14) Gai. 3, 225   (15) sic $A\Theta$, percussit BC   (16) § 9 fin.
similis Dig. 47, 10, 9 § 2 (Ulp. l. 57 ad ed.)   (17) Cod. 9, 35, 11
(18) § 11. 12 ex Dig. 47, 10, 11 pr. § 1 (Ulp. l. 57 ad ed.)

That word covers not only burning and breaking but also tearing, squashing, spilling, and every sort of ruining or making worse. There is authority that if someone adds something to another's wine or oil to spoil its natural quality he becomes liable under this section. 14. This much is certain: just as someone becomes liable under the first section where he has killed a slave or quadruped intentionally or by fault, so here the liability for any other loss is also based on wicked intent or fault. Under this section the person causing loss is liable to pay the value of the thing in the preceding thirty days, not the year. 15. The word 'highest' is omitted. But Sabinus rightly held that the valuation was to be made just as though the word 'highest' had been included. In his view the plebeian assembly at Rome, which passed this law on the proposal of the tribune Aquilius, was content just to use the word in the first section. 16. The conclusion was reached that the statutory action lies only where someone causes loss immediately by his bodily force. Where people cause loss in other ways the practice is to give actions based on the policy of the statute. These policy actions are given against one who shuts up another's slave or animal so that it dies of starvation, drives a draught animal so hard that it is injured, harasses an animal till it throws itself over a cliff, or induces another's slave to climb up a tree or go down a well so that in climbing up or down he is killed or injured. But suppose someone pushes another's slave from a bridge or river bank, and the slave drowns. Here it is easy to conclude, from the fact that he pushed him in, that he has caused the loss by his bodily force. So he is liable directly under the Aquilian Act. Suppose there is no bodily force and no physical thing is harmed, but a person still somehow suffers loss. Here neither the action on the very words of the Aquilian Act nor an action based on its policy lies. It has been held that the person responsible is liable to an action on the case. An example is where someone out of pity frees another's slave from chains and lets him escape.

4.4 CONTEMPT

'Iniuria', the Latin name of this delict, in its general sense denotes all wrong conduct. Its specialized senses are, first, contempt, in Latin 'contumelia', from the verb 'contemnere', which the Greeks call 'hubris'; second, fault, which the Greeks call 'adikema' and which is the sense the word has in the Aquilian delict; third, unfairness and injustice, which the Greeks call 'adikia', such as you suffer when a praetor or a judge gives a wrong judgment against you. 1. Contempt is committed not only when someone is struck with a fist or with clubs, or even flogged; but also when a vocal attack is made on him; when his goods are seized like a debtor's by someone who knows he owes him nothing; when someone writes, makes up, or publishes a defamatory book or poem, or intentionally procures its writing, composition or publication; or when someone follows about a lady or a youth or a girl, or indulges in sexual harassment; also of course in many other ways. 2. Someone can be the victim of contempt not only in his own person but also through his children if they are still within family authority, also through his wife — that being the view which has prevailed. If you commit a contempt against someone's daughter, who is married to Titius, an action can be brought against you not only for the daughter herself but also for both the father and the husband. By contrast when a husband is subjected to a contempt, his wife has no action. It is reasonable that wives should be defended by husbands, not vice versa. A father-in-law can have an action for a contempt to his daughter-in-law when the husband is within family authority. 3. The law holds that no contempt can be committed against a slave, but that the delict can be committed to an owner through a slave. This does not happen as with wives and children but only where something more gross occurs, manifestly in contempt of the owner. For example, where one person flogs another's slave. There is an edictal action for that. No action lies to the owner where someone abuses a slave vocally or strikes him with a fist. 4. When a contempt is committed against a slave held in common, the valuation should focus not on the size of each owner's share but on their personal standing. It is to them personally that the contempt is offered. 5. If Titius has a usufruct in the slave and Maevius the ownership, the law prefers to treat Maevius as the victim. 6. If the contempt is committed to a free man honestly serving as your slave, no action will be given to you but he will be allowed to sue for himself. The exception is where he is struck in contempt of yourself. Then you do have the action. The law is the same for a slave belonging to another but living as yours, so that the action for contempt lies when the wrong to him is done in contempt of you. 7. Under the Twelve Tables the penalty for this delict was, for a damaged limb, retaliation; and for a broken bone, a sum of money appropriate to the great poverty of the people of those times. Later the praetors began to allow victims to put their own value on the wrong. The judge could condemn for the victim's valuation or for such lesser sum as seemed right to him. The penalties of the Twelve Tables have fallen into disuse, while the praetors' system — also called honorarian — is frequently applied in the courts. The valuation of contempts rises and falls according to the victim's social standing and honour. The same sliding scale is also not unreasonably used for slaves, requiring one decision in respect of a slave entrusted with management, another for one in the middle rank, and yet another for one in the lowest rank or kept in fetters. 8. There is also a Cornelian Act on Contempts. It introduced an action where the plaintiff had been struck or beaten or his home violently entered. The word 'home' includes someone's own house in which he lives, or one which he rents, or has free of charge, or even one where he is a guest. 9. A contempt can be aggravated: in conduct, as where someone is wounded by another or struck with clubs; in place, as where he is subjected to a contempt in the theatre or the city square or in front of the praetor; in person, as where a magistrate suffers a contempt, or a senator at the hands of a common person, or a parent or patron at the hands of children or freedmen. A contempt to a senator or to a parent or to a patron is differently valued from one committed against an outsider or a person of low degree. Sometimes the nature of a wound will aggravate the contempt, as where the victim has been struck in the eye. It matters little whether such a contempt is done to the head of a family or to a son. Either way it counts as aggravated. 10. Note finally that the victim of every contempt can sue criminally or civilly. If he sues civilly, a penalty will be imposed on the basis of the valuation already described. If he sues criminally, the judge can impose a discretionary penalty. Note also that, as the Emperor Zeno's enactment said, persons of illustrious degree or higher may maintain and defend criminal actions for contempt through agents. The details appear in the pronouncement itself. 11. Liability for contempt is not confined to the person who himself commits it, i.e. to one who strikes the blow. It extends also to one who intentionally sets out to get or procure someone to punch a victim's face. // 12. This action is

fecit vel qui curavit, ut cui mala pugno percutere-
12 tur. Haec actio dissimulatione aboletur: et ideo,
si quis iniuriam dereliquerit, hoc est statim passus
ad animum suum non revocaverit, postea ex paenitentia remissam iniuriam non poterit recolere.

V[1]
DE OBLIGATIONIBUS QUAE QUASI EX DELICTO NASCUNTUR.

[2]Si iudex litem suam fecerit, non proprie ex maleficio obligatus videtur. sed quia neque ex contractu
obligatus est et utique peccasse aliquid intellegitur,
licet per imprudentiam: ideo videtur quasi ex maleficio teneri, 'et in quantum de ea re aequum religioni
1 iudicantis videbitur, poenam sustinebit'. [2]Item is,
ex cuius cenaculo vel proprio ipsius vel conducto
vel in quo gratis habitabat deiectum effusumve aliquid est, ita ut alicui noceretur, quasi ex maleficio
obligatus intellegitur: ideo autem non proprie ex
maleficio obligatus intellegitur, quia plerumque ob
alterius culpam tenetur aut servi aut liberi. cui
similis est is, qui ea parte, qua vulgo iter fieri
solet, id positum aut suspensum habet, quod potest,
si ceciderit, alicui nocere: quo casu poena decem
'aureorum' constituta est. de eo vero quod deiectum
effusumve est dupli quanti damnum datum sit constituta est actio. ob hominem vero liberum occisum
quinquaginta 'aureorum' poena constituitur: si vero
vivet nocitumque ei[3] esse dicetur, quantum ob eam
rem aequum iudici videtur, actio datur: [4]iudex enim
computare debet mercedes medicis[5] praestitas cetéra-
que impendia, quae in curatione facta sunt, praeterea operarum, quibus caruit aut cariturus est ob
2 id quod inutilis factus est. [6]Si filius familias
seorsum a patre habitaverit et quid ex cenaculo
eius deiectum effusumve sit, sive quid positum sus-
pensumve habuerit, cuius casus periculosus est: Iuliano placuit in patrem nullam esse actionem, sed
cum ipso filio agendum. quod et in filio familias
3 iudice observandum est, qui litem suam fecerit. [6]Item
exercitor navis aut cauponae aut stabuli de dolo[7]
aut furto, quod in nave aut in caupona aut in sta-
bulo factum erit, quasi ex maleficio teneri videtur,
si modo ipsius nullum est maleficium, sed alicuius
eorum, quorum opera navem aut cauponam aut sta-
bulum exercerit: cum enim neque ex contractu sit
adversus eum constituta haec actio et aliquatenus
culpae reus est, quod opera malorum hominum utere-
tur, ideo quasi ex maleficio teneri vidétur. in his
autem casibus in factum actio competit, quae heredi
quidem datur, adversus heredem autem non competit.

VI[8]
DE ACTIONIBUS.

Superest, ut de actionibus loquamur. [9]actio autem
nihil aliud est, quam ius persequendi iudicio quod
sibi debetur.
1 Omnium actionum, quibus inter aliquos apud
iudices arbitrosve de quaque re[10] quaeritur, summa
divisio in duo genera deducitur: aut enim in rem
sunt aut in personam. namque agit unusquisque aut
cum eo, qui ei obligatus est vel ex contractu vel ex
maleficio, quo casu proditae actiones in personam
sunt, per quas intendit adversarium ei[11] dare aut[12]
dare facere oportere et aliis quibusdam modis: aut
cum eo agit, qui nullo iure ei obligatus est, movet
tamen alicui de aliqua re controversiam. quo casu
proditae actiones in rem sunt. veluti si rem corpo-
ralem possideat quis, quam Titius suam esse affirmet,

et possesor dominum se esse dicat: nam si Titius
2 suam esse intendat, in rem actio est. Aeque si
agat ius sibi esse fundo forte vel aedibus utendi
fruendi vel per fundum vicini eundi agendi vel ex
fundo vicini aquam ducendi, in rem actio est. eiusdem generis est actio de iure praediorum urbanorum, veluti si agat ius sibi esse altius aedes suas
tollendi prospiciendive vel proiciendi aliquid vel immittendi in vicini aedes. contra quoque de usu fructu
et de servitutibus praediorum rusticorum, item praediorum urbanorum invicem quoque proditae sunt
actiones, ut quis intendat ius non esse adversario
utendi fruendi, eundi agendi aquamve ducendi, item
altius tollendi prospiciendi proiciendi immittendi: istae
quoque actiones in rem sunt, sed negativae. quod
genus actionis in controversiis rerum corporalium
proditum non est: nam in his is[13] agit qui non possidet: ei vero qui possidet non est actio prodita, per
quam neget rem actoris esse. sane uno casu qui
possidet nihilo minus actoris partes optinet, 'sicut in
'latioribus digestorum libris opportunius apparebit'.
3 'Sed istae quidem actiones, quarum mentionem
'habuimus, et si quae sunt similes, ex legitimis et ci-
'vilibus causis descendunt. aliae autem sunt, quas
'praetor ex sua iurisdictione comparatas habet tam
'in rem quam in personam, quas et ipsas necessarium
'est exemplis ostendere'[14]. ecce 'plerumque' ita permittit
in rem agere, ut vel actor diceret se quasi usu cepisse, quod usu non ceperit, vel ex diverso possessor[15] diceret adversarium suum usu non cepisse quod
4 usu ceperit. Namque si cui ex iusta causa res
aliqua tradita fuerit, veluti ex causa emptionis aut
donationis aut dotis aut legatorum, necdum eius rei
dominus effectus est, si eius rei casu possessionem
amiserit, nullam habet directam in rem actionem ad
eam rem persequendam: quippe ita proditae sunt
iure civili actiones, ut quis dominium suum vindicet.
sed quia sane durum erat eo casu deficere actionem,
inventa est a praetore actio, in qua dicit is, qui possessionem amisit, eam rem se usu cepisse et ita vin-
dicat suam esse. quae actio Publiciana appellatur,
quoniam primum a Publicio praetore in edicto pro-
5 posita est. Rursus ex diverso si quis, cum rei
publicae causa abesset vel in hostium potestate esset,
rem eius qui in civitate esset usu ceperit, permittitur domino, si possessor rei publicae causa abesse
desierit, tunc intra annum rescissa usucapione eam
petere, id est ita petere, ut dicat possessorem usu
non cepisse et ob id suam esse rem. quod genus
actionis et aliis quibusdam[16] simili aequitate motus
praetor accommodat, 'sicut ex latiore digestorum seu
6 'pandectarum volumine intellegere licet'. Item si
quis in fraudem creditorum rem suam alicui 'tradiderit', bonis eius a creditoribus ex sententia praesidis
possessis permittitur 'ipsis creditoribus' rescissa 'traditione' eam rem petere, 'id est dicere eam rem tradi-
'tam non esse et ob id in bonis debitoris mansisse'[17].
7 Item Serviana et quasi Serviana, quae etiam hypothecaria vocatur, ex ipsius praetoris iurisdictione
substantiam capit. Serviana autem experitur quis de
rebus coloni, quae pignoris iure pro mercedibus fundi
ei tenentur: quasi Serviana autem qua[18] creditores
pignora hypothecasve persequuntur. inter pignus autem et hypothecam quantum ad actionem hypothecariam nihil interest: nam de qua re inter creditorem
et debitorem convenerit, ut sit pro debito obligata,
utraque hac appellatione continetur. sed in aliis differentia est: nam pignoris appellatione eam proprie
contineri dicimus, quae simul etiam traditur creditori, maxime si mobilis sit: at eam, quae sine traditione nuda conventione tenetur, proprie hypothecae

---

(1) *Cf. Dig.* 9, 3; 4, 9; 47, 5   (2) *pr.* § 1 *in. ex Gai l.*
3 rer. cott. (*Dig.* 44, 7, 5 § 4. 5; 50, 13, 6)   (3) *ei*] *P, om.*
BC (4) *§ 1 fin. similis Dig.* 9, 3, 7 (*Gai. l. 6 ad ed. prov.*)
(5) *medicis om.* B   (6) *§ 2. 3 ex Gaio l. l.* (*Dig.* 44, 7, 5
§ 5. 6)   (7) *dolo*] *libri cum* Θ, *damno Dig.*
(8) *Cf. Gai.* 4, 1..74   (9) *pr. fin. similis Dig.* 44, 7, 51

(*Cels. l.* 3 *dig.*)   (10) *quaque re*] *CP[a], qua* B   (11) *ei*]
scr. sibi   (12) *dare aut*] *BC, om. E*Θ   (13) *is om.*
B   (14) ‘ ’ *Iustinianis tribuit Ferrini*   (15) *pos-*
sessor del. Bachovius, cf. Θ   (16) *quibusdam et aliis*
libri   (17) ‘ ’ (§ 6) *Iustinianis tribuit Lenel*   (18) *qua*
del.

extinguished by dissimulation. If someone lets a contempt pass – having suffered it he dismisses it from his mind – he cannot later change his mind and rekindle the contempt he overlooked.

4.5 OBLIGATIONS AS THOUGH FROM DELICT

If a judge makes a case his own, his obligation does not strictly arise from wrongdoing. It does not arise from contract either. Because he certainly is in a way at fault, even if only from ignorance, his obligation is said to arise as though from wrongdoing. He has to pay penal damages in the sum that seems reasonable to the conscience of his judge. 1. A person is also said to incur an obligation as though from wrongdoing when something is thrown or poured from his apartment, whether his own, rented, or lived in free, with the result that someone is harmed. His obligation is not derived from delict proper because he often becomes liable through someone else's fault, a slave's or a child's. A similar case is the person who has things placed or hanging where people come and go, which might do harm if they fell. For him there is a penalty of 10 aurei. For the other case, of something thrown or poured, an action lies for twice the value of any loss caused. If a free man is killed, there is a penalty of 50 aurei. If he survives but is injured, an action is given for whatever sum the judge thinks reasonable. He must take into account doctor's fees which have been paid and all other expenses of the cure, also earnings lost or likely to be lost on account of the disability. 2. Where a son lives separately from his father and something is thrown or poured from his apartment or he has something placed or hung which would be dangerous if it fell, Julian says that no action lies against the father but that the claim must be brought against the son himself. The same applies where a son who is a judge makes the case his own. 3. Again, someone in charge of a ship, inn, or stable is considered as incurring a liability as though from wrongdoing when deceit or theft is committed in the ship, inn, or stable. This is correct where no wrong is committed by him personally but only by one of the people whose labour he uses to run the ship, inn or stable. His liability arises as though from wrongdoing because, first, this action was not set up against him on the basis of contract, and, secondly, he is to a certain extent guilty of fault in using the labour of unsatisfactory people. The action which is given here is an action on the case. It lies to but not against heirs.

4.6 ACTIONS

It remains to speak of actions. An action is nothing but a right to go to court to get one's due. 1. The main classification is into two: every action which takes an issue between parties to a trial before a judge or arbiter is either real or personal. A plaintiff may sue a defendant who is under an obligation to him, from contract or from wrongdoing. The personal actions lie for these claims. In them the plaintiff says that the defendant ought to give him something, or ought to, give or and do something. There are a number of other patterns. Or else he may sue a defendant who is not under any kind of obligation to him but is someone with whom he is in dispute about a thing. Here the real actions lie. Suppose someone in possession of a corporeal thing; Titius maintains it is his;

the possessor says it belongs to him. Here, if Titius pleads that the thing is his, the action is real. 2. The same if someone claims to be entitled to a usufruct over some land or a house; or a right of way for man and beast over his neighbour's land; or a right to lead water from his neighbour's land. The same again with actions for the urban servitudes: claiming e.g. the right of building higher, of prospect, projection, or attachment to a neighbour's wall. With usufruct, and rustic and urban servitudes, there are also symmetrical counter-actions. These allow a plaintiff to plead that his adversary does not have the usufruct, right of way, water, higher building, prospect, projection, or attachment. These are also real, but negative. There is no such action for disputes about corporeal things. There the party out of possession pleads as plaintiff, and no action exists for the possessor to assert that the thing does not belong to the plaintiff. It is true though, that there is one case in which the possessor assumes the role of plaintiff. More is said about this in the Digest. 3. The actions we have mentioned, and others similar, rest on statute or state law. There are others, real and personal, developed in the praetor's jurisdiction. We must give examples. A real action commonly given by the praetor is the one where the plaintiff alleges fictitiously that something has become his by usucapion, when in fact it has not; or, the other way around, that his opponent has not usucapted when in fact he has. 4. Suppose a thing has been delivered on a basis sufficient in law, e.g. sale, gift, dowry, or legacy, but the recipient has not yet become owner. If he now loses possession, he has no standard real action to claim it. The actions of the state law were given for ownership. It was obviously hard that there was no action here. So the praetor invented the one in which the plaintiff out of possession pleads that he usucapted the thing and, with that modification, vindicates it as his own. It is called the Publician action, because the praetor Publicius was first to put it in the edict. 5. An example of the other case is this. Suppose someone is away on state business or is a prisoner of war; he usucapts a thing belonging to a person back home. When the possessor returns from his absence on state business, the owner has a year to bring an action based on a rescission of the usucapion, i.e. he asserts that usucapion has not run in favour of the possessor and that on that basis he himself is owner. The same equitable considerations led the praetor to adapt this claim for some other plaintiffs. This is more fully treated in the Digest or Pandects. 6. Again, suppose a conveyance in fraud of creditors. When the creditors get possession of the debtor's assets under judgment of the governor, they are allowed to claim the thing conveyed with the conveyance set aside, i.e. they plead on the assumption that it was never delivered and thus remained one of the debtor's assets. 7. The Servian action and the quasi-Servian, called the action on a mortgage, are also praetorian. The Servian lies for claim to the goods of an agricultural tenant. These are security for the rent. The quasi-Servian action is used by creditors to enforce their pledges and mortgages. This action on mortgage draws no distinction between pledge and mortgage. Both terms can be used whenever a debtor and creditor agree that some item of property shall be security for the debt. In some contexts there is a difference. For 'pledge' properly applies to a thing which is immediately handed over to the creditor, especially to a movable, while we use 'mortgage', in its narrower meaning, where the thing is charged by agreement, without being handed over. // 8. There are also personal

8 appellatione contineri dicimus. In personam quoque actiones ex sua iurisdictione propositas habet praetor. veluti de pecunia constituta, ʿcui similis videʾbatur recepticia: sed ex nostra constitutione[1], cum ʿet, si quid plenius habebat, hoc in pecuniam conʾstitutam transfusum est, ea quasi supervacua iussa ʿest cum sua auctoritate a nostris legibus recedereʾ. item praetor proposuit de peculio servorum filiorumque familias et[2] ex qua quaeritur, an actor iura-

9 verit, et alias complures. De pecunia autem constituta cum omnibus agitur, quicumque vel pro se vel pro alio soluturos se constituerint, nulla scilicet stipulatione interposita. nam alioquin si stipulanti pro-

10 miserint, iure civili tenentur. Actiones[3] autem de peculio ideo adversus patrem dominumve comparavit praetor, quia licet ex contractu filiorum servorumve ipso iure non teneantur, aequum tamen esset peculio tenus, quod veluti patrimonium est filiorum

11 filiarumque, item servorum, condemnari eos. Item si quis postulante adversario iuraverit deberi sibi pecuniam quam peteret, neque ei solvatur, iustissime accommodat ei talem actionem, per quam non illud quaeritur, an ei pecunia debeatur, sed an iuraverit.

12 Poenales quoque actiones ʿbeneʾ[4] multas ex sua iurisdictione introduxit: veluti adversus eum qui quid ex albo eius corrupisset: et in eum qui patronum vel parentem in ius vocasset, cum id non impetrasset: item adversus eum, qui vi exemerit eum qui in ius vocaretur, cuiusve dolo alias exemerit: et alias in-

13 numerabiles. Praeiudiciales actiones in rem esse videntur, quales sunt, per quas quaeritur, an aliquis liber vel an libertus sit, vel de partu agnoscendo. ex quibus fere una illa legitimam causam habet, per quam quaeritur, an aliquis liber sit: ceterae ex ipsius

14 praetoris iurisdictione substantiam capiunt. [5]ʿSic ʾitaque discretis actionibus certum est non posse ʾactorem rem suam ita ab aliquo petere ʿsi paret eum ʾʾdare oportereʾ: nec enim quod actoris est id ei dari ʾoportet, quia scilicet dari cuiquam id intellegitur, ʾquod ita datur, ut eius fiat, nec res quae iam actoʾris est ʿmagisʾ eius fieri potest. plane odio furum, ʾquo magis pluribus actionibus teneantur, ʿeffectumʾ ʾest, ut extra poenam dupli aut quadrupli rei reciʾpiendae nomine fures etiam hac actione teneantur ʾʾsi paret eos dare oportereʾ, quamvis sit adversus ʾeos etiam haec ʿin remʾ actio, per quam rem suam

15 ʾquis esse petit. Appellamus autem in rem quidem ʾactiones vindicationes: in personam vero actiones, ʾquibus dare facere oportere intenditur, condictiones. ʾcondicere ʿenimʾ est denuntiare prisca lingua: nunc ʾvero ʿabusiveʾ dicimus condictionem actionem in perʾsonam esse, qua actor intendit dari sibi oportere: ʾnulla enim hoc tempore eo nomine denuntiatio fit.ʾ

16 Sequens illa divisio est, quod quaedam actiones rei persequendae gratia comparatae sunt, quaedam poenae persequendae, quaedam mixtae sunt.

17 Rei persequendae causa comparatae sunt omnes in rem actiones. earum vero actionum, quae in personam sunt, hae quidem quae ex contractu nascuntur fere omnes rei persequendae causa comparatae videntur: veluti quibus mutuam pecuniam vel in stipulatum deductam petit actor, item commodati, depositi, mandati, pro socio, ex empto vendito, locato conducto. plane si depositi agetur eo nomine, quod tumultus incendii ruinae naufragii causa depositum sit, in duplum actionem praetor reddit, si modo cum ipso apud quem depositum sit aut cum herede eius ex dolo ipsius agitur: quo casu mixta est actio.

18 Ex maleficiis vero proditae actiones aliae tantum poenae persequendae sunt, aliae tam poenae quam rei persequendae et ob id mixtae sunt. poenam tantum persequitur quis actione furti: sive enim manifesti agatur quadrupli sive nec

---

manifesti dupli, de sola poena agitur: nam ipsam rem propria actione persequitur quis, id est suam esse petens, sive fur ipse eam rem possideat, sive alius quilibet: eo amplius adversus furem etiam con-

19 dictio est rei. Vi autem bonorum raptorum actio mixta est, quia in quadruplo[6] rei persecutio continetur, poena autem tripli est. sed et legis Aquiliae actio de damno mixta est, non solum si adversus infitiantem in duplum agatur, sed interdum et si in simplum quisque agit. veluti si quis hominem claudum aut luscum occiderit, qui in eo anno integer et magni pretii fuerit: tanti[7] enim damnatur, quanti is homo in eo anno plurimi[8] fuerit, secundum iam traditam divisionem. ʿitem mixta est actio contra eos, ʿqui relicta sacrosanctis ecclesiis vel aliis venerabiliʾbus locis legati vel fideicommissi nomine dare distuʾlerint usque adeo, ut etiam in iudicium vocarentur: ʾtunc etenim et ipsam rem vel pecuniam quae relicta ʾest dare compelluntur et aliud tantum pro poena, et ʾideo in duplum eius fit condemnatio.ʾ

20 Quaedam actiones mixtam causam optinere videntur tam in rem quam in personam. qualis est familiae erciscundae actio, quae competit coheredibus de dividenda hereditate: item communi dividundo, quae inter eos redditur, inter quos aliquid commune[9] est, ut id dividatur: item finium regundorum, quae inter eos agitur qui confines agros habent. in quibus tribus iudiciis permittitur iudici rem alicui ex litigatoribus ex bono et aequo adiudicare et, si unius pars praegravari videbitur, eum invicem certa pecunia alteri condemnare.

21 Omnes autem actiones vel in simplum conceptae sunt vel in duplum vel in triplum vel in qua-

22 druplum: ulterius autem nulla actio extenditur. In simplum agitur veluti ex stipulatione, ex mutui datione, ex empto vendito, locato conducto, mandato

23 et denique ex aliis compluribus causis. In duplum agimus veluti furti nec manifesti, damni iniuriae ex lege Aquilia, depositi ex quibusdam casibus: item servi corrupti, quae competit in eum, cuius hortatu consiliove servus alienus fugerit aut contumax adversus dominum factus est aut luxuriose vivere coeperit aut denique quolibet modo deterior factus sit (in qua actione etiam earum rerum, quae fugiendo servus abstulit, aestimatio deducitur): item ex legato, ʿquod venerabilibus locis relictum est, se-

24 ʾcundum ea quae supra diximusʾ[10]. Tripli vero, ʿcum quidam maiorem verae aestimationis quantitatem ʾin libello conventionis inseruit, ut ex hac causa viaʾtores, id est exsecutores litium, ampliorem summam ʾsportularum nomine exegerint: tunc enim quod[11] ʾpropter eorum causam damnum passus fuerit reus, ʾid triplum ab actore consequetur, ut in hoc triplo et ʾsimplum, in quo damnum passus est, connumeretur. ʾquod nostra constitutio[12] induxit, quae in nostro coʾdice fulget, ex qua[13] dubio procul est ex lege con-

25 ʾdicticiam[14] emanareʾ. Quadrupli veluti furti manifesti, item de eo, quod metus causa factum sit, deque ea pecunia, quae in hoc data sit, ut is cui datur calumniae causa negotium alicui faceret vel non faceret: ʿitem ex lege condicticia a nostra constitutione ʾoritur, in quadruplum condemnationem imponens his ʾexsecutoribus litium, qui contra nostrae constitutio-

26 ʾnis[15] normam a reis quicquam exegerintʾ. Sed furti quidem nec manifesti actio et servi corrupti a ceteris, de quibus simul locuti sumus, eo differt, quod hae actiones omnimodo dupli sunt: at illae, id est damni iniuriae ex lege Aquilia et interdum depositi, infitiatione duplicantur, in confitentem autem in simplum dantur: ʿsed illa, quae de his competit, quae ʾrelicta venerabilibus locis sunt, non solum infitiatione ʿduplicaturʾ[16], sed et si distulerit relicti solutionem, ʾusque quo iussu magistratuum nostrorum convenia-

---

(1) *Cod.* 4, 18, 2   (2) et] *P*, om. *BE*   (3) τὴν δὲ de peculio ἀγωγήν *Θ*   (4) bene] *Wa*, pene *B*, praetor bene *PEWb*   (5) *Gai.* 4, 4. 5. 18   (6) quadruplum *BPE*

(7) tantum *libri*   (8) plurimi] pl. et magni pretii *libri*

(9) commune] *PE*, ex quacumque causa comm. *B cum Θ*   (10) § 19   (11) quod] id quod *libri*   (12) *Cod.* 3, 10, 2   (13) ex qua] *BW cum Θ*, quam *PE*   (14) condicticia *libri*   (15) *Cod.* 3, 2, 5   (16) *sic P*, duplicantur *BEa*

actions which emanated from the praetor's jurisdiction. There is the action on a money undertaking. Very similar was the action on a banker's guarantee. By our pronouncement we have abolished the latter, having first made it superfluous by transferring any extra scope it had to the money undertaking. The praetor also introduced the action on the personal fund of slaves and sons, and the action on the question whether the plaintiff swore an oath, and numerous others. 9. The action on a money undertaking lies against anyone who has undertaken to pay, whether for himself or another. This assumes of course that the undertaking is not by stipulation. Someone who promises in reply to a stipulator's question becomes liable at state law. 10. The praetor introduced the action on a personal fund, maintainable against fathers or owners, because the old state law did not automatically make them liable on contracts of sons or slaves. It is reasonable that they should be liable up to the limit of the personal fund. For sons and daughters and even slaves the fund operates in effect as private property. 11. Suppose a plaintiff is required by his opponent to swear the money claimed is due; he takes the oath, but still the money is not paid. The praetor very justly gives him an action solely on the question whether he took the oath, not whether the money is due. 12. In the exercise of his jurisdiction he also wisely introduced many penal actions, e.g. for falsifying the album, or summoning a patron or parent to court without special permission, or forcibly abducting a person summoned to court or intentionally procuring such abduction; and countless others. 13. Pre-judicial actions are classed as real. These ask whether a person is free, or whether a person is a freedman; and some inquire whether children should be recognized. Perhaps only one of these – on freedom – can claim a basis in state law. The rest are praetorian. 14. This distinction between real and personal actions means that a plaintiff definitely cannot claim something of his own from another by a pleading in the form 'If it appears that he ought to give.' What a plaintiff owns cannot be due to be given to him, because the legal construction of 'give to someone' is 'so give it as to make it his'. What is his already cannot be made more so. No doubt it was from hatred of thieves, to multiply their liabilities, that the law came to allow against them not only the claims for twofold or fourfold penal damages but also the pleading 'If it appears they ought to give'. This claim with its restorative function is allowed against the thief despite the fact there also lies against him the real action by which a person claims the thing is his. 15. We call real actions 'vindications'; the personal actions in the form 'ought to give or do' are actions of debt, in Latin 'condictiones'. Earlier the word 'condicere' signified the giving of notice. Nowadays there is no giving of notice in this context, but we inaccurately keep the name for the personal action in which the plaintiff says something ought to be given to him. 16. A second division of actions is this: some have a restorative function, some are penal, and some are hybrid. 17. All real actions are restorative; among personal actions those from contracts are almost all restorative. e.g. where a plaintiff claims money lent or due on a stipulation, or when he sues on loan for use, deposit, mandate, partnership, sale, or hire. It is true though that if someone alleges that a deposit had to be made by reason of riot, fire, collapse, or shipwreck, the praetor offers an action for double damages. The doubling happens if the claim is made against the actual depositee, or against the depositee's heir for wilful default. That action is hybrid. 18. Among actions for wrongs some are exclusively penal and others aim to

penalize and to restore. The latter are hybrid. An action for theft has an exclusively penal aim. The fourfold damages for manifest theft and double for non-manifest are all penalty. The plaintiff has separate actions for the restorative function, whether the thief has the thing or anyone else has it; he has the action asserting the thing is his and, on top of that, he has the action of debt against the thief. 19. The action for things taken by force is hybrid, because the fourfold award includes restoration. The penalty is threefold. The action on the Aquilian Act for loss is also hybrid, not only when brought for double against a defendant denying liability but sometimes even when brought for single damages, e.g. where a slave has been killed when lame or one-eyed, who was fit and more valuable within that year. As already explained, the condemnation is then for the highest price in the year. There is another hybrid action against those who delay giving over legacies and trusts to holy churches and other sacred places for so long that they have to be taken to court. They are then compelled to hand over the thing or the money left and as much again as penalty. That is how their condemnation comes to be for double. 20. Some actions are hybrid in a different sense, between real and personal. One is the action for partitioning an estate, which lies to coheirs for division. Another is the action for dividing common property, which lies to co-owners for division. Another is the action for determining boundaries, brought between adjacent landowners. In these three, the judge is allowed to distribute the thing among the litigants as seems fair and reasonable, and then, if one has more than his share, the judge can subject him to a money condemnation in favour of the other. 21. Actions all claim one, two, three, or fourfold damages. None goes higher. 22. Actions for single damages include those on stipulation, the loan called mutuum, sale, hire, mandate, and many others. 23. Actions for double include those for non-manifest theft, for wrongful loss under the Aquilian Act, for some instances of deposit; also for corruption of a slave. This last lies against someone whose encouragement or advice causes another's slave to escape, to behave in contempt of his master, to turn to luxurious living, or to become worse in way whatsoever. The calculation of damages includes the value of things which the absconding slave takes. Another action for double arises from legacies left to sacred places, mentioned above. 24. An action for threefold lies when someone puts in his writ of summons an exaggerated valuation of the sum at issue, enabling the officers of the court who administer litigation to demand higher fees. The defendant who has to pay them more can claim it threefold from the plaintiff. The threefold award includes restoration. This was introduced by our own pronouncement, now in our Codex, which puts it beyond doubt that a statute-based action of debt lies. 25. An action for fourfold lies for manifest theft, for intimidation, for money given to someone to bribe him to do or not do something to further vexatious litigation. Here again a statute-based action of debt lies under our enactment, which imposes this fourfold penalty on court officials who exact anything from defendants in breach of the rules in our pronouncement. 26. The actions for non-manifest theft and for corruption of a slave differ from the others mentioned with them in being invariably for double. The others, i.e. the Aquilian actions for wrongful loss and some for deposit, are doubled only on denial of liability. Someone who admits liability is only liable for single damages. The action for legacies to sacred institutions is doubled not only on denial but also when delay in paying lasts until the order of one of our magistrates brings the defaulter to court. // Someone

tur, in confitentem vero et antequam iussu magistra-
27 tuum conveniatur solventem simpli redditur. Item actio de eo, quod metus causa factum sit, a ceteris, de quibus simul locuti sumus, eo differt, quod eius natura tacite continetur, ut, qui iudicis iussu ipsam rem actori restituat, absolvatur. quod in ceteris casibus non ita est, sed omnimodo quisque in quadruplum condemnatur, quod est et in furti manifesti actione.
28 Actionum autem quaedam bonae fidei sunt, quaedam stricti iuris. [1]bonae fidei sunt hae: ex empto vendito, locato conducto, negotiorum gestorum, mandati, depositi, pro socio, tutelae, commodati, pigneraticia, familiae erciscundae, communi dividundo, praescriptis verbis, quae de aestimato proponitur, et ea, quae ex permutatione competit, et hereditatis petitio. quamvis enim usque adhuc incertum erat, sive inter bonae fidei iudicia connumeranda sit sive non, nostra tamen constitutio[2] aperte eam esse bonae fidei
29 disposuit. Fuerat antea et rei uxoriae actio ex bonae fidei iudiciis: sed cum pleniorem esse ex stipulatu actionem invenientes omne ius, quod res uxoria ante habebat, cum multis divisionibus in ex stipulatu actionem, quae de dotibus exigendis proponitur, transtulimus[3], merito rei uxoriae actione sublata ex stipulatu, quae pro ea introducta est, naturam bonae fidei iudicii tantum in exactione dotis meruit, ut bonae fidei sit. sed et tacitam ei dedimus hypothecam: praeferri autem aliis creditoribus in hypothecis tunc censuimus, cum ipsa mulier de dote sua experiatur, cuius solius providentia hoc induximus.
30 In bonae fidei autem iudiciis libera potestas permitti videtur iudici ex bono et aequo aestimandi, quantum actori restitui debeat. [4]in quo et illud continetur, ut, si quid invicem actorem praestare oporteat, eo compensato in reliquum[5] sit is cum quo actum est condemnari debeat. sed et in strictis iudiciis ex rescripto divi Marci opposita doli mali exceptione compensatio inducebatur. sed nostra constitutio[6] eas compensationes, quae iure aperto nituntur, latius introduxit, ut actiones ipso iure minuant sive in rem sive personales sive alias quascumque, excepta sola depositi actione, cui aliquid compensationis nomine opponi satis impium esse credidimus, ne sub prae-
31 textu compensationis depositarum rerum quis ex actione defraudetur. Praeterea quasdam actiones arbitrarias id est ex arbitrio iudicis pendentes appellamus, in quibus nisi arbitrio iudicis is cum quo agitur actori satisfaciat, veluti rem restituat vel exhibeat vel solvat vel ex noxali causa servum dedat, condemnari debeat. sed istae actiones tam in rem quam in personam inveniuntur. In rem veluti Publiciana, Serviana de rebus coloni, quasi Serviana, quae etiam hypothecaria vocatur: in personam veluti quibus de eo agitur, quod aut metus causa aut dolo malo factum est, item qua[7] id, quod certo loco promissum est, petitur. ad exhibendum quoque actio ex arbitrio iudicis pendet. in his enim actionibus et ceteris similibus permittitur iudici ex bono et aequo secundum cuiusque rei de qua actum est naturam aestimare, quemadmodum actori satisfieri oporteat.
32 Curare autem debet iudex, ut omnimodo, quantum possibile est, certae pecuniae vel rei sententiam ferat, etiam si de incerta quantitate apud eum actum est.
33 [8]Si quis agens in intentione sua plus complexus fuerit, quam ad eum pertinet, causa cadebat, id est rem amittebat, nec facile in integrum a praetore restituebatur, nisi minor erat viginti quinque annis. huic enim sicut in aliis causis causa cognita succurrebatur[9], si lapsus iuventute fuerat, ita et in hac causa succurri solitum erat. sane si tam magna causa iusti erroris interveniebat, ut etiam constantissimus quisque labi posset, etiam maiori viginti quinque annis succurrebatur: veluti si quis totum legatum petierit, post deinde prolati fuerint codicilli, quibus aut pars legati adempta sit aut quibusdam aliis legata data sint, quae efficiebant, ut plus petiisse videretur petitor quam dodrantem, atque ideo lege
33a Falcidia legata minuebantur. [9]Plus autem quattuor modis petitur: re, tempore, loco, causa. re: veluti si quis pro decem aureis qui ei debebantur viginti petierit, aut si is, cuius ex parte res est, totam eam vel maiore ex parte suam esse intenderit.
33b Tempore: veluti si quis ante diem vel ante condicionem petierit. qua ratione enim qui tardius solvit, quam solvere deberet, minus solvere intellegitur, eadem ratione qui praemature petit plus petere vide-
33c tur. [10]Loco plus petitur, veluti cum quis id, quod certo loco sibi stipulatus est, alio loco petit sine commemoratione illius loci, in quo sibi dari stipulatus fuerit: verbi gratia si is, qui ita stipulatus fuerit Ephesi dare spondes?, Romae pure intendat dari sibi oportere. ideo autem plus petere intellegitur, quia utilitatem, quam habuit promissor, si Ephesi solveret, adimit ei pura intentione: propter quam causam alio loco petenti arbitraria actio proponitur, in qua scilicet ratio habetur utilitatis, quae promissori competitura fuisset, si illo loco solveret. quae utilitas plerumque in mercibus maxima invenitur, veluti vino oleo frumento, quae per singulas regiones diversa habent pretia: sed et pecuniae numeratae non in omnibus regionibus sub isdem usuris fenerantur. si quis tamen Ephesi petat, id est eo loco petat, quo ut sibi detur stipulatus est, pura actione recte agit: idque etiam praetor monstrat, scilicet quia
33d utilitas solvendi salva est promissori. Huic autem, qui loco plus petere intellegitur, proximus est is qui causa plus petit: ut ecce si quis ita a te stipulatus sit hominem Stichum aut decem aureos dare spondes?, deinde alterutrum petat, veluti hominem tantum aut decem[11] tantum. ideo autem plus petere intellegitur, quia in eo genere stipulationis promissoris est electio, utrum pecuniam an hominem solvere malit: qui igitur pecuniam tantum vel hominem tantum sibi dari oportere intendit, eripit electionem adversario et eo modo suam quidem meliorem eius dicionem facit, adversarii vero sui deteriorem. qua de causa talis in ea re prodita est actio, ut quis intendat hominem Stichum aut aureos decem sibi dari oportere, id est ut eodem modo peteret, quo[12] stipulatus est. praeterea si quis generaliter hominem stipulatus sit et specialiter Stichum petat, aut generaliter vinum stipulatus specialiter Campanum petat, aut generaliter purpuram stipulatus sit, deinde specialiter Tyriam petat: plus petere intellegitur, quia electionem adversario tollit, cui stipulationis iure liberum fuit aliud solvere, quam quod peteretur. quin etiam licet vilissimum sit quod quis petat, nihilo minus plus petere intellegitur, quia saepe accidit, ut promissori facilius sit illud solvere, quod maioris
33e pretii est. Sed haec quidem antea in usu fuerant: postea autem lex Zenoniana et nostra[13] rem coartavit. et si quidem tempore plus fuerit petitum, quid statui oportet, Zenonis divae memoriae loquitur constitutio: sin autem quantitate vel alio modo plus fuerit petitum, omne, si quid forte damnum ex hac causa acciderit ei[14], contra quem plus petitum fuerit, commissa tripli condemnatione, sicut supra diximus,
34 puniatur. Si minus in intentione complexus fuerit actor, quam ad eum pertineret, veluti si, cum ei decem deberentur, quinque sibi dari oportere intendat, aut cum totus fundus eius esset, partem dimidiam suam esse petierit, sine periculo agit: in reliquum enim nihilo minus iudex adversarium in eodem iudicio condemnat[15] ex constitutione divae memo-
35 riae Zenonis. [16]Si quis aliud pro alio intenderit,

---

(1) *Gai.* 4, 62 (2) *Cod.* 3, 31, 12 § 3 (3) *Cod.* 5, 13, 1
(4) *conf. Gai.* 4, 61 (5) *sic P*, reliquo *BE* (6) *Cod.* 4, 31, 14
(7) qua] *B*, cum *PE* (8) *Gai.* 4, 53 (9) succurrebat *B*
(10) *Gai.* 4, 53a. 53b (11) *Gai.* 4, 53e (12) decem] *BP*, d.
aureos *E* (13) quo] *B*, quo sibi *P*, quod sibi *E* (14) *Cod.*

3, 10, 1. 2 (14) damnum...ei] *Ea*, damnum ut in sportulis...ei *BEb*, damnum...ei in sportulis *P*: καί τι ἐντεῦθεν ζημία συμβῇ τῷ ἐναγομένῳ. οἷον σπορτούλων πλειόνων δόσις Θ (15) condemnat] *PEΘ*, ei condemnat *B* (16) *Gai.* 4, 55

who admits liability and pays before being summoned, need only pay single damages. 27. There is a difference between the action for intimidation and the others mentioned with it. One who complies with the judge's order to restore the thing itself must be absolved. It is not the same in the other cases, where the defendant always has to pay fourfold, as in the action for manifest theft. 28. Some actions are based on good faith, some on strict law. Those based on good faith are: sale, hire, uninvited intervention, mandate, deposit, partnership, guardianship, loan for use, pledge, partition of an estate, division of common property, also the action with a special preface which is framed for sale or return, and the similar action for exchange, also the claim for an inheritance. Until quite recently it was in doubt whether this last counted as based on good faith. Our legislation makes clear that it does. 29. With these formerly stood the action for a wife's property. We, finding the action on a stipulation to have a wider scope, transferred the law of the action for a wife's property, with all its refinements, to the species of the action on stipulation propounded for recovering dowries. It was wise at the same time to convert to the basis of good faith the version of the action on stipulation which replaced the abolished action for a wife's property. Solely in its role as the instrument for demanding dowries, this is accordingly now a good faith action. To it we have also attached a tacit mortgage, but with priority over other mortgagees only when the woman herself is suing for her own dowry. This reform was introduced solely for her protection. 30. Where a trial is founded on good faith, the law gives the judge a free discretion to work out the sum to be restored to the plaintiff on the basis of what is fair and reasonable. This includes the principle that, if the plaintiff is under a duty to make some performance for the defendant, the latter should be condemned only for the balance after set-off. Even for trials founded on strict law, a written reply of the Emperor Marcus allowed a defendant to claim a set-off by using a plea of deceit. Our own pronouncement has made set-off more widely available where the counterclaim has a sound legal basis. We provided that real and personal claims, and any others, should be automatically reduced by it, with the single exception of the action on deposit. We considered it immoral that such an action should be resisted by invoking set-off and we were concerned about people being cheated out of things deposited on the pretext of counterclaims. 31. Next, discretionary actions. These turn on the discretion of the judge. The defendant is to be condemned only if he does not comply with an order, made in the judge's discretion, to satisfy the plaintiff by restoring the thing, or producing it, or making payment, or giving up a slave noxally liable. This category cuts across the classification into real and personal. Real examples are the Publician action, the Servian action concerning the property of agricultural tenants, the quasi-Servian, also called the mortgage action. Personal examples are the actions for intimidation, for deceit, and also the action on a promise for performance at a specific place. So also the action for production of a thing. In all these actions, and others similar, the judge is allowed to apply the principle of fairness and reasonableness to work out, according to the nature of the precise issue, exactly how the plaintiff's claim ought to be met. 32. When it comes to judgment, the judge must see that, so far as is possible for him to do it, he reduces even unliquidated claims to orders for fixed sums or specific things. 33. It used to be the rule that the plaintiff lost his case if he included in his principal pleading more than his claim warranted. He was unlikely to get a decree from the praetor for restitution to the status quo, unless he was below the age of twenty-five. Under that age the practice was to relieve the minor, just as it was usual in other situations, after examining the facts, to help him if his youth had led him into a mistake. It is true though that, if there was some obvious reason for a justifiable mistake which even a scrupulous man might have made, a person over twenty-five might also hope for a remedy. An example would be where he claimed the whole amount of a legacy, and then codicils were produced which revoked part, or else gave legacies to others with the effect that this plaintiff's claim broke the nine twelfths limit to which legacies had to be scaled back under the Falcidian Act. 33a. There are four types of overclaim, in amount, time, place, or basis. Excess in amount happens when a debt of 10 is claimed as 20, or someone with a share claims the whole or a larger share than he has. 33b. Excess in time happens where the claim is made before it is due, or before a condition has been satisfied. A late payer pays less; one who claims too early claims too much. 33c. Excess in place happens where a stipulation for performance at one place is enforced without mention of the place appointed for performance: he stipulates 'Do you solemnly promise to give at Ephesus?' and then at Rome pleads an unqualified 'ought to be given'. This is overclaim because the unqualified pleading takes from the promissor the advantage of performing at Ephesus. To deal with this, one of the discretionary actions is available for making the claim at a different place. Account is then taken of any advantage which the promissor would have had in performing at the named place. In relation to commodities like wine, oil and grain, such advantages are often very considerable. They often command different prices in different regions. Even cash is available at different rates of interest in different places. If one does claim at Ephesus – at the actual place stipulated – it is right to advance the unqualified pleading. The praetorian edict shows the same thing, for the very good reason that the promissor keeps any advantage he has. 33d. Very similar to overclaim in place is excess in basis. Suppose someone takes a stipulation from you in these terms, 'Do you promise to give me the slave Stichus or 10?' and then claims the one or the other, only the slave or only the 10. He overclaims because a stipulation in those terms leaves it to the promissor whether to give the money or the slave. One who pleads without qualification, that the other ought to give him the money or ought to give him the slave, deprives his opponent of this choice. He improves his own position and makes the other's worse. To cope with this, there is an action which allows the plaintiff to plead that he ought to be given either the slave Stichus or 10. That allows him to match his claim to the terms of his stipulation. Suppose that, having stipulated generally for a slave, he claims Stichus in particular, or for wine and he claims specifically Campanian, or for purple and he claims Tyrian. He too overclaims, because he deprives his opponent of a choice. The stipulation gave him freedom to perform other than as claimed. It is still overclaim if the plaintiff claims the very cheapest thing within the description, since it can often suit the promissor to give a more expensive one. 33e. The earlier rules have been restricted by reforms of Zeno and ourselves. Where there is overclaim in time, the pronouncement made by Zeno, of blessed memory, now states what must be done. Where there is overclaim in amount or in one of the other ways, then, as we have said above, all loss that is inflicted on the person against whom the excess claim is made is remedied by the imposition of a threefold penalty. 34. Underclaim entails no danger. Suppose 10 are due, and he claims 5; or he claims half a piece of land when all of it is his. The pronouncement of Zeno, of blessed memory, allows the judge to condemn the opponent for the unclaimed balance in the same trial. // 35. If a plaintiff's principal

'nihil eum periclitari' 'placet, sed in eodem iudicio 'cognita veritate errorem suum corrigere ei permitti-'mus,' 'veluti si is, qui hominem Stichum petere de-'beret, Erotem petierit, aut si quis ex testamento sibi 'dari oportere intenderit, quod ex stipulatu debetur.' 36 Sunt praeterea quaedam actiones, quibus non solidum quod debetur nobis persequimur, sed modo solidum consequimur, modo minus. ut ecce si in peculium filii servive agamus: nam si non minus in peculio sit, quam persequimur, in solidum pater dominusve condemnatur: si vero minus inveniatur, eatenus condemnat iudex, quatenus in peculio sit. quemadmodum autem peculium intellegi debeat, suo ordine 37 proponemus. Item si 'de dote' iudicio mulier agat, placet eatenus maritum condemnari debere, quatenus facere possit, id est quatenus facultates eius patiuntur. itaque si dotis quantitati concurrant facultates eius, in solidum damnatur: si minus, in tantum quantum facere potest. propter retentionem quoque dotis repetitio minuitur: nam ob impensas in res dotales factas marito retentio[1] concessa est, quia ipso iure necessariis sumptibus dos minuitur, 'sicut ex latio-38 'ribus digestorum libris cognoscere liceat'. Sed[2] si quis cum parente suo patronove agat, item si socius cum socio iudicio societatis agat, non plus actor consequitur, quam adversarius eius facere potest. idem est, si quis ex donatione sua conveniatur. 39 Compensationes quoque oppositae plerumque efficiunt, ut minus quisque consequatur, quam ei debeatur: namque ex bono et aequo, [3]'habita ratione 'eius, quod invicem actorem ex eadem causa prae-'stare oporteret, in reliquum eum cum quo actum est 40 'condemnaret'[4], sicut iam dictum est[5]. Eum quoque, qui creditoribus suis bonis cessit, si postea aliquid adquisierit, quod idoneum emolumentum habeat, ex integro in id quod facere potest creditores cum eo experiuntur: 'inhumanum enim erat spoliatum for-'tunis suis in solidum damnari.'

VII[6]
QUOD CUM EO QUI IN ALIENA POTESTATE EST NEGOTIUM GESTUM ESSE DICITUR.

[7]'Quia tamen superius[8] mentionem habuimus de 'actione, quae[9] in peculium filiorum familias servo-'rumque agitur: opus est, ut de hac actione et de 'ceteris, quae eorundem nomine in parentes domi-'nosve dari solent, diligentius admoneamus.' et quia, sive cum servis negotium gestum sit sive cum his, qui in potestate parentis sunt, fere eadem iura servantur, ne verbosa fiat disputatio, dirigamus sermonem in personam servi dominique, idem intellecturi de liberis quoque et parentibus, quorum in potestate sunt. nam si quid in his proprie observetur, separatim ostendemus[10].
1 [11]Si igitur iussu domini cum servo negotium gestum erit, in solidum praetor adversus dominum actionem pollicetur, scilicet quia qui ita contrahit 2 fidem domini sequi videtur. Eadem ratione praetor duas alias in solidum actiones pollicetur, quarum altera exercitoria, altera institoria appellatur. exercitoria tunc locum habet, cum quis servum suum magistrum navis[12] praeposuerit et quid cum eo eius rei gratia cui praepositus erit contractum fuerit. ideo autem exercitoria vocatur, quia exercitor appellatur is, ad quem cottidianus navis quaestus pertinet. institoria tunc locum habet, cum quis tabernae forte aut cuilibet negotiationi servum praeposuerit et quid cum eo eius rei causa, cui praepositus erit, contractum fuerit. ideo autem institoria appellatur, quia qui negotiationibus praeponuntur institores vocantur. 2a Istas tamen duas actiones praetor reddit et si liberum quis hominem aut alienum servum navi aut

tabernae aut cuilibet negotiationi praeposuerit, scilicet quia eadem aequitatis ratio etiam eo casu inter-3 veniebat. Introduxit et aliam actionem praetor, quae tributoria vocatur. namque si servus in peculiari merce sciente domino negotietur et quid cum eo eius rei causa contractum erit, ita praetor ius dicit, ut, quidquid in his mercibus erit quodque inde receptum erit, id inter dominum, si quid ei debebitur, et ceteros creditores pro rata portione distribuatur. et quia ipsi domino distributionem permittit, si quis ex creditoribus queratur, quasi minus ei tributum sit, quam oportuerit, hanc ei actionem ac-4 commodat, quae tributoria appellatur. Praeterea introducta est actio de peculio deque eo, quod in rem domini versum erit, ut, quamvis sine voluntate domini negotium gestum erit, tamen sive quid in rem eius versum fuerit, id totum praestare debeat, sive quid non sit in rem eius versum, id eatenus praestare 4a debeat, quatenus peculium patitur. In rem autem domini versum intellegitur, quidquid necessario in rem eius impenderit servus, veluti si mutuatus pecuniam creditoribus eius[13] solverit aut aedificia ruentia fulserit aut familiae frumentum emerit vel etiam fundum aut quamlibet aliam rem necessariam mer-4b catus erit. Itaque si ex decem ut puta 'aureis', quos servus tuus a Titio mutuos accepit, creditori tuo quinque 'aureos' solverit, reliquos vero quinque quolibet modo consumpserit, pro quinque quidem in solidum damnari debes, pro ceteris vero quinque eatenus, quatenus in peculio sit: ex quo scilicet apparet, si toti decem 'aurei' in rem tuam versi fuerint, totos decem 'aureos' Titium consequi posse. licet enim una est actio, qua de peculio deque eo q..?? in rem domini versum sit agitur, tamen duas habet condemnationes. itaque iudex, apud quem de[14] ea actione agitur, ante dispicere solet, an in rem domini versum sit, nec aliter ad peculii aestimationem transit, quam si aut nihil in rem domini versum intellegatur aut 4c non totum. [15]Cum autem quaeritur, quantum in peculio sit, ante deducitur, quidquid servus domino quive eius in[16] potestate sit debet, et quod superest, id solum peculium intellegitur. aliquando tamen id, quod ei debet servus, qui in potestate domini sit, non deducitur ex peculio, veluti si is in huius ipsius peculio sit. quod eo pertinet, ut, si quid[17] vicario suo servus debeat, id ex peculio eius non deducatur.
5 Ceterum dubium non est, quin is quoque, qui iussu domini contraxerit cuique institoria vel exercitoria actio competit, de peculio deque eo, quod in rem domini versum est, agere possit: sed erit 'stultissimus', si omissa actione, qua 'facillime' solidum ex contractu consequi possit, se ad difficultatem perducat probandi in rem domini versum esse, vel habere servum peculium et tantum habere, ut solidum 5a sibi solvi possit. Is quoque, cui tributoria actio competit, aeque de peculio et in rem verso agere potest: sed sane huic modo tributoria expedit agere, modo de peculio et in rem verso. tributoria ideo expedit agere, quia in ea domini condicio praecipua non est, id est quod domino debetur non deducitur sed eiusdem iuris est dominus, cuius et ceteri creditores: at in actione de peculio ante deducitur quod domino debetur et in id quod reliquum est creditori dominus condemnatur. rursus de peculio ideo expedit agere, quod in hac actione totius peculii ratio habetur: at in tributoria eius tantum, quod negotiatur, et potest quisque tertia forte parte peculii aut quarta vel etiam minima negotiari, maiorem autem partem in praediis et mancipiis aut fenebri pecunia habere. prout ergo expedit, ita quisque vel hanc actionem vel illam eligere debet: certe qui potest probare in rem domini versum esse, de in rem verso 6 agere debet[18]. Quae diximus de servo et domino,

---

(1) retentio] P, quasi retentio BE (2) sed] $BP\Theta$, sed et E (3) $Gai.$ 4, 61   (4) $sic\ BPE$, condemnare vel condemnat dett.   (5) § 30
(6) Cf. Gai. 4. 69..74 Dig. 14. 15 Cod. 4, 25.26   (7) Gai. 4, 69
(8) 4, 6, 36   (9) qua Gai.   (10) ostendemus] dett. cum Θ,

ostendimus B, ostendamus PE (11) § 1. 2 similes Gaio 4, 70. 71   (12) sic B et Gai. 4, 71, navi PE (13) eius] B, eam $P^a E$, eius eam P^b (14) de del. (dett.)   (15) § 4c et 5 similes Gaio 4, 73. 74   (16) eius in] P^b, in eius Gai., in $BP^a E$ (17) quis BP (18) certe...debet] $PE\Theta$, om. B

pleading claims the wrong thing, he puts himself in no danger. When the truth appears we permit him, even in the course of the same trial, to amend his mistaken pleading. Suppose he should have claimed the slave Stichus but claimed Eros; or he said the thing ought to be given him under a will, when in fact it was due under a stipulation. 36. There are also some actions in which we do not insist on the whole of what is due to us but sometimes obtain the whole and sometimes less. Suppose, for instance, that we bring an action in respect of the personal fund of a son or slave. If the fund is as large as our claim, the father or owner is condemned for the whole amount. If it is less, the judge limits his condemnation to that amount. We will deal in the appropriate place with the question how the personal fund ought to be assessed. 37. Again, if a woman brings an action for her dowry, it is right that the husband should be condemned only to the limit of his ability to pay – that is, for as much as his wealth will bear. If his wealth equals the amount of the dowry, he is condemned for the whole sum; but if it comes to less, only to the limit of his ability. A claim to recover a dowry can also be reduced by a right of retention. Such a right is allowed to the husband for money expended on the dotal property: by operation of law a dowry is diminished by necessary expenditure on it. More details on this can be found in the Digest. 38. If someone sues a parent or patron, or if a partner sues another in an action on partnership, he again obtains no more than the opponent can pay. The same where an action is brought against a donor for a gift. 39. Another reason a plaintiff can end with less than he is owed is set-off. As has been said, fair and reasonable account is taken of the plaintiff's own duties arising from the same cause. Condemnation is for the balance. 40. Suppose a man surrenders his estate to his creditors but subsequently acquires something which makes him once again a man of property. The creditors can bring a fresh action against him, but only for what he can now afford to pay. It was a savage practice to condemn a man for the whole amount when he had already been stripped once of all his worldly wealth.

4 7 DEALING BY PERSONS WITHIN AUTHORITY

We mentioned before the action about the personal fund of sons and slaves. Now we need to go into more detail about it and the other actions against parents and owners in respect of the activities of dependent persons. Since the law is much the same whether the dealing is with a slave or a free dependant, to save time we shall focus on slaves and owners. We can assume the same rules for free dependants and their parents and shall deal separately with any points which apply only to them. 1. Where someone deals with a slave on the order of his owner, the praetor gives an action against the owner for the full amount. The obvious reason is that one who contracts in those circumstances relies directly on the credit of the owner. 2. For the same reason the praetor gives two other actions for full liability, the exercitorian and the institorian. The former lies where someone makes one of his slaves master of a ship, and then a contract is made with the slave in the course of the ship's business. The person in charge of the everyday business of a vessel is, in Latin, the 'exercitor'. That is how the action gets its name. The institorian action lies where someone puts a slave in charge of a shop or business, and then a contract is made with the slave in the course of his management. Here the name is from 'institor', the Latin for the manager of a business. 2a. The praetor gives these two actions even where the ship, or shop, or other business, is put under the management of a free man or of a slave of a

person other than the appointor. Clearly all these cases come within the same just rationale. 3. The praetor also brought in another action, the tributorian. If to his owner's knowledge a slave trades in goods from his personal fund, and a contract is made with him in that course of dealing, the law which the praetor lays down is that those goods and anything earned from them should be distributed in proportionate shares between the owner, if anything is owed to him, and the other creditors. He leaves this distribution to be made by the owner himself. He then gives this action, called the tributorian, to any creditor who wants to complain of having had too little 'attributed' to himself. This explains the name. 4. Besides these he also introduced the action on the personal fund and conversion to the owner's use. This lies even when the slave does some business other than at his owner's behest. It makes the owner answer in full for anything turned to his own advantage; for anything not so converted, he must answer to the limit of the personal fund. 4a. There is a conversion to the owner's use whenever the slave dutifully makes an outlay for him. For example, he borrows money and then he pays off the owner's creditors, or repairs deteriorating buildings, or buys household food, or even goes into the market for land or some other worthwhile thing. 4b. Suppose your slave borrows 10 from Titius, pays 5 to your creditor, and uses up the remaining 5 in some other way. For the first 5, you should be condemned in the full amount; for the rest, only up to the limit of the personal fund. Obviously, if all 10 had been converted to your advantage, Titius could have successfully sued you for the whole sum. There is only a single action aimed at the personal fund and conversion to the owner's advantage, but the amount of its condemnation is calculated on two bases. The practice is for the judge to look first for the conversion to the owner's use and only to move to the valuation of the personal fund if it seems that nothing, or not the whole amount, has been so converted. 4c. When the amount of the personal fund is worked out, a deduction has first to be made of anything owed by the slave to the owner or to a person under the owner's authority. Only the balance counts as the fund. Occasionally a debt to a person within his owner's authority is not deducted, as where the internal creditor is himself part of the fund. If a head slave owes something to his sub-slave, that debt is not deducted. 5. It is certainly true that someone who has contracted in reliance on the owner's order and someone who can use the exercitorian or the institorian can also turn to the action on personal fund and conversion. But it will be most unwise of him to abandon an action by which he can very easily recover the full amount of his claim and to embrace instead the difficulties of proving the conversion or the existence and sufficiency of the fund. 5a. One who can use the tributorian action can also turn to the action on personal fund and conversion. For him it is sometimes better to bring the one, sometimes the other. The advantage of the tributorian is that there the owner does not have a special position. A debt to the owner is not a prior charge; he has the same ranking as the other creditors. In the action on the personal fund the deduction of debts to the owner does have priority. The owner's condemnation to the creditor is only for the balance. The advantage of the action on the personal fund is that it extends to the entire fund. The tributorian only reaches the part of the fund which is traded. It is of course possible for someone to trade only a third or a quarter or even a smaller fraction of his personal fund, leaving the greater part in land, slaves, or money lent out at interest. Every plaintiff should therefore choose the action which is best for him in the circumstances. One who can prove a conversion to the owner's advantage should definitely sue in respect of that conversion. //

eadem intellegimus et de filio et filia aut nepote et
7 nepte, patre avove cuius in potestate sunt. Illud
proprie servatur in eorum persona, quod senatus
consultum Macedonianum prohibuit mutuas pecunias
dari eis, qui in parentis erunt potestate: et ei qui
crediderit denegatur actio tam adversus ipsum filium
filiamve nepotem neptemve, sive adhuc in potestate
sunt, sive morte parentis vel emancipatione suae potestatis esse coeperint, quam adversus patrem avumve,
sive habeat eos adhuc in potestate sive emancipaverit. quae ideo senatus prospexit, quia saepe one-
rati aere alieno creditarum pecuniarum, quas in luxu-
riam consumebant, vitae parentium insidiabantur.
8 Illud in summa admonendi sumus id, quod iussu
patris dominive contractum fuerit quodque in rem
eius versum fuerit, directo quoque posse a patre
dominove condici, tamquam si principaliter cum ipso
negotium gestum esset. ei quoque, qui vel exercitoria vel institoria actione tenetur, directo posse condici placet, quia huius quoque iussu contractum intellegitur.

VIII [1]
DE NOXALIBUS ACTIONIBUS.

[2] 'Ex maleficiis servorum, veluti si furtum fecerint'
aut bona rapuerint aut damnum dederint 'aut iniu-
'riam commiserint, noxales actiones proditae sunt,
"quibus domino damnato permittitur' aut litis aesti-
'mationem sufferre aut hominem[3] noxae dedere.'
1 Noxa autem est corpus quod nocuit, id est servus: noxia ipsum maleficium, veluti furtum damnum
2 rapina iniuria. Summa autem ratione permissum
est noxae deditione defungi: [4]'namque erat iniquum
'nequitiam eorum ultra ipsorum corpora dominis dam-
3 'nosam esse.' Dominus noxali iudicio servi sui
nomine conventus servum actori noxae dedendo liberatur. nec minus perpetuum eius dominium a domino
transfertur: si autem damnum ei cui deditus est re-
sarcierit quaesita pecunia, auxilio praetoris invito
4 domino manumittetur. [5]'Sunt autem constitutae
'noxales actiones aut legibus aut edicto praetoris:
'legibus veluti furti lege duodecim tabularum, damni
'iniuriae lege Aquilia: edicto praetoris veluti iniuriae-
5 'rum et vi bonorum raptorum. [5]Omnis autem noxalis
'actio caput sequitur. nam si servus tuus noxiam
'commiserit, quamdiu in tua potestate sit, tecum est
'actio: si in alterius potestatem pervenerit, cum illo
'incipit actio esse, aut si manumissus fuerit, directo
'ipse tenetur et extinguitur noxae deditio. ex diverso
'quoque directa actio noxalis esse incipit: nam si
'liber homo noxiam commiserit et is servus tuus esse
'coeperit (quod casibus quibusdam effici primo libro
'tradidimus[6]), incipit tecum esse noxalis actio, quae
6 'ante directa fuisset. [5]Si servus domino noxiam
'commiserit, actio nulla nascitur: namque inter do-
'minum et eum qui in eius potestate est nulla obli-
'gatio nasci potest. ideoque et si in alienam potesta-
'tem servus pervenerit aut manumissus fuerit, neque
'cum ipso neque cum eo, cuius nunc in potestate sit,
'agi potest. unde si alienus servus noxiam tibi com-
'miserit et is postea in potestate tua esse coeperit,
'intercidit actio, quia in eum casum deducta sit, in
'quo consistere non potuit: ideoque licet exierit de
'tua potestate, agere non potes,' quemadmodum si
'dominus in servum suum aliquid commiserit, nec si
'manumissus vel alienatus fuerit servus, ullam actio-
7 'nem contra dominum habere potest. 'Sed veteres
'quidem haec et in filiis familias masculis et feminis
'admiserunt. nova autem hominum conversatio huius-
'modi asperitatem recte respuendam esse existimavit

'et ab usu communi haec penitus recessit: quis enim
'patitur filium suum et maxime filiam in noxam alii
'dare, ut paene per corpus pater magis quam filius
'periclitetur, cum in filiabus etiam pudicitiae favor
'hoc bene excludit? et ideo placuit in servos tantum-
'modo noxales actiones esse proponendas, cum apud
'veteres legum commentatores invenimus saepius dic-
'tum ipsos filios familias pro suis delictis posse con-
'veniri.'

IX [7]
SI QUADRUPES PAUPERIEM FECISSE DICITUR.

Animalium nomine, quae ratione carent, si quidem[8] lascivia aut fervore aut feritate pauperiem fecerint, noxalis actio lege duodecim tabularum prodita
est (quae animalia si noxae dedantur, proficiunt reo
ad liberationem, quia ita lex duodecim tabularum
scripta est): puta si equus calcitrosus calce percusserit aut bos cornu petere solitus petierit. haec autem actio in his, quae contra naturam moventur,
locum habet: ceterum si genitalis sit feritas, cessat.
[9]denique si ursus fugit a domino et sic nocuit, non
potest quondam dominus conveniri, quia desinit dominus esse, ubi fera evasit. pauperies autem est damnum sine iniuria facientis datum: nec enim potest
animal iniuriam fecisse dici, quod sensu caret. haec
quod ad noxalem[10] actionem pertinet.
1 Ceterum sciendum est aedilicio edicto prohiberi
nos canem verrem aprum ursum leonem ibi habere,
qua vulgo iter fit: et si adversus ea factum erit et
nocitum homini libero esse dicetur, quod bonum et
aequum iudici videtur, tanti dominus condemnetur,
ceterarum rerum, quanti damnum datum sit, dupli.
praeter has autem aedilicias actiones et de pauperie
locum habebit: [11]numquam enim actiones praesertim
poenales de eadem re concurrentia alia aliam con-
sumit.

X [12]
DE HIS PER QUOS AGERE POSSUMUS.

[13]'Nunc admonendi sumus agere posse quemlibet aut
'suo nomine aut alieno. alieno veluti procuratorio tutorio
'curatorio, cum olim in usu fuisset alterius nomine agere
'non posse' nisi pro populo, pro libertate, pro tutela.
praeterea lege Hostilia permissum est furti agere
eorum nomine, qui apud hostes essent aut rei publicae causa abessent quive in eorum cuius tutela essent.
et quia hoc non minimam incommoditatem habebat,
quod alieno nomine neque agere neque excipere actionem licebat, coeperunt homines per procuratores
litigare: nam et morbus et aetas et necessaria pere-
grinatio itemque aliae multae[14] causae saepe impedimento sunt, quo minus rem suam ipsi exsequi
1 possint. Procurator neque certis verbis neque
praesente adversario, immo plerumque ignorante eo
constituitur: cuicumque enim permiseris rem tuam
2 agere aut defendere, is procurator intellegitur. [15]'Tu-
'tores et curatores quemadmodum constituuntur, primo
'libro expositum est.'

XI [16]
DE SATISDATIONIBUS.

'Satisdationum modus alius antiquitati placuit, alium
'novitas per usum amplexa est.'
'Olim enim'[17]'si in rem agebatur, satisdare 'posses-
'sor compellebatur', ut, si victus nec rem ipsam re-
'stitueret nec litis aestimationem[18], potestas esset peti-
'tori aut cum eo agendi aut cum 'fideiussoribus' eius.'
quae satisdatio appellatur iudicatum solvi: unde autem sic appellatur, facile est intellegere: namque sti-

(1) Cf. Gai. 4, 75..79 Dig. 9, 4 Cod. 3, 41   (2) Gai. 4, 75
(3) hominem] PΘ, hunc hominem ABE, om. Gai.   (4) Gai.
4, 75   (5) Gai. 4, 76..78   (6) 1, 3, 4. 1, 16, 1
(7) Cf. Dig. 9, 1   (9) sic dett., quid libri boni   (9) pr.
fin. similis Dig. 9, 1, 1 § 10. 3 (Ulp. l. 18 ad ed.) •   (10) no-
xalem] PE, nox. hanc AB

(11) § 1 fin. similis Dig. 50, 17, 130 (Ulp. l. l.)
(12) Cf. Gai. 4, 82..87 Dig. 3, 3 Cod. 2, 13   (13) Gai.
4, 82   (14) multae] dett. cum Θ, m. iustae (m. et iustae B)
libri   (15) Gai. 4, 85
(16) Cf. Gai. 4, 88..102 Dig. 2, 8 Cod. 2, 57   (17) Gai.
4, 89   (18) eius ins. libri

k*

6. All this applies equally to free dependants – sons, daughters and grandchildren – and the heads of their families – fathers or grandfathers. 7. But the Macedonian Resolution applies only to these. It prohibits the lending of money to persons within family authority. The lender is denied every action. He may not sue the son himself – or, as the case may be, the daughter, or the grandchild – either during dependence or after independence by the head of the family's death or by emancipation. He may not sue the head of the family, not while he retains the borrowing dependent in his authority, and not after an emancipation. The senate made this Resolution because the lives of parents were often threatened by offspring burdened with debts from borrowing money wasted on high living. 8. Note finally that where a contract is made by the order of a father or owner and something has been converted to his use, an action of debt lies directly against him, as though from the outset the deal had been with himself. The law is the same with someone who is liable to the exercitorian or institorian. The action goes directly against them, because they too are treated as having given their order for the making of the contract.

4.8 NOXAL ACTIONS

Noxal actions lie when slaves commit delicts – theft, robbery, loss, or contempt. These actions give the condemned owner an option to pay the damages as assessed in money or to make noxal surrender of the slave. 1. The word 'noxa' denotes the noxious body, here the slave; 'noxia' indicates the wrong itself, the theft, robbery, loss, or contempt. 2. There is a very good reason for the option of noxal surrender. It would be unjust to allow wicked slaves to inflict on owners any loss beyond their own value. 3. In noxal proceedings over one of his slaves an owner discharges himself by making noxal surrender. The transfer certainly passes perpetual ownership of the slave. But once the slave has brought in enough money to make good the loss suffered by the person to whom he is surrendered, he is manumitted by order of the praetor even without the owner's consent. 4. Some noxal actions were established by statutes, some by the edict of the praetor. Statutory instances are the action for theft under the Twelve Tables, and for wrongful loss under the Aquilian Act. Examples from the praetor's edict include contempt and robbery. 5. Noxal actions depend on current status. If your slave commits a delict, the action lies against you so long as he remains within your authority. If he moves to another, the action then lies against that other. If he is manumitted, he becomes directly liable himself, and the option of noxal surrender is extinguished. Conversely, it is possible for a direct action to become noxal. Where a free man commits a wrong and then becomes your slave, which, as explained in Book 1, can happen in some circumstances, the previously direct action now lies against you noxally. 6. If a slave commits a wrong against his owner, no action arises. It is impossible for any obligation to come into being between an owner and someone within his authority. If the slave moves to another or is manumitted, no action lies either against himself or against the person who now has authority over him. It also follows that if another's slave commits a wrong against you and afterwards comes under your authority, the action is extinguished. It has been drawn into a relationship in which it cannot exist. Even if the slave moves out of your authority, you cannot sue. The same if an owner does something to one of his slaves. The slave can never have an action against the owner, not even after if he is manumitted or alienated. 7. The old jurists applied these rules to dependants in family authority as well, both males and females. As attitudes changed it was rightly thought that such harshness could not be tolerated. Hence the practice of treating children in the same way as slaves has been abandoned. What father allows his son to be given in noxal surrender, much less his daughter? It would hurt the father almost more than the son. With daughters, sexual propriety provides another good reason for the change. A final reason for confining noxal actions to slaves is that in the old legal commentaries we quite often find it said that sons who commit delicts can themselves be sued.

4.9 LIABILITY FOR ANIMALS

Suppose a horse given to kicking kicks, or a bull given to goring gores. The Twelve Tables gave a noxal action for 'pauperies', the loss caused by unreasoning animals, whether from mischievous temperament, excitement, or wildness. As the Twelve Tables provided, noxal surrender of the animal releases the owner. But the action lies only over animals which turn fierce contrary to nature. It does not cover those born wild. So, if a bear gets away from its owner and does harm, he, now the former owner, cannot be sued, since he stopped being owner when the wild creature escaped. Pauperies is loss caused without wrongfulness on the part of the perpetrator. An animal cannot be said to commit a wrong, since it does not understand what it is doing. So much for the noxal action. 1. But note that the edict of the aediles forbids us from bringing into a place where people usually come and go any dog, hog, boar, bear, or lion. It also provides that, if the edict is infringed and a free man comes to harm, the owner shall be condemned for whatever sum seems just and reasonable to the judge; and in respect of other things he shall be condemned for double the amount of loss inflicted. Besides these aedilitian actions, the action for pauperies will also lie. When actions lie concurrently in one situation, one exclusively penal action never consumes another.

4.10 LITIGATION THROUGH OTHERS

We should note that a person can bring an action for himself or for someone else, as agent, guardian, or supervisor. The practice in earlier times was not to allow litigation through representatives except on behalf of the people, to assert a man's freedom, or as guardian. The Hostilian Act added permission for actions for theft to be brought for prisoners of war and those away on state business; also for anyone under the guardianship of such a person. The great inconvenience of this restriction on representation of plaintiff or defendant led people think of litigating through agents. Illness, age, unavoidable journeys, and many other causes can often make it difficult for a man to assert his own rights. 1. An agent can be appointed without special words and without the other side having to be present. Indeed it is frequently done without the latter's knowledge. Any person whom you authorize to claim or defend your rights is considered to be your agent. 2. The way in which guardians and supervisors are appointed has been described in Book 1.

4.11 SECURITY

Modern usage has developed a different system for giving security from that employed in the old days. When a real action was brought, the possessor used to be compelled to give security so that, if he lost and did not restore the thing or pay the valuation, the plaintiff could claim either against him or against his guarantors. This was called 'security for paying the judgment'. It is easy to see why.

pulatur quis, ut solveretur sibi quod fuerit iudicatum. ['multo magis is', qui in rem actione conveniebatur, 'satisdare' cogebatur, 'si alieno nomine iudicium accipiebat. ipse autem qui in rem agebat, si suo nomine petebat, satisdare non 'cogebatur'. procurator vero si in rem agebat, satisdare iubebatur ratam rem dominum habiturum: periculum enim erat, ne iterum dominus de eadem re experiatur. tutores et curatores eodem modo quo et procuratores satisdare 'debere verba edicti faciebant. sed aliquando his 'agenti-
1 'bus' satisdatio remittebatur. [1]Haec ita erant, si 'in rem agebatur. sin vero in personam, ab actoris 'quidem parte eadem 'optinebant, quae diximus in 'actione qua in rem agitur. ab eius vero parte cum 'quo agitur si quidem alieno nomine aliquis inter-'venerit, omnimodo satisdaret[2], quia nemo defensor 'in aliena re sine satisdatione idoneus esse creditur. 'quod si proprio nomine aliquis iudicium accipiebat, 'in personam,' iudicatum solvi satisdare non cogebatur.
2 'Sed haec hodie aliter observantur. sive enim 'quis in rem actione convenitur sive personali suo 'nomine, nullam satisdationem propter litis aestima-'tionem[3] dare compellitur, sed pro sua tantum per-'sona, quod iudicio permaneat[4] usque ad terminum 'litis, vel committitur suae promissioni cum iureiurando, 'quam iuratoriam cautionem vocant, vel nudam pro-'missionem vel satisdationem pro qualitate persone
3 'suae dare compellitur. Sin autem per procura-'torem lis vel infertur vel suscipitur, in actoris qui-'dem persona, si non mandatum actis insinuatum est 'vel praesens dominus litis in iudicio procuratoris sui 'personam confirmaverit, ratam rem dominum habi-'turum satisdationem procurator dare compellitur: eo-'dem observando et si tutor vel curator vel aliae tales 'personae, quae alienarum rerum gubernationem re-
4 'ceperunt, litem quibusdam per alium inferunt. Sin 'vero aliquis convenitur, si quidem praesens procura-'torem dare paratus est, potest vel ipse in iudicium 'venire et sui procuratoris personam per iudicatum 'solvi satisdationis sollemnes stipulationes firmare vel 'extra iudicium satisdationem exponere, per quam 'ipse sui procuratoris fideiussor existit pro omnibus 'iudicatum solvi satisdationis clausulis. ubi et de hypo-'theca suarum rerum convenire compellitur, sive in 'iudicio promiserit sive extra iudicium caverit, ut tam 'ipse quam heredes eius obligentur: alia insuper cau-'tela vel satisdatione propter personam ipsius expo-'nenda, quod tempore sententiae recitandae in iudicio 'invenietur[5], vel si non venerit, omnia dabit fideius-'sor, quae condemnationi continentur, nisi fuerit pro-
5 'vocatum. Si vero reus praesto ex quacumque 'causa non fuerit et alius velit defensionem subire, 'nulla differentia inter actiones in rem vel personales 'introducenda potest hoc facere, ita tamen ut satis-'dationem iudicatum solvi pro litis praestet aestima-'tione. nemo enim secundum veterem regulam, ut iam 'dictum est, alienae rei sine satisdatione defensor ido-
6 'neus intellegitur. Quae omnia apertius et per-'fectissime a cottidiano iudiciorum usu in ipsis rerum
7 'documentis apparent. Quam formam non solum 'in hac regia urbe, sed et in omnibus nostris provin-'ciis, etsi propter imperitiam aliter forte celebraban-'tur, optinere censemus, cum necesse est omnes pro-'vincias caput omnium nostrarum civitatum, id est 'hanc regiam urbem, eiusque observantiam sequi[6].'

XII[7]
DE PERPETUIS ET TEMPORALIBUS ACTIONIBUS ET QUAE AD HEREDES VEL IN HEREDES TRANSEUNT.

[8]'Hoc loco admonendi sumus eas quidem actiones, 'quae ex lege senatusve consulto 'sive ex sacris con-

'stitutionibus' proficiscuntur, perpetuo solere' 'antiqui-'tus competere', donec sacrae constitutiones tam in 'rem quam personalibus actionibus certos fines dede-'runt': 'eas vero, quae ex propria 'praetoris' iurisdic-'tione pendent, plerumque intra annum' 'vivere (nam 'et ipsius praetoris intra annum erat imperium)'. 'ali-'quando tamen et in perpetuum extenduntur,' 'id est 'usque ad finem constitutionibus introductum': 'quales 'sunt hae, quas bonorum possessori ceterisque qui 'heredis loco sunt accommodat. furti quoque mani-'festi actio, quamvis ex ipsius praetoris iurisdictione 'proficiscatur, tamen perpetuo datur': 'absurdum enim
1 'esse existimavit eam aream terminari'. 'Non omnes 'autem actiones, quae in aliquem aut ipso iure com-'petunt aut a praetore dantur, et in heredem aeque 'competunt aut dari solent. est enim certissima iuris 'regula ex maleficiis poenales actiones in heredem[9] 'non competere, veluti furti, vi bonorum raptorum, 'iniuriarum, damni iniuriae. sed heredibus huiusmodi 'actiones competunt nec denegantur, excepta iniuria-'rum actione et si qua alia similis inveniatur. ali-'quando tamen etiam ex contractu actio contra he-'redem non competit,' 'cum testator dolose versatus 'sit et ad heredem eius nihil ex eo dolo pervenerit. 'poenales autem actiones, quas supra diximus, si ab 'ipsis principalibus personis fuerint contestatae, et he-
2 'redibus dantur et contra heredes transeunt'. [10]Su-'perest ut 'admoneamus', quod si ante rem iudicatam 'is cum quo actum est satisfaciat actori, officio iudi-'cis convenit eum absolvere, 'licet' iudicii accipiendi 'tempore in ea causa fuisset, ut damnari debeat: et 'hoc est, quod 'ante' vulgo dicebatur omnia iudicia 'absolutoria esse.

XIII[11]
DE EXCEPTIONIBUS.

[12]'Sequitur, ut de exceptionibus dispiciamus. com-'paratae sunt autem exceptiones defendendorum eo-'rum gratia, cum quibus agitur: saepe enim accidit,' 'ut', 'licet ipsa persecutio[13] qua actor experitur iusta 'sit, tamen iniqua sit adversus eum cum quo agitur.'
1 Verbi gratia si metu coactus aut dolo inductus aut errore lapsus stipulanti Titio promisisti, quod non debueras promittere, palam est iure civili te obligatum esse et actio, qua intenditur dare te oportere, efficax est: sed iniquum est te condemnari ideoque datur tibi exceptio metus causa aut doli mali aut in
2 factum composita ad impugnandam actionem. Idem iuris est, [14]'si quis quasi credendi causa pecuniam sti-'pulatus fuerit neque numeravit. nam eam pecuniam 'a te petere posse certum est: dare enim te 'oportet, cum ex stipulatu[15] tenearis: sed quia ini-'quum est eo nomine te condemnari, placet excep-'tione 'pecuniae non numeratae' te defendi debere,' 'cuius tempora nos, secundum quod iam superioribus 'libris scriptum est[16], constitutione nostra[17] coartavimus.'
3 Praeterea debitor si pactus fuerit cum creditore, ne a se peteretur, nihilo minus obligatus manet, quia pacto convento obligationes non omnimodo dissol-vuntur: qua de causa efficax est adversus eum actio, qua actor intendit 'si paret eum dare oportere'. sed quia iniquum est contra pactionem eum damnari,
4 defenditur per exceptionem pacti conventi. Aeque si debitor deferente creditore iuraverit nihil se dare oportere, adhuc obligatus permanent, sed quia ini-quum est de periurio quaeri, defenditur per excep-tionem iurisiurandi. in his quoque actionibus, quibus in rem agitur, aeque necessariae sunt exceptiones: veluti si petitore deferente possessor iuraverit rem suam esse et nihilo minus eandem rem petitor vindicet: licet enim verum sit quod intendit, id est rem eius esse, iniquum est tamen possessorem con-

---

(1) *Gai.* 4, 90. 96. 98..102   (2) satisdari debet *Gai.* (3) sic *BΘ*, pro litis aestimatione (extim. *P*) *PE* (4) permanet *BP*ª*E*   (5) invenitur *BP*ª, inveniatur *P*ᵇ, veniret *E*   (6) consequi *B*
(7) *Cf. Gai.* 4, 110..114   (8) *Gai.* 4, 110..113   (9) here-

dem] *Gai. Θ*, heredem rei *libri*   (10) § 2 *ex Gaio* 4, 114 (11) *Cf. Gai.* 4, 115..125 *Dig.* 44, 1 *Cod.* 8, 35   (12) *Gai.* 4, 115. 116   (13) persecutio] *PE*, actio *B*   (14) *Gai.* 4, 116ª   (15) *sic W Gai.*, stipulatione *BPE*   (16) 3, 21 (17) *Cod.* 4, 30, 14

// The form of the plaintiff's stipulation was that there must be paid to him whatever should be adjudged. The defendant in a real action was all the more bound to give security if he was defending the action for a third party. For his part the plaintiff in a real action was not compelled to give any security if he was claiming on his own behalf. An agent in a real action would be ordered to give security for ratification by his principal, because there was a risk that the principal might sue again on the same matter. The provisions of the edict made guardians and supervisors give security in the same manner as agents, but in actions brought by them the security was sometimes waived. 1. Those were the rules for real actions. For personal actions, the same applied on the plaintiff's side. On the defendant's side, someone defending for a third party would have to give security in all events. Nobody defending a case other than his own is considered reliable without security given. A defendant joining issue for himself in a personal action did not have to give security for paying the judgment. 2. These things are differently ordered nowadays. If someone is made defendant on his own account, whether the action is real or personal, he is not compelled to give any security for paying the value as assessed. For his continued appearance at the trial until the conclusion of the litigation, he is bound in his own person by a promise supported by oath, called 'cautio juratoria'. Or he may be asked either to make an unsecured promise or to give security. It depends on his personal status. 3. If a suit is started by or against an agent, then, on the plaintiff's side, unless a commission to sue is registered on the record or the principal comes in person and confirms the position of his agent before the court, the agent has to give security for the principal's ratification. The same applies where a guardian, or supervisor, or some other such person having the stewardship of another's property, sues through a representative. 4. On the defendant's side, if he is prepared to appoint an agent in person, he can come to court and confirm the position of his agent through the proper form of stipulation for paying the judgment; or else, without coming, he can arrange the giving of security so as to become his own agent's guarantor in respect of all the provisions of the stipulation for paying the judgment. In this case, whether he is promising in court or out of court, he must also agree to a mortgage of his property to bind himself and his heirs. On top of that, he must arrange a stipulation on his own account to the effect that at the time when judgment is delivered he will be present in court or, if he is not, a guarantor will pay whatever the judgment orders unless there is an appeal. 5. If the principal defendant is for some reason not available, and another person wants to take on the defence, he can do so in both real and personal actions provided he gives security for paying the judgment in the amount assessed. As has been said, according to the ancient rule nobody defending another's case is relied on without security. 6. This system can be studied clearly and completely from the daily practice of the courts as evidenced in the records of actual litigation. 7. We have ruled that it is to apply not only in this imperial city but also in all our provinces, even if in ignorance they have been working some other published scheme. It is essential that all provinces should follow the capital, should follow, that is, this imperial city and the practice here adopted.

4.12 PERPETUAL AND TEMPORARY ACTIONS DESCENT OF RIGHTS AND LIABILITIES

We begin by noting that in the old days actions based on acts, resolutions of the senate, or imperial law were all perpetual. Imperial pronouncements then imposed fixed periods of limitation on both real and personal actions. Praetorian actions, on the other hand, used mostly to last one year. The praetor himself held power for just one year. But some praetorian actions were and are treated as perpetual, i.e. they last for the imperial period of limitation. Among these are the ones which the praetor gives to estate-possessors and others equivalent to heirs. Similarly the action for manifest theft is perpetual, despite the fact that it emanated from the praetor's jurisdiction. He thought it absurd that it should expire in one year. 1. Not all actions which lie against a man at law or by praetorian grant also descend against or are given against his heir. No rule is more certain than that penal actions arising from wrongs do not lie against heirs. So the actions for theft, things taken by violence, contempt, and wrongful loss do not. But they do descend to heirs and are not refused them. The exception is the action for contempt and any other like it. Sometimes, however, even an action arising from contract does not descend against an heir, as where the testator has been guilty of fraud and the heir has reaped no advantage from that deceit. The penal actions which we have just mentioned do descend to and against heirs if the original parties got beyond joinder of issue. 2. Notice that if the defendant satisfies the plaintiff before judgment, the judge has an inherent duty to absolve him even if the facts at the time issue was joined justified condemnation. This is the meaning of the old maxim 'Every trial absolves.'

4.13 PLEAS IN DEFENCE

Next come pleas in defence. These were evolved to defend people facing actions. It often happens that the claim being pursued by the plaintiff is recognized in law but is unjust as against the particular defendant. 1. Suppose, for example, that you made an ill-advised promise in reply to a stipulation by Titius; you did it because you were intimidated or deceived or mistaken. It is clear that at law you are now bound and that the action which says that you 'ought to give' can be brought against you. But it is unjust that you should be condemned. So you are allowed a plea in defence to undermine the action, the plea of intimidation, or of deceit, or one framed on the particular case. 2. It is the same where in the preparations for a loan the lender takes a stipulation from you for the money and then fails to give you the cash. He can definitely make a claim against you for that money. You 'ought to give' it. You are bound by virtue of the stipulation. But it is unjust that you should be condemned. So you have a defence; you are given the plea of money not paid. As we said in an earlier book, a pronouncement of our own has restricted the time limit for this plea. 3. Suppose a debtor comes to an agreement with his creditor that no claim shall be made against him. He still remains bound. Obligations are not always discharged by a simple agreement. The action in which the plaintiff's main pleading says 'If it appears that he ought to give' holds good against him. But because it is unjust that he should be condemned in contradiction of the agreement he has a defence by the plea of agreement. 4. A debtor still remains under an obligation even if at his creditor's invitation he takes the oath that he owes nothing. But since it would be improper to investigate the question of perjury the debtor has a defence by the plea of oath taken. Pleas are equally necessary in real actions. Suppose the possessor, at the claimant's invitation, swears the thing is his, and the claimant none the less vindicates it. Even if his pleading is true – that the thing is his – it is wrong for the possessor to be condemned. // 5. Again, if an action

5 demnari. [1]Item si iudicio tecum actum fuerit
sive in rem sive in personam, nihilo minus obligatio
durat et ideo ipso iure postea de eadem re adversus
te agi potest: sed debes per exceptionem rei iudi-
6 catae adiuvari. ʻHaec exempli causa rettulisse
ʻsufficiet. alioquin quam ex multis variisque causis
ʻexceptiones necessariae sint, ex latioribus digestorum
7 ʻseu pandectarum libris intellegi potest.ʼ Quarum quaedam [2] ʻex legibus vel ex his, quae legis vicem
ʻoptinent, vel ex ipsius praetoris iurisdictione sub-
8 (7) ʻstantiam capiunt.ʻ Appellantur autem exceptiones aliae perpetuae et peremptoriae, aliae tempo-
9 (8) rales et dilatoriae. Perpetuae et peremptoriae
sunt, quae semper agentibus obstant et semper rem
de qua agitur peremunt: qualis est exceptio doli
mali et quod metus causa factum est et pacti conventi, cum ita convenerit, ne omnino pecunia petere-
10 (9) tur. Temporales atque dilatoriae sunt, quae ad
tempus nocent et temporis dilationem tribuunt: qualis est pacti conventi, cum convenerit, ne intra certum tempus ageretur, veluti intra quinquennium. nam
finito eo tempore non impeditur actor rem exsequi.
ergo hi, quibus intra tempus agere volentibus obicitur
exceptio aut pacti conventi aut alia similis, differre
debent actionem et post tempus agere: ideo enim et
dilatoriae istae exceptiones appellantur. alioquin, si
intra tempus egerint obiectaque sit exceptio, neque
eo iudicio quicquam consequerentur propter exceptionem nec post tempus ʻolimʼ agere poterant, cum temere rem in iudicium deducebant et consumebant,
qua ratione rem amittebant. ʻhodie autem non ita
ʻstricte haec procedere volumus, sed eum, qui ante
ʻtempus pactionis vel obligationis litem inferre ausus
ʻest, Zenonianae constitutioni [3] subiacere censemus,
ʻquam sacratissimus legislator de his qui tempore
ʻplus petierunt protulit, ut et indutias, quas, si[4] ipse
ʻactor sponte indu1serit vel natura actionis continet,
ʻcontempserat, in duplum habeant hi, qui talem in-
ʻiuriam passi sunt, et post eas finitas non aliter litem
ʻsuscipiant, nisi omnes expensas litis antea accepe-
ʻrint, ut actores tali poena perterriti tempora litium
11 (10) ʻdoceantur observare.ʼ Praeterea etiam ex
persona dilatoriae sunt exceptiones: quales sunt pro-
curatoriae, veluti si per militem aut mulierem agere
quis velit: [5]nam militibus nec pro patre vel matre
vel uxore nec ex sacro rescripto procuratorio nomine
experiri conceditur: suis vero negotiis superesse sine
offensa disciplinae possunt. ʻeas vero exceptiones,
ʻquae olim procuratoribus propter infamiam vel dantis
ʻvel ipsius procuratoris opponebantur, cum in iudiciis
ʻfrequentari nullo perspeximus modo, conquiescere
ʻsancimus, ne, dum de his altercatur, ipsius negotii
ʻdisceptatio proteletur.ʼ

XIV
DE REPLICATIONIBUS.

[6]ʻInterdum evenit, ut exceptio, quae prima facie
ʻiusta videatur, inique noceat. quod cum accidit, alia
ʻallegatione opus est adiuvandi actoris gratia, quae
ʻreplicatio vocatur, quia per eam replicatur atque
ʻresolvitur vis[7] exceptionis. ʻveluti cumʼ pactus est
ʻaliquis cum debitore suo, ne ab eo pecuniam petat,
ʻdeinde postea in contrarium pacti sunt, id est ut
ʻpetere creditori liceat: si agat creditor et excipiat
ʻdebitor, ut ita demum condemnetur, si non convene-
ʻrit, ne eam pecuniam creditor petat, nocet ei ex-
ʻceptio, convenit enim ita: namque nihilo minus hoc
ʻverum manet, ʻlicetʼ postea in contrarium pacti sunt.
ʻsed quia iniquum est creditorem excludi, replicatio
1 ʻei dabitur ex posteriore pacto convento. [6]ʻRursus
ʻinterdum evenit, ut replicatio, quae prima facie iusta
ʻsit, inique noceat. quod cum accidit, alia allegatione
ʻopus est adiuvandi rei gratia, quae duplicatio voca-

2 ʻtur. [6]Et si rursus ea prima facie iusta videatur,
ʻsed propter aliquam causam inique noceat,
ʻrursus allegatione alia opus est, qua actori adiuvetur,
3 ʻquae dicitur triplicatio. [6]Quarum omnium ex-
ʻceptionum usum interdum ulterius quam diximus
ʻvarietas negotiorum introducit': ʻquas omnes apertius
ʻex latiore digestorum volumine facile est cognoscere.ʼ
4 Exceptiones autem, quibus debitor defenditur,
plerumque accommodari solent etiam fideiussoribus
eius: et recte, quia, quod ab his petitur, id ab ipso
debitore peti videtur, quia mandati iudicio redditurus
est eis, quod hi pro eo solverint. qua ratione et si
de non petenda pecunia pactus quis cum reo fuerit,
placuit proinde succurrendum esse per exceptionem
pacti conventi illis quoque qui pro eo obligati essent,
ac si et cum ipsis pactus esset, ne ab eis ea pecunia peteretur. sane quaedam exceptiones non solent
his accommodari. ecce enim debitor si bonis suis
cesserit et cum eo creditor experiatur, defenditur per
exceptionem ʻnisi[8] bonis cesseritʼ: sed haec exceptio
fideiussoribus non datur, scilicet ideo quia, qui alios
pro debitore obligat, hoc maxime prospicit, ut, cum
facultatibus lapsus fuerit debitor, possit ab his quos
pro eo obligavit suum consequi.

XV[9]
DE INTERDICTIS.

Sequitur, ut dispiciamus de interdictis ʻseu actionibus, quae pro his exercentur. erantʼ autem interdicta
formae atque conceptiones verborum, quibus praetor
aut iubebat aliquid fieri aut fieri prohibebat. [10]ʻquod
ʻtum maxime faciebat, cum de possessione aut quasi
ʻpossessione inter aliquos contendebatur.ʼ
1 Summa autem divisio interdictorum haec est,
quod aut prohibitoria sunt aut restitutoria aut exhibitoria. prohibitoria sunt, quibus vetat aliquid fieri,
veluti vim sine vitio possidenti, vel mortuum inferenti,
quo ei ius erit inferendi, vel in loco sacro aedificari,
vel in flumine publico ripave eius aliquid fieri, quo
peius navigetur. restitutoria sunt, quibus restitui aliquid iubet, veluti cum [11] bonorum possessori possessionem eorum, quae quis pro herede aut pro possessore
possidet ex ea hereditate, aut cum iubet ei, qui vi
possessione fundi deiectus sit, restitui possessionem.
exhibitoria sunt, per quae iubet exhiberi, veluti eum,
cuius de libertate agitur, aut libertum, cui patronus
operas indicere velit, aut parenti liberos [12], qui in
potestate eius sunt. sunt tamen qui putant proprie
interdicta ea vocari, quae prohibitoria sunt, quia
interdicere est denuntiare et prohibere: restitutoria
autem et exhibitoria proprie decreta vocari: sed tamen optinuit omnia interdicta appellari, quia inter
2 duos dicuntur. [13]ʻSequens divisio ʻinterdictorum
ʻhaecʼ est, quodʼ quaedam ʻadipiscendae possessionis
ʻcausa comparata suntʼ, quaedam ʻretinendaeʼ, quae-
3 dam ʻrecipirandae.ʼ [13]Adipiscendae possessionis
ʻcausa interdictum accommodatur bonorum possessori,
ʻʻquod appellaturʼ quorum bonorum, eiusque vis et po-
ʻtestas haec est, ut, quod ex his bonis quisque, quorum
ʻpossessio alicui data est, pro herede aut pro pos-
ʻsessore possideat, id ei, cui bonorum possessio data
ʻest, restituere ʻdebeat. pro herede autem possidere
ʻvidetur, qui putat se heredem esse: pro possessore
ʻis possidet, qui ʻnullo iureʼ rem hereditariam vel etiam
ʻtotam hereditatem sciens ad se non pertinere possi-
ʻdet. ideo autem adipiscendae possessionis vocatur
ʻinterdictum, quia ei tantum utile est, qui nunc pri-
ʻmum conatur adipisci rei possessionem: itaque si
ʻquis adeptus possessionem amiserit eam, hoc inter-
ʻdictum ei inutile est. interdictum quoque, quod ap-
ʻpellatur Salvianum, adipiscendae possessionis causa
ʻcomparatum est, eoque utitur dominus fundi de rebus
ʻcoloni, quas is pro mercedibus fundi pignori futuras

(1) § 5 *ex Gaio* 4, 106   (2) *Gai* 4, 118   (3) *Cod.* 3, 10, 1
(4) si *om. libri, suppl.* Mommsen   (5) *cf. Cod.* 2, 12, 7
   (6) *Gai.* 4, 126..129   (7) vis] *Gai* Θ, ius PE, *inc.* B

(8) nisi] B, si PE, εἰ μή Θ   (9) *Cf. Gai.* 4, 138..170
Dig. 43, 1 *Cod.* 8, 1   (10) *Gai.* 4, 139   (11) cum *om. edd.*
cum Θ   (12) *sic* E, eius *ins.* BP   (13) *Gai.* 4, 143. 144. 147

against you, whether real or personal, goes to trial, your obligation none the less survives. At law another action can be brought on the same matter. You must be protected. You have the plea of previous decision. 6. These examples must suffice. The more detailed account in the Digest or Pandects will show you how frequent and various is the need for pleas in defence. 7. Some defence pleas come from statutes or their equivalents, some from the praetor's jurisdiction. 8 (7). Also, they are either perpetual and peremptory or temporary and dilatory. 9 (8). The former are those which constitute a permanent bar to the plaintiff and block the cause of action for ever. Examples are the plea of deceit, the plea of intimidation, and the plea of agreement where the agreement not to sue is absolute. 10 (9). The latter are those which obstruct a claim for a while and produce a delay, for instance the plea of agreement when the agreement is not to sue for a time – say, for five years. When the period expires, nothing stops the plaintiff pursuing the matter. Suing within the period, you may be met with the plea of agreement or another of that kind; if so, you will have to postpone the action till the time has passed. That is why such pleas are called dilatory. In the old days the plaintiff who sued and met such a defence would not only take nothing from that trial but would also be barred from a later suit. Over-eager to go to law, he had consumed his claim, and he lost it completely. It is not our wish to have so strict a system nowadays. Our ruling is that anyone who makes bold to bring an action before the time fixed by an agreement or annexed to an obligation shall be subject to the pronouncement of Zeno which that most revered legislator passed concerning those who are guilty of overclaiming in respect of time. The effect of this is both to give those who suffer such an injustice twice the allowance of time flouted by the plaintiff, whether conceded by himself or inherent in the nature of the action, and also, when the period does expire, to prevent their having to defend the action unless they are paid all the expenses of the litigation beforehand. Our purpose is that fear of this penalty shall teach plaintiffs to respect the time allowances which are built into litigation. 11 (10). Some dilatory pleas arise from the character of the parties, as for instance the pleas against agents, as where a party wants a soldier or a woman to bring an action for him. A soldier may not sue in the capacity of agent, not even for his father, his mother, or his wife, nor even with an imperial writ. He can appear in cases of his own without being in breach of discipline. Other pleas used to be advanced against agents on the ground that they or their principals were disqualified by a mark of disgrace. We perceived that such pleas were rare in practice, and we abolished them to stop arguments over them delaying debate of the main business.

4.14 REPLICATIONS

It can happen that a plea which looks on its face to be just would itself create an unreasonable bar. There then has to be a further pleading to support the plaintiff. That is called a replication, because by it the force of the plea in defence is turned back and undone. Suppose a creditor agrees with his debtor not to sue for his money; then, later, they make an agreement to the contrary, that the creditor may sue. If the creditor brings his action and the debtor relies on a plea that he should be condemned only if there was no agreement not to sue, that plea will bar the creditor. An agreement to that effect was made. After all the plea remains true, despite the subsequent agreement to the contrary. But it would be unreasonable to bar the creditor. So he is allowed a replication based on the subsequent agreement. 1. A replication which on its face seems right may itself create an unreasonable

result. In such a case there has to be another plea on the defendant's side. That is called a duplication. 2. And if that in turn seems right on its face but would unreasonably bar the plaintiff, yet another pleading has to be inserted on his behalf. That is a triplication. 3. In practice the diversity of human affairs sometimes prolongs these exchanges even further than we have described. The full picture can be gathered from the Digest. 4. Pleas available for the defence of a debtor are often extended to his guarantors. This is quite right, since claims against them are in effect claims against him. In an action based on mandate, he will have to restore to them whatever they have paid out for him. So it has been held that where a creditor comes to an agreement with his debtor not to sue him for the money the guarantors bound on the debtor's behalf must be allowed the benefit of the plea of agreement. It is as though the agreement not to claim the money had been made with the guarantors themselves. Some pleas, of course, cannot be extended to guarantors. If a creditor sues a debtor who has made a surrender of his goods, the debtor has a defence by the plea 'unless he has surrendered his goods'. The benefit of that plea cannot be given to the guarantors. There is a very good reason. The main purpose of someone who takes sureties from a debtor is precisely to have someone to sue if the debtor becomes insolvent.

4.15 INTERDICTS

We look next at interdicts or the actions used instead of them. Interdicts were forms or sets of words used by the praetor to order or to prohibit. The commonest occasion for such interventions was disputes over possession or quasi-possession. 1. The main classification is between prohibitory, restitutory, and exhibitory. By prohibitory interdicts the praetor forbids something: force against a person in unvitiated possession; force against someone burying a body where he has a burial right; building on sacred land; interference with navigation on a public river or from its banks. By restitutory interdicts he orders something to be handed over: to an estate-possessor, possession of every item from the estate held by another as heir or as mere possessor; to someone forcibly ejected, possession of the disputed land. By exhibitory interdicts he orders production: of a person whose free status is disputed; of a freedman from whom a patron wants his customary services; of children to the head of their family. Some say that 'interdict' should properly be confined to prohibitions, on the ground that to interdict is to denounce and forbid. They say that exhibitory and restitutory interdicts should properly be called decrees. Prevailing practice calls them all interdicts, taking the word in the sense of 'dicere inter', to 'pronounce between' two parties. 2. The next classification: for obtaining, retaining, or recovering possession. 3. One for obtaining possession is 'quorum bonorum', available to an estate-possessor. It works like this. The praetor has awarded estate-possession to someone. As heir or as bare possessor, another person is in possession of some of the assets from the estate. The interdict orders that those things be handed over to the person who has been awarded possession. Being possessed as heir means holding in the belief that one is heir; possessing as bare possessor means holding some or all the assets of the estate with no claim of right and in the knowledge that you are not entitled to the inheritance. The interdict is for obtaining possession because it can only be used for getting possession for the first time. If you have once had possession, it is no good to you. The Salvian interdict is another example. This is used by a landowner to obtain things pledged for his tenant's rent. // 4. Two interdicts

4 'pepigisset. ¹Retinendae possessionis causa com-'parata sunt interdicta uti possidetis et utrubi, cum 'ab utraque parte de proprietate alicuius rei contro-'versia sit et ante quaeritur, uter ex litigatoribus 'possidere et uter petere debeat.' namque nisi ante exploratum fuerit, utrius eorum possessio sit, non po-test petitoria² actio institui, quia et civilis et natu-ralis ratio facit, ut alius possideat, alius a possidente petat. et quia longe commodius est possidere potius quam petere, ideo plerumque et fere semper ingens existit contentio de ipsa possessione. commodum au-tem possidendi in eo est, quod, etiamsi eius res non sit qui possidet, si modo actor non potuerit suam esse probare, remanet suo loco possessio: propter quam causam³, cum obscura sint utriusque iura, con-4a tra petitorem iudicari solet. Sed interdicto qui-dem uti possidetis de fundi vel aedium possessione contenditur, utrubi vero interdicto de rerum mobi-lium possessione. 'quorum vis et potestas plurimam 'inter se differentiam apud veteres habebat: nam' uti possidetis interdicto is vincebat, qui interdicti tem-pore possidebat, si modo nec vi nec clam nec pre-cario nanctus fuerat ab adversario possessionem, etiamsi alium vi expulerit aut clam abripuerit alie-nam possessionem aut precario rogaverat aliquem, ut sibi possidere liceret: ⁴utrubi vero interdicto is vincebat, qui maiore parte eius anni nec vi nec clam nec precario ab adversario possidebat. 'hodie tamen 'aliter observatur: nam utriusque interdicti potestas 'quantum ad possessionem pertinet exaequata est, ut 'ille vincat et in re soli et in re mobili, qui posses-'sionem nec vi nec clam nec precario ab adversario 5 'litis contestationis tempore detinet.' ⁵'Possidere 'autem videtur quisque non solum, si ipse possideat, 'sed et si eius nomine aliquis in possessione sit, licet 'is eius iuri subiectus non sit, qualis est colonus et 'inquilinus: per eos quoque, apud quos deposuerit 'quis aut quibus 'commodaverit', ipse possidere vide-'tur: et hoc est, quod dicitur retinere possessionem 'posse aliquem per quemlibet, qui eius nomine sit in 'possessione. quin etiam animo quoque retineri pos-'sessionem 'placet', id est ut, quamvis neque ipse sit 'in possessione neque eius nomine alius, tamen si non 'relinquendae possessionis animo, sed postea rever-'surus inde discesserit, retinere possessionem videtur. 'adipisci vero possessionem per quos aliquis potest, 'secundo libro exposuimus⁶. nec ulla dubitatio est, 'quin animo solo possessionem adipisci nemo potest. 6 ⁵'Reciperandae possessionis causa solet interdici, 'si quis ex possessione' fundi vel aedium 'vi deiectus 'fuerit: nam ei proponitur interdictum unde vi, per 'quod is qui deiecit cogitur ei restituere possessionem', 'licet is ab eo qui vi deiecit vi vel clam vel precario 'possidebat. sed ex sacris constitutionibus, ut supra 'diximus⁷, si quis rem per vim occupaverit, si aliena 'dem in bonis eius est, dominio eius privatur, si aliena, 'post eius restitutionem etiam aestimationem rei dare 'vim passo compellitur. qui autem aliquem de pos-'sessione per vim deiecerit, tenetur lege Iulia de vi 'privata aut de vi publica: sed de vi⁸ privata, si sine 'armis vim fecerit, sin autem cum armis eum de pos-'sessione expulerit, de vi publica'. ⁹'armorum autem 'appellatione non solum scuta et gladios et galeas 7 'significari intellegimus, sed et fustes et lapides. ⁹Ter-'tia divisio interdictorum haec est, quod aut simpli-'cia sunt aut duplicia. simplicia sunt, veluti in qui-'bus alter actor, alter reus est: qualia sunt omnia 'restitutoria aut exhibitoria: namque actor est, qui 'desiderat aut exhiberi aut restitui, reus is, a quo 'desideratur, ut restituat aut exhibeat. prohibitorio-'rum autem interdictorum alia simplicia sunt, alia duplicia. simplicia sunt, veluti cum prohibet praetor 'in loco sacro vel in flumine publico ripave eius ali-

quid fieri (nam actor est, qui desiderat, ne quid fiat, 'reus, qui aliquid facere conatur): duplicia sunt veluti 'uti possidetis interdictum et utrubi. ideo autem du-'plicia vocantur, quia par utriusque litigatoris in his 'condicio est nec quisquam praecipue reus vel actor 'intellegitur, sed unusquisque tam rei quam actoris 'partem sustinet.' 8 'De ordine et veteri exitu interdictorum super-'vacuum est hodie dicere: nam quotiens extra ordi-'nem ius dicitur,' qualia sunt hodie omnia iudicia, non 'est necesse reddi interdictum, sed perinde iudicatur 'sine interdictis, atque si utilis actio ex causa inter-'dicti reddita fuisset.'

XVI¹⁰
DE POENA TEMERE LITIGANTIUM.

Nunc admonendi sumus magnam curam egisse eos, qui iura sustinebant, ne facile homines ad litigandum procederent: 'quod et nobis studio est'. idque eo maxime fieri potest, quod temeritas tam agentium quam eo-rum cum quibus ageretur ¹¹modo pecuniaria poena, modo iurisiurandi religione, modo metu infamiae 1 coercetur. 'Ecce enim iusiurandum omnibus qui 'conveniuntur ex nostra constitutione¹² defertur: nam 'reus non aliter suis allegationibus utitur, nisi prius 'iuraverit, quod putans se bona instantia uti ad con-'tradicendum pervenit.' ¹³'at adversus infitiantes ex 'quibusdam causis dupli 'vel tripli' actio constituitur, 'veluti si damni iniuriae aut legatorum 'locis venerabili-'bus' relictorum nomine agitur. statim autem ab initio 'pluris quam simpli est actio veluti furti manifesti qua-'drupli, nec manifesti dupli: nam ex his causis et aliis 'quibusdam, sive quis neget sive fateatur, pluris quam 'simpli est actio. item actoris quoque calumnia coerce-'tur': 'nam etiam actor pro calumnia iurare cogitur ex 'nostra constitutione. utriusque etiam partis advocati 'iusiurandum subeunt, quod alia nostra constitutione¹⁴ 'comprehensum est. haec autem omnia pro veteris 'calumniae actione inducta sunt, quae in desuetu-'dinem abiit, quia in partem decimam litis actorem 'multabat, quod nusquam factum esse invenimus: sed 'pro his introductum est et praefatum iusiurandum et 'ut improbus litigator etiam damnum et impensas litis 2 'inferre adversario suo cogatur'. ¹⁵'Ex quibusdam 'iudiciis damnati ignominiosi fiunt, veluti furti, vi bo-'norum raptorum, iniuriarum', de dolo, item 'tutelae, 'mandati, depositi', directis non contrariis actionibus, 'item pro socio,' quae ab utraque parte directa est et ob id quilibet ex sociis eo iudicio damnatus igno-minia notatur. 'sed furti quidem aut vi bonorum 'raptorum aut iniuriarum' aut de dolo 'non solum 'damnati notantur ignominia, sed etiam pacti, et 'recte: plurimum enim interest, utrum ex delicto ali-'quis an ex contractu debitor sit.' 3 Omnium autem actionum instituendarum prin-cipium ab ea parte edicti proficiscitur, qua praetor edicit de in ius vocando: utique enim in primis ad-versarius in ius vocandus est, id est ad eum vocan-dus est, qui ius dicturus sit. qua parte praetor pa-rentibus et patronis, item liberis parentibusque pa-tronorum et patronarum hunc praestat honorem, ut non aliter liceat liberis libertisque eos in ius vocare, quam si id¹⁶ ab ipso praetore postulaverint et im-petraverint: et si quis aliter vocaverit, in eum poe-nam 'solidorum quinquaginta' constituit.

XVII
DE OFFICIO IUDICIS.

Superest, ut de officio iudicis dispiciamus. et qui-dem in primis illud observare debet iudex, ne aliter iudicet, quam legibus aut constitutionibus aut mori-

---

(1) Gai. 4, 148   (2) petitori B, petitoris P, petituris E (3) propterea quod scr.   (4) cf. Gai. 4, 150   (5) Gai. 4, 153. 154   (6) 2, 9, 4   (7) 4, 2, 1   (8) de vi] Θ, si B, vi PᵇE, om. Pᵃ   (9) Gai. 4, 155..160

(10) Cf. Gai. 4, 171..183   (11) cf. Gai. 4, 171   (12) Cod. 2, 58, 2 pr. (a. 534?)   (13) Gai. 4, 171. 173. 174   (14) Cod. 3, 1, 14 § 1   (15) Gai. 4, 182   (16) id] PE, om. B

for retaining possession are 'uti possidetis' and 'utrubi'. They lie where two parties are in dispute about ownership, and the preliminary question is which of them is in possession and which must be plaintiff. Without first identifying the possessor, it is impossible to begin the vindication. Logic and law both require one party to possess and one to claim from that possessor. It is far better to be possessor than to be plaintiff. So there is often, in fact almost always, a hot dispute as to possession itself. The possessor's advantage is that even if the thing does not belong to him it stays with him unless and until the plaintiff proves it his. If the matter remains doubtful, the practice is to give judgment against the plaintiff. 4a. The interdict 'uti possidetis' is for disputes about land and buildings; the interdict 'utrubi' for movable goods. For the classical jurists there was a considerable difference in their working. In 'uti possidetis' the winner was the party in possession at the date of the interdict itself, as long as his possession had not been obtained from his opponent by force, stealth or licence. It was irrelevant that the possessor had forcibly driven out a third party, had secretly usurped a third party's possession, or had obtained a third party's licence to possess. With 'utrubi' the winner was the one who had possessed for the greater part of that year, not counting possession obtained from the opponent by force, stealth or licence. The law is different now. The working of the two interdicts has been harmonized. The winner, for both land and movables, is the party who possesses when issue is joined, still discounting possession obtained from the opponent by force, stealth or licence. 5. A person possesses not only when he himself holds but also when someone holds for him, even if outside the family, e.g. an agricultural or urban tenant. One who deposits a thing or lends it for use possesses it through the depositee or the borrower. That is what is meant by the saying that a person can retain possession through anyone who possesses for him. We hold that possession can be retained by intent alone. That is to say, even if a person is not himself in possession and nobody is in possession on his behalf, he is still the possessor provided he left without intending to give up possession and with the intention of coming back. As for obtaining possession though others, we have said in Book 2 who can do it for you. It is certainly impossible to obtain possession by intent alone. 6. Recovery of possession is illustrated where a person has been dispossessed of land or a house by force: 'unde vi' issues in his case. It compels the ejector to restore possession to him even if he himself acquired possession from the violent ejector by force, stealth or licence. As we have said, imperial pronouncements have laid down that where a person seizes a thing by force he forfeits his ownership, or, if the thing was not his, must restore it to the victim of his violence and, over again, pay its value. A violent dispossessor is also liable under the Julian Act on Private or Public Force: private, if unarmed; if armed, public. Not only shields and swords and helmets but also even clubs and stones count as arms. 7. The third classification: they are single or double. In single interdicts one party is plaintiff and the other is defendant. All restitutory and exhibitory interdicts are of this kind. The plaintiff is the party who wants the thing produced or handed over, the defendant the one from whom these demands are made. But with prohibitory interdicts some are single and some double. Single examples are the praetor's injunctions against activities on sacred land or on a public river or its banks: there is a plaintiff trying to stop the activity and a defendant trying to do it. Double examples are 'uti possidetis' and

'utrubi'. They are double because the position of both sides is the same; neither litigant can clearly be characterized as plaintiff or defendant. Instead both share each role. 8. Nowadays it is unnecessary to set out the list of interdicts and all their old procedure. Under the special judicature, now generalized to all litigation, no interdict need issue at all. Instead decisions are reached without any actual interdict, as though an action had been given based on the idea behind the interdict in question.

4.16 PENALTIES FOR OVER-EAGER LITIGANTS

We should notice what pains the guardians of the law have taken to see that people do not turn lightly to litigation. This is our concern as well. The main checks on the eagerness of plaintiffs and defendants are money penalties, oaths to bind the conscience, and the fear of disgrace. 1. Under our own pronouncement every defendant is put to an oath. He cannot avail himself of his defence unless he first swears that he was brought to deny the claim in the belief that he had good grounds for doing so. Next, in some actions the claim is doubled or tripled if the defendant denies liability. These include the actions for wrongful loss and for legacies to sacred places. Some actions lie from the outset for multiple damages, for instance the action for manifest theft for fourfold or non-manifest for twofold. In these and in some others the defendant is liable for more than single damages whether he admits liability or denies it. There are also restraints against vexatiousness on the plaintiff's side. Under our pronouncement the plaintiff too must take an oath against abuse of the court's procedure. Another pronouncement obliges the advocates on both sides to take the oath. These provisions replaced the old action for vexatious litigation, which had fallen out of use. It imposed on plaintiffs a penalty of one tenth the value of their claim, but we found that this was never exacted. Instead we introduced the oath already mentioned and the rule that a vexatious litigant must pay his opponent's costs and all the loss caused him by the suit. 2. In some actions a condemned defendant incurs disgrace: theft, goods taken by force, contempt, deceit, the direct but not the counter-actions for guardianship, mandate, and deposit, also partnership. In this last case the action is direct whoever brings it, so that any partner condemned incurs disgrace. In the actions for theft, goods taken by force, contempt, and deceit, not only those condemned but also those who settle incur disgrace. This is quite right. The crucial question is whether a man's liability arises from wrongdoing or from contract. 3. The beginning of every action is controlled by the part of the praetor's edict providing for summons to court. That is of course always the first step, getting the defendant before the person who will decide the case. The praetor there gives an assurance of respect for parents and patrons, and ascendants and descendants of patrons and patronesses. He does not allow their children and freedmen to summon them to court without first seeking and obtaining praetorian permission. For a summons in breach of this rule there is a penalty of 50 solidi.

4.17 POWERS AND DUTIES OF JUDGES

We still have to discuss the judge. Above all he must be sure not to depart from the statutes, imperial pronouncements, and custom. // 1. Suppose he is

1 bus[1] proditum est. Et ideo si noxali iudicio addictus est, observare debet, ut, 'si condemnandus videbitur dominus, ita debeat condemnare: 'Publium "Maevium Lucio Titio decem aureis condemno aut 2 "noxam dedere." Et si in rem actum sit, sive contra petitorem iudicavit, absolvere debet possessorem, sive contra possessorem, iubere eum debet, ut rem ipsam restituat cum fructibus. 'sed si in prae-'senti neget se possessor restituere posse et sine fru-'stratione videbitur tempus restituendi causa petere, 'indulgendum est ei, ut tamen de litis aestimatione 'caveat cum fideiussore, si intra tempus quod ei da-'tum erit non restituisset.' et si hereditas petita sit, eadem circa fructus intervenient, quae diximus intervenire in singularum rerum petitione. illorum autem fructuum, quos culpa sua possessor non perceperit, in utraque actione eadem ratio paene fit[2], si praedo fuerit. si vero bona fide possessor fuerit, non habetur ratio 'consumptorum neque non perceptorum': post inchoatam autem petitionem etiam illorum ratio habetur, qui culpa possessoris percepti non sunt vel per-3 cepti consumpti sunt. Si ad exhibendum actum fuerit, non sufficit, si exhibeat rem is cum quo actum est, sed opus est, ut etiam causam rei debeat exhibere, id est ut eam causam habeat actor, quam habiturus esset, si, cum primum ad exhibendum egisset, exhibita res fuisset: ideoque si inter moras usucapta sit res a possessore, nihilo minus condemnatur. praeterea fructuum medii temporis, id est eius, quod[3] post acceptum ad exhibendum iudicium ante rem iudicatam intercessit, rationem habere debet iudex. quod si neget is, cum quo ad exhibendum actum est, in praesenti exhibere se posse et tempus exhibendi causa petat idque sine frustratione postulare videatur, dari ei debet, ut tamen caveat se restituturum: quod si neque statim iussu iudicis rem exhibeat neque postea exhibiturum se caveat, condemnandus sit in id, quod actoris intererat ab initio rem exhibitam 4 esse. Si familiae erciscundae iudicio actum sit, singulas res singulis heredibus adiudicare debet et, si in alterius persona praegravare videatur adiudicatio, debet hunc invicem coheredi certa pecunia, sicut iam dictum est[4], condemnare. eo quoque nomine coheredi quisque suo condemnandus est, quod solus fructus hereditarii fundi percepit aut rem hereditariam corrupit aut consumpsit. quae quidem similiter inter plures quoque quam duos coheredes 5 subsequuntur. Eadem intervenient et si communi dividundo de pluribus rebus actum fuerit. quod si de una re, veluti de fundo, si quidam iste fundus commode regionibus divisionem recipiat, partes eius singulis adiudicare debet et, si unius pars praegravare videbitur, is invicem certa pecunia alteri condemnandus est: quod si commode dividi non possit, vel homo forte aut mulus erit de quo actum sit, uni totus adiudicandus est et is[5] alteri certa pecunia 6 condemnandus. Si finium regundorum actum fuerit, dispicere debet iudex, an necessaria sit adiudicatio. quae sane uno casu necessaria est, si evidentioribus finibus distingui agros commodius sit, quam olim fuissent distincti: nam tunc necesse est ex alterius agro partem aliquam alterius agri domino adiudicari. quo casu conveniens est, ut is alteri certa pecunia debeat condemnari. eo quoque[6] nomine damnandus est quisque hoc iudicio, quod forte circa fines malitiose aliquid commisit, verbi gratia quia lapides finales furatus est aut arbores finales cecidit. contumaciae quoque nomine quisque eo iudicio condemnatur, veluti si quis iubente iudice metiri agros

7 passus non fuerit. Quod autem istis iudiciis alicui adiudicatum sit, id statim eius fit cui adiudicatum est.

XVIII[7]
DE PUBLICIS IUDICIIS.

Publica iudicia neque per actiones ordinantur nec omnino quicquam simile habent ceteris iudiciis, de quibus locuti sumus, magnaque diversitas est eorum 1 et in instituendis et in exercendis. Publica autem dicta sunt, quod cuivis ex populo exsecutio eo-2 rum plerumque datur. Publicorum iudiciorum quaedam capitalia sunt, quaedam non capitalia. capitalia dicimus, quae ultimo supplicio adficiunt vel aquae et ignis interdictione vel deportatione vel metallo: cetera si qua infamiam irrogant cum damno[8] pecuniario, haec publica quidem sunt, non tamen capitalia. 3 Publica autem iudicia sunt haec. lex Iulia maiestatis, quae in eos, qui contra imperatorem vel rem 'publicam aliquid moliti sunt, suum vigorem extendit. 'cuius poena animae amissionem sustinet et memoria 4 'rei et post mortem damnatur. Item lex Iulia de 'adulteriis coercendis, quae non solum temeratores 'alienarum nuptiarum gladio punit, sed etiam eos, qui 'cum masculis infandam libidinem exercere audent. 'sed eadem lege Iulia etiam stupri flagitium punitur, 'cum quis sine vi vel virginem vel viduam honeste 'viventem stupraverit. poenam autem eadem lex irro-'gat peccatoribus, si honesti sunt, publicationem par-'tis dimidiae bonorum, si humiles, corporis coercitio-5 'nem cum relegatione. Item lex Cornelia de si-'cariis, quae homicidas ultore ferro persequitur vel 'eos, qui hominis occidendi causa cum telo ambulant. 'telum autem, ut Gaius noster in[9] interpretatione legis 'duodecim tabularum[10] scriptum reliquit, vulgo quidem 'id appellatur, quod ab arcu mittitur: sed et omne 'significatur, quod manu cuiusdam mittitur: sequitur 'ergo, ut et lapis et lignum et ferrum hoc nomine 'contineatur. dictumque ab eo, quod in longinquum 'mittitur, a Graeca voce figuratum, ἀπὸ τοῦ τηλοῦ: 'et hanc significationem invenire possumus et in Graeco 'nomine: nam quod nos telum appellamus, illi βέλος 'appellant ἀπὸ τοῦ βάλλεσθαι. admonet nos Xeno-'phon[11]. nam ita scripsit: καὶ τὰ βέλη ὁμοῦ ἐφέρετο, 'λόγχαι, τοξεύματα, σφενδόναι, πλεῖστοι δὲ καὶ λίθοι[12]. 'sicarii autem appellantur a sica, quod significat fer-'reum cultrum. eadem lege et venefici capite damnan-'tur, qui artibus odiosis, tam[13] venenis vel susurris 'magicis homines occiderunt vel mala medicamenta 6 'publice vendiderunt. Alia deinde lex asperrimum 'crimen nova poena persequitur, quae Pompeia de 'parricidiis vocatur. qua cavetur, ut,[14] si quis paren-'tis aut filii aut omnino adfectionis eius, quae nuncu-'patione parricidii continetur, fata properaverit, sive 'clam sive palam id ausus fuerit, nec non is, cuius 'dolo malo id factum est, vel conscius criminis existit, 'licet extraneus sit, poena parricidii punietur et neque 'gladio neque ignibus neque ulla alia sollemni poena 'subicietur, sed insutus culleo cum cane et gallo galli-'naceo et vipera et simia et inter eius ferales angu-'stias comprehensus, secundum quod regionis qualitas 'tulerit, vel in vicinum mare vel in amnem proiciatur, 'ut omni elementorum usu vivus carere incipiat et[15] 'ei caelum superstiti, terra mortuo auferatur. si quis 'autem alias cognatione vel adfinitate coniunctas per-'sonas necaverit, poenam legis Corneliae de sicariis 7 'sustinebit[16]. Item lex Cornelia de falsis, quae 'etiam testamentaria vocatur, poenam irrogat ei, qui 'testamentum vel aliud instrumentum falsum scripserit

---

(1) moribus] PE, a maioribus B, τῇ τῶν σοφῶν νομο-θεσίᾳ Θ   (2) fit] B, habetur PE   (3) quod] P, qui BE: καὶ τοὺς καρποὺς δὲ τοῦ μέσου χρόνου, τουτ-έστι τοὺς μετὰ προκατάρξιν μέχρι καταδίκης Θ, quod vix recedit a nostra lectione   (4) 4, 6, 20   (5) is] B, is invicem PE   (6) quoque] que B
(7) Cf. Dig. 48, 1   (8) infamiam (-mia A^u) i. cum damno] A^u PEΘ, vel inf. i. c. d. B, vel dampnum vel in-

famiam i. cum damno A^l, vel damnum vel infamia i. A^{bg}   (9) in] A om. rel.   (10) Dig. 50, 16, 233 § 2 (11) Anab. 5, 2, 14   (12) id est: et tela simul mitte-bantur, hastae, sagittae, fundae, permulti et lapides (13) tam] AE, om. B, tam..magicis om. R   (14) si quis...auferatur ex Cod. 9, 17, 1   (15) et] RA, ut B Cod.   (16) sic P, subsistit RB, substituetur A

assigned a noxal action. Once he concludes that the owner should be condemned he must give this form of judgment: 'I condemn Publius Maevius to pay Lucius Titius 10 or to make noxal surrender to him.' 2. If he hears a real action and finds against the claimant, he must absolve the possessor; or, if he decides against the possessor, he must order him to restore the thing in question and its fruits. If the possessor says that he cannot restore there and then, and asks for time, his request should be granted unless it is evasive and provided he undertakes, backed by a guarantor, that the money valuation will be paid if he fails to restore the thing within the time allowed. If the claim is to an inheritance, the rule as to fruits is the same as we have mentioned for claims to individual things. The calculation takes similar account of fruits which should have been taken but for the possessor's neglect. That is the position where the possessor is a shark. Against an honest possessor no account is taken of fruits already consumed or never received. Only when the action starts does the account of fruits not taken or consumed begin to run. 3. When an action for production is brought it is not enough for the defendant to produce the thing itself. He must go further. He must make a 'full cause' production. That means he must let the plaintiff have the thing as he would have had it if it had been produced as soon as he claimed production. If the possessor has usucapted the thing in the meantime he must still be condemned; and account must be taken by the judge of intervening fruits, i.e. those between joinder of the action for production and judgment. If the defendant says he cannot produce the thing then and there and asks for time, it should be allowed to him, if the request is not evasive and if he enters an undertaking to deliver up the thing. If he neither produces the thing immediately on the judge's order nor enters into an undertaking to produce it later, he must be condemned for the value of the plaintiff's initial interest in securing its production. 4. Suppose the judge has before him an action for the division of an inheritance. He must assign individual things to individual heirs, and if that gives one more than his fair share he must, as has been said, condemn that heir to pay a balancing sum back to his co-heir. A similar condemnation of one heir to another should be made where one has had the fruits of the inheritance entirely to himself or has damaged or consumed an estate asset. Of course the same applies when there are more than two heirs. 5. These techniques also apply in the division of common property when a plurality of things is involved. When such an action is brought in respect of one thing, one piece of land for instance, the judge, so far as it admits of convenient division into parcels, must assign individual parcels to individual heirs. Then, if one heir gets too much, he must make a balancing condemnation. If the thing cannot be conveniently divided, a slave or a mule perhaps, he must assign the entire thing to one and condemn him to pay a sum of money to the other. 6. Suppose he hears an action for determining boundaries. He must work out whether he should make any adjusting assignment. One case where that is definitely necessary is where the estates should be marked off by clearer boundaries than previously. A part of one man's estate then has to be assigned to the owner of the other, and the latter should be condemned to pay back a sum of money. Another reason for condemning a party in this type of action is if he has deliberately interfered with the boundaries, for example by stealing boundary stones or cutting down boundary trees. And another is contempt of the court, as where the judge orders the land to be measured and a party does not allow it. 7. The judge's allocation of property in these actions immediately confers title on the recipient.

4.18 CRIMINAL TRIALS

Criminal trials are not ordered by forms of action. They are quite different from the ones we have been dealing with so far. This is especially true of the way in which they are initiated and conducted. 1. They are called criminal – in Latin 'publica' – because as a rule any member of the public can set them in motion. 2. Some are capital and some not. The ones which are capital are those which entail the ultimate penalty or else end in banishment from hearth and home or transportation or condemnation to the mines. The rest, which lead to disgrace and money fines, are still public but are not capital. 3. The list is as follows. First, the Julian Act on Treason. This strikes hard against those who conspire against the emperor and the the state. It punishes them with loss of life and execration of their memory after death. 4. Next, the Julian Act on the Suppression of Adultery. This puts to the sword not only those who treat with contempt the marriages of others but also those who dare to indulge their unspeakable lust with males. The Julian Act also punishes criminal sexual intercourse, where, without violence, a man seduces an unmarried girl or a respectable widow. The Act's punishment for such offenders is, for the highly placed, confiscation of half their wealth, for common people, corporal punishment and banishment. 5. Next, the Cornelian Act on Assassins. This puts to the sword of vengeance murderers and those who carry arms with murderous intent. Here the word used for 'arms', namely 'telum', ordinarily means, as our own Gaius writes in his commentary on the Twelve Tables, an arrow shot from a bow, but it also denotes anything flung from the hand. So it includes missiles of stone, wood, or iron. The word is formed from the idea of something propelled from a distance, from the Greek phrase 'apo tou telou'. We can find the same idea in the Greek equivalent, for what we call a 'telum' they call a 'belos', from their word for throwing. Xenophon writes, using this word, 'They bore missiles with them, spears, arrows, slings and many stones.' The word for assassins is 'sicarii' and comes from 'sica' which is a metal dagger. The act also punishes poisoners capitally: people who use their detestable knowledge to kill men by poison or by magic spells or sell lethal poisons to the public. 6. Next, a separate act visits a rare punishment on the terrible crime of parricide. This is the Pompeian Act on Parricide. It provides that anyone who dares openly or secretly to hasten the end of an ascendant or son or any relative within the term 'parricide', and anyone who intentionally procures such a death, and any co-conspirator even if outside the family, shall suffer the punishment for parricide: he is not put to the fire, nor to the sword, nor to any other custom-hallowed death, but is sewn into a sack with a dog, a cock, a snake, and a monkey; and, sealed in with those bestial intimates, he is thrown, as the nature of the place allows, into a nearby sea or river. In this way while he still lives he loses the use of every element; the sky is taken from him before he dies, and the earth is denied him when he is dead. On the other hand, if anyone kills a relation by blood or marriage outside the parricide degrees, his is dealt with under the Cornelian Act on Assassins. 7. Next, the Cornelian Act on Forgery, also called the Cornelian Act on Wills. This punishes a person who writes a forged will or other document, // or

'signaverit recitaverit subiecerit quive signum adul-
'terinum fecerit sculpserit expresserit sciens dolo malo.
'eiusque legis poena in servos ultimum supplicium est[1],
'quod et in lege de sicariis et veneficis servatur, in
8 'liberos vero deportatio. Item lex Iulia de vi pu-
'blica seu privata adversus eos exoritur, qui vim vel
'armatam vel sine armis commiserint. sed si quidem
'armata vis arguatur, deportatio ei ex lege Iulia de
'vi publica irrogatur: si vero sine armis, in tertiam
'partem bonorum publicatio imponitur. sin autem per
'vim raptus virginis vel viduae vel sanctimonialis vel
'aliae fuerit perpetratus, tunc et peccatores et ei, qui
'opem flagitio dederunt, capite puniuntur secundum
'nostrae constitutionis[2] definitionem, ex qua haec
9 'apertius possibile est scire. Lex Iulia peculatus
'eos punit, qui pecuniam vel rem publicam vel sacram
'vel religiosam furati fuerint. [3]sed si quidem ipsi iudi-
'ces tempore administrationis publicas pecunias sub-

'traxerunt, capitali animadversione puniuntur, et non
'solum hi, sed etiam qui ministerium eis ad hoc ad-
'hibuerunt vel qui subtracta ab his scientes suscepe-
'runt: alii vero, qui in hanc legem inciderint, poenae
10 'deportationis subiungentur[4]. Est inter publica
'iudicia lex Fabia de plagiariis, quae interdum capitis
'poenam ex sacris constitutionibus irrogat, interdum
11 'leviorem. Sunt praeterea publica iudicia lex Iulia
'ambitus et lex Iulia repetundarum et lex Iulia de
'annona et lex Iulia de residuis, quae de certis capi-
'tulis loquuntur et animae quidem amissionem non
'irrogant, aliis autem poenis eos subiciunt, qui prae-
'cepta earum neglexerint.'
12 'Sed de publicis iudiciis haec exposuimus, ut
'vobis possibile sit summo digito et quasi per indicem
'ea tetigisse. alioquin diligentior eorum scientia vobis
'ex latioribus digestorum sive pandectarum libris deo
'propitio adventura est.'

---

(1) est] *E*, et *R*, om. *AB*   (2) *Cod.* 9, 13, 1   (3) sed…susceperunt] *conf. Cod.* 9, 28, 1   (4) *sic R* subiguntur *A,* subiungentur *B*

seals one, or reads one out for witnessing, or substitutes a false one for a true one; also a person who knowingly and with evil intent makes or engraves or casts a duplicate seal. The punishment under this statute is, for slaves, the ultimate penalty, as also under the statute on assassins and poisoners; for free persons, transportation. 8. Next, the Julian Act on Public or Private Force. This counters those who use force either with or without arms. If someone is shown to have used armed force, the punishment of transportation is imposed on him by the Act for public force; if unarmed force, he suffers confiscation of one third of his wealth. If force is used to rape a virgin or widow, whether religious or lay, the culprits and any accomplices are punished capitally under our own pronouncement. The details are best taken from its own terms. 9. Next, the Julian Act on Embezzlement. This punishes those who steal money or property which is public, sacred, or religious. If judges, of all people, take public money during their time of office, they are punished capitally, and with them any who have helped or have knowingly received what they have taken. Others within this Act are punished by transportation. 10. To this list of crimes also belongs the Fabian Act on Kidnapping. Some cases under that Act entail capital punishment by virtue of imperial amendments; some have a lesser penalty. 11. Besides these there are: the Julian Act on Bribery, the Julian Act on Extortion, the Julian Act on Interference with the Corn Supply, and the Julian Act on Improper Application of Public Funds. These all have their own specific provisions. They do not inflict loss of life but subject those who ignore their terms to lesser punishments. 12. We have not said much about crime. Our finger has pointed, like an informer's; yours have touched the subject's surface. But, God willing, you will go on to study these matters more deeply in the great books of the Digest or Pandects.

Vocabulary

This is not a comprehensive glossary. It is no more than an attempt to explain why we chose to translate some Latin terms as we did. In principle we have only included terms in the vocabulary if we experienced some difficulty over the translation. The key words are from our English text. The Latin equivalents are given after them in brackets. Where an entry includes a term which is itself explained in the vocabulary it is always marked [qv]. We rely largely on the text itself to do the explaining; each entry gives references which explain or otherwise show the meaning of the term in question. It may be helpful to explain the system of citation. There are four books, and each book has numbered titles. Book 3, title 23 is on sale. That is written in this way: J.3.23. The 'J.' stands for Justinian's *Institutes*. Each title is broken into numbered sections or, though they are not indented, paragraphs. The first section of a title is not '1' but the '*principium*', which means 'beginning'. So if you want to refer to less than the whole of a title you have to give three sets of figures: J.3.23.5. A longer consecutive passage is cited in this way: J.3.23.2-5. To cite paragraphs 2 and 5, omitting 3 and 4, you write J.3.23.2,5. And to cite passages from more than one title you separate the references with semi-colons: J.3.23.3-5; 4.6.28; 4.12 pr. When a *principium* is cited, no point separates the number of the title and the letters 'pr', and it is convenient also to omit the point that would normally indicate that 'pr' is an abbreviation. Since every reference in the vocabulary is to Justinian's *Institutes* we dispense with the 'J.'

Accession (*accessio*)

This noun is the standard word used to denote this means of acquiring ownership but in the *Institutes* it appears only once, at 2.1.26. The topic is discussed in a rather informal way by describing how something loses its identity by becoming part of a thing belonging to another. The Latin verb used is '*cedere*'. We made the legal outcome clearer at times by giving a stronger indication of the party who became owner. See 2.1.20-34.

Act (*lex*)

This translation is always used for specific statutes, e.g. the Hortensian Act at 1.2.4. It seemed the natural English equivalent. Acts with double names or two names are given using a hyphenated form, e.g. the Aelian-Sentian Act at 1.6 and the Julian-Plautian Act at 2.6.2. The model here was the American Taft-Hartley Act. 'Plebeian statutes' (*plebi scita*) at 1.2.4 in the discussion of sources are never subsequently distinguished from acts (*leges*). They are certainly not what we now call 'plebiscites'. See e.g.1.2.4; 1.5; 2.22; 4.18.

Action on the case (*actio in factum*)

This may tie the praetorian remedy too closely to the English form of action, but it is a better translation than 'action on the facts' which sounds too informal. Originally an action granted by the praetor when no standard action was available, it is not clear exactly how Justinian wished the term to be understood in his works. See e.g. 4.1.11; 4.3.16; 4.5.3. See also POLICY ACTION and SPECIAL JUDICATURE.

Action of debt (*condictio*)

Although this suggests an English comparison which cannot be pressed too far, we thought it better to translate than to anglicize. Something like 'condiction' makes the action sound more mysterious than it needs to. Again the word 'debt' implies owing in a wide enough sense to cover the many contractual and non-contractual causes for which the *condictio* lay. See 2.1.26; 3.14; 3.15 pr; 3.27.6,7; 4.1.19; 4.6.15.

Action for production (*actio ad exhibendum*)

There are no translation problems here except perhaps how to deal with the words '*causam rei debeat exhibere*' at 4.17.3. We rendered this standard legal jargon as 'he must make a "full cause" production'; the text itself sufficiently explains its meaning. See 4.6.31; 4.17.3.

Action, real or personal (*actio in rem, in personam*)

This translation is convenient but loses the sense of 'against' conveyed by the Latin '*in*'. A personal action is one which lies against a specific person under an obligation to the plaintiff, e.g. as a result

of making a contract with him or committing a wrong against him. A real action is one which asserts a recognized and already constituted relationship between the plaintiff and a thing, typically ownership, as in the vindication [qv]. The terms have so many substantive and procedural implications for Roman and indeed for modern law that we were tempted to retain the Latin here. But this ran against our principle of making every term accessible to those without any Latin. The word 'real' [qv] is used in a totally different sense in connection with parents and children, but the contexts are sufficiently distinct to avoid any confusion. See 4.6.1-20. See also Introduction pp.14-15.

Action with a special preface (*actio praescriptis verbis*)

The disappearance of the forms of action meant that there was no special preface to these actions in Justinian's time. The translation is a literal one. The name of the action was coined from the preface required in certain non-standard *formulae*. See 3.24.1,2. See also SPECIAL JUDICATURE.

Action for a wife's property (*actio rei uxoriae*)

A literal translation. The action allowed a widow or a divorced woman to recover at least part of the value of her dowry. The word 'property' is technically misleading because title to the dowry vested in the man, subject to the duty of returning it in certain circumstances. Justinian made considerable changes in the law. See 4.6.29,37.

Address, see Resolution

Adrogation (*adrogatio*)

There is no convenient way translate this word or its agent noun 'adrogator'. Modern law has no word for the adoption of independent people, because it does not recognize the Roman distinction between dependent and independent people. See 1.11; 1.22.1; 3.10.

Agent, see General agent

Agnate (*agnatus*)

Agnates are relatives in the male line from a common male ancestor. If that common ancestor is alive and the tie of agnation has not been artificially broken, they are all in his family authority [qv]. People of either sex can be agnates, as can those who are adopted into a family. We have described as 'full agnates' those siblings who have the same

father or adoptive father (*consanguinei*). See 1.15; 1.23.3; 3.2; 3.5.4,5; 3.6.8.

Ascendant (*parens*)

This is the strict meaning of the word in the law of succession; it applies to persons of both sexes in this sense. But it quite often signifies the head of the family [qv], necessarily always male. See 3.6 pr-6.

Aulus Agerius

This is the stock name for the plaintiff, the person who brings the action (*actor*, *agere*). Numerius Negidius is the stock defendant, who denies the claim (*negare*) but may still have to pay (*numerare*). They only appear once, at 3.29.2, where the traditional wording of the Aquilian stipulation is given. We kept the Latin because anything on the lines of Peter Plaintiff and David Defendant sounded precious.

Aureus

The standard gold coin of the early Empire. From Constantine onwards it was called the *solidus*. For Justinian the terms seem to be synonymous. The Latin names have only been retained where specific fines and money limits are mentioned, and at 3.7.2,3 where Justinian's rate of conversion from the classical *sestertius* is given. When sums of money are mentioned as mere examples we simply give the figure even when the text says *aurei*. e.g. 'Suppose a man dies with an estate of 100.' See 1.20.5; 2.7.2; 3.7.3; 3.15.2; 4.5.1; 4.16.13.

Authority (*potestas*)

This seemed more natural than 'power'. However, we did not want to make the relationship between father and son sound too informal; so both sons and slaves are described by the slightly stilted phrase 'within authority' or sometimes 'in authority' (*in potestate*). The context will show that the latter does not mean 'having authority' but merely varies the preposition 'within'. We refer to 'family authority', but the full Latin term for this – *patria potestas* – is rarer than might be expected. For the sake of clarity we have sometimes said 'family authority' where the text only says *potestas*. Also, the Latin often says *filius* where *filius familias* is intended. We had to decide from case to case whether the English required 'son in family authority'. See 1.8; 1.9; 1.12; 4.7.

Bronze and scales, by (*per aes et libram*)

We adhered to a literal translation. The ancient and

obsolete ceremony for making a will involving these instruments is described at 2.10.1. We treated the *emancipatio* here and at 2.10.2 as though it were *mancipatio*. *Mancipatio* as a conveyance is of course not mentioned in this work. At 1.12.6 the ceremony of emancipation is described as having involved pretended sales and intervening manumissions.

Capital (*capitalis, capite*)

'Capital' punishment did not necessarily involve execution. Any penalty involving loss of liberty or citizenship or both was 'capital' since it involved a first or second degree status-loss (*capitis deminutio*). See 4.18; 1.12.1-3; 1.16.

Capitulated alien (*dediticius*)

Although at public law such a description was to be taken literally, in private law the term applied to the lowest class of freedman. Justinian abolished the status. See 1.5.3; 3.7.4.

Charge (*merx*)

The money payment required in the contract of hire (*locatio conductio*). Charge seemed more general than fee or rental. It allowed us to say that there must be 'no charge' in loan for use (*commodatum*). The title on hire is too short to require anything more complicated. See 3.24; 3.14.2. See also HIRE.

Child (*impubes, pupillus, liberi, infans*)

A variety of technically different people are described as children – children by age and children by relationship irrespective of age. The context is all important. The age of puberty, fixed by Justinian at 14 for boys and 12 for girls, marked the end of childhood for most legal purposes, including the need for a guardian [qv]. We used 'child' for persons under puberty. Those outside family authority needed guardians, in relation to whom they were wards (*pupilli,-ae*), but we frequently used 'child' rather than 'ward'. An *infans* by Justinian's time was anyone under seven; we used 'very young child', 'infant' or even 'baby' as seemed most appropriate. *Liberi* can sometimes be translated as children, not meaning young children but issue of any age. It includes descendants [qv] beyond sons and daughters. 'Child' is an economical term for sons and daughters because it conveniently includes both sexes. See 1.13; 1.21;1.22; 2.12.1; 3.19.9,10; 4.1.18.

Classical (*vetus, antiquus*)

For Justinian 'old' or any similar expression applied to law or lawyers means 'classical', unless the rule or institution is clearly more ancient, connected for example with the Twelve Tables [qv].

Codicil (*codicilli*)

A convenient translation though the Roman codicil could exist independently of the will and was originally an informal document. There is some danger of creating a misleading impression that Roman and modern codicils were the same. See 2.25.

Code

There is no Roman equivalent of a modern code in the sense of a more or less comprehensive and systematic restatement of the law or a major part of it. The *Corpus Iuris* in general and the *Institutes* in particular provided both some of the raw materials and most of the structure for the eventual creation of codes in the West. We do use the word in connection with the Twelve Tables [qv], which though very early and crude were probably meant to be something like a code. See Introduction p.11. See also CODEX.

Codex

It would have been misleading to translate this in the usual way as 'code' [qv]. It means a collection of imperial pronouncements [qv]. Apart from one reference to the Theodosian Codex of AD 438, the Codex referred to in this work is the first edition of Justinian's Codex of 529. The pronouncements in question all appeared again in the second edition of 534, which is the one which survives. See 2.16.1; 2.20.27; 3.1.16; 3.3.4; 4.6.24. See also Introduction pp.9-11.

Cognate (*cognatus*)

This normally means a blood relation, including one adopted out of the family or emancipated. So a cognate, unlike an agnate [qv], can be related to another through the female line. People adopted into a family also become cognates. See 1.15; 1.16.6; 3.5; 3.6.

Complaint of an irresponsible will, see Irresponsible will

Compulsory heir, see Heir

Contempt (*iniuria*)

This translation expresses what came to be the

key-note of this very broad delict but conceals the fact that the broad delict had an even broader name. '*Iniuria*' means no more than 'wrong'. In English law 'trespass' underwent a similar specialization. See 4.4.

Contracts by conduct, see Obligation contracted by conduct

Criminal trial (*iudicium publicum*)

The translation expresses the substantive rather than the procedural nature of these trials. Private citizens normally acted as accusers. Any citizen could represent society in this way, which is why they are called 'public' proceedings – 'public' not in the sense of 'open' but 'of the people'. The reference at 4.18 pr to the absence of 'forms of action' is properly intelligible only against the background of the old formulary procedure. See 4.18. See also SPECIAL JUDICATURE.

Cut-in legatee (*legatarius partiarius*)

As the text explains this kind of legatee comes in for a share of the whole estate with the heirs. He differs from ordinary legatees, who take some specific thing or sum out of the estate. To call him a 'sharing legatee' would not sufficiently convey the idea of his being brought in with the heir or heirs. See 2.23.5,6.

Descendants (*liberi*)

They can sometimes be translated as children, but descendants is technically more correct. The difference is often important in the law of succession. A good example can be see at 1.14.5.

Digest or Pandects (*digesta seu pandectae*)

Justinian often refers the student to this work for more detail, though without telling him where to look. We decided not to modernize the translation of either name. We dealt somewhat shortly with the ornate and self-congratulatory language in which the *Digest* is mentioned. See Introduction pp.10-11.

Down-payment (*arra*)

In Justinian's time this may well have been a substantial sum. Originally it was probably no more than a token, for which our translation would have been inappropriate. Others use 'earnest', which should now be avoided as obsolete. 'Deposit' is too easily confused with the contract of the same name. See 3.23 pr.

Edict (*edictum*)

This usually refers to the praetor's edict, more rarely to that of the curule aediles, but sometimes it means a kind of imperial pronouncment [qv]. See 1.2.6,7. See also Introduction pp.11, 17.

Emperor (*divus*)

Instead of translating the supreme honorific title as 'divine' or 'deified' or even 'late', we chose simply to refer to e.g. 'the Emperor Antoninus Pius'. Some religious and political meaning is lost, though for a Christian like Justinian it is difficult to know how much.

Endorsement, guardian's (*auctoritas tutoris*)

This expression is used to prevent confusion with 'authority' (*potestas*) [qv]. There is a slight drawback, from the association with modern documents. As is made clear at 1.21.2 a guardian must give his endorsement on the spot and cannot do so by letter. Apart from this no formalities were required. See 1.21; 2.8.2.

Estate-possession (*bonorum possessio*)

This has to be given a translation with a sufficiently technical ring to it. It also has to be neat enough for frequent repetition. 'Possession of goods' or even 'of the estate' is too informal and too cumbersome. We could not find a better term of art, especially for naming the sub-forms 'estate-possession in support of the will' (*secundum tabulas*) and 'estate-possession counter to the will' (*contra tabulas*). We did not generally show the presence of the word '*unde*' in dealing with the people entitled to a grant of estate-possession. For Justinian such references must have become mere labels. See 3.9; 2.13.3; 2.17.6; 3.1.9,12; 3.2.3; 3.3 pr; 3.5.5.

Exchange (*permutatio*)

This sounded more modern than 'barter' and made it clearer why this contract could be difficult to differentiate from sale. See 3.23.2.

Fair and reasonable (*bonum et aequum*)

The meaning is clear enough but the phrase is difficult to translate satisfactorily. 'Fair' is better than the rather bland 'good'. 'Reasonable' is an enormously important word in modern law. '*Aequum*', with its idea of balance, is one of its ancient equivalents. By Justinian's time *bonum et aequum* had long been a standard expression, to be taken as a whole.

Family authority, see Authority

Freedman, freedwoman (*libertinus,-a; libertus,-a*)

Our translation is used for both Latin words, the second of which is used with special reference to the patron [qv]. Other possibilities such as 'ex-slave' are clumsy. See 1.5; 1.17; 3.7; 3.8; 3.11.

Freedom, liberty (*libertas*)

The expression 'grant of freedom' is often used in connection with the freeing of slaves even where the Latin has no obvious reference to 'grant'. The Latin 'manumittere' often becomes 'to grant freedom', avoiding difficult constructions and giving the convenient term 'grantor' instead of the ugly 'manumitter'. See 1.5; 1.6; 1.14.1; 2.14 pr, 1; 3.7; 3.11.

Frustrated will, see Will

Full agnate see Agnate

General agent (*procurator*)

On the basis of a text such as 2.9.5 this seems accurate. But the person who accepts a mandate from another cannot be called an agent in the full modern sense of the word. We avoided referring to the contract of mandate as agency. See 4.10; 4.11; 3.26.

Grant of freedom, see Freedom

Guarantor (*fideiussor*)

The older books speak of 'surety' but in modern terminology such a person is a guarantor. In Justinian's law there is only one kind. See 3.20; 4.14.4.

Guardian (*tutor*)

This person is distinguished from the *curator*, who is called a supervisor [qv]. Since guardianship ended in the normal way when children reached 12 or 14, it seemed reasonable to refer to him or her as a 'child' rather than as a 'ward' wherever possible. The English word 'tutor' is used in some jurisdictions for 'guardian' but is likely to mislead. For most people a 'tutor' is a type of teacher. See 1.13-1.26; 2.20.25,27; 3.19.20;.3.27.2; 4.11 pr. See also ENDORSEMENT, GUARDIAN'S.

Guardianship, see Guardian

Honorarian (*honorarius*)

We had to resort to this anglicization because at 3.13.1 the text explains that 'honorarian obligations' is an alternative description of 'praetorian obligations', thus using up the best translation. But even when the word is introduced at 1.2.7 an explanation of it is offered, which suggests that it sounded like unfamiliar jargon in Justinian's time.

Head of the family (*paterfamilias, pater, parens*)

This person is often simply called 'father' (*pater*); or else '*parens*' which means ascendant [qv]. In theory your oldest living male ascendant in the male line, barring the operation of adoption or emancipation, in practice he would usually be your father or grandfather. We have spelled this out where necessary. See 1.8; 1.9.

Heres (*heres*)

The main problem here was the *suus heres*. We have translated that as 'immediate heir'. Literally it means a person's own heir, but it would have been difficult to sustain repeated instances of that translation. To have called them 'family heirs' would have expressed the contrast with some 'outsiders' but not all. A member of your family not within your authority [qv] is not your immediate heir. 'Immediate' is meant to convey the sense of their ranking first on intestacy because they are in some way entitled even while the head of their family [qv] is still alive. 'Compulsory' is used for '*necessarius*'. An *extraneus heres* is called an 'outside heir' or an 'outsider' – i.e. one outside the deceased's authority. See 1.6.1,2; 2.14; 2.19; 3.1.

Hire (*locatio conductio*)

This translation adequately covers what is said in the short title on this contract. 'Lease' and 'contract of employment' were not called for. The poverty of English in this field makes it difficult to name the two parties' actions. We did it by calling the *actio locati* the 'action for hiring out' and the *actio conducti* the 'action for taking on hire'. All attempts at happy equivalents for *locator* and *conductor* seem doomed. See 3.14.2; 3.24. Hire is distinct from both kinds of loan. See also CHARGE.

Immediate heir, see Heir

Interdict (*interdictum*)

By Justinian's time these no longer involved their own distinct procedure, as is explained in 4.15.8. There is a problem in relation to the names of the individual interdicts. Their opening words were used as their names. Translations do not work. We have left the names in Latin: *quorum bonorum*, *uti possidetis*, *utrubi*, and *unde vi*. This was almost the only context in which we followed that option. See 4.15. See also SPECIAL JUDICATURE.

Irresponsible will (*inofficiosum testamentum*)

The complaint of an irresponsible will involved a *color insaniae*; its form was that of a fictitious claim that the testator had been insane when he made his will, though in fact the burden of the complainant's case was the disappointment of his legitimate expectations. The testator was 'irresponsible' in not considering his family responsibilities. The word often used is 'unduteous', but that is barely English. The 'quarter' rather vaguely referred to in this context is a quarter of the complainant's entitlement on intestacy. See 2.18; 3.1.14.

Latin (*Latinus*)

This identifies a type of freedman [qv] and has no geographical significance. Justinian abolished the category. See 1,5.3; 3.7.4.

Law of all peoples (*ius gentium*)

This is a slightly less confusing translation than 'the law of nations', which to modern readers suggests public international law. The law of all peoples consisted in the rules and institutions of private law which the Romans believed every people should and did have in its own system, as opposed to the law peculiar to one people. See 1.2 pr-2, 11; 2.1.11. See also STATE LAW.

Law of nature (*ius naturale*)

The way in which this is described as applying to animals at the end of 1.2 pr is difficult to translate. We may have been too free. Again at 2.1.11 there is another well known problem as to whether the distinction between the law of nature and the law of all peoples has been forgotten or a new kind of observation is being made. The adjective '*naturalis*' is used quite often, especially in 2.1; 'Natural justice' (*naturalis aequitas*) occurs at 2.1.40 and 3.1.9. The adjective creates a link with the law of nature, the law which exists independently of being put there by man, or simply with 'the nature of things'. But we have not always translated *naturalis* as 'natural'. See 1.2 pr,2; 1.3.1-2; 2.1. See also LOGIC and REAL.

Law of the state, see State law

Loan (*commodatum, mutuum*)

Apart from retaining its Latin name at 3.14.2 where it is first mentioned and contrasted with *mutuum*, *commodatum* is usually translated as 'loan for use'. But *mutuum* cannot easily be called 'loan for consumption', since that phrase is not really appropriate for money. We get through money but do not consume it in the sense that we consume food and drink. We left it as 'the loan called *mutuum*'. Both are distinct from hire [qv]. See 3.14 pr,2; 3.24.2; 2.8.2; 4.1.16; 4.6.17,22.

Logic (*naturalis ratio*)

This was one way of translating this difficult expression, e.g. at 1.10 pr. We also used 'first principles' at 2.1.35 and 'reasonable' at 2.1.12. 'Natural reason' seemed rather lame and fails to identify any modern type of argument.

Long-term possession, see Usucapio

Manumission, see Freedman and Freedom

Military fund, see Personal fund

Mortgage (*hypotheca*)

'Mortgage' is familiar in English while 'hypothec' is not. However, as the text hints at 4.6.7 mortgage and pledge (*pignus*) are much less distinct than in English law. See 2.6.14; 2.8 pr; 4.6.7,29; 4.11.4.

Mutuum, see Loan

Natural, see Law of nature; Logic; Real

Novation (*novatio*)

Here we accepted 'novation' as an anglicization which has become an established legal term in English. The text does not make it completely clear that it entailed the extinction of an existing obligation and its replacement by another. See 3.29.3.

Nullified will, see Will

Numerius Negidius, see Aulus Agerius

Obligation contracted by conduct (*obligatio re contracta*)

The translation brings out the symmetry with the series of contracts by words (*verbis*), by writing (*litteris*), and by mere agreement (*consensu*). It also matches the description of delictual obligation as arising *ex re*. Though the conduct involved in this class of contracts is always the delivery of a thing as is said in 3.22.1, a translation at a higher level of generality seems to be required. The usual 'real contracts' is merely evasive. See 3.13; 3.14; 4.1 pr. See also Introduction p.13.

Outsider (*extraneus*)

A person not in the family, usually in the more specific sense of one not within the authority of the head of the family [qv]. See HEIR.

Patron (*patronus*)

This word is quite appropriate for the former master of a freed slave. It has the correct overtones of continuing power over the freedman, including the power to do him good. See 1.17; 3.7; 3.8. See also FREEDMAN.

Personal action, see Action, real or personal

Personal fund (*peculium*)

The fund was *de facto* the property of the son or slave. The translation tends to suggest that the fund was always of money, whereas in fact it was often of a business or stock in trade. Many legal complications arose from the limited liability of the head of the family [qv] in relation to the personal funds of his dependants. The 'military fund' (*peculium castrense*) was different in that for most purposes it did belong outright to the son in family authority. It consisted in what he acquired while on army service. Justinian extended the possibilities for sons and daughters to acquire property for themselves. See 2.9; 2.11; 3.17; 3.28; 4.7.

Plea in defence (*exceptio*)

These were once clauses which had to be inserted in the *formula*, but by Justinian's time they had become the standard names for substantive defences. 'Exception' is not English. The particular defences are rendered as the pleas of deceit (*doli*), intimidation (*metus causa*), agreement (*pacti conventi*), previous decision (*rei iudicatae*), money not paid (*non numeratae pecuniae*), and oath taken (*iusiurandi*). The word replication (*replicatio*) has been retained for the plaintiff's riposte to a plea in

defence. See 2.1.30, 32-34; 3.15.3; 3.21; 4.13; 4.14. See also SPECIAL JUDICATURE.

Plebeian statute, see Act

Pledge, see Mortgage

Policy action (*actio utilis*)

The main difficulty is the translation of the adjective '*utilis*'. Where the praetor gave an action on the case [qv] on the basis that the plaintiff's claim fell within the policy – the *utilitas* – of an established action although outside the letter of its detailed rules, the action was described as '*utilis*': a *utilitas* action (as opposed to one justified by the hitherto existing rules reflecting that policy). The adjective cannot be given its normal meaning of 'useful' or 'advantageous'. Similarly, if we used 'politic' here it could not bear its ordinary meaning; it would mean nothing but 'policy-based'. So these are *utilitas*-based actions. As with all terminology emanating from the days when there were forms of action, it is not clear what force the term bore for the lawyers of Justinian's time. See 2.1.34; 2.23.4; 4.3.16.

Principal pleading (*intentio*)

For classical lawyers this had technical significance as the crucial clause of the *formula* which expressed the plaintiff's main contention. By Justinian's time the notion of *intentiones* as having set words and a definite grammatical form had gone. The concept of the plaintiff's central contention remained. See 4.6.33. See also SPECIAL JUDICATURE.

Pronouncement (*constitutio*)

We chose this as the generic term for all the authoritative utterances of the emperor. 'Proclamation' had too oral a ring. The traditional translation is 'constitution', but this is now merely confusing since modern lawyers are immediately led to think of constitutional law. The repetition of the word 'pronouncement' caused problems. Occasionally, where we were sure that the particular pronouncement could be said to have a legislative character, we said 'imperial legislation' instead. The commonest form of pronouncement was the *rescriptum*, a written answer from the emperor. Dissuaded from 'writ', we chose 'written reply' or, for short, simply 'reply'. Occasionally, as in relation to adoption, 'writ' did, however, seem preferable. When the written answer is expressly referred to as a '*subscriptio*' at 2.12 pr, we were reduced to the clumsy 'answer appended to a petition'. The word 'ruling' was used for '*decisio*', as

in Justinian's *Fifty Rulings*, the *decisiones* by which he settled some long-standing controversies. References to Justinian's own legislative pronouncements are very prominent. See 1.2.6; 1.5.3; 2.6 pr; 2.7.1-4; 2.20.2,23, 27, 34-36; 3.2.3-4,7-8; 3.15.1; 4.1.16(18); 4.6.8,24,25,30,33. See also Introduction p.11.

Private law, see Public law; State law

Promissor, see Stipulation

Property-purchaser, see Will

Puberty, see Child

Public law (*ius publicum*)

The major distinction between public law and private law is mentioned at 1.1.4. But the text then makes clear that the subject of the book is private law. The criminal trials [qv] touched on at the end are the exception.

Real (*naturalis*)

This adjective has been used to describe non-adoptive relationship between parents and children. English does now say 'real father' and 'real mother' to identify the biological parent. 'Real children' involves only a slight extension. 'Natural' in English has the wrong connotation, 'illegitimate'. '*Naturalis*' can mean this (e.g 1.10.13) but normally means precisely those born of lawful marriage. 'Real' in this sense is to be contrasted with 'real' as a direct anglicization of '*res*', as in actions real and personal [qv]. We have avoided one instance of this by using the expression 'obligations contracted by conduct' [qv] for 'real contracts'. See 1.11; 1.12.8; 2.13.4; 2.18.2; 3.1.9-14; 3.5; 3.10.

Reason, legally sufficient (*iusta causa*)

We have found that 'just cause' fails to alert people to the sense of '*iusta causa*' and have therefore often translated it in this more formal way. 'Good reason' is, however, sometimes satisfactory. See 2.6; 1.6.4,5.

Religious thing (*res religiosa*)

This is an ugly anglicization. It means graves and their attachments. 'Funerary property' would have been cumbersome and would not have conveyed the sense of the land's being subject to divine law,

in classical times dedicated to the gods below. It has to be distinguished from a sacred thing (*res sacra*), e.g. a church consecrated to God, in pagan times to the gods above. See 2.1.7-9.

Resolution of the senate (*senatus consultum*)

We have sometimes abbreviated this to 'resolution'. The alternative would have been to anglicize to 'senatusconsult'. Our principle was against that approach. Specific resolutions are given capitals: for example the Tertullian Resolution at 3.3. The Emperor's speech to the senate – his *oratio* – which came to be regarded as having legislative force in itself has been rendered as 'address'. See 1.2.5; 2.17.7; 2.23.4,6,7; 3.1.14; 3.3; 3.7.4; 3.8 pr; 3.12.1; 4.7.7.

Right of rehabilitation (*postliminium*)

There is no English equivalent which would recapture the sense of 'returning over the threshold'. We have been as short as possible with the laboured explanation of the meaning of the word at 1.12.5. See 1.12.5; 1.20.2; 2.1.17; 3.12.5.

Ruling, see Pronouncement

Sacred thing, see Religious thing

Sestertius, see Aureus

Solidus, see Aureus

Son in family authority, see Authority

Special judicature (*iudicia extraordinaria* or *extra ordinem*)

This was special only when originally introduced as an imperial alternative to the normal system of formulary litigation (*iudicia ordinaria*). The ordinary system was based on a list of model claims in the praetor's edict, which the plaintiff had to adjust to his own case. If his lawyer thought he could substantiate none of them, he could argue for a new one before the praetor. Whether established or new, the claim was sent on by the praetor for trial by a lay judge. The *formula* was the document which carried the issue to the judge and told him what he had to do. The special procedure supplanted this system, in particular dispensing with any list of model claims. Professional judges became normal, and the whole case was heard before them. Much of the vocabulary of the older system survived. See 3.12 pr; 4.15.8. See also Introduction p.17.

State law (*ius civile*)

This goes against centuries of 'civil law' and may seem to make us guilty of translator's hubris. We thought it was necessary to put life back into the expression, to give it something approaching its original meaning. Living in a 'Department of Civil Law' we know that the words are often misunderstood, often accepted without thought. At 1.2.2 there is a sign of the process that made 'civil law' mean 'Roman law'. Although he cites the example of Athenian state law, Justinian regards Roman state law as state law par excellence. Our translation does admittedly have slightly anachronistic overtones of the modern state and of public law [qv]. See 1.2.1,2; 1.3.4; 1.13.1; 2.6 pr; 2.10.2; 4.6.3. See also Introduction p.8.

Statutory (*legitimus*)

The Latin can be a straightforward adjective describing a rule or institution based on an act [qv] or resolution [qv]. Sometimes the relevant act has been amended by imperial pronouncements [qv]. Quite often the relevant legislation is that of the Twelve Tables (qv). Sometimes the word means lawful, without specific reference to a statute. See 1.15; 1.17; 1.18; 3.2; 3.3; 3.4; 4.6.3.

Stipulation (*stipulatio*)

We retained to a large extent the traditional way of describing this contract. The creditor, the stipulator, still stipulates for something from the debtor, the promissor. See 3.15-20.

Stipulator, see Stipulation

Substitute (*substitutus, substituere*)

We have tried to use this noun and verb in preference to the more abstract 'substitution'. We wanted to convey the idea that this area of law is a good deal less arcane in the Latin than many translations and discussions suggest. 'Substitutes for children' instead of 'pupillary substitution' is a translation in this vein. See 2.15; 2.16.

Supervisor (*curator*)

A supervisor is distinguished from a guardian (*tutor*) [qv]. It is not easy to find one word for a person whose role was to look after the interests of people under different disadvantages and requiring different protection: the insane (*furiosus*), the wasteful (*prodigus*), those still immature – over puberty but under 25 (*minor viginti annis*). 'Curator' and 'superintendent' sound to the modern reader like people in charge of institutions. 'Supervisor' is itself not very happy. See 1.21; 1.23; 1.24; 1.25; 4.11 pr.

Trust (*fideicommissum*)

There are marked differences between the Roman and the modern trust, but the translation is the best available and establishes a historical continuity. In Roman law trusts arose only on succession, not *inter vivos*. See 2.23; 2.24.

Twelve Tables (*lex duodecim tabularum*)

This early restatement of the law dating from around 450 BC is often cited in the text. Only fragments quoted by later writers are extant. Reverence for it in Justinian's time does not imply greater knowledge than we have. The adjective 'statutory' often refers to the Twelve Tables. We have occasionally referred to it as a 'code'. Though early, it is the nearest thing in Roman law to what we now think of as a code [qv]. See 1.15 pr; 1.17; 1.23.6; 1.26 pr; 2.1.29; 2.1.41; 2.6.2; 2.22 pr; 2.13.5; 3.1-7 pr; 4.4.7; 4.9.4.

Usucapion (*usucapio*)

This ugly word and the equally unlovely verb 'usucapt' simply could not be avoided. We translated '*longi temporis praescriptio*' as 'long-term possession', but we thought it unsafe to make '*usucapio*' into 'prescription'. See 2.6.

Verbal release (*acceptilatio*)

This is the opposite of a stipulation but we thought it better not to use the anglicization 'acceptilation' despite the loss of symmetry. See 3.29.1.

Vindication (*vindicatio*)

This word refers back to the old *rei vindicatio* of the formulary system. Most actions had self-explanatory names, action for theft, for deposit and so on. Some had special names, e.g. the *condictio* and the *vindicatio*. In plain language this might have been 'the action for ownership'. Its principal pleading [qv] said 'If it appears that the...is owned by Aulus Agerius by Quiritary title'. We translated *condictio* as 'action of debt' [qv] but, because 'vindicate' is after all an English word and remains technical in Scots law, we retained 'vindication'. See 4.6.15; 4.1.19. See also ACTION, REAL OR PERSONAL and Introduction pp.14-15, 17.

Ward, see Child; Guardian

Wasteful, see Supervisor

Will (*testamentum*)

This is in itself unexceptionable, but a few related terms require comment. We described as 'nullified' (*ruptum*) a will invalidated by a later event not affecting the testator's status, and as 'frustrated' (*irritum*) the will invalidated by a subsequent loss of capacity. These are vivid but somewhat arbitrary, as are the Roman distinctions. The 'property-purchaser' (*familiae emptor*) was a friend of the testator who under the ancient type of will 'by bronze and scales' [qv] formally bought the estate from the testator while he was alive and was given instructions as to how to distribute it on the testator's death. See 2.10.10; 2.17.

Within authority, see Authority

Written reply, see Pronouncement

SIGNORUM EXPLICATIO.

V = codex bibliothecae capitularis Veronensis XXXVIII (36), cui insunt varia opuscula Sulpicii Severi (v. Reifferscheid, bibliotheca patrum p. 110). ad supplendum huius libri hiatum postea adglutinata sunt tria folia rescripta, quorum scriptura antiquior continet ex Iustinianis institutionibus indicem titulorum usque ad 3, 5 (= *ind. V*), prooemii finem inde a verbis § 5 *ab imperiali*, libri primi titulum I et II inde u § 4 extr. scripta sunt litteris maiusculis. contuli Veronae 1868.

E = codex bibl. reg. Berolinensis, olim Rosnyanus, Lat. fol. n. 269 saec. IX, continens finem institutionum inde a verbis 4, 18, 5 in. *eos qui hominis*. contuli ipse.

U = Vercellensis 122 saec. IX vel X, qui continet prooemium. contuli Vercellis a. 1868.

A = lex Romana canonice compta (de qua cf. Maassen, Ueber eine lex Romana canonice compta. Wien 1860. 8.) una cum collectione Anselmo dedicata: illam continet codex Parisiensis 12448 (antea Harleianus 386) saec. X (= A^i), quem habui Berolini, huius adhibui codices Vercellensem (= A^u) et Bambergensem P I 12 saec. IX (= A^{bg}), quos ipse contuli. insunt huic collectioni institutionum tituli 1, 1 .. 4. 8. 9. 10. 12; 2, 1. 2. 6 (titulos 3 et 6 om. Ans. ded.) 14 § 5..12; 3, 6 pr. .. § 9. 15. 19; 4, 1..4. 8. 9. 18.

B = codex bibliothecae publicae Bambergensis D II 3 saec. IX vel X, integrum institutionum corpus continens. contuli Berolini.

T = codex Taurinensis bibliothecae regiae Athenaei D III 13 (olim H VI 4) saec. IX vel X. habet haec: 1, 13, 3 *te in patris* .. 14, 3 *posse dari*, 19 med. *post obitum* .. 25, 13 *potest excusare*, 26, 3 *endum est quasi* .. 2, 7, 3 *nuptias appellabatur*, 2, 8 pr. *lex in soli* .. § 2 fin. *eandem summam*, 9, 2 *quod sui iuris* .. 16, 1 fin. *pupillaris sub*, 8 *usque ad* .. 19, 6 *divus quidem*, 20, 2 fin. *cuius constitutionis* .. 8 in. *sive disiunctim*, 23, 5 med. *singulis quoque* .. 3, 24, 5 in. *omnia secundum*, 25, 9 *praevaluit* .. 4, 1, 16 med. *furem furti actionem*.

inde a verbis 3, 23, 3 fin. *nondum emptor* manus prima ob superinductionem saec. XIV ut videtur factam saepe incerta est (conf. Zeitschrift für Rechtsgeschichte VII pag. 45 sq.). contuli Berolini.

C = folia 21 libri institutionum saec. X vel XI, iam dispersa in codicibus monasterii montis Casini n. 160. 169. 175. 200. 270. 295. 326. 394, quibus teguminis loco addita sunt. continent 2, 5, 3 *potest ad* .. 6, 7 in. *autem ad*, 10, 12 *fiat* .. 16, 2 *testamenta alterum*, 22, 1 in. *si Titii pars* .. 23, 1 fin. *ius diceret*, 23, 9 med. *an expediat* .. 3, 1, 2 *existimantur ut*, 1, 13 in. *naturalis parentis* .. 15 fin. *patris sui*, 23, 1 med. *aestimaverit sub* .. 24 pr. *quidem locati*, 27, 7 in. *ex quibus causis* .. 29, 2 med. *res erit* (et secundum Bluhmium etiam 24 pr. ... 27, 7), 4, 1, 3 med. *furtum manifestum* .. 16 med. *concedatur et adversus*, 3, 9 *occiderit qui* .. 6, 5 *esset usu ceperit*. collata sunt Schradero a Bluhmio, mihi maiore ex parte a vv. dd. R. Schoene et O. Hirschfeld.

P = codex bibliothecae publicae Parisiensis 4421 saec. XI. contuli Berolini a. 1869.

E = codex bibliothecae publicae Bambergensis D II 4 saec. XI vel XII. contuli ipse.

W = codex bibliothecae civitatis Coloniae Agrippinae X, 8, olim Wallraffianus, saec. XII. contuli ipse.

Θ = Theophili paraphrasis Graeca institutionum.

dett. = libri deteriores, quorum lectiones laudantur in editione Schraderi.

inc. = incerta lectio.

ind. = index titulorum, qui extat in codicibus V et B.

Ubi librorum scriptura emendata est, siglis eorum ad indicandam emendationem litterulam *b* addidi: primitiva scriptura his locis litterula *a* significatur. ubi in ipsis libris notatur diversitas scripturae, hanc significavi litterula *v*, contextum libri litterula *i*. interrogationis signum librorum siglis additum semper ad proxime praecedens referendum est.

Index

This index allows the reader to look up Latin or English terms. The Latin terms are cross-referred to the English, and the principal texts are then given under the latter. Where the Latin and English are substantially identical (e.g. *actio*, action), only the English is given. References to the pages of the Introduction are given in **bold** type.